NOTABLE WOMEN
AND
A FEW EQUALLY NOTABLE MEN

Nine Plays by Ruth Wolff

Broadway Play Publishing Inc
www.broadwayplaypub.com

NOTABLE WOMEN—AND A FEW EQUALLY NOTABLE MEN
Plays—Copyright ©1965-2010 by Ruth Wolff
Dramatizing Lives—Unpublished Work Copyright ©2010 by Ruth Wolff
We Open in Florence—Copyright ©1977 by Ruth Wolff

No part of this publication may be photocopied, reproduced, stored in a retrieval system, or transmitted, in any form or by any means, electronic, mechanical, recording, or otherwise, without the prior permission of the publisher. All rights, including but not limited to the professional, motion picture, radio, television, videotape, videodisc, foreign language, tabloid, recitation, lecturing, publication and readings, are reserved. Additional copies of this book are available from the publisher.

The amateur and stock acting rights to the plays included in this volume are controlled exclusively by Broadway Play Publishing Inc (except for THE ABDICATION, whose rights are controlled by Dramatic Publishing, P O Box 129, Woodstock IL 60098). Without permission of the publishers in writing no performance of the plays may be given. Royalty must be paid every time a play is performed whether or not it is presented for profit and whether or not admission is charged. A play is performed any time it is acted before an audience, whether by professionals or amateurs. For all other rights please contact the author c/o Broadway Play Publishing Inc.

First printing: March 2010, second printing: April 2011
I S B N: 978-0-88145-449-9

Book design: Marie Donovan
Page make-up: Adobe InDesign
Typeface: Palatino

CONTENTS

About the Author .... *v*
Dramatizing Lives — The Art of Writing the Biographical Play 1
THE ABDICATION 41
THE PERFECT MARRIAGE 123
HALLIE 179
EMPRESS OF CHINA 235
SARAH IN AMERICA 301
ELEANOR OF AQUITAINE 341
GEORGE AND FREDERIC 419
JOSHUA SLOCUM SAILING ALONE AROUND THE WORLD 485
THE SECOND MRS WILSON 525
We Open in Florence 589

ABOUT THE AUTHOR

Ruth Wolff's play THE ABDICATION premiered at the Bristol Old Vic starring Gemma Jones. The Eureka Theatre of San Francisco presented its American premiere. Produced in almost every one of the United States, it has been performed worldwide in many languages with notable productions in Canada (in French), in Italy (in Italian) and in The Hague and Belgium (in Dutch). It was produced in London in 2005. Its acting edition is published by Dramatic Publishing. With screenplay by Ms. Wolff, the Warner Bros. film of THE ABDICATION starred Liv Ullmann and Peter Finch.

The Kennedy Center produced her play SARAH IN AMERICA starring Lilli Palmer as Sarah Bernhardt, directed by Sir Robert Helpmann. The play was also produced at the Pasadena Playhouse featuring Katherine Helmond and at Hofstra University featuring Tovah Feldshuh. Ms. Wolff's film about the early life of Sarah Bernhardt, THE INCREDIBLE SARAH, starred Glenda Jackson and Daniel Massey.

Her play EMPRESS OF CHINA premiered at the Pan Asian Repertory Theatre in New York in 1984 directed by Tisa Chang and starring Tina Chen. With the same star and director, a new production was presented at New York's West End Theatre in 2003. Other productions include those at the Cincinnati Playhouse, the Tinfish Theatre in Chicago, the East Coast Theatre Company in Sydney, Australia (2004) and (in Italian) at the Todi Festival in Italy. The acting edition is published by Broadway Play Publishing Inc.

Ms Wolff's play THE SECOND MRS. WILSON, about the critical last year of the Wilson White House, premiered September 2001 at the Barter Theatre, the State Theatre of Virginia. Her play AVIATORS premiered in 2005 at the New Jersey Repertory Theatre and was subsequently produced at the Barter Theatre. The play is published by Broadway Play Publishing Inc.

JOSHUA SLOCUM SAILING ALONE AROUND THE WORLD premiered at The Rhode Island Shakespeare Theatre. GEORGE AND FREDERIC premiered at the University of Utah. Wolff's adaptation of THE GOLEM appeared Off-Broadway.

Staged readings include: THE PERFECT MARRIAGE (East Hampton Playwrights Theatre), HALLIE (Smith College, Vassar College, Writer's Theatre) and ELEANOR OF AQUITAINE (O'Neill Theatre Center and Playwrights Horizons).

Among her other plays are: ARABIC TWO, FOLLY COVE, STILL LIFE WITH APPLES, BUFFALOES, THE SHAKESPEARE ROAD, THE ARDENT PHILANTHROPIST, THE SKY POOL, THE FALL OF ATHENS and HOTEL VICTORY.

Her film commissions include *Lieutenant Battle* (Universal), *Wives* (Warner Bros.), *Shadows On The Moon* (Imperial Development) and *Wild Nights*.

A native of Massachusetts who now lives in New York, Ms Wolff was educated at Smith College and Yale University. Her essays have appeared in The New York Times and other publications. She is a recipient of a Rockefeller Fellowship and a Kennedy Center Bicentennial Commission, is a fellow of the McDowell Colony and a member of the Dramatists Guild, the League of Professional Theatre Women and the Writers Guild of America, West.

For June, Jane, Amy
and all the other Notable Women
whose encouragement and support
have meant so much to me over the years

and

For all the treasured Notable Men in my life
—most particularly Martin, Evan, Nathaniel and Noah

Dramatizing Lives
The Art of Writing the Biographical Play

THE BIOGRAPHICAL PLAY

All plays are about people.

Biographical plays are about people who actually lived.

Some playwrights choose to portray themselves, their neighbors, their relatives (disguised or not), or the people they see on the subway. But others turn to known figures, people who have distinguished themselves in some splendid or horrific way, whose stories are known though we have never met them, and whose lives beg to be lived again—embodied in actors on the stage. It's this latter type of play which I've often chosen to write and which, here, I attempt to analyze, define and explore.

From the beginning, personifying on the stage the life of someone from the far or recent past has been an extremely rich source for drama. The towering heroes and heroines of the Greeks—Oedipus, Electra, Antigone, etc.—were figures of legend, but so familiar to the early audiences that what was legendary must have seemed real to them. In the Middle Ages, plays and playlets were spun around the lives of Biblical characters and the saints. Elizabethan drama is studded with superb Shakespearean portrayals of various Richards, Henrys and other royals. The examples go on and on, from everybody's Saint Joan, through Sherwood's Lincoln, Bolt's Sir Thomas More and Shaffer's Mozart, to portraits of today's greats and not-so-greats.

Lives are lived and they inspire playwrights to base plays on the events, intricacies, confrontations, triumphs and absurdities those who lived those lives experienced along the way. The substance is there already, so it's a great temptation to turn that substance into art on the stage. After all, people have an insatiable curiosity about the lives of other people. Sometimes the interest is prurient. But often it's an unspoken plea for illumination: life is such an elaborate and confusing maze, how did those folks make their way through it? Looking at other people's lives, as dramatized on stage, can be both a relief and a pleasure. Providing that illumination and that pleasure is the vocation of those who write the biographical play.

A play based on a life is a very different thing from a biography. A biographical play is a play first and a biography second. The biographer's task is to ferret out all possible information about the subject, searching highways, byways, original materials, archives, living relations, friends and enemies, even opening graves if necessary in the pursuit of "the whole truth, nothing but he truth". Once that is found, the biographer takes all the notes and discoveries (the biographer always hopes there will be new discoveries, sexual if possible, scandalous as next best choice) and puts them in some order, usually chronological. The biographer comes up with some insights and writes the book—a book as long as the material warrants or the publisher will allow. The volume is then interlaced with prints, charts, drawings, photographs and an appealing cover which give flesh to the major contribution of the biographer: the written word.

The playwright's art is quite different. Having taken the journey of writing a biographical play more than nine times, I realize more and more how different my journey is. In the first place, the more I know, the more I have to throw out. This doesn't keep me from the knowing. In fact, I am insatiable. It is my hunger to know, to penetrate the secrets of other people's lives, which is both my curse and my delight. Yes, I read as much as I can, explore as much as I can, tread the steps the subjects trod, experiencing a shiver of mystical contact. But at the end of all those journeys, I must create a *play*—a thing to be viewed on a stage, a thing which must unfold in no longer a time than an average corpus can confine itself to an average theater seat. Two hours.

Therefore, the center of my work is not the research. The center of my work is what I create. This may sound vain. It has taken me years to be able to come out of the closet with this statement. The playwright writing a biographical play uses the matter of another person's life and molds it into an original creation.

The biographer presents the life, the whole life, with all its high, low and lag times. The playwright's work seldom encompasses a whole life—although a great span can be suggested. There can be highs, there can be lows, but there can never be lags in a play. Even the most dramatic life is immensely untidy, with contradictions, irrelevancies and twists which a biographer can insert into a paragraph or footnote. But the playwright must give the life dramatic shape, must give the drama structure. In the service of this great and primary demand, characters are jettisoned, lovely moments are passed by. Nothing serves a drama less than including an event solely because "it really happened". If it does not serve the dramatic structure, if it does not suit the major theme, the scene must go.

In biographical book writing a major sin is to invent dialogue. Nothing sets reviewers' teeth on edge quite as much as seeing words in quotes which the subject of the biography didn't say. In a play, however, just about *everything* is something the subject didn't say. Yes, there are pastiches, there may be quotes, and there are plays based on transcripts or tape recordings. But in a play written from scratch, most of what comes out of the characters' mouths is something the playwright invented. We know not what Richard III said when his nag was shot out from under him. It was *Shakespeare* who said, "My kingdom for a horse."

Just as playwrights invent dialogue for characters who once lived, so they invent scenes. In fact, this is the center and the joy of the playwright's craft. Unlike the biographer, who must stick to the known, the playwright takes the leap into the unknown—to write the scenes which may have happened but which no one witnessed, the scenes which everyone involved in lied about or never revealed. We speculate—within the bounds of reason. Or, if we leap outside the bounds of reason, we let the audience know we are indulging in flights of imagination. Such flights can be more insightful than blind adherence to dull "facts". For playwriting is not documentary writing. Playwrights have a license to use their imaginations. In fact, if they don't use their imaginations, their licenses to be playwrights should be revoked.

In a way in which biography can never be, biographical playwriting is a personal expression. In THE ABDICATION, Christina of Sweden is as much my personal view of the subject as, in painting, Picasso's is of Gertrude Stein—or Dora Maar. In SARAH IN AMERICA, Sarah Bernhardt is my view of the actress; it is not the way she sees herself or the way others may see her. In other plays, when Mary Shelley, George Sand and Tzu-Hsi, Dowager Empress of China, speak, they are speaking in my voice as much as in their own. As I speak for and through them, truths may be uttered which may not have been uttered in their lifetimes, but which I intuit as I put flesh to their bones. Playwrights can give meaning and structure to lives which the subjects who lived them were never able to achieve.

Because a playwright's work lives best when embodied in the flesh of actors, we are very fortunate if the actor's view of the character we've created (yes, *created*) jibes with our view. But we shouldn't be embarrassed to say this is our view and insist on that being the way the character be portrayed.

I believe that exploring the mysteries of people who lived is fascinating and worth embodying in scenes and dialogue on stage. I feel sorry for those who find the term "historical play" a pejorative term. It shows a great limitation of vision. For when we playwrights write about the Past, we are still seeing with our own eyes and what we say has meaning to, and is vibrantly of, the Present.

Contemporary cutting edge drama may have its place in the sun for a passing moment, but such plays can soon seem dated. On the other hand, plays which take place in another time, which aspire to the "classic" or the universal, not being wedded to the moment, can have a longer staying power. They can be revived again and again, particularly if their themes are relevant for all time.

In many ways, writing a biographical play presents the same challenges as writing a play not based on a living or formerly living character. Many playwrights who seem to be writing so-called "original" plays are actually basing their characters or situations on people they know or knew, or on events which truly happened. In these plays of personal direct observation, the characters are fictionalized and reimagined so that the original disappears and seems to be a creature entirely of the playwright's invention. In a biographical play, the mask comes off. The subject admits to his or her true identity and the playwright states clearly that what is written is, indeed, intended to be a portrait of someone. For the playwright sitting down to write a biographical play, that is the first challenge: What Somebody will it be about?

CHOOSING A SUBJECT

People are always asking me, "How did you come to write about so-and-so?" I always attempt to come up with a cogent answer. But the real answer is: "I have no idea." It's a mystery to me why, out of hundreds of thousands of people to write about, my mind will suddenly decide to zero in on this one. Usually I've been aware of the person's existence for a long time. Years. Decades. At some point that dim awareness crystallizes into a more focussed interest. I'll have an instinct that something of dramatic significance is there.

Love and its complexities is a favorite theme of mine and so of course I was drawn to the romantic atmosphere of the medieval Courts of Love and their patroness, Eleanor of Aquitaine. This led me to read more about her. I was attracted to everything Eleanor was—but I had no idea how to make a play of it. Then it came to me that the importance of Eleanor was her life, her entire life, in which she refused, from beginning to end, to be limited by being born female. Since this was a theme with many modern soundings, I knew I had to write the play ELEANOR OF AQUITAINE. I knew, too, that the play had to be about her entire life, from age sixteen to her death at eighty-two.

What first drew me to think about Christina of Sweden as a subject was very simple: I wondered why anyone would abdicate a throne. Having power, being rightful queen, seemed like an enviable and exalted position. How could anyone give it up? I explored her life and began to realize her abdication had to do with her inability to resolve the conflicting masculine and feminine aspects of her nature—once again, an extremely contemporary theme. When I realized that this aspect of her story—and the story of her love for Cardinal Azzolino—had never really been told dramatically, I felt compelled to write THE ABDICATION.

Sometimes I'm attracted to a subject for a particular reason—but then, on further exploration, a different theme evolves and surprises me. The idea of writing about George Sand appealed to me because she was a "liberated woman". However, when I looked into her life more deeply, I found out just how tied, how immensely domestic and unliberated much of her life really was. In focusing GEORGE AND FREDERIC on Sand's relationship with Chopin and with her daughter, Solange, I found I wasn't writing about the revolutionary woman, but about woman *after* her feminist revolution. It's a much more complex and interesting subject and it echoes what's happening today, after *our* feminist revolution. George Sand declared herself a free and independent woman—and *then* what happened? Her daughter, having witnessed her mother's life, declared herself a free and independent woman. Somehow the daughter's declaration of sexual independence didn't resonate with the same pure fire of liberation as did her mother's. Sand found herself mouthing reactionary moral phrases. There were, in other words, consequences to her practice of complete freedom. That's exactly the situation many women find themselves in today (and always will).

In choosing to write about Tzu-Hsi, the Dowager Empress of EMPRESS OF CHINA, I was deliberately trying for a change of pace. I had been writing about love, love, love and I wanted to write about a Major Villainess, someone totally evil. Of course, when I began to write about her I discovered she had many motivations which were not at all evil—for example, her desire to preserve the glories of the China of the past. As she tried to hold her country together through the challenges of the new twentieth century, I had tremendous sympathy for her—like the sympathy one has for Macbeth. And while, in the play, there are scenes about her stubbornness, her cruelty and her voracious need for power, there are also scenes which arouse our compassion as Tzu-Hsi watches the world she upheld with pride slip away.

Although I'd been interested in Sarah Bernhardt as long as I could remember, the first impetus to write about her as a subject came to me from the outside. A film producer who had seen the movie of THE ABDICATION asked if I'd like to write a film on Bernhardt for Glenda Jackson. I said I'd like to very much. The producer wanted the story to cover Bernhardt's early career and rise to stardom. That was fine with me. But there was one point on which we differed: I felt that Bernhardt's tours, especially her American tours, were what made her the star whose fame was global. I felt that the French anger at the Americanization of Sarah and her winning back not only the French but the world at large would make a fine climax for the movie. For largely budgetary reasons, the producer decreed: "No American tours." So I wrote THE INCREDIBLE SARAH without showing the tours—and when I finished the movie I decided to write a one-person play *only* about the tours: SARAH IN AMERICA.

Hallie Flanagan is the only historical figure I've written about whom I actually knew. In her extreme age—and my extreme youth as a sophomore at Smith College—I sat around her dining room table and absorbed some of her spirit in my first playwriting course ever. She never talked about her fight against the House Un-American Activities Committee which had put an end to the Federal Theatre, but we all knew about it. Much later, in times when America's arts budgets were being cut, I remembered her fight and decided her trial should be dramatized for the stage.

THE PERFECT MARRIAGE had its impetus when, one day in Paris, I happened upon a biography of Shelley and became fascinated by the romance between him and Mary Shelley. What they went through! And yet I had the sense that theirs was a "perfect" marriage. It seemed to me their story was far too melodramatic and full of pathos to be accepted by a contemporary audience. I decided to give their tale a comedic twist and have it all take place in the afterlife. It allowed me to say some things about contemporary marriage that I wanted to say and to tell their story at the same time.

With THE SECOND MRS. WILSON I'd heard the phrase that Edith Wilson had been "America's First Woman President" so many times I couldn't help but want to explore that subject. What I discovered led to my having an extremely compassionate view of both the much-maligned Edith and the misunderstood Woodrow Wilson. Again, it was the story of a marriage. But when the play was produced, it was against the background of present day events—and what struck the audience profoundly was the political arguments between Wilson and Henry Cabot Lodge, between internationalism and isolationism. In the present climate, it's the intricacy of the United States' involvement in world affairs which makes the subject of this play immensely contemporary.

I never take on the writing of any biographical play unless the life seems to me to have contemporary meaning. Personal meaning. If I'm attracted by a life, but have nothing to say through it, I don't write the play.

CRITERIA FOR CHOOSING A SUBJECT

When deciding whom to write about, it's perfectly obvious that some people are better subjects than others. They lived more exciting lives—lives that practically beg to be dramatized. They make the playwright's work easy if they have a leading idea to their lives, perhaps some Magnificent Obsession, or if they have some major scene in their lives which everything else leads to, or around which everything else revolves. A passionate life is good fodder. A glorious death is even more of a help. Some people's lives fall so clearly into these categories that dramatists can't keep their hands off of them.

Lincoln Center Library for the Performing Arts, in New York City, has a file on historical characters whose lives have been the subjects of plays, films and television dramatizations. The person who has inspired more dramatizations than anyone else, the all time winner, is Elizabeth I of England. Joan of Arc weighs in second. Next comes Abraham Lincoln, and after him comes Jesus Christ. All these were good guys. A ruthless dictator and a power-hungry emperor—Hitler and Napoleon—are tied for the next spot. After them comes Oscar Wilde. The file is divided into works written before 1974 and those written after. The person who leads the recent list—the person who has inspired more dramatizations than anyone else since 1974—is Marilyn Monroe.

It's fascinating to see from those lists whose popularity has waxed and whose has waned. Queen Victoria had fifteen pieces written about her before 1974, but only one after. The interest in Saint Joan fell from forty-one to two. Byron was a great early favorite, with twelve dramatizations before 1974, but only five after. The Brontës got more popular. Churchill, the Roosevelts (especially Teddy), Emily Dickinson, George Washington, Mark Twain and Vincent Van Gogh have proven irresistible to dramatic writers—as have Benedict Arnold, John Wilkes Booth, Rasputin and Catherine the Great.

Comparisons are odious, so it makes no sense to write about somebody who's been written about many times before—unless, of course, one has something entirely new to say. It would be better to be the one person who wrote well about Hrotswitha of Gandersheim than to be one of fifty who flailed about around Queen Elizabeth I.

The advantage to choosing a subject who has already established his or her popularity or notoriety is the recognition value. On the other hand, choosing someone whose life is well-known means fighting everyone's preconceptions. An audience often comes to a biographical play with a strong idea of what the leading character's character should be like. Much of what they believe not only comes from previous fictions, but can be totally wrong. Even with people who aren't universally known, the view of them in the public's mind can be so strong that all of the writer's effort has to be spent erasing an existing image. Sometimes the preconception is so powerful that the public simply won't accept another view.

I had this challenge with THE SECOND MRS WILSON, which is the inside story of the last critical year of the Wilson White House. When I say the title, people invariably respond: "Oh, yes. She's the one who ran the country." It's a sentence hung on Edith Wilson like a noose made of pearls. It makes her seem like a bitch who made a grab for power. In my view, that is entirely untrue. I believe she was an intelligent, though not politically astute, woman who was forced to function as guardian at the gate and protector of her husband's interests. Woodrow Wilson was the fallen leader and Edith Wilson was the one who was fighting beside him to help him achieve his goals.

It's true that there was confusion and inefficiency while Edith kept government officials from seeing the President and when, as intermediary, she interpreted their wishes to him and his to them, but I believe Edith Wilson's motives were honest and straightforward. However, that's not the Edith the people who mouth that one sentence about her want to see. They want to see a manipulating, ball-busting, power-mad bitch. And while I have one character in the play actually call her the "B" word, that's not the woman I'm presenting.

Sometimes the preconceptions about a character come from another dramatic work. When I wrote THE ABDICATION, my only previous acquaintance with Christina of Sweden was from seeing a revival of the 1932 film, *Queen Christina*, whose script was written by S N Behrman. Even though there's a play about her by Strindberg, I haven't read it and the play isn't what shaped the ideas about Christina in the public's mind. It was the film which colored our views. It presents an extremely romantic image of Greta Garbo as a Queen who gave up her throne for love of the Spanish Ambassador.

It's a delicious movie—and completely fabricated. Behrman, M G M, and Garbo's mentor, Salka Viertel, fixed forever in the minds of the public this splendid image of Queen Christina—so beautiful, so romantic—so utterly false. Except for the fact that Christina and Garbo were both Swedish and both ambisexual, they were two very different souls, particularly in the beauty department, nor did Christina give up the throne for love. Sticking to niceties like the facts wasn't an aim of those early movie-makers. They just wanted to entertain—and they did.

I don't have any quibble with these fictional interpretations based on scintillas of verities—I enjoy them along with everybody else. I don't have any quibble, that is, as long as everyone knows that any relation of this Christina to the actual Christina is extremely tenuous, or as long as people can accept another Christina into their heads. When I wrote THE ABDICATION (play and screenplay), those who had seen *Queen Christina* were surprised at seeing a rough, tortured and not particularly attractive Christina. Yet because the earlier film was so patently romanticized a vision, audiences were ready to accept a different characterization, one both more complex and more real.

My vision of Christina as a woman who abdicated the throne and then fell in love with a Cardinal might be shocking, but it is true. Yet I do hope I treat her with sympathy. What disturbs me is today's fashion for debunking heroes. While, in the past, writers overglamorized heroes, today the opposite is in fashion. There is a cynical approach to treating other people's lives which I find despicable, if not actually dishonest. The effect is not just to show them "warts and all", but to show them as one big wart, to "cut 'em down to size". If there is something dirty or mean to be said, many current biographers, on stage, on film and in print, go out of their way to say it. If there is some dark cranny which hasn't come to light, expose it, is their motto. If there's nothing actually evil or scandalous to uncover, damning people by reporting on bad language or cranky moods can be used to do them in.

Of course, sometimes the debunking approach actually results in a revival of interest. In AMADEUS Peter Shaffer drags that sweet little Mozart right off his piano bench and hurls him at us as a slobbering scatological woman-chaser out of whose corrupt persona flows beatific music. A large part of the popularity of the play is based on the difference between public expectation and the playwright's conception. The play would probably have been less popular if the expectation had been scatological and the playwright's conception beatific.

Where there's a choice for the writer, I choose sympathy over denigration. Why bother to spend time treating someone's life only to destroy him or her for posterity? It's time, I think, for compassion, for a dose of the Greek moderation and balance. It's not a matter of white-washing or putting people on pedestals, it's a matter of understanding the depth of the human struggle and giving those who excel in sheer survival their true worth.

THE COMMIT POINT

So while some choose whom to write about out of repulsion, I choose out of attraction. I begin by having a vague feeling that there might be elements in the life worth dramatizing. I read a little about him or her and realize that there's something in the life which has been speaking to me, something about the life which has meaning, and not just for the time in which they lived, but for now. From that preliminary reading I get a feeling for some scenes, some juicy emotions, some depths, some complexities, some dramatic moments. The mine looks promising, but should I begin working it?

I've reached the commit point, the "go, no-go" decision. Everything I do in the future on this project will be based on that. Committing to what will eventually prove to be a rotten idea can waste decades of one's life—so this decision is crucial. Days and weeks of serious soul-searching now will be worth their weight in future time and effort. Leaping into a subject with one's eyes closed, with only an instinct that there's something there, can prove disastrous months, even years, down the line. While THE ABDICATION and SARAH IN AMERICA were produced almost immediately after they were written, EMPRESS OF CHINA took ten years to get to production. Some plays can take longer than that.

Yet at this early stage instinct and intuition are important. Objectively, I want to know that I have an affinity with the subject, that the events (internal and external) in the life are absorbing and dramatic. But, most importantly, I have to know I have some idea that I have something personal to say—not so much about the life—but *through* the life. This life is the medium through which I want to express something highly subjective and individual. I am not *using* the life, I am fusing it with my own ideas and giving it birth again, through my voice and my sensibility. This is not a distortion. It's that there is a point of affinity which makes the character's existence reach out to my existence and vice versa. That person's life spoke to me—and when I dramatize it, and when he or she speaks through that dramatization, it will be in a voice which is theirs and mine at the same time.

Once I've decided that it's going to be a "go", the real work begins. The research.

RESEARCHING WITH THE CREATIVE MIND

I don't think there's any sentence I hear more often, or one I hate more in reaction to a play of mine, than when someone comes up and says: "Gee, you must have done a lot of research." Yes. Yes, I probably did a lot of research. But anyone can do research. The art, the achievement, comes in what the playwright does with that research. One can research Egyptian history forever, one still won't have ANTONY AND CLEOPATRA.

Every now and then I think this remark about research comes out of awe or simple curiosity—but mostly I feel it as a put-down. What they're saying is: Anyone who reads can write the play. I beg to differ. The creation of a play based on someone else's life is just as much a creative act as creating a play out of any other matter. Like a painter looking at a human subject, the subject exists but it is the creation on the canvas—or here, in the play, the written dialogue and scenes—which is the work of art.

The research phase for a play is quite a different thing from the research phase for a fact book or thesis. It's a crucial part of the creative process. It's not just reading; it's reading with the creative mind. In this case, the playwright/reader is not the passive receptor taking notes but the active creator constantly on the lookout for the moments, the incidents, the psychologies which give insights and which inspire the elements to be transformed from "fact" to "drama" in order to make the play.

Only I can do the research because I'm creating as I'm researching. I'm forming the play even as I'm absorbing the material. I'm looking at it from my own unique point of view, choosing, discarding, connecting, getting small revelations, feeling moments of illumination, letting my mind soar to imagined moments from tiny hints glimpsed here and there. If someone else did the research, I'd miss all this. Someone else can do the research for a writer doing a documentary or even for a straight factual biography, but not for a writer writing a play.

So I dive into books, letters, scrapbooks, documents, primary and secondary materials. In the beginning, I'm just swimming around in a morass of material, enjoying myself in a completely receptive, only vaguely purposeful state. I read one book, then another, then another, then that leads to another. Sometimes the list seems to stretch out endlessly. I'll be reading about one person, but another's biography would give another point of view, so I look at that. There may be many views of one person or event to be looked at.

For THE SECOND MRS WILSON, where all the action takes place inside the White House during the last year of the Wilson administration, the only person who didn't write about that time of crisis was Woodrow Wilson. His wife, his doctor, his press representative, the hostile leader of the Senate, even his Chief Usher all wrote books about that period. I read them all, weaving my way through conflicting stories—and through obfuscations and enmities and rationalizations. Penetrating the inner sanctum of Woodrow Wilson's silence from views of him given by others was like decoding a mystery-filled novel by Henry James, where one subject is illuminated from many different points of view.

But, in preparation for writing, biography isn't all I read. I have to read up on the period—what was going on in the world in which that character lived. And I must, of course, have some working knowledge of the character's field of expertise. If it's politics, I read politics. If it's music, I read about music. If it's Chinese civilization at the turn of the twentieth century, I read about that.

If the person lived in the modern era, there are newspaper reports with reviews, quotes, publicity releases. It was fascinating to contrast the front page newspaper stories during the days of Woodrow Wilson's illness with what was discovered later to be the facts of his stroke. And, of course, with Sarah Bernhardt, every time she sneezed a hundred reporters rushed to report the event. I dive in and start reading anything I can get my hands on.

But one has to know how to look at the material. Sometimes sources give conflicting opinions. The Encyclopedia Britannica gives an extremely negative entry to Tzu-Hsi, the Empress of China. In their eyes, she was a worthless despot. The Encyclopedia Americana, on the other hand, credits her with holding together the Manchu Empire and attempting some measure of reform. Similarly, there are those who maintain that George Sand destroyed Frederic Chopin and others who say that Chopin ruined Sand. Amidst all these conflicting views, I begin to form my own feelings on the subject—feelings independent of the material.

LIES, HINTS AND SILENCES

As it happens, most of the people I've written about were fairly literate, so I read what they wrote about themselves. They may have written reams—journals, letters, autobiographies, or works of literature with an autobiographical slant. I read, knowing most of what I read will be useless; I'm just looking for the nuggets.

It might be supposed that one could find the "truth" by going to original journals and letters. But from long experience I've decided something about journals and letters: they lie. Letters tell others what we want them to know, sometimes what the recipient wants most to hear. I'm quite certain people don't reveal themselves fully in letters.

Christina of Sweden and Cardinal Azzolino wrote to each other voluminously—in French, the common language in which this Swede and this Italian could communicate. Their correspondence was discovered two centuries later by the Swedish Minister to Rome and published in 1889. With long and difficult labor, I read every word of this rare volume in the original French. It contains only the letters of Christina to Azzolino. The letters are exceedingly decorous and formal. She writes endlessly about property and paintings and certain managerial offices she is requesting him to perform for her. All perfectly proper, all queenly.

Then, after hundreds of pages, there is this one phrase in one of her letters: "Since duty forbids you from becoming my lover, let me always remain your slave." This one sentence, this crack in the facade, is the gem on which one can build mountains of suppositions. The proof of Christina's love for Azzolino is not in the content but in the voluminous quantity of letters she wrote him—letters about everything *but* love—except for this one sentence. The proof of his love for her is this: When she died, he was her executor. The first thing he did after her death was to burn his letters to her. What we would know if we had those!

To me, that's an eloquent story—those silences, those evasions. The same thing happens with Mary Shelley's journal. It breaks off completely at the time of her deepest marital troubles. If one read only the journal, and not outside sources, one wouldn't suspect she had deep problems. With Wilson, too, it's the conspiracy of silence, the sketchy brevity of his inner circle's accounts of his health during the critical days of his illness, which gives us the clue to its gravity. All those in his inner circle wrote that he was seriously ill, but not one said he had a stroke and was in a coma. Not one tells us how long he was unconscious, they don't even say that he was.

Letters reveal the semi-public face of the writer, but journals reveal the private. Yet journals, too, can deeply deceive. Why are journals written? Sometimes they are written as an objective chronicle of what happened—which makes them dry and almost useless because the subjective is utterly missing. Sometimes they're written as a record for posterity—meaning they're written for others to read. In this case, they are tricky to interpret because they are usually self-serving and often not accurate. Journals kept for others to read are extremely selective, with some things recorded, others excluded. Obviously, the most interesting material can be what's excluded.

Some people use their journals to create a whole other self—a person no one knows, the person they'd like to be but aren't—or the person they are but don't want anybody else to know. In this case, the persona of the journals can reveal (or hide) a totally different person from accounts given by others.

Some people use journals to justify their actions. Others use them to work out their problems, to confess. The confessional journal (particularly if kept secretly) is the most delicious, the most useful, the most in touch with the writer's inner life. But such a journal tends to catch the writer only in specific moods—rage, joy or melancholy only. On the other hand, someone known for depression may not record it. Virginia Woolf's next-to-last entry in her diary—only a few days before her suicide—ends: "And now to cook the Haddock." Journals can sound absolutely reasoned, balanced and in control of circumstance when their authors are in great mental disarray. Hallie Flanagan had a nervous breakdown and was told by her psychiatrist to write the story of her life. Her brief account under those circumstances is both unemotional and moving. The writing of it is not only a good source for those writing about her—it was also her cure.

So one mustn't be deceived about what one finds in letters and journals. The self is a highly protective creature; letters and journals are its armor. Even at their most confessional, they can be written not to reveal, but to conceal. People may write down what they feel, but it certainly isn't *all* they feel.

And it's necessary to remember that in the past, just as today, most important scenes happened not in letters, but face to face, with no one but the participants present. Though we live in an age of constant emails, of Facebook and Twitter, of recorded phone calls and hidden cameras, there are still, thank heaven, some scenes which happen absolutely *à deux*. Who really knows what lovers said to each other, or what occurred in that devastating argument just before they parted?

It is my job, the playwright's job, to fill in the silences. It is as much by what's *not* in the letters and journals as what *is*, that one creates the play. It's in this rich area of conjecture that the playwright exercises intuition and imagination. It is to reveal the color and the content of those lacunae that much of biographical playwriting exists. In fact, imagining the emotions and events within these silences is the heart of the dramatist's work. Unlike the documentarian, venturing into the unknown and making it palpable is the playwright's preserve.

Here the dramatic writer has a great advantage over the scholar. For, while the scholar is stuck with "facts", the playwright not only can, but must, fill in the substance of the areas of obscurity and conjecture. Where the biographer reverts to dots, blanks, footnotes and "we don't knows", the dramatist leaps off into the darkness and illuminates it. If the playwright's instinct and empathy are correct, what is filled into those silences will be truer than "truth", more insightful than "fact".

In a creative, almost unconscious way, I always have my sensors out, alert for magical insights. Often, in the research phase, I can be going through items or artifacts and suddenly one will leap out, bringing a sudden feeling of contact and illumination. This happened while I was going through pieces of memorabilia from Sarah Bernhardt in the Arsenal, the theater collection of the Bibliothèque Nationale in Paris. Suddenly I realized I was holding in my hand the original printed notice of a sale of jewelry by "Madame Sarah Bernhardt Damala". Just one year after she married her only husband, she was forced to sell her jewels to pay for his other women and his cocaine. Bernhardt's use of Damala's name after hers struck me as both very valiant and very poignant. They were *her* jewels, after all; he had nothing to do with the purchase of them. Out of what anger, what disappointment, what betrayed love, was she selling her valuables? Holding that small card in my hand made Bernhardt seem to me extremely close and real.

TRAVEL AND TOURISM

Another delight of the research phase is going on journeys of discovery, pilgrimages to some site connected with the person whose life I'm trying to probe and understand. I enjoy these trips, but I must confess that they provide such a flood of detail that they're much more valuable for book or film writing. For the writing of a play they can end up being almost useless. One can have a wonderful touristy time, spend a lot of money, have marvelous feelings of communing with the spirit of the person—then find one can use, from the trip, almost nothing at all.

I visited George Sand's country house a year after I wrote GEORGE AND FREDERIC. It's a gracious manor house in a walled enclave within Nohant, a small village south of Paris. There they were—her writing desks, and the very piano on which Chopin used to play for her in the evenings. There were the puppets she sewed with her own hands so the family could put on shows. The countryside had a mystical beauty. The deep moist green of the fields was magical, and at night the sky and everything beneath it seemed to glow. I stood in front of Sand's grave under a tree in her own garden and communed with her. ... And, from this superb journey, I used, in the play, nothing at all.

It was the same with Eleanor of Aquitaine. I stood in front of her tomb in the Abbey of Fontevrault. It's one of the most beautiful and unusual abbeys in France, and was then being restored. Inside the soaring Romanesque nave, with its stones freshly scrubbed to a pale ivory, there was nothing, absolutely nothing—except, on the spacious empty floor, four stone coffins with carved stone figures lying on top of them: Eleanor, her husband Henry II, her son Richard the Lionheart, and her youngest son King John.

I stood in awe, gazing at those four stone coffins with the carved horizontal figures on them, overwhelmed that the bones of the people with whom I'd spent so much time, and whom I felt I knew so well, were actually within. There they were. The four of them. Their presence was palpable. I was deeply moved. ... But as far as the play was concerned, this visit supplied me with nothing.

I have stood outside Sarah Bernhardt's house in Paris and inside Woodrow Wilson's house in Washington D.C. and although I have found those visits moving and infinitely interesting, what they added to what I could incorporate into the plays about Sarah or Woodrow was virtually nothing.

ATTACHMENT TO AND USE OF RAW MATERIALS

There can be great pleasure in visiting the sites, reading the life, pouring through the scrapbooks and appreciating the memorabilia of one's subject—but there's a danger also. One can fall too much in love with the materials. This happened to me with SARAH IN AMERICA. It fascinated me that

Bernhardt had touched the American landscape in so many places, that she'd actually played Keokuk, that she'd visited a steel mill in Pittsburgh, that she'd stood at Niagara Falls. In New York I spent hours turning the pages of the scrapbooks of Sarah Bernhardt's American tours and reading the crisp and fading newspaper clippings pasted in from publications across the country.

I was so enamored of her itinerary that I mentioned as many places as I could in the play. Until we opened out of town, none of us realized that the travel anecdotes which so delighted us in rehearsal had no meaning when delivered to an audience on the other side of the proscenium. I told my director, Sir Robert Helpmann, that we had to cut back. We had to stick to the dramatic line of Bernhardt's personal trials and tribulations and to her growth as an actress and human being, so that her journey in the landscape would be subordinated to her personal journey.

However, we were now stuck with the director's highly realistic and mechanized production. When writing the play I'd envisioned a very simple set with only the movement of light to suggest scene changes. Helpmann, however, saw it another way. When Bernhardt mentioned Pittsburgh, he saw, and we had, red lights and factory whistles and real red smoke rising. When she mentioned Niagara, we had blue lights and fans and tons of dry ice sending torrents of mist surging down, inundating the entire rear wall of the stage. For my one-person play we had three turntables, a dozen stage hands rushing to and fro backstage—and people collapsing with smoke inhalation in the audience.

When I pleaded, "Please, cut Pittsburgh and Niagara! They don't work dramatically!" I was told, "Do you know how much we spent to get those two effects up there? We can't cut them now!" So Lilli Palmer as Sarah Bernhardt went to Pittsburgh and Niagara every night of that run—and as soon as the play closed I grabbed back the script and tore out those pages and wrote new ones, based on what I felt Sarah was feeling. In subsequent productions the new scenes worked—because they were based on psychological truth not on "facts" hung on no inner armature.

Now I know I have to be ruthless about throwing wonderful things away. I'll find some superb incident, or anecdote, or quote—and I can't fit it in. I know I must junk it, resist it at all costs. If it repeats a point I've already made, if it is poignant but has no real significance, if it is charming but not integral to what I'm saying, I have to jettison it. A narrative biography can include everything, but a play can't use digressions. In a play, a digression is like a crack in a vase. Even if it's only the littlest crack, everything in the vessel will flow out.

Some plays are more closely related to their materials than others. Of the plays I've written, most take an imaginative leap and quote almost nothing from any basic material. Two, however, have texts based solidly on existing materials and these required me to be even more ruthless and decisive in excising than the others. In JOSHUA SLOCUM SAILING ALONE AROUND THE WORLD there was the tremendous challenge of telling the whole story of his circumnavigation, which he told in his long book, but telling it in two acts totalling ninety minutes. I had to sense what would hold in performance and what would not. There are some portions of his tale which are stand-out stories but which would take so long to relate that they didn't fit the pace of the flow and compacting them would eviscerate their meaning. They had to go—for the feeling of this play had to be that Slocum was ever moving onward.

In HALLIE I based the play squarely on the texts of the Federal Theatre's hearings before the House Committee on Un-American Activities. The hearings took days, and many many hours, and covered many many pages. My drama had to come in within the two hours' traffic of the stage and to be without the digressions and convolutions which characterize official happenings—but I also wanted to quote enough from the original hearings so the Committee Members would damn themselves out of their own mouths.

Shaping these two plays was a different task from shaping most of the plays I've written, but the principles were the same. The main point is this: One has to know what one's trying to say in the play and say no more and no less than that. If one takes the research phase directly into the writing phase without vision or organization—or even with too much love—one will be betrayed.

I know I've come to the end of the research phase when my notes start repeating themselves, or when I haven't taken a note in a week. Like Brick, in *Cat on a Hot Tin Roof,* who knows he's drunk when he gets a click in his head, I get a click that says I'm drunk with the material—and I'm ready to write.

FORGETTING, STRUCTURING, AND INVENTING

Actually, what I'm ready to do is organize. The organization part—the structuring—is of supreme importance in any play. But unlike the early creative phase with any other kind of play, where the mind usually creates scenes and structures from the beginning, with the biographical play one is not only doing that but has also absorbed acres of dross. What must happen now is most important—and perhaps most shocking. One must begin to forget.

The process of forgetting all the myriad facts one has absorbed is comparable to a painter squinting at a landscape in order to erase the details and see only the important forms, the essence. During this part of the process I must move away from the material, let it become a haze until it forms and takes shape again, not into notes and facts, but into a play. In order to do this I must shut my eyes and see only what I want to see. I have to let some things speak to me and some remain silent. I am not trying to become an authority on the subject, I am not preparing for a quiz, I am taking from the basic material only what I need in order to do what I hope I do best: create. It is during this process of forgetting, of abstracting, that what was mere material begins to be transformed from objective lumps of clay into (I hope) art.

And so, as I build the structure, I am letting some things go and choosing others. I am selecting and I am inventing.

Selectivity and invention are the essence of biographical play writing—the choosing and creating of telling moments and details. The way something needs to happen in order to be dramatic is seldom the way it happens in life. Plays have structure; life doesn't. Life is messy; plays are, by comparison, neat. Life is repetitive; a play can't be. In life, situations are seldom solved, character hardly ever develops. The essence of drama is solution (or at least resolution) and change.

Life is frequently understatement, evasion, confusion, avoidance of scenes more often than having them. Drama can be these sometimes, but not all the time. Characters must engage, situations must develop, climaxes and resolutions must occur. In this sense, drama is the antithesis of life, for life often seems formless, and drama must have form. That's why people find so much satisfaction in watching drama—it's like watching life, but life which has form. It's the gratification of the spectator's unconscious desire for form and meaning in events which provides drama's greatest pleasure.

In the process of making Art out of Life, I adapt, rearrange, refocus, invent, create. It isn't easy, even for the masters. Shakespeare's history plays soar— but slightly less consistently than his comedies and tragedies. Even in *his* hands, real lives don't hang together as well as made-up stories do.

With some subjects, there's an obligatory scene—Joan at her trial, for example—and one knows damn well one's going to have to have it. If it's a well-known scene, it's the hardest thing to write—because everybody already knows it. They're going to compare their idea of the scene with the idea put forth in this drama. That may be the point, of course: the writer may be counting on the viewer's pre-knowledge as a reference in order to show a variation of a hackneyed moment. One can come at such a scene obliquely (in fact, in this day and age one had better!), but one can't avoid it. Deal with the later life of Van Gogh and the ear-slicing-off scene has to be there. Avoid it and audiences and critics will notice nothing else.

Some lives are shaped so dramatically that the form of the play comes easily and seems best told straightforwardly, naturalistically, chronologically. With others, the dramatic solution may be more complex. When I decided to write about Christina of Sweden, two aspects of her life interested me. One was her life in Sweden, leading up to why she abdicated. The other was her great love for Cardinal Azzolino after her abdication, in Rome. I puzzled for a long time over how to tell both of these quite different stories. If I told one first and the other second, the drama seemed to have a break in the middle and neither story related to the other.

I solved the problem by setting the play in the form of Christina's confession to the Cardinal, with flashbacks to her earlier life, from childhood to her abdication. In this way I had two time frames running simultaneously. It gave the play a richness and chiaroscuro which a simple chronological line wouldn't have. It also allowed me to show only the salient dramatic moments in both stories—and to completely avoid the dross.

Also, in this play, I broke up the leading character into three parts: the adult Christina and two rival parts of her younger self, Chris and Tina, who represent, roughly, her masculine and feminine sides. This technique, too, allowed me to move away from "facts" to concentrate on my individual interpretation of Christina's character.

With EMPRESS OF CHINA I made a decision to have all the action take place within the walls of the Forbidden City and, in order to show the conflict between the Empress and her nephew, the Emperor Kuang-Hsu, to have the scenes alternate between their courts. I also consciously decided to have, in each scene, some physical object—a prop or set piece—as a major plot or symbolic element. Between the opening image of Shen-tai on the rack and the closing image of Tzu-Hsi dressed as a peasant fleeing in a cart are such elements as the clocks, the bicycle, the artificial flowers tied to a barren tree, etc. These were consciously and purposely created to key each scene to a particular image and provide the possibility for a simple production whose sets, costumes and props would create ideas in space.

In SARAH IN AMERICA I wanted to present an actress on tour from ages thirty-six to seventy-two. In early productions I had a silent maid who was there for the prime purpose of helping the actress change costumes. Since all the other characters are imagined, I began to feel this was a stylistic inconsistency. And after one particular production, where the actress playing the maid took to folding and unfolding large white napery behind the star's big scenes, I finally eliminated this silent character.

My major aim in SARAH IN AMERICA was to write a one-person play, not a narrative. Many one-person plays have the actor come on stage made up to look like the character and costumed in the character's clothes and stand there and address the audience—simply telling the life in retrospect in story form: "This is what I did, and then I did that, and then I did the other..." This is impersonation, not dramatization. My aim was to *dramatize*—to have the action unfold on the present plane, with the events happening as we watched. The only difference between SARAH IN AMERICA and a large-cast multi-scened play is that in my play all the characters except Bernhardt are imaginary. Using the accepted convention of some types of monologues, she talks to people—but they aren't physically there.

I should add that this was a heck of a lot harder to write than a conventional "and then I did" narrative performance, and that some who saw this play had no comprehension of what I was attempting. Some people didn't have enough imagination to "see" or "hear" the absent characters. Of course the burden on the actress—to create those invisible characters, to shift swiftly from one emotion to another without outside impetus, and to do without the crutch of being able to constantly hold an audience's attention through direct communication—is immense. But in my opinion the challenge—in the performance and in the imagination required of the audience—increases the enjoyment and is worth the effort involved.

In ELEANOR OF AQUITAINE there's an even longer portion of a life covered—from 16 to 82. Here the style I invented was to have the scenes flow one into the other, like a lap dissolve in film, so there is the sense of life hurtling onward. Eleanor is in the middle of one time and place and suddenly she is in another time and place entirely. This technique helps fortify the theme—of event after event happening to her swiftly and unexpectedly over a whole life—and of her trying to gain control over her existence, like a rider trying to keep a runaway horse on course.

With each of these choices of style I was creating by using the raw material as clay, but I was making my own sculpture, my own work of art, out of that clay. There was not a mere transcribing of events, there was deliberate interpretation, and that interpretation was based on my feelings of how best to communicate my ideas to an audience in a theatre.

TRANSFORMING LIFE INTO ART

There are other techniques normally used in writing biographical plays. One is leaving out characters or combining several characters into one. Another is compacting time. Another is cutting out events, especially repetitions. Another is changing the sequence of events to make them more effective. To avoid soliloquy or direct address, thoughts that a character had alone (recorded in a diary, for example) may be communicated in a scene to someone else. One is constantly inventing scenes which may have taken place but for which there is no evidence. One can also have scenes which one definitely knows did not occur.

This last will have every academic authority writing letters to the New York Times but, for purposes of the drama, creating such scenes is entirely justifiable. Not only justifiable, but necessary. History records that Elizabeth the First never went to the tower to confront Mary of Scotland just before Mary was beheaded but Schiller has her go there and it's the best scene of his play—the confrontation scene—the one which climaxes the drama and puts closure to the relationship. It's the scene one's waiting for throughout the play; if it didn't happen, the play would be dry and unsatisfying—like life.

Such a totally invented scene is not justified if its contents have nothing to do with truth or its substance is completely at odds with reality (unless, of course, a fantastical interpretation is the point). In this case, while Mary and Elizabeth never said what they say in this scene *to each other*, what they say was surely what they were thinking on their own or saying to those in their separate courts. To have them confront in person may not be "truth" but it is good play writing.

I have the same kind of scene in THE SECOND MRS WILSON. In the play, after Wilson's stroke, Mrs Wilson asks Senator Henry Cabot Lodge to come to the White House. In a major confrontation scene, Lodge and Wilson face off against each other, giving their opposing views on the subject of the United States joining the League of Nations. It's a tense and dramatic scene—one where the opponents are truly engaged, *mano a mano*. I've watched audiences be completely absorbed in this combat. The positions in this confrontation were uttered by the two men in an earlier White House meeting, but I have them enunciated here, face to face, at a time when Wilson was seeing nobody. Should I have stuck to "truth" and not had them confront at this moment in person? Or should I stick to *dramatic* truth and not commit the one crime drama must never be guilty of—the only hanging sin—being dull? I made my choice.

THE THEME

All plays must be written around a central idea. Sometimes that idea or theme is apparent to the playwright from the beginning and is the reason for writing the play. At other times the theme of the play evolves more slowly. At some point in the creation of a play—the earlier the better—the writer knows or feels what the whole thing is really about. Sometimes that knowledge is objective, sometimes it's an instinct, but it must be present.

There is an inner necessity about a dramatic presentation which cries out for organization around a theme. Anything which does not fit this theme, no matter how interesting, is outside the realm of the play. If the lack of a *raison d'être* for a scene isn't apparent during the writing process, it will become painfully apparent in performance when, in the audience's presence, the play falls to pieces before the writer's eyes.

We've all been subjected to dramatizations which are dogged detailed renderings of the events of a person's life but which don't hang together as drama. This is because a play is constantly, subliminally, asking the question: "Why?" *Why* was Joan condemned to burn at the stake? *Why* did Galileo recant? *Why* did Joshua Slocum sail alone around the world and Christina abdicate the throne of Sweden? It's not just the events, but the *significance* of the events which the best drama presents.

If that significance isn't totally clear during the research phase, it's worth days, weeks, even months during the structuring phase to let that significance rise up to the writer's consciousness and be able to be felt or stated. Every play must have a leading idea. This leading idea becomes a "to prove" against which every scene must resonate in an onward scene-by-scene development. Writing about a life without an organizing theme is possible ("and then she did this, and then she did that...") but very soon the dramatization will dissolve into meaninglessness. A sequence of events may seem like a structure, but unless that sequence is suffused with meaning, the structure will crumble. The edifice will not stand.

There is nothing more important than grappling with this challenge—finding the *significance* of the events and actions. Not paying attention to this aspect at this phase can mean *years* of problems down the line.

THE EMOTIONAL MATRIX

Important as it is to write having in mind a leading theme or idea, it's equally important to write within an emotional matrix. Gertrude Stein said, "Remarks are not literature." To which Theodore Kalem, former drama critic of *Time* magazine, added, "Information is not drama." Unlike an encyclopedia entry, a biographical play must, at every moment, be infused with both meaning and emotion. The audience has to not only see what's going on with the characters, but feel it.

A biographical play isn't just a presentation of the life, it's a presentation of the life infused with and transformed by the dramatic imagination. As such, it reaches the audience not only through the mind, but through the heart. To do that requires an imaginative leap and often far more perception than is required of an author of narrative biography. Narrative biographers often avoid speculating about emotions or motivations. They are allowed to equivocate: "Maybe Mister X felt guilty about this action—or he may have been utterly callous. We don't know." In drama, a decision must be made. An audience will want to *know* whether Mister X is feeling guilt or is utterly callous.

If the writer doesn't make a choice and give a clue to Mister X's feelings, the audience will make that decision on its own, perhaps one the playwright didn't intend. Any emotion the playwright doesn't specify will be filled in by the actors and the audience who are constantly judging and coming to conclusions. The skilled playwright presents the characters' emotions so that, while the subtler points may be open to interpretation, the major motivations will be clear.

JOURNEYING UNAFRAID INTO TERRA INCOGNITA

Narrative writers can also leave holes where they don't have facts or skip swiftly over events which are central. I am surprised at how often, when reading a biography, I'll be curious about what happened and how (I'm not even now talking about the deeper issue of "why"), and there'll be next to nothing written about it. Not one of the accounts I read about Wilson's stroke in September of 1919 was specific about how long he was unconscious. Most don't even indicate that he *did* have a stroke. I can understand reticence on the part of the inner circle, who might have feared being accused of a cover-up. But what about later writers? Isn't that a very obvious question to want answered? And if it isn't going to be answered, shouldn't the narrative writer raise the question and answer it with an "I don't know?"

It's within the "I don't know's" that the dramatic writer has to let go of the original material's holes and equivocations and float free, where more truth may be found by departing from fact than by slavishly sticking to it. In that way, the imagination creates a scene which is both invented and dramatically true. For example: In ELEANOR OF AQUITAINE the facts are that, sometimes dressed as an Amazon, Eleanor went with her husband, Louis VII of France, on a Crusade. On the way, because one of Eleanor's knights disobeyed a command, many of Louis' troops were killed in battle. Louis' minister blamed Eleanor for the slaughter and insisted that Louis make her toe the line. Eleanor refused to be humiliated into accepting a lifetime of humble obedience and felt that if these were the terms for continuing the marriage then it must be dissolved.

Having Eleanor and Louis thrash this out as a marital argument seemed to me both trite and out of character for Louis, who was later made a saint and who deeply loved Eleanor. Instead, I decided to have Louis, doing penance for the loss of his men, take a vow of silence. Eleanor comes to him to ask him what she should do about his minister's demand that she bend herself completely to his will from now on. Louis doesn't answer. She says that if she must become a shadow, a non-person, she will seek a divorce. Is that what he wants? He doesn't speak a word. She asks for a sign, any sign, to communicate to her his wishes. But Louis, torn between his faith and his love, says nothing and continues praying. Taking his silence for rejection, Eleanor leaves, walking out of his life forever.

I had no factual basis for Louis' vow of silence, but it works dramatically and keeps me from having to duplicate the same kind of confrontation scene which Eleanor later has with her second husband, Henry II. The incidents belong to history; the method of portraying them in scenes is mine. In ways like this, drama departs from reality, saying the same things, but with more interest, more meaning and more emotion. Once again: In theatre, the greatest crime isn't inaccuracy, the greatest crime is to be boring.

ONE'S OWN VOICE

Every playwright knows that in making a play out of someone else's life, we're making that life our own. What's presented is not the life, it's the author's point of view about that life. So two dramatizations of the same life can be wildly dissimilar. My view of Eleanor of Aquitaine as the gracious independent sovereign who presides over the Courts of Love is diametrically opposite from James Goldman's Eleanor, the suburban hausfrau harpy in THE LION IN WINTER. Shakespeare's Cleopatra is not Shaw's. Shakespeare's is grand, tragic, magnificent; Shaw's is spoiled, kittenish, afraid. While Shaw has his young Cleopatra exhibit a certain amount of wilfulness and command toward the end of his play, I don't think his queen could ever grow into Shakespeare's Cleopatra any more than Shaw could grow into Shakespeare.

Any play by Shaw, comedy or tragedy, will be filled with wit. His Saint Joan is like no one else's. She may end up on the stake, but there's plenty of banter on the way to the flames. Ingrid Bergman told me that Shaw was furious because she'd acted a Saint Joan and it wasn't *his* Saint Joan. He summoned her to Ayot St Lawrence and confronted her with the matter. She was unapologetic, telling him he hadn't portrayed the "real" Joan, that his Joan was far too clever. "You've made her say a lot of things the real Saint Joan wouldn't have dreamt of saying," Ingrid told Shaw.

I had this same situation with Bergman. She was the first actress to want to play Christina on stage in THE ABDICATION. She invited me to her country house in Choiselle, south of Paris. I flew over to France and stayed in a small guest house by her pool. Every morning Ingrid would come across the grass from the big house bringing me coffee and slices of fresh baguette on a tray. We would sit by the pool and discuss the play. In Ingrid's view, I hadn't portrayed the "real" Christina. Ingrid had a tiny book with a red cover which contained Christina's Maxims. How could I have failed to use any of them in my dramatization, she wanted to know. The book was a collection of pious homilies; not only could no one live by them, I don't think Christina did herself. Unless quoted cynically, which was not what Ingrid had in mind, these sayings had absolutely nothing to do with what I was trying to express in THE ABDICATION.

Ingrid Bergman was one of the most beautiful and gracious people to walk the earth; I was very lucky to have had some personal contact with her. Possibly because of my youth and her beauty I never got the courage to say, "Ingrid, this is *my* Christina. Yours is yours. Your vision of the 'real' Christina may be just as valid as mine, but since this is my play, this is the Christina I'm portraying."

While I didn't dare use the possessive pronoun then, I use it now. If an actor or actress comes to me with an open reference book saying I've left out this or that, or that I've put in something other than what their book says, or why don't we just change such-and-such to make it more like their idea of the character, I reply courteously, "This is my vision of that character. If you want some other vision, write your own play."

Every writer has his or her own tone. The better the writer, the stronger and more unique the tone. There's nothing you can do to change it any more than you can change the type of blood which flows in your veins. It pours out—

and Shakespeare comes out Shakespeare, Molière comes out Molière, Ibsen comes out Ibsen, Williams comes out Williams—no matter whose persona they pretend to be adopting. Shakespeare's heroes and heroines will always have deep soundings. Molière's will always have a comic sense. Giraudoux's characters will always have distinctly oblique motivations. When Giraudoux's Judith raises her knife to kill Holofernes, it won't be because she hates him but because she loves him. Turning historically recorded motivations topsy-turvy is Giraudoux's dramatic method, his surprise.

My own voice is a civilized voice, a humanist's voice, a voice tinged with irony, obliquity and compassion, a voice reflecting a balanced perspective, often juxtaposing tragedy and comedy, suddenly, side by side. I have (and I know it is unpopular in these times) a vision which looks upward. No matter how far away my characters may be from achieving their ideals in this world, there is always a projection of those ideals within them. And no matter what I may think of their goals personally, the plays always reflect my admiration for their attempts.

Every actor who plays a role will play it differently. But somewhere within that portrayal is the voice of the playwright, and no matter how strong or how good the actor, in the best plays, the playwright's voice shines through. I have seen THE ABDICATION performed quite a few times, but possibly the best performance of Christina I ever saw was in the French language production in Montreal. Here, the actress playing the role was not afraid to be unattractive—an indication given both in the text and the character description.

I appreciate actors and actresses who take the clues for their performances from the text and not from outside sources. When an actor prepares, it is up to the playwright to indicate all the actor needs to know.

CONTEMPORANEITY

Just as a biographical play is an expression of the author's mind and sensibility, so it is an expression of the *now*. No matter what era it's dealing with, the best biographical play isn't a "historical" play, it's a contemporary play. If it comes out of a living author's mind, it comes out of the present and is a reflection of the present world view. While its ideas are of this very moment, at it's best a historically-based play portrays psychologies and interrelationships which are eternal. It may deal with the past, but the better it is, the more timeless it is, the more it has to say to the present.

During the German occupation of Paris in World War II the Nazis never seemed to catch on that Anouilh's ANTIGONE, which was playing in the theater nightly, was not about some ancient Greek heroine fighting tyranny, it was a call for rebellion against the Nazi regime. At that same time, Albert Camus, fighting in the French Resistance, was writing his CALIGULA, another tale of tyranny. It was produced not long after the Allies reached the French capital and the lessons of the play were not lost on the newly-liberated French.

The final dress rehearsal for THE SECOND MRS WILSON at the Barter Theatre, the State Theatre of Virginia, took place on September 11, 2001. We were all thoroughly shaken by the tragic events unfolding that morning. Those events influenced audience reaction to the play. When Wilson, the internationalist, said, "America is no longer isolated. Enemy planes can now reach our shore," his words took on a whole new meaning, unfortunately an all-too-current meaning. And when Lodge, the isolationist, said, "We do not want our boys dying in far flung battlefields for causes they don't understand," his thoughts echoed many Americans' as they contemplated our involvement in Vietnam or the Middle East. It was after World War I that this country began to be considered the world's number one nation. A play written in the early 90s portraying events from 1918 to 1923 resonates with meanings for today.

While dealing with events in history, the historical play can prove itself, paradoxically, to be a play for all time, a play which seems, in every age, completely contemporary.

TODAY OR YESTERDAY

In dealing with the past, then, how much responsibility does the playwright have to set the character within his or her particular time? How much of the flavor of the past time needs to be captured? It depends on what the playwright is trying to do.

Some eras have customs which hold people more tightly within their period than do others. Conservative times. Times with strong rules. In America, witch-burning belongs to a specific century. Yet Arthur Miller used THE CRUCIBLE, a play deep within its own period and customs, to make a moral statement about the witch-hunts of our times and it has become his most-produced play. Another play, THE BARRETTS OF WIMPOLE STREET, is more shackled to its period. It is hard to picture an Elizabeth Barrett Browning of today submitting as long as she did to the possessiveness of a tyrannical father.

In the sexually permissive age in which we now live many plays which punish lovers just for having love affairs seem antediluvian. Those plays can only be done if firmly attached to their period. Moral outlook is the unspoken unacknowledged sensor through which the collective audience views a stage work. If the general moral outlook is the same, a play can fit with any century. If the general moral outlook is in conflict with the present, the play and the attitudes of its characters seem dated and passé.

Of all the plays I've written, perhaps the one furthest from my culture and experience is EMPRESS OF CHINA. All of its characters are Chinese—which I am not. It takes place in a court whose customs I never experienced. How dare I choose a Chinese Empress as a subject! I dare because I felt that, beyond the customs and traditions of an exotic empire was a woman—a woman whose feelings were not so different from any ruler's feelings—and a ruler's feelings are not so different from any human's. On a larger scale, perhaps. With larger consequences. But I felt a kinship with Tzu-Hsi's struggle and I felt that, in my individual view of her and of the events of that time, I could "get it right." The play has been presented many times, by Asian and Caucasian companies and to audiences of varied persuasions. Their responses have been gratifying. People respond to the human drama unfolding. The customs of the distant court are only incidental. What matters is the human interaction, and this is universal, in any time, any place, and with any race.

The timelessness of plays may be reinforced in the design of the sets and costumes. In THE ABDICATION my aim was to show a modern problem through a historical character. For that reason, I stipulated an abstract modern set design which would release the characters from their specific time. I fought for that in its premiere production at the Bristol Old Vic in Bath, England, but I lost. In that production the action of the play seemed really to be taking place in an antechamber of the Vatican—with realistic costumes and a set with a Tiepolo ceiling and Bernini-like sculpted angels. Because of that setting, the play looked, in its first incarnation, like a musty revival. And the audience had to work harder to understand the play's contemporary reference.

The play's Italian production by Il Gruppo Arte Drammatica and its United States premiere at the Eureka Theater in San Francisco, two very different productions, recovered the play's contemporaneity. The Italian production was designed by Mario Ceroli, a prominent sculptor. The light airy proscenium set featured simple Scandinavian wooden slats with profiles of figures in wood. The Eureka production featured a very simple black space stage consisting of various platforms in different shapes and sizes. Both productions were modern, as was the production in The Hague, which featured a tilted circular platform with only a bench-like box as a set piece. These designs released the play from its specific period—as I had intended. Following my set description, these deliberately non-period productions raised the play to the plane of ideas and brought it into direct communication with the audience. It was what I was trying to do in that particular play.

LANGUAGE

One knotty problem in setting characters in time is language. Should they speak the way we do now or the way we imagine they did then? Suppose one wrote a play which took place in Elizabethan England? Should it be written in some simulacrum of Elizabethan English? While much of what Shakespeare wrote may seem stilted and "poetic" to us, I suspect some of the superb musical quality of his characters' poetry was part of Elizabethan everyday speech and therefore seemed, to them, heightened but not unnatural. Our imitation of it, however, would seem distinctly *un*natural. Must a writer writing today about the past have to attempt that time's rhythms, vocabulary, and language?

In other words, in dealing with any past period, what should one use—their language or ours? The answer is a compromise. Expressions, words, sentence constructions and methods of address from the past can be used to give flavor, but it's absurd to use what seems to us to be stilted language—because the language of people who lived in the past wasn't stilted to them. We have to use what sounds right to us. The point isn't to call attention to archaic ways of speech, but to use language as a window so we see through the speech to the ideas, characters and emotions within.

There's a delicate balance between making a play seem faithful to the time it's portraying and making something comprehensible and not absurd. It's a question of taste and common sense. Slang dates itself faster than any other word usage and, if used to indicate a specific period, should be used sparingly unless it's meant deliberately for comic effect. Use of the slang of another day can help anchor a character to a period. On the other hand, when a character in the past uses today's slang it stands out like a sore thumb and that kind of anachronistic word usage should be avoided.

The way characters speak should feel appropriate to them—but it should also feel appropriate to us. In WINTERSET, Maxwell Anderson tries to make fictional poetic drama out of the aftermath of the Sacco and Vanzetti case. His high-flown language sets our teeth on edge today not only because we've left behind the age of Anderson and Christopher Fry and all "poetic" drama, but because Anderson's poetry doesn't seem appropriate to working-class characters. At the time when those lines were written, however, audiences and critics had a reverence for this kind of poetry or heightened prose.

Finding the right verbal expression for a historical play might seem like a challenge but its solutions are almost automatic to an author exercising common sense and instinct. Speech changes with class, education and circumstance. More formal speech is used by the more educated classes and by all classes in formal situations. Less formal speech is used by less educated classes and in less formal situations. And, of course, speech is the expression of what a person is thinking. If the thought is graceful, the expression should be. If the thought is halting and lame, the expression should be, too. This obtains whether the time frame is the past or the present. The only rule is to be at ease with language and avoid obvious anachronisms.

Language is only an external characteristic. Basically, the human animal doesn't change over time. Society's rules may change but human psychology doesn't. The basic loves, hates, jealousies, fears—that's what plays are about, and they're timeless. Everything else, all the surface details, pale to insignificance beside the human eternal drama being portrayed. The language used should be that which helps communicate what's going on, rather than distancing audiences from it. It should be a language which doesn't call attention to itself, but which disappears even as it illuminates, so the audience takes for granted the medium and gets the message.

AUTHENTICITY

What, then, does the writer of the biographical play owe to the god of authenticity? Unless it's the point of the story, one doesn't go out of one's way to disregard basic verities—to have Napoleon win the battle of Waterloo or the South win the War between the States. Criticism from know-it-alls goes with the territory. And while no one gives kudos for accuracy, the knives are out for any departures from accepted facts. For that reason I enjoy Jean Anouilh's confession in the introduction to his play, BECKET. He tells us that in the play he makes a big point of establishing a rivalry between Henry II and Thomas à Becket based on the fact that Henry is Norman and Becket is Anglo-Saxon, two rival groups. In this introduction, however, he reveals that he later discovered both were Norman—and that almost no one noticed his error. In fact, he says, this rather basic deviation from truth enhanced rather than marred the effectiveness of the drama.

In this day and age one cannot count on such not-noticing. Genuine authorities and critics who have become sudden authorities on a play's subject will rise up wielding verbal brickbats for any obvious misstatements of the facts.

The sophisticated viewer will, however, understand the parameters of artistic license. The playwright, too, will understand and not stretch the bounds of believability beyond their limits. The first and most obvious departure from authenticity results from the stage's necessity for severe compression. Everything is going to happen within two hours—sometimes less, sometimes more. Years can pass within those two revolutions of the clock. And the players can visit all the earth and the moon on that one small platform. This compression—the limitation of real time and space—is the overwhelming challenge to truth on the stage. Given this severe limitation, it's a miracle that a writer of biographical plays ever manages to give even the *illusion* of accuracy. If someone lived eighty years, or 700,800 hours, and this is to be dramatized, what will be represented is 1/350, 400th of a life—the distilled essence.

By coming to the theatre, the audience enters into an unspoken pact with the playwright. With both parties accepting severe compression as a given, the playwright's essential responsibility is to tell the truth *as the playwright sees it*. As their side of the agreement, the audience trusts the playwright to be fair, not to deliberately lie. If the writer has a particular bias toward the material, that bias should be presented and accepted as personal vision.

Among my least favorite most-frequently-asked questions is: "Did such-and-such really happen?" If I answer yes, the questioner stands ready with the accusation that this isn't my personal creation, it's "only history.". If I answer no, the questioner stands ready to accuse me of daring to invent. Writing a play isn't the same as writing an academic treatise or reporting for a newspaper. The main point isn't to inform; the main point is to entertain. The aims of playwriting are: to entertain, to move, to give insight—in that order. And while this doesn't give the playwright license for unlimited invention, it does give license to heighten and make dramatic scenes which were dry and dull in actuality. It also gives license to imagine and invent scenes which may or may not have occurred.

Unlike real life, every second on stage must be interesting. Dramatic. There must be a sequence of climaxes, constant absorption in the events unfolding, and a satisfactory and moving resolution. How much should the writer twist reality in order to satisfy these basic rules of the theatre?

One can write scenes which never happened and scenes which one imagines but for which one has no proof. But the playwright is breaking faith with the audience if what happens is the opposite of what really did happen or is outside the laws of probability. Unless that reversal is the point of the drama, this kind of invention is a breach of trust beyond the special exigencies of theater writing. One invents within the bounds of possibility. This keeps the playwright's pact with the audience, and with the theater as an art dedicated to truth.

There is a very strange effect which takes place in fact-based plays which has the effect of fictionalizing. Nothing sits more uneasily in a play than a remark the character actually said—particularly if that remark is well-known. How, on stage, should Lincoln be shown pondering what to say in his Gettysburg Address? Should he begin, "Let me see—'Eighty-seven years ago'—no, I think it sounds better if I say: 'Four score and seven years ago'—Eureka! That's it!"? Or suppose John Paul Jones, hard-pressed in battle, suddenly cries: "I have not yet begun to fight!" Instead of giving the play authenticity, these now-hackneyed remarks leap off the stage and shock the audience out of their enthralled absorption in the drama. Bells go off in their heads. They rejoice: "I know that line! He *really* said that!"—as opposed to all the other stuff, which he didn't *really* say, the stuff the playwright wrote—and the writer is in trouble.

One can never recreate actuality. It's always an approximation. What can one do? It isn't *really* Lincoln up there. But if the work is true to the spirit of the character, something profound can happen which is closer than actuality, it is the essence of a character's being, the essence of his or her inner, perhaps never overtly expressed, truth.

Invented dialogue is anathema to honest narrative biography. But in a play, invented dialogue is often all one has. In a question-and-answer period after a performance of SARAH IN AMERICA someone asked me, "How much of the dialogue we heard was said by Sarah Bernhardt and how much was written by you?" I had to answer: "Everything was written by me except Bernhardt's two mottoes: '*Quand même*' and 'The secret of my life is will.' Also, most of the monologues in the performance scenes are actual quotations from the plays she played in. Outside of that, every word in her mouth is one I invented."

Excepting HALLIE and JOSHUA SLOCUM SAILING ALONE AROUND THE WORLD, this is the case with all of the plays I've written. I truly have *written* them—meaning that everything—except, possibly, a few sentences which are quotes—is something created by me. And that, for every playwright in this field, is as it should be. Scenes which, in a book about someone's life, might be described in descriptive paragraphs are, in a play, given dialogue, immediacy, *life*. That is, after all, the purpose of the drama.

NARRATION VS. DRAMATIZATION

In this process of bringing a character to life, it's much easier to be a narrative biographer than a writer of biographical plays. That's because it's much simpler to write *about*, to describe something, rather than to make the word flesh as one must on the stage. The narrative biographer can write: "She was witty, intelligent, exciting, constantly amusing—to be near her was to thrill to her vibrant originality and consummate enjoyment of life."

But try to put that into a scene. No adjectives, no description, nothing but dialogue—dialogue that is "witty, intelligent, exciting, constantly amusing and abundantly full of vibrant originality and the consummate enjoyment of life." It's not the world's easiest assignment.

Biographical books, films and plays each have their own different relationships to fact, truth and reality. Narrative biography requires the greatest attention to accuracy of fact. Yet a biographical book is only words—words with a few still pictures. Film documentaries can include words as narrative—but they also include portraits, or still and moving pictures of the subject, plus images of anything which can be photographed: sites associated with the subject, possessions, film or photos of the times. Filmed documentary, constrained by limitations of time and materials, must be more selective than biography on the page—and while it can, in dealing with those who lived in this century, often present actual images of the person speaking and moving about, it doesn't present the person in three dimensions. Dramatized biography on film uses an actor to impersonate the subject, but it can also show the real or recreated personal venues in which he or she lived on a vast and realistic two-dimensional canvas.

Stage biography presents the person in three dimensions. The person shown is incarnated in the shape of an actor. The presentation is, of necessity, a simulacrum, a "fiction". Yet the sense of being directly in the presence of the subject can be exceedingly strong and convincing. Book, film and stage biography each has its own separate relationship to "reality." It is the skill of the writer, the interpreter, which is responsible for determining which of these forms makes the subject come most alive.

Which of these forms, then, is closest to "truth"? Again, it depends on the insights of the interpreter. Some subjects, for one reason or another, cry out to be recreated in one medium or another. Some, for example, immediately seem "filmic". The number of characters or scenes or the desire for visual atmosphere may make incarnation in a movie the natural choice. Other subjects lend themselves to interpretation on the stage—in general those with fewer necessary characters and where words and ideas are more important than images. But "truth" has to do with the insight, wisdom and skill of the creating mind, not with the medium chosen to present the life story.

There is a paradox that stage dramatization, while existing in time and in space and in scenes unfolding in the present moment—and therefore more closely an approximation of life than any other delineation—still is not "reality". It is as if the individual forever keeps the self to the self, not allowing the precious stuff of his or her being to be stolen, ever. That great individuals are so possessive of their selves is possibly why we try so hard to steal the essence of that self and incarnate it in drama.

HAZARDS

There are certain hazards peculiar to the writing of biographical plays and fair warning must be given. The first of these, Murphy's Law of Biographical Playwriting, is: Whatever character one chooses to write about, someone else will be writing about it at the same time. Ideas seem to float on the air and be contagious. Just decide to write about somebody whom nobody else has ever heard of, who has been caught for centuries in the obscuring mist of time, and the minute one makes a decision to portray that soul, someone else will make the same decision.

This has happened to me more often than I care to think about. All one can do is ride it out. Sometimes one gets there first and best, sometimes one doesn't. Anyone who can't face this competition shouldn't write in the field of stage biography. There's no counting on luck and no escape from this danger. All one can count on is one's staying power and the hope that one has written the best play.

There are other perils, as when the public preconception of the physical characteristics of a subject is so strong that it's useless to fight it and no actor or actress fits those preconceptions. The Rhode Island Shakespeare Company perfectly cast the one man in my one-man play, JOSHUA SLOCUM SAILING ALONE AROUND THE WORLD. Like Slocum, the actor was rail thin and balding and, for the performance, grew a small grey beard just like Slocum's. However, this actor was also emotionally unbalanced and, in one of those "I can't believe this is happening" moments, he walked out the day before the opening performance.

In true show business tradition, we decided the show must go on. The director, Bob Colonna, stepped into the part. He did a splendid job—with wit, strength, variety and a marvelous freshness. The audiences at the Newport, Rhode Island performances (to whom we explained our emergency) were spellbound by his performance. However,—Colonna was a shorter, more heavy-set man. While we'd hoped to tour this production, we couldn't. There'd have been no way that anyone who was familiar with Slocum could accept this actor in this part.

A further risk in this field is the threat of getting sued under the laws which protect a living person's rights of publicity and privacy. Interestingly enough, a person has a right to control his or her public image mostly in conjunction with products, with commercial exploitation, but, except in rare instances, a public person does not have the right to control a dramatization based on his or her life. People have the right to privacy, to be left alone or not have embarrassing information revealed about them—but the more public they become, and therefore the more prone to dramatic treatment, the less privacy they have. By becoming public figures their lives become largely public domain.

If lies or details about their life they'd prefer not to have revealed are dramatized, a subject could sue for defamation, but the writer could maintain that, as a dramatization, the portrayal is a work of the imagination and is thus protected under the First Amendment. In point of fact, it is the strength of the First Amendment, guaranteeing freedom of speech and expression, which overrides almost all objections of any living subject to having their persona exhibited in a drama. A litigious subject could sue and drain the writer's financial resources, but if the writer has made the usual disclaimers—that the work does not purport to be an exact rendering of the facts or of the person's character and that the person had given up all rights to privacy by becoming a public figure—there is a very good chance that, as a creative work, the work would be allowed to live its uncensored life. However, this area is still not clearly and absolutely defined in law, so for a writer without the resources or energy to mount a long and costly legal defense, prudence would be the best policy.

For this and other reasons, therefore, the best subject is a dead subject. This is partly because time gives perspective on the life, but also because there aren't many people still around who will want to criticize, to profit from the dramatization or to throw in their two cents to tell how it "really was." Film producers routinely buy off such authorities by hiring them as "consultants", but there's seldom that much money around to do that with a stage play. There are added complexities when dealing with living subjects which the playwright must recognize and be willing to face.

When I sat around Hallie Flanagan's dining room table in her house at Paradise Pond, she was a frail older woman trembling with Hodgkin's disease, but she insisted that it shouldn't bother us, she said it didn't bother her. When, years after college, I came to write about her fight to save the Federal Theater from extinction, I remembered her indomitable spirit.

The Hallie who helmed the Federal Theater had that same spirit, but was a woman in strong middle life—not the one I'd known. The play I wrote was an objective trial drama, a court confrontation. I considered adding something of Hallie's personal life—but what kept me from doing it was meeting her daughter. It had a censoring effect. It made me hesitant to deal with Hallie's character as a mother and wife. Although I could have written more scenes portraying this side of her life, the reality of meeting someone who had actually lived the life I was writing about made the thought of my portraying it feel like an invasion of privacy. Nor did I want to be told, by a member of her family, that I didn't get things quite right. Hallie's daughter appreciated HALLIE, but I wonder how she'd have felt about a more personal view of her mother, particularly if I'd added scenes of herself when younger as a character in a play. I felt Hallie's daughter had a right not to be disturbed by my or by an actor's interpretation.

But, for me, by far the worst hazard in writing the biographical play is that anybody who can read thinks they can write your play for you. More often than I like to remember I've gotten that sinking feeling as someone—actor, director, producer—approaches me with an open book and asks, "Why didn't you put this in?" I answer, politely, "Because, to my story, that was irrelevant."

At some rare times someone does have an insight which would enrich the play, and then I'm happy to listen. But, in the main, I want the actor or actress to understand and go with the interpretation of the character which I'm presenting through the dialogue and action. After years of work and thought, I feel what I've evolved is a complete portrait, all that anyone would need to fulfill the demands of the role. However, many actors, on being cast, ask, "What books should I read?" Reluctantly, I make suggestions. Some feel they want to immerse themselves in support material to fill out their performances. I feel all the clues they need to the character are in the play.

It's when they read too much and begin not doing my play, but some character from a book, that drives me mad. In fact, probably the worst actor one can get for the part is one who says, "Oh, I've always loved so-and-so, I know their life backwards and forwards, I can't wait to portray it." Such previous knowledge and devotion invariably means trouble. I can only repeat "This is *my* Bernhardt, *my* Sand, *my* Christina of Sweden." Vain as that sentence may sound, it's only if the actor understands and gives her- or himself over to the playwright's interpretation of the character, that the collaboration will succeed.

Another problem arises when leading actors blackmail the playwright by saying, "I'll do your play, but only if you include these scenes." Having become instant authorities through outside reading, they now have favorite moments from the life of the character—moments which either have no relevance, or which are interesting in and of themselves but stop the action of the play. This has happened to me a few times and only once, to get Lilli Palmer to appear in SARAH IN AMERICA, did I assent—not to a threat, but to a very strong request. Palmer said she'd do the play but wanted inserted two longish anecdotes about Bernhardt's son. I wrote them in even though I found them totally outside the parameters of my play and knew they stopped the action. Each night when I heard these set pieces, I cringed. As soon as Palmer's appearance in the play was over, I tore those anecdotes out of the script and it regained its flow.

When Vanessa Redgrave optioned THE ABDICATION she spent many hours with me discussing her ideas for script changes. I must admit, to have an actress of her ability star in one's play would be such a privilege that I was sorely tempted. As it turned out, for other reasons, she never did get to perform in the play, so I never had to put my principles to the acid test.

THE CHARACTERS AND THE PLAYWRIGHT

It's a strange phenomenon, writing about real people. As a playwright, I work very hard to possess the characters, but sometimes they possess me instead. I can wake up in the middle of the night and see Mary Shelley at the foot of the bed, and Chopin on the chair, and Tzu-Hsi emerging from the closet and I want to shout, "Go away! Get out of here! Leave me alone!" But they smile wickedly and remain, haunting me.

I remember one day in Lilli Palmer's dressing room after a performance of SARAH IN AMERICA in Washington. Someone asked her if she'd seen the exhibit on Sarah Bernhardt in the Kennedy Center Library. Lilli, who was at that moment removing her red Bernhardt wig, cried: "If anyone mentions Sarah Bernhardt to me again, I will scream!" Lilli was feeling possessed by Bernhardt, overwhelmed by Bernhardt. She was losing her *self* in her total immersion in the performance and had a great need to escape Bernhardt's stranglehold when off stage.

I feel closer to some characters than others. If I were asked which one I feel closest to, I'd say Mary Shelley. She wasn't a queen or an empress or an actress or a writer who dressed as a man and took many lovers. She was a writer who married and bore children and loved her husband in spite of all their travails. Second closest to me (or what I'd like to be) is probably Eleanor of Aquitaine— the woman who was the epitome of grace, the chatelaine of the Courts of Love. Eleanor was twice wedded to men who only wanted the lands which were her birthright, but eventually, rather like Eleanor Roosevelt, she came to self-realization and independence, with dignity and powers of her own.

I feel there are definite parts of an earlier (and quite imaginary) me in George Sand and Christina of Sweden—both "pants parts," people who, in spite of the fact that they were women, felt best while striding through life assuming the powers that are thought of as male. Each of the other people I've written about, male and female, has some characteristic with which I am in sympathy. And while I may not always know why I chose each in the beginning, I realize now that all of them embody one basic theme: They are women and men who refuse to accept what life has doled out to them, who insist on taking life into their own hands and making out of it as much as they can. That's my personal theme, too.

I am not always in love with my characters. There are moments when I come to hate them. I hate the way they possess me, when I'm writing or in the process of production, to the point of obsession. I hate the way they hide their inner lives. Sometimes they seem to be taunting me to find out the truth, then turning away just as I snatch at it.

There are moments, however, when they come alive for me—by surprise. There'll be a flash of mystic communion, a bright light of revelation. Sometimes that revelation comes from a moment of contact with a shard of evidence left directly by the person, as when I was listening to an ancient recording of Sarah Bernhardt reciting PHÈDRE—and suddenly I *knew*, beyond words, beyond explanations, just what the special quality, the sacred flame of Bernhardt was.

There was another such moment—a day in the Musée Carnavalet in Paris—when I saw the casts of the hands of George Sand and Frederic Chopin lying in a glass case. I was momentarily stunned, Sand and Chopin were so intimately *there*. The casts had been taken from life and clearly showed the lines of the skin, the veins. But what moved me more than anything else, what led to revelation, was the comparative size of those hands. Chopin, the invalid, had a hand so large and strong it could reach an octave and a half and seemed to have the strength to pound right through a piano. And Sand, the capable indomitable earth mother, had one of the tiniest most fragile hands I'd ever seen. Yet Chopin was the invalid and Sand was the manager of their lives and their household. Those hands, beside each other, said volumes to me—more than any books about the couple I'd ever read.

Sometimes moments of revelation happen during the writing—as when I was outlining the scenes for THE SECOND MRS WILSON. I felt, in all I had read about the period after his stroke, that there was a *hole* somewhere—a piece of the psychological puzzle that was missing. Then, in one moment, it all came clear to me: the person who was keeping people from seeing Wilson was not Edith, was not his doctor, it was Wilson himself. No account I'd ever read of that period ever said this, but I suddenly was absolutely certain that as soon as the President became conscious and realized the extent of his frailty, and the danger of his being removed from office because of it, he must have given orders that he be seen by as few people as possible. And while Edith took all the blame for acting as Cerberus, barking at all who approached the door of the

President, my contention is that the one who had stationed her there was the President himself.

Illuminating, too, was the result of my quest to solve the riddle of the Shelley's marriage. My early instinct—that it was a splendid pairing in spite of all its *sturm und drang*—for a long time did not yield answers in terms of a dramatizable solution. It was when I conceived of the idea of sentencing them to remain alone together forever in the Afterworld that they finally confronted each other and defined, at last, the quality of their love. Realizing the eternal and indestructible essence of their love, Mary tells Shelley: "You held me to my highest self" and "Everyone disappointed except you. ... No matter how awful it was with you, it was always glorious." In other words, it was their never-wavering devotion to the qualities in each other, their deeply valuing each other in spite of everything, which was the unshatterable precious stone at the heart of their tumultuous relationship. When I reached this insight I felt I at last understood not only this couple, but something central and incontrovertible about successful married life.

CONCLUSION—A PERSONAL VIEW

It isn't easy writing about the lives of other people. There's a tremendous amount of work to do before one can even begin to approach the writing of the play. There are dangers before and after the writing which other playwrights don't begin to have to face. Yet, I enjoy it. In fiction, any of a thousand events could or could not happen. A character could die or not die, have an affair or not have an affair, go to outer space or not go to outer space. There's no factual necessity to the story.

When one deals with a real life, one begins with facts—some knowable and some unknowable. One's whole focus is to give motivations to what one knows happened and speculate about what one doesn't know. One is always focusing not on the *what* but on the *why*. Why people did what they did, why events turned out the way they turned out, is, to me, endlessly fascinating.

The biographical play is not some secondary species. A biographical play is an *original* play. The point of view and the treatment and the vision are original. Critics may like to devalue the playwright's contribution, but, at its best, the biographical play transforms its material into art—free-standing, original art. That transformation is All—it forges in the smithy of the writer's soul a new thing, a dramatic work which stands on its own, is referenced to nothing, needs no footnotes or outside echoes to present itself with its own dignity and its own existence. Like a portrait painted by a master, it is the transformation of the life of another; it has a life of its own.

We are in a period which doesn't value history and which, therefore, will be condemned to repeat history's mistakes. We are also in a cynical period, one which has no use for heroes. I don't consider the portrayal of an anonymous dying druggie to be more worthy of a playwright's attention than the portrayal of someone who made a unique contribution to civilization and is therefore worthy of being remembered through a dramatic work. We are, in these early years of the Twenty-first Century, obsessed by theater works about those who are self-centered, physically or psychologically injured, even deranged. I prophesy that most of the plays written about such people will disappear or be of only sociological interest in future decades. These plays will be looked on as quaint aberrations. At the risk of not seeming to be contemporary, I have always had a wider and more inclusive vision of human value and human time. If a person's fame, abilities or ideas have lasted until now, they will probably last into the future. In an evanescent field, I like the possibility of writing about people who might still be of interest in another time.

I like writing biographical plays because I enjoy mysteries. I like puzzling out and giving shape and meaning to a life. I'm not so vain as to think my personal experiences could make high drama. Those who deal in thinly disguised autobiography run the danger of repeating themselves, running out of material and, finally, boring their public.

On the other hand, all biographical art is, in some sense or other, autobiographical. Just as I am every one of the men and women I've written about, so each of them is also a part of a protean me. But I prefer appearing in disguise. I want to say what I want to say through other people—others whom I believe felt as I do and who, already immortal, deserve to come alive again on the stage, interpreted by a compassionate humanistic pen. They serve me and I serve them. We are partners together. And if the themes are universal enough, then their dramas are timeless. They have already lived, they live now, they will live again.

I confess to a distrust of the immediate, to an impatience with characters so small that they are mere blips on the face of history. They live, but the meanings of their lives do not last. While it might seem that in these plays I am looking at the past, the truth is I am looking at today and what came before today as though looking back from a very distant future. Looking back from that unknowable future, what we call the present and what we call history seem to exist at the same time.

I like the idea of living lots of lives instead of just the one I was born to. I like being able to be a great composer, an actress, a president, a seductress, a queen. I like living in the Middle Ages, in the Age of Louis XIV, in Peking or in Paris at the turn of the twentieth century. I love finding myself in a castle in Sweden, a tent in Asia Minor, a church in Rome. I like being anyone, male or female, at any time, in any place, in any circumstance. In spite of the slings and arrows, the difficulties in writing for the theater of our time, it is a thing of splendor to live a life confined only by the limits of one's imagination.

As the bodies of those who once lived molder, as their voices are stilled and their deeds fade, it is we who give them life again, give them breath. Who knows, as playwrights, having added art to life, we might be so fortunate as to have people remembered not from the dry pages of history books but from the way we portrayed them. Then we could consider ourselves, along with Shakespeare (for it is he, not Henry V who said it), among "We few, we happy few..."

THE ABDICATION

For stock and amateur rights please contact Dramatic Publishing Company, 311 Washington Street, P O Box 129, Woodstock, Illinois 60098, 815-338-7170, fax 815-338-8981, e-mail: dpcplays.com..

THE ABDICATION premiered at the Theatre Royal, Bath, England, on 26 May 1971, produced by the Bristol Old Vic Company. The American premiere was presented by the Eureka Theatre, San Francisco. The play has been presented worldwide and in most of the United States. Notable productions abroad include: Il Gruppo Arte Drammatica *(Italy)*, De Haagse Comedie *(Netherlands)* and Théâtre de Quat'sous *(Montreal)*.

Ruth Wolff wrote the 1974 Warner Bros. film based on the play. It starred Liv Ullmann and Peter Finch.

CHARACTERS & SETTING

BIRGITO
DOMINIC
CHRISTINA OF SWEDEN
CARDINAL AZZOLINO
TINA
OXENSTIERNA
CHRIS
CHARLES
EBBA
MAGNUS

Time: The main action of the play takes place in Rome, 1655.

Place: An antechamber in the Vatican

Setting: A raked platform surrounded by vertical panels which can rise, fall or pivot to create a space in which scenes flow easily from present action to other places, other times.

The setting should be abstract, less concerned with physical reality than with evocation of character, mood and state of mind.

ACT ONE

(At rise:)

(The antechamber is deserted except for an empty ceremonial chair which dominates the space. Music. The lights come up slowly on the empty chair.)

(After a moment, BIRGITO, *a dwarf, enters warily from stage right. He explores the room, then approaches the chair, moving around it, running his fingers over it, then he hops up onto it.)*

*(*DOMINIC, *a young priest, enters busily from the interior of the Vatican, stage left, carrying documents.* BIRGITO *sees him, hops down and attempts to hide behind the chair.)*

DOMINIC: Who is there? *(No answer)* I said who is there! *(He goes toward the chair.)* Come out! Come out of there!

*(*DOMINIC *reaches behind the chair and pulls* BIRGITO *out.* BIRGITO *struggles in his grasp. A* HOODED FIGURE *enters from the outside, wearing a traveling cape.)*

CHRISTINA: Let him go!

(In spite of himself, DOMINIC *obeys instantly.)*

DOMINIC: Who—?

*(*BIRGITO *bites* DOMINIC *on the hand.* DOMINIC *cries out and drops his papers.)*

DOMINIC: He bit me!

CHRISTINA: *(To* BIRGITO, *as she emerges from the shadows)* How does he taste?

*(*BIRGITO *makes a wry face.)*

CHRISTINA: In that case, don't make a habit of it.

(She begins to stride toward the interior.)

DOMINIC: Just a minute, sir! Where do you think you're going?

CHRISTINA: To see the Pope.

DOMINIC: You can't just break in and expect him to—

*(*CHRISTINA *throws back her cape revealing herself to be a woman wearing men's clothes and carrying a riding crop.)*

CHRISTINA: I am Christina of Sweden.

DOMINIC: *(Stunned)* Impossible —

CHRISTINA: You will not know me by my costume, or by secret rings, or by documents. You will know me by the angle of my chin.

DOMINIC: But she is not expected for three days —

CHRISTINA: Nevertheless, she is here, and to hell with the expectation.

DOMINIC: But Madame —

CHRISTINA: Tell the Pope I have arrived to throw myself at his feet and become his newest and most ardent Catholic! Tell him I was so eager to see him that I galloped on ahead of all my retinue. Tell him I have sworn not to take my first communion till I receive it from his hand. Tell him I — *(She breaks off. She looks suddenly lost, vulnerable, deeply troubled.)*

(BIRGITO approaches her, recalling her to herself.)

CHRISTINA: *(She turns to DOMINIC impatiently:)* Well? ...Go!

(DOMINIC hesitates. CHRISTINA laughs.)

CHRISTINA: Don't worry. We won't steal anything. ... Though I did rather fancy that Raphael we passed in the hall.

(DOMINIC pauses for a moment, then exits, stage left. CHRISTINA says to BIRGITO:)

CHRISTINA: Caught them off guard, didn't I?

(BIRGITO smiles with satisfaction. CHRISTINA strides about the room.)

CHRISTINA: Well, Birgito, what do you think? Will the Vatican suit us?

(BIRGITO performs some mocking stunts, parodies of piety and reverence.)

CHRISTINA: Are you glad we gave up Sweden for Rome?

(BIRGITO shivers with cold, then pantomimes languishing under the sun.)

CHRISTINA: Yes, yes, how glorious! To be out of the cold and under the Italian sun at last! In the land of Leonardo, Michelangelo, the ruins of the Caesars! You know, sometimes I thought we'd never make it. But here we are — safe, sound, and about to be greeted by the Pope! How I've longed to meet him —

(BIRGITO questions how he should greet His Holiness. Should he shakes hands? Bow? Salute?)

CHRISTINA: You kiss his ring! ... And then — you leave me alone with him.

(Again the look of troubled longing comes over her but she banishes it quickly, brightening to say:)

I wonder what kind of reception they're planning for me? I heard that when some duke or other converted and came to live in Rome they gave three days and nights of continuous parties. Imagine the celebration they'll give for a queen! ... I can't wait for it to begin —! *(She throws her arms in the air as if she were going to dance.*)

(DOMINIC, *re-entering, interrupts her.*)

DOMINIC: Madame—

CHRISTINA: Is the Pope coming?

DOMINIC: He is in his apartments.

CHRISTINA: Oh, then I'm to be brought to him. Good. Is this the way—? (*She starts to exit stage left.*)

(DOMINIC *hurries to block her path.*)

DOMINIC: Madame, please—! Not yet—

CHRISTINA: Oh?

DOMINIC: There are formalities—

CHRISTINA: Oh, let's dispense with those! Tell the Pope I permit him not to stand on ceremony.

DOMINIC: This ceremony, I'm afraid, is necessary.

CHRISTINA: Ceremony is *never* necessary. I thought, when I gave up the crown, I'd be through with all that nonsense.

DOMINIC: This ceremony is hardly nonsense.

CHRISTINA: Well, what is it?

DOMINIC: Before you can see the Pope, you must confess.

CHRISTINA: Confess!

DOMINIC: A ritual cleansing.

CHRISTINA: I could better use a bath!

DOMINIC: For the good of your soul—

CHRISTINA: My soul has survived abdication, conversion, and a thousand miles of being jostled about in square-wheeled carriages. I shall not make the rest of the journey on my knees!

DOMINIC: But Madame—

CHRISTINA: Besides, I've already poured out my soul in letters to His Holiness. Why does he want me to whisper it all over again into his ear?

DOMINIC: Oh, you won't be confessed by *him*!

CHRISTINA: Who then?

DOMINIC: Another.

CHRISTINA: Some ancient cleric hiding behind his curtains muttering, "Yes, my daughter. No, my daughter..."?

DOMINIC: Please, Madame—

CHRISTINA: I shall not expose my soul to some faceless creature—!

(CARDINAL AZZOLINO *enters from stage left. He is a handsome, forceful man in his mid-forties.*)

AZZOLINO: Do it eye-to-eye, then.

DOMINIC: Father—

AZZOLINO: She's quite right. The curtains are put on the confessional to make things easier for the penitent. But I can see that Christina, the former Queen of Sweden, is not one for the easiest way.

CHRISTINA: I expected the Pope to take me in his arms and bless me. I did not expect to be held in his antechamber—

AZZOLINO: I quite understand.

CHRISTINA: I am a Queen!

AZZOLINO: An *ex*-Queen—if you will forgive the distinction.

CHRISTINA: I have rank—

AZZOLINO: Great rank—as do we all in the eyes of God.

CHRISTINA: And what have I in the eyes of the Pope?

AZZOLINO: He has not seen you.

CHRISTINA: Then I insist you give him the opportunity immediately!

AZZOLINO: (*Coolly*) Dominic, tell his Holiness he may retire for the evening. It is obvious that his daughter will not be ready to be received by him tonight.

CHRISTINA: In the name of God—!

AZZOLINO: You see, Brother Dominic, she has religion after all. It just remains for us to discover *what* religion.

(CHRISTINA *makes a gesture of protest.* BIRGITO *rushes forward, ready to challenge* AZZOLINO.)

AZZOLINO: What have we here?

CHRISTINA: My best friend and companion of the road, Birgito.

(BIRGITO *crosses himself hastily.*)

AZZOLINO: Where are your maidservants?

CHRISTINA: I prefer the company of men. Birgito serves me well. I've named him after the only Swedish saint. She was a lady, of course, and as beautiful as virtue, while he is a man, and as ugly as sin. Outside of that, they are identical!

(BIRGITO *pantomimes holiness.*)

CHRISTINA: He's asking you if you see the resemblance.

AZZOLINO: "Asking" me?

CHRISTINA: He cannot speak—except in gestures. ... Oh, don't try to overhear him, only I can understand.

(BIRGITO *makes signs to her.*)

AZZOLINO: What does he say?

CHRISTINA: He says we should go back to Sweden!

(AZZOLINO *laughs and says to* BIRGITO:)

AZZOLINO: After such a long journey, at least you will consent to spend the night.

(BIRGITO *looks to* CHRISTINA *for advice. She nods. He indicates he will accept the invitation.*)

AZZOLINO: Dominic, show Birgito to the Queen's apartments.

DOMINIC: Yes, father—

(DOMINIC *and* BIRGITO *start out.*)

AZZOLINO: And, Dominic—

DOMINIC: Yes, father?

AZZOLINO: Please be on your best behavior. Remember, you are escorting a saint...

(*Posing as a holy relic,* BIRGITO, *escorted by* DOMINIC, *marches out upstage.*)

AZZOLINO: I apologize for Brother Dominic. His request for you to confess apparently surprised you.

CHRISTINA: It did.

AZZOLINO: When he's been at it longer, he'll be more diplomatic.

CHRISTINA: I hope so.

AZZOLINO: It's a mere formality. If you prefer, we can wait till you are less tired—

CHRISTINA: I am never tired.

AZZOLINO: I only thought you might like to—

CHRISTINA: I always look like this. Rest does not improve me. ... Tell me, Cardinal—. You *are* a Cardinal? I don't misread the costume?

AZZOLINO: I am a Cardinal.

CHRISTINA: This—formality—before I can see the Pope. Is it usual Vatican procedure?

AZZOLINO: Frequently.

CHRISTINA: Do you never make exceptions?

AZZOLINO: Sometimes.

CHRISTINA: Then surely I can be one.

AZZOLINO: I am afraid not.

CHRISTINA: Why?

AZZOLINO: There are doubts.

CHRISTINA: About what?

AZZOLINO: The sincerity of your conversion.

CHRISTINA: I gave up a *crown* to become a convert!

AZZOLINO: So it seems...

CHRISTINA: No one in the history of the world has ever made such a sacrifice!

AZZOLINO: So anxious were you to become a Catholic.

CHRISTINA: So anxious.

AZZOLINO: Then why did it take you a year to make the journey from Stockholm to Rome?

CHRISTINA: The roads were muddy.

AZZOLINO: And the ballrooms of Hamburg, Antwerp and Brussels? Were they muddy, too?

CHRISTINA: They were divine!

AZZOLINO: The *Church* is divine.

CHRISTINA: Ah, but in quite a different way—

AZZOLINO: In your letters to the Pope you said you would travel as a pilgrim, incognito!

CHRISTINA: I tried to.

AZZOLINO: With an entourage of two-hundred-and-fifty-five!

CHRISTINA: Can Catholics not have footmen?

AZZOLINO: Within reason. They dress within reason, too. The women do not go about dressed as men.

CHRISTINA: I wear what I please! Will you measure my faith by my clothes and my servants?

AZZOLINO: I will measure your faith—by your faith.

CHRISTINA: Which you obviously find wanting.

AZZOLINO: Since your abdication, you've been cavorting over the face of Europe—

CHRISTINA: I was enjoying myself for the first time in my life!

AZZOLINO: And what made you suddenly decide to cut short the merry-making and descend on the Vatican?

(CHRISTINA *looks at* AZZOLINO. *She will not answer the question.*)

CHRISTINA: I insist on seeing the Pope. At once!

AZZOLINO: That is impossible.

CHRISTINA: But he led me to believe he would greet me as a daughter the moment I arrived!

AZZOLINO: And so he hoped to.

CHRISTINA: Then why am I still standing here?

(AZZOLINO *takes a packet of letters from his pocket and shows it to her.*)

AZZOLINO: Because of these.

CHRISTINA: And what are those?

AZZOLINO: Letters—from priests and bishops all along your route.

CHRISTINA: You had me spied upon!

AZZOLINO: There was no need. Your actions were all too open... You associated with people of the basest character. You roamed the streets, carousing every night. You commanded for your pleasure entertainments of the most disreputable nature. Some say you took part in them—

CHRISTINA: Anything else?

AZZOLINO: What more would you like? *(Thumbing through the letters)* Sacrilege... Debauchery... Perversion...

CHRISTINA: Go on, it's getting better.

AZZOLINO: Tales are told of you in every dining-hall and tavern in Europe. The circumstances of your life are like some bawdy joke! Look at this: *(He holds up a book.)* "The Pleasures and Depravities of Christina, Queen of Sweden." Translations are being sold in seven languages. Your escapades are single-handedly keeping a continent of gossips alive!

CHRISTINA: Then why didn't you stop me from coming?

AZZOLINO: To judge for ourselves.

CHRISTINA: And if I prove that every word in that pile of trash is arrant slander?

AZZOLINO: We still would have our suspicions. Need I tell you why? Your father laid waste half of Europe to win it for the upstart religion. He gave his life forcing millions to convert to the Protestant cause. Why on earth would his daughter suddenly decide to abandon all that and descend on Rome?

CHRISTINA: I came to see the paintings.

AZZOLINO: Surely you could have made the grand tour without going so far as giving up your throne and assuming a religion which is outlawed in your country! After all, we do permit even Lutherans to see the Sistine Chapel. Why bother with conversion. What advantage do you hope to find here?

CHRISTINA: "Advantage!" That's not the word of a priest, it's the word of a politician.

AZZOLINO: *(Struck)* Surely you're not naive enough to believe your coming here will have no political consequences!

CHRISTINA: I come as a private individual, seeking God.

AZZOLINO: *Which* God?! A mere seven years ago you personally signed the treaty which dealt a nearly mortal blow to Papal influence in Europe. Now you arrive here on our doorstep—

CHRISTINA: I thought, under the circumstances, you would be glad—no, not glad, grateful, *overjoyed* to have me! This Church's popularity has not been at so low an ebb since its early days in pagan Rome! You need me!

AZZOLINO: Some think we do. There are those in the College of Cardinals who think your conversion is a wonderful coup for Catholicism. They think it will bring thousands of lost sheep back into the fold. They refuse to believe a word against you. They are eager to welcome you into the faith.

CHRISTINA: Thank them.

AZZOLINO: There are others, however, who believe the stories against you. Or at least believe the *people* believe them. They feel your presence will bring discredit to the Holy City. They are determined to keep you out.

CHRISTINA: Why not have a battle of Cardinals in Saint Peter's Square?

AZZOLINO: *I* am the battlefield. I have been assigned to question you.

CHRISTINA: Which side are you on?

AZZOLINO: I am neutral.

CHRISTINA: There is no such thing!

AZZOLINO: Then let us say—I will be fair.

CHRISTINA: *(Bitterly)* Thank you very much. ... Will you be the one to pass final judgment?

AZZOLINO: I shall make recommendations to the Pope.

CHRISTINA: And will he act on them?

AZZOLINO: I think so.

CHRISTINA: Then my fate is in your hands.

AZZOLINO: In your own, I would say.

CHRISTINA: I refuse to submit to this! I came here as a haven and a refuge!

AZZOLINO: You came here after God-knows-what political intrigues, debaucheries and perversions and expect the Pope to welcome you, showing he approves!

CHRISTINA: You insult me to suggest I came all this way to rebel against the Holy Father!

AZZOLINO: I need some evidence that if you are to be the Vatican's eternal guest, you will abide by its rules and not be a constant embarrassment!

CHRISTINA: What do you think I would do? Break your china? Ride my horse through Saint Peter's nave?

AZZOLINO: You cannot become a Catholic for your own convenience!

CHRISTINA: For whose, then?

AZZOLINO: If you have done these things and are repentant, you will be accepted.

CHRISTINA: If I have done these things and am *not* repentant?

AZZOLINO: You will not.

CHRISTINA: And what if I have *not* done these things?

AZZOLINO: That's why I want to hear your story.

CHRISTINA: And what if I don't choose to tell?

AZZOLINO: Then—you are free to go.

CHRISTINA: Go? ...Where—?

AZZOLINO: Back to Sweden, perhaps.

CHRISTINA: You know that is impossible.

AZZOLINO: You seemed to enjoy Antwerp.

CHRISTINA: There is nothing for me there—

AZZOLINO: Spain, then? Or France?

(CHRISTINA *doesn't reply.*)

AZZOLINO: Well, where can a lady go when she has given up a Protestant throne to become a Catholic? When she arrives to spend the rest of her life in Rome, but the Pope refuses to let her in? Who would care to entertain a woman without God or country? What place would she have in the world, such a woman, who has been used to so much, and who expected—what— in Rome, some kind of spiritual crown?

CHRISTINA: You forget. I was received into the Church three weeks ago, at Innsbruck. I am already a convert!

AZZOLINO: Then go where other converts go.

CHRISTINA: Where do they go?

AZZOLINO: Why—anywhere.

CHRISTINA: Anywhere... *(Lost and confused, she looks at him.)*

AZZOLINO: *(After a moment)* ...There is no "anywhere" for the former Queen of Sweden, is there?

CHRISTINA: No.

AZZOLINO: Then she must be accepted by the Pope.

(Silence. CHRISTINA understands.)

CHRISTINA: ...What is your name?

AZZOLINO: ...Azzolino.

CHRISTINA: How long have you been a Cardinal, Azzolino?

AZZOLINO: Long enough.

CHRISTINA: Have you ever confessed a Queen?

AZZOLINO: No.

CHRISTINA: Does the prospect disconcert you?

AZZOLINO: I assume you're mortal.

CHRISTINA: Come, Azzolino! Let's get ourselves some good French wine, and when I've drunk enough, I'll tell you the story of my life!

AZZOLINO: I wish to hear the story of your life without wine!

CHRISTINA: *(Laughing)* Not even a little sacramental sip?

AZZOLINO: Your eternal soul is at stake and you laugh!

CHRISTINA: What do you want?

AZZOLINO: Seriousness! Obedience!

CHRISTINA: Seriousness and obedience!

> *(The lights change. TINA appears. She is CHRISTINA as CHRISTINA remembers herself at an earlier age, meek and docile, dressed in a gown the color of ivory, a pale and waxen image. With TINA is AXEL OXENSTIERNA, her very just, very correct Prime Minister. They are rehearsing for the*

coronation. TINA *carries the orb and scepter and wears the ceremonial cape.* OXENSTIERNA *carries the crown.)*

TINA: *(Dimly in the background, unseen by* AZZOLINO*)* Yes, Oxenstierna. Yes, Oxenstierna.

CHRISTINA: Have I come all this way once more to play the Doll Queen?!

AZZOLINO: I beg your pardon?

OXENSTIERNA: Good girl, Your Majesty. Chin up high—

TINA: Yes, Oxenstierna. Yes, Oxenstierna.

CHRISTINA: *(Imitating the voice of* TINA*)* "Yes, Azzolino. Yes, Azzolino." Is this what you want?

AZZOLINO: I don't understand you.

OXENSTIERNA: Smile once to your left, once to your right—

CHRISTINA: I became Queen at six, you know. All I could do was smile and obey my Prime Minister.

OXENSTIERNA: Pause by the throne and curtsey to the left.

(CHRISTINA *mockingly imitates what* TINA *is doing.)*

AZZOLINO: I am not asking you to become a puppet!

CHRISTINA: Aren't you?

AZZOLINO: But there are certain standards of conduct—

OXENSTIERNA: Good girl, your majesty, now to the right—

CHRISTINA: What will you give me if I do as you wish?

OXENSTIERNA: How would you like to stay up until midnight?

AZZOLINO: All I can offer is absolution—

TINA: Thank you, Oxenstierna.

CHRISTINA: Why should I need absolution?

OXENSTIERNA: Now bend your left knee and lower your head—

TINA: Yes, Oxenstierna. Yes, Oxenstierna.

(OXENSTIERNA *places the crown on her head.)*

CHRISTINA: I was the best behaved child you could ever wish to know!

AZZOLINO: *(Holding the book)* That isn't what they say about you here.

(CHRIS *dashes in. The more jaunty side of* CHRISTINA, *she, too, is dressed in ivory—but as a dashing young man. She snatches the crown from* TINA's *head, puts it on her own and says:)*

CHRIS: I'm going to fall flat on my face! *That* will entertain the multitudes!

OXENSTIERNA: *(To* CHRIS*)* Christina—!

AZZOLINO: They say you grew up like a boy—rebellious and rude—

CHRIS: *(Snatching the orb and scepter)* What do I do with these—a juggling act?

OXENSTIERNA: Christina, you must rehearse your coronation—

CHRIS: *(Holding the orb)* You know, Oxy, this reminds me of your head! Here, catch! *(She throws it at him.)*

AZZOLINO: They say you had the language of a guttersnipe—

CHRIS: I warn you, I'm going to have to piss in the middle of the ceremony! *(She pantomimes vulgarly with the scepter, then twirls the crown around it.)*

*(*TINA *runs after her, trying to recapture the royal symbols.)*

TINA: Stop it! Stop it!

*(*CHRIS *laughs.)*

OXENSTIERNA: You must behave yourself!

(A fight develops between CHRIS *and* TINA. OXENSTIERNA *throws up his hands and exits.)*

AZZOLINO: Well, which of these creatures are you?

CHRISTINA: None of them! Both of them! Neither!

*(*CHRIS *and* TINA *disappear.)*

AZZOLINO: This chapter says you're the harlot of the northern hemisphere.

CHRISTINA: How picturesque!

AZZOLINO: This chapter says you are a man in disguise.

CHRISTINA: And a harlot, too! Some trick!

AZZOLINO: Why did you never marry?

CHRISTINA: *(Sarcastically)* I was too busy.

AZZOLINO: Why did you give up the crown?

CHRISTINA: *(With heavy irony)* To devote myself to lust.

AZZOLINO: Answer my questions!

CHRISTINA: So you can report my answers to the Pope? Is he somewhere in the darkness now, listening?

AZZOLINO: Like God, he does not have to listen in order to hear.

CHRISTINA: *(Shouting)* Listen, God! Pope! Cardinals! Bishops! Washerwomen!

AZZOLINO: Christina—

CHRISTINA: Today's confession is tomorrow's gossip! I'm saving them the trouble of whispering behind their hands!

AZZOLINO: The confessional is sacrosanct. One does not shout in it.

CHRISTINA: What does one do in it?

AZZOLINO: One tells what troubles one most deeply.

CHRISTINA: *(Her tone belying her words)* Nothing troubles me.

AZZOLINO: *(Deeply)* Why did you give up the crown?

CHRISTINA: It was too heavy.

AZZOLINO: Why did you never marry?

CHRISTINA: I am allergic to gold rings.

AZZOLINO: Why did you become a Catholic?

CHRISTINA: To come to a better climate!

AZZOLINO: Is it true that—

CHRISTINA: Oh, yes! Everything is true! What do they accuse me of? Murder? Rape? The seven deadly sins? Anything you like! ... I caused the storm that wrecked the Spanish fleet! I personally infected Holland with the plague! Next week Vesuvius and I have a surprise in store for the citizens of Pompeii! Oh, yes. I'm guilty! Guilty!

AZZOLINO: I've had enough of this! The Pope will have to give the assignment to somebody else. I am tired of dealing with refugees from the Courts of Europe who flock here for the wrong reasons. The Vatican is not some kind of holy wayside inn! I do not take the Church and what it has to offer lightly.

CHRISTINA: Nor do I, Azzolino.

(Pause)

AZZOLINO: Then I give you one more chance.

CHRISTINA: *(Echoing him)* To open my heart to you?

AZZOLINO: To tell me the truth!

(Pause)

CHRISTINA: I have nothing to tell.

AZZOLINO: In that case, I am wasting my time. *(He holds up the documents.)* These will stand. *(He starts to stride out.)*

    (TINA enters)

TINA: Let's play the truth game!

CHRISTINA: I don't want to play the truth game!

TINA: Charles—!

(AZZOLINO *turns back to* CHRISTINA.)

AZZOLINO: Your entire future is at stake and you call it a game—?!

CHRISTINA: *(Laughing)* Azzolino—! Azzolino—!

TINA: Ebba—!

AZZOLINO: I don't understand you!

CHRISTINA: How touchy you are!

TINA: Magnus—!

CHRISTINA: I was thinking of something I used to play when I was young.

TINA: We each have to tell the absolute truth!

CHRISTINA: A truth game. I was rather good at it.

AZZOLINO: Now *that* astounds me.

CHRISTINA: I used to play it with my cousin Charles,

(CHARLES *appears.*)

CHRISTINA: —my dear friend, Ebba,

(EBBA *appears.*)

CHRISTINA: —and that most handsome of all young gentlemen, Magnus Gabriel de la Gardie!

(MAGNUS *appears.*)

MAGNUS: Anyone who lies has to pay a forfeit! Anyone who lies has to forfeit a kiss!

(MAGNUS *runs after the girls. They squeal with laughter.*)

CHRISTINA: *(In the spirit of the game)* What would you like to know the truth about?

AZZOLINO: *(Lightly)* Everything!

(CHRISTINA *laughs.*)

MAGNUS: What's the biggest lie you've ever told?

EBBA: About my age. I always say I'm two years older.

MAGNUS: I lied about where I was last Christmas Eve.

CHARLES: Where were you?

MAGNUS: Behind the stables.

CHARLES: What were you doing?

MAGNUS: Wouldn't you like to know!

(CHARLES *reacts puritanically, then continues:*)

CHARLES: My biggest lie—was about mathematics. Once—I cheated.

TINA: Charles!

MAGNUS: What about you, Christina?

TINA: I never lie.

AZZOLINO: Was that the truth?

CHRISTINA: Was and is. Absolutely!

AZZOLINO: Didn't you ask each other any harder questions?

CHRISTINA: Of course—

TINA: Now we each have to tell—our greatest virtue.

MAGNUS: My courage.

EBBA: My looks.

TINA: Charles—?

CHARLES: I can't think of anything—

MAGNUS: Forfeit! Forfeit!

TINA: No. It's true. There's nothing to say. Charles is Charles. That's all there is to it!

CHRISTINA: Charlie has no character at all! Charlie is absent! Charlie is invisible!

AZZOLINO: Who is this fellow who's invisible?

CHRISTINA: The present King of Sweden, Charles the Tenth!

EBBA: Now it's your turn, Christina.

AZZOLINO: You abdicated to *him*?

CHRISTINA: Does that surprise you? It seems to be an advantage for a King—to have no character.

MAGNUS: What's your greatest virtue, Christina?

TINA: I am always in command of myself. I never let my emotions get out of control.

CHRISTINA: *(Under her breath)* Good girl, good girl...

TINA: Now each of us has to tell—our greatest fault!

EBBA: My greatest fault is—at a ball, I can never decide which partner to choose, I have so many!

CHARLES: My greatest fault is—my greatest fault is—...I really don't know!

CHRISTINA: He never did.

MAGNUS: My greatest fault is my eagerness to throw myself into the thick of the battle, thus risking the life of the leader of my men.

TINA: How brave you are!

EBBA: How brave!

CHRISTINA: How insufferable!

CHARLES: Now it's your turn, Christina.

TINA: My greatest fault—is my overwhelming desire for perfection, and my inability to reach it often enough.

(CHRIS *suddenly appears behind* TINA.)

CHRIS: Rubbish! Why don't you tell them how you're afraid of the dark! About your nightmares!

TINA: I don't have nightmares!

CHRIS: Liar! Why don't you tell them how you're afraid to sleep without someone being near?

TINA: The game is over!

CHRISTINA: The game is over!

CHRIS: The hell it is! *(She whips out a fencing sword and challenges* EBBA.) So you can't decide among those dancing partners. Is that why you have to kiss them *all*?

(EBBA *squeals and runs away from her.*)

(Chris challenges Charles.)

CHRIS: What's behind those profound silences? Great thoughts? Or is your mind a total blank?

(CHARLES *backs away.*)

(CHRIS *challenges* MAGNUS.)

CHRIS: And you! Are you as brave as you look, or is it just the uniform? Confess! Confess!

CHRISTINA: *(Dryly)* I used to love confession...

MAGNUS: If you were a man, I'd show you if it's just the uniform.

CHRIS: *(Whipping out a second sword)* All right, then show me!

EBBA: Christina—!

CHARLES: What are you doing?!

TINA: Stop!

CHRIS: *En garde!*

MAGNUS: *En garde!* And then I have a few hard truths to ask *you*, my lady!

CHRIS: You'll have to hit me first!

TINA, EBBA, CHARLES: Stop! Please! *(etc)*

(CHRIS *and* MAGNUS *duel. He is confident at first, but she beats him several times and he hardens.*)

MAGNUS: I'll damn well run you through!

CHRIS: Oh, will you! I shouldn't count on it, Magnus— *(She manages a strategic hit.)*

AZZOLINO: You were good!

CHRISTINA: The best!

(OXENSTIERNA *enters.*)

OXENSTIERNA: Children! Children! You're waking the entire household!

TINA: I'm sorry, Oxenstierna. We'll be quiet—

CHRIS: We will not be quiet! I am Queen! I will make as much noise as I like! *(She lets out a loud, long, savage bellow.)*

TINA: *(Over* CHRIS's *sustained cry)* I don't see how you can act like that!

(TINA *runs out sobbing, followed by* OXENSTIERNA. CHRIS *laughs.*)

CHRIS: *(To* MAGNUS—*still fencing)* Had enough?

MAGNUS: No!

AZZOLINO: I must say you were strong—

CHRISTINA: You have to be strong to rule a country. You must be the center, the absolute *power*—!

AZZOLINO: Power—! But surely that's not—

CHRISTINA: Not like a woman?

MAGNUS: *(Winded)* Hey! You're almost as good as a man!

CHRIS: "Almost!" *(With one deft thrust* CHRIS *flips the sword from* MAGNUS's *hand and points her sword at his throat.)* Say I'm better!

MAGNUS: All right! ... All right! ... You're better!

(CHRIS *lets* MAGNUS *up.*)

CHRIS: Come back tomorrow. I'll beat you again!

MAGNUS: *(Ironically)* I'll look forward to it. *(He exits.)*

(CHRIS continues practicing triumphantly.)

CHRISTINA: There! Didn't I show him!

AZZOLINO: Did you really enjoy winning?

CHRISTINA: Of course!

AZZOLINO: Wouldn't it have been better the other way 'round?

CHRISTINA: How do you mean?

(CHRIS disappears.)

AZZOLINO: No man likes being beaten by a woman. It's human nature.

CHRISTINA: Then human nature will have to change!

AZZOLINO: Is that why the first thing you did after your abdication ceremony was to jump into pants, buckle on a sword and begin calling yourself "Count"?

CHRISTINA: I wanted to throw off who I was and become who I always wanted to be.

AZZOLINO: A man.

CHRISTINA: Someone who could be taken seriously.

AZZOLINO: Who could take seriously someone disguised in the clothing of the other gender?

CHRISTINA: When you first saw me, from a distance, didn't you mistake me for a man?

AZZOLINO: Not for a moment.

CHRISTINA: Ah... So there's no escape after all...

AZZOLINO: From what are you trying to escape, Christina?

CHRISTINA: *(Looks at him for a moment, then:)* I'm saying no more. I'd forgotten how skilled you people are at drawing out admissions. Inquisitor!

AZZOLINO: *Confessor.*

CHRISTINA: Are the instruments of torture ready, "confessor"? ... Or is confession the greatest torture of all?

(Before AZZOLINO has a chance to respond, there are sounds outside. BIRGITO runs in gesticulating excitedly to CHRISTINA. He is followed by DOMINIC, who is also very agitated.)

AZZOLINO: What's the matter?

DOMINIC: I can't understand it! He won't accept any of the rooms I show him.

(BIRGITO *pantomimes something to* CHRISTINA.)

AZZOLINO: How many has he seen?

DOMINIC: Twelve.

AZZOLINO: You've shown him twelve rooms and none are satisfactory?

(BIRGITO *gestures to* CHRISTINA.)

CHRISTINA: They are satisfactory, but they are not sufficient.

AZZOLINO: How many rooms do you require?

CHRISTINA: Twenty.

AZZOLINO: For your attendants?

CHRISTINA: For myself.

DOMINIC: *(Aside to* AZZOLINO*)* I thought the fellow was mad. He gets it from his mistress.

CHRISTINA: Birgito and I get restless at night, so we prowl from room to room. Whenever I find a bed I like, I lie down. Birgito pulls along his pile of bedding and sleeps on the floor beside me.

DOMINIC: I never heard of such a thing. We can't possibly—

(AZZOLINO *silences him with a gesture.*)

AZZOLINO: *(To* CHRISTINA, *a new tone in his voice)* We will do our best to accommodate you.

(DOMINIC *looks at him questioningly.*)

AZZOLINO: See that their needs are taken care of.

DOMINIC: Twenty rooms!?

AZZOLINO: More, if necessary.

DOMINIC: Very well, father.

AZZOLINO: And make sure that every room has fresh flowers.

DOMINIC: I'll do my best.

(DOMINIC *exits in consternation, followed by a triumphant* BIRGITO.)

CHRISTINA: Thank you.

AZZOLINO: Why do you sleep in twenty rooms?

CHRISTINA: It's more restful—

AZZOLINO: Why are you afraid of the dark?

CHRISTINA: That was long ago—!

AZZOLINO: Why did you become a Catholic?

CHRISTINA: To cure me of insomnia!

(*Ominous lights whirl out of the darkness in the background.*)

AZZOLINO: I can assure you of beds, but not of sleep.

CHRISTINA: I thought this was the house of miracles.

AZZOLINO: For some it is.

CHRISTINA: Then it will have to be for me...

AZZOLINO: Why can't you sleep, Christina?

(CHRISTINA *covers her face with her hands, overwhelmed by the nightmare which is growing around her.*)

    (TINA *appears out of the whirling lights and cries out:*)

    TINA: Mama! Mama! Mama!

(CHRISTINA *puts on a shawl, becoming her own mother.*)

CHRISTINA: Yes, child?

    TINA: Mother, what is that big black box beside your bed?

CHRISTINA: Your father.

    TINA: Mother, it's a box!

CHRISTINA: He is inside.

    TINA: He can't breathe!

CHRISTINA: The dead don't breathe. The dead don't speak. The dead don't see. The dead don't— (*She suddenly breaks off.*) I refuse to play this part! I hate my mother!

AZZOLINO: Why did you hate your mother?

CHRISTINA: She kept my father's body in a box. She refused to bury him! ... She made me sleep with her, next to the big black box.

    TINA: I don't want to! I'm afraid!

AZZOLINO: Don't be afraid, Christina. Tell me everything.

(CHRISTINA *meets the challenge in* AZZOLINO's *eyes. Accepting the dare, she continues:*)

CHRISTINA: I am not afraid! (*She immerses herself in the dream. Turning to* TINA, *she says:*) Your father—has disappointed me—very much, Christina.

    TINA: How?

CHRISTINA: By dying.

    TINA: Oh.

CHRISTINA: Do you know what you learn by that? ... You can't trust men! ... They make you promises and then—they leave you! Come back! Come back! Now I have nothing but this! *(She looks at a small imaginary casket in her hands.)*

    TINA: Mama! What a pretty golden casket! What's inside it?

CHRISTINA: Your father's heart...

    TINA: My father's heart... Give it to me! He loved me!

CHRISTINA: He loved *me*! He loved *me*! And now I have no friend!

    TINA: *I'll* be your friend...

CHRISTINA: *(Looking at* TINA *scornfully)* You? You —! *(Her eyes breathe hate.)* A child is no friend! A child is nothing! ...I need someone to understand me. Someone to keep me company, to make me smile...

    (Suddenly BIRGITO *appears wearing an exaggerated court costume.)*

    TINA: Oh, Mama! Who is that awful man behind you?

CHRISTINA: It's Gonzago.

    TINA: Why is he here?

CHRISTINA: To make us laugh! Dance, Gonzago! Dance!

    (He dances with grotesque and malformed steps.)

    TINA: But he's so ugly! How can you bear to have him near you?

CHRISTINA: Dwarfs bring you luck! They keep out evil spirits. Have one with you always when you are with child. Or else you may bring forth a creature with skin like scales, or charred, or hairy. Or one with a giant head, but no eyes or mouth. Or one—

*(*CHRISTINA *breaks off. She tears off the shawl.)* I won't go on! She's an hysterical female! I despise everything about her! Why wasn't *she* the one who died?!

    (She breaks violently away as the DWARF *grabs* TINA *and whirls her off.)*

*(*CHRISTINA *wakens from the nightmare.)*

CHRISTINA: Oh, God, I didn't mean to say that!

AZZOLINO: *(Giving her the mercy of a response, yet knowing she does mean it)* Of course...

CHRISTINA: I don't mean it! I don't mean it...

AZZOLINO: Perhaps you'd like to rest—

CHRISTINA: No! *(She pulls herself together.)* I can face my own nightmares, Cardinal Azzolino. I am not my mother.

AZZOLINO: Is she still alive?

CHRISTINA: Not to me.

AZZOLINO: Why not to you?

CHRISTINA: You should ask her that. She despised me from the moment I was born. I soon learned to return the affection—in kind.

AZZOLINO: And yet you keep a dwarf, like she did—

CHRISTINA: It's the same one. She gave him to me as a farewell present. I think she thought I would throw him back in her face. I wouldn't give her the satisfaction.

AZZOLINO: Do you keep him to bring you luck as well?

CHRISTINA: No.

AZZOLINO: Why, then?

CHRISTINA: ...To remind me of my inner self.

AZZOLINO: You see your inner self—like that?

CHRISTINA: How do you see your self?

(AZZOLINO *looks at* CHRISTINA *for a moment. He doesn't answer.*)

CHRISTINA: *(She bursts out with:)* Thank God I have no daughter! I couldn't bear anyone to feel about me as I felt about her!

AZZOLINO: She made you hate all women—

CHRISTINA: Hate women! *(She laughs.)*

  (EBBA *and* CHRIS *enter, hand in hand.*)

CHRISTINA: You've read every line of that book, haven't you, Azzolino? Surely you know the worst thing I'm accused of isn't hating women! *(She laughs again. She looks at* CHRIS *and* EBBA.*)* Have you ever found a woman of such beauty, such intelligence, that she was, in every form, in every gesture, exactly what a woman ought to be?

AZZOLINO: Yes. The Virgin Mary.

CHRISTINA: I'll match my Ebba to her any day!

> EBBA: *(Laughing)* Christina, you must give up hunting!
>
> CHRIS: Why, Ebba?
>
> EBBA: It's making you into a lean young boy! You look like a fellow who is just about to have to shave!
>
> CHRIS: I know.
>
> EBBA: You must come boating with us tomorrow. And let the *men* handle the oars. You and I will just sit still.

CHRIS: I'll copy you.

EBBA: I'll come and choose your dress.

CHRIS: And will you comb my hair for me?

EBBA: Of course I will. But you can't do much with it until it grows! Why did you slice it all off?

CHRISTINA: Because I'll never be like you!

EBBA: What?

CHRIS: I'll never be like you, Ebba.

EBBA: Dear Christina...

CHRIS: Isn't it ironic that I should have the crown and you have everything else?

EBBA: I haven't so much.

CHRIS: Oxenstierna said that when I fell in love, I would feel beautiful—

EBBA: And so you will—

(CHRISTINA *moves toward* EBBA.)

CHRISTINA: But I love you—. And when I think of you, I feel so ugly.

(CHRIS *retreats and eventually disappears.*)

CHRISTINA: Knowing your beauty makes me know my ugliness the more. Watching you walk, with such grace, I realize how awkward I am—how clumsy—

EBBA: It's not true, Christina...

CHRISTINA: I ought by rights to hate you, but I can't.

EBBA: And I don't want you to—

CHRISTINA: Exploring myself—is such a barren country. Exploring you—what natural wonders! When I touch you, I realize what a woman should be.

EBBA: So I was born...

CHRISTINA: Aren't men's bodies strange, Ebba? So oddly made! How can we ever know what they're feeling? When I touch you, I know your body's secrets. Know how it echoes me. When you share my bed—

AZZOLINO: This is mortal sin—!

CHRISTINA: I love you, Ebba...

AZZOLINO: Stop!

(CHRISTINA *looks up.*)

(EBBA *disappears*.)

CHRISTINA: You said you wanted to know everything about me—

AZZOLINO: You're telling me all this with no remorse—

CHRISTINA: Do you want to hear the truth, or only what you want to hear?

AZZOLINO: The truth.

CHRISTINA: I loved that woman more than I have ever loved a man.

AZZOLINO: Have you ever tried to love a man?

CHRISTINA: I've found none worthy.

AZZOLINO: Perhaps you didn't look hard enough.

CHRISTINA: Well, get out your lantern, Cardinal, and let's go search! Perhaps there's one waiting just around the corner! Tell me, have *you* ever found a man you could love as I loved Ebba?

AZZOLINO: You can't turn every question back on me—

CHRISTINA: Love is so rare! Must we deny it when we find it? Is it to be called hideous just because the object is the same sex? Don't you love the Pope—?

AZZOLINO: This is blasphemy!

CHRISTINA: Blasphemy! Well, then, sell me an indulgence! There is no sin so large that the wrath of the Church cannot be bought off. Isn't that true?

AZZOLINO: You will not continue!

CHRISTINA: *(Furiously)* Indeed, I will not continue, Azzolino! ... I thought you wanted to hear my life. But you only want the pale acceptable edges of it. I came here to embrace a new religion. Instead, I find myself on trial for my life! I do not regret my life, Azzolino—except for the last few hours of it. I have had enough of standing in this ante-chamber, denied the courtesies that would be granted an ordinary kitchen maid! You can take your drafty corridor and save it for the next Queen who happens to come your way. Am I pure enough to be let in? I refuse to answer! But see how the world will laugh when they find out *I* walked out on the Pope! *(She strides toward the upstage exit.)*

AZZOLINO: *(Calmly)* That is an extremely brave gesture—for a woman who has nowhere to go.

(CHRISTINA *exits*.)

(DOMINIC *enters*.)

DOMINIC: Your voices could be heard all the way from the chapel!

AZZOLINO: Have the choir sing louder.

DOMINIC: Isn't it going well, father?

AZZOLINO: I wouldn't exactly say so. No.

DOMINIC: Word seems to have leaked out that she's here. There's quite a crowd gathering in the square.

AZZOLINO: Friendly or hostile?

DOMINIC: Mostly, I think, they have come to stare.

AZZOLINO: How is His Holiness?

DOMINIC: Resting—

(AZZOLINO *paces, troubled.*)

DOMINIC: Is she anything like what they say?

AZZOLINO: She is an extremely complex woman. Sometimes she seems vulgar and belligerent, other times, vulnerable and afraid.

DOMINIC: Why did she give up the throne?

AZZOLINO: I don't know yet.

DOMINIC: Why did she become a Catholic?

AZZOLINO: Dominic, would you like to take over the questioning?

DOMINIC: No, father. No. But the Cardinals are very anxious for your decision. I've been sent to find out what's happening.

AZZOLINO: I'm not ready to make my report yet.

DOMINIC: I wish you hadn't been chosen for this task—

AZZOLINO: Whom do you think should have been assigned? Altieri, who would use her for his own advancement? Merano, who would intimate that if a large enough gem were thrust into his palm, the doors would be flung wide?

DOMINIC: No, no. But have you any idea what you'll recommend?

AZZOLINO: Not the slightest. I don't even know if she'll come back.

DOMINIC: If she is alienated from the faith, you could damage your career in the Church forever!

AZZOLINO: Yes. And if I admit her and it turns out to be a calamity, there'll be exactly the same result.

DOMINIC: I think it's unfair of the Pope to test you this way! You're as much on trial here as she is!

AZZOLINO: Don't you think I know that? Don't you think I know how many in the College of Cardinals are waiting for me to make a misstep? Barberini would like me to admit her, with the thought that her presence in the Vatican will darken my entire future. Fabiani would like me to exclude her, in which case she might seek protection in the court of Spain, which, pretending we've committed mortal insult to a Catholic, would then have an excuse to cut off all financial support of the Vatican—and I'd be to blame.

DOMINIC: And the Pope?

AZZOLINO: The Pope hopes I will be as wise as Solomon and somehow come up with a solution which will satisfy everybody!

DOMINIC: Your whole career in the Church could hinge on what you decide.

AZZOLINO: What's the matter, Dominic? Don't you think I'm up to the challenge?

DOMINIC: Of course you are, father—

AZZOLINO: Then show your faith in me by calming down.

DOMINIC: How can I be calm? The entire Holy City is in turmoil! The Cardinals say they must have your answer—

AZZOLINO: So they can serve her up to the crowd neatly labeled "saint" or "sinner"—

DOMINIC: Father—

AZZOLINO: *(Sharply)* When I have an answer, they will get it!

DOMINIC: I don't think they'll wait much longer—

AZZOLINO: They will wait as long as it takes! The woman has spent her entire life on display to the public! Now, for a few hours she is alone with herself. She is no longer a Queen, or a freak, or a heathen, or a candidate for canonization, she is a human being! A very troubled human being—

DOMINIC: But you owe them a decision—

AZZOLINO: Hang what we owe them! What about what we owe to her?!

(CHRISTINA *re-enters.*)

CHRISTINA: I cannot find Birgito—

(*At this moment* BIRGITO *rushes in from stage left as if being chased from there.*)

DOMINIC: What were you doing in the Pope's private quarters!

CHRISTINA: Do not touch him! Come here, Birgito.

(BIRGITO *runs to* CHRISTINA *and gestures excitedly.*)

CHRISTINA: Quietly now—! Quietly! Begin again—. What have you found?

(CHRISTINA *watches his gestures intently.*)

AZZOLINO: *(To* DOMINIC:*)* Go. Keep everyone patient, if you can. I depend on you.

(DOMINIC *exits.*)

(CHRISTINA *begins to react to* BIRGITO *with increasing surprise and concern.*)

CHRISTINA: No—! No—! It can't be—! *(To* AZZOLINO:*)* Is this true?

AZZOLINO: I don't know what he's saying.

CHRISTINA: He says—the Pope is ill. Is it true?

AZZOLINO: ...Yes.

CHRISTINA: How long has he been ill?

AZZOLINO: Several months now.

CHRISTINA: Is it serious?

AZZOLINO: ...Extremely.

CHRISTINA: ...Do you mean—he's not expected to recover?

AZZOLINO: It is in the hands of God...

CHRISTINA: *(Shaking her head in disbelief—near tears)* To come all this way and find him dying—. It can't be true—

AZZOLINO: Christina—

CHRISTINA: I need him to live—!

AZZOLINO: Whatever happens to His Holiness the *Church* remains.

CHRISTINA: *(Collecting herself)* ...Why wasn't I told of this?

AZZOLINO: No one was told. The enemies of the Church are only too ready to take advantage of such circumstances.

CHRISTINA: Am I considered an enemy?

AZZOLINO: He must be protected—

CHRISTINA: From me? How lovely!

AZZOLINO: I didn't mean—

CHRISTINA: In the event that he should die, who will succeed him?

(AZZOLINO *is silent.*)

CHRISTINA: *(After a moment, she repeats:)* I said, who will succeed him?

(AZZOLINO *turns toward* CHRISTINA *and looks her directly in the eye.*)

CHRISTINA: *(Looks at* BIRGITO *who confirms her suspicion by pointing at* AZZOLINO *and nodding)*. Aha!

(AZZOLINO *turns away.*)

CHRISTINA: Go and pack our bags, Birgito. It is obvious we came to Rome at the wrong time.

(BIRGITO *exits upstage.*)

CHRISTINA: So you have ambitions!

(AZZOLINO *turns to her but does not answer.*)

CHRISTINA: Ambition is an evil demon, Cardinal. You must guard against it.

AZZOLINO: I am not ambitious. I am simply one of those best qualified to lead.

CHRISTINA: And you are vain, too!

AZZOLINO: No. Merely honest.

CHRISTINA: If you were honest, you would have told me of your ambition from the start.

AZZOLINO: There's nothing to be ashamed of in ambition. Not all of us were born to privilege the way that you were. Some of us have had to work our way up without money, title, rank—

CHRISTINA: Is that why you decided to enter the Church? You were born poor?

AZZOLINO: Not poor exactly. But I wasn't rich. The Church is a good place for those with talents but no social station.

CHRISTINA: Not born to be a secular prince, you found there was plenty of opportunity for advancement in God's kingdom.

AZZOLINO: I have ability—!

CHRISTINA: At what, if you don't mind my asking?

AZZOLINO: At diplomacy, finance, international relations—

CHRISTINA: It's interesting that you don't mention prayer.

AZZOLINO: *(Stung)* Perhaps my greatest quality as a priest is not to constantly cloak myself in piety!

CHRISTINA: Your virtues are duly noted. Now, Cardinal—what is your greatest fault?

AZZOLINO: *(With a smile)* My overwhelming desire for perfection.

CHRISTINA: How often do you reach it?

AZZOLINO: Probably no oftener than you.

(CHRISTINA *laughs.*)

CHRISTINA: Well, you'll have to reach it now if you plan to become the Holy of Holies. Or possibly you could leave it all to your sister-in-law.

AZZOLINO: I have no sister-in-law.

CHRISTINA: What a pity! I understand the Pope before this found *his* indispensable. What was her name? Olympia Maidalchini? They say that half the red hats in the College of Cardinals were earned in her bed!

AZZOLINO: How dare you—!

CHRISTINA: I dare, dear possible Pope, because I am leaving! Do you think I don't know what's happening in this corridor?

AZZOLINO: What is happening?

CHRISTINA: A bid for the papal crown, with me as a pawn.

AZZOLINO: That isn't so!

CHRISTINA: What's the matter, Cardinal? Don't you like the truth game? *(Mockingly, she makes the fencing gesture of "touché".)*

AZZOLINO: You are mistaken.

CHRISTINA: Am I? You forget, I've played these power games myself. I know exactly what you need to ensure your election.

AZZOLINO: And what is that?

CHRISTINA: An extraordinary feat. A demonstration of your remarkable powers. And by amazing good fortune, the perfect opportunity has fallen right into your lap. You can confront the most spectacular convert the Church has ever known—and keep her out!

AZZOLINO: This is absurd—

CHRISTINA: Think what they'll all say: "What a holy man he is, this Cardinal! Unimpressed by titles and earthly vanities! Interested only in preserving the purity of the Church! Hosanna to Azzolino! He must be Pope!"

AZZOLINO: So that is what you think— *(Pauses)* Very well—go to him. Go in to His Holiness.

CHRISTINA: ...What?

AZZOLINO: He's there. At the end of that corridor. *(He gestures toward stage left.)*

CHRISTINA: But—

AZZOLINO: Go. His door's unlocked. There's nothing on this earth to stop you.

(CHRISTINA turns toward the exit, but hesitates.)

AZZOLINO: Don't be frightened. He's an old man, and very frail. I am sure you can put your case to him most convincingly. It's very possible he will press you to his heart.

(CHRISTINA looks again toward the exit, but still, for some reason, makes no move to go to it.)

AZZOLINO: Why do you hesitate?

CHRISTINA: I don't know...

AZZOLINO: You've been waiting a long time for this moment. Go on—

CHRISTINA: ...What will happen when I've been received by him?

AZZOLINO: Your life in Rome will begin.

CHRISTINA: My life in Rome...

AZZOLINO: Concerts...balls...entertainments...fireworks...music...laughter...

CHRISTINA: Music! ...Laughter! ...Yes! Oh, yes!

AZZOLINO: And you will have lost your chance forever—

CHRISTINA: My chance—?

AZZOLINO: To find out why you came.

(CHRISTINA *does not speak.*)

AZZOLINO: ...Stay, Christina. Stay and talk with me.

(CHRISTINA *looks at him.*)

AZZOLINO: ...I think you need us very much...

(*This reaches her. She turns to him. From the distance comes the sound of vespers, gentle and stirring.* CHRISTINA *pauses to listen.*)

CHRISTINA: Father, if you only knew—(*She breaks off.*)

AZZOLINO: What is it?

CHRISTINA: It seems so strange—to call somebody "father".

AZZOLINO: You don't remember yours—?

CHRISTINA: Oh, yes. I do! We used to go walking together, my hand in his.

AZZOLINO: And you missed him when he died?

CHRISTINA: I would sometimes walk, like this— (*She extends her hand, as if holding the hand of a taller, unseen person.*) —as if he were still there. I do it even now sometimes. (*She closes her hand on air. Her face expresses the memory of loss of holding nothing.*)

AZZOLINO: I lost my father, too, when I was young.

CHRISTINA: Strange. I never thought of Cardinals having fathers.

AZZOLINO: We do. And brothers and sisters and even aunts and uncles.

CHRISTINA: But no sons.

AZZOLINO: No. No sons. At least—not officially.

(*She laughs.*)

CHRISTINA: What a shame! Then holiness could be hereditary.

AZZOLINO: Like royalty.

CHRISTINA: Like royalty.

AZZOLINO: You sigh whenever I mention it. Was it all so difficult?

CHRISTINA: You ask that only because you haven't yet had power yourself.

AZZOLINO: That's why I want so very much to know how you could give it up.

CHRISTINA: What do you think power is?

AZZOLINO: The ability to make things happen the way one wishes.

CHRISTINA: And you think that's possible? It's an illusion! There are always events, circumstances, strange turns of mind or fate or character—and one is never able to make things turn out the way one wants them to! Never!

AZZOLINO: Is it so impossible that one would voluntarily give up a crown?

CHRISTINA: ...The crown... it is so little... Do you know, Azzolino, I once gave up the sun...

> (*Music begins.*)
>
> (*An extraordinary golden headdress of the sun appears, dimly approaching from the distance. It is being borne by* BIRGITO *as the court page. But it is so big he cannot be seen.*)
>
> (TINA *runs in and, amazed, watches the sun as it comes closer and closer, growing brighter and brighter.*)
>
> TINA: Oh! What is it?
>
> (*It comes nearer.*)
>
> TINA: How beautiful it is!

CHRISTINA: How beautiful...

> TINA: I've never seen anything like it!
>
> (BIRGITO *puts it on her head.*)
>
> TINA: Oh, who could have sent me such a gift?!
>
> (MAGNUS *enters.*)
>
> MAGNUS: I did.
>
> TINA: Magnus! Magnus Gabriel de la Gardie!
>
> (BIRGITO *exits.*)
>
> TINA: I didn't know you were back from France! No one told me!
>
> MAGNUS: I'm my surprise for you.
>
> TINA: (*Touching the headdress*) And this...
>
> MAGNUS: I wanted to bring something worthy of you. So there was only one thing to bring: the sun.
>
> TINA: Thank you, Magnus! I'll treasure it forever! ... You know, I

expected nothing from you. And at the same time—

CHRISTINA: —I expected nothing less.

TINA: Tell me all about the court of France—

MAGNUS: It's said that Louis has *three* mistresses!

TINA: *(Blushing)* I mean—tell me what they wear.

MAGNUS: The men wear ruffles and breeches. They're always competing about who has the shapeliest legs!

(TINA *laughs, slightly embarrassed, and continues:*)

TINA: And what about the women? Do they dress the same as we do?

MAGNUS: Far more elaborately. Brocades and silks. Bright colors. And a new style—

TINA: What new style?

MAGNUS: —with what they do in front.

TINA: What do they do?

MAGNUS: They wear tight laces—that pull their waists in very small down here— *(He demonstrates, touching her waist.)* —and push the rest way out in front up here, like this... *(He cups his hands beneath her breasts lightly.)*

TINA: Oh! *(She stands stock still, not daring to move as his hands remain touching her.)*

MAGNUS: Their necklines are cut straight across like this, to here— *(He traces a line across her bosom.)* Sometimes so low their nipples pop out! *(Demonstrating, he touches the points of her breasts and she pulls back involuntarily.)* What's the matter?

TINA: Nothing...

MAGNUS: *(With a grin)* I was only trying to show you—

TINA: Yes, I know—

MAGNUS: Do you mind?

TINA: Of course not! It's just—that I'm Queen. And so I have to do— I have to be—. Everything I do must be—

MAGNUS: I understand perfectly.

TINA: But I want you to know—

MAGNUS: Don't think another thing about it. I understand! *(He goes.)*

(TINA *dances alone, pretending to be the Goddess of the Sun in her headdress.*)

CHRISTINA: He "understood". I was sure *I* "understood". I was beside myself with joy!

(OXENSTIERNA *enters.*)

TINA: Oxenstierna, I have a surprise for you! I'm going to make him my husband!

OXENSTIERNA: Who?

TINA: Magnus Gabriel de la Gardie! Hasn't he a beautiful name? I love to say it! I'm announcing it tonight!

OXENSTIERNA: But you can't—! You have to consult—!

TINA: I have consulted with my heart. My heart knows best.

OXENSTIERNA: That's not like you to say.

TINA: I know. I am not like myself. I begin to think there may be some hope for me.

CHRISTINA: I ran to look for Magnus—

(OXENSTIERNA *exits.*)

TINA: Magnus—!

AZZOLINO: Did you find him?

CHRISTINA: *(A strange note in her voice)* Yes, I found him.

AZZOLINO: Where was he?

CHRISTINA: In the garden—educating Ebba Sparre with exactly the same lesson!

(MAGNUS *appears with* EBBA *in the distance.* TINA *comes upon them. They do not see her.* MAGNUS *traces on* EBBA *the same lines he traced on* TINA. *But* EBBA, *laughing, reacts warmly and sensuously to his touch.*)

(TINA *watches, extremely disturbed.*)

CHRISTINA: With the very same caresses I was ready to share a *throne* for, he was proposing to Ebba Sparre!

(EBBA *and* MAGNUS *kiss and joyously run off.*)

(TINA *tears off the headdress of the sun and runs out.*)

AZZOLINO: What did you do?

CHRISTINA: *(Defiantly)* I made him my commanding officer!

(CHRIS *and* MAGNUS *enter from opposite sides.* CHRIS *gives him orders coldly.*)

CHRIS: Have you inspected the troops?

MAGNUS: Yes, your majesty.

CHRIS: Is all in order?

MAGNUS: Yes, your majesty. It is.

CHRIS: Very well. *(She turns to go.)*

MAGNUS: Your majesty—

CHRIS: *(Coldly)* Yes?

MAGNUS: ...You never call me by my name any more.

CHRISTINA: *(Under her breath)* Magnus Gabriel de la Gardie...

MAGNUS: And ... you never—speak to me as a friend.

CHRIS: *(After a moment, like a glacier)* ...How is your lovely wife?

MAGNUS: Coming along nicely, thank you.

CHRIS: *(Bitterly)* Tell her she must come see me—after she has calved.

(MAGNUS goes out.)

AZZOLINO: *(Almost to himself)* And you still feel the pain...

CHRISTINA: *(Emotionally)* Not in the least. It is healed. Scar tissue.

(EBBA, big with child, walks in slowly, sewing.)

CHRISTINA: It's her affair, isn't it, if she wants to turn herself into a cow?!

CHRIS: My God, is there nobody left who can keep their legs together?! I said I didn't want to see you that way! *(She turns her back on EBBA.)*

EBBA: We can't go on not talking to each other—

CHRIS: How can you bear to look like that?

EBBA: Like what?

CHRIS: Like a stuck pig.

EBBA: What's wrong?

CHRIS: You've spoiled yourself. You've been ruined. And you go around like that—for everyone to see?

EBBA: Christina! I'm married.

CHRIS: *(Tortured)* So you are.

EBBA: When you're married, you'll do the same—and with the same result.

CHRIS: I never want to look that way! Never!

(CHRIS exits.)

EBBA: Christina!

CHRISTINA: *(To* AZZOLINO*)* Do you know how many times my mother blew up like a whale and then blew down again? Again and again and again! And I'm her only living child! ... Some were washed away before they formed. Some were formed and never had a heartbeat. Some came out and saw the world— and died. *(She confronts* EBBA.*)* How can you sit there sewing?

    EBBA: What would you have me do?

CHRISTINA: Why don't you get up and scream?

    EBBA: Why?

CHRISTINA: For the pain on your baby's birth day.

    EBBA: Women have managed it before.

CHRISTINA: The creatures are so large. Those solid heads. And such a small place to come out of.

    EBBA: Nature's with you at the proper moment.

CHRISTINA: Is she? Always?

    EBBA: Well, I suppose that one can't guarantee it—

CHRISTINA: How do you know it won't be born a dwarf—or an idiot? How do you know it won't come out a monster—like me?

    EBBA: Christina! What are you saying?

CHRISTINA: How do you know it won't come out a monster—like me?

    EBBA: You're talking nonsense! I won't listen to you!

    (EBBA *disappears.*)

AZZOLINO: Why do you call yourself a monster?

CHRISTINA: I came here to forget!

AZZOLINO: I thought you came to understand—

CHRISTINA: No—! I won't go on—! What tricks are you using to make me say these things? Things I have never spoken to a soul before! Words I thought never to say come pouring out—

    (TINA *runs in, distraught.*)

    TINA: What's wrong with me? What's wrong? Oxenstierna!

CHRISTINA: No! There will be no more telling!

AZZOLINO: Things buried and not faced will rise up to haunt you later.

    (OXENSTIERNA *enters.*)

    TINA: Why do I feel so terrible? So strange?

CHRISTINA: I was twelve. I didn't know the terror I felt that night was simply—

becoming a woman. I had been to myself so perfect until then. Now that was gone.

> TINA: What's wrong with me?
>
> OXENSTIERNA: This is the way it's supposed to be. It means—that you can have a baby.
>
> TINA: I'm going to have a baby!
>
> OXENSTIERNA: No, no. You *can* have a baby. Your body is grown up enough to make a baby. But you won't have one for many years. First you must get married.
>
> TINA: That's right. Every child should have a father, shouldn't it. I will marry and God will hear about it and send me down a baby.
>
> OXENSTIERNA: That's not how it is.
>
> TINA: How is it?
>
> OXENSTIERNA: I will send someone to explain it to you.
>
> (OXENSTIERNA *exits.*)

CHRISTINA: He never did.

> (CHRIS *enters.*)
>
> CHRIS: I'll explain it to you!

CHRISTINA: I said that we will not go on!

AZZOLINO: You must. Once you start to pursue an idea, you must see it through to the end.

CHRISTINA: You remind me of my philosopher—

AZZOLINO: Descartes? I understand you invited him to Stockholm and then would only see him at three in the morning.

CHRISTINA: That's when I most needed him.

> (CHRIS *tries to whisper in* TINA's *ear, but* TINA *pushes her away.*)
>
> TINA: Stop it! I won't listen!

AZZOLINO: He died in your palace. Of the cold, so they say.

CHRISTINA: We could *all* die of the cold in my country. Or of the drought. The drought of music, science, art—

> TINA: I don't think you should tell me! I think I am too young to know!
>
> (CHRIS *chases* TINA, *then pins her down whispering in her ear. Unwillingly,* TINA *listens, her eyes wide open in disbelief.*)
>
> (*Trying determinedly to keep her mind off the exchange behind her,*

CHRISTINA *talks louder and faster.)*

CHRISTINA: Who is your favorite painter?

AZZOLINO: Giotto.

CHRISTINA: One of the tame ones. My favorite is Rubens.

AZZOLINO: He of the overweight goddesses.

CHRISTINA: I have six of his paintings of Venus—

AZZOLINO: The goddess of love.

TINA: That can't be the way it's done! You're lying!

CHRIS: I'm not.

TINA: But that's awful!

CHRIS: There's more to it—

TINA: No—!

(Once more, CHRIS *tries to whisper to* TINA, *who doesn't want to hear.* CHRISTINA, *too, doesn't want to hear. Trying to blot out the memory behind her, she speaks loudly and wildly.)*

CHRISTINA: My philosopher and I stayed up till dawn, discussing everything. Does the sun go around the earth or the earth go around the sun? Can faith be reconciled with reason? Do men and women have free will? How do I know I exist—?

TINA: Does it hurt?

CHRIS: I really don't know.

TINA: It must be terrible.

CHRIS: I can't get anybody to speak about it. I have to find out more—

CHRISTINA: *(Loudly, swiftly, becoming almost gibberish)* Everything can be explained by mathematics! If we know the relation between all the points of a curved line and all those of a straight line, it is easy to find the relation between the points of a curve and all other given points and lines, and from this to learn the diameter, the axis, the center—

TINA: It terrifies me! Terrifies me!

CHRIS: Don't be a coward!

TINA: You mean—you'd do it?

CHRIS: Me? Submit to that from a man? The sovereign queen of Sweden go down on her back and be ploughed like a field? Never!

CHRISTINA: They tutored me night and day on Aristotle and Plato. They taught me mathematics and geometry until I could do them in my sleep. They made sure I knew Latin, French, Spanish, Greek, economics, poetry, diplomacy—but what they were really raising me for was for *breeding*!

> CHRIS: They want me to marry Charles! It would be like going to bed with a mongoose!

(CHRIS *and* TINA *exit.*)

AZZOLINO: Surely you could have tried to like him?

CHRISTINA: What do you know about these things? Such questions are resolved for you! You escaped from it all the day you took your vow of celibacy!

AZZOLINO: Even celibacy involves a decision.

CHRISTINA: And what about when it's simply a fact? When virginity hangs upon you like a lead weight and you long to push it off, but you're too frightened of what you'll find when it's gone?

AZZOLINO: Do you think young priests just put on a cassock one day and all earthly longings vanish into the air?

CHRISTINA: Then how do they bear it?

AZZOLINO: They devote themselves to good works and cold baths.

CHRISTINA: You're mocking me—!

AZZOLINO: A little. I'm sorry.

CHRISTINA: How do *you* bear it?

(AZZOLINO *doesn't reply.* CHRISTINA *says, mischievously:*)

CHRISTINA: Or is it no trouble for you?

AZZOLINO: *(Harshly)* I pray!

CHRISTINA: *(After a moment, seriously)* ...Yes. Forgive me. *(She looks into his eyes)* You must need to pray harder than most— *(Pause)* How old were you when you decided to become a priest?

AZZOLINO: Fifteen.

CHRISTINA: It seems such a waste, somehow—

AZZOLINO: A waste—!

CHRISTINA: A man with your strength—your capacity for life. Now *Charles* should have been a priest!

AZZOLINO: Don't you think I have a talent for it?

CHRISTINA: An almost frightening talent.

AZZOLINO: Frightening?

CHRISTINA: *(Staring at him)* You have such power—to make me open doors in my mind that I thought were locked forever. I thought giving words to these thoughts would kill me, and yet you make me go deeper and deeper—

AZZOLINO: For your sake, not for mine—

CHRISTINA: *(A cry of pain)* How much further must I go—!

(AZZOLINO *does not answer, but looks steadily at* CHRISTINA.)

CHRISTINA: *(She turns away and moves about restlessly.)* Since you became a priest, have you ever imagined things you shouldn't imagine? Or wanted to see—things you should never see?

AZZOLINO: What sort of things?

CHRISTINA: Because of your vows—have you never thought of what you might be missing?

AZZOLINO: One cannot allow oneself to think.

CHRISTINA: ...I think...I think all the time...

AZZOLINO: That is why you must speak... You need to tell me more, don't you?

CHRISTINA: *(Bursting out)* Oh, why do you make me go on—?

AZZOLINO: Tell me, Christina—

CHRISTINA: No—

>   (EBBA *appears in the darkness saying:)*

>   EBBA: No—

AZZOLINO: You must tell me *all*—

CHRISTINA: I can't—!

>   EBBA: Christina, I can't—! I can't—!

CHRISTINA: There are terrible things—things you should never hear—

AZZOLINO: I must hear.

>   EBBA: Christina! It's impossible.

CHRISTINA: Even the most terrible thing of all?

AZZOLINO: Yes.

>   EBBA: No! How can you ask such a thing?

CHRISTINA: *(To* EBBA*)* Who else could I ask?

>   EBBA: Not me!

CHRISTINA: *(To* AZZOLINO*)* Who else could I turn to?

AZZOLINO: Tell *me*!

(Pause)

CHRISTINA: I want to know what it's like...

    (Pause)

    EBBA: Find out for yourself!

CHRISTINA: But then it will be too late!

    EBBA: For what?

CHRISTINA: To know if it's what I want. How can I know unless I can watch?

    EBBA: Dear God—

CHRISTINA: For the friendship I have given you. For the love I've felt for you. Help me, Ebba. I beg you. Help me.

    EBBA: My poor Christina—!

CHRISTINA: I will be quiet. I will hide in a corner in the dark. Magnus will never know. ... Please..

AZZOLINO: And she let you watch?

CHRISTINA: She took pity on me. If only she knew what I really felt—! As if to be there, hidden, was what I wanted! To watch—him—

AZZOLINO: Magnus Gabriel de la Gardie...

CHRISTINA: To watch—him—enter and begin to caress his wife...

    (Night. MAGNUS *enters to* EBBA *and begins to make love to her. In the shadows,* CHRISTINA *watches.)*

CHRISTINA: How that sight went through me—!

    (As MAGNUS *and* EBBA *are about to consummate their union,* CHRISTINA *cries out:)*

CHRISTINA: Aah—!

    *(*MAGNUS *thrusts* EBBA *away.)*

    MAGNUS: Who's there? *(Silence)* I said—who is it?

*(*CHRISTINA *steps forward into the light.)*

CHRISTINA: Christina—

    MAGNUS: Christina! *(Coming toward her threateningly)* What are you doing here?

    EBBA: Magnus! Please! I let her!

    MAGNUS: What was this to be? A public demonstration? *(He comes toward* CHRISTINA.*)*

CHRISTINA: *(Retreating)* Magnus, please—I'm sorry—

    MAGNUS: Don't be sorry.

EBBA: What are you going to do?

MAGNUS: Why—exactly what she wants.

(MAGNUS *takes* CHRISTINA *by the hand. She tries to pull away, but he holds her firmly.*)

MAGNUS: I've enough for two. Come on, Christina. Come to bed with us—

CHRISTINA: No—no—!

MAGNUS: You want to find out what it's like? Well, I'll show you!

EBBA: Magnus! Stop it!

MAGNUS: Come lie between us. Or wouldn't you know which way you'd want to turn? ... Well, what's the difference? Left side, right side, you're game for anything, aren't you? Come, Christina! Here's a space for you!

CHRISTINA: Let me go!

EBBA: She is the *Queen*!

MAGNUS: I know what she is. And *Queen* says all of it. She isn't *woman*, that is sure. (*He thrusts her away.*)

EBBA: Please, stop—

MAGNUS: Poor ignorant Christina. Wants to learn. Won't someone teach her? Teach her but not touch her, eh, Christina? Teach her from a distance. Why not for real?

(CHRISTINA *stands mute, as if in shock.*)

MAGNUS: Why hasn't any man ever wanted her? Why couldn't she attract even a stable boy? Why does everyone hold back from her—even Charles?

EBBA: Because she's *Queen*—

MAGNUS: Most Queens end up bedded. She never will. (*To* CHRISTINA:) Do you know why?

(*She pulls back.*)

MAGNUS: You're cold inside—

CHRISTINA: (*As if remembering*) Cold...

MAGNUS: —Like the frozen tundra. Even when you wear the golden headdress of the sun, it shines with the ice of the northern lights.

CHRISTINA: (*Remembering*) Ice...

MAGNUS: You pretend to be in love with me. But when I touch you,

you feel nothing, do you! *(He is holding her.)* Nothing gives way inside you. Nothing cries out to be surrendered! To be taken! You were born without the quality of woman! You couldn't get it now, not for all your kingdom or your wealth! *(He thrusts her away.)* I don't care where you go, how hard you look or who they pair you up with, no one will ever love you. No one will ever love you, Christina. You don't know how to love!

CHRISTINA: You can't say such a thing—!

(MAGNUS *kisses* EBBA *passionately, defiantly.*)

CHRISTINA: *(To* AZZOLINO:*)* How could he say such a thing—?

(MAGNUS *takes* EBBA *brusquely and strides out*).

CHRISTINA: I love. I *do* love—!

AZZOLINO: Whom do you love, Christina?

(She looks at him for a moment, confused, upset, unable to answer. Then she cries out after MAGNUS:*)*

CHRISTINA: You are relieved of your command, Magnus Gabriel de la Gardie! You are made *nothing*! *(She covers her face with her hands. She is extremely agitated.)*

AZZOLINO: *(With great compassion)* Go on. Don't stop. Tell me the rest...

CHRISTINA: I dismissed de la Gardie from his post.

(OXENSTIERNA *enters.*)

CHRISTINA: Do you think I did right?

AZZOLINO: It was your prerogative—

CHRISTINA: I didn't ask what was my prerogative! I asked if I did right!

OXENSTIERNA: Your majesty—

(CHRIS *enters. Her scene with* OXENSTIERNA *parallels* CHRISTINA's *scene with* AZZOLINO.*)*

AZZOLINO: Well, I—

CHRIS: I was wrong!

OXENSTIERNA: What?

CHRISTINA: I was at fault.

CHRIS: *I* was at fault, do you hear me!

OXENSTIERNA: Yes, I hear you.

CHRISTINA: I didn't know what I was doing!

CHRIS: I let my emotions carry me away!

OXENSTIERNA: It can happen.

CHRIS: I don't want it to happen!

OXENSTIERNA: As you grow older, you will grow more sure.

CHRISTINA: You mean—more like a stone—

OXENSTIERNA: I mean—the unformed heart and mind often waver.

CHRIS: In men as well as women?

OXENSTIERNA: Well, perhaps less in a man.

CHRISTINA: I didn't ask to be this sex!

CHRIS: Why does God will it on me and then punish me for it!

OXENSTIERNA: You can acquire the firmness of a man.

CHRIS: How?

OXENSTIERNA: —By acquiring a husband.

CHRIS: A husband...

CHRISTINA: A husband. A mate. The solution to everything!

OXENSTIERNA: For the sake of the state, you must begin to think about an heir.

CHRISTINA: Make sons, make daughters, make sons, make daughters...

OXENSTIERNA: What joy you'd bring to all the people—if you would take a husband.

CHRIS: Would I, Oxenstierna? And what joy would I bring to myself?

(CHRIS *runs out.*)

CHRISTINA: They kept insisting that I marry Charles!

AZZOLINO: He was no match for you.

CHRISTINA: Who on God's earth could be a match for me?

AZZOLINO: He would have to be a man—quite rare.

(AZZOLINO *and* CHRISTINA *look at each other for a moment, their eyes holding.*)

OXENSTIERNA: Christina, —Charles admires you deeply.

CHRISTINA: He's never mentioned it.

OXENSTIERNA: He becomes tongue-tied in front of you.

CHRISTINA: And in front of everyone else, does he suddenly become the court wit?

OXENSTIERNA: There are customs. ... Differences of rank. ... He is afraid to speak.

CHRISTINA: I see. And if I were a woman without title, would he come charging in and sweep me off my feet?

OXENSTIERNA: You know he cannot ask you for your hand!

CHRISTINA: I know. But I will tell you a secret, Oxenstierna. If he did, —I would gladly give it to him.

OXENSTIERNA: You would—?

CHRISTINA: I would have it cut off at the wrist and sent to him in a velvet box. ... But as for giving him one more inch of my body—no! No! I will never do it!

OXENSTIERNA: What are you saying?

CHRISTINA: I am Queen of Sweden. By reason of my exalted rank and privilege, I am allowed anything I want. I am allowed to marry a man I do not love. I am allowed, by night, to submit to God-knows-what idiotic fumblings and horrors, and by day to rule the fumbler and the entire world. I am allowed, after these exquisite nocturnal pleasures, to blow up like a cow, and stumble around, fingers, face, breasts and paunch enormous. And after months of this comic self-entertainment I am allowed to bring forth, in unimaginable pain, a dwarf, a monster, a vegetable, or, if by chance I am supremely fortunate, —another creature like myself.

OXENSTIERNA: Ordinary women do this daily.

CHRISTINA: I am not ordinary! If there is one thing you have taught me since I could hear, it is the specialness of me. Kings rule—and indulge between the sheets in every sort of pleasure. And then they go off to battle and joyfully await news of the arrivals of their sons. I would be happy to be a King and do all those things. But I will not submit to being boarded by a jackass in order to blow up like a mountain and erupt again and again in excruciating torment for the State! Find me a man who will bear my children!

OXENSTIERNA: Christina—

CHRISTINA: Find me a battalion of men who will each let me have my way with them and watch me ride out of their lives forever at the dawn. Find me a chance encounter on a hill where *I* pursue and *he* takes the consequences.

OXENSTIERNA: Christina, you're asking the impossible—

CHRISTINA: I am Queen! I can have anything I want!—And I tell you I will not submit my body and my mind to what is asked of me.

OXENSTIERNA: But if you love—

CHRISTINA: I loved once. I was betrayed.

OXENSTIERNA: You will again.

CHRISTINA: I will never give myself to a man. Never! ... I will never give myself to a man—(*Suddenly she turns and faces* AZZOLINO *squarely.*)—unless it be to you.

(AZZOLINO *looks at* CHRISTINA. *Their eyes hold.*)

(*Blackout*)

END ACT ONE

ACT TWO

(At rise:)

(A brilliant mid-morning. The bells are beginning to chime the hour.)

(By the second chime, BIRGITO enters from upstage carrying a richly brocaded box tied with a golden ribbon. He is excited about its contents and waits expectantly for AZZOLINO — who arrives with DOMINIC from stage left just as the clock strikes ten.)

AZZOLINO: Where is your mistress?

(BIRGITO gestures that she has sent him to deliver this present. He holds it up for AZZOLINO to untie.)

(AZZOLINO undoes the ribbon. The sides of the box fall away, revealing an exquisitely carved ivory goblet. ... AZZOLINO admires it coolly. It is very beautiful but it does not explain why CHRISTINA is not here.)

(DOMINIC takes the goblet and inspects it with admiration. Then suddenly, as he examines it closely, his eyes open wide with shock.)

(He thrusts the goblet back at AZZOLINO who now examines it again — and sees exactly what it is that DOMINIC is scandalized about.)

(He is turning to BIRGITO to demand some kind of explanation, when, from upstage, CHRISTINA appears.)

(AZZOLINO and DOMINIC stare at her in astonishment. No longer is she wearing the clothes of a man. She is dressed, instead, in a beautiful gown — whose décolletage leaves no doubt as to her gender.)

CHRISTINA: *(Delighted at the effect she is making)* I have come to continue my confession.

(Seeing that DOMINIC is staring at her open-mouthed, AZZOLINO makes a gesture that dismisses him. DOMINIC exits. Following AZZOLINO's example, CHRISTINA sends BIRGITO away. Now only AZZOLINO is left staring.)

CHRISTINA: What's the matter?

AZZOLINO: That dress —

CHRISTINA: You protested about my other clothing. I wanted to show you that my heart is in the right place.

AZZOLINO: So I see...

CHRISTINA: *(She is not suddenly beautiful. She is the same person she was, but is making this feminine attempt.)* Are you aware that all Rome is talking about our sessions together?

AZZOLINO: Yes. I am aware of it.

CHRISTINA: Christina and the Cardinal, alone, day after day. Doesn't the gossip disturb you?

AZZOLINO: Not at all.

CHRISTINA: How thoroughly self-possessed you are, Cardinal.

AZZOLINO: *(Wryly)* It comes with the hat.

CHRISTINA: I thought you might feel you were being compromised.

AZZOLINO: No.

CHRISTINA: Then why haven't you thanked me for my gift?

AZZOLINO: If I were choosing a gift for the Vatican, I don't think I'd pick *The Rape of the Sabine Women*.

CHRISTINA: But Azzolino, think of all those converts!

AZZOLINO: Most of our converts wear clothes!

CHRISTINA: I'll have them painted on! Bring the goblet to my apartments tonight, after eleven—

AZZOLINO: What are you doing?

CHRISTINA: Courting you.

AZZOLINO: I am serious.

CHRISTINA: So am I. Quite.

AZZOLINO: You are misbehaving.

CHRISTINA: Yes, Cardinal.

AZZOLINO: You are going beyond the bounds of decency!

CHRISTINA: Yes, Cardinal. I am.

AZZOLINO: Do you know what that means?

CHRISTINA: A passport to hell? I thought I'd earned that already.

AZZOLINO: There are degrees in hell—

CHRISTINA: Well, I've always wanted nothing but the best.

AZZOLINO: You are incorrigible!

CHRISTINA: I am like a child.

AZZOLINO: You are playing a game—

CHRISTINA: To be honest, I'm not sure whether I am or not... Do you refuse my gift?

AZZOLINO: Of course!

CHRISTINA: You could sell it and feed several thousand starving orphans.

AZZOLINO: *You* sell it, then, and bring me the gold.

CHRISTINA: I see. Gold is holy and flesh is not.

AZZOLINO: That wasn't flesh you gave me, it was ivory.

CHRISTINA: Well, then, between flesh and ivory, which is more holy?

AZZOLINO: Ivory is infinitely less destructible.

CHRISTINA: Yet the spirit—which is holiness—is far more likely to reside in flesh.

AZZOLINO: Why did you never marry?

CHRISTINA: The Inquisition continues—!

AZZOLINO: Why did you never marry?

CHRISTINA: Why didn't *you*?

AZZOLINO: Christina, you are driving me out of all patience!

CHRISTINA: Most people take marriage for granted. What was there about you and I that we did not?

AZZOLINO: You and I—

CHRISTINA: Is marriage a natural state—or the most unnatural?

> (OXENSTIERNA *appears.*)
>
> OXENSTIERNA: Marriage is the natural state.
>
> (CHRIS *appears.*)
>
> CHRIS: Not to me.
>
> OXENSTIERNA: It is God's way of renewing the generations.
>
> CHRIS: My pig "renewed the generations" yesterday. And as far as I know she was never a bride.
>
> OXENSTIERNA: Christina, by your refusal to marry you are making the entire country uneasy.
>
> CHRIS: Why? Because they are deprived of their vicarious enjoyment of my wedding night?
>
> OXENSTIERNA: They are anxious about the succession! They want you to have children—
>
> (CHARLES *enters.*)

CHRIS: *(Grimly)* Do they, indeed—

OXENSTIERNA: Your majesty, Charles is here.

CHRIS: *(Not looking at him)* Ah, yes—Charles—

OXENSTIERNA: Will you see him?

CHRIS: If you insist.

(OXENSTIERNA *smiles encouragingly at* CHARLES *and backs out discreetly, leaving them alone. Pause.* CHARLES *clears his throat. He is awkward and cannot get out what he has to say.*)

CHARLES: ...Have you noticed—that all our friends are married?

CHRIS: *(Distantly)* Are they?

CHARLES: They all seem—very happy.

CHRIS: Oh? They do?

CHARLES: With all of them married, doesn't it make you—want anything?

CHRIS: It makes me want to widen my circle of acquaintances!

CHARLES: *(Putting his fingertips lightly on her arm)* Christina—

CHRIS: *(Crying out)* Don't touch me! *(Then, collecting herself, coldly)* I have not given you leave to touch me.

CHARLES: Forgive me. What permission do I have?

CHRIS: To speak.

CHARLES: I—*(He can't go on.)*

CHRIS: I have given you leave to speak. What do you have to say?

CHARLES: *(He sputters. He starts. He can't get it out.)* ...Nothing—! *(He flees from her presence.)*

CHRISTINA: Poor Charlie...

(CHRIS *goes out the other way.*)

AZZOLINO: You should have helped him.

CHRISTINA: Tell me, Azzolino, if you were he, would you have blundered like that?

AZZOLINO: I hope not!

CHRISTINA: When I said I hadn't given you leave to touch me, would you have snatched your hand away?

AZZOLINO: No. ... If one wants something badly enough, then—*(He breaks off)*

CHRISTINA: *(Steadily)* Then what?

AZZOLINO: *(Quietly)* Then one lets nothing stand in one's way.

CHRISTINA: My mind exactly...

>(CHRIS *enters, calling out:*)
>
>CHRIS: Oxenstierna! Oxenstierna!
>
>(OXENSTIERNA *comes running.*)
>
>OXENSTIERNA: *(Eagerly)* Yes, your majesty—?
>
>CHRIS: I have some good news for you.
>
>OXENSTIERNA: Ah, at last!
>
>CHRIS: You say the people want me to ensure the succession.
>
>OXENSTIERNA: Yes—
>
>CHRIS: Well, tell them their sovereign is happy to oblige. I want you to be the first to know: I am going to have a son.
>
>OXENSTIERNA: God in heaven—!
>
>CHRIS: Next Tuesday.
>
>OXENSTIERNA: What are you saying?
>
>CHRIS: I am going to present the country with my heir!
>
>(CHARLES *enters.*)
>
>CHRIS: Here he is!

CHRISTINA: *(To* AZZOLINO:*)* How do you like that for immaculate conception?

>CHRIS: It was an extremely easy delivery. I'm quite surprised.
>
>OXENSTIERNA: Christina, what the country wants—
>
>CHRIS: —is a King if I should die. Hereby I provide one.
>
>OXENSTIERNA: By decree—!
>
>CHRIS: The perfect way! Then we all know what we're getting. Congratulate me! I am the first woman in history to have a son two years older than herself!
>
>CHARLES: I don't want to be your son! I want to be your husband!
>
>CHRIS: How bold he is this morning!
>
>(TINA *runs in.*)
>
>TINA: Let's play house! You can be my baby son!
>
>CHARLES: I don't want to be your son!
>
>CHRIS: Ungrateful boy!
>
>CHARLES: What shall I do?

(OXENSTIERNA *throws up his hands and exits.* TINA *puts* CHARLES's *head in her lap.*)

TINA: There, there, don't cry. Drink your milk now... (*She feeds him from an imaginary cup.*)

CHARLES: Oh, God, what shall I do?

CHRISTINA: He was a lovely baby. Except, poor boy, he was always drunk.

AZZOLINO: Perhaps you drove him to it!

CHRISTINA: As a matter of fact, he's turned out quite well—in spite of everything...

CHRIS: You are going to be the bravest and strongest of all sons—

CHARLES: In the name of God, Christina—!

CHRIS: You will ride into battle close beside me. And when I die—

CHARLES: I don't want to profit from your death!

CHRIS: Of course you do. That's what it means to be a son.

CHARLES: I want to have a son *with* you! *Our* son! Someone who will love us and live on after us—

CHRISTINA: ...Azzolino, are you ever sorry that you have no son?

AZZOLINO: Are you?

CHARLES: I want to marry you, Christina.

CHRIS: What's gotten into you? I've never seen you so audacious!

CHARLES: I'm at my wit's end, Christina. I don't know what to do—

AZZOLINO: Why did you abdicate?

CHRISTINA: I was bored.

CHRIS: I don't mean to hurt you, Charlie. I'm very fond of you—

CHARLES: But not enough to marry me—

AZZOLINO: Why did you abdicate?

CHRISTINA: To become a Catholic.

AZZOLINO: Why did you become a Catholic?

CHRISTINA: To find you.

AZZOLINO: The truth!

CHRISTINA: The truth, dear Cardinal, does not exist.

CHRIS: You'd be much better off as my heir—

AZZOLINO: I am charged with the salvation of your soul!

CHRISTINA: *(Suggestively)* I know a way that you could save it—

AZZOLINO: I'm not your suitor, I'm your priest!

> CHARLES: I don't want to be your heir, I want to be your husband!
>
> *(At this show of strength,* TINA *exits.)*

CHRISTINA: You men just will not fit yourselves into the proper categories!

> CHARLES: *(To* CHRIS*)* I want to be a father, too—
>
> CHRIS: Then do it with somebody else. How many times do I have to repeat:—I have no intention of bearing children!
>
> (OXENSTIERNA *and* MAGNUS *enter.)*
>
> CHRIS: What are *they* doing here?
>
> CHARLES: I asked them to come and second me.
>
> CHRIS: So you still don't have the courage—
>
> MAGNUS: Christina, I know that when I married I offended you. But that shouldn't turn you against marriage forever.
>
> CHRIS: My dear Magnus, you give yourself too much credit. You're speaking of a childish infatuation. There's no need to use such a tragic tone.
>
> OXENSTIERNA: Tell us frankly, Christina. Is it simply that you don't like Charles? Shall we look for other candidates?
>
> CHRIS: I tell you no!

AZZOLINO: Why did you abdicate?

CHRISTINA: They kept trying to get me married!

AZZOLINO: There have been virgin queens. Elizabeth of England—

CHRISTINA: I could have been greater than she if I had wanted to. My renunciation of power was a far greater act than just her hanging on.

AZZOLINO: Why did you abdicate?

> MAGNUS: Why won't you marry?
>
> CHRIS: The matter is settled. Am I never to hear the end of this?
>
> CHARLES: Why are you so dead set against marriage?
>
> CHRIS: Let me be, I tell you!
>
> OXENSTIERNA: Never before have I known you to put your own wishes before those of your people—
>
> MAGNUS: Why won't you marry?

CHRIS: Stop it!

AZZOLINO: Why wouldn't you marry?

CHRISTINA: Stop it! Stop it!

(There is a blinding flash of light. TINA appears, dressed all in white, wearing a halo and looking like the Virgin Mary. She says, in beatific tones:)

TINA: I am dedicating my maidenhead to God!

CHRISTINA: It was the only thing I could say that would get them to stop pestering me.

MAGNUS: What are you talking about?

TINA: I am dedicating my maidenhead to God.

CHARLES: It's a joke!

OXENSTIERNA: She's only joking!

MAGNUS: Tina, you really are absurd—

(They burst out laughing at her. She exits in a holy glow. They follow.)

CHRISTINA: They're Protestants, you see. To them, virginity has no value. ... It never occurred to them I'd find a place where it has.

AZZOLINO: So that's why you wanted to become a Catholic! To justify your desire not to marry!

CHRISTINA: Nuns don't marry, and nuns are praised in the Church.

AZZOLINO: And so are mothers.

CHRISTINA: And yet the greatest mother of them all produced her child *without* fornication. Is it possible the idea was as repellent to her as it was to me?

AZZOLINO: You can't compare yourself to the Blessed Virgin—!

CHRISTINA: Mary understands me. No matter how bizarre I may seem to the rest of the world, Mary understands...

AZZOLINO: You used the Church!

CHRISTINA: Oh, no. The Church used me. It was delighted to think it might catch such a great fish in its net. All I had to do was whisper and it sent emissaries—to tempt me into the one true faith. It sent me priests, disguised as strolling fiddlers. Didn't they tell you how it was?

AZZOLINO: Yes. They told me.

CHRISTINA: No one but me knew who they were...

(Upstage, CHRIS pantomimes greeting an unseen fiddler.)

CHRISTINA: In public, we talked of worldly things...

CHRIS: *(As if to the fiddler)* Tell me, fiddler, where do you come from?

(Silence. There is no answer.)

CHRISTINA: *(To AZZOLINO)* Do you remember where he came from?

AZZOLINO: ...Tuscany.

CHRIS: *(To the unseen fiddler)* How is the weather in Tuscany?

(CHRISTINA looks at AZZOLINO, waiting for an answer. After a moment, he answers:)

AZZOLINO: ...Warm.

CHRIS: Do you know the newest music of Lully? You must teach my court musicians—

(CHRIS freezes, waiting for an answer. AZZOLINO realizes that if he does not provide the answers, the scene will not go on. He replies:)

AZZOLINO: Gladly...

CHRIS: But first, you must show me the latest innovations in the dance.

(Music begins. CHRIS raises her hand and begins dancing with her unseen partner.)

CHRISTINA: In private, we talked of God. ... I told him how my old religion did not satisfy. I needed something solid, something sure. Something which wouldn't seem to disappear when I most needed it.

CHRIS: *(As she dances)* Tell me about the sacraments...

CHRISTINA: Tell me about the sacraments...

AZZOLINO: There are seven. Eucharist, baptism, confirmation, penance, extreme unction, marriage, holy orders—

CHRIS: Tell me about baptism...

(As in a dream CHRISTINA begins to dance, like CHRIS.)

CHRISTINA: ...about baptism...

AZZOLINO: Baptism brings grace, removing all previous sin from the soul.

CHRIS: Tell me about the catechism...

CHRISTINA: ...the catechism...

AZZOLINO: In it are the answers to all questions of the heart...

(CHRISTINA approaches AZZOLINO and begins to dance with him. CHRIS moves into the shadows and eventually disappears.)

CHRISTINA: Tell me about mortal and venial sin.

AZZOLINO: Venial sin is committed without knowing it is sin. Mortal sin is sin committed knowingly.

CHRISTINA: *(Holding him closer and closer)* Tell me about the visions of the saints — *(More and more aroused)* Tell me about joy! Love! God! Tell me about ecstasy! *(Holding him, she throws her head back in rapture.)* Oh, I do want to convert! Yes! Yes!

> (TINA, *suddenly appearing, kneels and says rapturously, as* CHRISTINA *continues to embrace* AZZOLINO:)
>
> TINA: I am in love with God! I accept the body and the blood of Christ, I accept the body and the blood, I accept the body —

(CHRISTINA *rapturously whispers these words along with* TINA, *all the while holding* AZZOLINO, *caressing him.*)

AZZOLINO: *(Quietly)* Let me go —

(CHRISTINA *looks at him, as if wakening. He repeats steadily:*)

AZZOLINO: *Let me go.*

(CHRISTINA *allows* AZZOLINO *to pull back.* TINA *disappears. Pause*)

AZZOLINO: What in the world possessed you —?

CHRISTINA: I was having visions.

AZZOLINO: You were being carried away by God-knows-what illicit fantasy!

CHRISTINA: Illicit fantasy! It was God, you know, who invented the sense of touch.

AZZOLINO: Not for the way you were using it!

CHRISTINA: Azzolino, do not play the innocent.

AZZOLINO: I am extremely displeased with you!

CHRISTINA: I see. And did Olympia Maidalchini please you more?

(AZZOLINO *is stopped.*)

CHRISTINA: You see. ... I know. ... I have spies, too. They tell me things.

AZZOLINO: What do they tell you?

CHRISTINA: Enough to make your pretence of purity look a little thin.

AZZOLINO: What do they say?

CHRISTINA: They say you shared her bed. Often. They say that's where you earned your bright red hat.

AZZOLINO: Do you believe them?

CHRISTINA: Yes. I believe them. And I rejoice in that belief! *(She moves closer to him.)* I think you have known the pleasures of the flesh — and I envy you your knowledge.

AZZOLINO: Christina, I am put here in this corridor to judge you—

CHRISTINA: I am jealous of you, Cardinal Azzolino! Jealous of you—for what you have had and I have not.

AZZOLINO: Your future in Rome rests in my hands alone—

CHRISTINA: I am jealous of what you know...

AZZOLINO: I am trying to judge you fairly. But you're making it impossible!

CHRISTINA: What about you? What about your eyes, the way they look right through me. What about your voice—

AZZOLINO: I am not responsible for those!

CHRISTINA: Are you not, dear Azzolino? On the contrary, I think you know exactly what you're doing. You know very well the effect your presence here is having on me. It's what you want. Admit it!

(Pause)

AZZOLINO: Christina... You are not the first to think you are in love with your confessor—

CHRISTINA: And what about the confessor? Does he never fall—?

AZZOLINO: Will you kindly keep your mind on the matters we're discussing!

CHRISTINA: *Us!* That's what we're discussing!

AZZOLINO: I mean serious matters.

CHRISTINA: *(Laughing)* Serious matters!

> (CHRIS *appears carrying a silver bowl heaped with snow, and a bottle of wine. She pours the wine onto the snow then scoops up handfuls and devours it.*)
>
> (OXENSTIERNA *enters urgently, followed by* MAGNUS *and* CHARLES, *as if at court in a Council of State.*)
>
> OXENSTIERNA: Serious news, your majesty. ... France and Spain are going to war!
>
> CHRIS: Oxenstierna, have you ever eaten snow drenched in wine?
>
> *(She offers him the bowl. He pushes it aside.)*
>
> MAGNUS: We must strengthen our armed forces.
>
> CHRIS: You swallow it by handfuls. It can cure any fever, any pain—
>
> CHARLES: Should we give priority to the army or the navy?
>
> CHRIS: I like the sailors' uniforms the best.
>
> OXENSTIERNA: Christina—
>
> CHRIS: Let's put the army into navy uniforms!

OXENSTIERNA: Christina, please! There are important decisions to be made—

CHARLES: Should we support France or Spain?

CHRIS: *(Dreamily)* The Spanish Ambassador kissed the *inside* of my hand...

MAGNUS: The French army is stronger.

CHRIS: I shall give the French Ambassador another chance. *(She holds out her other palm to be kissed.)*

CHARLES: We must seek an alliance with one or the other—

CHRIS: Which are the better lovers?

OXENSTIERNA: You don't seem to understand. The country is in danger!

CHRIS: Listen—

(They draw near her. She confides:)

CHRIS: In another hundred years—we'll all be dead!

OXENSTIERNA: Christina—

CHRIS: I don't hear music—

CHARLES: You must come to a decision—

CHRIS: We must have music!

OXENSTIERNA: A responsible decision!

CHRIS: Have you heard that bawdy song they're singing about me in the taverns?

(BIRGITO enters as a Page, with a stringed instrument.)

MAGNUS: This is no time for songs—

CHRIS: It goes like this—

OXENSTIERNA: We are on the brink of *war*—!

CHRIS: *(Singing)*
The Queen of Sweden sleeps alone
And swears she'll never marry.
Is she a monster, dame or man,
Oh, which sex does she carry?
Come tarry,
Come tarry,
Come board the monster, dame or man,
And see which sex she'll carry.

(As CHRIS exits, CHRISTINA suddenly cries out:)

CHRISTINA: I'll tell you what sex Christina is! She isn't *any*!

(Pause)

OXENSTIERNA: Christina, the country must be governed. We are here to help you. Tell us what you want.

CHRISTINA: To be loved.

OXENSTIERNA: Your people love you!

CHRISTINA: Send them to my bedroom!

OXENSTIERNA: Christina—

CHRISTINA: The contact of another human being—that comfort—that's all that's wanted. And if one has it, all problems, everywhere, are solved. It's being left apart, alone, singular, that causes all the world's worst troubles. We should send our armies out to embrace each other! *There's* the way to peace—

CHARLES: How can this come from you, who wanted no-one!

CHRISTINA: No one or *any*one. What's the difference—?

OXENSTIERNA: Christina, the nation is waiting. ... This won't solve our problems of State!

CHRISTINA: The biggest problem of the State is *my* problem.

OXENSTIERNA: You must be responsible!

CHRISTINA: To the State, or to myself?

OXENSTIERNA: You are Queen!

CHRISTINA: So you've been telling me for over twenty years! But if only, just for once, I could *not* be Queen!

CHARLES: What would you be?

CHRISTINA: A woman of the streets! A gypsy! A sorcerer! I could become a highwayman, a gambler, a fusilier! I could run away to sea, become a vagabond, a pirate! I could be anything—anything!

(OXENSTIERNA, CHARLES *and* MAGNUS *disappear.*)

CHRISTINA: I could be the Queen of Rome!

(*A burst of organ music. Bright golden light.* TINA *and* CHRIS *run in with a papal crown and a golden cloak.*)

TINA: Make way—!

CHRIS: Make way—!

TINA & CHRIS: Excelsior!

TINA: To the Glory of God, Christina the Pope!

CHRIS: Pop*ess*.

(They crown CHRISTINA *and plunge to their knees beside her.)*

TINA & CHRIS: Bless us, father...

CHRISTINA: *(Dispensing blessings in sing-song litany)* Pax vobiscum...

CHRIS: What is your title?

CHRISTINA: I am the Virgin Christina!

TINA: What is your kingdom?

CHRISTINA: I am the Queen of masques and pageants. I am High Priestess of the Happy Holy Days! Where people celebrate, I reign!

CHRIS: What is your congregation?

CHRISTINA: All those who search for joy. All those who cry each moment of the day, "I cannot bear the life I'm living!" I am the patron saint of the confused and lonely, the priestess of the weeping and afraid, the shepherdess of the unwillingly wanton. I am Christina! High Pontifess of Joy!

CHRIS: Hosanna!

*(*TINA *flees in horror.)*

AZZOLINO: Exactly as I thought—

CHRISTINA: If you want pain and penance, worship at *his* altar. But if you look for laughter, follow me!

*(*CHRIS *exits triumphantly, carrying the papal crown.)*

AZZOLINO: You *are* here under false colors! You came to Rome to set up a separate kingdom for yourself!

CHRISTINA: *(Waking from her visions)* What—?

AZZOLINO: You saw yourself on a raised dais, sitting next to the Pope on an equal throne!

CHRISTINA: I didn't mean—

AZZOLINO: You *did* expect to be the Queen of Rome. You still expect it! Once that door is opened to you, you expect to reign along with him!

*(*CHRISTINA *looks at* AZZOLINO, *her eyes widening in horror and self-realization. Suddenly, she blurts out:)*

CHRISTINA: Yes! It's true!

AZZOLINO: You came to Rome because there's no Queen here to rival you!

CHRISTINA: It's true! It's true!

AZZOLINO: You joined the Catholic Church because—

CHRISTINA: *(Crying out helplessly)*—I didn't know what else to do!

AZZOLINO: *(Indicating the letters)* The accusations here—are they false or true, Christina?

CHRISTINA: *(Wildly)* All false! All true! What do they say? I gave myself to Men? Women? Dogs? ... *(Suddenly she looks at him directly and says deeply:)* I gave myself to no one! I have—never—loved! Not even God. *(She falls to the floor in deep contrition.)* Oh help me to come to Him. No one has ever loved me. Can He love me? ...Help me, Azzolino. I don't know what to do... *(She sobs, face to the ground in deep humility.)*

AZZOLINO: You have come to Him. You have confessed to Him. He will not turn away. *(He puts his hand over her head in benediction.)* God, grant peace of soul to your daughter, Christina. Look upon her with compassion, absolve her from all sin, bring her to Thy light. ... *(He touches her head.)* May the Lord bless you and keep you, may He cause His countenance to shine upon you and be gracious unto you, may He lift His countenance upon you, and give you peace. Amen.

(She rises, as if a great weight had been removed. After a long time, she speaks.)

CHRISTINA: ...In this place, I have told you things I have never told another human being.

AZZOLINO: You were speaking *through* me to God—

CHRISTINA: ...What will you say when they ask you if Christina is worthy of being received into the Church?

(A long silence)

AZZOLINO: ...I will answer—yes.

CHRISTINA: Do you really believe I am?

AZZOLINO: Sometimes God reveals His wonders slowly. If you are not a true believer now, belief may come—

CHRISTINA: "May come"—!

AZZOLINO: It *will* come. I am certain!

CHRISTINA: In other words, you plan to lie, for my sake—

AZZOLINO: No. ... To give you the benefit of the doubt.

CHRISTINA: —because you have come to *care*—!

AZZOLINO: I care for your *soul*!

CHRISTINA: Never mind. I need no further declaration!

AZZOLINO: Christina, don't misunderstand me—

CHRISTINA: Oh, this *is* the house of miracles! You needn't say another word!

AZZOLINO: Christina! Stop!

CHRISTINA: *(With joy)* I give you my full attention. My full mind. My full heart.

AZZOLINO: ...I want to admit you to the Church, but you must help me.

CHRISTINA: In every way I can.

AZZOLINO: You must study the laws of the Church.

CHRISTINA: If you will teach me.

AZZOLINO: You must do your best to live by them.

CHRISTINA: With all my heart.

AZZOLINO: Not flaunting them, not going against them—

CHRISTINA: Of course not.

AZZOLINO: ...Not asking others to go against them—

CHRISTINA: Azzolino, what are you trying to say?

AZZOLINO: Christina, this is very hard for me—

CHRISTINA: Go on—

(Pause)

AZZOLINO: *(With great difficulty)* ...You know the laws under which I live—

CHRISTINA: Some of them.

AZZOLINO: You know—I have vowed—to consecrate my life to the service of God.

CHRISTINA: I know.

AZZOLINO: Then you must realize that my thoughts—must always be with Him. That it is impossible for me to feel towards any other—the devotion that I owe to Him, or to accept from any other—such feelings towards me.

CHRISTINA: I don't understand you—

AZZOLINO: For me to even *listen* to what you have been saying is a serious violation of the rules I've sworn to live by.

CHRISTINA: *(Appalled)* What are you saying—?

AZZOLINO: *(With gentleness and sympathy)* You must promise me, Christina, that if I admit you here—you will never again allow yourself to display to me—or to behave towards me—as you have been doing.

CHRISTINA: *(Anguished)* You dare propose such a bargain—?!

AZZOLINO: Christina—

CHRISTINA: You want me to stifle what I feel?!

AZZOLINO: There is no other way—

CHRISTINA: *(A despairing cry)* But I have found my happiness in you!

AZZOLINO: You must find it in God. If you love the Church—

CHRISTINA: I love the Church because you brought me to it!

AZZOLINO: You cannot say that—!

CHRISTINA: But it's true! Has nothing happened between us during these hours? Have you no feelings for me?

AZZOLINO: You cannot ask that of a priest!

CHRISTINA: I ask it of *you*. I feel for *you*.

AZZOLINO: You cannot love me *and* the Church!

CHRISTINA: But I do!

AZZOLINO: Then you must stop. Or if you cannot, then at least you must keep silent.

CHRISTINA: You want me to stop up my brain, my eyes, my mouth? Become once more the Doll Queen?

AZZOLINO: You must never speak of these things again!

CHRISTINA: You may find safety in lies, Cardinal Hypocrite. I do not.

AZZOLINO: Christina, if I vouch for you—will you behave?

CHRISTINA: What will you do if I don't? Burn me as you've burned so many others?

AZZOLINO: The Church demands obedience!

CHRISTINA: The Church demands a blind soul. Death in life.

AZZOLINO: It asks that those who wish its grace follow its commandments.

CHRISTINA: Do *you* believe in its commandments? Can you, a thinking, compassionate being, accept what it asks you to relinquish of free will, of life?

AZZOLINO: *(In a rage)* Are you trying to separate me from my faith? Who are you, —the Devil?

CHRISTINA: Is that what you think—?

AZZOLINO: Christina, you know if you are not accepted here, no place will take you.

CHRISTINA: I know that.

AZZOLINO: You know your only chance for a life of dignity is here.

CHRISTINA: I know. I know.

AZZOLINO: Then in the name of heaven, help me to help you. Promise me that you will obey the laws of the Church.

CHRISTINA: They ask too much!

AZZOLINO: If you want the Church to bring you to God—

CHRISTINA: I don't need the Church to bring me to God. I was *born* with Him within me!

AZZOLINO: If you want us to intercede for you with Him—

CHRISTINA: I don't need you to intercede for me with Him! I shall do as I've always done—speak directly to Him myself!

AZZOLINO: This is heresy!

CHRISTINA: *(Addressing heaven)* God,—You and I are the best of friends, aren't we! Nothing, not even the Church, can come between us!

AZZOLINO: If you want to be within this faith—

CHRISTINA: Let it receive me as I am or reject me—!

AZZOLINO: You must submit to its will!

CHRISTINA: I will not! I will love you if I choose! I defy the Pope and the Church and Heaven!

AZZOLINO: You will not be admitted! Ever! As God is my witness, you will never be let in! *(He exits left in a fury.)*

(CHRISTINA *manages to hold herself proudly erect until he has gone. Then she begins to sway—and collapses on the floor.*)

>*(Above her unconscious form,* TINA *appears as in a vision.)*
>
>TINA: I am the most wonderful Queen that Sweden has ever had! For one thing, I am extremely pretty. All the mothers of the kingdom want their daughters to look exactly like me. My blonde hair, my blue eyes, my gentle disposition. I am the example of goodness for the entire world to follow. I rule my people with a gentle hand and the country lives in peace and joy, held together by sheer love of me!
>
>(CHRIS *appears.*)
>
>CHRIS: I am the best Queen who ever lived. Kings included. Everyone's amazed when they see me review the troops. I am the country's finest soldier. I rule with a firmness and dispatch that makes me the equal of any man living. In fact, I challenge you to find a man as reasonable and clear-headed as I. There is none extant. Last week I was paid the highest compliment ever. Parliament is thinking of declaring me King!

(CHRISTINA *stirs, tortured by these visions. She raises herself and murmurs:*)

CHRISTINA: I am going to give up the crown...

TINA: What did she say?

CHRIS: *(In amazement)* She wants to give up the crown!

TINA: How can you consider such a thing?

CHRIS: You must be mad!

CHRISTINA: I'm lonely...

TINA: You're *supposed* to be lonely. It's the privilege of your station.

CHRISTINA: And I'm tired...

CHRIS: You don't get enough fresh air...

CHRISTINA: I have too much to do—

TINA: You should leave it all to Oxenstierna. All you have to do is *sign*.

CHRISTINA: I'd rather be no Queen at all than a Doll Queen!

TINA: But to be Queen is to be everything—!

CHRISTINA: I'd rather be nothing and be at peace—!

CHRIS: You'd give up the power—?

CHRISTINA: Gladly—

TINA: The glory—?

CHRISTINA: Oh, God, yes!

CHRIS: You're a coward! A weakling!

TINA: What will people say?

CHRISTINA: I don't care!

CHRIS: You're only thinking of your personal pleasure!

CHRISTINA: "Pleasure!" Oh, my God—!

TINA: A Queen must sacrifice her life for her duty!

CHRISTINA: And what if she tries to do her duty and always, always fails!

TINA: That's not true!

CHRIS: Of course it isn't true!

CHRISTINA: *I am unfit for this occupation!* —The months go by. I don't know where they're going. In the days, I face one crisis after the next. In the nights, I scream out with dreams whose horrors multiply when I awaken. Shall I choose the hard way or the soft way? Shall I rule with a hand of iron or a heart of love? I think of love. I want to break into the maleservants' bedrooms. Treaties are read to me, I hear only the voices of the speakers. I am asked to choose emissaries, I choose them by the color of their eyes. I feel that Nature is setting traps for me—and I shall not escape—!

CHRIS: Close your eyes. See yourself as a man. Say: "I'll deal with this as a man would."

TINA: She's a woman—

CHRISTINA: Sometimes I've prayed to turn into a man. And then for a moment I feel strong and able. I stride through events and move them. I am Power. I am Strength. And then I fade... The moon is in an unfavorable quadrant. The tides are out of phase. My will seems to wither, like decaying flowers. I cry out to be loved and loving, but if it were to happen, I'd be all the more confused. *(She turns to them.)* Look at me! I am a grotesque! A freak! Look at my man-woman brain, my man-woman heart, my man-woman body! Look at me! Two sexes! Both at once and neither! I'm being torn apart! I must give up the crown—

CHRIS & TINA: No—!

CHRISTINA: I *must*!

CHRIS: But what is it you want?

CHRISTINA: ...I want—not to be a woman. I want to tear out and destroy everything that's feminine in me. ... Or, if I must still be a woman—I want not to be a Queen.

TINA: But if you're not a Queen, what are you?

CHRISTINA: Myself! ... Oh, God, set me free!

CHRIS: Pull yourself together!

TINA: Compose yourself!

CHRISTINA: God, let me be not a Queen or not a woman!

CHRIS: You must be both.

TINA: Both.

CHRISTINA: No!

CHRIS & TINA: *You must be both!*

CHRISTINA: I can't—! *(She cries out in despair and covers her face with her hands, near total breakdown.)*

(CHRIS and TINA come to her.)

CHRIS: Rest, you must rest.

TINA: Come. We'll comfort you.

(They begin to lead her out.)

CHRIS: Lean on us.

TINA: You must rest. Rest...

(They lead her gently off.)

(The lights change. It is several days later. AZZOLINO *is pacing the corridor. After a moment,* DOMINIC *enters from upstage.)*

AZZOLINO: What is her condition?

DOMINIC: Feverish.

AZZOLINO: Have you sent physicians to her?

DOMINIC: Yes. But she sends them away.

AZZOLINO: Who is attending her, then?

DOMINIC: Only her dwarf.

AZZOLINO: Why doesn't she send for me?

DOMINIC: I don't know, father.

AZZOLINO: She ought to send for me—

DOMINIC: As you have said—she is very proud.

AZZOLINO: Well, I can't wait any longer. It's essential that I see her—*(He starts to exit upstage.)*

DOMINIC: Father—

AZZOLINO: Yes?

DOMINIC: His Holiness—thinks it best if you don't. I was asked to tell you.

AZZOLINO: But I am her confessor! She may need me.

DOMINIC: Still, it is his—wish—that you not go.

AZZOLINO: Are you telling me the Pope has *forbidden* me to see Christina?

DOMINIC: Yes, father. I'm sorry.

AZZOLINO: I can't obey— *(He starts to go.)*

DOMINIC: Please, father, don't. He's doing it for your sake. He is concerned about the rumors.

AZZOLINO: What rumors?

DOMINIC: Haven't you heard?

AZZOLINO: For heaven's sake, Dominic, speak out!

DOMINIC: Stories, father. Stories. They're circulating all over Rome. About how you and she—. How she and you—

AZZOLINO: By God, I must give credit to people of small imagination! How quickly their limited minds outstrip the facts! ... A Queen comes to the Vatican. I am sent to question her. And all at once we are together not in a corridor, but in a bed! Is there no other possible encounter between a man and woman except the sexual? In spite of centuries of learning, of cultivation of the spirit, mind and soul, does it always come down to that one animal fact? How dare they say we are that much—or that little—to each other?! What do they know? Imbeciles! Cretins! God save me from the common mind!

(AZZOLINO *dismisses* DOMINIC *who exits stage left.*)

(*Alone,* AZZOLINO *takes the ivory goblet and contemplates it. Then suddenly he puts it aside.*)

AZZOLINO: God save me from myself... (*He falls on his knees in prayer.*)

(*After a while,* CHRISTINA *enters slowly, risen from the sickbed.*)

CHRISTINA: Why didn't you come to me?

(AZZOLINO *rises.*)

CHRISTINA: I waited.

AZZOLINO: But you did not send for me.

CHRISTINA: No...I came to you instead.

(*Pause*)

AZZOLINO: How do you feel?

CHRISTINA: I'm still breathing, thank you.

AZZOLINO: Prayers were said for you.

CHRISTINA: *(With a half smile)* On your instruction?

AZZOLINO: Yes.

CHRISTINA: *(With irony)* I am touched by your concern.

AZZOLINO: *(In the same vein)* I am not quite as cruel as you make me out to be. Although I was, perhaps, a little severe at our last meeting. I'm sorry.

CHRISTINA: Well! An apology. That's more than I expected.

AZZOLINO: I shouldn't have forced the questioning beyond your endurance.

CHRISTINA: Oh, is *that* how you think you were severe with me?

AZZOLINO: Wasn't it?

CHRISTINA: Oh, no.

AZZOLINO: How, then?

CHRISTINA: ...Tell me, have you informed the powers-that-be of your decision yet?

AZZOLINO: I haven't made a decision.

CHRISTINA: Ah...then let me help you.

AZZOLINO: *You?!*

CHRISTINA: Why not? Fever clears the head.

AZZOLINO: But—

CHRISTINA: You said I couldn't enter the Church and go on loving you.

AZZOLINO: Yes—

CHRISTINA: Bitter alternatives. Because I want them both. But if I must choose one, as you have made it clear I must, then, Azzolino—I choose you.

AZZOLINO: Christina—!

CHRISTINA: What are you going to do? Order your guards to throw me out?

AZZOLINO: I don't know what I'm going to do with you!

CHRISTINA: Do what you like! I have made my decision!

AZZOLINO: Christina! What do you expect of me?

CHRISTINA: I expect you to go on and on hiding yourself behind your crimson robes! *(She prances about the room imitating a priest in an attitude of prayer kicking up his heels.)* I expect you to keep hitching up your skirts as if I were a mouse nipping at your heels. "Go away! Oh, go away! How can you say these shocking things to me? After all, I am a Cardinal!"

AZZOLINO: What is this exhibition?!

CHRISTINA: I'm showing you yourself.

AZZOLINO: This is—

CHRISTINA: Sacrilege! Of course it is! That's your first line of defense, isn't it? "Sacrilege! Blasphemy! This is mortal sin!" Go, wrap your red robe tighter.

AZZOLINO: Christina—

CHRISTINA: I wouldn't mind if the phrases were yours. But they aren't. They come with the costume!

AZZOLINO: These robes are a symbol—

CHRISTINA: Yes. Of Azzolino the father. But, tell me, where is the symbol of Azzolino the *man*?

(AZZOLINO *starts to leave.*)

CHRISTINA: Go on! Walk out! Are you so afraid of me?

(AZZOLINO *turns back.*)

CHRISTINA: You wanted the truth. Well, there's more to hear yet!

AZZOLINO: I beg you not to say things we will *both* have to do penance for afterwards.

CHRISTINA: I cannot tell you how grateful I would be, if *you* had any cause for penance! I would go from here to Jerusalem on my knees, if I could get you to admit to one guilty thought.

AZZOLINO: Christina, don't—

CHRISTINA: You refused my nude carvings. I don't blame you. They are lascivious. But do you know what I lay in bed imagining?

AZZOLINO: No—

CHRISTINA: The most lewd sculpture in the world... You and I, made of spun sugar, and fully clothed, standing three inches high on a cake. Wouldn't it be obscene, that sculpture?

AZZOLINO: Why obscene?

CHRISTINA: Because we'd be two, then. Two together. And two together is a couple and a couple is coupling and that, of course, between a Queen and a Cardinal, is obscene.

AZZOLINO: It is not as obscene for the Queen as it is for the Cardinal.

CHRISTINA: And yet, the Queen is a virgin—and the Cardinal is not.

AZZOLINO: That is not the issue! You and I—

CHRISTINA: Why not you and I? Why not? Why not? Are we so despised by God that we are to be denied what others take with ease? Is there some mystery about us? And if so, are we something more in His eyes? Or something less—?

AZZOLINO: *(Increasingly disturbed by her)* Christina, I beg you—

CHRISTINA: If God sent me this love, can it be wrong for me to feel it and express it—? ...Through my confession, you know me as no human being on earth has ever known me. There is only one kind of knowing left. Know me that way! *(She falls to her knees.)*

AZZOLINO: Get up, in the name of heaven—

CHRISTINA: Look how low I have been brought by you. I, who said I never could be humbled! Here I am on my knees—and happy to be here!

AZZOLINO: I beg you to rise—*(He turns away.)*

CHRISTINA: What is it? Do you hate me so much? Can't you bear to look at me? To touch me? Am I that much of a monster?

AZZOLINO: Get up!

CHRISTINA: Never unless you raise me!

(AZZOLINO *raises* CHRISTINA *to her feet. They face each other in silence, nearly touching. There is a pause, then he speaks with quiet intensity:*)

AZZOLINO: ...You think, because I wear these robes, that I am inhuman. You think that I am something removed from the world. Suspended. Serene. Insulated against "ordinary" cravings and desires.

CHRISTINA: You forget. I know about Olympia.

AZZOLINO: Oh, yes. Olympia. How do you see the episode with her? A youthful aberration? A coldly cynical affair? I strayed once, confessed, was absolved—and am forever beyond that? ... Would you like to hear the truth of it?

CHRISTINA: No—

AZZOLINO: Are you afraid you might find out what I really am, beneath the drapery? *(He goes on his knees to her.)*

CHRISTINA: What are you doing?!

AZZOLINO: I have listened to your confession. Now, "Cardinal Christina", you will listen to mine! *(He grasps the hem of her gown.)*

CHRISTINA: Let go!

AZZOLINO: Bless me, father, for I have sinned—

CHRISTINA: Get up! Get up! Let go of me!

AZZOLINO: *(He tightens his grip on her.)* You *will* listen!

(Half in horror, half in terror, CHRISTINA *stands still.)*

AZZOLINO: Bless me, father, for I have sinned. I have possessed a woman. I have given myself to the pleasures of the flesh. I have been consumed by lust. I am a fallen priest.

*(*CHRISTINA *turns away.* AZZOLINO *holds her fast.)*

AZZOLINO: For a priest to have a woman, that is not uncommon, is it? It is *how* he has her, isn't it, that determines the degree of sin. ... A whore for a sudden need—that isn't pretty, perhaps, but it might be pardonable. A long continuing alliance with a woman—that is not sanctioned, but surely it must find *some* approbation in the eye of God. ... But neither of these is the way I loved. *(He tightens his grip on her as his tone becomes more impassioned.)* The way I had a woman was to be had *by* her. My love wasn't love, it was a consuming fire. An unconquerable obsession! A need for her—beyond my need for God. ... That was my experience of love: I was debased, my mind and spirit enslaved. I was possessed by living demons! While I loved, I was no use to God, the Church, myself, or anyone! To be with her, embraced by her, within her, I would even have surrendered up my life.

*(*CHRISTINA *starts to speak.* AZZOLINO *interrupts her.)*

AZZOLINO: I am not finished! ... I prayed to God for some deliverance. I lived on bread and water for a hundred days. I did not allow myself to sleep. I wore a hair shirt which pierced my flesh with the points of a thousand needles. I scourged myself. And after *years* of self-inflicted penance—I was cured. I vowed never again to let myself fall. ... To keep my thoughts within their necessary borders, to remind myself of those days in hell, I would submit myself to any torture—

CHRISTINA: Azzolino—

AZZOLINO: God is here, I want to be able to serve him! I want to feel His call again, in innocence, as I did when I was a boy. I do not want to lose myself again, Christina.

(*Facing upstage,* AZZOLINO *opens his robe to her, revealing that his flesh is lacerated.* CHRISTINA *reacts with horror. Then she says, with gentleness and pity:*)

CHRISTINA: But these are recent wounds!

AZZOLINO: Yes.

CHRISTINA: Why on earth would you be doing this?

AZZOLINO: (*After a long pause*) ...Because of you.

(CHRISTINA *is stunned.*)

AZZOLINO: I knew, even before you knew, how much there could be between us.

CHRISTINA: And you never told me...

AZZOLINO: I thought I had made myself impervious. I had kept my vows for ten long years. ... And then you came. You. Strange, tormented creature. ... Confused, courageous, brilliant creature. ... Fearing what I feared, loving what I loved. You set up in me such echoes—

CHRISTINA: Azzolino—

AZZOLINO: You asked me once what was my greatest fault. Now I will tell you. My greatest fault is, in spite of years on my knees, in spite of all the teachings of the Church, in spite of the sacred trust of this uniform—in spite of all these things—I love. And worse than this, I do not think it is a sin. I do not even think it is a weakness! I glory in it! I do love! I do want! I do desire!

CHRISTINA: ...Do you desire—me?

AZZOLINO: (*After a very long time*) ...Yes. I do.

(AZZOLINO *and* CHRISTINA *face each other, overwhelmed at their mutual confession.*)

CHRISTINA: (*After a long silence, overcome*) ...Dear merciful God—!

> (EBBA *appears.*)
>
> EBBA: Can you imagine, Christina! They say you love me!
>
> (CHARLES *appears.*)

CHARLES: Why can't you love me, Christina? Why? Why!

(MAGNUS *appears*.)

MAGNUS: You'll never love anyone! And no one will ever love you! You don't know how to love!

(EBBA, CHARLES *and* MAGNUS *disappear*.)

(CHRISTINA *closes* AZZOLINO's *robe*.)

CHRISTINA: I never meant to cause you pain—

AZZOLINO: I know that.

CHRISTINA: If only I had known what you were suffering, for me—

AZZOLINO: Part of penance is to suffer in silence.

CHRISTINA: My dear Azzolino—

AZZOLINO: ...Tears?

CHRISTINA: *(Through them)* No. Oh, no...

AZZOLINO: And you the woman I love most for her courage.

CHRISTINA: Azzolino, —if we loved—it would be a love of equals—taking nothing, giving all...

AZZOLINO: I know... *(He touches her face.)*

CHRISTINA: *(After a long pause)* ...I want to give myself to you.

AZZOLINO: Christina, we would be damned—

CHRISTINA: And if we were? We'd float through hell together forever, like Paolo and Francesca. What an exquisite punishment! Eternally joined together in the act of love!

AZZOLINO: Christina—

CHRISTINA: If I don't have you, I will have no one. ... Once! Just once—!

AZZOLINO: It is never once. Once is always only the beginning.

CHRISTINA: Then let's begin and give ourselves to love! Let's enjoy all that God has given humans to enjoy! Let's celebrate Him! Let's fulfill His commands! Say *Yes* —to Him, to Life, to Love, to Everything!

AZZOLINO: How magnificent you are—!

(*Suddenly he comes to her. They kiss.*)

CHRISTINA: ...I love you, Azzolino.

AZZOLINO: Christina... Dear Christina...

CHRISTINA: We must have a secret pact together. A set of rules for you and me alone. Truth will be whatever you and I believe together. Nothing else matters.

Nothing else is real.

AZZOLINO: I want to tell you everything I've ever thought and felt and known —

CHRISTINA: Oh, yes. I must hear everything. Were you wild as a boy? What pets did you have? A dog? A horse?

AZZOLINO: A lizard.

(CHRISTINA *laughs, then says quietly, very simply:*)

CHRISTINA: Will you be my true good friend? I've never had one.

AZZOLINO: If you'll be mine.

CHRISTINA: Till death.

(AZZOLINO *and* CHRISTINA *touch, as comrades.*)

CHRISTINA: I asked philosophers — what is happiness? No answer made any sense to me. That was because I'd never felt it — not until this hour.

(AZZOLINO *and* CHRISTINA *start to kiss again.*)

(BIRGITO *enters.*)

CHRISTINA: What is it, Birgito?

(BIRGITO *pantomimes swiftly, seriously.*)

CHRISTINA: I don't understand — (*Then, beginning to understand what he is telling her, she looks stunned.*) No —. It isn't possible —

(BIRGITO *continues pantomiming. She cries out:*)

CHRISTINA: It can't be happening *now*! Not *now*!

(BIRGITO *continues to pantomime.*)

CHRISTINA: I don't want to hear —! Go away! Go away!

(CHRISTINA *rushes at* BIRGITO. AZZOLINO *stops her.* BIRGITO *runs out.*)

AZZOLINO: What is it? What did he say?

CHRISTINA: Is God so jealous of me?

AZZOLINO: (*Strongly*) What did Birgito say?!

CHRISTINA: Nothing! It was a dance! A meaningless pantomime! (*Agitated,* CHRISTINA *buries her head in her hands.*)

(OXENSTIERNA *enters and says:*)

OXENSTIERNA: The King is dying.

CHRISTINA: (*Under her breath*) The King is dying.

AZZOLINO: What —?

(CHRISTINA *looks at* AZZOLINO *and says, slowly, carefully:*)

CHRISTINA: ...The Pope is dying...

(DOMINIC *enters from stage left, highly disturbed.*)

DOMINIC: *(Urgently)* Father—

AZZOLINO: I am coming.

DOMINIC: The Pope is dying.

OXENSTIERNA: The King is dying.

CHRISTINA: *(Crying out defiantly as* AZZOLINO *and* DOMINIC *exit)* Everybody dies!

(*Once they have gone,* CHRISTINA's *thoughts erupt into bizarre, unearthly visions, part memory, part nightmare.*)

OXENSTIERNA: Your father's dead. You must get ready for the coronation.

CHRISTINA: No, I don't want to!

OXENSTIERNA: You must get ready for the coronation—

(TINA *and* CHRIS *enter carrying the symbols of office.*)

CHRISTINA: I don't want it! I don't want the crown!

(TINA *and* CHRIS *chase her, trying to force it on her.*)

CHRISTINA: Take it away! Take it away!

(*They force the crown on her, pinning her down forcefully as she struggles to escape.*)

CHRISTINA: You are killing me!

(*A blast of trumpets rings out.*)

OXENSTIERNA: God save her sovereign majesty—Christina, Queen of Sweden!

(CHARLES *enters and kneels to her.*)

CHRISTINA: *(Struggling in the grip of* CHRIS *and* TINA*)* Charlie! Dear Charlie! Save me! Take the crown! *(She tries to give the crown to him, but cannot reach him. She shouts at* CHRIS *and* TINA*:)* Let me go!

(*They hold her fast.*)

CHRISTINA: Let me go!! *(Suddenly she breaks away.)*

(CHRIS *and* TINA *exit.*)

(CHRISTINA *instantly takes the crown off her head and crowns* CHARLES, *saying to him:*)

CHRISTINA: Thank you! Thank you for setting me free!

OXENSTIERNA: You must get ready for the abdication...

CHRISTINA: *(Triumphant)* I've done it!

OXENSTIERNA: You must get ready for the abdication...

CHRISTINA: It's finished! Now I'm going to live!

OXENSTIERNA: You must get ready for the abdication...

CHRISTINA: The abdication is over! I did it, Oxenstierna! And look what was in store for me! ...I fell in love! I found a man! *The* man—

OXENSTIERNA: *(Sternly)* You must get ready for the abdication...

(OXENSTIERNA *and* CHARLES *exit.*)

(*Suddenly, the meaning of* OXENSTIERNA's *words comes through to her. She murmurs:*)

CHRISTINA: No—no—*(She looks around. She is alone. She cries out:)* Birgito!

(*Instantly,* BIRGITO *appears.*)

CHRISTINA: Birgito, I am being asked to give him up. I can feel it. Worlds out there that suddenly need him. And I am being asked to let him go. What must I do? Renounce him for the sake of God? Is this the purpose of my life? To abdicate everything?! I won't! I won't! I can't!

(CHRISTINA *goes wild.* BIRGITO *tries to comfort her. She throws her arms about him.*)

CHRISTINA: How can I bear it, Birgito? How am I to bear it?

(*For a moment,* BIRGITO *and* CHRISTINA *cling to each other.*)

(AZZOLINO *enters.*)

(BIRGITO *exits.*)

(AZZOLINO *stands for a long time in silence. Then he says:*)

AZZOLINO: ...The Pope has asked to see you...

(CHRISTINA *looks at* AZZOLINO.)

AZZOLINO: You swore you'd take communion only from his hand. There is still time.

CHRISTINA: He wishes, then, to give it?

AZZOLINO: With all his heart, Christina.

CHRISTINA: Because of what you told him of me?

AZZOLINO: Because of what you are...

(*Pause.* AZZOLINO's *and* CHRISTINA's *eyes hold.*)

CHRISTINA: ...Did he speak to you—about yourself?

AZZOLINO: Yes. He blessed me. ... Spoke of the kingdom I could inherit. ... Urged me to consecrate my life anew to God.

CHRISTINA: Renouncing me for Him—like rival lovers...

AZZOLINO: Christina—

CHRISTINA: *(Crying out)* I hate your God! He's nothing but a trickster! Gives with the right hand just to have the pleasure of taking away with the left! *(Intensely)* Moments ago I thought my life had meaning. I thought I understood why I gave up all I had, why I came. For love—for the solution of that final mystery! But that was not God's plan, was it! His plan—His great wide cosmic plan—was to snatch you away just before the mystery is solved! *(At the end of her being)* What kind of God is that? Are we His playthings? Does He throw us happy moments just to snatch them all away? Is that why we exist? So He can taunt, tease, torture, *murder* us?!!!

AZZOLINO: Christina, I can't bear to see you this way—

CHRISTINA: Go blind, then, and thank your God for another miracle!

AZZOLINO: *(Angrily)* That we breathe, think, feel, hear, see, is enough of a miracle! That He continues to let us do so when we squander most of His gifts most of the time is the greatest miracle of which I can conceive!

(Pause)

CHRISTINA: ...Azzolino—what are we going to do?

AZZOLINO: What can I say to comfort you?

CHRISTINA: You let me go so easily—!

AZZOLINO: *(Struggling within himself)* If you think that—you have understood nothing of me...

CHRISTINA: Then how can this happen—to us?

AZZOLINO: *(After a pause, gently, and with great pain)* ...All lovers feel—that they are exceptions. That they make their own rules, create their own laws. That they live—as you and I have lived in this corridor—in their own special universe. ...But God's kingdom is greater—and, in the end, it must be served...

(A long silence. At last CHRISTINA *says:)*

CHRISTINA: ...Are we not the earth's strangest couple? Saying no to each other—and having that the greatest gift we each can give?

AZZOLINO: I have one more: just one last time to say—I love you.

(CHRISTINA *looks at* AZZOLINO *as if he had given her the universe.*)

(Slowly, AZZOLINO *raises his hand and makes a cross above* CHRISTINA, *in benediction. In response, she makes a cross of benediction over him.)*

(For a moment, AZZOLINO's and CHRISTINA's fingertips touch, communicating all desire, all passion, all holiness. Then they slowly lower their hands and he says:)

AZZOLINO: Won't you go in and receive the Pope's blessing?

CHRISTINA: Do you think I'm worthy of it?

AZZOLINO: I think you are. I think you've been through enough of a trial to enter heaven.

CHRISTINA: Have I? Well, if ever I do get there, I must ask God a question.

AZZOLINO: What question?

CHRISTINA: *(After a long pause, a tortured cry from the heart)* ...Why—?

(CHRISTINA looks at AZZOLINO once more, searching for answers. Their eyes hold, communicating for the last time the depth of their feeling.)

(Then CHRISTINA turns toward stage left and exits.)

(AZZOLINO watches her go.)

(Blackout)

END OF PLAY

THE PERFECT MARRIAGE

THE PERFECT MARRIAGE was presented in staged readings at the East Hampton Playwright's Theatre and at the Roundabout Theater in New York City. Other staged readings were presented at the Penguin Theater in Stony Point, NY, and at Santa Barbara City College.

CHARACTERS & SETTING

PERCY BYSSHE SHELLEY
ARCHANGEL/DEVIL
MARY SHELLEY
WOMAN *(as* HARRIET, CLAIRE, ELISE *&* JANE*)*
MAN *(as* SOLDIER, HOGG, BYRON, POLICEMAN *&* PRINCE*)*

The action takes place in the afterworld before and after 1851.

Setting: Limbo is a grey abstract space of unformed shapes and shadows.

When the space is transformed into Hell, these unformed shapes become flames. Heaven is suggested by radiant shafts of light.

When the environment changes to suggest scenes from the past, the transformations should happen simply. The lights change. A prop appears from above, or a shape moves aside, revealing it.

The action should flow from the eternal present to the past with great ease. There should be a lightness, a transparency, about the shapes which is almost ethereal.

This is a place we have never seen, never been in, before.

ACT ONE

(Time: 1851)

(Place: Limbo)

(At rise:)

(We are in a space whose lights, shadows and forms are constantly slowly changing.)

(PERCY BYSSHE SHELLEY, thirty, blond, handsome, sensitive, calm now, but still with something of the wild poet about him, is standing downstage looking intently and expectantly down on earth.)

(Upstage, an opening begins to emerge in the void. Through it appears a glint of golden light).

(From downstage, the ARCHANGEL enters and says urgently to SHELLEY:)

ARCHANGEL: Now's your chance to enter heaven, Shelley. For God's sake, take it.

SHELLEY: Calm down, Archangel.

ARCHANGEL: Hurry—!

SHELLEY: I thought you liked having me here—

ARCHANGEL: Let's say I've gotten used to you. Most guests only stay a few hours. You've stayed thirty years!

SHELLEY: I suppose that seems a bit excessive.

ARCHANGEL: Oh, no. I've enjoyed your company. But please, Shelley, go while you can.

SHELLEY: I want to wait for Mary. *(Peering down on earth)* ...Look at her. Our son Percy is by her bed. She's just about to give up the ghost—

ARCHANGEL: You ought to leave—!

SHELLEY: What's the rush?

ARCHANGEL: I'm afraid, if you wait for her, that something will happen which will end your chance of getting into heaven forever.

(The opening grows larger, the glow grows brighter.)

SHELLEY: You're such a worry wart, Archangel.

ARCHANGEL: This is the first time anything like this has happened!

SHELLEY: The first time a man has waited in limbo for his wife?

ARCHANGEL: Most dash up like mad to get away from her.

SHELLEY: They weren't married to Mary. I'll enter Paradise with her—or I won't enter at all.

ARCHANGEL: I've told you a thousand times: *There are no couples in heaven.*

SHELLEY: We'll be the first, then.

ARCHANGEL: In heaven, each soul is supremely at one with itself—so there's no need for pairing. In heaven, *one*'s the perfect number.

SHELLEY: I'll prove that *two* is.

ARCHANGEL: Enter now. Alone, Shelley. Before it is too late!

SHELLEY: *(Observing the scene below)* She's said her last goodbyes. Her eyes are closing. ... She's breathing her last. ... She's made the break! *(He turns to the ARCHANGEL.)* Now you'll see. When it comes to love, no one can surpass Mary and Shelley! We'll go through those gates together—

ARCHANGEL: I tell you it is not allowed!

(The opening closes. The golden light disappears.)

ARCHANGEL: Too late.

SHELLEY: Poor Archangel. Don't look so afraid for me. I know exactly what I'm doing. The gates will be thrown open for the two of us together because of the perfection of our love. ... I was unknown when I died, do you realize that? Now my poems are known the whole world over! And it's entirely her doing! Mary! My wonderful, devoted Mary.

ARCHANGEL: What age would you like her to appear when she arrives?

SHELLEY: ...The age that she was when I died. ... Twenty-four.

ARCHANGEL: Done.

SHELLEY: *(Watching her approach from afar)* Beautiful... But even at *fifty*-four she was handsome, wasn't she? She was illuminated by a love for me which shone through her entire being.

ARCHANGEL: What is this love you earth-people make so much of?

SHELLEY: Watch us together, Archangel. You want to know what love is? It's Mary and me.

ARCHANGEL: She's here.

SHELLEY: I'll give her a moment to get used to the place before the splendid shock of our reunion. *(He hides himself.)*

(MARY—*intelligent, handsome*—*enters. She looks twenty-four, but has the poise and depth of an older woman, a woman of substance.*)

ARCHANGEL: Welcome, Mary Shelley.

MARY: *(Looking around her)* So there *is* a heaven.

ARCHANGEL: There is. This isn't it.

MARY: Where am I, then?

ARCHANGEL: A sort of—waystation.

MARY: I thought my *life* was that. So this is more of the same.

ARCHANGEL: No one stays here long. That is—not usually. It's just—a judgment place.

MARY: I see. Before up or down.

ARCHANGEL: The assigning of a final destination won't be hard in your case. Your life, as far as I can make out, was exemplary.

MARY: More's the pity.

ARCHANGEL: I beg your pardon?

MARY: Nothing. Tell me, sir—

ARCHANGEL: Archangel.

MARY: Ah. Archangel. Tell me—is what awaits me here pleasant or unpleasant?

(SHELLEY *appears.*)

SHELLEY: That's for you to decide.

MARY: Shelley—!

SHELLEY: Hello, Mary.

MARY: How can *you* be here? You don't believe this place exists!

SHELLEY: It does.

MARY: You're not, I hope, the entire population.

SHELLEY: Not exactly.

MARY: Good. If all one saw in the afterlife was one's old acquaintances, it'd hardly be worth the trip.

ARCHANGEL: *(Aside to* SHELLEY*)* Are you sure this is your Mary?

SHELLEY: The trip disoriented her. Just wait until she gets her bearings.

ARCHANGEL: Your husband waited for you—

MARY: He needn't have bothered.

SHELLEY: "Bothered—!"

ARCHANGEL: He's the one responsible for making you twenty-four again.

MARY: Am I twenty-four? I don't feel like it. *(To* SHELLEY*)* I feel like your grandmother.

SHELLEY: You're not. You're lovely. I waited for you because you and I are going to be the first couple to enter heaven together.

MARY: It must be something that's forbidden.

ARCHANGEL: It is.

MARY: Of course. That's why he wants it.

SHELLEY: Don't you want to be there with me?

MARY: Whatever for?

(SHELLEY *looks at* MARY *in shock.*)

ARCHANGEL: Excuse me, Mrs Shelley, when you were alive, you wrote glowingly of your husband.

MARY: I extolled him to the heavens.

ARCHANGEL: You said in print that the marriage was superb.

MARY: Absolute bliss.

ARCHANGEL: You threatened to kill yourself when you found yourself a widow—

MARY: I was given to melodrama. I freely admit it.

ARCHANGEL: You called him "The Divine Shelley"!

MARY: Archangel, I spent a lifetime canonizing him. Surely you can't expect me to devote my afterlife to that same rot!

SHELLEY: Are you saying you didn't mean what you wrote?

MARY: Not a word.

ARCHANGEL: Then why did you write it?

MARY: Can't you imagine the hundreds of reasons why, on earth, we shade the truth?

SHELLEY: You meant what you wrote! I know you did!

MARY: How long I've been looking forward to heaven! Do you know how I imagined it? As the place devoid of lust, greed, envy, hunger, vanity, ambition. But most of all, as the place of independent souls. With no need for procreation, no fear, there must be no loneliness, no dependency, no need for coupling. It's true, isn't it? That everyone there lives in absolute contentment? It's the life I've been looking forward to—a life lived blissfully alone.

ARCHANGEL: There, you see? *She* understands the system.

SHELLEY: The system is wrong!

MARY: Not there yet and already he's reorganizing the Celestial Kingdom.

SHELLEY: Marriage is in disrepair on earth. How can there be a perfect couple there until a standard is set in heaven?

MARY: Things have stumbled along pretty well up till now.

SHELLEY: Not well at all! Think of the discontent of couples on our planet. Who's to blame for it?

MARY: Who is?

SHELLEY: This flaw. An example of a perfect couple has to be established in heaven. If it isn't, coupling on earth eventually will end. Mankind will end.

MARY: You're claiming you and I could be responsible for the annihilation of the human race?

SHELLEY: A standard must be set!

MARY: Let some other couple set the standard.

SHELLEY: But we're the best.

MARY: How much you seem to have forgotten!

SHELLEY: No, *you're* the one who, for some reason I can't fathom, has blotted all we had out of your mind!

ARCHANGEL: You each will testify—

MARY: I don't want to testify! My marriage was tumultuous, tragic, absurd—and short. Insultingly short. I don't want to listen to him trying to prove it was perfection!

ARCHANGEL: I'm afraid you'll have to. Once he's brought the matter up, it must be settled. And once the testimony has begun, it must be seen through to its conclusion.

MARY: Is there no way for me to just—ascend?

ARCHANGEL: Not as long as his suit is pending.

SHELLEY: I only want to enter heaven if we can go together.

MARY: I only want to enter if I can go alone!

ARCHANGEL: *(To* SHELLEY*)* I must say, I'd hold more hope for your attempt if you both testified on the same side of the question.

SHELLEY: It's for the future of the human race, Mary.

MARY: If the future depends on us, I fear the race is lost.

(The lights change. The formal trial begins.)

ARCHANGEL: The perfect marriage should be based on truth.

SHELLEY: We had truth.

MARY: More than anyone could stand of it.

ARCHANGEL: The perfect couple should be selfless.

MARY: One of us was, to a fault.

ARCHANGEL: Understanding—

MARY: What we had surely passeth all understanding.

ARCHANGEL: Utterly faithful—

SHELLEY: Now there we'd score!

MARY: Dear God, this must be the place of blessed forgetfulness!

SHELLEY: We had the perfect beginning.

(MARY *looks at* SHELLEY.)

SHELLEY: You'll have to admit no two ever had quite so splendid an encounter at their start.

ARCHANGEL: Where *was* your first encounter?

SHELLEY: At a grave. Her mother's grave... Mary used to go there with bread and butter and a book...

> (*The lights change. Mary Wollestonecraft's grave appears.*)
>
> (MARY *stares at it a moment, then reluctantly moves toward it. She reclines against the tombstone with a book and a sandwich.* SHELLEY *approaches and says to her:*)
>
> SHELLEY: What are you reading, Mary?
>
> MARY: (*Hiding it, then answering*) A Vindication of the Rights of Women.
>
> SHELLEY: Do you think it will make more sense if you read it on its author's grave?

MARY: (*In the present, to the* ARCHANGEL) Must I relive my life just as I thought I'd finally escaped it?

ARCHANGEL: All must be spoken.

> MARY: (*Reluctantly returning to the past*) My mother died when I was born. Reading her work is my way of getting to know her. How bold and clear her mind was, how free her thinking.
>
> SHELLEY: Do you think you think like her?
>
> MARY: Yes, I believe so.
>
> SHELLEY: And a little like your father?

MARY: A little like him, too. Being the daughter of Mary Wollestonecraft and William Godwin is no light responsibility! I have so much to live up to!

SHELLEY: Do you fashion your thoughts to please?

MARY: No! ...Do you fashion your thoughts to *dis*please?

SHELLEY: Touché, Mary Godwin!

MARY: Rebellion for the sake of rebellion is a mark of youth.

SHELLEY: Youth! I'm six years older than you are!

MARY: I was born mature.

SHELLEY: Yes, I think you were. You have an advantage over me. Your father's a philosopher. You were born to riches of the mind. All I was born to was a title.

MARY: Is it true what they say? That your father will have nothing to do with you?

SHELLEY: Sir Timothy's refusing to speak to me is the pride of my life! All the old fogey wants is to raise me to be as bigoted as he is! Can you imagine? The old codger stopped talking to me just because I was booted out of Oxford!

MARY: Why were you?

SHELLEY: I tacked the tenets of atheism on the Chapel door!

(MARY *smiles*.)

SHELLEY: I hate anything which dictates how a man must think—particularly organized religion.

MARY: *(Aside)* Make a note of that, Archangel.

SHELLEY: I hate kings, war, poverty, injustice and political oppression. I love the possibilities of the human mind. I love words, vision, truth, freedom, sailing paper boats along the river! I love friendship, poetry, painting, music—

MARY: *(Suddenly interrupting)* Do you love *me*?

SHELLEY: I beg your pardon?

MARY: I've seen you looking at me across my father's table, Mr. Shelley. Do you think I don't know what those looks mean?

SHELLEY: What an extraordinary child!

MARY: Don't patronize me! You know I've loved you from the moment that I saw you. You know you cannot enter a room without my feeling faint. If you didn't know all this, why did you come to this churchyard?

SHELLEY: *(Taken aback)* To see what you were reading.

MARY: You *know* what I was reading.

(SHELLEY *takes the book. Inside it are loose pieces of paper.*)

SHELLEY: My poems...

MARY: I have feelings about you which I've never before experienced. I don't know what to say about them, what to do. I think these feelings happen once, once only, in a lifetime. To me, they're happening with you. They mean, come what may, I'm yours, soul and body, forever.

SHELLEY: You're just sixteen—!

MARY: I'm young, but I'm an old soul, Shelley. In each of my existences I've been seeking the perfect companion—and it's you.

(SHELLEY *starts to speak.* MARY *stops him.*)

MARY: I know I should wait for you to speak and then stammer "good gracious!" or "I don't know!" But I *do* know. I know I'm yours forever. I'm condemned to that, Shelley.—And to whatever you have to say to me right now.

SHELLEY: *(After a moment, staring at her in wonder)* How bold you are! Innocent and bold!

MARY: Do you despise me?

SHELLEY: Child Mary!

MARY: You're making fun of me! I never should have spoken out! You'll tell all London—!

SHELLEY: You know everything and nothing!

MARY: Dear Heaven, have you come here to destroy me?

SHELLEY: I came to say—I love. Don't speak, don't cry, don't faint, precious Mary. I came as a stranger to your father's house—and I saw you there, surrounded by this woman that he's married and her children. An alien at your own hearth. But your instinct for the truth is far straighter than your father's—and he knows it.

MARY: Don't say that—!

SHELLEY: We are not going to lie to each other, Mary. Ever! Whatever we say to each other must be—as much as we can make it—the truth. Someday that may be all we'll have—but if we have that, we'll have everything.

MARY: Then you see us, somehow, with a life together?

SHELLEY: I loved you from the moment that I saw you. I've been searching all my life for the perfect woman. From that very first moment, I knew it was you. ... Before the earth began, it was ordained that you and I should cleave together. I will match your boldness with my boldness, your intelligence with mine. Fire to fire, sense to sense, our minds, our hearts, in every way that beings can come together, we shall come together. If this is what you want, and if you want to give it freely, take my hand.

(MARY *stands for a moment looking at* SHELLEY. *Then slowly, bravely, she puts her hand into his extended hand.*)

MARY: Yours till death, Shelley.

SHELLEY: Yours till death, Mary.

(The tombstone disappears. The lights change.)

(MARY *and* SHELLEY *let their hands fall apart, becoming once more separate beings.*)

SHELLEY: The perfect first encounter! There was blood there! All the planets urging us together!

ARCHANGEL: But the woman was the pursuer—

SHELLEY: I loved that most about her. That her ardor equalled mine. That she wasn't afraid to speak!

ARCHANGEL: I must admit one could do worse than to take this first encounter as a model. Yes, I do believe your opening moments were absolutely splendid.

MARY: There's one small something he forgot to mention.

ARCHANGEL: Yes, what is it?

MARY: The Divine Shelley was married at the time.

(The WOMAN AS HARRIET *enters. She is pregnant.)*

SHELLEY: I never hid it.

ARCHANGEL: You didn't mention it—

SHELLEY: We both knew. It was a subject so mutually understood it wasn't worthy of discussion.

MARY: There was, at the time, more than one question on the subject of Harriet, young Romeo's wife.

SHELLEY: Harriet wanted marriage. I never wanted marriage.

MARY: This "perfect first encounter" took place between a sixteen year old virgin and a married man with a young son and a pregnant wife.

ARCHANGEL: In that light, your beginning does begin to sound somewhat less than ideal—

SHELLEY: When I met Mary I was already living apart from Harriet.

MARY: Yes, but after you met me you remarried her.

SHELLEY: Only because she wanted a church wedding! *(To the* ARCHANGEL*)* Harriet had no mind, no soul. We eloped as babies. Would you insist I be shackled for life because of a mistake I made at nineteen?

ARCHANGEL: *(To* MARY*)* You could have refrained from pledging yourself to another woman's husband.

MARY: I was dazzled. You know how it is with virgins.

(A look from the ARCHANGEL. *He doesn't know.)*

ARCHANGEL: *(To* SHELLEY*)* Did you and Harriet separate against Harriet's will?

SHELLEY: I wanted a partnership of souls. Harriet was incapable of it.

ARCHANGEL: But did she give you up freely?

MARY: She threatened to kill herself.

SHELLEY: *I* threatened to kill *my*self! What could I do? When love dies, so does a marriage. And my marriage to Harriet had died long before I met Mary.

MARY: This man, who is trying to prove to you the consummate beauty of the conjugal condition, is saying that marriage is an arrangement no more binding than an agreement to play croquet on Tuesdays!

ARCHANGEL: Did you part against Harriet's will?

MARY: Yes! They parted against Harriet's will!

> *(A wide-brimmed straw hat hung with bright ribbons appears. The* WOMAN AS HARRIET *takes it and puts it on.)*

MARY: She was the first, the very first shadow between us. Harriet in her wide-brimmed hat with ribbons! Harriet with her laughter—like a child!

> *(The* WOMAN AS HARRIET *dances across the space.)*

> WOMAN AS HARRIET: Shelley! Shelley! I adore it! I shall wear it to Hyde Park on Sunday!

> SHELLEY: *(His emotions clouded)* Will you, Harriet?

> WOMAN AS HARRIET: I shall be the talk of the town! My pretty hat, my pretty son, my pretty husband, and my pretty new baby—

> *(She comes toward him, but* SHELLEY *crosses to* MARY.*)*

MARY: *I* stilled the laughter. *I* was the shadow for *her.*

> *(Seeing them together, the* WOMAN AS HARRIET *cries out:)*

> WOMAN AS HARRIET: Don't leave me, Shelley! I can't live without you! ... This new child I'm bearing is yours, I swear it! ... You'll be back. This attraction to Mary Godwin is just a passing flirtation, I know. You'll

come back to me,—won't you?

(Ignoring the WOMAN AS HARRIET, SHELLEY *turns to* MARY.)

SHELLEY: Come, Mary! Come with me to France, to Switzerland! You will be my muse, my love—

MARY: But, Shelley, you are taken.

SHELLEY: No soul is ever "taken". Lent for a bit, perhaps. But every soul, always, must belong to itself and must be free. The oaths of the marriage contract are a snare. You and I will never need them. For you and me there will be only one bond: Love.

MARY: But Harriet—

(As if in another place, the WOMAN AS HARRIET *cries out:)*

WOMAN AS HARRIET: I'm prettier than she is! When I walk in the park, you should see how all the soldiers flirt with me!

(The MAN AS SOLDIER *enters. The* WOMAN AS HARRIET *flirts with him. She exits. He follows.)*

SHELLEY: A husband and wife ought to continue united only so long as they love each other. Any law which forces them to live together one moment after the decay of their affection is intolerable tyranny! There is no love, therefore I am not married. It's that simple.

ARCHANGEL: So you and Mary ran off—

SHELLEY: She tied her fate to mine and, one dark night, fled with me across the Channel.

(The night sky over the English Channel appears. We see the dark clouds and hear the wind and the waves.)

MARY: The first time happens only one time to a woman. And Shelley was the perfect lover for a first time. ... Ask anybody.

(SHELLEY holds open a great dark cloak for MARY. For a moment, she hesitates, but the force of memory compels her to enter. He wraps her in the cloak and, looking at her tenderly, says:)

SHELLEY: You aren't afraid of love, are you, Mary?

MARY: *(Softly)* No, Shelley.

SHELLEY: Where there is no love, the union of two bodies is sinful. But where the heart, the soul, the mind have joined, as ours have joined, then the bodies must join, too.

(MARY and SHELLEY join hands. She is aroused, overwhelmed by his touch.)

SHELLEY: We shall be, you and I, the perfect couple. I pledge to you nothing less than the ideal life—without jealousy, without hypocrisy, without slavery. I don't want you to lose yourself in my life. I want a life of clear thought, mutual respect, for each of us complete and total freedom. Do you understand me, Mary? A wondrous new way of living—each of us totally each other's and totally free.

MARY: The grand illusion!

ARCHANGEL: *(To MARY)* How could you do it—run off with another woman's husband?

MARY: ...He had the gift of tongues. He knew the language of the heart. He made his own rules—and every one seemed clear and fine to me.

ARCHANGEL: But still—

(SHELLEY comes toward her.)

MARY: And then—he touched me. I didn't know what feeling was until he touched me! And suddenly—this feeling overcame me—like a madness. I didn't know what it was. It was—desire.

ARCHANGEL: So he was as good at loving as they say—

MARY: Better.

SHELLEY: Best!

(SHELLEY starts to embrace MARY. She pulls away.)

MARY: Keep your distance! I thought that in this region the sense of touch would be mercifully absent!

SHELLEY: Sorry, Mary. No such relief.

(SHELLEY comes toward MARY again.)

MARY: No, don't! I won't be seduced in this world as I was in the other!

SHELLEY: You loved the seduction. Admit it!

MARY: Your touch and your poetry. One or the other could always bring me down.

SHELLEY: *(Quoting himself seductively)*
"I fear thy kisses gentle maiden,
Thou needest not fear mine—"

MARY: Enough—!

SHELLEY: *(To the ARCHANGEL)* She still responds. After nearly forty years—!
...To the perfect first encounter, add the perfect elopement.

MARY: Yes, if the perfect number on the perfect elopement is three!

(The sparkle of light dancing off water appears. The WOMAN AS CLAIRE enters and starts to disrobe.)

WOMAN AS CLAIRE: Shelley, come swim with me! The Channel's ice! It's thrilling!

MARY: On our first, our "unwed honeymoon" trip together, he insisted we bring along my stepsister, Claire.

SHELLEY: I thought you'd like a companion—

MARY: So you could go bathing with her in the nude?

SHELLEY: We invited you along.

MARY: It was too cold—!

WOMAN AS CLAIRE: It's divine! Oh, Shelley! Dive off the rock with me!

(The WOMAN AS CLAIRE *pulls* SHELLEY *toward the water.)*

SHELLEY: But I can't swim!

WOMAN AS CLAIRE: Then drown yourself in delight!

SHELLEY: But Mary—

WOMAN AS CLAIRE: Never mind her. She never dares anything. I do. Come on, Shelley—!

(She and SHELLEY *splash and play in the water.)*

MARY: Our whole lives together we were always accompanied by someone else. Some shadow figure. Lurking. Observing. There was Claire Clairmont, the daughter of this woman that my father married after my mother died. Claire lived beneath our roof almost every minute of our marriage. And whom do you think Shelley invited to come live with us when we returned from the continent? Harriet! His wife!

(The ocean scene fades. SHELLEY *comes to* MARY, *in the past.)*

SHELLEY: I can't understand why she refused. I thought she'd want to have our second baby where I could look after her.

MARY: Is being alone with me so difficult?

SHELLEY: I want us to be seen. I am so proud of us! I want others to share our happiness.

MARY: Not only his happiness, but me! We had hardly been back in England a month when he offered to share me with his best friend.

(The MAN AS HOGG *enters wearing a foolish, formal hat.)*

MARY: The Perfect Triangle!

*(*MARY *stands to the side.)*

MAN AS HOGG: Welcome home, Shelley!

SHELLEY: Thomas Jefferson Hogg! You may be the only person

speaking to us in all of England!

MAN AS HOGG: I could never not speak to *you*, Shelley.

SHELLEY: *You* don't agree with the general belief that I'm a lascivious, perverted, atheistic womanizer, do you?

MAN AS HOGG: I think you live by a higher morality, Shelley, I really do.

SHELLEY: My father's so furious at me he says he'll never speak to me again as long as he lives. Thank heaven I still have a few pounds a year from my dear dead grandfather. My father's cut off my allowance totally!

MAN AS HOGG: Because you ran off with Mary?

SHELLEY: He thinks I'm a freak of nature because I got two women pregnant at the same time!

MAN AS HOGG: It's not common in England.

SHELLEY: And as for *Mary's* father, the free thinker, he won't even permit us to come to tea! We might curdle the milk!

MAN AS HOGG: If I were he, nothing could keep me from seeing Mary.

SHELLEY: You like her?

MAN AS HOGG: I think I'm in love with her.

SHELLEY: That's wonderful!

MAN AS HOGG: I've been smitten since you first introduced us. That face, illuminated by that mind. How can I resist?

SHELLEY: Why should you resist? If she'd enjoy it, nothing would please me more than to share my treasure.

(MARY, *having overheard, enters the scene. She is pregnant.*)

MARY: Shelley—!

SHELLEY: I don't want you ever to feel owned by me, Mary. You didn't know about love. I introduced you to it. But that doesn't mean you should spend a lifetime being exclusively mine. If a stranger appeals to you—or a friend—you're free to give yourself wherever your fancy takes you.

MARY: And you also?

SHELLEY: Of course. Me also. If we're free and open about it, whatever we choose to do, the other will cheer us on!

(*The* MAN AS HOGG *tries to embrace* MARY. *Seeing this, the* WOMAN AS CLAIRE *enters and flirts with* SHELLEY.)

MAN AS HOGG: Mary, my own precious darling—

WOMAN AS CLAIRE: Shelley, my own precious dove—

MARY: Jefferson, please! I'm fat as a pig—and pigs are highly unromantic!

MAN AS HOGG: But after you have the baby, you and I—

MARY: *(Vaguely)* Oh, yes, after I have the baby.

MAN AS HOGG: You promise?

MARY: *(Lying)* Yes, I promise.

(The MAN AS HOGG releases MARY. The WOMAN AS CLAIRE and SHELLEY disengage at the same time.)

ARCHANGEL: Did you mean it?

MARY: How do I know if I meant it?

SHELLEY: You loved my unorthodox ways, my idea of a life without petty jealousy—

MARY: It seemed appealing. In theory.

SHELLEY: Let it be noted that Mary loved her new style freedom!

MARY: Let it be noted that my baby died.

(A gravestone rises up. The MAN AS HOGG and the WOMAN AS CLAIRE exit.)

SHELLEY: I had forgotten about the loss of that baby.

MARY: I hadn't. I never forget any of them. Any of the lost babies. *(To the ARCHANGEL)* Our firstborn child—a girl—arrived too soon and died within a fortnight. I'd fed her earlier in the evening. In the night I went to her crib—and she was dead.

SHELLEY: How could I have forgotten?

MARY: Once you said the problem with life is: What we know, we can never cease to know. That's not the problem here. Here it seems one can cease to know anything one wishes.

SHELLEY: I may have forgotten some of the bad parts. But you seem to have forgotten all of the good!

MARY: All this is being dredged up at your instigation, Shelley. Remember that, if more reveals itself than you would wish to recall.

SHELLEY: *(Dredging it out of his memory)* I recall that almost a year to the day that you lost that first baby you gave birth to William—

MARY: So you remember our precious Willmouse—

SHELLEY: A miniature replica of both of us.

ARCHANGEL: Surely *then* you were happy.

MARY: Could a happy woman have invented Frankenstein and his monster?

ARCHANGEL: How old were you when you conceived that image of terror and destruction?

MARY: I was nineteen.

ARCHANGEL: Nineteen, madly in love, mother to a beautiful son, and possessed by such nightmares?

SHELLEY: It was an inspiration of genius!

MARY: It was the result of dark unnamed fears—

SHELLEY: It was a magnificent creative act!

MARY: It was about a man who sought perfection and destroyed himself in the seeking of it. ... The perfect picture of Shelley.

SHELLEY: It was a purely imaginative creation!

ARCHANGEL: How did this work come about?

MARY: It never would have happened without my dear stepsister, Claire. I had a poet, she had to have a poet. She threw herself at Lord Byron—what did it matter that she'd never met him!

> (*The* WOMAN AS CLAIRE *enters excitedly waving a letter.*)
>
> WOMAN AS CLAIRE: I've heard from him! Lord Byron! He answered my letter! He's invited me to come see him! I'm going to become his mistress at Lake Geneva!
>
> SHELLEY: I somehow think we shouldn't let her go alone.

MARY: We were forced to accompany Claire to see Byron at his villa on Lake Geneva.

SHELLEY: Where it never stopped raining.

> (*Silhouettes of the Alps appear. It begins to rain. The* MAN AS BYRON *appears, proud, posing, limping. The* WOMAN AS CLAIRE *runs toward him, enticing him with her umbrella. The* MAN AS BYRON *is absolutely appalled. He turns away. Upset, she goes out.*)
>
> MAN AS BYRON: (*To* SHELLEY) She says Mary had a child out of wedlock, *she* has to have a child out of wedlock. ... Anything I can do to oblige.
>
> (MAN AS BYRON *limps out after* WOMAN AS CLAIRE.)
>
> (*The wind howls, the lightening flashes.*)

SHELLEY: They slept together in every room of the villa!

MARY: Claire had to be certain that she had conceived.

> *(The MAN AS BYRON limps in, exhausted. The WOMAN AS CLAIRE runs in after him.)*

> WOMAN AS CLAIRE: We haven't done it in the pergola!

> MAN AS BYRON: Stop mauling me, Woman!

> SHELLEY: *(To save MAN AS BYRON)* Listen, everybody! Let's have a contest! Let's try to scare each other to death.

> MAN AS BYRON: *(With a glance at WOMAN AS CLAIRE)* I'm already terrified!

> SHELLEY: Let's see who can make up the most frightening story!

> MAN AS BYRON: Present events excluded, I imagine?

> *(They gather by the fire. The WOMAN AS CLAIRE tries to cuddle up to the MAN AS BYRON. He is unfeeling.)*

MARY: We each took turns telling the most terrifying tale we could think of.

> *(The rain pounds down. The lightening flashes.)*

SHELLEY: The rest of us soon lost interest in our stories. But Mary's seemed to grow longer and more exciting daily. It was the story of a man who probed the secret of creating life.

MARY: In my mind's eye, I could see the scientist bend over the creature he had fashioned out of clay and straw—

> *(The shadow of the monster begins to rise. The WOMAN AS CLAIRE stops pawing the MAN AS BYRON. All are enthralled. MARY says, in the Doctor's voice:)*

> MARY: "I, Frankenstein, shall create, out of inanimate matter, a being who can move and breathe!"

> *(The shadow rises higher.)*

MARY: I saw the hideous yet pitiable creature come to life. I heard him speak—

> *(The shadow image of the monster begins to grow to enormous proportions. MARY speaks in his voice, a voice echoing with emotion.)*

> MARY: "Do not turn from me, Frankenstein. I am thy creature. Will no entreaties cause thee to turn a favorable eye upon me? Your fellow men spurn and hate me. My only dwelling place is a cave of ice. Everywhere I see bliss, from which I alone am irrevocably excluded. Misery made me a fiend. Make me happy and I shall be virtuous. But am I not alone? Miserably alone?"

(The WOMAN AS CLAIRE *and the* MAN AS BYRON *exit. The image of the monster fades.)*

ARCHANGEL: How could you come to write of such a creature?

MARY: I seemed to understand his cravings, his loneliness—

ARCHANGEL: Surely you were not lonely.

MARY: His yearning for communication—

ARCHANGEL: You had Shelley in whom you could confide.

MARY: His desperate need for love—

ARCHANGEL: You had Shelley's love.

MARY: Yes, but I did not have it in the future! As the monster did not have it as I wrote! I seemed to know, then, what he was feeling! It was as if my soul foresaw the horror and darkness which would one day descend on me—

SHELLEY: When you lost me.

MARY: What?

SHELLEY: You're saying the darkness descended when you lost me. In that case, you are also saying that I was the light. *(He comes to her.)* Who loved the ghost tale more than any of your listeners? Who loved its compassion, the complexity of its approach to human life? Who told you to write it long and deep, to write it as a novel?

MARY: You did, Shelley.

SHELLEY: What kept you going in the months succeeding?

MARY: Your faith in my work.

SHELLEY: We returned to England, and she wrote.

MARY: It was the worst time of my life, I was possessed by demons.

SHELLEY: It was the best time of your life. You were possessed by work!

MARY: Yes. *(To the* ARCHANGEL*)* I had watched Shelley create, as if by divine visitation, and for once this miracle was happening to me. I wrote and wrote. I was obsessed by creating. In the next room, Claire gave birth to Byron's daughter, Allegra, and I wrote. Little Willmouse crawled in and out between my legs, and I wrote. Shelley writing, me writing—

SHELLEY: The two of us scribbling at white heat. Hardly anyone in England was speaking to us. We were outcasts, but we didn't care—

MARY: It was our own world we were creating!

SHELLEY: Nothing could diminish it! By sheer strength of mind we had created our own universe, our bastion impervious to assault.

> (The WOMAN AS HARRIET's beribboned hat, soaking wet, appears. SHELLEY sees it and cries out:)

SHELLEY: No! Not this! I had forgotten!

MARY: I told you not to begin.

SHELLEY: I can't go on!

ARCHANGEL: You must.

> (With tremendous unwillingness, SHELLEY takes the battered, dripping wet hat and says, after a long pause:)

SHELLEY: Harriet has drowned herself in the Serpentine...

> (The WOMAN AS HARRIET's corpse is carried in by the MAN AS POLICEMAN.)

SHELLEY: Her body has just been found. It had been three weeks in the water. It's thought she'd been living with an army officer and he deserted her. When she was found, she was six months pregnant with his child.

(SHELLEY turns to the ARCHANGEL:)

SHELLEY: Her death was not my fault!

MARY: No. It was mine.

ARCHANGEL: Yours?

MARY: Without me, Shelley never would have left her.

> (The WOMAN AS HARRIET's corpse suddenly revives and says:)

WOMAN AS HARRIET: Oh, he would have left me for someone. Shelley was a man notably devoid of husbandly tendencies.

SHELLEY: I had *fatherly* tendencies.

> (The WOMAN AS HARRIET's corpse lies back down. The MAN AS POLICEMAN carries her out.)

ARCHANGEL: (To SHELLEY) What happened to the children? You had two, did you not, by Harriet?

SHELLEY: (Remembering) Charles and Ianthe...

> (Suddenly, in the past) Mary, Harriet's parents won't let me see my children! They say I deserted them, that a decision about where they'll live permanently will have to be made in court. A *court* will decide who is most suitable to care for my children!

MARY: Is there nothing we can do?

SHELLEY: One thing. Yes. Just one.

MARY: Shelley, what is it?

SHELLEY: *(Extremely hesitantly)* I've spoken to my solicitors—it's their advice—they urge—they strongly recommend—

MARY: *(To the* ARCHANGEL*)* He, whose desire for freedom, whose shall we say monstrous desire for perfection, led to tragedy upon tragedy, he whose desire for the ideal set lives, like dominoes, tumbling down one after the other, now faced the most appalling tragedy of all—

SHELLEY: *(Bursting out)* Mary—we must get married...

(MARY *stares at* SHELLEY.)

SHELLEY: We'll never be given custody unless we do. ... Oh, they do get one, don't they, the rulemakers and hypocrites. They do lie in wait for one!

ARCHANGEL: You are saying, then, that the embracing of legitimacy was occasioned purely and simply by pressure from your peers, that in reality you held the marriage laws of God and of the State in contempt.

SHELLEY: Our principles were *greater* than those laws, not less!

ARCHANGEL: Are you challenging Divine Command? ...Be careful or you'll lose your case, Shelley!

MARY: He challenged everything. There was not one principle, of law or nature, which Shelley took for granted. He opened his eyes, saw the world, and rejected everything.

SHELLEY: Except you.

MARY: And so, once more, the anti-matrimonialist was married. And so my father, the free-thinker, invited us to his table at last.

SHELLEY: And so our friends, with smug satisfaction, were able to call us "Mister and Mrs".

MARY: And so I bore a daughter, my little Clara, delivered in legitimacy.

ARCHANGEL: *That* must have been a happy moment.

MARY: Yes. That was. *(To* SHELLEY:*)* Do you remember what happened next?

SHELLEY: *(Suddenly, in the past)* Mary! They won't let me have the children! Harriet's and mine! ...After four months in chancery, I am legally pronounced unfit to be the father of my own children!

MARY: Why?

SHELLEY: They say you and I haven't baptized Willmouse and Clara.

MARY: We'll baptize them.

SHELLEY: They say I don't believe in God.

MARY: We could teach Harriet's children to believe in God.

SHELLEY: They say I believe in the eventual demise of the British Empire.

MARY: And so you do—

SHELLEY: But does that make me unfit for raising children?

MARY: Shelley—

SHELLEY: They accuse me of being an anarchist pamphleteer!

MARY: You are a poet.

SHELLEY: So I said. But it seems I don't have sufficient volumes in print to prove it. And in spite of the fact that since their births I have been supporting my offspring totally, they declare I am too indigent to give them support!

MARY: And so they say—

SHELLEY: *(Rising to a white hot rage)* They say *no*! I may not have my children! My only crime has been to sue for permission to care for my own babies, and all I've accomplished is to have myself proven publicly to be unfit, indigent, idle, insane, a moral degenerate, a pervert and, worse than this, one who does it in rhyme! ...Oh, what a vindication for my father, who has thought all this for years, and now finds it proclaimed for all to see in the official public record! *(Out of breath, he chokes on his words.)*

MARY: Be calm! You'll make yourself ill!

(Exhausted, SHELLEY *says hoarsely:)*

SHELLEY: But this isn't the worst, Mary.

MARY: *(Fearfully)* Go on.

SHELLEY: The worst is they are dropping hints about taking away *our* children. Yours and mine.

MARY: What are you saying?

SHELLEY: Doesn't it follow that if I am unfit to care for Charles and Ianthe, then Willmouse and Clara must be in mortal danger of exposure to their father, too?

MARY: They wouldn't—. They couldn't—

SHELLEY: Come in the middle of the night and seize them? Oh, Mary, I no longer know what justice is in England. I am so hated in this country, it doesn't seem like mine.

MARY: We'll have to go away! Leave England!

SHELLEY: Can they drive us from our home?

MARY: We'll go south. To Italy. You'll feel better there. Your thoughts will be freer there. Our money will go further there. And we'll be safe—

(MARY *takes* SHELLEY's *hand.*)

SHELLEY: We deserve the sun, don't we? For a time?

MARY: We do, my darling.

SHELLEY: Start packing. I'll go and tell Claire.

MARY: Claire! Must we always inhabit the same space as Claire?

SHELLEY: We'll deliver Claire and little Allegra to Byron.

MARY: Byron will take Allegra and leave us Claire.

(*The past fades.* MARY *says:*)

MARY: It happened exactly as I'd predicted. We left England as soon as we could get our things together. Fleeing, fleeing our home. Yet it never occurred to us that we were going into exile. ... Did you ever imagine you would leave me a widow in Italy, Shelley? Did you think for a minute, as we sailed from Dover, that you would never see England again?

(*As if these were concepts outside* SHELLEY's *comprehension, his brow clouds for a moment.*)

(*The* WOMAN AS CLAIRE *enters, followed by the* MAN AS BYRON. *She is hysterical.*)

WOMAN AS CLAIRE: What are you saying?!

MAN AS BYRON: I'll take care of the little creature, but I don't want you anywhere near her.

WOMAN AS CLAIRE: But she's our love child—!

MAN AS BYRON: Lady, you have a strange idea of love.

WOMAN AS CLAIRE: *(Whining)* How can you keep Allegra from her own mother?

MAN AS BYRON: Do you want me to support her or don't you?

WOMAN AS CLAIRE: Shelley lets Mary keep *her* children!

(*The* MAN AS BYRON *stomps off. The* WOMAN AS CLAIRE *has a crying, whining fit.*)

SHELLEY: Come on, Claire. Allegra will be fine with him. You'll stay with us.

(SHELLEY *comforts the* WOMAN AS CLAIRE. MARY *observes with apprehension.)*

MARY: We travelled to Modena, to Bologna, to Pisa, and finally settled in a house at Bagni di Lucca.

(Images of the lush green Italian countryside appear.)

MARY: To care for our little ones, we had our new Swiss maid, Elise.

SHELLEY: How happy we were!

ARCHANGEL: It sounds idyllic.

MARY: *(With irony)* Oh, yes. Idyllic. We felt, under the Italian sun, we were nibbling away at the edges of happiness.

SHELLEY: We were quite confident in our immediate future.

MARY: But we were wrong.

SHELLEY: Wrong?

MARY: Is it possible you don't remember?

(SHELLEY looks puzzled.)

MARY: More Divine forgetfulness! *(During the following, she picks up a doll.)* Shelley went with Claire to Venice to plead with Byron to let her see Allegra. Leaving our precious Willmouse with Elise, I set out with the baby to join them. Clara was just one year old. Precociously bright, enchanted with everything around her. Everything—a moth, a leaf, a candle-flame—filled her with delight...

(She stops, looking at the doll. SHELLEY, too, stares at the doll. Dimly, the past begins to come back to him.)

SHELLEY: Enough!

MARY: Oh, no, I must continue! *(She goes on.)* Clara was cutting new teeth and the ride in the carriage seemed to disturb her. She contracted a fever. And dysentery. She wouldn't nurse. By the time Shelley met me at Este she was pale as an eggshell and seemed even more delicate. We could not find a doctor to treat her.

(MARY looks at SHELLEY, but he looks away.)

MARY: We rushed to Venice. They sent for the doctor. I sat in the hotel lobby with Clara in my arms. The doctor came immediately—rushing into the room in a great black cloak. But my baby—was already dead.

SHELLEY: We buried her in Venice...

(A tombstone rises. It reads: "Clara Shelley, 1817-1818".)

MARY: It is easier to die yourself, you know, like my mother did, than to live to watch the death of your daughter.

(MARY *returns the doll to its place. It disappears.*)

SHELLEY: *(To* MARY, *softly)* You couldn't speak. For days and days. We kept pulling you to the sights of Venice—

(*Phantom projections of San Marco, the Campanile, the Doge's Palace, etc. appear, superimposed over the tombstone.*)

MARY: But I couldn't see and I couldn't speak—

(MARY *stands before the tombstone.* SHELLEY *says, in the past*)

SHELLEY: "My dearest Mary, wherefore hast thou gone,
And left me in this dreary world alone?
Thy form is here indeed,—a lovely one—
But thou art fled, gone down the dreary road,
That leads to Sorrow's most obscure abode;
Thou sittest on the hearth of pale despair, Where
For thine own sake I cannot follow thee."
Mary... You're dying with her death. Speak. Speak to me.

(MARY *says nothing.*)

SHELLEY: This grief will destroy you. You mustn't blame yourself.

MARY: I'm not blaming myself.

SHELLEY: I feel it all as deeply as you. But we must share the sorrow. Tell me what you're thinking—

MARY: *(Turning on him)* I am thinking—if only we hadn't had to go on this wild journey to help Claire—! Claire! Impetuous Claire! Inescapable Claire!

(*The* WOMAN AS CLAIRE *enters and cries:*)

WOMAN AS CLAIRE: Mary is jealous of our friendship, Shelley! If I can't talk with you, I'll write you—in care of the Inn—under the name "Joe James"! I'll come see you at the Inn, Joe James!

(SHELLEY *reaches out to* MARY, *but she pulls away.*)

SHELLEY: Mary, my love, don't draw away—. Let me comfort you.

MARY: I couldn't bear his touch.

SHELLEY: And yet I loved you. I grieved more for the loss of you than for the loss of the child. *(To the* ARCHANGEL*:)*...We went south, farther south—

MARY: As if moving nearer the sun would solve our problems! By winter, there we were—Elise and Willmouse, Shelley and me—and Claire—in Rome.

SHELLEY: *(Suddenly)* Rome.

MARY: Ah, it begins to come back to you. Venice. And now Rome.

(A carved wooden horse appears. SHELLEY *takes it and caresses it.)*

SHELLEY: *(It seems to come back to him as he speaks.)* Willmouse was only three—and so beautiful we had him sitting for his portrait. He loved words. Italian and English. Even more than toys, words were his delight. One day in May he said his stomach hurt. A childhood thing. A nothing. But we had been through so much recently, I sat with him day and night. He was getting well. He was chattering to me in flawless Italian. Then he went into convulsions and, quietly, he died.

(A second tombstone rises. It reads: "William Shelley - 1816-1819".)

MARY: Less than six months after we lowered one tiny body into the ground, we were lowering in another!

SHELLEY: Mary—

MARY: No babies... *(She is keening back and forth and moaning.)* No babies...

SHELLEY: *(At the grave)*
"My lost William—
Where art thou, my gentle child?
Let me think thy spirit feeds,
With its life intense and mild,
The love of living leaves and weeds
Among these tombs and ruins wild—
Thy little footsteps on the sands
Of a remote and lonely shore;
The twinkling of thine infant hands,
Where now the worm will feed no more;
Thy mingled look of love and glee
When we returned to gaze on thee—"

MARY: *(Crying out)* Out of all this he made poems. *Po—e—try!!!*

(The tombstones disappear.)

(MARY buries her head in her hands. SHELLEY *cries to the* ARCHANGEL:*)*

SHELLEY: Don't make her go on! I never should have started this.

MARY: He wants to stop now because he has begun to remember more of the shadows. Not just what befell us, but what we brought upon ourselves.

SHELLEY: Never mind. I concede defeat. Let's forget the whole business.

ARCHANGEL: No! You must see it through to the bitter end.

MARY: Right! Let's say aloud the things we went to our graves not uttering!

SHELLEY: We have nothing to say—

MARY: But we do, Shelley! Let's say the big thing, the thing we have never spoken before!

> *(The lights change.* MARY *continues.)*

> *(As* MARY *speaks, the* WOMAN AS ELISE, *dressed as a maid, enters carrying a tray of Italian coffee.)*

MARY: In the winter of that unbelievable year, a few months after the death of William, we found ourselves in Naples.

> *(*SHELLEY *accepts coffee from the* WOMAN AS ELISE. MARY *does not.)*

*(*MARY *continues, matter-of-factly, as the* WOMAN AS ELISE *exits.)*

MARY: Shelley thought if I saw Pompeii, Vesuvius, Capri, my heart and mind might be relieved of the darkness which threatened to drive me mad.

SHELLEY: I thought it would help!

MARY: He wanted to do everything he could. So he came to me one day saying—

> SHELLEY: *(In the past)* Mary, you remember how we swore at the start we'd always be open and straightforward with each other?

> MARY: Yes, Shelley.

> SHELLEY: I want to speak with you and I feel I owe you the truth.

> MARY: Yes?

> SHELLEY: Mary,—I'm about to become a father.

MARY: *(To the* ARCHANGEL*)* I wasn't pregnant.

> SHELLEY: I want to do the best by the child, by its mother, and by you.

> MARY: Under the circumstances, doing your best by me hardly seems possible.

> SHELLEY: By the child, then. What I want—is to register, at its birth, that I'm its father—and that you are its mother.

> *(*MARY *stares at* SHELLEY.*)*

> SHELLEY: You wouldn't want a child of yours to have another mother, would you?

> *(The* WOMAN AS CLAIRE *calls mockingly, flirtatiously:)*

> WOMAN AS CLAIRE: Joe James! Joe James! Come see me at the Inn, Joe James!

> SHELLEY: *(To* MARY*)* I know it's painful for you—

> MARY: *(Wildly)* To bring forth a child without going through childbirth, painful? On the contrary!

SHELLEY: Thank you, Mary. Elise will be very grateful.

(MARY *looks at him for a moment, then suddenly bursts out laughing.*)

MARY: Elise. *Elise!*

(MARY *laughs hysterically. The* WOMAN AS ELISE *appears in a maid's apron, saying seductively, with a Swiss accent:*)

WOMAN AS ELISE: Shall I light your lamp, Mister Shelley? ...Shall I close the window? ...I've brought you some fresh cheese—

(*The* WOMAN AS ELISE *exits.*)

MARY: *(Sardonically)* This is splendid! What openness! What honesty! You're telling me you're having an affair with our maid! This is everything I dreamt of from the start! For each of us, total freedom!

SHELLEY: Mary, you pulled away—

MARY: *Mea culpa*, poet of my dreams. *Mea culpa!* Eros visits you relentlessly and must be indulged—in spite of death and melancholy—

SHELLEY: It was the passion of a moment, over even as it was satisfied.

MARY: Oddly enough, I know that. And in spite of the fact that you probably think me too "womanly" to comprehend, I'm not jealous of Elise.

SHELLEY: I knew you'd understand—

MARY: *(Lost)* What I don't understand is why, in spite of all this "understanding", you and I cannot be happy.

SHELLEY: Circumstance. Bloody circumstance.

MARY: I wonder.

SHELLEY: What do you mean?

MARY: I wonder if we're cursed.

SHELLEY: Cursed?

(*The image of the monster appears, holding Harriet's hat, dripping wet.*)

MARY: Sometimes I think I see the ghost of Harriet. She still blames me for stealing you from her.

SHELLEY: That's nonsense! Superstition!

(*The monster disappears.*)

MARY: *(Quietly)* I think we are fated to have a dark future, Shelley. And there's nothing, nothing we can do about it.

(*Silence.* SHELLEY *turns away.*)

(MARY *says to the* ARCHANGEL:)

MARY: A child was born to Elise. Elena Adelaide Shelley. And duly registered as mine and Shelley's. Fifteen months later, totally oblivious to her overabundance of mothers, she died.

ARCHANGEL: Was the existence of this child ever acknowledged in your lifetimes?

MARY: Never.

ARCHANGEL: No hint of it ever became public?

SHELLEY: Several years later, a scandalous rumor began to be whispered about.

ARCHANGEL: Which was—?

MARY: That in those months when we lived in Naples, Shelley had had a child by Claire.

SHELLEY: It was Elise's doing. Petty blackmail from a kitchen maid!

ARCHANGEL: *(To* MARY*)* Didn't you ever think of leaving him?

SHELLEY: On the contrary! She never said one word against me!

ARCHANGEL: Why not?

MARY: Come now, Archangel, you must have some idea about human nature. Don't you realize how great a force there is to bring a perfect marriage down? I wouldn't give the world the satisfaction! We'd defied them all to pursue the ideal life and by Heaven I wasn't going to admit we never found it!

SHELLEY: But we did!

MARY: He's mad. Not only dead, but deranged. *(To the* ARCHANGEL*)* Let me tell you about our life together. ... He blithely rumpled sheets anywhere the fancy took him. I wallowed in melancholy and self-pity when, you're right, the only self-respecting thing to do would have been to leave. We betrayed not only the laws of God and the State, but the sacred pact we made with each other. We were sad, wretched, hopeless, lost—

SHELLEY: In short, the perfect marriage.

ARCHANGEL: You must be joking!

SHELLEY: Not at all. *(He turns to* MARY:*)* What did you do when I asked you to pretend to be the mother of my illegitimate child?

MARY: I consented.

SHELLEY: And when the rumors started saying I was sleeping with Claire, with Elise, with any of the others, what did you do?

MARY: I came to your defense.

SHELLEY: After my death, did you ever say one word against me?

MARY: Never.

SHELLEY: Why not?

MARY: What purpose would it serve?

SHELLEY: In other words, you were protecting me!

ARCHANGEL: You were widowed at twenty-four. Why did you never remarry?

MARY: My brief exposure to the institution was enough to make me swear off the thing forever.

ARCHANGEL: For thirty years?

MARY: I didn't expect to survive. When each day dawned, I thought, I hoped, it would be my last.

SHELLEY: So you could see me again!

MARY: That was farthest from my expectations. This reintroduction is not what I expected at all.

SHELLEY: What did you expect?

MARY: My freedom!

ARCHANGEL: Why did you devote your entire life to him?

MARY: By building up his life, I built up mine. He was my greatest fiction! Isn't it a magnificent joke on everybody that the splendid picture of the Shelleys was nothing more than a phantom of Mary Shelley's brain?

SHELLEY: You're lying! If you devoted yourself to me, it was because you truly loved me!

MARY: Loved! I was your slave. My devotion to you so possessed my soul I couldn't breathe. Why should it be, Shelley, that from the moment we went off together, I lived your life? You had ideals and I set out to live them. Even after your death, I couldn't escape. For thirty years, with you dead, every action I undertook, every thought I conceived, I looked to you first, for your approval. ... That's not life. That's the waste of a separate soul. That's not existence.

SHELLEY: I had no idea you felt like this...

MARY: Shelley, my sweet, there's so much about us you don't know. I've been holding back the truth for decades! *(To the* ARCHANGEL*)* This is delicious! It's worth dying, just to get a chance to get this out! *(To* SHELLEY*)* I want you, I want everyone, to know —

SHELLEY: No! There's no need to go on. It's clear what I thought was love was mesmerism. What I thought was a free give and take of souls was a poisonous spell. I was blind in life and hypnotized after death. It's not your fault. It's the fault of the One who arranged this whole charade. ... He betrayed the entire human race from the Beginning — on the day He invented a system which depends on the desire of male and female to cleave together two by two.

ARCHANGEL: You must not insult your Creator—

SHELLEY: Who can believe in a God who invents for earth a system of two's and then remains single? Why should we believe in a Creator who creates us in His own image, but forces us to pair while He remains the bachelor God? Childbirth in pain, loss of children in pain, loss of each other in pain—and this is the Creator from whom we're to expect divine justice?

ARCHANGEL: You are risking eternal damnation!

SHELLEY: Bring on your worst! I fear nothing from your selfish, self-centered God—this God who makes himself the only one who can endure the solitary existence. Where is the loving and forgiving God you say created the universe? What did He invent? Pairing. The ultimate torture. The ultimate trap. ... The idea of eternity with Mary was all that kept me sane. Now I see that not only my hopes on earth, but my hopes in death, are a fraud. Who can accept a God whose eternal peace is nothing but an illusion? Who can accept a Creator whose offer of happiness is nothing but the ability to forget?

ARCHANGEL: I'm warning you—!

SHELLEY: Who can accept a God who creates us desperate for love then makes our finding of it so impossible? *(He calls upward:)* Tormenter! Torturer! Liar! Heathen!

ARCHANGEL: You are condemned to hell forever!

(There is a great crash of thunder. A gaping pit opens, belching smoke and flames. SHELLEY *tumbles into it, vanishing below.* MARY *looks down after him, then cries:)*

MARY: Oh, no! You can't escape from me that easily!

*(*MARY *dives in and disappears after* SHELLEY. *The* ARCHANGEL *peers in after her, then says to us:)*

ARCHANGEL: That woman is a glutton for punishment!

(Blackout)

END ACT ONE

ACT TWO

(Time: Immediately following ACT ONE)

(Place: Hell)

(At rise:)

(There are great flames, ungodly cries, otherworldly sounds of threat, horror and abomination. The air is sulphurous, frightening—and exciting.)

(Somewhere in the flames a WOMAN leaps upward again and again, trying to reach a branch on which there is fruit which continually eludes her grasp. Elsewhere in the shadows, a MAN tries to push a huge boulder up a hill. But no matter how close he comes to succeeding, it always rolls back down.)

(Suddenly SHELLEY descends into the flames. He looks around him and then says exultantly:)

SHELLEY: Hell! Glorious hell! This is the place for me! No more sweet dreams, the soft balm of forgetting. No more illusions. This is where I belong. The region of the self-deceived.

(SHELLEY looks at the MAN pushing the rock.)

SHELLEY: You'll never get it to the top. Why do you keep pushing?

(SHELLEY looks at the WOMAN trying to reach the fruit.)

SHELLEY: You'll never eat again. Why keep leaping after the grape?

(Still going about their futile tasks, the MAN and WOMAN disappear. SHELLEY calls after them:)

SHELLEY: Fools! You want to know the way to conquer hell? *Accept it!* If flames are presented to you, burn! If the ocean is presented to you, drown! Shout, "This is my just reward! Thank you, magnificent Dark Spirit!"

(The DEVIL appears.)

DEVIL: It's nice to be appreciated.

SHELLEY: Ah, the master of the revels himself!

DEVIL: Welcome to my domain.

SHELLEY: I'm delighted to be here.

DEVIL: If so, you are the first.

SHELLEY: Devise whatever fiendish torture you may! Nothing can be excruciating enough for a simpleton who put his faith in romantic love.

DEVIL: Was that your crime?

SHELLEY: Anyone mad enough to think there's such a thing as eternal love *deserves* to go to hell!

DEVIL: Then you'll feel right at home here.

SHELLEY: How absurd are the saved, with their misguided optimism and their inextinguishable hopes. Their dreams. This is the place for me! Sharp insights. Inescapable pain! I can't wait!

DEVIL: I hope I'll be able to satisfy your expectations.

SHELLEY: Were you ever married?

DEVIL: I *invent* tortures, I don't *submit* to them.

SHELLEY: Marriage is the most ridiculous of all human institutions. You want to break a totally sane man? Expose him to marriage. You want to cure a lover of love? Sentence him to two weeks in the married state. Of all human mysteries yet devised, none is so impenetrable as marriage, where the word "yes" to a proposal seems the most splendid of victories, and is, in reality, the prelude to an endless series of infinite defeats.

DEVIL: We have no marriage here.

SHELLEY: What a shame! You're depriving yourself of the most delectable of torments.

DEVIL: Am I?

SHELLEY: What have you in store for me?

DEVIL: Most punishments are self-devised.

SHELLEY: I can't imagine what torture you could invent worthy of the abominations I've committed. I spent a lifetime writing hymns of praise to a woman who seemed so extraordinary I went against all my principles and committed wedlock. I spent my entire afterlife waiting for her to arrive. I actually proposed us to heaven as the quintessential couple! Adam and Eve—without the snake. What a fool I was! Bring on your worst instruments of torture!

DEVIL: Happy to oblige. *(He makes a gesture.)*

*(*MARY *enters.)*

SHELLEY: Mary!

MARY: Shelley.

DEVIL: *(Aside to* SHELLEY*)* Do you think this torture will suffice?

SHELLEY: What are you doing here? I thought you'd be ecstatic never to see me again.

MARY: You think you can escape me just by going to Hell?

SHELLEY: *(To* MARY*)* Haven't you had enough?

MARY: I want to go through and out the other side of you forever.

SHELLEY: I thought you'd done that.

MARY: Not completely. I have to cut you out of every corner of my spirit and my brain.

DEVIL: An exorcism! How delightful! How do you propose to do it?

MARY: By forcing him to cast light on all the darkest crannies of our past together.

SHELLEY: *(To the* DEVIL*)* Tell her to go.

MARY: I won't! Not until I find out everything.

DEVIL: *(To* MARY*)* When you want to leave, you might discover the exit door is closed.

MARY: It's worth the risk.

SHELLEY: I've told you all there is to tell.

MARY: Oh, no, you haven't!

DEVIL: What hasn't he told you?

MARY: He hasn't told me—

DEVIL: What?

SHELLEY: What haven't I told you?

MARY: —how you really felt about Jane Williams.

DEVIL: Don't tell me you followed him to Hades just to find out how he felt about one more female!

MARY: Jane wasn't just "one more female". What he had with Jane was far more serious than the rest...

DEVIL: Then let us hear. It will help me decide what circle to consign him to.

SHELLEY: Throw me to the lowest!

MARY: I'm not here to settle your future in Hell, I'm here to find out what my life was! I must know: ...Did you love Jane? Did you—really—love Jane?

SHELLEY: Of course I loved Jane. Madly, badly, gladly. Now off with me to the deepest depths!

DEVIL: *(Commandingly) Tell me your story!*

(Sudden silence.)

(The WOMAN AS JANE *enters. She has long blonde hair. She is followed by the* MAN AS EDWARD. *He is wearing a sailing jacket. As commanded,* MARY *begins:)*

MARY: Jane and Edward Williams came to live with us that last summer in our villa on the Gulf of Spezia. Edward had just retired from the army. He'd been an officer, stationed in India. Jane was—Jane was Jane. Beautiful, talented Jane...

> *(As* MARY *watches,* SHELLEY *enters the scene, carrying pen and paper.)*
>
> SHELLEY: *(His eyes never leaving* WOMAN AS JANE*)* Edward, my friend, I can't tell you how happy I am that you've come to visit. And brought such treasure with you.
>
> MAN AS EDWARD: I am lucky, aren't I? Isn't she beautiful?
>
> SHELLEY: Beautiful...
>
> MAN AS EDWARD: I hope she still loves me now that I'm no longer in uniform.
>
> WOMAN AS JANE: Edward, would you be a dear and go up to the house and bring me my guitar?
>
> MAN AS EDWARD: Of course, my sweet.
>
> *(The* MAN AS EDWARD *exits.)*
>
> SHELLEY: I'm sure you love your husband, in or out of uniform.
>
> WOMAN AS JANE: Of course I do.
>
> SHELLEY: You seem to be a woman capable of very strong emotions.
>
> WOMAN AS JANE: Are you flirting with me, Mister Shelley?
>
> SHELLEY: Would you find that dangerous?
>
> WOMAN AS JANE: I'm not afraid of danger. What I'm afraid of is that you're not sincere.
>
> SHELLEY: I am sincerity incarnate!
>
> WOMAN AS JANE: Prove it.
>
> SHELLEY: You are beauty! You are love! You are Venus!
>
> WOMAN AS JANE: And you—are married.
>
> SHELLEY: What do you bring that up for?
>
> WOMAN AS JANE: Because you're not free to love me.
>
> SHELLEY: But I am! Listen: *(Passionately reciting the poem he is writing)*
> "I never was attached to that great sect,
> Whose doctrine is that each one should select

    Out of the crowd a mistress or a friend,
    And all the rest, though fair and wise, commend
    To cold oblivion—and so—
    With one chained friend, perhaps a jealous foe,
    The dreariest and the longest journey go."

MARY: I was the one chained friend!

SHELLEY: I never chained you. You chained yourself. And not to me alone. You chained yourself to Percy Florence!

   (*The* WOMAN AS JANE *disappears.*)

MARY: *(To the* DEVIL*)* We had a child. A three-year-old son—named for his father and for the city in which he was born.

SHELLEY: Every day she was afraid that he would die!

DEVIL: Mothers!

MARY: We'd lost so many! I was determined we were going to keep this one alive!

   (*A cradle appears.* MARY *rocks it.*)

   SHELLEY: Mary, let's go to the Uffizi.

   MARY: I have to stay with Percy.

   SHELLEY: We'll take him with us.

   MARY: It looks like rain.

   SHELLEY: We'll cover him up.

   MARY: I won't subject him to the dampness by the Arno.

SHELLEY: *(To the* DEVIL*)* Of all disasters—famine, disease, poverty, pestilence, earthquake—the one which most curbs life is the pram in the hall!

DEVIL: *Kinder, Kirke, Küche*—Woman's Work. All *my* inventions!

SHELLEY: *Bambino, bambino, bambino*—he's all she ever thought of!

   MARY: Are you saying you don't love your own child?!

   SHELLEY: I love Percy, but I've lost you to him.

   MARY: He needs me.

   SHELLEY: He circumscribes our lives.

   MARY: Only till he's grown.

   SHELLEY: Twenty years! What am I to do till then, join a monastery?

   MARY: Concentrate on writing.

   SHELLEY: If I want a quiet place to write, I have to find a rock in a field.

MARY: *I* can't write at all.

SHELLEY: I know. But there must be some way we can continue to live!

(The cradle disappears.)

(The WOMAN AS JANE *enters.)*

MARY: *You* continued to "live"!

SHELLEY: I tried my best to get you to do the same!

DEVIL: *(To* SHELLEY*)* How did you do that?

(The WOMAN AS JANE *crosses and, beckoning seductively to* SHELLEY, *exits.)*

SHELLEY: *(Distracted)* By offering her the opportunity to go off with other men!

DEVIL: Delicious!

SHELLEY: I offered her Thomas Jefferson Hogg.

MARY: He never had me.

SHELLEY: I know. He complained to me about that bitterly.

DEVIL: Did you never try to fix her up with Byron?

SHELLEY: He found her much too intelligent to take to bed. I offered her a Prince—

(The MAN AS PRINCE *enters and says seductively to* MARY *in an Italian accent:)*

MAN AS PRINCE: Come with me, Mary, to my villa in the country. We will stroll hand in hand through my vineyards. We will make love with each other on silken sheets.

*(*SHELLEY *calls to* MARY *in encouragement.)*

SHELLEY: Go on! You'll feel better for it!

MARY: Sorry, Prince, I can't go. My husband gave his permission.

(The MAN AS PRINCE *disappears.)*

SHELLEY: Other women would give their eye teeth to have such an understanding husband!

MARY: You told me to go off with other men because you knew I couldn't do it!

SHELLEY: That's your inadequacy, not mine.

MARY: You blame me for being faithful!

SHELLEY: Fidelity is nothing more than cowardice—disguised as virtue.

MARY: It's not my fault that I could never love anyone else, never look at anyone else.

SHELLEY: And what about the times you couldn't look at *me*?

MARY: No—

DEVIL: What was it? Boredom? The slow tapeworm of marital disaffection?

MARY: I couldn't bear it that I seemed not to want him as once I wanted him! He was my star, my guide. Why did I grow cold?

DEVIL: Considering all you've told me, who wouldn't?

SHELLEY: It was time. Only time.

MARY: I think time's more cruel to women. The little defeats of daily life. The births and deaths. And the fear. The constant fear—

DEVIL: What fear?

MARY: That he would leave me . ... He left Harriet. He could leave me.

> (*The* WOMAN AS JANE *enters with a guitar and begins to sing. It is clear she is singing only for* SHELLEY.)
>
> WOMAN AS JANE:
> "I arise from dreams of thee
> In the first sweet sleep of night
> When the winds are breathing low,
> And the stars are shining bright:
>
> I arise from dreams of thee,
> And a spirit in my feet
> Hath led me—who knows how?
> To thy chamber window, Sweet!"
>
> MARY: *(To the* WOMAN AS JANE*)* Who wrote those lyrics?
>
> WOMAN AS JANE: Why, your husband.
>
> MARY: I never heard them before.
>
> WOMAN AS JANE: Shelley wrote them especially for me.
>
> (SHELLEY *and the* WOMAN AS JANE *murmur quietly together.*)

DEVIL: Well, if he's to burn down here, at least he got some fun before it. Looks like it was a pleasurable summer—at least for *some* people.

MARY: That depends on your definition of pleasure. Shelley's *days* were fine, but let me tell you about his nights—

SHELLEY: Are we to be spared nothing? We're in Hell. The real one. Why relive our hells on earth?

DEVIL: *(To* SHELLEY*)* That summer a hell on earth? Even though you had this buxom beauty? Very curious.

MARY: He couldn't sleep. When he did, he would sleepwalk and come bursting into my room—

(In spite of himself, SHELLEY enters the past, moving as if in a nightmare.)

SHELLEY: Mary, get up! The sea is flooding the house and all is coming down!

(MARY runs to him and tries to shake him out of it.)

MARY: Shelley! Wake up! Wake up!

SHELLEY: Mary, I saw myself, myself outside myself, walking on the terrace.

MARY: Shelley, please. It's just a dream—

SHELLEY: Then I was strangling you! I was leaning over your bed and strangling you!

MARY: It's just a dream, Shelley—

SHELLEY: Then the sea rose up and I was in its midst. I was crying out, but I couldn't hear what I was saying. What is it? What does it mean, Mary?

MARY: Rest, Shelley, rest—

SHELLEY: There is no rest!

(SHELLEY paces, nearly mad. MARY, helpless, cries out:)

MARY: Jane! He needs you!

(The WOMAN AS JANE appears.)

MARY: Only you can cure him, Jane.

(The WOMAN AS JANE soothes SHELLEY's brow. MARY looks on, jealous.)

MARY: *(To the DEVIL)* She was always there to bring him what he needed. Jane and her magic mesmerizing gift. ... I could have killed her!

DEVIL: Quite understandable.

(SHELLEY, feeling better, looks at JANE with love and gratitude. The DEVIL says to MARY:)

DEVIL: Why couldn't *you* comfort him?

MARY: For the fifth time in our eight short years together, I was pregnant.

(MARY enters the past. Distraught)

MARY: Shelley! I'm afraid I'm losing the baby! Shelley!

SHELLEY: I sat her in ice—held her in ice—trying to stop the bleeding—

MARY: My mother died this way, drowning in her own blood!

SHELLEY: Your mother died in childbirth, not in miscarriage.

MARY: Giving me life, she died.

SHELLEY: Stay still!

MARY: Where do they go—all my lost babies?:

(Images of babies, some only embryos, appear in the flames. We hear their cries.)

DEVIL: They're here. All here. Why should you want them? They were demon-children, conceived in your husband's desire for other women.

MARY: Not true!

DEVIL: That's why they came to earth and left so quickly.

MARY: You're lying!

DEVIL: It's really quite efficient, damning tiny tots in infancy. Saves them and me immense amounts of trouble later on.

MARY: You're so cruel!

DEVIL: That, lest you forget, Madame, is my business.

(MARY tries to get up. SHELLEY holds her down by force.)

SHELLEY: Stay still, Mary—

MARY: Shelley, let me die. If I die, I can release you.

SHELLEY: For what?

MARY: For the life you want. I'm not enough. I wanted to be all women to you. I seem to be only a fragment. An icy fragment.

SHELLEY: My Mary—

MARY: We have become each other's prisons. We have become the limitations of each other's lives. I am your chains—

SHELLEY: No!

DEVIL: *(To SHELLEY)* Couldn't you have made that sound more convincing?

SHELLEY: *(Trying again)* No! No, Mary.

MARY: And we were the two who were going to found a new kind of affection—stronger, freer, purer than any other. It all began so beautifully. What happened?

SHELLEY: We invented a monster.

(The monster begins to rise in the flames.)

MARY: Who is he? What is his name?

SHELLEY: His name is—Perfect Love.

(The monster rises to overwhelming height, gives a hideous cry, then disappears.)

DEVIL: So you admit Perfect Love is a monster.

SHELLEY: I admit it.

DEVIL: That where it exists it is a prison and a trap.

SHELLEY: It is.

DEVIL: That to escape that trap—

SHELLEY: —I fell in love with far horizons.

>(*The sails of a small boat appear in the flames.*)

MARY: Shelley! Stop! I feel we're in some danger!

SHELLEY: What danger? He can't kill us, we're already dead. He can't damn us; I, at least, am already damned! If you don't want to be damned, leave now. Leave!

DEVIL: (*Suddenly, commandingly:*) Continue! (*To* MARY) You said you wanted to see this through to the end and you will!

>(SHELLEY *goes toward the sail.*)

MARY: Can't a woman change her mind?

DEVIL: Not in Hell. (*The* DEVIL *gestures toward* SHELLEY.)

>SHELLEY: Mary! Come see my new boat!

MARY: He couldn't swim. He had a fateful fascination with the water.

>SHELLEY: It's called the *Don Juan*. I'm painting that out.

MARY: It's bad luck to change the name of a ship—

>SHELLEY: I christen thee *Ariel*. Sprite. Symbol of Freedom!

MARY: I don't want to relive this—

>SHELLEY: Edward's going to teach me how to sail her. We're taking her out on her maiden voyage—

>(*The* MAN AS EDWARD *appears and boards the boat.*)

MARY: (*To the* DEVIL) I don't want to go through all this again—

>SHELLEY: We're sailing her to Leghorn for a week—

MARY: We all know what happened. Why live it over?

DEVIL: Because I wish to see it.

MARY: You must have an appetite for the macabre.

DEVIL: My dear, I thrive on it!

>(SHELLEY *boards the boat beside the* MAN AS EDWARD. *The* WOMAN AS JANE *comes and stands beside* MARY *on the shore.*)

SHELLEY: Cast off!

MARY: *(Suddenly)* Shelley! Don't go—!

SHELLEY: Hoist the mainsail!

WOMAN AS JANE: Goodbye, Edward! *Buon Viaggio*! Shelley, don't forget my ribbons and my music! Bring us back some spices and some silk!

SHELLEY: *(To* MARY*)* And what shall I bring you?

MARY: Nothing. Or perhaps—Plato's *Republic.*

SHELLEY: Fine. Plato's *Republic*—and some silk.

(The boat starts moving off. MARY *cries out:)*

MARY: *(Suddenly)* Shelley—!

(The boat, with SHELLEY *and the* MAN AS EDWARD *on it, moves off.)*

*(*MARY *turns to the* DEVIL*:)*

MARY: I was as much in love with far horizons as he was. Why couldn't I have been on the boat, too?

(The boat disappears in the flames.)

MARY: Strange, about Shelley. I had no premonitions.

DEVIL: You begged him not to go.

MARY: Mere superstition. To appease the gods with a show of worry. So they could confound me—and bring him safely home. ... Shelley and Edward were away a week.

(The WOMAN AS JANE *waves a letter.)*

WOMAN AS JANE: I've received a letter from Shelley! "Dear Jane: I fear you are solitary and melancholy at Villa Magni. How quickly those hours pass in which we live together so intimately, so happily."

MARY: *I've* received a letter from Shelley: "Dear Mary: I have found the translation of the Plato you requested."

DEVIL: Jane's letter is far more intimate than yours.

MARY: *(To herself)* Mine is a letter from a husband.

WOMAN AS JANE: *(To herself)* Mine is a letter from a lover.

DEVIL: Were Jane and Shelley lovers?

*(*MARY *doesn't answer.)*

(The WOMAN AS JANE *puts on a protective shawl and runs to the shore.)*

WOMAN AS JANE: They're coming back today!

MARY: A storm was brewing. Jane and I went down to the shore together—to wait. We stood for hours, soaked to the skin.

> *(They stand on the shore, the storm swirling around them.)*

WOMAN AS JANE: They'll never make it back! The *Ariel* can't take this!

MARY: Edward's a good sailor—

WOMAN AS JANE: They never should have set out in a storm—

MARY: Perhaps they decided to wait—

WOMAN AS JANE: Shelley swore he'd be back today. You know how Shelley is when he swears—

MARY: *(Giving her a look)* I know how Shelley is, Jane, thank you. *(She looks off toward the shore.)* Percy! Don't play so near the water! Go back into the house! Go in, go in! *(She looks out to sea.)* I think I see a sail—! ...No.

WOMAN AS JANE: No.

MARY: Their sail never appeared on the horizon. ... Ten days later, their bodies were washed ashore. ... They wouldn't let me see my Shelley's body. The fish had eaten all the exposed flesh away. Gone! That face. Those hands. ... They only knew who he was from the book of Keats' poems lying folded back in his pocket, and, rattling against the bone of his wedding finger, a golden ring I'd given him on his birthday, inscribed *"Il buon tempo verra"* — "The good times will come." ...They had to burn the bodies. Jane and I received the remains of our husbands in two separate urns.

> *(Two urns appear. The* WOMAN AS JANE *takes one and goes off.* MARY *takes the other.)*

MARY: I buried Shelley in Rome. ... After all the hopes—ashes.

DEVIL: How long had you had together?

MARY: Eight years. Only eight short years. I was twenty-four. He was just on the brink of turning thirty.

DEVIL: And the waves took him.

MARY: The waves took him.

DEVIL: You must have been relieved.

MARY: "Relieved!"

DEVIL: This isn't heaven, Mary. Here, we don't pretty up the blunt realities of the human heart. Shelley drowned—and with him drowned the reason for your sorrows.

MARY: Not true!

DEVIL: You no longer had to worry whether he would leave you. He had left.

MARY: I was distraught!

DEVIL: You were relieved!

MARY: How could I be? He left so many unanswered questions.

DEVIL: What questions?

(MARY *looks around her and says, suddenly, in a panic:*)

MARY: Where is Shelley?

DEVIL: Would it bother you if you never saw him again?

MARY: Where has he gone! *(She searches in panic.)* Shelley—!

DEVIL: Why do you want to see him?

MARY: I told you—to get to the other side of him once and for all.

DEVIL: Then you must be delighted to be rid of him, finally, forever.

MARY: Forever? No! Bring him back!

DEVIL: Why should I?

MARY: I can't have him damned because of me. I'll have him on my conscience for all eternity!

DEVIL: Believe me, conscience doesn't last that long.

MARY: I have to see him!

DEVIL: Exit, Mary. While you have the chance, ascend.

MARY: Make him reappear!

DEVIL: I can't. ... Only *you* can.

MARY: How?

DEVIL: By asking your questions.

MARY: What questions?

DEVIL: The ones you followed him to hell to ask.

MARY: I already asked—

DEVIL: Not those foolish ones. The others.

MARY: I can't—! I won't—! Not for you to use them to condemn him!

DEVIL: Very well. You have seen your husband for the last time.

MARY: No! *(She searches desperately.)* Shelley—! *(She can't find him.)*

DEVIL: Will you ask your questions?

MARY: *(Finally, giving in)* ...Yes.

DEVIL: All of them?

(Reluctantly, MARY nods.)

DEVIL: Very well. Begin.

(MARY looks at DEVIL, puzzled.)

DEVIL: *Begin.*

MARY: To whom?

DEVIL: To the flames.

(Bewildered, MARY addresses the flames.)

MARY: Shelley, did you love me?

DEVIL: Not the nonsense questions!

MARY: Were you going to leave me?

DEVIL: You are wasting my time! Ask the things you really have to know. The things that *I* must know.

(MARY knows what he is getting at. For a long time she is silent, then, at last:)

MARY: Shelley—why did you set sail when they warned you not to?

(There is no answer.)

MARY: When the wind rose up, why didn't you reef your sails?

(Again, no reply.)

MARY: Why did you head into the storm?

(SHELLEY's voice is heard, echoing out of the flames.)

SHELLEY: *(O S)* I wanted to go to the edges of experience!

MARY: Shelley—!

DEVIL: Ask more.

MARY: Shelley, what were you trying to escape? ... Was it me?

(SHELLEY appears in the flames, dimly.)

SHELLEY: There was something I was seeking... *(He disappears.)*

DEVIL: Ask him what it was.

(MARY hesitates.)

DEVIL: Go on. Ask.

MARY: What were you seeking?

(There is no response. MARY cries:)

MARY: Shelley! What were you seeking?

(SHELLEY appears in the flames.)

SHELLEY: ...Death.

(The flames around SHELLEY *dissolve. He stands, solid and real, before them.)*

DEVIL: At last!

MARY: The truth!

DEVIL: Love always forces more admissions than does torture. I couldn't have pried that out of him myself. Thank you, sweet dame.

MARY: You drowned yourself.

SHELLEY: I challenged the waves and they took me on.

MARY: You were seen from another boat. Edward fought to hold on as you capsized, but you never even tried. You let yourself go down—

SHELLEY: I let the sea decide.

MARY: You drowned yourself—to get away from me.

SHELLEY: ...Yes, Mary.

MARY: You had that much hatred for me.

SHELLEY: Hatred? No. ... Love. I killed myself to free you.

(MARY starts to laugh.)

MARY: Shelley, it didn't work! Here we are, side by side!

SHELLEY: Not for long. Soon we'll be apart at last. You'll have Heaven. I'll have Hell.

DEVIL: He's right. It's true, suicides are my province.

MARY: And murderers? Aren't they your province, too?

DEVIL: Of course.

MARY: Then here I stay. If he killed himself for me, I'm guilty of his murder. ... So there, Mister Lucifer, start thinking of what circle *I* should be consigned to.

SHELLEY: Mary—

MARY: I won't have you punished for my crimes. If anyone's to burn in Hell, let it be me.

SHELLEY: No. Let it be me!

MARY: Let him go off to Heaven—

DEVIL: You're unbelievable! You fear my wrath so little you'll each endure any torture for the other?!

MARY: He can't bear suffering. I'm used to nothing else.

SHELLEY: She's mad.

MARY: Whatever you have in store, let it fall on me! Release him!

SHELLEY: *(To* MARY*)* You're taking on a fate that has no end! Leave me to bear it on my own—

MARY: No!

DEVIL: Enough! ...Why you think the decision is in your hands, I can't imagine. The only one who makes decisions here is me. ... I'm exhausted with your petty squabbling. You try my patience with your whining, "I'm not free! I must be free!" All on earth are free. You just don't take your freedoms. You're given independence and what do you invent? Marriage! Marriage—with or without contract—is human folly taken to the extreme. ... *Can't you let each other go?* You claw at each other with the ecstasy of lovers. You flaunt the glory of the triangle but the truth is your marriage was a secret place for two which kept everybody out. You committed high treason to the entire human race by excluding everybody but each other. Very well. You like coupledom so much, you may have it. Eternally. I hereby sentence you to be chained together forever in Hell

SHELLEY: Let her go!

DEVIL: So you can have the satisfaction of a second martyrdom for her sake?

SHELLEY: She doesn't belong here!

DEVIL: I think you will find that, however perverse her reasons, she will always decide she belongs with you.

(Great chains descend. The MAN *and* WOMAN, *now Lucifer's Slaves, enter and begin to chain* MARY *and* SHELLEY *together back-to-back.)*

SHELLEY: *(To* MARY*)* You could go free!

MARY: And have you on my conscience forever?

DEVIL: I told you—conscience does not last!

MARY: It will with me.

DEVIL: So be it.

(The DEVIL *makes a gesture. The* MAN *and* WOMAN *finish chaining* MARY *and* SHELLEY *together, then exit.)*

DEVIL: No other presence will ever disturb your private exchanges. No other voice will ever reach your ears. You will see no one but each other, hear no one but each other. No one will ever appear to disturb your perfect double solitude. You will remain alone—together—forever. From this time forth, even forevermore.

(The DEVIL *disappears in a burst of flame.)*

*(*MARY *and* SHELLEY *are alone, surrounded by flames. They are silent. The place seems very vast, very threatening. At last,* SHELLEY *speaks:)*

SHELLEY: So we're to be each other's hells.

MARY: I'm sorry if the thought of only my voice through all eternity disturbs you.

SHELLEY: That isn't what I meant. *(Pause)* I think we're fated to see with perfect clarity, for all time.

MARY: What do you see?

SHELLEY: ...How very much you despise me.

MARY: I never said that.

SHELLEY: But it's true. Isn't it true?

MARY: No, I—

SHELLEY: The only way we can stay sane in this place is to be completely honest with each other. You hate me, don't you!

MARY: Don't be absurd!

SHELLEY: It's not absurd! You deeply hate me!

MARY: Stop!

SHELLEY: I won't! You're thinking it! I want to hear you say it! Say it!

MARY: *All right!* Yes, it's true! I despise you! You deprived me of so much of my life! The joy of watching together as our son grew into manhood. The joy of our becoming a superannuated couple, of your taking my ancient elbow and guiding me across a street. *(Intensely)* Why did you leave me? *Why did you leave me?*

SHELLEY: I told you: to set you free!

MARY: I didn't want to have to be given my freedom! I wanted to be free by Divine Right.

SHELLEY: I know that.

MARY: I don't want to be known as well as you know me—

SHELLEY: I understand.

MARY: I don't want to be forever understood—

SHELLEY: Mary, what do you want?

MARY: To be where you can't see me.

SHELLEY: Why?

MARY: *(Quietly, seriously)* Because all you ever wanted of me was perfection, and I couldn't manage it. You wanted me to be splendid. And I couldn't bring it off.

SHELLEY: Did you want any less of me? And didn't I fail?

MARY: You didn't fail in my eyes.

SHELLEY: You didn't fail in mine. ... I used to eavesdrop on your life when mine was over. I used to listen to your prayers.

MARY: I prayed to die.

SHELLEY: You never spoke the smallest criticism of your poor dead husband.

MARY: It would have seemed the greatest infidelity. Worse, even, than giving myself to another man.

SHELLEY: You should have remarried. There were at least a dozen worthy suitors.

MARY: *(Finally, a great admission)* ...Everyone disappointed — except you.

SHELLEY: Mary —

MARY: No matter how awful it was with you, it was always glorious.

SHELLEY: My Mary!

MARY: But why is it, Shelley, that in love you didn't lose your whole existence, and I did?

SHELLEY: You didn't.

MARY: I wanted to be my own separate being.

SHELLEY: But you always were.

MARY: Never!

SHELLEY: Mary, what's your favorite color?

MARY: ...Blue.

SHELLEY: Mine also. ... Your favorite hour of the day?

MARY: Dawn.

SHELLEY: And so is mine. ... Your favorite painter —

MARY: Leonardo.

SHELLEY: Exactly my choice also.

MARY: What are you saying?

SHELLEY: I'm saying that we weren't bending ourselves to each other, we *were* each other! I never told you what to think — you thought it by yourself. That I thought it, too, that's the miracle. Be it Heaven or Hell or regions unnamed, we're one soul, Mary, through life and now through all eternity. We love each other. You love me! Say it!

MARY: *(Finally)* Yes! I love! As much right now as at the very first moment I saw you. As much as I did each time we made love, or when you kissed my brow after the birth of a child.

SHELLEY: For all the heartache I brought you, forgive me.

MARY: I thank you for it. No one else ever loved me enough to make me take the hard way. You held me to my highest self. When you were gone, all I could think of was to try to live up to your ideal of me.

SHELLEY: You have surpassed it. You have become more than I ever dreamed. Mary—

(SHELLEY *takes* MARY's *hand.*)

MARY: Are you touching me?

SHELLEY: I am.

MARY: Do you feel anything?

SHELLEY: No.

MARY: Neither do I. ... Shelley! We've lost the sense of touch! You're here, but I feel nothing! There's no comfort!

SHELLEY: Then we'll exist on memory.

MARY: Remembering all we lost? All we never had?

SHELLEY: We had everything. We had each other. We still do—and it's magnificent! ...In fact, this Hell is positively superb! We will go on in perfect harmony through all eternity!

MARY: A lifetime wasn't long enough to spend with you. Even forever will be too brief.

SHELLEY: Forever... *(He considers it, then asks:)* ...But how will we spend the time?

MARY: I will recite all your poems to you. And you will recite to me all six of my novels.

SHELLEY: Your novels—

MARY: You know them by heart, of course.

SHELLEY: I—

MARY: I know all *your* works by heart.

SHELLEY: Yes, but—

MARY: You sat in limbo for thirty years and didn't have time to read my books?

SHELLEY: The library's upstairs.

MARY: No matter. You'd probably think the books were woman's scribbles, not worthy of your attention.

SHELLEY: Not true! I was waiting for you to arrive and recite them to me in person!

MARY: Liar!

SHELLEY: I always loved the way you recited your work.

MARY: I always hated the way you recited yours. So pretentious! As if you were saying: "This is a higher art; it has meter!"

SHELLEY: Poetry is not meter! It is concise, precise thought!

MARY: And Prose is drivel?

SHELLEY: You're intentionally misinterpreting—!

MARY: I'm saying what you're thinking!

SHELLEY: You're twisting my words—!

MARY: You're insulting my intelligence!

SHELLEY: You're deliberately baiting me—

MARY: Are we going to go on squabbling—?

SHELLEY: Till Hell freezes and the Heavens turn to flame—!

MARY: Only if you retain your stubborn, superior way of intimating that my work is pedestrian while yours—

(Suddenly a great voice is heard.)

ARCHANGEL: *(O S) Silence!*

(Stunned, MARY and SHELLEY are silent.)

ARCHANGEL: *(O S)* Speak no words but the answers to my questions. ... Do you hear my voice?

MARY & SHELLEY: Yes.

ARCHANGEL: *(O S)* Do you see each other?

MARY & SHELLEY: Yes.

ARCHANGEL: *(O S)* Do you see the flames?

MARY & SHELLEY: Yes.

ARCHANGEL: *(O S)* Then you have passed the test.

(From above, the ARCHANGEL appears. As he does, the flames dissolve. In their place appear grey unformed shapes. We are once again in Limbo.)

ARCHANGEL: All that you witnessed in this region was the making of your own imaginations. ... Given the choice, you both created the same Hell. You inhabited it together, experienced it together, yet it existed only for the two of you.

(The chains fall away. MARY *and* SHELLEY *step out of them. The chains rise up and disappear.)*

ARCHANGEL: You were wrong to say there was no one watching. Someone was. The One, the All-Powerful. He has empowered me to speak on his behalf. ... Being singular, He has compassion for his children who walk the earth in pairs. For some reason that escapes me, the ones who test the borders of existence are the ones that He respects the most. ... Marriage is His ultimate challenge. In its complexity and mystery, He most admires those who are able to balance on the tightrope between doubt and love, fidelity and freedom, the other and the self. ... For reasons that are beyond my ken, your story charmed Him. No one ever insisted on entering Heaven as a couple before. He has looked upon you, and He has seen that it is good. ... *I* think He will be letting Discord into Heaven. But He says He will be admitting a model for earthly life. I think it will be a tremendous threat to peace in the Celestial Kingdom. But He says peace is not the avoidance of conflict, it is the resolution of opposing ideas. Therefore, I welcome you as the first couple ever to enter Heaven together.

(Suddenly bright light spreads and overwhelms the greyness. Limbo disappears. In its stead there magically appear bright clouds, golden rays of sun, magnificent halations.)

(A great opening appears upstage with light coming through it. The ARCHANGEL *gestures toward the opening.)*

ARCHANGEL: You've won your suit, Shelley. You've achieved what you waited for for thirty years! The way is open to you as a couple. Enter.

*(*SHELLEY *pulls back.)*

ARCHANGEL: What's the matter?

SHELLEY: Something's happening to me—something terrible! ... I think I'm beginning to belong to you, Mary.

MARY: "Belong...?"

SHELLEY: In the way that we said we never would. In the way that I thought I never could. I can feel it growing, through my body, through my soul, like a choking weed—the overwhelming desire—to be faithful.

MARY: *(Loving)* Oh, Shelley—

ARCHANGEL: There *are* miracles, after all.

SHELLEY: *(To* MARY*)* It happened when you tussled with me eye-to-eye and word-to-word. I suddenly got this awful feeling—I'm going to love you and only you for all time!

MARY: My poor dear man...

SHELLEY: Imagine! Me! Monogamous!

MARY: Don't worry. I won't tie the noose too tightly.

(*The* ARCHANGEL *makes a gesture and chains of flowers descend. The* MAN *and* WOMAN, *now dressed in contemporary clothes, enter, wrap* MARY *and* SHELLEY *loosely together in the chains of flowers, then stand aside, together.*)

ARCHANGEL: In recognition of your reunion, the Master of all is giving you a special gift. He is restoring to you the sense of touch.

(*The* ARCHANGEL *raises his arm in benediction.* MARY *takes* SHELLEY's *hand. He reacts.*)

MARY: Do you feel anything?

SHELLEY: (*Lying*) Nothing.

(MARY *kisses him passionately.*)

MARY: I begin to remember what it was like. Don't you?

SHELLEY: (*Still lying*) I feel nothing at all.

MARY: You will.

SHELLEY: Mary, what if it all comes back? What if everything begins again?

MARY: Let it begin! The beauty, the horror, the passion, the conflicts, the ecstasy!

(MARY *starts to lead* SHELLEY *toward the entrance to Heaven.*)

ARCHANGEL: (*To* MARY *and* SHELLEY, *referring to the* MAN *and* WOMAN:) Henceforth all couples shall know what you know, and feel what you feel. You shall be their vision and their example. As your love goes, so shall go the love of all.

(SHELLEY *looks back at the* WOMAN, *who gives him a come-hither look.*)

(MARY *sees* SHELLEY *responding to the* WOMAN.)

MARY: I hope they can survive it.

(MARY *yanks* SHELLEY *toward Heaven. They walk toward it,* MARY *looking resolutely onward,* SHELLEY, *pulled by her, looking longingly back—*)

(*Blackout*)

END OF PLAY

HALLIE

HALLIE was seen in staged readings at Smith College, Vassar College and The Writer's Theatre, New York.

CHARACTERS & SETTING:

HALLIE FLANAGAN DAVIS
KATE
PHILIP DAVIS
PETERS, *the recording secretary*
CHAIRMAN MARTIN DIES, *Texas, Democrat*
REPRESENTATIVE JOE STARNES, *Alabama, Democrat*
REPRESENTATIVE J PARNELL THOMAS, *New Jersey, Republican*
REPRESENTATIVE ARTHUR D HEALEY, *Massachusetts, Democrat*

Time: December 6, 1938

Place: Washington, DC. The Hearing Room of the House Special Committee to Investigate Un-American Activities

Setting: When the audience enters, they see on stage the masks of Comedy and Tragedy, three dimensional and at least as tall as a human being. At the start of the performance, these masks rise up and remain above the stage, defining the upper limits of the stage picture.

When the masks rise, the Hearing Room, the main space for the action, is in darkness. Lights come up on the forestage, which is used as an antechamber to the main space.

Once the Hearing Room is illuminated, we see an inlaid wood or marble floor surrounded by space. On this floor, upstage right, is a dais on which is an important-looking table. Behind it are four important-looking chairs. Downstage left is a smaller table at which there is one chair, with a chair behind it. Downstage right is a very small table with one chair.

There are no walls. The area is surrounded by a cyclorama. Changes of mood are created by changes in light. Although the time and place are specific, there is the feeling this debate, witnessed by the masks of Comedy and Tragedy, is taking place in every place and for every time.

Sections of this play are adapted from the testimony recorded at sessions of the House Un-American Activities Committee.

ACT ONE

(At rise: The masks of Comedy and Tragedy rise and remain suspended over the proceedings.)

(The Hearing Room is in darkness. The lights come up on the forestage.)

(HALLIE FLANAGAN DAVIS enters, stage left, followed by KATE, her assistant. HALLIE, wearing a hat and suit and carrying a briefcase, is a red-haired energetic woman of forty-nine, intelligent, self-possessed and self-confident.)

(KATE, a capable young woman, a bit overwhelmed by her surroundings, is laden down with charts and documents.)

HALLIE: Do you have the figures on the most people we ever had employed at one time?

KATE: Yes, Hallie.

HALLIE: Do you have that broken down state by state?

KATE: Yes, I do.

HALLIE: And the operating budget? How tightly we run the ship?

KATE: I can even tell them how many paper clips we used last year.

HALLIE: Yes, but can you tell them how many of those paper clips were Communists?

KATE: Sorry, I don't have that information.

HALLIE: I have a feeling that's the only type of question they're going to ask.

KATE: I don't like this place. It gives me the shivers.

HALLIE: Well, my dear, it's *meant* to give you the shivers.

KATE: Don't you feel intimidated?

HALLIE: Not at all. I've been trying for months to get them to let me testify. I'm glad the day is here at last!

KATE: But they've been making mince meat of the heads of the other arts projects.

HALLIE: Well, Kate, I don't think they're going to make mince meat of me. There's a certain excitement about fighting for a just cause which gets my Irish up.

KATE: You're not Irish.

HALLIE: No, but my first husband was, and he had to leave me *something*! Besides, the charges are nonsense. All I have to do is clearly let them know that.

KATE: And I'll be there to hand you all the substantiating material you need.

HALLIE: Thanks, Kate.

KATE: Is Philip coming down from Vassar?

HALLIE: No, I told him not to. He shouldn't cancel classes on my account. Besides, it's best if he stays with the children.

(PHILIP *enters. He is an attractive dark-haired man of thirty-eight.*)

PHILIP: The children and I voted, and it was decided that I come here.

HALLIE: Philip—!

PHILIP: You didn't really think I was going to miss your star performance, did you?

HALLIE: I told you—

PHILIP: *(Kissing her)* I don't always follow orders.

HALLIE: You *never* do!

PHILIP: I'd say that runs in the family. ... Hello, Kate. How's our leader?

KATE: Ready for battle.

HALLIE: First I want to refute the charges that were made against the theater and against me personally. Then I want to show them the positive things that we've done. Then I want to convince them that we must continue to exist, even after the relief aspect is over.

PHILIP: Nothing like asking for the moon!

HALLIE: You know my motto: Make no small plans.

PHILIP: I pity the panel. When Saint Joan gets her armor on, nothing can stop her.

HALLIE: I'm not underestimating them, Philip. But this is America, as my grandfather used to say. Justice will triumph!

PHILIP: That's the spirit!

HALLIE: The others who've testified didn't really have all their information. I do. All I have to do is present it to them clearly and comprehensively. After all, this isn't a kangaroo court, this is the House of Representatives.

PHILIP: I hope your optimism is justified.

(PETERS, *the recording secretary, enters, and says, with seriousness:*)

PETERS: Are you Hallie Flanagan?

HALLIE: I am.

PETERS: The Committee would like you to take your place. They want to begin.

HALLIE: I'll be happy to.

PHILIP: I'm your cheering section. I'll be in the visitors' gallery. If anyone treats you in an ungentlemanly fashion, I'll let 'em have it.

HALLIE: Fine, Professor. Just be sure that you do it in Greek.

(PHILIP *kisses her then exits.* HALLIE *and* KATE, *the documents in their arms, follow* PETERS *off stage left.*)

(*The lights come up on the Hearing Room. Three of the congressmen,* DIES, STARNES *and* THOMAS, *enter.*)

(MARTIN DIES, *Democrat, Chairman of the Committee, is a tall rangy Texan of thirty-eight. An intense man with piercing eyes, he is the youngest of the three but has been in Congress the longest.* DIES *is never without his Corona cigar. He takes the center position, behind a giant ashtray.*)

(REPRESENTATIVE J PARNELL THOMAS, *age forty-four, Republican from New Jersey, crosses up center and takes his place at the Chairman's left.* THOMAS, *new to Congress, is a thin, sharp-eyed, buttoned-up northeasterner. A former stockbroker whose clothing and speech are precise and who never has a hair out of place, he constantly holds a gold pencil.*)

(REPRESENTATIVE JOE STARNES, *also age forty-four, Democrat from Alabama, is serving his second term in Congress. A slightly over-weight, near-sighted man who is always playing with and then cleaning his glasses, he has unruly greying hair and an open collar. He speaks with a deep southern accent. He takes the chair downstage, to* DIES'*s right.*)

DIES: I hope we can do this Flanagan woman's testimony in one day. We've got a hell of a lot to get through before the Christmas recess.

STARNES: Aren't you going to stay in Washington over the holidays?

DIES: And miss my annual New Year's Eve Texas barbecue? Not on your life.

(REPRESENTATIVE ARTHUR D HEALEY *enters carrying a newspaper.* HEALEY, *forty-nine, Democrat from Massachusetts, is a thin, nondescript man, grey suit, graying hair, who tends, even here in this room, to fade into the background. Without a word, he puts the newspaper in front of* DIES, *then takes his place upstage center, to* THOMAS'*s left.*)

DIES: Well, what do you know! The Post has us back on the front page again! (*He eyes the page, then frowns.*) They seem to think we're getting nowhere fast with this investigation. (*He reads aloud:*) "Begun in August and now it's December. When will Dies and his committee wrap things up?" ...Just get these fellows!

If we whiz through, they say our witnesses don't get a fair hearing. If we take time to be thorough, they start complaining, as if every minute that passes was gas being charged up at the pump! What do these guys want?

THOMAS: I think they'd like some evidence which will lead to charges and convictions.

DIES: I have a feeling, gentlemen, that that possibility is not too far away.

(There is the sound of people entering the Hearing Room. Preceded by PETERS, HALLIE *and* KATE *enter from the left.* PETERS *gestures to the small table downstage left where* HALLIE *is to sit.* KATE *takes a seat slightly behind and downstage of her.* PETERS *goes to the Recording Secretary's table downstage right.)*

*(*DIES *bangs his gavel.)*

DIES: This session of the House Special Committee on Un-American Activities will come to order! *(He looks out toward the audience.)* I'd like quiet in the room, please. You people in the gallery and you gentlemen in the press box, we can do without these constant expressions of approval and disapproval.

*(*DIES *gestures to* PETERS, *who approaches* HALLIE *with a bible and indicates that she should put her hand on it.)*

PETERS: Do you solemnly swear that the testimony you are about to give is the truth, the whole truth and nothing but the truth, so help you God?

HALLIE: I do.

*(*PETERS *takes his place behind the small table downstage right, ready to begin recording.* DIES *says to* HALLIE:*)*

DIES: Please be seated.

*(*HALLIE *sits.)*

HALLIE: Mister Chairman, have I the right to address the chair?

DIES: Yes, after I ask you a few preliminary questions.

HALLIE: I—

DIES: Please! I haven't even lit my cigar yet!

(He begins to light his cigar. As he is doing so, THOMAS *says:)*

THOMAS: I would like to have a nickel for every minute we've spent these past weeks waiting for our Chairman to light his cigar. *(He taps his gold pencil impatiently on the table.)*

STARNES: And I would like to have a nickel for every time you've tapped your damn gold pencil!

DIES: Gentlemen, mind your manners! ... You see what happens, Mrs Flanagan, when we have a committee made up of one Republican *(He indicates* THOMAS*)*, two Democrats *(He indicates* STARNES *and* HEALEY.*)* and one Neutral. *(On the last, he indicates himself.)*

THOMAS: Especially when the Neutral was born a Democrat. The way I see it, that's three of you to one of us.

DIES: That, John, is the meaning of bi-partisan in a Democratic Congress. *(Having finished lighting his cigar, and drawing on it with satisfaction, he addresses* HALLIE:*)* Mrs Flanagan, since we'll be asking you your history, you have a right to know ours. This special committee has been set up by the House of Representatives, under my chairmanship. Our assignment is to investigate charges of un-American activity in government-supported projects, in your case, the Federal Theater.

HALLIE: Yes, I understand that.

DIES: Yesterday we heard testimony from Mrs Woodward, the Director of W P A Arts Projects. We expect to hear from Mister Alsberg, the head of the Writer's Project, later this week.

HALLIE: Yes. I know.

DIES: *(Waving his hand toward a pile of documents on the table before him)* In these last weeks we've received many documents and have listened to many witnesses who make serious accusations—

HALLIE: Those are exactly what I am here to refute.

DIES: You can't refute them until we have presented them—

HALLIE: Chairman Dies, I am not exactly ignorant of what has been going on before this committee for the past several months. If you recall, I wrote you time after time asking for the opportunity to appear—

DIES: Well, now we are graciously extending to you that opportunity—

HALLIE: For that, I am most grateful. ... Now, may I address the chair?

DIES: Mrs Flanagan—we haven't even begun. Don't try to put the last act before the first act! ... Now—*(He looks at his papers.)* Your name is Hallie Flanagan?

HALLIE: My name is Hallie Flanagan.

DIES: *(To* PETERS:*)* Are you getting all of this down?

(PETERS *nods.*)

DIES: Miss or Mrs?

HALLIE: Mrs Philip Davis. *(She looks up toward the gallery.)*

DIES: *Miss* Flanagan, then.

HALLIE: No. Flanagan was the name of my first husband.

STARNES: Oh, you've had two husbands?

HALLIE: My first husband died. My second husband, Mister Philip Davis, classics professor, is in the gallery. *(She gestures toward him.)*

STARNES: That young man?

HALLIE: I'm not dead yet, Congressman Starnes.

DIES: How do you wish to be addressed?

HALLIE: I am usually addressed as "Mrs Flanagan".

DIES: Very well. Will you please state what your position is, Mrs Flanagan?

HALLIE: I am national director of the Federal Theater Project under the Works Progress Administration.

DIES: How long have you held that position?

HALLIE: For three and a half years. Since the beginning of the project on August 29, 1935.

STARNES: *(Interrupting)* Mister Chairman, may I ask a question?

DIES: *(Beginning to be annoyed)* Let me just get through with these preliminaries. ... All right, Representative Starnes, what is your question?

STARNES: Mrs Flanagan, who appointed you as national director?

HALLIE: Mister Harry Hopkins.

STARNES: Mister Harry Hopkins, the Secretary of Commerce?

HALLIE: That was before he became Secretary of Commerce. It was soon after he was appointed Director of the Works Progress Administration by President Roosevelt.

THOMAS: And they say cronyism is dead.

HALLIE: I don't see why President Roosevelt shouldn't appoint the man he trusts most in the world to head the project which was closest to him.

DIES: Please, Mrs Flanagan, we're not here to discuss President Roosevelt's pet projects.

HALLIE: As you well know, people from all occupations were walking the streets. I think the President's idea—not to put them on relief, but to put them to work and have the government pay them for that work—is an idea of genius!

THOMAS: Providing you're not in charge of figuring out how to finance it. *(He taps his pencil.)*

DIES: You may as well know, Mrs Flanagan, you are not exactly in the presence of the New Deal fan club.

STARNES: Mrs Flanagan,—did Mister Hopkins approach you or did you approach Mister Hopkins in relation to this appointment?

HALLIE: Mister Hopkins approached me. Projects were being set up under the W P A for writers and for artists. Mister Hopkins asked if I would direct the project for theater.

STARNES: Do you know who recommended your name to Mister Hopkins?

HALLIE: I do not.

STARNES: Mister Hopkins didn't tell you who recommended your name to him?

HALLIE: He did not.

STARNES: I am merely wondering, Mrs Flanagan, meaning no disrespect, that if he wanted to appoint a director for the Federal Theater Project, why would he choose a woman—and one none of us has heard of?

HALLIE: Perhaps because he knew my work, because he knew me.

STARNES: Ah, he knew you?

HALLIE: We went to the same college.

STARNES: You went to the same college...

HALLIE: And he knew my work.

STARNES: And just what—

DIES: Excuse me, Joe, but are these questions leading anywhere?

STARNES: I am trying to establish her qualifications—

DIES: Then ask a direct question! ...Mrs Flanagan, will you tell us briefly the duties of your position.

HALLIE: Yes, Mister Chairman. I am concerned with combating un-American inactivity.

DIES: We will get to that in a moment—

HALLIE: Please listen. I said I am combating un-American inactivity.

DIES: Inactivity?

HALLIE: The inactivity of professional men and women who, when I took office, were on relief. My job was to expend the funds which Congress had designated as relief for the unemployed in the field of theater. My mandate was to set up projects in any city where twenty-five or more professionals were found to be on relief.

STARNES: Mister Chairman, I think before her statement is made, we should find out more about Mrs Flanagan's history. Where she went to college and so forth—

DIES: We are going to get to that! *(To* HALLIE:*)* You say you are director of all these activities?

HALLIE: Yes. The project is national in scope.

(HALLIE *gestures toward* KATE. KATE *sets up an easel and puts on it a map of the United States showing the location of Federal Theater projects throughout America.* HALLIE *rises to illustrate:)*

HALLIE: Outside of our main headquarters here in Washington, we have three main offices: one in New York, one in Chicago, one in Los Angeles.

THOMAS: Why there?

HALLIE: These are where there are most unemployed professionals in theater. From those centers, we direct projects in all the states. Until we were cut back, we had ten thousand people all over the country employed in—

THOMAS: Mrs Flanagan, what would you say was the primary purpose of setting up the Federal Theater Project?

HALLIE: *(Taking her seat)* To give relief to professional theater people.

THOMAS: To put them back to work?

HALLIE: Yes.

THOMAS: And yet you have many non-relief people on your rolls.

HALLIE: We did have some. Where we needed certain talents and couldn't find—

THOMAS: Mrs Flanagan, when the W P A hires ditch diggers, it hires *unemployed* ditch diggers.

HALLIE: Theater people aren't ditch diggers, Mister Thomas.

THOMAS: You mean they're better?

HALLIE: I mean they're different.

STARNES: You mean they're too good to be ditch diggers?

HALLIE: Many of our people *did* dig ditches, but they didn't do it very well.

THOMAS: So the only way they could tap into government money was by having us fund theater—

HALLIE: That's what they were trained for. They were professionals.

THOMAS: When they couldn't seem to make a living at it?

HALLIE: Representative Thomas—

THOMAS: In last week's testimony of your cousin, Miss O'Shea—

HALLIE: Miss O'Shea is not my cousin—

THOMAS: In last week's testimony—

DIES: We are not ready yet to go into previous testimony—

HALLIE: *(Riffling through her papers)* I heard about Miss O'Shea's testimony and I'd like to refute—

THOMAS: I am just trying to clarify—

STARNES: I think first we should get into her background—

DIES: One at a time, gentlemen!

STARNES: I think first we should get into her background—

DIES: All right. First things first.

HALLIE: *(Aside)* If you feel the need to go into ancient history—

DIES: I beg your pardon?

HALLIE: Nothing. What would you like to know?

STARNES: *(Looking at pages in front of him)* You are a graduate of Grinnell College?

HALLIE: I am.

STARNES: Just where is this Grinnell?

HALLIE: In Iowa. The state where I was born.

STARNES: And you had some experience, I believe, in Radcliffe or in Chicago?

HALLIE: I took my master's degree at Radcliffe.

STARNES: That was in what year?

HALLIE: That was in 1923. I then became production assistant to Professor Baker in his 47 Workshop at Harvard and assisted in the production of plays.

STARNES: Was it there you met Harry Hopkins?

HALLIE: No. That was at Grinnell.

STARNES: That far back—

THOMAS: Weren't you at Vassar when he pulled you out of there to become the head of the Federal Theater?

HALLIE: I am a professor of English at Vassar.

THOMAS: I thought you were in Theater—

HALLIE: I am in charge of the experimental theater.

STARNES: Experimental?

HALLIE: We try not to do the same old things in the same old ways, Congressman.

THOMAS: You seem to speak of it in the present. Are you holding down two jobs, Mrs Flanagan?

HALLIE: I am a professor on leave. I still spend a day or two a month at Vassar. But only on leave from my Federal job.

STARNES: It says here you are one of the first women in America to receive the Guggenheim Foundation scholarship. Is that correct?

HALLIE: Yes, that is correct.

STARNES: You went abroad for twelve or fourteen months to study the theater?

HALLIE: I did.

STARNES: What date was that?

HALLIE: That was in 1926 and 1927.

STARNES: You spent most of that time in what country?

HALLIE: In Russia.

STARNES: In Russia...

THOMAS: How much time did you spend in Russia, Mrs Flanagan?

HALLIE: I spent two and a half months in Russia out of fourteen months, but let me say, gentlemen, that—

THOMAS: Isn't it true that you spent more time there than you did in any other country?

HALLIE: I did, because there are many more theaters in Russia than there are in any other country.

THOMAS: I have here a clipping from *The New York Times* of September 22, 1935 in which you say the continental theater is tiresome and boring but the Russian theater is vital and alive. Tell me, Mrs Flanagan, what is it about the Russian theater that makes it more vital and alive than the theaters of the continent and the theaters of the United States?

HALLIE: I don't see that that point is relevant. I have consistently maintained that the Federal Theater is an American theater, founded on American principles, and it has nothing to do with the Russian theater.

DIES: You are not answering the question, Mrs Flanagan.

HALLIE: All right—the Russians, if we are to go into this here—have a long and exciting history of theatrical development, with great variety and interest. For instance, I went to their ballet a great deal. They have many beautiful ballets, based on fairy tales, and they—

STARNES: All those fairy tales have a little moral to them, don't they? What we call a moral?

HALLIE: I was sent by the Guggenheim Foundation to make a comparative study of—

STARNES: That is not answering the question.

THOMAS: I think the witness ought to be allowed to finish her answer.

STARNES: I think the witness's answer should be responsive to the question.

THOMAS: You are interrupting her all the time. I should like to hear what the witness has to say.

STARNES: I have no disposition to interrupt the witness in answering questions provided the answers are responsive to my questions.

THOMAS: I appreciate that.

STARNES: But when the answer is not responsive to the question, I reserve the privilege of calling the witness's attention to that fact.

THOMAS: Yes, but you interrupt the witness when you don't like the answer. I would like to hear the answer.

STARNES: I would like to, too, —if it is responsive!

DIES: *(Banging his gavel)* The correct procedure is that which is followed in court. The witness's testimony is supposed to be responsive; and then if the witness has any explanation to make, she may make it.

STARNES: Part of the witness's statement was responsive and part absolutely was not.

THOMAS: You interrupt her and I object to that.

STARNES: *(Rising)* I think that remark is a little uncalled for.

THOMAS: *(Rising)* You interrupt her!

DIES: Gentlemen, let us proceed now.

(STARNES *and* THOMAS *sit down.*)

HALLIE: Do you want me to continue with a discussion of the Russian theater?

DIES: No. For heaven's sake, let's go on. ... Congressman Healey, do you have any questions for the witness?

HEALEY: Not at the moment. *(He takes a drink of water.)*

DIES: Congressman Thomas?

THOMAS: Mrs Flanagan, are you a member of any Russian organization at the present time?

HALLIE: I am not.

THOMAS: Have you ever been a member of any Russian organization?

HALLIE: I have not.

DIES: Representative Thomas—!

(THOMAS *subsides.* DIES *picks up a book.*)

DIES: Mrs Flanagan, do you believe that theater is a weapon?

HALLIE: I believe that theater is a great educational force. I think it is entertainment. I think it is excitement. I think it may be all things to all men.

DIES: I'd like to quote from a book you wrote called *Shifting Scenes*.

HALLIE: Oh, I haven't read that book in ten years. I'm honored by having it read!

DIES: In here, you say the theater is a weapon—a weapon for teaching class consciousness.

HALLIE: That book is about theater in Russia. And, in Russia, that's what much of theater is.

DIES: But not in the United States?

HALLIE: No.

(DIES *takes up a magazine.*)

DIES: And yet here, in an article by you from Theater Arts Monthly, you say, "The theater being born in America today is a theater of workers. Its object is to create a national culture by and for the working class of America."

HALLIE: And so it was. But I had nothing to do with setting up workers' theaters.

DIES: But this is a quotation from you, in an article by Hallie Flanagan headed, *A Theater is Born*.

HALLIE: But, Mister Chairman, that theater was not born through me. I was reporting—

DIES: With approval—

HALLIE: Mister Chairman, let us not get into a controversy over this because it is so simple—

DIES: Mrs Flanagan, it is not simple at all. You are aware that the reason you are here is because there have been accusations of un-American activities on the Federal Theater Project. Over the past months we have heard witness after witness charge that a large number of people in the Federal Theater are members of the Workers' Alliance—a known Communist front organization. Do you deny this?

HALLIE: Yes, I deny it. Most of the personnel employed in the Federal Theater are members of professional unions and, as such, are expressly forbidden to join any other unions.

DIES: What if they do it anyway? Have you explored this possibility?

HALLIE: You know that, under government law, this is a question I am forbidden to ask.

DIES: So you do not know, and yet you feel confident enough to deny the accusation.

HALLIE: I do, Mister Chairman.

DIES: The accusation has also been made that meetings for Communist front organizations have been held on government property in Federal Theater offices.

HALLIE: Not to my knowledge.

DIES: But you can't have been everywhere, can you?

HALLIE: I have trusted associates who would tell me—

DIES: The charge has been made that Communist flyers are posted on Federal Theater bulletin boards.

HALLIE: That is something I have never seen.

DIES: The charge has been made that the Daily Worker and other Communistic propaganda have been disseminated on the project in project time. Do you know whether or not that is true?

HALLIE: Representative Dies, I have never seen such literature disseminated. Anyone who did such a thing on project time would be dismissed.

DIES: In other words, if such has been done, it has been done without your knowledge and without your consent?

HALLIE: That is absolutely true.

DIES: It would be against express orders on your part?

HALLIE: Against express orders, Congressman.

DIES: You don't say, though, it has not been done?

HALLIE: I could not say of my own knowledge.

DIES: We want to establish the fact—which will clear you of that charge—if such charges are made against you before this committee—that you did not order it done.

HALLIE: To the contrary. I said it should not be done.

STARNES: It remains to be proved whether it actually *was* done.

HALLIE: Mister Chairman, I have prepared a brief which clearly shows—

(HALLIE *hands the brief to* KATE *who tries to give it to* DIES *. He waves it away.*)

DIES: *(Getting out of his seat and pacing)* Mrs Flanagan, how many performances has the Federal Theater given in the three years of its existence?

HALLIE: I'm sorry, I don't have an exact figure. I would say it is in the tens of thousands.

DIES: And how many people in the United States have seen your performances?

HALLIE: The recorded figure, Mister Chairman, is something like twenty-five million people. Twenty-five million people sometimes paying as little as a quarter, or a loaf of bread, or a handful of nails—

DIES: In other words, you have reached something like twenty-five percent of our population with your plays?

HALLIE: That is true.

DIES: Well, that is certainly a powerful voice, a powerful method of communication.

HALLIE: Perhaps the largest ever.

DIES: And yet your alleged cousin alleges: "They couldn't get any audiences for anything except Communistic plays, plays which teach class consciousness."

HALLIE: That is untrue! We have done nine hundred and twenty-four plays of every shape and content and variety.

(KATE *hastens to put up a chart of plays.* HALLIE *stands before it and says:*)

HALLIE: Comedies, tragedies, history plays, religious plays, vaudevilles, circuses, children's plays, living newspapers—

THOMAS: I want to hear more about these living newspa—

DIES: Later. Proceed, Mrs Flanagan.

HALLIE: We have performed all over the United States, before people of all ages, all levels of income and all religious and political persuasions.

(KATE *puts up a chart of audiences. The* CONGESSMEN *don't look at it.*)

HALLIE: We have performed before social clubs, welfare and civic organizations, educational organizations, religious groups, business groups, trade unions, professional unions, political clubs. We have performed in prisons, in pool halls, in school auditoriums, on islands, in tents, on the backs of trucks!

(KATE *puts up a chart of Federal Theater employees.*)

HALLIE: There have never before been this many people working in the theater in this many places in any country at any time. Ever! That we should even attempt something like this, on so vast a scale, has a certain Marlowesque madness.

DIES: You mention Marlowe. Is he a Communist?

HALLIE: I'm very sorry. I was referring to Christopher Marlowe.

DIES: Tell us who this Marlowe is, so we can get the proper reference, because that is all we want to do.

HALLIE: Put it in the record that he was the greatest dramatist in the period immediately preceding Shakespeare.

DIES: Put that in the record, because the charge has been made that your theater is Communistic and we want to help you.

HALLIE: Thank you.

DIES: *(Returning to his seat)* Of course, we had what some people call Communists back in the days of the Greek theater.

HALLIE: Quite true.

DIES: I believe Mister Euripides was guilty of teaching class consciousness also, wasn't he?

HALLIE: *(Sitting down)* I think that was alleged against all of the Greek dramatists and against practically every great dramatist.

DIES: So we can't say when it all began, can we.

HALLIE: No, Congressman. We cannot.

DIES: Then why would this Mister Banta, who testified before us last week, tell us that the Federal Theater and its plays are rife with Communism?

HALLIE: You know he is a sick man. I have facts on Mister Banta's physical and mental condition in relation to a hospital stay—

STARNES: Mister Hopkins has been in the hospital, too, hasn't he?

HALLIE: Yes, but it was for no mental difficulty.

THOMAS: That might be a matter of opinion.

HALLIE: I would like to put into the record Mister Banta's files from the clinic—

DIES: You employed him even though you now claim he was mentally deranged?

HALLIE: He was greatly in need. We wanted to aid him.

DIES: Is mental deficiency any ground for disqualifying a person on the Theater Project?

THOMAS: Some think it is a qualification.

HALLIE: I do not know of my own knowledge whether he is crazy or not. I only know about his actions, which look to me to be highly questionable.

THOMAS: *(Rising and taking the floor)* Well, tell us, would you, how you select those you choose to employ.

HALLIE: We select them from the relief rolls, from those who have been just about licked by this Depression. As you're aware, it's hit those in the theatrical profession pretty hard—

THOMAS: Why them more than others?

HALLIE: I did not say them more than others. But if the others were hit, then those in the entertainment field could not be paid for their work because the others could not afford to pay for entertainment.

THOMAS: So you interviewed the great lot of unemployed in the theater profession.

HALLIE: We did, Congressman. They came flooding to us, to our open auditions.

THOMAS: Have you any idea how many of them had been previously unemployed?

HALLIE: I don't understand—

THOMAS: Mrs Flanagan, we've heard stories of people who hadn't performed in years suddenly dusting off their old tap shoes and flocking in to be put on the dole of the United States Government. So we want to know: How many of these so-called theater professionals were actually unemployed in theater *before* the great Depression?

HALLIE: I have no figures on that.

THOMAS: Theater workers are usually unemployed, are they not?

HALLIE: They often are. That is why the formation of the Federal Theater has been such a—

THOMAS: I'm indicating that if they were unemployed in the theater perhaps they deserved to be.

HALLIE: I don't see how that follows.

THOMAS: If they were people of talent, they wouldn't be on relief! If they are on relief, it shows they are not people of talent. There are many commercial producers who resent the government supporting a theater of amateurs and misfits.

HALLIE: Those are the same producers who cry "Unfair!" when these amateurs and misfits turn out a popular hit! Have you ever seen one of our performances, Mister Congressman?

THOMAS: Have you ever seen our burden of work, Mrs Flanagan?

HALLIE: If you came, you would *see* the talent. I have some photographs to show you—

(KATE *tries to give him a pile of photographs; he doesn't take them. She puts them on the table before the other* CONGRESSMEN.)

THOMAS: I have no doubt—

HALLIE: There are many people of great ability who are unable to find work and this theater gives them hope and dignity.

THOMAS: But you said some of those you employ are not on relief.

HALLIE: That's true. We have special permission to take in a quota of 25% who are not on the relief rolls.

THOMAS: To add a little quality?

HALLIE: To supplement the talents of those who are on relief! ... If we need an ingenue for a production in a particular place and all we have on relief are senior character actors we can't have the ingenue played by a grandmother! And there's another thing as well: Many people of great talent, who do not have bread to put in their mouths, are too proud to go on relief and therefore cannot work for us. We let them in on our non-relief quota.

THOMAS: Yes, I understand you take in all kinds.

HALLIE: All kinds.

STARNES: And all colors. *(He rises.)* I hear one of the first plays produced by the Federal Theater in New York was a Negro play, a Negro play done in Harlem.

(THOMAS *takes his seat.*)

HALLIE: It was Shakespeare's *Macbeth*, with an all Negro cast.

STARNES: Shakespeare's hard enough to understand done white, why would you want it done colored?

HALLIE: It was an inspiration of the director.

STARNES: A twenty-year-old white man who had never directed before!

HALLIE: Orson Welles.

STARNES: A boy. With no experience—

HALLIE: He played The Shadow on the radio. And he was the Voice of Chocolate Pudding—

STARNES: The Voice of Chocolate Pudding... And you trusted him?!

HALLIE: He is a genius.

STARNES: Was he on relief?

HALLIE: He was not on relief. But no one else could have come up with such an original idea for the production! Welles set the play in Haiti in the 19th century. The witches were witch doctors—with jungle drums. A scene in Shakespeare which has seldom worked before at last worked marvelously!

(KATE *tries to put photos before* STARNES. *He doesn't look at them*)

STARNES: All too marvelously, as I understand it. Isn't it true that there was an actual murder performed by the cast of this voodoo *Macbeth*?

HALLIE: No, that is not true!

STARNES: Is it not so that they got all good reviews but one?

HALLIE: That is true.

STARNES: And the bad one was from the New York critic Percy Hammond?

HALLIE: Yes, Representative Starnes.

STARNES: And isn't it true that the Negroes in the company were much offended? And didn't they take to the basement of the theater with their drums? And didn't Percy Hammond die within a week of writing that notice?

HALLIE: He died, but not because of drums. Because of a heart attack.

STARNES: It is disturbing to me that we have black magic in the Federal Theater!

(KATE *gets up and waves the* Macbeth *photographs in* STARNES' *face.*)

KATE: And it is disturbing to me that you never look at these things! You keep making disparaging remarks. But you don't look at what's been achieved here! *Macbeth* in a savage jungle. Look at how much they've managed to do with just a few costumes and lights. Look at these other productions! If you'd just open your eyes and see what Hallie and her people have managed to do on a shoestring!

THOMAS: *(Rising)* A shoestring! Young lady, in its three years this theater has cost the Federal Government forty million—!

KATE: It's worth it! Every penny! Why don't you look—?

DIES: *(Rising)* One more outburst like that and you'll be held in contempt of Congress and ejected from this room. Now that's a warning. We have business to do here and we don't need you to tell us how to do it!

HALLIE: It's all right, Kate.

(*She guides* KATE *back to her seat. All the others take their seats.* STARNES *cleans his glasses.* DIES *relights his cigar.* THOMAS *is tapping his gold pencil.*)

KATE: *(Aside to* HALLIE:*)* If he doesn't stop tapping his pencil, I'll kill him!

HALLIE: I don't think that would help us.

KATE: *(Aside to* HALLIE:*)* And what is that fourth guy thinking? Why doesn't he ever speak? Is he for us or against us?

DIES: Are you ladies interested in having this hearing continue, or do you want to go on with your coffee klatsch over there?

HALLIE: Please continue.

DIES: Thank you! *(He draws on his cigar and says:)* Mrs Flanagan, the charge has been made that many of the plays done by the Federal Theater Project are propagandistic. Is that true or untrue?

HALLIE: I can't say we have never done a propaganda play. But I should like to go into the definition of propaganda. Propaganda is education, education focused on certain things.

DIES: Like Communism —

HALLIE: To the best of my knowledge, we have never done a play which was propaganda for Communism. We have done a play which was propaganda for better housing, for better medicine, for —

DIES: Mrs Flanagan, who chooses the plays for the Federal Theater?

HALLIE: All the plays produced by the Federal Theater are passed on by the Federal Theater Policy Board.

DIES: Do these people all sit at one place?

HALLIE: No, but they have regular meetings.

DIES: Suppose you wanted a play put on and rest of them did not?

HALLIE: It would not be put on.

DIES: So you have a rather democratic way of deciding what plays to do? Democratic in the larger sense.

HALLIE: We do.

DIES: Then how do you account for the fact that so many of the plays contain propaganda?

HALLIE: I do not believe that they do.

THOMAS: There are many plays which have been brought to our attention —

HALLIE: As I understand it, there are twenty-six plays which have been brought to your attention. Twenty-six out of nine hundred and twenty-four, that does not seem to me to be a large number.

DIES: Even *one* would be too many, Mrs Flanagan. How do you choose these plays?

HALLIE: On their artistic value.

DIES: On their artistic value only? Are you here to testify that they have no social significance or propaganda value?

HALLIE: I would not like to say they have no social significance, but our primary motive in putting them on is their artistic value.

THOMAS: Even with the so-called "Living Newspapers"?

STARNES: Would you explain, for the edification of those of us who have not been privileged to see one, just what a "Living Newspaper" is?

HALLIE: A Living Newspaper is a play written about a contemporary subject, one which is of great interest to a large segment of the public. It is a dramatization of current events—

DIES: Usually involving controversy.

HALLIE: Yes. From Aristotle on down, drama has always been composed of conflict or controversy.

THOMAS: Do you think these plays are non-partisan?

HALLIE: Well, as much as possible—. Yes, I think so.

STARNES: And you say they're based on current events?

HALLIE: Whatever concerns us today.

STARNES: You mean you could take today's paper and make a dramatization of it?

HALLIE: Absolutely.)

STARNES: *(Picking up a newspaper)* You could take this front page here—December 6th, 1938—and make a play?

(STARNES *hands the paper to* PETERS, *who hands it to* HALLIE.)

HALLIE: My goodness, this is strange news, isn't it? "Germany and France Sign Non-Aggression Pact."

STARNES: You can make a play out of that?

HALLIE: Yes. I'm sure I can. First I'll have a character we call The Loudspeaker announce that headline.

STARNES: That doesn't sound very dramatic.

HALLIE: We'll get to the dramatic parts. I'll have an actor come on as Bonnet, the French minister. He'll tell what France expects of this treaty. Then I'll have another actor come on as Von Ribbentrop, the German minister. He'll explain why Germany is suddenly so anxious to have peace with France.

STARNES: No thrill a minute there.

HALLIE: Just wait! Mussolini comes on. He calls Hitler on the phone and shouts that this treaty is a betrayal of the Rome-Berlin axis. He yells, what about Italy's claims for a piece of France? Has Hitler turned his back on those?

STARNES: You'd make up a play which stars Hitler and Mussolini? You'd give over our government-supported American stages to Nazi lies?

HALLIE: The stage is a very powerful instrument for truth, Representative Starnes. Hitler's hypocrisy in offering this treaty to France would be very clear to an audience. If it's not clear, we'll have a Reporter appear, saying what's in this editorial: "It is obvious to all except France that the only reason Hitler wants peace on Germany's western border is that he wants to be free to pursue the conquest of Poland to the east."

(HALLIE *puts down the paper. A moment of silence. For a moment, outside reality has entered.*)

STARNES: Well, I don't know why we'd have to pay to see that on stage if we could get it in the paper. I don't know that I hold with these "Living Newspapers".

THOMAS: Neither do I. *(He rises and takes the floor.)* Mrs Flanagan, I have here the script of *Injunction Granted*. In this play, members of the Workers Alliance come into the halls of the legislature in the State of New Jersey and sit there and take over the government.

HALLIE: That actually happened.

THOMAS: I know it actually happened! I was there! Mrs Flanagan, *I* am one of the members of the New Jersey Legislature you were condemning!

HALLIE: We were not condemning—

THOMAS: Right here—you have the leader of the Workers' Alliance say: "Brothers, we have taken over this house to protest against the inaction of our elected leaders!" ... I happen to know there was nothing in the way of inaction!

HALLIE: Just a minute. I beg your pardon. That speech was a quotation.

THOMAS: Yes. A quotation from one of the members of the Workers' Alliance who were sitting in our seats!

HALLIE: They were demonstrating against six years of mass unemployment.

THOMAS: Do you know, Mrs Flanagan, that certain members of the State legislature offered jobs to members of the Workers' Alliance and those jobs were not accepted!

HALLIE: I didn't know that. If you had written to us and given us that factual material, we would have tried to get that into the play. We try to include the views of all sides—

THOMAS: That's very well for you to say in retrospect. But while the play was running, audiences heard a state senator say, "God damn it, we're not going to subsidize pensions for workers and that's that!" Do you think that is the right kind of propaganda to put out against the legislators who were elected by the people of that State?

HALLIE: If a senator can say it in the legislature, why should he object to our having him say it on stage?

THOMAS: I want an answer to my question.

HALLIE: I do think that what an elected legislator says in the legislature he can also be seen to say on a stage. But you should also remember the other work — the classics, our history plays, children's plays, religious plays, musical plays —

THOMAS: Mister Chairman, it is my personal opinion that the witness has evaded question after question.

DIES: Mrs Flanagan, attempt to answer the question.

HALLIE: What is the question?

THOMAS: Mrs Flanagan, do you, as National Director of the Federal Theater Project, think that it is proper for the Federal Theater Project, an agency of the Federal Government, to put out this kind of propaganda against the elected legislators of a particular State?

HALLIE: It is not propaganda against the elected legislators. It is propaganda for fair labor relations. And I must insist that doing plays dealing with real problems in America today is one thing the Federal Theater should do. This play was intended to prove that during the time when there was mass need and mass unemployment, the people were not getting sufficient help from their legislative bodies.

THOMAS: Then you're saying that we should use the Federal Theater Project, through its plays, to encourage populist rebellions. That is practically what you just said. Do you admit it or don't you?

HALLIE: I think that Living Newspapers, which I have discussed fully and would like to discuss more, may be one phase of proper activity for any theater.

THOMAS: But you don't answer the question.

HALLIE: Yes, I am answering it.

THOMAS: Do you admit it or don't you admit it?

HALLIE: I do think it is a proper use of Government Funds.

THOMAS: Thank you. I am glad I finally have your answer.

(THOMAS *takes his seat.* DIES *turns to* HEALEY.)

DIES: Congressman Healey, did you say something?

HEALEY: No.

(HEALEY *takes a drink of water.* DIES *turns to* STARNES:)

DIES: Congressman Starnes, do you have some questions?

STARNES: I certainly do, Mister Chairman. (*He rises, cleans his glasses, then peers through them at some papers.*) ...Mrs Flanagan, are you currently rehearsing in New York City a play called *Sing for Your Supper*?

HALLIE: Yes, that is correct.

STARNES: Do I understand you have been in rehearsal for thirteen months—longer than any other you've ever put on?

HALLIE: It's true, but there are reasons.

STARNES: I'd certainly like to hear them.

HALLIE: As you know, we pay the wage set by you in Congress—between twenty and thirty dollars a week. Since that is considerably less than the wage set by Equity, we cannot work our people the same number of hours. Consequently, it takes us at least twice as long as it takes a commercial manager to put on a play.

STARNES: You are, then, blaming Congress for this problem?

HALLIE: No, sir. I am merely making an observation. Then, in this particular case, this peculiar thing keeps happening. In order to be fair to our people, we have to have our rehearsals open. And as fast as we get the acts ready, our performers are seen and snapped up by Broadway.

STARNES: But that's what you're in business to do, isn't it? Get actors off the government rolls and back being supported by private enterprise.

HALLIE: That's true. But as soon as they're snapped up, we have to start all over again.

STARNES: So you end up rehearsing for over a year!

HALLIE: May I ask whether delays are un-American?

STARNES: What is your point?

DIES: I think her point is that this committee is charged with determining whether there is un-American activity in the Federal Theater and this is beside the point!.

STARNES: *(Taking his seat)* We have touched on everything in the world, whether it has been un-American or not, for hours now.

HALLIE: Not by my wish.

STARNES: If we have touched on one thing that is un-American, we might as well touch on one more.

DIES: Do you think it's on the point?

STARNES: I certainly do! ...The charge has been made that there is inefficiency, extravagance and corruption in the Federal Theater Project and I want to know what Mrs Flanagan is doing about it.

DIES: That is an administrative detail—

STARNES: An administrative detail! When hundreds of thousands of Federal funds may be being wasted? I would just like to know what could be more un-American than that!

DIES: We can't widen the scope of this inquiry—

STARNES: I believe that precedent has been set and I—

HALLIE: I am prepared to answer his questions. I would like to answer his questions.

DIES: And I would like us to be able to adjourn for lunch!

STARNES: I think it is not inappropriate to ask whether this little lady is capable of running the immense thing she has going here.

(In spite of herself, KATE jumps up and cries:)

KATE: Capable of running it! She created it!

DIES: We will not have interruptions from the floor.

KATE: You should see what it's like in that office! All Mrs Flanagan has to handle! "Mrs Flanagan, the trained dog in the circus has died and the clown has no act, but he's starving. Should we pay him?" "Mrs Flanagan, the power lines have been blown down in a storm in Texas, a troupe is stranded. Where can they get generators so they can perform?" "Mrs Flanagan—"

DIES: Little lady, if you don't take your seat and be silent, I'll declare you in contempt of Congress and have you forcibly ejected!

(KATE sits in her seat, fuming.)

STARNES: This is exactly what I find so disturbing in the Federal Theater. Its constant air of insubordination! No Federal agency is so full of sitdown strikes as these art folks. A few months back a troop of dancers imprisoned their administrative director in his office overnight.

HALLIE: To the protest the cuts. Every time you cut our budget, people lose their means of livelihood.

STARNES: And so they strike.

HALLIE: If you can think of a better way to make their wishes known, I'd like to hear it.

STARNES: They could write to their Congressmen.

HALLIE: And starve before they get relief, what with all the red tape.

STARNES: Red tape is the government's way of assuring fairness for all.

HALLIE: I'm sure it seems fair—except when you're entangled in it!

STARNES: What I know is, you're a government agency, but you don't follow government orders.

HALLIE: But we do! We follow them to the letter.

DIES: What about in the matter of *The Cradle Will Rock*?

HALLIE: I followed orders.

DIES: Your subordinates did not.

HALLIE: I tried—

DIES: As an administrator, you must do more than try—you must make sure that orders from above are followed. Orders came down that that show must not open—and it opened!

HALLIE: But not under the auspices of the Federal Theater—

DIES: A runaway production. Even worse!

STARNES: What is this play?

HALLIE: It's a musical written by Marc Blitzstein.

STARNES: What's it about?

HALLIE: Prostitution of—

STARNES: Aha!

HALLIE: Prostitution of the soul. Its message is: One mustn't sell one's talent and dignity to the bosses.

DIES: Like the United States Government.

HALLIE: *Any* bosses. The place where it takes place is called Steeltown, U S A.

DIES: I understand it's about the conflict between labor and management.

HALLIE: Partly.

DIES: Didn't you think it unwise to put on such a vehicle in such precarious times?

HALLIE: I did not.

DIES: There is a great deal of labor unrest. You could have been inciting to riot—

HALLIE: No, Mister Chairman. All we were doing was inciting to thought.

DIES: When that play was in rehearsal there was yet another sit-down strike on the Federal Theater Project.

HALLIE: It was the only way they had to protest a thirty percent cut in the budget. Seventeen hundred of our people were about to be dismissed. They were upset.

DIES: We knew they were upset. That's why we declared a cooling off period.

HALLIE: Is that what you call it? The play was to open June 16th. One week before that you sent a memorandum that no new play, musical or art exhibition could open before July first.

DIES: But you opened anyway, on June 16th—in express contravention of government orders!

HALLIE: I tried to get an exception for this show—

DIES: You didn't get it. All the government was asking for was a postponement—

HALLIE: John Houseman and Orson Welles didn't think so.

STARNES: Once more we hear from the Voice of Chocolate Pudding!

HALLIE: They thought the play was going to be cancelled. They thought the order for postponement was censorship.

DIES: Censorship!

HALLIE: In a new guise. They thought the government, for its own reasons, was trying to silence their production.

DIES: It is not their prerogative to think.

HALLIE: They think it is.

DIES: I was told that guards were posted to enforce government orders—keep the audience out and to keep any government-owned sets and props inside the theater.

HALLIE: Yes. And what a pretty sight that was! Government Cossacks sent to keep the government-funded performance from opening. Our people had to meet in the powder room in the basement of the Maxine Elliot Theater to try to decide what to do.

DIES: Were you in that powder room?

HALLIE: I was not.

DIES: Then how do you know any of this?

HALLIE: I was told—

THOMAS: I object. She was not present. She can't testify about an event she did not witness.

STARNES: I want to find out what happened.

HALLIE: The artists felt obliged to honor their commitment to their audience—

THOMAS: Probably a bunch of left wing radicals—

HALLIE: They felt obliged to open as scheduled. That is a sacred trust between performer and audience. It is a trust they felt that they should keep.

DIES: Or perhaps this whole affair was a grandstand play, and what they *really* wanted was publicity.

HALLIE: *(Pointedly)* If so, they wouldn't be the first to take on a cause in order to get their names in the papers, would they?

(KATE *leans over and whispers to* HALLIE:)

KATE: Careful, Hallie. Don't try to score points. If you win, you lose with these guys.

HALLIE: Finally, late in the afternoon, they found private moneys which would allow them to open. But Actors Equity sent a ruling that actors who had been rehearsing under a Federal Theater contract could not appear on stage for another management.

DIES: That should have stopped them.

HALLIE: Not Houseman and Welles. They sent a young woman out to hire a piano—and a truck and driver to move it to a theater—and they set out to find a vacant theater. For three hours this young woman drove around the streets of New York with a piano waiting to find out whether or not they would find a place to perform. ... Just as the truck driver was threatening to dump the piano into the street, Welles and Houseman found an empty theater. The Venice Theater, an old vaudeville house twenty blocks north of the Elliot. ... By that time, the audience had begun to mill about outside the Elliot.

DIES: The Commie hordes.

HALLIE: A theatre audience! All together they started to walk twenty blocks up the street. I wasn't there. But they told me it was a splendid procession! Up Broadway. First the truck carrying the piano—and, with it, poor young Marc Blitzstein, who had no idea of what was going to happen. Then the actors, without sets, without costumes. They hadn't even been allowed to take their wigs! And then hundreds of people—people who had been promised a performance—

STARNES: And did they get it?

HALLIE: Yes. They got it. A performance such as has never been seen before or since! On the bare stage of the Venice Theater, with an old oleo drop of Naples in the background, there sat Marc in his shirtsleeves and suspenders at this upright piano. The house was filled to the rafters. When the lights went on, everyone cheered. Marc told me later he was trembling. He knew he'd have to play and sing the entire opera by himself and he wasn't sure that he could make it! He began, with shaking hands, to play the overture. Then suddenly, when he came to the first solo—the solo of the young girl—he heard a voice—a voice coming from a box toward the front of the theater. It was Olive Stanton—singing her role—from her seat.

Equity said they couldn't sing from any stage for another management? Well, she'd sing from the house! A small voice at first. Then she gained more assurance and her voice got louder. When the time came for the next singer to sing—another voice from far back in the theater was heard. And another, and another! Oh, not all the actors arrived. Some were afraid to defy the government edict—

DIES: You mean, were prudent enough to be respectful!

HALLIE: But others filled in for those who were not there. And when it came time for the people to sing—the Negro chorus had assembled in the balcony, and, from there, at the appointed measure, rolled forth a tremendous—"Amen!" At every cue, they sang out: "Hallelujah! Amen!"

THOMAS: And the evening was a success?

HALLIE: It was a triumph!

DIES: This evening—which should not have taken place at all, which was ordered not to take place—was a triumph!

HALLIE: Yes, it was. It was the people on stage and the performers in the house and the audience all united in one great common experience—

STARNES: Of major insubordination!

HALLIE: Of exaltation! Of joy!

DIES: Doing just what the Federal Theater has always done—thumbing its nose at authority, supporting anarchy, displaying defiance!

HALLIE: Defiance, yes. But not political! Artistic!

STARNES: And artists can do anything they want to? Artists can thumb their noses at whoever they want?

HALLIE: I'm afraid they think it their prerogative. In fact, they think it their God-given duty.

DIES: And you agree?

HALLIE: As I said, on this occasion, I removed myself from the fray the moment they decided to withdraw the production from the aegis of the Federal Theater.

DIES: But you approved.

HALLIE: I remained neutral.

DIES: Then you did not approve. You found their actions reprehensible.

HALLIE: No, not reprehensible.

DIES: Then you found them heroic.

HALLIE: (*Pause, then:*) ...Yes! Yes. I did! As head of the Federal Theater I was forced to be silent and caution them about the consequences of their actions. But as Hallie Flanagan, I applauded them in my mind! I applaud the idea of "the show must go on no matter what!" It's the life force! It's the irrepressible cry of the human spirit! It's what theater is: a celebration of the splendor of indomitable life!

(*There is the sound of one person applauding from the gallery. All look in that direction.* KATE *says to* HALLIE:)

KATE: Philip...

(HALLIE *blows him a kiss.*)

DIES: (*Frowning*) ...I think we'll break for lunch now.

HALLIE: You understand, neither I nor anyone on my staff, encouraged them in any way—

DIES: That's quite enough, Mrs Flanagan. We'll continue later.

(DIES, STARNES *and* THOMAS *begin to pick up their papers.*)

HALLIE: I don't want you to think the Federal Theater is full of rebels and renegades. These particular people got carried away for that moment. There are thousands in the Federal Theater who ask only to continue their work. If you penalize the rest—

DIES: Mrs Flanagan, we are not a judge and jury. We do not mete out punishment.

HALLIE: Our people are afraid of cuts. You cut thirty percent before. If you cut another thirty percent, we'll have less than half of the personnel we started with. Think of the human result—

DIES: We're not thinking of a cut of thirty percent.

HALLIE: Thank goodness.

DIES: We're thinking of cutting it all.

HALLIE: All—?

DIES: We're thinking of a cut of the Federal Theater's entire budget.

HALLIE: But that would end the theater!

DIES: So it would.

HALLIE: But you can't—

DIES: What do you think this hearing is all about, Mrs Flanagan?

HALLIE: It's about charges of Communism in—

DIES: It's about a recommendation we will make to the Appropriations Committee of the House of Representatives.

HALLIE: The Appropriations Committee—

THOMAS: I am a member of that committee—

DIES: It all comes down to a matter of dollars and cents—

HALLIE: *(Riffling through her papers)* But it's more than a matter of dollars and cents! What our men and women are doing is important! Vital! I have a statement. I want to read my statement!

DIES: After lunch.

(DIES, STARNES *and* THOMAS *pick up their papers and go out stage right.* HEALEY *hesitates for a moment, as if he were about to speak to* HALLIE. *Then he changes his mind and exits after his colleagues.*)

HALLIE: Suddenly I'm not hungry.

(*She and* KATE *pick up their papers and exit stage left.* PETERS *turns out the lights and exits in the direction of the* CONGRESSMEN.)

(Blackout)

END ACT ONE

ACT TWO

(At rise: The same day, after lunch. HALLIE and PHILIP are in the anteroom, on the forestage, stage left. HALLIE has taken her hat off. PHILIP is trying to hand her a sandwich.)

PHILIP: Hallie, you have to eat something—

HALLIE: My problems aren't going to be solved by a tuna sandwich.

PHILIP: You need energy—

HALLIE: I need some new ideas before the curtain goes up on the second act! They're making me feel like a criminal. *Mea culpa*. I've committed Art. Lock me up, boys!

PHILIP: Politicians never quite trust you art folks.

HALLIE: If I were directing this production, I'd give the committee masks. Dies as a grizzly bear, Starnes as a walrus, and Thomas as a snake.

PHILIP: What about Healey, the one who doesn't speak?

HALLIE: A giraffe.

PHILIP: How about a camel? All that water! ... What do you think he's thinking?

HALLIE: With a little luck—and a strong kidney—he may sometime let us know.

PHILIP: I think you're holding your own as well as can be expected.

HALLIE: They keep interrupting! When they had that parade of "friendly witnesses", they let them go on forever. With me, I get a sentence out and— pow!—they interrupt!

PHILIP: They'd let you go on forever—if you were saying what they want to hear.

HALLIE: It never occurred to me they might be considering cutting the entire budget. They can't—! Hopkins has to come to our defense. He has to!

PHILIP: Hallie—

(KATE enters carrying a slide machine and a box of slides.)

KATE: They want evidence, do I have evidence! I pulled out slides from everything we've ever done!

HALLIE: Did you manage to connect with Harry Hopkins?

(KATE *shakes her head.*)

KATE: I tried his office. I tried his home. I even tried his doctor's office. I just can't find him anywhere.

HALLIE: Did you leave messages?

KATE: All over the place.

HALLIE: I'm sure he'll get over here if he receives them. I want him to hear for himself what's going on. I know he'll come out with a strong statement in defense of the Federal Theater.

KATE: I tried Mrs Roosevelt. She, too, is among the missing. Absolutely everyone seems to be not in. Or not in to us.

HALLIE: I can see Mrs Roosevelt being too busy to take a call, but Harry wouldn't avoid me, would he?

PHILIP: Maybe he feels he has to stay out of controversy. There's word that Roosevelt's grooming him for the Presidential race, possibly even as the man to take his place at the top of the ticket.

HALLIE: Then there's nothing I can do except handle things on my own.

PHILIP: There is one thing you could do—

HALLIE: What—?

PHILIP: Hold a press conference.

HALLIE: I don't need to. There are reporters in the gallery already.

PHILIP: They're only getting the story of what the committee wants to ask you. I think you should get the press in here, now, before the afternoon session. You should tell them all the things you want to say in defense of the Theater.

HALLIE: I can't, Philip. You know the rules. All contact with the papers must be handled by the central office of the W P A.

PHILIP: But they're nowhere to be seen—

HALLIE: You know how upset they got the last time I spoke out—

PHILIP: Are you living your life to not upset the W P A?

HALLIE: I can't go against specific orders—

PHILIP: It seems to me you've followed orders long enough!

HALLIE: *(With an edge to her voice)* Well, that's a new position for my philosopher-husband. What is it? You think I'm not handling things correctly?

(*Sensing trouble,* KATE *says:*)

KATE: I'll go keep trying to reach Harry Hopkins— (*She exits.*)

PHILIP: I just think—this is the time and the place to speak your piece, so say it all. Damn the torpedoes, full speed ahead!

HALLIE: Give them the opportunity to call me "that bitch"? "That hysterical female"?! No, no! That's exactly what they're waiting for! That's why, no matter how much I'm provoked, I'm bound and determined to speak with reason and without passion.

PHILIP: If you think that'll do it.

HALLIE: You think I'm not being my usual outspoken self, is that it?

PHILIP: I think you could use a bit more candor—

HALLIE: Why don't I just tell them what I know? "Yes, gentlemen, I think there well may be those in the Federal Theater whose sympathies lie in the Communist direction." Is that what you want me to say?

PHILIP: Of course not.

HALLIE: In this day and age the Liberal line and the Party line can sometimes sound almost identical. That doesn't mean the Theater's Communist.

PHILIP: Why don't you tell them that?

HALLIE: Because I don't think their brains are large enough to comprehend it!

PHILIP: Try them.

HALLIE: If I admit to knowing there's one single Red sympathizer in the Federal Theater, I'll be ousted from this job.

PHILIP: Then you won't have to go on day after day killing yourself.

HALLIE: You'd like that, wouldn't you? You'd like to have me back home playing mother and wife.

PHILIP: You know I have never once ever made that kind of demand on you.

HALLIE: You don't need to. It's in your eyes. And in the eyes of your kids and mine. I told you at the start that homemaking was not my forte.

PHILIP: And I heard you—

HALLIE: Yes, but we were honeymooning on the isles of Greece at the time. There was the blue sea all around and you thought: "She doesn't really mean it." Philip, I do mean it. I love being a mother, but I can't be mother one hundred percent of the time!

PHILIP: I know that. I don't want you to stay home and play Mama. All I'm trying to say is: This is your opportunity to get yourself a public forum, so take it.

HALLIE: You mean—throw caution to the winds and give up the greatest chance I've ever had—the hope, the smidgen of a hope, that this could be the beginning of an American National Theater.

PHILIP: You don't understand what I'm saying.

HALLIE: You think I'm going to lose, so I may as well throw caution to the winds and speak everything I have to say.

PHILIP: I'm on your side, Hallie.

HALLIE: You want me to be Joan of Arc! But Philip, I don't want to be burned at the stake. Never mind me—the Theater! I want it to go on! I love this great, unruly mess of a Theater! I don't want to see it end! Not just for myself, but for all the people in it. I'm on a tightrope here. That's why I'm treading so carefully.

PHILIP: Well—you have to do what you think best.

HALLIE: I may be naive, but I still think I can get a fair hearing. I think maybe at the last moment, when it comes to a vote, the giraffe will get up and speak. I think he'll turn them around. I think *I* can turn them around.

PHILIP: Then of course you have to try—

(KATE *re-enters.*)

KATE: They're ready for you in the hearing room.

HALLIE: *(To* PHILIP*:)* You'll see, they'll understand everything when I read my brief—

PHILIP: Hallie—I don't think you're going to be allowed to read it.

HALLIE: If you think I'm going to lose, go back to Poughkeepsie! I don't want you up in the gallery waiting to be proven right! Go!

PHILIP: Hallie—

HALLIE: I need every ounce of mental energy I have to keep from falling into the traps they're setting for me. I don't want negative vibrations in that room coming from you!

PHILIP: I only want to help you, as I've always wanted to help you!

HALLIE: There are some moments, Philip, some terrifying awful moments, when the only thing one can do is go it alone.

(HALLIE *puts on her hat and follows* KATE *out stage left.* PHILIP *stands looking after her for a moment, then exits in the opposite direction.*)

(The lights come up on the Hearing Room.)

(STARNES, THOMAS *and* DIES *enter, each laden with scripts and documents. They move toward the dais.)*

DIES: Then we're agreed: Whatever we do, no more squabbling. We've got to present a united front here. We don't want to be made fools of by a redhead in a hat. The eyes of the world are upon us.

STARNES: In that case, Congressman, I suggest you flick that cigar ash off of your tie.

THOMAS: Won't look good to the electorate.

DIES: Are you suggesting that I'm up here exposing my ass for personal gain?

STARNES: Can you think of any other reason to expose one's backside?

DIES: I don't suppose you ever heard of a little thing called patriotism?

THOMAS: It is possible to defend the flag without wrapping oneself in it.

DIES: I resent your insinuations—

THOMAS: How many more days are you going to drag out these hearings?

STARNES: Probably till he gets his picture on the front page of every newspaper in these forty-eight states!

DIES: I'll tell you how long: Till I get every Commie off the government payroll!

STARNES: Watch out, ladies and gentlemen! The Chairman is about to ride into battle again!

DIES: I don't know why the hell the two of you got yourselves onto this committee!

STARNES: Maybe to protect the House of Representatives from the excesses of an ambitious fledgling like you.

DIES: How can you say such a thing?

STARNES: *(With a grin)* Under my First Amendment Rights.

(HEALEY *enters.*)

STARNES: Ah, Healey, glad you decided to return!

THOMAS: Don't know how we could survive without your words of wisdom!

(HEALEY *gives them a look, but says nothing.*)

STARNES: What are you thinking?

HEALEY: I'm thinking I haven't made up my mind yet.

DIES: We have to end government support of Communists!

THOMAS: We have to use government monies for general welfare and defense.

STARNES: We can't use government funds to support a bunch of artsy-fartsy failures!

DIES: Those are not the issues here. I thought we were going to present a united front!

THOMAS: Oh, we're united. Just not necessarily under your banner.

DIES: Maybe you gentlemen don't love your country enough to want to deliver it from its enemies. I do!

(They put their stacks of documents on the table in front of them and take their seats.)

(HALLIE and KATE enter from stage left and take their places in the witness area. KATE puts a projector in place on the table.)

(DIES lights his cigar and says:)

DIES: Good afternoon, Mrs Flanagan.

HALLIE: Good afternoon, Congressman Dies.

DIES: I see you've been busy during your lunch hour.

HALLIE: Apparently so have you, Mister Chairman.

DIES: You are an expert witness, Mrs Flanagan. My colleagues and I feel we have to be on our toes.

HALLIE: Thank you. Gentlemen, my assistant and I have brought some slides which might help you appreciate the scope and quality of the productions of the Federal Theater—

(KATE stands at the table, ready to show the slides.)

DIES: Mrs Flanagan, your desire for us to see the results of your art is understandable, but my colleagues and I want to focus on the matter of subversive activities in the Federal Theater.

HALLIE: That should be a brief exploration.

DIES: Why?

HALLIE: Because there are no subversive activities in the Federal Theater.

DIES: Mrs Flanagan, are you familiar with the legend of the Trojan Horse?

HALLIE: I am.

DIES: The enemy wheeled the horse into the city of Troy. It looked like a splendid gift. But enemy soldiers were inside. They crept out in the dark of night and conquered the city.

HALLIE: It's a very dramatic story.

DIES: My question is this: Is the Federal Theater that Trojan Horse? Is it already inside our city? Are its enemy soldiers even now infiltrating our land?

HALLIE: Congressman Dies—

DIES: Mrs Flanagan, the last few years have seen difficult times in this country. There has been poverty and political unrest. There have been strikes, bombings, arson, lynchings! We may be seeing the beginning of a revolution! A revolution from within—fueled by secret Bolshevik plots to overthrow this government, plots which even now are being hatched—

HALLIE: Not by the Federal Theater.

DIES: That remains to be seen.

HALLIE: Chairman Dies, the Federal Theater is not a political institution, it's a cultural one! Most of the time we do musical comedies, fairy tales, classics. We've done plays by Shakespeare, Moliere, Ibsen, O'Neill. Important playwrights! Mister Eugene O'Neill gave us the rights to produce nine of his plays! Let me show you the slides of our production of *Ah, Wilderness*—

(KATE *looks for the slides of that show.*)

STARNES: There's a lot of bad language and strange goings on in that Mister O'Neill!

HALLIE: Mister T S Eliot gave us the right to present the world premiere of his *Murder in the Cathedral*. I'd like to show you pictures of that—

DIES: Have you ever done any anti-Fascist plays?

HALLIE: We did Sinclair Lewis's *It Can't Happen Here*. That's a play which warns that totalitarian takeovers are possible anywhere. We gave that play seventeen simultaneous openings in sixteen different cities!

THOMAS: I thought you said the Federal Theater wasn't political—

HALLIE: I mean it's not political in the sense of its not having a particular philosophy to expound—

DIES: Have you ever done any plays that are definitely anti-Communist?

HALLIE: Mister Chairman, we never do a play because it holds any political bias—

DIES: You did one play in which Earl Browder, the head of the American Communist party appeared as a character.

HALLIE: *Triple-A Plowed Under*. That was about the crisis with the farmers—

DIES: In that play did Earl Browder expound his theory of Communism?

HALLIE: No, he did not.

DIES: But he appeared. And he spoke. Do you think that a legitimate use of the Federal Theater?

HALLIE: It seems to me we would be on very dangerous ground if we denounced as subversive any play in which any character opposing our own political faith appeared. You might as well say the March of Time, because it quotes from Stalin, is Communist, or because it quotes from Hitler is Fascist. I do not think that is a tenable position.

DIES: I have only asked a simple question about whether Browder expounded his views. If he did not, then the answer is no.

THOMAS: We are trying to discover if you think the theater should be used for the purpose of conveying ideas along social, economic or political lines—

HALLIE: I would hesitate on the political—

THOMAS: Eliminate the political. Upon social and economic lines?

HALLIE: I think it is one logical, reasonable and I might say imperative thing for our theater to do.

STARNES: To put forth propaganda for one particular viewpoint? *(He riffles through his pile of scripts.)* What about this play—*The Revolt of the Beavers*?

THOMAS: My God, Starnes, that is a play for children!

STARNES: The Chief of Police of the City of New York refused to let his policemen see this play—and they had been given free tickets!

THOMAS: Imagine passing up the opportunity to see beavers revolting!

HALLIE: I'm sorry the Chief of Police thought his big burly policemen could be corrupted by actors in beaver suits. ... I would like to show you a slide of that production.

(KATE *rises to put on a slide.* HALLIE *rises to say:*)

HALLIE: You will see whether these furry creatures look like a threat to the United States Government.

DIES: Mrs Flanagan, for us to see your slides, we would have to pull down the blinds and dim the lights. I suggest we save that treat for the end of this session—if there is time.

HALLIE: Yes, Mister Chairman.

(HALLIE *and* KATE *take their seats.*)

DIES: I don't suppose you could summarize the plot of *The Revolt of the Beavers*?

THOMAS: Must we?

HALLIE: I certainly can. It's about a colony of little beavers: Oakleaf, Beanpole, Blubber, Birch, and Old Man Wind!

THOMAS: Sounds like the roster of the U S Senate!

HALLIE: Oakleaf leads a revolution against the tyrant chief when the chief refuses to give him any bark. The beavers organize and throw the tyrant out of Beaverland. Then, of course, they get all the bark they want. Does that sound subversive?

STARNES: This play is accused of poisoning the minds of youth.

DIES: *(Reading a clipping)* Here's what Mister Brooks Atkinson of the New York Times said of this play: "Many children unschooled in the technique of revolution now have an opportunity, at Government expense, to improve their tender minds. Mother Goose has been studying Marx." Next we'll have Jack and Jill leading the class revolution!

HALLIE: I'm sorry Mister Atkinson was disturbed by this play. I took my and my husband's children and they enjoyed it immensely.

STARNES: I didn't know you had children—

HALLIE: Do you think being a mother disqualifies me from running the Federal Theater?

STARNES: Your children would be bound to be prejudiced.

HALLIE: Then listen to these comments from children in the public schools:

(KATE *hands* HALLIE *a sheaf of papers in children's handwriting.*)

HALLIE: "The play teaches us never to be selfish because you don't get anything out of it." ... "I thought the grown people acted their parts as children very well, especially as beavers on roller skates." ... "The play says if you are unkind at any time in your life, you will always regret it." ...I think that's not a bad idea, gentlemen.

DIES: Just because the children didn't know what they were seeing didn't mean they weren't seeing it. One of the most dangerous things about propaganda is that no one knows it *is* propaganda. Ideas, planted in young and impressionable minds, may erupt again when those minds are fully grown.

THOMAS: Can we get off the subject of these beavers?! ...Mrs Flanagan, can you say you have never done a play which was propaganda?

HALLIE: On the contrary, we've done quite a few plays which were propaganda. Propaganda for democracy, propaganda for better medicine, in *One-Third of a Nation* it was propaganda for better housing—the one third which is ill-housed, ill-fed and ill-clothed.

DIES: Yes, and that was a scurrilous attack on this government, blaming us for the plight of millions of do-nothing laborers who would prefer to live in squalor if they can't live all their lives on the dole!

HALLIE: Congressman Dies, the worst thing about *One-Third of a Nation* is that it was true.

STARNES: What about *Stevedore*? What was that propaganda for?

HALLIE: I'm not sure we produced that one—

STARNES: I have a script for it, so you must have produced it. Do you think it's correct for a government theater to produce a play which is teaming with profanity?

HALLIE: Could you be specific?

(*As* STARNES *searches through a manuscript,* HALLIE *says, aside, to* KATE:)

HALLIE: How could he have gotten hold of these scripts?

STARNES: Right here, on page twenty-four. "God damn dem, anyhow. What dey think I am? Do I look like somebody who'd jump over a back fence and rape a woman?" ... I am not going to read all the things in here, but there are numerous examples of absolutely vulgar statements and the frequent use of the Lord's name in a profane way. ... I am not undertaking to indict you, but what I'm asking you is this: Do you think it is proper that the taxpayers' money of America should be used to produce, before an American audience, a play that contains such vulgarity and such profanity?

HALLIE: I have no defense for blasphemy. But in this particular case, I suspect you are quoting out of context—

STARNES: Then you will agree with me that the play should not have been produced?

HALLIE: I don't know that I'd say that about any play unless it were incompetent, malicious or untrue.

STARNES: You mean you think we should allow *anything* to be said on our stages? Without any government control—?

HALLIE: Yes—

(HEALEY *moves to pick up his glass and it spills.*)

STARNES: (*To* HEALEY:) What does that mean? That you're shocked that we should allow this type of play?

HEALEY: It means I've spilled my water.

(PETERS *moves to help him mop it up.* THOMAS *impatiently taps his pencil.*)

STARNES: Will you stop tapping your goddam pencil!

THOMAS: Will you stop cleaning your goddam glasses!

DIES: (*Banging his gavel*) Gentlemen! Gentlemen! ... Let's get back on track here. Mrs Flanagan, are you saying you think it's proper for the Federal Theater to do plays which deal with very current controversial issues?

HALLIE: I have said so before and I say it again: Yes.

DIES: Even if it means taking sides on an issue?

HALLIE: I think we strive for objectivity, but I think the whole history of plays in the theater would indicate that any dramatist holds a passionate brief for the things he is saying. Practically any play from the beginning of time has been loaded with some dramatist's ideas and emotions.

THOMAS: But, Mrs Flanagan, these are plays that all of us—all of us American people—help to finance. Do you not think that, since the Federal Theater Project is an agency of the Government and since all of our people support it through their tax money—people of different classes, different races, different religions, some who are workers, some who are businessmen—don't you think that no play should ever be produced which undertakes to portray the interests of one group over another?

HALLIE: I think that if every play that you did expressed one opinion, it would be a loaded theater, and quite out of keeping with a theater subsidized by Government funds. However, if you are considering the whole scope of the Federal Theater, you would have to take into consideration the many plays done, the many types of plays. I think that you gentlemen would have to go to some of these plays!

THOMAS: Mrs Flanagan, we are not arguing with you. We are simply asking you. You are the source of our information.

HALLIE: Have any of you gentlemen ever seen one of our plays?

DIES: Mrs Flanagan, my colleague is not asking this in a sarcastic manner. This is for the purpose of eliciting information from you, who are the servant of our administration in this important matter.

HALLIE: Quite true.

DIES: And to you we come for information.

(KATE *suddenly jumps up and cries:*)

KATE: If you're coming to her for information, why not receive it? You think she's insulting you by asking you to consider what the Federal Theater is really about! This is what it's about! *(She snaps on the projector and begins to show slide after slide of stage productions.)* And this! And this!

(DIES *bangs his gavel.*)

DIES: Miss, you are in contempt and will leave this room!

KATE: I will be happy to leave this room! So I don't have to watch testimony before Deaf, Dumb and Blind here! *(She indicates the panel.)*

HALLIE: *(Aside, ironically)* Thanks for your help, Kate.

KATE: *(To the* CONGRESSMEN:*)* You're not looking at the evidence. How can you do that? The Federal Theater has done nearly a thousand plays. You're only considering a few.

DIES: Lady, if there were only *one* unacceptable one, that would be one too many.

(Sounds of murmuring are heard from the balcony.)

DIES: I think we'd better clear this room.

KATE: So no one can see how unfair you're being!

DIES: *(Banging his gavel:)* Out! Everyone! ...Especially you, young lady.

KATE: *(To* HALLIE:*)* Oh, Hallie, I'm sorry. I just wanted to help—*(She picks up the slides and slide projector.)*

HALLIE: Don't worry. I'll be all right here.

DIES: Gentlemen of the press, you leave too, please. I'll talk to you later. Myself. After this session is over.

(KATE *exits. The balcony is cleared, the murmuring ceases.* HALLIE *is alone at the witness table.* DIES *says to her:)*

DIES: Well, that's better, isn't it. Just us, without an audience.

HALLIE: That's not the way we like things in the theater.

DIES: Well, that's the way we like things in this room.

HALLIE: So no word gets out—?

DIES: Every word gets out. Every word we say here becomes part of the public record.

HALLIE: Excellent. Then we must make sure that everything that should be said is in that record. *(She picks up her brief.)* I have here a statement—

DIES: Mrs Flanagan, we were asking you if you don't think you're treading on dangerous ground when you use an agency of the Government—no matter how laudable it may be in private life—to portray the interests of any class or group in a more advantageous light than any other.

HALLIE: Chairman Dies, if our plays deal with the problems of ordinary folk rather than the problems of society gentlemen and ladies, it's because the ordinary folk have so many problems at this moment. That doesn't prove we're Communists!

DIES: Come now, Mrs Flanagan. Don't most of your plays make the workers into heroes, while the employers are portrayed as venal and absurd?

HALLIE: *(Stonewalling)* Could you give me a specific example?

DIES: I am asking you if that is done.

HALLIE: If you give me quotations, I will be glad to answer.

DIES: Can you name one single play—not one of these historical plays or classical plays—one single play where the audience is left with the idea that organized labor doesn't get the best of the other fellows?

HALLIE: Why, Congressman, I could sit in this room till the end of day and give you dozens of plays. *Spirochete*, for example.

DIES: What's that about?

HALLIE: Syphilis.

DIES: I'm not talking about that!

HALLIE: It's a play educating the public about a social disease. That's a perfectly clear example, isn't it? And we have other plays, about the Bonneville Dam, and the founding of California, and the history of vaudeville—

DIES: Mrs Flanagan, the Federal Theater reaches twenty-five million people. Therefore, it is a very powerful vehicle of expression, isn't it, and of propaganda. And do you know of any way in which that power could be more seriously abused than to portray one class over another class?

HALLIE: But I have been giving you a long list of illustrations of the fact that we do not do so.

DIES: I am not asking you that. I say, isn't that a fact?

HALLIE: I am asking you for illustrations where we have done that. I claim you are stating a hypothetical case, Congressman.

DIES: Then will you say that you have not produced a play in which, throughout the play, one class is not portrayed in a more advantageous role than another?

HALLIE: No. And that is not what you asked. You asked if I could give you a single play in which we have not done that and I could give you a myriad. For instance, in *Power*, the central character is the consumer. The whole play is to show how power came into being, what makes it, and what is the best possible use of it.

DIES: And what impression is that play designed to bring to the mind of the audience—that public ownership of power is a good thing?

HALLIE: Yes, I think it does speak highly for the public ownership of power.

DIES: You know, every time I turn on the gas, or flick on a light, that gas and that light are there—and they are provided by private companies. But let us assume, for the sake of argument, that public ownership is desirable. Do you not think it improper that the Federal Theater, using the taxpayers' money, should present a play to the audience which champions one side of a controversy?

HALLIE: No, Mister Chairman, I do not consider it improper. I have just said that I felt a small percentage of our plays do hold a brief for a certain cause in accordance with general forward-looking tendencies, and—

DIES: Who determines what is a forward-looking tendency?

HALLIE: Why, our play policy board, which chooses these plays.

DIES: Well, suppose your forward-looking policy board approves of the public ownership of *railroads*. Are we all to be treated to a play which demands we take the railroads out of the hands of the Union Pacific, the New York Central, the—

HALLIE: We never choose plays that way, Mister Chairman. We choose a play on the basis of whether or not it is a good play.

DIES: Well, then, suppose someone came to you with a play which championed the public ownership of railroads—and it was a good play—would you do it?

HALLIE: Let me put it this way—if they came to me with a play which championed the *private* ownership of railroads, we would do that, too.

DIES: All right. You have established the precedent of exhibiting a play championing the cause of public ownership of utilities, is that correct?

HALLIE: Yes, but—

DIES: And you have said if a good play arrived advocating the public ownership of railroads, you would consider it fine to show that to twenty-five million people, too. Is that true?

HALLIE: Yes, but you have to take into account our wide variety of plays—

DIES: Now suppose someone came in with a play showing that public ownership of all the property in the United States was a good thing—and it was a good play, you would also exhibit that, would you not?

HALLIE: Well, that is a very clever move on your part to maneuver me into a certain position.

DIES: I do not pretend to any cleverness. I would not undertake to match my cleverness with you on this subject because you are thoroughly acquainted with it.

HALLIE: No, I would not do such a play—because that would be recommending the overthrow of the United States Government, and I do not want that, gentlemen, whatever some of your previous witnesses may have intimated.

DIES: So you censor your own theater. You are saying *we* are not capable of deciding what is proper to be exhibited in our theaters, but *you* are capable of making that judgment for us, is that right?

HALLIE: *(Getting rattled for the first time)* No, that is not right! ...I can't go into these hypothetical questions. I came up here under the distinct understanding that I was to refute testimony given by witnesses before your committee. You are proposing a long series of hypothetical questions.

DIES: You say you are here to refute testimony of other witnesses. You can't refute any of the testimony that appeared in this record dealing with Communist activities on the project, can you, because you admit you were not there, you did not see it, you did not know it. So you can't refute that, can you?

HALLIE: I want to take it up charge by charge.

DIES: But you have already stated that if Communist activities took place, you did not see them.

HALLIE: I say—to my own knowledge, in the offices which I have frequented, it has not been true. I cannot have been in every office all the time.

DIES: So you yourself are not in a position to deny under oath any of the testimony that has appeared in this record dealing with Communist activities on the project, are you?

HALLIE: Oh, yes, I am. I certainly am. I have affidavits—

DIES: But those affidavits depend for their truth or falsity upon what someone else said.

HALLIE: They are affidavits of people under oath I have employed.

DIES: I am talking about what you are prepared to say yourself. The statement has been made in the testimony that you are in sympathy with Communistic doctrines. Are you in a position to deny that?

HALLIE: Yes, I am.

DIES: Even though this cousin of yours, Miss O'Shea—

HALLIE: For the last time, I am not now, I never have been, and I never want to be a cousin of Miss O'Shea!

DIES: I take your point.

HALLIE: Mister Chairman, I am an American and I believe in American democracy. I believe the Works Progress Administration is one great bulwark of that democracy. I believe the Federal Theater, which is one small part of that large pattern, is honestly trying in every possible way to interpret the best interests of the people of this democracy. I am not in sympathy with any other form of government in this country.

DIES: That is your statement. You are absolutely not in sympathy with Communism. You are opposed to it, you know nothing of it personally. But you can't deny, of course, of your own personal knowledge, that there is no Communist activity on your project.

HALLIE: If there is, it is without my knowledge or consent.

DIES: But can you prove there is not?

HALLIE: I can definitely refute certain specific charges—

DIES: But can you swear no pamphlets were distributed, no speeches were made, no meetings were held on the project during pay time? Can you refute that under oath?

HALLIE: I cannot refute that under oath, because I have not been present.

DIES: Exactly.

HALLIE: I cannot prove these things didn't happen. But can you prove they did?

DIES: I have sworn affidavits.

HALLIE: And so do I! Stating the opposite! Why don't you feel that mine are equally as valid?

DIES: Mrs Flanagan—

HALLIE: You have no more evidence than I do! You won't allow *my* hearsay, why will you allow these other people's?

DIES: You forget, Mrs Flanagan, I have something quite concrete—I have these plays. The contents of these plays. And we have already come up with example after example where—

HALLIE: Mister Dies, The Federal Theater is not a Communist Organization!

DIES: Mrs Flanagan, —how do you know? ...You have no idea how many Communists there are around us. The Communists have wheeled the Trojan Horse inside our city. It is here. That we don't know the enemy is within doesn't mean that they aren't all around us.

HALLIE: You're saying they're here even when we can't see them? Even though you have no proof they're here?

DIES: Especially so. They are the hidden enemy. It is their job to keep their infiltration secret. The more they are invisible, the more you know they're there.

HALLIE: But that is madness!

DIES: Are you accusing me of being mad?

HALLIE: You ask me if my offices are run by Communists. I say they aren't. You ask me how I can tell. I say I've never seen them. You tell me that is exactly the proof that they're there! That means, no matter what I say today or if I spoke till Kingdom Come I could never convince you we are guiltless!

DIES: Exactly.

HALLIE: But that's not justice! Ever since this trial began—

DIES: These hearings—

HALLIE: This trial! Ever since this trial began I've been hoping to set the record straight, but now I see that I could never do that. You don't want it. You want to believe what you want to believe.

DIES: Be careful, Mrs Flanagan—

HALLIE: I have been being careful. I was not speaking out before because I thought I shouldn't say everything I was thinking. But now I will stop censoring myself. I know now that your minds were made up before this trial began! Such a process would never be allowed in a court of law. In a court, the defendant has a right to face his or her accusers. In a court, the defendant has a lawyer to defend him. In a court, everything the defendant wants to say must be heard!

DIES: Are you accusing us of injustice?

HALLIE: You accuse me of being un-American, I say that *you* are. This procedure is the most un-American procedure that could exist!

DIES: And what you do you think is American—running a theater supported by the government which exists to criticize that government? You think we should *pay* to have you say these things to us? To have you say the things you say on your stages?

HALLIE: Yes! Oh, yes! This theater was founded to be free, adult, uncensored. This theater was founded on that most basic right of the Constitution: the right of free speech. If you censor that speech, if you make it say only what you want it to say, then that is Communism, that is totalitarianism.

STARNES: And what should we do? Have it say only what *you* want it to say? Things like— *(He starts to read from a playscript again.)*— "You're too goddam uppity, you big hump of horse rump—." That is absolutely obscene! The Government of the United States should not be paying money to show people this obscenity!

HALLIE: But if you censor that, you put in place the machinery to censor everything! Then only those things which some authority wants said will be said.

STARNES: Then who shall pass on what can and cannot be said by our government theater? You?

HALLIE: The people! They will vote by deciding when and when not to come.

STARNES: The dirtier it is, the more they'll come. Artists know they can get an audience if they go beyond the bounds of human decency. That's why they do it.

HALLIE: Some artists do it. Not all. But if they go to excess it's to shock us out of our complacency, awaken us, make us think.

STARNES: This stuff corrupts the innocent.

HALLIE: I fear for those who are innocent of making their own decisions.

STARNES: You think, given a choice, they'll come to the better stuff and leave this rot alone?

HALLIE: I do.

STARNES: Well, you've got a damn sight more faith in human nature than I do, Mrs Flanagan. People have to be led. And we have no control over what you're saying in your theater.

HALLIE: Why should you?

STARNES: Damn it, because we're paying for it, that's why! If we're paying for it, we have the right to have it say what we want it to say.

HALLIE: What "we"? You gentlemen do not agree on everything. And you're not afraid to express yourselves. Why can't the theatre show diversity and difference of opinion, too? Let it be free—

STARNES: To shame and defame—

HALLIE: Look at me. Do I look like a revolutionary, a pornographer, a corrupter of the public morals? You and I are responsible citizens with differing ideas—

STARNES: I will defend to the death my right to disagree with your ideas.

HALLIE: What you are *supposed* to defend to the death is *my* right to disagree with *your* ideas.

THOMAS: Why should we give our moneys to this theater? Why to it and not some other place where we would be better served?

HALLIE: To whom? To the sick, the poor, the hungry? I am not against giving moneys to the sick, the poor, the hungry. But the artists, too, are sick and poor and hungry. You want to give it to ditch diggers because ditch diggers are safe. Ditch diggers are silent. We speak for them. We give them voices.

THOMAS: There are much more important things which need the government's support—

HALLIE: The things of war? Is that where you want to spend your money? In one year, the Federal Theater costs the price of one battleship. And it exists, not to *take* lives, but to make them things of value.

DIES: That, Mrs Flanagan, is a matter of opinion.

THOMAS: These artists think the world owes them a living. They think they're better than everybody. Why should they live on the dole while everybody else is responsible for making their own way?

HALLIE: Because the things they do aren't always recognized to be things of monetary value. Van Gogh never sold a painting in his lifetime. Mozart was buried in a pauper's grave. Artists need to be nurtured.

THOMAS: For how long? These people get onto the Federal Theater Project and they want to stay.

HALLIE: Not so. Our whole reason to exist is to get our people off the relief rolls and onto other projects.

THOMAS: Is it? Don't you hope that most of them will stay? Haven't you said that you hoped this would be the beginning of a National Theater?

HALLIE: Almost every civilized country on the face of the earth has one, why can't we have one?

THOMAS: A national theatre headed by you, is that your ambition?

HALLIE: If I'm the one thought capable—

THOMAS: Don't you think that's vanity?

HALLIE: No more vanity than running for office and hoping to win.

DIES: None of this is apropos—. *(He begins gathering up his papers.)*

HALLIE: *(Holding up her brief)* I have a statement to make. You promised I could make my statement—

DIES: There isn't time now.

STARNES: I want to get this into the record: *(Reading:)* "That red bastard! Nigger-lover! I'll bet you're a hot mama. Think I'm your size, brown sugar?"

HALLIE: I want to get my statement into the record—

DIES: Mrs Flanagan. It is time to adjourn. I will vote to cut the budget of the Federal theater.

STARNES: So will I.

THOMAS: And I.

(HALLIE *turns toward* HEALEY, *who has been looking at the photographs on the table.*)

HALLIE: And you, Congressman Healey? Don't you have something to say? How are you going to vote?

HEALEY: Mrs Flanagan, I've listened closely to all you've had to say here. I've studied all your charts. I even saw a few of your productions—and enjoyed them. And what I think is this: I think there has been more Communist influence in this theater than you know or than you wish to tell us. That doesn't frighten me the way it frightens my colleagues. I think our ideas can stand up to those fellows'. And just because a theater presents propaganda for the little guy doesn't mean it's un-American. I am *for* theater. I am even for *uncensored* theater. ... But in these perilous times, I just don't think the government should be getting involved in making decisions on what art should be funded and what shouldn't. I think we should leave all that to the private sector.

HALLIE: But private sources have even more strings on them than government—

HEALEY: Nevertheless, I don't think arts funding is a government job.

HALLIE: So no one can accuse the government of supporting any ideas whatsoever!

HEALEY: I understand your concern. And I have every sympathy for your project. ... But I will vote to cut the budget of the Federal Theater.

DIES: Well, we are all in agreement. Recommendation to the Finance Committee of the United States House of Representatives to cut—

HALLIE: You're burning down an entire building to get a mouse out of the basement!

DIES: This Government needs that money for much more urgent matters.

HALLIE: But what about the eight thousand artists still on relief?

THOMAS: They'll just have to stop being so lazy and get down to work.

HALLIE: But this *is* their work.

THOMAS: I mean *real* work, Mrs Flanagan.

DIES: We are going to get the government out of show business if it's the last thing we do.

(They rise and begin picking up their papers.)

HALLIE: Wait! I have things to say! I want to speak on behalf of the Federal Theater!

DIES: Mrs Flanagan—there *is* no Federal Theater.

(They start to leave.)

(From outside, PHILIP enters. HALLIE looks at him wordlessly. Then, suddenly taking courage, she says to the CONGRESSMEN in a commanding voice:)

HALLIE: I said wait!

(They turn. HALLIE begins to speak:)

HALLIE: It may seem like a game to you, this thing called Theater. It may seem like play—and therefore nothing at all. Nothing to support with funds which might better go for bread or guns or ditches. What use is it? Since I've given my life to this art, you won't mind if I try to tell you.

Everyone who works in the theater has a secret: They know that the spotlight cast upon a stage is a magic light. It is the light of truth. I have seen things which seemed perfectly true in a book, perfectly true in life, be put on stage and this light cuts right through to the lie within them.

In the light of the stage, things which seem impossible to bear are lit with the light of compassion. Things which seem like transitory joys are joyous forever because they exist night after night in the light of the stage.

I have stood at the back of a theater and seen people who were tired, dispirited, lonely, lose themselves in the action which they saw before them. I have seen them laugh and cry. And in the release of that laughter and those tears, their spirits were renewed and lifted.

Is this nothing? Can you say that this is worth less than apples? Less than ditches? Less than guns?

It will survive, the stage. Whether or not you approve it. It exists *for* your pleasure but not *at* your pleasure. The artists whose voices you silence today will speak again. Loudly. Clearly. And no decree can stop them.

When you and I are gone. When these temples to democracy are gone, the words which have been written and spoken on our stages will still be sounding.

Why should the arts exist? The arts are the soul of the country. They sing for us. They cry for us. They shout for us. They are our voice! And whether you hear or not, that voice cries out! Even with a fist in the throat, that voice sounds, and that voice is eternal!

(*The* CONGRESSMEN *look at each other, embarrassed by her impassioned outburst.*)

(PHILIP *comes toward* HALLIE *and stands looking at her in great admiration. She picks up her briefcase. Together they walk out.*)

(DIES *turns to the* CONGRESSMEN *and says:*)

DIES: These theater folk really know how to over-dramatize things, don't they!

(*Nodding in agreement, the* CONGRESSMEN *exit.*)

(*The spotlight brightens on the masks of Comedy and Tragedy. They descend and hold the center of the stage.*)

(*Blackout*)

END OF PLAY

EMPRESS OF CHINA

EMPRESS OF CHINA premiered on April 25, 1984 in New York City produced by the Pan Asian Repertory Company. In 2003 Pan Asian presented a new production off-Broadway. Its many United States productions include those at the Cincinnati Playhouse (Cincinnati) and the Tinfish Theater (Chicago). Notable foreign productions include East Coast Repertory Company *(Sydney, Australia)* and, in Italian, at the Todi Festival *(Todi, Italy)*.

CHARACTERS & SETTING

SHEN TAI, *actor*
LI LIEN-YING, *chief eunuch*
TZU-HSI, *dowager empress*
KUANG-HSU, *emperor*
KANG YU-WEI, *tutor*
LUNG-YU, *wife*
THE PEARL CONCUBINE
JUNG LU, general
SERVANTS

Time and place: The action takes place in the Forbidden City, Peking, China, between 1898 and 1900.

The scenes unfold in various locations in the Forbidden City: The Empty Chamber, The Hall of Supreme Harmony, The Palace of Tranquil Old Age, The Garden, The Ocean Terrace, The Imperial Viewing Platform, and The Gate of Spiritual Valor.

Setting: A cube of space set in a black or white void.

A unit set made of platforms and vertical elements which, with slight alteration or by use of projections, may be transformed to make the same space accommodate different places and scenes.

For each scene, the specific place is suggested by the appearance of one or two significant objects—a screen, a throne, a gate, an instrument of torture, etc. All should be accomplished with great simplicity.

The vertically hung circular Drum of Remonstrance is visible throughout the play.

The production should be sharply modern, with any richness of detail and color occurring only in the props and costumes.

The setting should be abstract, less concerned with physical reality than with evocation of character, mood and state of mind.

ACT ONE

(At rise: The Empty Chamber. Prison.)

(In the center of the barren chamber a young man, SHEN TAI, naked above the waist, is suspended, spread-eagle, in chains. Beneath his chin is the sharp silver blade of an axe, so positioned that, should he fall asleep, should he move from a head-erect position in any way, he will decapitate himself.)

(SHEN TAI is a Chinese man in his late twenties, a muscular descendant of simple peasant ancestry, now desperately weary, parched and starving from days of being suspended in air.)

(His head begins to nod. He warns himself hoarsely:)

SHEN TAI: Stay awake! ...Stay awake, you ass!
 I don't think you realize what a magnificent position you are in. ... You don't have to stand. You don't have to sit. You don't have to worry about eating. Or drinking.
 What an amazing privilege! To be prisoner within the walls of the Forbidden City! Very few commoners ever enter here. Of course, even fewer leave.
 (Fearfully) They say the Empress Dowager's favorite punishment is the death of a thousand cuts. The executioner skins the victim, slice by slice, keeping him alive to witness his own demise as long as possible
 I wonder if that will happen to me? ...It's certainly worth staying alive to find out!
 (He thinks he hears a noise.) What's that? ... Who's there? *(There is no reply. He calls out:)* I have faith in the mercy of the Empress Dowager!
 (Silence. He calls out again:) The Empress Dowager is exalted above all women! She is the Motherly, Auspicious, Orthodox, Heaven-Blessed, Brightly Manifest, Calm, Sedate, Perfect, Illustrious, Exalted—

(Suddenly, from somewhere outside the chamber, a high male voice announces imperiously:)

LI: *(O S)* Do not look upon the Empress!

(The Empress?! SHEN TAI is astonished, frightened, curious. He hardly has time to compose himself when LI LIEN-YING, the chief eunuch, a crafty old man with hairless face and soft lips, enters.)

LI: Do not look upon the Empress!

SHEN TAI: The Empress? Here?

LI: Do not speak!

(SHEN TAI *closes his mouth.*)

LI: You are a creature of less than no importance. You are excrement! A turd!

SHEN TAI: Gracious thanks.

LI: Silence! Why she considers soiling her eyes by gazing upon you, I do not know!

(*From behind the screen comes the deep hard voice of an older woman, echoing majestically:*)

TZU-HSI: *(O S)* I adore filth!

LI: Do not hear!

SHEN TAI: How can I not—?

TZU-HSI: *(O S)* Remove his ears!

SHEN TAI: I heard nothing! Nothing!

LI: Do you know why you are here?

SHEN TAI: No, Excellency.

LI: I am Li Lien-Ying, chief eunuch. Not "Excellency".

SHEN TAI: Yes, Eunuch.

LI: "Honorable Sir!"

SHEN TAI: Yes, Honorable Sir—or Madame.

LI: What—?

SHEN TAI: I said nothing.

LI: Is it true you have insulted the Empress?

SHEN TAI: No, it is not true.

LI: Is it true you have dared personify her in performances in public squares?

SHEN TAI: No insult was meant—

LI: Is it true you have assumed her dress, her voice—?

TZU-HSI: *(O S)* Why do you think you can portray me? Have you ever seen me?

LI: Do not answer!

TZU-HSI: *(O S)*: By what right do you usurp my life, my breath?! Do you think you can equal me?!

(*Suddenly, the Dowager Empress* TZU-HSI *appears. The effect is overwhelming. She is a woman in her sixties, wiry, strong, with steel-cold eyes, black-dyed hair, and foot-*

long sharpened shafts for fingernails. Her silken gown is elaborately embroidered.)
(Overwhelmed by her presence, SHEN TAI *stares at her, stunned, for a moment, then regains his senses and looks firmly away.)*

SHEN TAI: I see nothing! I hear nothing!

LI: Fall to your knees in the presence of the Empress Dowager, Tzu-Hsi!

*(*TZU-HSI*—pronounced "Soo-Shee"—approaches the helplessly spread-eagled* SHEN TAI, *and says imperiously:)*

TZU-HSI: I release him from the obligation of falling on his knees.

LI: Thank her for her mercy.

SHEN TAI: Thank you—

LI: Do not speak to her!

SHEN TAI: *(Confused and upset)* I thank the Empress!

*(*TZU-HSI *walks slowly around him, examining every inch of him like a specimen, then says:)*

TZU-HSI: I will allow him one question.

LI: You have one question.

(Silence. SHEN TAI *considers his question. Then, at last, he asks:)*

SHEN TAI: Will I live?

*(*TZU-HSI *breaks out in a sudden laugh.)*

TZU-HSI: He is superb! The direct mind of a peasant! *(To* SHEN TAI:*)* You will live if I say you will live. And I will decide after I see you perform.

SHEN TAI: I am only a poor travelling player—

TZU-HSI: Good. Poverty sharpens artistic perception.

SHEN TAI: I did not train at the academy. I learned my craft in the streets. I was an orphan. Half-starved. If you knew how poor—

LI: Do not sully the Empress's ears with tales of misfortune in the country!

TZU-HSI: Discuss it with my nephew, the Emperor. These things do not concern me. I am retired. *(To* LI:*)* Release him.

*(*SERVANTS *enter, release* SHEN TAI, *and exit.)*

LI: Do you have a name?

SHEN TAI: Shen Tai.

TZU-HSI: Soft. Appropriate for a man who plays women.

LI: Perhaps he served his clientele in other ways—

SHEN TAI: Offstage I am a man! *(Aside:)* Unlike you.

(Before LI *can respond,* TZU-HSI *says:)*

TZU-HSI: I will see your performance, Shen Tai.

SHEN TAI: I have no costumes—

TZU-HSI: I have costumes. The remains of an actor who displeased me.

*(*TZU-HSI *points toward a large trunk.* SHEN TAI *opens it. It is full of costumes and props.)*

TZU-HSI: I used to enjoy sex, food and theatre—in that order. Now I enjoy theatre, food—and food. *(She claps her hands and calls out:)* Bring my food!

*(*SERVANTS *bring in trays containing dish after dish of a sumptuous banquet.* SHEN TAI *looks on hungrily.* TZU-HSI *deliberately taunts him as she chooses her favorite food.)*

TZU-HSI: I love theatre most—although I do not know why the art is usurped by those who have no training for it, no rights to it. But then, there are many rights which now are being usurped in the country—and not to its good.

*(*SHEN TAI *is trying on a robe.)*

TZU-HSI: Why am I being kept waiting?!

(Hurriedly, SHEN TAI *fastens it.* TZU-HSI *suddenly feels despondent.)*

TZU-HSI: Li, I think this entertainment will not amuse me.

LI: My dear Empress, there is no amusement quite as amusing as being on the throne.

TZU-HSI: True. Off of it, everything I do seems merely like filling time. ... Why am I being kept waiting?

*(*SHEN TAI *puts on a ridiculous headdress. The effect is insulting.)*

TZU-HSI: I am being pilloried! *(She rises in fury.)*

SHEN TAI: Empress, do not condemn me for the ineptitude of my acting! I am only a poor—

TZU-HSI: In the name of Buddha, begin!

*(*SHEN TAI *begins. He takes a pose as a young and innocent maiden. He begins in a high falsetto. His gestures are wildly exaggerated. The effect is absurd.)*

SHEN TAI: I am a young and innocent maiden, the daughter of a poor but honest Manchu official. Already, at sixteen, I am known for my radiant, shining, unbelievable, unsurpassable, incredible beauty. *(He looks at her, hoping his flattery will impress her.)*

TZU-HSI: I want to see it exactly as you play it!

SHEN TAI: My beauty is so renowned that I am summoned with other maidens to the Great Within on the Emperor's birthday. Because of my radiant, shining, unbelievable, unsurpassable, incredible beauty—

TZU-HSI: *(Aside)* It's lucky I have a good digestion!

SHEN TAI: Because of my great beauty, I am chosen to be concubine by the Emperor himself!

(Hungrily, SHEN TAI eyes TZU-HSI's plate as she enjoys her dinner.)

TZU-HSI: Starvation is good for you. It will help you keep your girlish figure. Continue.

SHEN TAI: Bidding farewell to my beloved family, I go to live forever within the walls of the Forbidden City. Here I am known as the Orchid Concubine. The Emperor loves me above all others. And in a while, as a reward for my modesty, charm, humility, and quiet virtue, heaven smiles upon me. I am permitted to present the Emperor with—his only son.

(He bows, awaiting her response. She rises, eyes aflame.)

TZU-HSI: *(With fury)* Is that how you portray me?

SHEN TAI: Yes, Empress, as a woman of grace and beauty—

TZU-HSI: You lie! Do you think I believe your audience comes to see that?!

SHEN TAI: It is how I see you—as the great benevolent Regent of China for four decades! As a woman of supreme wisdom and kindness. As—

TZU-HSI: Enough! Do not insult me by trivializing my life! Do you think I could have ruled for five minutes as that sweet, puking idiot you portray? ... About my father, you are right. He was poor. And honest? Of course he was honest. He was dead! *(She comes toward him.)* I shall show you how I was chosen to be concubine.

(TZU-HSI takes his place; SHEN TAI begins to sit in hers.)

LI: Do not sit in the presence of the Empress!

(SHEN TAI rises precipitously. TZU-HSI says commandingly:)

TZU-HSI: This is the *true* story of my life. Pay attention! ...I am sixteen. On the Emperor's birthday, I am summoned with other maidens to the Great Within. Here he will choose his bride and concubines. It is the only opportunity I will ever have to make a life. I *must* be chosen! But first, I must be certified a virgin.

My lover, the warrior Manchu Bannerman Jung Lu, has given me a precious sapphire. When I am lying on the table of the woman who examines maidenheads, she finds it. I am passed through.

Although another is chosen as wife, the Emperor chooses me himself as concubine. He chooses me because, when all others look modestly down, I look up. He likes what he sees.

When months go by and still I have not been chosen to come to his chamber, I bribe the Chief Eunuch to be sure the Emperor will walk down a path where he can hear me singing. That very night, he writes my name on his slate. At darkness I am carried to his bed, naked, wrapped only in a yellow quilt.

There follows a night like no other night he has known. My screams of fear, my modest protestations, the exquisite shudder of my first ecstasy! ...First love can be extraordinary—if one has experience!

By morning, I am his favorite and inseparable concubine. ... But hardly because of my modesty and virtue! And as for my making a son for my impotent, dissolute husband by heaven smiling! You must be mad!

SHEN TAI: Empress—

TZU-HSI: Silence! I will not be insulted by your view of me! There is no virtue in virtue! There is no value in innocence! I prefer guile! I will not allow you to continue this sweet and treasonable portrayal!

SHEN TAI: I will portray the Empress in whatever way she wishes—

TZU-HSI: The perfect mentality for a slave!

SHEN TAI: I am at your command—

TZU-HSI: I command you to stand erect and be of use to me! I command you to portray me correctly—or die! And while you are perfecting your portrayal, I command you to give acting lessons to my nephew, the Emperor. His walk is not authoritative. His voice is higher than mine!

SHEN TAI: I will give him Emperor lessons.

TZU-HSI: And while you are in his court, you will hear everything, see everything. After that, you will tell me everything. The Kuang-Hsu Emperor has no abilities at all—except at times the ability to keep his own counsel. You must report to me *everything*.

SHEN TAI: Then I will live?

TZU-HSI: Your life is of no importance to me. Nor is your death. *(She sees him looking at the food.)* Would you care to eat the dishes I have not eaten?

SHEN TAI: Yes, Empress! You are generous, Empress!

(Hungrily, SHEN TAI dives into several dishes that TZU-HSI has not touched. Suddenly, he begins to vomit.)

TZU-HSI: You do not like the taste of maggots?

(SHEN TAI looks at TZU-HSI.)

TZU-HSI: You're fortunate you chose that dish. *(She points to a second dish.)* This one is seasoned with little springs which uncoil inside your intestines. *(She points to a third dish.)* This one is laced with ground cat hairs—which have an interesting effect upon the stomach walls. *(She returns to the one he ate.)* All you have is a few worms happily crawling through your inner passages.

(At the thought, SHEN TAI once more begins to vomit.)

(TZU-HSI turns and begins to exit, followed by the eunuch. Behind her she hears the sound of SHEN TAI vomiting.)

TZU-HSI: I like that sound. It is a good sound. It is the sound of a future friend. *(She goes out.)*

(Lights change.)

(The Hall Of Supreme Harmony. Court of the Emperor Kuang-Hsu.)

(In the room is displayed the Emperor's exquisite clock collection. It is a sunny morning. KUANG-HSU, the Emperor, a pleasant but effeminate-looking man in his middle twenties, is deep in studies with his tutor, KANG YU-WEI, an intense man in his mid-thirties, an activist and scholar.)

TUTOR: It is more splendid to be living at this time than at any other since the creation of the planet, my Emperor! This is the time when the future meets the past. Ideas which have been dreams for centuries can now become reality.

KUANG-HSU: But, my tutor, how can *I* make some contribution?

TUTOR: By being the one to bring China into the modern world.

KUANG-HSU: It is a great responsibility.

TUTOR: You can achieve it. You can be the means of abolishing suffering and bringing the country into the age of equality and peace.

KUANG-HSU: Tell me once more what life will be like when we achieve this...

TUTOR: In the One World, people will live high in the air in great palaces with air cooling and heating from electricity. Some people will live in flying vessels. Others will live on great ships—with gardens inside.

KUANG-HSU: And you really think all this can happen in my lifetime?

TUTOR: All this and more. There will be machines which harness the energy of the sun so people will be spared all backbreaking labor. There will be new methods for preserving health and spiritual well-being. This Age of Disorder will be replaced by the Age of Ease and Happiness for all.

KUANG-HSU: It must be we Chinese who invent these things!

TUTOR: That I cannot promise.

KUANG-HSU: But we invented silk and paper and gunpowder—

TUTOR: True, Emperor. But today the train, the telegraph, and the steam engine are more to the point.

KUANG-HSU: Why are these not *our* discoveries?

TUTOR: It is the Western mind—which constantly looks forward—

KUANG-HSU: —while ours constantly looks back.

TUTOR: I think we are going to have to change direction.

KUANG-HSU: How can we ever catch up?

TUTOR: What they have, we can borrow. It isn't a matter of getting there first, it's a matter of getting there at all. The British, in the past ten years, have so mechanized their industry that they are able to manufacture in minutes what it takes us—

(*At this moment,* KUANG-HSU'*s* WIFE, LUNG-YU, *enters carrying brushes and paper. She is a homely creature several years older than he.*)

WIFE: Books in English again. Aunt will not like it.

KUANG-HSU: She will only know, dear wife, if you tell her.

WIFE: If you do not want to make her angry, do not do things she does not like! (*She sits, practicing calligraphy.*)

KUANG-HSU: Stop the lesson. A cloud has entered the room.

(*Like a radiant presence, the* THE PEARL CONCUBINE *enters. She is as intelligent as she is beautiful.*)

KUANG-HSU: Never mind. Here is the sun.

(KUANG-HSU *and* THE PEARL CONCUBINE *smile at each other.*)

THE PEARL CONCUBINE: A gift—from the British legation.

(*A* SERVANT *enters carrying a magnificent golden clock with a mechanical bird on top.* KUANG-HSU *is enthralled, but his* WIFE *shakes her head disapprovingly. He looks away.*)

TUTOR: You are permitted to like it. Your aunt is not in the room!

THE PEARL CONCUBINE: Oh, look! It tells the time of day by the chirping of a golden bird. It tells the weather, too! And the seasons! And it tells the year. The Western year. (*She giggles.*) It's only one thousand eight hundred and ninety-eight!

KUANG-HSU: I shall change it to the year of my dynasty. As I do, I shall study its workings.

(*The* SERVANT *exits.*)

WIFE: Aunt says you have all the makings of a clockmaker.

KUANG-HSU: And you have all the makings of an aunt!

THE PEARL CONCUBINE: Come, my love—

KUANG-HSU: How fortunate for me that I found the Pearl Concubine.

Otherwise I would be disappointed in the race of women.

(TZU-HSI *enters unannounced.*)

TZU-HSI: Which is nothing to what the race of women is in you!

(*All humble themselves in deep kow-tow, including* KUANG-HSU. *In a forceful aside, the* TUTOR *says to him:*)

TUTOR: You do not bow to her! You are the Emperor!

(KUANG-HSU *rises. The others rise.*)

TZU-HSI: Look at this lovesick boy on whose shoulders has fallen the Mandate of Heaven! Look at him—ruler of the world! In love! How can you expect to control others if you can't control your own passions? Love clouds the mind, drains the will, and deadens the senses. Be detached!

WIFE: He is detached—from me.

TZU-HSI: Is that why you haven't borne him a child?

WIFE: I have been practicing calligraphy as you told me.

(TZU-HSI *inspects the* WIFE's *work.*)

TZU-HSI: This looks like the work of silkworms. (*She spies the clock.*) Who is this one from?

KUANG-HSU: The British.

TZU-HSI: What do they want in return? Peking?

KUANG-HSU: To talk.

TZU-HSI: We do not have dialogues with inferiors.

KUANG-HSU: We could discuss our mutual problems—

TZU-HSI: We have no mutual problems. Our problem is them! They force us to sell them our tea and to buy their opium. They insist we all become good Protestants and Catholics. They want our goods, our lands, our souls. All we want is their absence. They petition. We say no. That is all.

THE PEARL CONCUBINE: It is not all, Empress, when, since the war, we owe them so much indemnity.

TZU-HSI: Listen to her! Why don't you appoint her Ambassador Extraordinary? She could seduce the entire allied army and they might leave us in peace!

THE PEARL CONCUBINE: Is it not possible that the West might show us how to—

TZU-HSI: Silence! I will acknowledge your existence when you produce a son.

KUANG-HSU: That isn't fair!

TZU-HSI: Why not? I had it said to me at her age.

(A clock chimes.)

KUANG-HSU: It is two o'clock by the clock which was given to me by the Czar of Russia.

TZU-HSI: And what did you give him? Half of Manchuria?

(Another clock chimes.)

KUANG-HSU: It is two o'clock by the clock given to me by the French premier—

TZU-HSI: For which you gave his traders rights to the entire China Sea.

(Another clock chimes.)

KUANG-HSU: It is two o'clock by the clock given to me by—

(TZU-HSI stops the pendulum of the clock that is chiming.)

TZU-HSI: *You* set the time! *You* regulate the hours for the empire! *You* determine the hours with the help of no other instrument but the sun!

KUANG-HSU: Their clocks are exact—

TZU-HSI: And every one is different! You betray your foolishness in thinking *they* hold the secret of time! The contrivances of their civilizations are mere toys against our art, our manners, our philosophy. These can be broken— *(She raises a hand as if to smash the clock.)*

KUANG-HSU: No—!

TZU-HSI: But our ways survive.

(She claps her hands. SHEN TAI enters, now very respectably dressed and groomed, very much her humble servant.)

TZU-HSI: I introduce to you the renowned and highly skilled actor, Shen Tai, whom I have hired to give you Emperor lessons.

TUTOR: Emperor lessons!

TZU-HSI: You may be attempting to give him an Emperor's mind, but more to the point is that he learn now to walk and talk and carry himself as an Emperor. *(She turns to KUANG-HSU:)* Or do you think you already *are* like an Emperor?

KUANG-HSU: *(Humiliated)* No, Aunt.

TZU-HSI: Perhaps, when Shen Tai finishes with you, you will actually be able to *rule!* *(She turns to SHEN TAI:)* Begin the lesson!

SHEN TAI: We'll start with the Emperor's walk. ... An Emperor walks with his head up.

KUANG-HSU: Do it. I will copy you.

(SHEN TAI demonstrates. KUANG-HSU tries it, not succeeding as well as SHEN TAI.)

SHEN TAI: An Emperor walks with his shoulders back.

KUANG-HSU: I see.

(KUANG-HSU *tries it. He does not do it as well as* SHEN TAI.)

SHEN TAI: An Emperor carries himself like a god!

KUANG-HSU: I'll try...

(THE PEARL CONCUBINE *approaches* SHEN TAI.)

THE PEARL CONCUBINE: Where did you learn to walk like an Emperor?

SHEN TAI: I made it up. I am an actor. I can be anything, perform anything!

(SHEN TAI *does an acrobatic trick that ends with his landing on the throne.*)

TZU-HSI: *There* is an Emperor! Ask him to demonstrate any quality of a majestic leader.

KUANG-HSU: (*Considers for a moment, then:*) ...Can you teach me—how the English do their waltz?

(TZU-HSI *throws up her hands, screams in frustration, and exits. The others exit, doing their very strange interpretation of a waltz.*)

(*Lights change.*)

(*The Palace of Tranquil Old Age.* TZU-HSI's *audience chamber.*)

(*The General,* JUNG LU, *strides into the room. He is a strong, solid ex-soldier in his mid-sixties, a plain man with plain forceful thoughts.* LI *rushes in after him.*)

LI: How did you get past the outer gate?

JUNG LU: The guards recognized me. ... I must speak to the Empress.

LI: Have you decided you are no longer banished? Perhaps she will not be of the same opinion.

JUNG LU: I am aware of the risk I run.

LI: She hasn't spoken your name in many years.

JUNG LU: I'm sure she has spoken yours often enough to make up for it.

LI: We are very intimate.

JUNG LU: A eunuch's intimacy!

LI: You stink, Jung Lu!

JUNG LU: At least my stink is the honest sweat of a long journey, while yours—

LI: Yes? Mine?

JUNG LU: Tell me, do you still carry your private parts in a bag around your waist so you won't reach heaven in a mutilated condition?

LI: You will one day get too frank, Jung Lu!

JUNG LU: It was what she valued most about me.

LI: Stolid and devoted as ever!

JUNG LU: Yes.

LI: Then how could you have betrayed her in the bed of an inferior?

JUNG LU: That is a long time past now.

LI: It may not be past for the Empress.

(*Silence. To this,* JUNG LU *has no rejoinder. At last he says:*)

JUNG LU: How much do you want for arranging to let me see her?

LI: I am Keeper of the Treasury. What more could I want?

JUNG LU: You *always* want more!

LI: Yes. That is the joy of wealth. Unlike desire for sex, desire for wealth can never be sated.

JUNG LU: Name your price. I have not traveled six days to stand outside her chamber!

LI: I will take—the knife she gave you.

JUNG LU: The knife—

LI: What use is it to a general without an army?

(JUNG LU *touches the jewelled knife at his waist, hesitating.*)

LI: Don't tell me you have a sentimental attachment to it!

(TZU-HSI *suddenly appears.*)

TZU-HSI: Such sentiment would be ill-advised.

JUNG LU: Empress—!

TZU-HSI: I will take the knife. After all, the audience is with me, is it not?

(JUNG LU *hands* TZU-HSI *the knife. Coolly, she hands it over to* LI.)

TZU-HSI: I reward fidelity.

JUNG LU: (*Bowing deeply*) Empress—

TZU-HSI: Do not patronize me with pretended humility!

JUNG LU: (*Rising*) Are you well?

TZU-HSI: Love is the only incurable disease, and I am blessed never to have been afflicted.

JUNG LU: It is your privilege, if you wish, to rewrite the past.

TZU-HSI: Every other person is a prison. ... Why have you intruded yourself into my presence?

JUNG LU: I—

TZU-HSI: You are flabby, by the way.

JUNG LU: And greying. But still faithful.

TZU-HSI: If you presume I wish you to be faithful, you presume too much!

JUNG LU: Empress, I know you as no other man has known you—

TZU-HSI: Arrogant!

JUNG LU: Before you were sixteen, you were secluded in your father's house. Since you were sixteen, you have hardly been outside these walls.

TZU-HSI: I know the story of my life!

JUNG LU: Walled up in this palace, one's view of the world can become distorted—

TZU-HSI: On the contrary. A distance from the world can bring perspective.

JUNG LU: In a way, for me, my banishment has been a boon.

TZU-HSI: For me, a blessing!

JUNG LU: It let me see things. Let me travel in the country. And I come to you now, myself—because I am the only one who has ever dared to bring you bad news.

TZU-HSI: This man is not to be borne! He happily absented himself for years! And now he returns to give me the tribute of announcing disaster! I will not listen!

JUNG LU: Empress, your fate is intimately tied to the fate of the country. And the country is ill, deeply ill.

TZU-HSI: And so would you be, if you had foreign soldiers stationed on your soil and could not get rid of them! So would you be if the heavens sent disease and famine, and your enemies sent greedy traders, wily missionaries—

JUNG LU: Why do our people listen to the missionaries? Because the missionaries feed them! I have seen a man sell his soul for a bowl of soup! I have seen others sell their daughters for a dram of opium! You have a country *drugged*—because it is too horrifying to be awake! If only you could *see* your people—

TZU-HSI: Do you make a religion of suffering humanity? Is a man good because he suffers?

JUNG LU: Suffering makes him angry.

TZU-HSI: Fine! In anger is energy! In energy is hope!

JUNG LU: It makes him wild.

TZU-HSI: Exactly the kind of man I like!

JUNG LU: Why do you joke?

TZU-HSI: Because you come here full of news and tell me nothing I do not already know!

JUNG LU: You know, but you don't *see*! Try to see what lies beyond these walls. See—hordes of bandits roaming the countryside. A savage force, neither a part of us nor a part of the West. They wear red headbands. They call themselves The Society of Righteous and Harmonious Fists. The English call them the Boxers.

They are fanatics, bound in secret societies. Obsessed with rituals, spells and incantations. They claim to be able to live through the hail of bullets! I myself have seen them pass swords through their palms and not bleed!

They prey on missionaries, traders, and anyone else they like. And the viceroys can do nothing, because the people believe in them and protect them.

TZU-HSI: And so should I—if they could live through bullets!

JUNG LU: Empress, it's this new danger I've come to tell you about. There is a spirit of rebellion—

TZU-HSI: The Drum of Remonstrance stands in the palace courtyard—to be sounded in protest against a house which is unworthy to rule. In the three hundred years of this Dynasty, that drum has never even been approached! The Ch'ing Dynasty still possesses the Mandate of Heaven.

JUNG LU: For how long?

TZU-HSI: China has been through times of disaster before. They are decreed by Heaven—as a cleansing process. Afterwards, the country and the Dragon Throne will be stronger than ever.

JUNG LU: I have warned you—

TZU-HSI: Go back and cultivate your lilies.

JUNG LU: Something must be done!

TZU-HSI: Some things have changed since you left, don't you realize? I am no longer Regent. My nephew is on the throne. I have no say. I devote myself to my mulberry trees, my water picnics.

JUNG LU: You must act!

TZU-HSI: I am not in power!

JUNG LU: (*Steadily*) The day you cease to be in power will be the day you cease to live.

(JUNG LU's *and* TZU-HSI's *eyes meet, piercingly.*)

(*Lights change.*)

(The Hall of Supreme Harmony. The TUTOR *shows a group of scrolled documents to* KUANG-HSU *as* THE PEARL CONCUBINE *looks on.)*

TUTOR: These decrees will bring China into the modern era—

KUANG-HSU: My aunt will never allow me to sign them.

TUTOR: She doesn't need to know—

KUANG-HSU: She has the right to see every decree I publish!

THE PEARL CONCUBINE: Yes. But the law says nothing about *when.*

KUANG-HSU: Still, I—

TUTOR: Emperor, the people are crying out for help! You can change the ways of centuries—just by putting characters on parchment and affixing your official seal!

*(*KUANG-HSU *turns to the* THE PEARL CONCUBINE.*)*

KUANG-HSU: Do you think I can?

THE PEARL CONCUBINE: I think you can work miracles.

KUANG-HSU: Then yes. I want to try. *(He opens the decrees one by one.)* By this decree, I set up a commission to study giving the people the right to vote and a constitution. By this, I declare the barbarous practice of foot-binding to be forever outlawed in this land. By this, I establish schools to teach science and engineering.

TUTOR: By this, you encourage free speech—

KUANG-HSU: Will my people be able to talk to me directly? Face to face?

TUTOR: It will be encouraged.

KUANG-HSU: And will I be able to go out and see them?

TUTOR: Your best witness is your own eyes.

KUANG-HSU: Mine and my Pearl's.

THE PEARL CONCUBINE: We'll travel through the provinces together—

KUANG-HSU: By train!

TUTOR: And there's something else. Something you must see to personally.

KUANG-HSU: Anything!

TUTOR: You must have a son.

*(*THE PEARL CONCUBINE *and* KUANG-HSU *exchange a look.)*

KUANG-HSU: You sound just like my aunt!

TUTOR: Does this request seem indelicate from me? I'm sorry. I have my dreams for China's future—and yet, I know the ways of her people are rooted in the past. There would be no faster way for you to ensure their loyalty and love than by giving them a son.

KUANG-HSU: Do you think one can create a child by decree, the way one can create a railroad?

(SHEN TAI enters. THE PEARL CONCUBINE greets him extravagantly, to save KUANG-HSU's emotional response.)

THE PEARL CONCUBINE: Look! Here is Shen Tai, come to continue your Emperor lessons! How is the Emperor progressing, Shen Tai?

SHEN TAI: Imperially!

THE PEARL CONCUBINE: Shen Tai was telling me all about his life the other day. He was once almost eaten by a wolf.

SHEN TAI: But I ate him first.

THE PEARL CONCUBINE: Shen Tai is very resourceful.

KUANG-HSU: I hope to make it unnecessary forever for my people to dine on wolves. ... What are you going to teach me today?

SHEN TAI: How to strengthen your voice.

KUANG-HSU: Well, that's a beginning—

SHEN TAI: We take the voice from the nose—and place it in the chest, thus—

(He intones a sound through the nose, then lowers it deeply into the chest. KUANG-HSU tries it, but cannot manage the lower register. The effect is comic.)

SHEN TAI: Perhaps it would be better with words.

(Before anyone can stop him, he picks up one of the decrees and begins to read aloud:)

SHEN TAI: "I, the Kuang-Hsu Emperor, decree that the universities shall teach the Western sciences of—"

(The TUTOR snatches the secret document from his hand.)

TUTOR: Extemporize!

(In a very deep voice, SHEN TAI begins swiftly and nervously to extemporize:)

SHEN TAI: I, the Kuang-Hsu Emperor, the Fatherly, Auspicious, Heaven-Blessed, Brightly Manifest, Calm, Sedate, Perfect—

(KUANG-HSU, attempting the majestic low voice, repeats:)

KUANG-HSU: "I, the Kuang-Hsu Emperor, the Fatherly, Auspicious, Heaven-Blessed, Brightly Manifest, Calm, Sedate, Perfect—" (Suddenly he cuts off and cries out:) It does not sound like me!

(Lights change.)

(The Garden. As LI stands in the background, the WIFE stands holding a basket of *paper flowers.* TZU-HSI *is attaching them one by one to the bare branch of a tree.)*

TZU-HSI: In all the world, I am the only one to have peach blossoms in February!

WIFE: This is true, Empress. ... But what if it rains?

TZU-HSI: Then you'll make new ones! The weather serves *us*, we do not serve *her*! Nature must be forced.

WIFE: I learn so much from you:

TZU-HSI: And from you I learn so little! You were supposed to tell me everything that happens in your husband's quarters.

WIFE: But I see him so seldom! He works in secret with his tutor all day long and late into each evening.

TZU-HSI: And on what—on *what*—are they expending these tremendous labors?

WIFE: I do not know. I am not in his confidence.

TZU-HSI: You do, sometimes, do you not, share his bed?

WIFE: Not as often as I should. The Pearl Concubine has so ensnared him—

TZU-HSI: Then you must work to ensnare him even more!

WIFE: I don't know how!

TZU-HSI: I have no time to give you lessons in pleasure at this moment! I do not care about your pleasure—or his. I want only to know his mind—his *mind*—and you can penetrate that through his senses.

WIFE: I will do whatever you tell me.

TZU-HSI: A man is at your mercy twice—when his desire is high and when his desire is sated. When desire is flaming in him, discretion vanishes. He does not know what he is saying, does not care. Withhold your favors until he rises to a madness. Then any secret that he has is yours. ... Or, if madness rules and words become impossible, then wait until after the act, after the final shudder. When his seed is spent and his body begs for rest, then he is off his guard. Then, too, you can coax his inner mind to speak to you.

WIFE: Yes, Empress.

TZU-HSI: Then you understand?

WIFE: Yes, Empress. Only one thing—

TZU-HSI: Yes?

WIFE: What is this "final shudder" of which you speak?

(TZU-HSI *stares at her.*)

TZU-HSI: Repeat the question.

WIFE: I should like to know what it is so I may recognize it and follow your instructions when it happens.

TZU-HSI: Then you do not know?

WIFE: No, Empress. It is something I have never witnessed.

TZU-HSI: When you go to the Emperor's bed, what do you do there?

WIFE: I am not chosen often.

TZU-HSI: When you *are* chosen, what do you do?

WIFE: I am carried there. I lie subject to his mouth and fingers. When he falls asleep, I am carried out.

TZU-HSI: And that is all? That is *all*?

WIFE: What else should there be?

(TZU-HSI *screams in rage. Stunned, the* WIFE *begins to sob.*)

WIFE: How have I failed to please you?

TZU-HSI: Must I always be surrounded by innocence and ugliness?! Leave my sight!

(*Sobbing, the* WIFE *runs out.* TZU-HSI *breaks out in wild, ironic laughter.* LI *joins in heartily.*)

TZU-HSI: She is a virgin! The wife I personally planted in the Emperor's bed remains an unviolated little girl! She might as well have been sleeping with you!

LI: Does his impotence surprise you?

TZU-HSI: I suspected it. But the Pearl Concubine looks so content—!

LI: Perhaps her contentment is based on something else—like "true love".

TZU-HSI: How revolting!

LI: *(Smiling)* The unfortunate Emperor must be suffering the effects of his dissolute youth.

TZU-HSI: All of which he spent in your company! I can imagine how you must have enjoyed watching him on the pleasure barges and in the opium dens of this city.

LI: I had to see he was entertained during your regency. Especially when you insisted on extending your regency for so inordinate a time.

TZU-HSI: He was an infant until way past his majority. I sometimes think he needs a wet nurse now! China has been unfortunate in her males.

LI: But supremely fortunate in you. How blessed we are that there appeared a female gifted with your qualities.

TZU-HSI: Gifted! It was no gift, it was the me I *made*! ...When I first came to the palace, I was ready to be the perfect feminine complement to my masculine lord. And then there came those nights in my master's bed. His fears, his inabilities, his weeping! And the impotence of his nights was nothing compared to the impotence of his days!

One night I had a dream. I was in a chariot being driven by my husband. We were racing down a mountainside at the speed of the wind! Fast, ever faster, the horses hurtled forward! We were out of control! I cried out to my husband to rein the horses in! He sat transfixed, he could do nothing! In another moment we would plummet over the precipice! I grabbed the reins. I took control I saved the chariot! *I* kept the country on its path. *I*. Not him. When there was a decision to be made, I made it. When there was a son to be made, I made that, too. Where are the women today who would dare what I dared? They do not exist!

(Lights change.)

(The Empty Chamber. Night. The prison has become SHEN TAI's *room. The instruments of torture, while still there, have been pushed aside. At the moment,* SHEN TAI *is burrowing deep into the trunk, trying on costume after costume. He comes up with an elaborate piece of warrior's armor and proudly dons it. He is delighted with himself.)*

SHEN TAI: If only my friends could see me! I am actually living in the palace! I—humble I—am permitted to look upon the Empress's face! I give lessons to the Emperor. And I'm better at playing his part than he is! Who knows how far I might rise if I do all the Empress expects of me? What a stroke of fortune! What more could a poor peasant ask?

(He turns. THE PEARL CONCUBINE *has slipped quietly into his chamber.* SHEN TAI *is astounded.)*

SHEN TAI: You! Here?

*(THE PEARL CONCUBINE *is nervous but determined. She has come on a mission. She will get it done.)*

THE PEARL CONCUBINE: I came—to thank you for your instruction of the Emperor.

SHEN TAI: Oh, don't mention it—*(Then, when she doesn't speak:)* He is progressing well, don't you think?

THE PEARL CONCUBINE: Very well.

SHEN TAI: Next, I'm going to teach him how to lead his troops into battle!

THE PEARL CONCUBINE: That could be—a very useful lesson. ... I have no way to show my gratitude.

SHEN TAI: No need. No need at all. ... Actually, I'm surprised you're here. I wouldn't think you'd even notice me.

THE PEARL CONCUBINE: Not notice you! When you're the only man in the compound?

SHEN TAI: What about the tutor?

THE PEARL CONCUBINE: He is not allowed to stay the night. Three thousand eunuchs—and you're the only male allowed to spend the night within the walls!

SHEN TAI: That must be very hard on all the concubines.

THE PEARL CONCUBINE: Very. Our turns in the Emperor's bed come up so seldom.

SHEN TAI: But you're the favorite. Your turn must come up often.

THE PEARL CONCUBINE: Often—*(She hesitates, then says it:)*—but not often enough.

SHEN TAI: *(Sympathetically)* Oh. *(Then suddenly he understands.)* Oh! *(He grins.)* So that's why you're here! ... Well, if it's a good time you want—!

(SHEN TAI *moves toward* THE PEARL CONCUBINE. *Instinctively, she moves back, then remembers her resolve.*)

THE PEARL CONCUBINE: Yes. A good time.

SHEN TAI: I'll see that you get it!

(SHEN TAI *grabs* THE PEARL CONCUBINE *roughly. It frightens her. She holds him away.*)

THE PEARL CONCUBINE: You are—well? You are not—impure? You are strong, and know, perhaps, that you could even be a—father?

SHEN TAI: Ask the girls in Shantung province.

THE PEARL CONCUBINE: I will trust your word.

SHEN TAI: *(Confidentially)* The Emperor's not much of a love maker, is he?

THE PEARL CONCUBINE: I will hear no criticism of my lord!

SHEN TAI: All right, all right, no criticism! But I'll show you what it's like to be made love to by a real man!

(SHEN TAI *grabs* THE PEARL CONCUBINE *purposefully. She is frightened.*)

THE PEARL CONCUBINE: Wait! One moment!

SHEN TAI: What do you mean, one moment! It'll be too late in one moment.

(SHEN TAI *grabs* THE PEARL CONCUBINE *firmly and begins to make love to her. She cries out.*)

SHEN TAI: What's the matter with you?

THE PEARL CONCUBINE: Nothing.

SHEN TAI: *You* came to *me*, remember?

THE PEARL CONCUBINE: I remember. *(Remembering her resolve, she girds herself for his advances.)*

SHEN TAI: Well, go ahead. Cry out if you want to. If you'll enjoy it better. I heard about you concubines. You pretend to lose your maidenheads every time! *(Roughly, he lays her down.)*

(Lights change.)

(The Palace Of Tranquil Old Age. LI *hurries in and hands* TZU-HSI *a document.)*

LI: Empress—

TZU-HSI: So this is the document my nephew and his tutor have been working on for months in secret! *(She opens the exceedingly long decree and bursts out laughing.)* I have never read anything so amusing in my life! My nephew thinks he will establish the Celestial Kingdom on Earth with one stroke of his brush! ...Why doesn't he just rename China "Europe" and be done with it! *(She throws the document to the floor.)* Idealistic garbage! Tell him I shall not let him make a fool of himself by making these provisions public!

LI: *(Rolling up the decree)* Empress, you know by law you have the right to *see* every document the Emperor publishes, but not the right to take action.

TZU-HSI: My advice is action enough. He has the spine of a jellyfish.

LI: It seems the jellyfish has developed a backbone.

TZU-HSI: What do you mean?

LI: These reforms went into effect today.

TZU-HSI: Without my knowledge or consent?!

LI: Your nephew had them sent to all the provinces two weeks ago. They were sealed, with instructions to open them this morning.

TZU-HSI: The very moment they were sent to me?

LI: Exactly.

TZU-HSI: How dare he—! *(She sputters in rage.)* This is a deliberate act of his against me!

LI: But still within the law. Exactly within the letter of the law.

TZU-HSI: I know these tricks! He cannot play them as well as I! ... Why didn't you tell me?

LI: I only discovered it this morning, when some viceroys asked for clarifications—

TZU-HSI: This insolence could not be his own idea.

LI: I agree. He would have to be led.

TZU-HSI: His tutor—

LI: Yes. I'm certain.

TZU-HSI: Summon him to me!

LI: I have taken that liberty. He is just outside. *(He claps his hands.)*

TZU-HSI: How well you know my mind, Li. Can you guess what I have in store for him?

LI: I am eager to see it.

(The TUTOR enters and bows politely. He feels confident and sure of himself.)

TZU-HSI: I have read—the Emperor's—new edicts. They are immensely edifying.

TUTOR: They are meant to be.

TZU-HSI: So we are to study all the ways of the West and do all we can to imitate them?

TUTOR: We shall take advantage of all they have discovered.

TZU-HSI: And shall we have our eyes rounded and our skin painted chalk white?

TUTOR: We shall take what applies and adapt it for our own usage.

TZU-HSI: Are you a prophet?

TUTOR: An historian.

TZU-HSI: Do you know everything?

TUTOR: Enough to help me see.

TZU-HSI: What did I have for breakfast?

TUTOR: I do not know.

TZU-HSI: And he claims to be a font of wisdom! Mark him down, Li!

(LI brushes a character on parchment.)

TUTOR: I know the temper of the people—

TZU-HSI: How old is this chrysanthemum?

TUTOR: *(Annoyed at her irrelevant questions.)* Three days.

TZU-HSI: Three hundred *years*! It has gone from seed to plant to seed to plant for three whole centuries! Mark him down, Li!

(LI makes another mark.)

TUTOR: The answer depends on whether one takes the long view or the short view —

TZU-HSI: Does it? And does that apply not only to flowers but to civilizations?

TUTOR: Yes, of course —

TZU-HSI: What color is my hair?

(TUTOR *looks at* TZU-HSI's *raven locks and considers the meaning of the question. Then he answers:*)

TUTOR: Your hair is white.

TZU-HSI: Does this look white to you?

TUTOR: You meant what color is it really!

TZU-HSI: I meant what color do you *see*! You have not the wisdom of a child! Mark him down!

(LI *does so.*)

TUTOR: You are trying to trap me!

TZU-HSI: As the West is trying to trap China! You cannot borrow their ways without having them possess our minds!

TUTOR: They believe in the good of the greatest number —

TZU-HSI: That is nonsense.

TUTOR: They believe in happiness for the common man —

TZU-HSI: They are deluded.

TUTOR: They believe in equality for all —

TZU-HSI: They are stupid! Humans are not equal to each other. They never shall be! There are the wise and the foolish, there are the noble and the debased. Out of what misguided sentimentality can you believe that the noble ones must constantly lower themselves to cater to the welfare of the mob? Must we constantly be looking down? Is it not for them to look up — and to do their best to follow?

TUTOR: Our people are dying —

TZU-HSI: So they are. And in good conscience we must accept the sacrifice of those who must suffer in order to bring society to a higher state of being

TUTOR: That is abomination!

TZU-HSI: It is truth. When will you idealists free yourselves from your maudlin romanticism about the "little people"? What seems abomination on the level of the individual is the highest morality on the level of the state.

TUTOR: You have no faith in goodness —

TZU-HSI: Goodness is cowardice.

TUTOR: You have no faith in progress—

TZU-HSI: I am proud of from whence I have come.

TUTOR: And what is to be? A country overrun by savages in red headbands?

TZU-HSI: If they will free us of the foreigners.

TUTOR: We will never be free of the foreigners. That time is over! What is at stake is the survival of China!

TZU-HSI: *I* will decide what is best for the survival of China!

TUTOR: May I remind you that it is your *nephew* who is on the throne!

(*An icy pause, then* TZU-HSI *says, exceedingly calmly:*)

TZU-HSI: Are you shouting at me?

TUTOR: I am trying to make you understand—!

TZU-HSI: Li, he was shouting.

(LI *begins to write.*)

TUTOR: I care as much as you care—

TZU-HSI: (*Sweetly*) Do you know you can be banished from the land for shouting in the Imperial Presence?

TUTOR: You are joking.

TZU-HSI: I am not joking. I hereby banish you for shouting.

TUTOR: There is no such law!

TZU-HSI: There is.

(TZU-HSI *signs her name to the paper* LI *has been writing.*)

TUTOR: The ink on that edict is not yet dry!

TZU-HSI: It is as dry as the ink on yours. And just as valid. You underestimate me. My brain is not white. My brain is as black as the color of my hair. You do not know how black my brain is! ...You are unfit to be a tutor and unfit to remain in this land. Go! Do not attempt to see the Emperor. From the moment you leave my sight, your life is in peril! Go!

(*The* TUTOR *bows and goes.*)

TZU-HSI: Did you see him go cold? What a battle! It was almost like flogging him! Almost as satisfying!

(TZU-HSI *claps her hands.* SHEN TAI *enters and bows deeply.*)

TZU-HSI: Why did you not inform me of the edicts which were being drawn up in my nephew's chambers?

SHEN TAI: I did not know—

TZU-HSI: It was your duty to know. It is the reason you were put there! It is the reason I bothered to spare your life.

SHEN TAI: They worked in greatest secrecy—

TZU-HSI: You have not been tortured in weeks, perhaps you miss it!

SHEN TAI: No, Empress.

TZU-HSI: Perhaps you want to perform for me.

SHEN TAI: Yes! Of course! I do!

TZU-HSI: Perform!

SHEN TAI: What do you want to see?

TZU-HSI: Those heroes in red headbands.

SHEN TAI: The ones the foreigners call the Boxers?

TZU-HSI: I understand they are invincible.

SHEN TAI: Yes, Empress.

TZU-HSI: I understand they can pass knives through their palms without bleeding.

SHEN TAI: Yes, Empress.

TZU-HSI: Show me this trick.

SHEN TAI: But I am not a Boxer!

TZU-HSI: You are what I say you are! Show me!

SHEN TAI: Yes, Empress.

(TZU-HSI *holds out her hand and* LI *gives her the jeweled knife. She hands it to* SHEN TAI *who holds it, trembling.*)

SHEN TAI: First they put themselves into a trance—

TZU-HSI: I have no time for trances!

SHEN TAI: They whirl around three times—

TZU-HSI: No whirling! Show me what I want to see!

SHEN TAI: They make themselves impervious to pain—

TZU-HSI: I tell you, *show me!*

(SHEN TAI *closes his eyes and stabs himself through his palm. He cries out in agony.*)

TZU-HSI: You must not cry out! Again!

(SHEN TAI *stabs himself again, stifling his cries although the pain is excruciating. The blood begins to flow.*)

TZU-HSI: And you must not bleed! Again! Again! Again!

(*In agony* SHEN TAI *stabs himself again and again as the blood flows profusely.* TZU-HSI *revels in his pain, with almost sexual enjoyment.*)

(*Lights change.*)

(*The Garden. A sunny day.* KUANG-HSU *and* THE PEARL CONCUBINE *are playing a game on a marble board. He plays and wins. He laughs.*)

THE PEARL CONCUBINE: You win again!

KUANG-HSU: I feel lucky. Do you know—weeks have passed and Aunt hasn't dared confront me! This time I have out-maneuvered her!

THE PEARL CONCUBINE: Why haven't you heard from your tutor?

KUANG-HSU: He must be in the provinces, carrying out my decrees. Come, let's have a picnic on Aunt's artificial lake! We'll take my new motorized boat and cruise out to the Ocean Terrace—

THE PEARL CONCUBINE: No, Kuang-Hsu—

KUANG-HSU: What's the matter?

THE PEARL CONCUBINE: I am—uneasy—near this lake of hers.

KUANG-HSU: You, who fear nothing, fear the lake?

THE PEARL CONCUBINE: Last night I dreamed of a woman who drowned trying to embrace the reflection of her child in the water—

KUANG-HSU: Phantoms! Superstitions! I'll protect you!

THE PEARL CONCUBINE: Do you fear nothing?

KUANG-HSU: Not any more! Oh, Pearl, I myself am going to bring China triumphant into this next century! Who would have thought I could accomplish this! For the first time in my life, I feel strong! I feel—manly! I feel—at this moment—I could even make love...

(KUANG-HSU *comes to* THE PEARL CONCUBINE. *She whispers.*)

THE PEARL CONCUBINE: Oh, try, my love. Please try...

(KUANG-HSU *and* THE PEARL CONCUBINE *embrace.*)

(*Lights change.*)

(*The Empty Chamber. Night.* SHEN TAI *lies asleep on his mat. His hand is bandaged. Every time he moves he moans in his sleep. After a moment, a figure silently appears. It is the* TUTOR. *His face and clothing bear marks of the fugitive life which, in the past weeks, he has lived.* SHEN TAI *stirs and wakens with a start.*)

SHEN TAI: Who is there?

TUTOR: Don't be afraid—

SHEN TAI: You! How can you be here? You have been banished!

TUTOR: What can I achieve outside the borders of the country?

SHEN TAI: But here you are in danger—

(*He moves and in doing so hurts his injured hand, which makes him cry out.*)

TUTOR: What have they done to you?

SHEN TAI: Nothing.

TUTOR: That doesn't look like nothing.

SHEN TAI: I did it to myself. She said do it—and I did it! I almost believed it wouldn't bleed, wouldn't hurt! ... How could I have done such a thing?

TUTOR: It's *her*. She holds all China in her prison chamber! Nothing will release us from that bondage—except her death.

SHEN TAI: I think she plans to live forever.

TUTOR: Many who have had such plans—have found themselves deceived.

SHEN TAI: In a play, words like that would have dark mysterious significance.

TUTOR: And in life, my friend—in life?

(SHEN TAI *looks at him in amazement. The* TUTOR *goes on:*)

TUTOR: Listen to me. I am a scholar. I have spent all my life with books. I thought all things could be achieved by good actions and good thoughts, by debate, by reason. But now I know: there is no place for reason while she is alive to act against it. She is the great disease from which the country must be cured!

SHEN TAI: Do I hear what I hear? I think you mean *murder*!

TUTOR: *Deliverance*. The entire country is waiting to be released—and you are the sword.

SHEN TAI: Me!

TUTOR: You are the only one who has access to her.

SHEN TAI: I can't.

TUTOR: You have played murderers—

SHEN TAI: But afterwards the victims get up!

TUTOR: And will the Emperor get up if she wills otherwise?

SHEN TAI: But he's her nephew!

TUTOR: And once she had a son...

(*Silence. Then* SHEN TAI *cries out:*)

SHEN TAI: I can't—! I can't—!

(SHEN TAI *makes a violent gesture and in doing so disturbs his injury. He cradles his hand. Quietly, the* TUTOR *says:*)

TUTOR: Have you ever seen the remnants of a man who is no longer a man?

(*Slowly the* TUTOR *pulls aside his robe and shows his mutilation.* SHEN TAI *stares in horror.*)

TUTOR: She said I was only banished. But her men were waiting outside the walls.

SHEN TAI: Horrible—

TUTOR: This is what she does to us. To us all. She mutilates our country. For our *country*—for China. You *must*—

(SHEN TAI *stares at* TUTOR.)

TUTOR: I have a plan, Shen Tai. It cannot fail...

(*Lights change.*)

(*The Palace of Tranquil Old Age. Night.* TZU-HSI *is examining herself in a hand mirror. Her hair, unpinned for the night, falls black and straight to a length lower than her waist. After several moments, the* WIFE *enters.*)

TZU-HSI: You are late!

WIFE: I wasn't sure you'd still want me to come. You seemed so displeased with me.

TZU-HSI: No one else does my hair as well as you do. If it's your one skill, I don't see why I shouldn't take advantage of it.

(*The* WIFE *begins to brush. Suddenly* TZU-HSI *cries out:*)

TZU-HSI: Ow! You've pulled out a strand! Put it back! Put it back!

(*Nonplussed, the* WIFE *stands holding the offending strand for a moment. Then, obediently, she tries to put it back into* TZU-HSI's *hair.*)

TZU-HSI: What's the matter? Do you think I am too vain?

WIFE: No, Empress.

TZU-HSI: The body is the house in which the soul lives. We must take infinite care of the body.

WIFE: Then you'll be happy to hear the news I have to tell you. I passed Shen Tai on my way in. He has a gift for you.

TZU-HSI: He has been negligent in his attentions to me lately.

WIFE: He says he'll share with you a secret of the actor's profession: a dye which will blacken the hair without blackening the scalp.

TZU-HSI: And he expects me to be grateful for such a gift? I who have the blackest hair in the entire country?! *(Then she adds diffidently:)* And the blackest scalp.

WIFE: He says the dye is so secret only he can administer it. He won't even let me watch.

TZU-HSI: Where is my new hair attendant?

WIFE: He said he would enter when you are alone.

TZU-HSI: Then leave me!

(The WIFE exits.)

TZU-HSI: I may as well pursue youth as assiduously as other old ladies.

(Sitting in her high-baked chair, TZU-HSI studies her face in the mirror. It is here that she first glimpses SHEN TAI as he enters.)

(SHEN TAI is dressed exactly as TZU-HSI is dressed. The same robe, the same long nails, the same hair. He looks startlingly like her.)

TZU-HSI: Well! What a costume for a hair attendant! ... Turn around! Turn around!

(SHEN TAI does so.)

TZU-HSI: Excellent. ... Can you do my walk?

(SHEN TAI walks.)

TZU-HSI: Can you do my voice?

SHEN TAI: *(In her voice)* "Well! What a costume for a hair attendant!"

TZU-HSI: Excellent! If you had my soul, you'd be me!

(SHEN TAI begins to wrap her in a special protective cape he has brought with him. It goes over her shoulders, over the back of TZU-HSI's chair, and down to her feet, covering her completely.)

SHEN TAI: I have no desire to be you, Empress.

TZU-HSI: Truly? I thought the whole world must envy me.

SHEN TAI: Empress, after months of observing in the shadow of your presence, I am ready to present to you—the *true* story of your life.

TZU-HSI: So at last you think you know me.

SHEN TAI: Yes.

TZU-HSI: You haven't made me virtuous and boring?

SHEN TAI: No.

TZU-HSI: Well, then, let me see.

(SHEN TAI moves across the room to begin.)

Tzu-Hsi: What about my hair?

Shen Tai: I will take care of it—at the end.

(Tzu-Hsi *sits back. Lights change.*)

(*Across the room,* Shen Tai *begins, affecting her voice, her mannerisms. This time, his style is graceful and very credible.*)

Shen Tai: I am the Orchid Concubine, serene and beautiful. My lord is Emperor. (*With movement and gesture, he pantomimes the Orchid Concubine.*)

Tzu-Hsi: Very good! Very good!

Shen Tai: I present him with his only son! (*He pantomimes.*) My lord is happy. ... But soon he dies. ... I survive.

My son is named Emperor. He is still an infant. I am made co-regent with my husband's widow.

She is called the Empress of the East. I am called the Empress of the West.

Tzu-Hsi: I always hated that title.

Shen Tai: My son grows—
My son marries—
After wiping his mouth with a certain napkin, my son is blessed with a visitation of the Heavenly Flowers. The smallpox! My son dies.
His pregnant wife throws herself into the nearest well.
I survive...

Tzu-Hsi: (*Without emotion*) My life abounds with tragedy.

Shen Tai: I choose the new Emperor. A three-year-old. My nephew.
He prefers the Empress of the East.
The Empress of the East suffers a fatal attack of indigestion.
I survive.

(Tzu-Hsi *shifts in her chair but the cape holds her.*)

Shen Tai: I am sole regent.
The Emperor grows.
I marry him to my niece.
He assumes the throne...
Happy, I retire to the Palace of Tranquil Old Age.

Tzu-Hsi: What do you do there?

(*A pause. Then* Shen Tai *takes a small vial from his pocket and says:*)

Shen Tai: I think of taking my own life.

Tzu-Hsi: Now that would be an end to your play! Everyone loves a scene of dying. But *why* do you consider taking your own life?

Shen Tai: Because I have plotted! I have lied! I have stolen power! I have murdered!

TZU-HSI: And you leave that out of your play? You are a fool, Shen Tai.

SHEN TAI: Whenever there was anyone in your way to power, they found themselves conveniently removed.

TZU-HSI: You are beginning to bore me! *(The encumbering cape annoys her, but she cannot free herself from it. She realizes she is captive.)* Why should I be afraid to take fate into my own hands? My hands are worthy. Not to act is cowardice. And I have never been afraid.

SHEN TAI: Not even now?

TZU-HSI: Go ahead! Dispatch me!

SHEN TAI: So many died!

TZU-HSI: Do you honor them for being innocent and dying? Death is a step up for them! *(She looks at the vial.)* Is that the hair dye?

SHEN TAI: A few drops anywhere on the skin—

TZU-HSI: Hurry, then! Do it! You will give me a great opportunity—

SHEN TAI: What opportunity?

TZU-HSI: To rule again, after my demise.

(Puzzled at this, SHEN TAI stares at TZU-HSI, while still holding the vial threateningly above her.)

TZU-HSI: Surely you know that murdered spirits return to inhabit the bodies of their murderers. I shall come back as a demon inside you. You in my costume. You shall sit on the throne and I will reign another forty years!

SHEN TAI: The Kuang-Hsu Emperor will reign!

(SHEN TAI comes to pour the liquid on TZU-HSI's scalp. She throws back her head and laughs.)

TZU-HSI: I wish you well in the reign of the Kuang-Hsu Emperor! Happy future in the dynasty of the joke! Do you wonder what has happened in the country since the Emperor's reforms went into effect? I'll tell you.

In Canton, the university has thousands of students signed up to learn the new subjects—but no one qualified to teach them. In Shanghai, where he reorganized the government, thousands of former employees are now out begging in the streets. In the interior, rather than help the foreigners lay tracks as they were ordered, workers threw themselves in front of the trains!

Everywhere there is chaos and confusion! Instead of curing the country's ills, the reforms have compounded them.

SHEN TAI: I had no idea—

(TZU-HSI looks SHEN TAI squarely in the eye.)

TZU-HSI: Heaven help this country when I die. It is *I* who for almost half a century have held it together! If you wonder where you can find the soul of this country, *I* am the soul of this country! In power or out of power, on the throne or off the throne, alive or dead, this country is *me*!

(SHEN TAI *falls to his knees before her.*)

SHEN TAI: Empress, I beg your forgiveness! You are supreme! Unsurpassable! All glorious! It is only that they are too blind to see!

TZU-HSI: Untie me, my twin, my other self. It is time, at last, for us to pay a visit to my devoted nephew.

(SHEN TAI *begins to release her.*)

(*Lights change.*)

(*The Hall of Supreme Harmony. Night.* KUANG-HSU *is pacing aimlessly.* THE PEARL CONCUBINE *tries to calm him.*)

KUANG-HSU: Within these walls I know nothing! Nothing! What is happening in the country? Why do I not hear one word!

THE PEARL CONCUBINE: Can you not sleep?

KUANG-HSU: Something must have happened to my tutor. To send no messenger in all this time! And she—my aunt—says nothing. What is she thinking?

THE PEARL CONCUBINE: It doesn't matter what she's thinking—

KUANG-HSU: I should have told her about my plans. I shouldn't have tried to act in secret. I cannot bear the silence any longer!

(TZU-HSI *enters, accompanied by* SHEN TAI, *who is still in her costume.*)

TZU-HSI: I am here, my nephew. And I bring you noise.

KUANG-HSU: Aunt—! Forgive me—

TZU-HSI: Forgive you? I congratulate you!

KUANG-HSU: Then you are no longer angry with me?

TZU-HSI: Angry with you? I am proud of you—for the first time in your life.

KUANG-HSU: I meant no harm—

TZU-HSI: Of course you didn't. What's a small assassination?

KUANG-HSU: Assassination!

TZU-HSI: Don't worry. Shen Tai confessed everything. I'm delighted by your cleverness. Yours and your tutor's.

KUANG-HSU: What has happened to my tutor?

TZU-HSI: Justice has happened to your tutor. I'm sure you don't mind.

KUANG-HSU: Are you saying he plotted your death?

TZU-HSI: Please, I want *you* to take all the credit—

KUANG-HSU: I knew nothing of this! Nothing! I would never plot against you—

TZU-HSI: If you had, I would have admired you.

KUANG-HSU: I would never—

TZU-HSI: I brought you up as my own son and this is how I am rewarded?

KUANG-HSU: No, Aunt—

TZU-HSI: Do you know the law of the Imperial Household for one who raises his hand against his mother?

(TZU-HSI *strikes* KUANG-HSU *across the face.* THE PEARL CONCUBINE *cries out:*)

THE PEARL CONCUBINE: Help! Guards!

(*No one enters.*)

TZU-HSI: It would seem you are without reinforcements. (*She gestures to* KUANG-HSU *imperiously.*) Sit and write what I dictate to you.

KUANG-HSU: Whatever you say, Aunt. (*He sits on the throne and prepares to write.*)

TZU-HSI: (*Dictating*) "I, the Kuang-Hsu Emperor, hereby revoke my former edicts."

KUANG-HSU: No!

TZU-HSI: "Revoke my former edicts!"

(*Helplessly, he writes:*)

KUANG-HSU: "Revoke my former edicts..."

TZU-HSI: "... And establish, once again, our ancient and time-honored ways."

KUANG-HSU: "... Our ancient and time-honored ways..."

TZU-HSI: "Furthermore, for reasons of failing health, I find I am no longer able to carry on the task of being Emperor."

KUANG-HSU: No—!

TZU-HSI: If this plot against my life is revealed, you will be executed! I am giving you a chance to survive!

THE PEARL CONCUBINE: You can't be so cruel—!

TZU-HSI: Stand away from him!

KUANG-HSU: (*Writing, feeling stunned and unreal*) "No longer able to carry on the task of being Emperor—" (*He stops.*) I can't—! I can't—!

THE PEARL CONCUBINE: (*To the* TZU-HSI:) How can you do this?

TZU-HSI: He is fortunate I am letting him live! ... Why should you complain, you two? I am going to let you take up residence on the Ocean Terrace in the middle of the lake in the north garden. A lovely retreat. There, surrounded by water, you will be able to do anything you like—except leave.

(KUANG-HSU *is speechless. He and the* THE PEARL CONCUBINE *look at each other.* THE PEARL CONCUBINE *says fiercely to* SHEN TAI:)

THE PEARL CONCUBINE: If you were given the task of destroying her, why did you not do it?

(SHEN TAI *turns away from her.*)

TZU-HSI: Shen Tai is my loyal servant! *(Then she says:)* We must have witnesses! *(She cries out:)* Come, everyone! Bear witness!

(*From separate directions, the* WIFE, LI, *and* JUNG LU *arrive.*)

TZU-HSI: I want you all to witness a momentous occasion. In fact, it is so momentous, I want to witness it myself. Shen Tai, take my place!

(SHEN TAI *stands above* KUANG-HSU, *where* TZU-HSI *stood.* TZU-HSI *moves back to observe them.*)

TZU-HSI: Now, once more. Let me see this great moment.

(*She claps her hands.* SHEN TAI, *imitating* TZU-HSI, *dictates to* KUANG-HSU:)

SHEN TAI: Write what I dictate to you! ..."I, the Kuang-Hsu Emperor, hereby revoke my former edicts—"

(KUANG-HSU, *humiliated and upset, sits motionless.*)

TZU-HSI: *(To* SHEN TAI:*)* Continue—

SHEN TAI: "Furthermore, for reasons of failing health, I find I am no longer able to carry on the task of being Emperor."

(LI *smiles and gives a congratulatory nod to* TZU-HSI.)

TZU-HSI: *(To* KUANG-HSU*)* Write!

KUANG-HSU: I have already written—*(He is weeping.)*

TZU-HSI: Well, then, write this—

(*With great satisfaction, she gestures to* SHEN TAI, *who pulls himself up imperiously to deliver this sentence in her voice, with her gestures.*)

SHEN TAI: "Unmindful of her age, my dear aunt has once more consented to take over the heavy burden of office—"

(KUANG-HSU *is unable to write. In* TZU-HSI's *voice,* SHEN TAI *admonishes him.*)

SHEN TAI: Write, I said! "My dear aunt has once more consented to take over the heavy burden of office!"

(KUANG-HSU *breaks down weeping on the throne.* SHEN TAI, *as* TZU-HSI, *stands imperiously over him.*)

(TZU-HSI *applauds* SHEN TAI.)

TZU-HSI: I am magnificent!

(TZU-HSI *gestures* SHEN TAI *away and takes the place where he was standing. With her folded fan, she touches* KUANG-HSU *on the shoulder and firmly forces him to relinquish the throne. She takes her place before the throne and stands above the rest proudly. A gong sounds. Everyone bends in a deep kow-tow to her except* KUANG-HSU *and the* THE PEARL CONCUBINE. TZU-HSI *snaps her fan.* KUANG-HSU *grovels in deep kow-tow, pulling the* THE PEARL CONCUBINE *down with him.* TZU-HSI *beams.*)

TZU-HSI: Magnificent! (*With great satisfaction, she seats herself majestically on the throne.*)

(Blackout)

END ACT ONE

ACT TWO

(At rise: The Hall Of Supreme Harmony. A golden auspicious dawn.)

(The Hall, which was once KUANG-HSU's *has become* TZU-HSI's *and has increased in splendor. An Imperial Screen masks the throne.)*

(A gong sounds. Followed by a procession of SERVANTS, LI *and* JUNG LU *enter from opposite sides and flank the Imperial Screen.* LI *wears an elaborate official robe.* JUNG LU *wears magnificent military regalia.)*

(A gong sounds three times, LI, JUNG LU *and the* SERVANTS *prostrate themselves in deep kow-tow.)*

(Two SERVANTS *slowly pull away the screen.* TZU-HSI *is revealed on the Dragon Throne in a magnificently embroidered robe.)*

(All at once KUANG-HSU's *clocks begin to chime.* TZU-HSI *cries out:)*

TZU-HSI: Destroy those! The world will go on my time from now on!

(The SERVANTS *remove the clocks and exit. From outside we hear the sound of the clocks being shattered.* TZU-HSI *smiles.)*

*(*TZU-HSI *claps her hands.* LI *and* JUNG LU *rise to a kneeling position. She smiles at them and says:)*

TZU-HSI: You never thought you'd see me up here, did you? I *told* you I was the cleverest woman alive! ...Those who say absolute power corrupts obviously never had it.

LI: You are the most powerful woman in the world.

JUNG LU: Except, perhaps, for Queen Victoria.

TZU-HSI: Queen Victoria! The Queen of that tiny island? She's almost old enough to be my mother!

*(*JUNG LU *squirms.* TZU-HSI *commands:)*

TZU-HSI: Kneel at attention!

JUNG LU: I'm afraid my knees aren't what they used to be.

TZU-HSI: Truly? *(She smiles. Grandly she bestows a precedent-shattering boon:)* Very well. You may sit in my presence.

*(*LI *and* JUNG LU *look at her in astonishment.)*

TZU-HSI: I don't want it said I am not ready for the twentieth century.

(LI *and* JUNG LU *rise, then, very uncomfortably, take seats.*)

JUNG LU: If you're *really* ready for the new century, you'll agree to receive the British Ambassador.

LI: The throne does not speak to British!

JUNG LU: He has been chosen to speak for all the foreign delegations in Peking.

TZU-HSI: What are they complaining about now?

JUNG LU: A fresh outbreak of incidents against their nationals. Rail and telegraph lines cut. An English missionary murdered. A French priest tortured and killed.

TZU-HSI: If they were not here, they would not have these problems.

JUNG LU: And six more French nuns have been massacred.

LI: They were grinding up the eyes of Chinese children to use for medicines!

JUNG LU: Nonsense! The Boxers always have some excuse for their atrocities.

TZU-HSI: Was it the Boxers again? They are so patriotic.

JUNG LU: The dead foreigners don't think so.

TZU-HSI: Why don't the foreigners take their thoughts back to Europe where they belong?

JUNG LU: The legations would like to discuss these matters with you.

LI: The Empress cannot see them! They won't perform the kow-tow! They'll ask embarrassing questions! They'll ask for forks! (*He pronounces kow-tow in the Chinese manner: ker'-toe.*)

JUNG LU: You *must* receive Sir Claude MacDonald—

TZU-HSI: Did I say I wouldn't? (*She smiles. She calls out:*) Send in the British Ambassador!

(SHEN TAI, *gotten up like a British potentate, with sash and monocle, and looking like something out of* Pinafore, *pedals in smoking a cigar and riding a bicycle.*)

SHEN TAI: (*With an exaggerated British accent:*) I must have tea or I shall perish! (*He falls off the bicycle with a crash.*) Oh, my poor darling bicycle! My poor darling cigar!

TZU-HSI: Sir Claude, since you're down there already, you might as well perform the kow-tow. (*Pronounced ker'-toe.*)

SHEN TAI: Oh, the kow-tow! The kow-tow! (*Howling it with exaggerated British pronunciation*) I simply cannot do it! (*He tries and drops his monocle.*)

TZU-HSI: Why have you come here, Sir Claude?

SHEN TAI: It's my duty to the heathen hordes. I absolutely positively *must* civilize you.

(SHEN TAI *hands* LI *a fork.* LI *sets it aside with extreme distaste.*)

TZU-HSI: Really? And how do you intend to do that?

SHEN TAI: By trade. ...Would you like a little linsey-woolsey?

(SHEN TAI *pulls a length of homespun cloth from his pocket and tries to hand it to* TZU-HSI. *She pushes it away.*)

TZU-HSI: We have silk, what do I want with linsey-woolsey?

SHEN TAI: How about a little opium?

(SHEN TAI *tries to give* TZU-HSI *a pipe.*)

TZU-HSI: I prefer to stay awake.

SHEN TAI: How about a little Christ? *(He pulls out a crucifix.)*

TZU-HSI: We have Buddha, thank you.

SHEN TAI: How can you be saved by someone who was such a fatty?

TZU-HSI: How can you be saved by someone who allowed himself to be hammered to death on two sticks?

SHEN TAI: But we have the One True Way. It is exceedingly generous on our part to share it with you.

TZU-HSI: Actually, *we* have the One True Way.

SHEN TAI: You can't, my dear. You're yellow! ...You can't be civilized until the day that you become White Christians.

TZU-HSI: White Christians! *(She rises.)* What you are saying is we should become prejudiced, intolerant and despotic—like you.

(SHEN TAI *tries to speak.* TZU-HSI *silences him with an angry gesture.*)

TZU-HSI: Why should we talk to you? You think us barbarous, immoral and uncivilized. You think us illiterate because all we speak is our own language!

You come here trying to make us into English. What if we did the same in reverse? What if we imported ten thousand British to work as cheap labor in our rice fields? What if we stationed Chinese troops in Piccadilly? What if we sent our priests to destroy your people's gods? Would you not do everything you could to get us out of your country?

(She becomes deeply serious.) A civilization of more than four thousand years is neither a child nor an imbecile! We are the land of Confucius and the three thousand mile wall. We are the land of grace, symmetry, peace, and wisdom. We are China. We were here long before you existed, and long after you are gone we shall remain.

(SHEN TAI *grovels on the floor in a deep kow-tow and, as Sir Claude, says:*)

SHEN TAI: Your majesty, your majesty—

TZU-HSI: Yes, Sir Claude?

SHEN TAI: Help me to become a Yellow Buddhist!

(*It is the climax of* SHEN TAI *and* TZU-HSI's *prepared performance. She laughs in triumph.* LI *applauds enthusiastically.*)

LI: You were splendid, Empress!

JUNG LU: It's easy to be splendid when you've written your opponent's part for him. But how would you respond if the Ambassador said what he really came to say? (*He takes the sash from* SHEN TAI *and himself becomes the Ambassador—perhaps attempting a fusty old accent.*) Your Majesty—we are disturbed at the growing number of incidents against our nationals. It is not safe for us to be in your streets.

TZU-HSI: (*Enjoying the game*) Dear English Person: Why *are* you in our streets?

JUNG LU: Our presence here is recognized by law.

TZU-HSI: Laws are changing. *I* am on the throne now.

JUNG LU: By what authority?

TZU-HSI: (*Taken aback*) I beg your pardon?

JUNG LU: By what authority have you usurped the throne?

LI: Jung Lu, you go too far!

JUNG LU: I want to know by what right you reign in the reign of the Kuang-Hsu Emperor!

TZU-HSI: He was ill. He resigned voluntarily.

JUNG LU: Is he still alive?

LI: Are you accusing the Empress of murder?

JUNG LU: I'm asking what the foreigners would ask! ...We want proof that he still exists! Nothing has been heard from him in many months.

TZU-HSI: Are you more interested in my nephew than in me?

JUNG LU: We have the right to deal with the legitimate ruler, and the legitimate ruler is not you!

(SHEN TAI *stares at this effrontery.* TZU-HSI *whirls on him.*)

TZU-HSI: What are you gaping at? Take that contraption and get out of here!

(SHEN TAI *takes the bicycle and hastily exits.*)

LI: (*To* JUNG LU) You have no right to address the Empress in this manner!

JUNG LU: The foreigners want to know you haven't dealt with Kuang-Hsu treacherously so they can believe you won't deal with them treacherously.

TZU-HSI: Do they see me as a double-headed dragon?

JUNG LU: They are afraid for their lives. They are begging you to provide them with armed protection against the Boxers!

TZU-HSI: Do they expect me to send my own soldiers against my own people? Let them protect themselves—or get out! ... They have ruined my day.

(Lights change.)

(The Ocean Terrace. The walls constantly reflect the surrounding water. All is delicate—like living within the shell of a pearly oyster. It is an incongruous prison— but a prison it is.)

(KUANG-HSU is alone. On his knees, he stares at his image in the water and cries out to it in great self-hatred:)

KUANG-HSU: Fool! ...Idiot! ...Blunderer! ...Is there anyone on Earth who can equal your stupidity! ...Why did you try to act without her knowledge! Why did you give her cause to hate you? Why couldn't you have been strong? *(He moves his hand furiously back and forth in the water as if trying to destroy his own image.)*

(THE PEARL CONCUBINE *enters with tea.*)

KUANG-HSU: If I told my aunt from the beginning of the reforms I planned—

THE PEARL CONCUBINE: She would never have allowed them to happen.

KUANG-HSU: I never planned her *murder*.

THE PEARL CONCUBINE: She knows.

KUANG-HSU: How could my tutor have gone ahead—

THE PEARL CONCUBINE: He should never have entrusted the deed to that absurd actor who now fawns all over your aunt. A man so fickle! So easily swayed—

KUANG-HSU: *I* was the greatest fool

THE PEARL CONCUBINE: You can't go over and over this...

KUANG-HSU: All my plans! All my glorious plans!

THE PEARL CONCUBINE: Someday they will all come to pass—you'll see.

KUANG-HSU: *(Tortured)* Where is the Eunuch?

THE PEARL CONCUBINE: He has not yet come.

KUANG-HSU: Each day he comes later and later!

THE PEARL CONCUBINE: It only seems so. Drink your tea.

KUANG-HSU: Where is he?

THE PEARL CONCUBINE: Can you not rest?

KUANG-HSU: Where is he?

(He paces, distraught, breaking out in a cold sweat, beginning to show the effects of his opium dependence. His WIFE *enters.)*

WIFE: What a lovely ride I've just had on the lake! Pity you're not allowed it.

THE PEARL CONCUBINE: I don't know why you continue to address him. He has refused to speak one word to you since the day we were placed on this island.

WIFE: I address him because, although he is practically out of his mind, he is not deaf. I address him because he hears everything I say!

KUANG-HSU: Get her away! Get her away! She is only here to report my every breath to my aunt!

WIFE: Oh, are you still breathing?

KUANG-HSU: *(Singing wildly to block her voice from his head.)* "There was an Emperor who had a shrew for a wife, a shrew for a wife. And he shut his head to her, for the rest of his life, the rest of his life—"

*(*LI *enters.)*

LI: The sounds that come from this island are delicious! Like the quacking of wild geese!

KUANG-HSU: You are late!

LI: I am not aware that we have any set time—or even that I have any obligation to come here.

KUANG-HSU: Have you brought it?

LI: Prison life has made you indelicate.

KUANG-HSU: Have you brought my pipe?

*(*LI *smiles enigmatically.)*

THE PEARL CONCUBINE: Answer him!

LI: *(Not answering)* Your aunt sends her felicitations—

KUANG-HSU: Is she coming to see me?

LI: She misses your splendid face. She has asked me to take your photograph.

*(*SERVANTS *enter with a box camera on a tripod.)*

THE PEARL CONCUBINE: I can imagine how much she craves to see his face!

KUANG-HSU: Oh, let me see! *(He examines the camera eagerly.)* There should be a silver-coated plate. And when I look in here, everything will be upside down.

... Oh yes. It's wonderful!

LI: If you'll stand in the light—

THE PEARL CONCUBINE: Don't do it. Don't play into her hands. If you pose for him you give a sign to the world that you consent to your intolerable imprisonment.

(KUANG-HSU *looks at her, then says to* LI:)

KUANG-HSU: I must refuse to have my photograph taken.

LI: You want your pipe...

(KUANG-HSU *realizes he must obey. He stands weak and wide-eyed while* LI *focuses the camera.*)

LI: Smile. You don't want the world to see the Emperor looking cross and petulant.

(KUANG-HSU *attempts to smile.* LI *takes the picture.*)

WIFE: I don't think the world will be impressed. (*She goes out.*)

(*The* SERVANTS *remove the camera and exit.*)

(KUANG-HSU *holds out his hand. With a slight smile,* LI *hands him the pipe.*)

THE PEARL CONCUBINE: (*To* LI:) This has been your way from the start—to corrupt him with pleasures.

LI: Only a woman can corrupt a man so deeply.

KUANG-HSU: There's nothing in this pipe!

(LI *smiles and, with infinite slowness, produces a small sack of opium from his pocket.* KUANG-HSU *snatches it and packs it into his pipe.*)

THE PEARL CONCUBINE: How you enjoy his pain, you and she! Watching it is your greatest pleasure!

LI: Why shouldn't he give me pleasure? I give pleasure to him.

THE PEARL CONCUBINE: You are a demon!

LI: (*Lighting* KUANG-HSU'S *pipe:*) Your master does not seem to think so.

(KUANG-HSU *lies back with his pipe, satisfied.* LI *exits.*)

(THE PEARL CONCUBINE *arranges the pillows on which* KUANG-HSU *is lying. He looks up from his opium to pathetically ask:*)

KUANG-HSU: How can you love me? How can you love me?

(THE PEARL CONCUBINE *stands looking out over the water, her hand gently touching the curve of her abdomen.*)

(*Lights change.*)

(The Hall of Supreme Harmony. TZU-HSI *is looking at the silver plate on which is the negative of* KUANG-HSU's *image.)*

TZU-HSI: Once immortality was carved in marble. Now it's in shadow images made from a silver plate. *(She looks at it, then draws her long nails across the surface, ruining it.)* I think, if there are going to be immortal images, they had better be of me.

(LI enters with the camera, borne by SERVANTS, who then exit. While TZU-HSI primps before a hand mirror, LI prepares to take her photograph.)

LI: You seem extremely happy today.

TZU-HSI: Having events in my own hands does wonders for my complexion.

LI: You look sixteen. How did you achieve this sudden onslaught of youth?

TZU-HSI: With great simplicity I have solved a problem which has been plaguing us for generations.

LI: Tell me—!

TZU-HSI: I have issued an ultimatum ordering the foreign delegations to leave Peking.

LI: A master stroke!

TZU-HSI: Within twenty-four hours.

LI: Empress, you are a genius! You look twelve! You look newborn!

TZU-HSI: Record it immediately!

(LI takes her photograph. She primps for a different pose. JUNG LU enters.)

JUNG LU: Is it true you've given the foreign delegations one day to leave the capital?

TZU-HSI: *(Posing)* It is true.

JUNG LU: How could you have done this?

TZU-HSI: I allowed them fifteen guards per legation. They asked permission to double that—and double that—and double that! Now there are more than two thousand "guards" making their way toward this city. It's an invasion!

JUNG LU: You said you would not protect them against the attacks of the Boxers...

TZU-HSI: I said they should protect themselves. That does not mean summoning armies to Peking! *(Against her will, she has lost her temper. She checks her face in the mirror and pouts.)* You've made me look—twenty-nine! *(To LI:)* We will resume tomorrow. This is not how I choose to be immortalized.

(SERVANTS enter and remove the camera. LI exits with them.)

JUNG LU: The legations are sending an envoy to talk to you.

TZU-HSI: They always want to talk, these Westerners!

JUNG LU: Will you see him?

TZU-HSI: Of course not. I've promised them safe conduct to their ships—

JUNG LU: Perhaps they want to ask for more time.

TZU-HSI: Time enough for their troops to get here? No! I want them out immediately!

JUNG LU: There is a rumor that they plan to ask for your resignation. *(She laughs.)*

TZU-HSI: Ask? Ask *whom*? Who do they think they are, these brazen intruders, to think they have the right to interfere in our affairs!

(LI enters, highly agitated.)

TZU-HSI: What is it?

LI: Empress—on his way here to the Forbidden City, the envoy from the foreign legations—has been killed.

TZU-HSI: I *said* they should not count on conversations!

JUNG LU: What happened?

LI: He and his entourage were set upon in the street—

JUNG LU: By the Boxers?

LI: More than likely.

TZU-HSI: It's the foreigners' own fault! Now they'll come to their senses and leave immediately.

LI: On the contrary, they seem to be gathering in supplies for a long stay. Apparently they fear that you cannot—or will not—honor your promise of safe conduct.

TZU-HSI: They dare doubt my word?

LI: The envoy and his entourage are dead. Even now the members of all the legations are gathering for safety in the British compound. There must be five hundred—almost half of them women and children.

TZU-HSI: And just what do they intend to do there?

LI: Await the arrival of their relief force.

TZU-HSI: And what do they expect *me* to do? Sit still while they march their combined forces to Peking? ...I have no alternative but to declare war against the legations.

JUNG LU: You cannot declare war against the official representatives of Great Britain, France, Germany, Italy, Austria, Belgium, Holland, Japan, and the

United States!

TZU-HSI: I shall crush them in one blow. Quickly. And drive them into the sea.

JUNG LU: And have upon your head the vengeance of all the great powers?

TZU-HSI: In this quarter of the earth, *China* is the only great power!

JUNG LU: These people have diplomatic immunity. It is against all civilized custom.

TZU-HSI: It is against all civilized custom for guests to treat their hosts with the condescension and contempt they have been heaping on us for centuries.

JUNG LU: I cannot be responsible if you declare an all-out war. How could I lead my army on a mission whose consequences would be so disastrous?

TZU-HSI: If your professional army can't accomplish the task, the Boxers will drive them out.

JUNG LU: That pack of wild dogs? Who knows if they are loyal to the throne?

TZU-HSI: They, at least, have the courage to defend me.

JUNG LU: Your regular army has the courage to defend you!

TZU-HSI: Then this is your chance. Get the task done!

(JUNG LU *exits.* LI *approaches her.*)

LI: Empress, may I venture an opinion? ...The Boxers are more fanatic about rooting out the foreigners than the regular army ever will be.

TZU-HSI: I know. But can the throne ally itself with beggars, thieves and cutthroats?

LI: Beggars who can live through bullets. Cutthroats with supernatural powers.

(TZU-HSI *says nothing.*)

LI: There is an old saying: "If you have two hands, why use only one?" ...The Boxers only await your word to put all their passion—all their hatred—behind the fight for China.

TZU-HSI: (*After a pause*) ...I will take advantage of this magic force—but no one must know. ... Send Shen Tai to me.

(LI *exits.*)

TZU-HSI: So small an unprotected bank of limp, pale Christians. Russian Christians who took from us—Central Asia. British Christians who took from us Burma, Hong Kong. French Christians who took from us—Indo-China. And Japanese Buddhists who took from us—Korea. They have all been a growing cancer for three centuries in China. But days from now—we will be cured!

(SHEN TAI *appears.* TZU-HSI *turns to him. Slowly she draws from her sleeve a thin band of bright red cloth.*)

TZU-HSI: Do you know what this is?

SHEN TAI: The headband of the Boxers.

(TZU-HSI *comes to* SHEN TAI *and ties it around his head.*)

TZU-HSI: You have played the hero, now you must *be* one.

SHEN TAI: I am not a soldier—

TZU-HSI: You are anything I say! You have the power to arouse multitudes. You have the power to harness this wild force and secretly make it serve my will.

SHEN TAI: What do you want me to do?

TZU-HSI: Arouse them! Direct them! Arm them!

SHEN TAI: I have no weapons.

(TZU-HSI *takes an emerald ring from her finger and gives it to* SHEN TAI.)

TZU-HSI: This will buy, I think, quite a few.

SHEN TAI: An emerald! Such beauty—!

TZU-HSI: It isn't beauty I give you, Shen Tai, it is power.

SHEN TAI: Power—

TZU-HSI: Isn't that what you have wanted all along?

(SHEN TAI *looks at* TZU-HSI, *then recognizes it.*)

SHEN TAI: Yes.

TZU-HSI: When you were powerless in the country, wasn't this what you dreamed of?

SHEN TAI: Yes, Empress!

TZU-HSI: Now I give you the power to liberate us all!

SHEN TAI: *(Aroused)* I can! I will! *(Slowly he begins to turn about, doing Kung-fu-like movements, hypnotizing himself into the trance of the Boxers. As he moves, he mutters magic incantations.)* Spirit of revenge, possess me! Spirit of the invincible, enter me and be my flesh! *(He whirls more and more swiftly until his arms grow strong, his legs sturdy, and his eyes burn with the fire of one possessed.)* Long live the Empress! *(Now the Boxer, he rushes out.)*

TZU-HSI: How miraculous it is that, just when I need them, this new force has arisen to deliver me. ... We are a strange alliance, the Boxers and I, but together—we will win.

(Lights change.)

(Ramparts of the Forbidden City. SHEN TAI, *standing on the ramparts, is illuminated in surrounding blackness. His head is thrown back, his red headband gleams. He cries out, exhorting unseen Boxer troops:)*

SHEN TAI: Fellow Boxers! Hear me! We are the avenging spirits! We are stronger than stone! Stronger than steel! I come to arouse you against the white plague which is upon us! Everywhere we are threatened by the round-eyed devils who have come from the west.

They outrage the spirit of our land. Their iron carriages disturb the terrestrial dragon and the land will not yield fruit to us! They have blackened the skies with their smoke and the heavens have gone dry! Their church spires pierce the realm of our gods, defiling their dwelling place! Everywhere their presence is a curse upon the landscape. Our gods are angry. They command us — get the blue-eyed devils out!

Only their blood can purify the streets of China! We Boxers are the force which shall make our nation clean! Bullets cannot harm us! We are indestructible!

Down with the foreign devils! Long live the Empress Tzu-Hsi!

(He runs out.)

(Lights change.)

(The Imperial Viewing Platform. A hot midsummer day. Sounds of battle are heard in the distance.)

(TZU-HSI stands enthusiastically viewing the action through a spy-glass as a SERVANT shields her from the sun with an umbrella. The WIFE stands fanning herself in the heat.)

TZU-HSI: I love the beginning days of a battle! When the weak still think they can win! Come look at our men!

WIFE: I cannot look —

TZU-HSI: When I was a girl, I used to dress myself in armor and pretend to lead regiments into battle. If I were a girl now, I'd be on the wall with my men.

WIFE: May I be excused?

TZU-HSI: You may not! If there is this much going on before your eyes, you will view it! ...How considerate of the foreigners to barricade themselves in the legation just beneath the Imperial Viewing Platform!

WIFE: It's so hot —

TZU-HSI: Good! The legations will be thirsty. They have only one small well.

(We hear the buzz of a mosquito. The WIFE swats at it.)

WIFE: I can't stand mosquitoes!

TZU-HSI: You! Mosquitoes! Precious comrades! That way! Feast on the legations! ...Look at them! With their pitiful supplies of food and ammunition. Look at their sandbags — made by the women out of their husbands' silk pajamas! ...Let us make a wager of how long it will take us to completely crush them! Two days? Three? ...Ask your husband if he would like to come witness this most glorious moment in all of China's history.

WIFE: He is ill, Empress.

TZU-HSI: Is he? I have never been so well!

(A woman's voice is heard outside.)

THE PEARL CONCUBINE: *(O S)* I *will* see her!

(As a GUARD tries to stop her, the THE PEARL CONCUBINE rushes in.)

TZU-HSI: What is this impudence!

THE PEARL CONCUBINE: I bring a message from the Kuang-Hsu Emperor.

(TZU-HSI dismisses the GUARD and SERVANT.)

TZU-HSI: Is he dying?

THE PEARL CONCUBINE: More slowly than you would like.

TZU-HSI: How did you get off the Ocean Terrace? Charmed the guards?

THE PEARL CONCUBINE: The Kuang-Hsu Emperor begs you to raise the siege of the legations.

TZU-HSI: Does he?

THE PEARL CONCUBINE: He begs that you escort them safely to the coast—

TZU-HSI: Is he their ally?

THE PEARL CONCUBINE: He thinks they should be treated with mercy.

TZU-HSI: His mind is befogged by the sweet haze *they* brought into China!

THE PEARL CONCUBINE: It is *you* who have brought him to this! It is you who have forced him into a dream life, without living! Isolated! A prisoner! Spare him these indignities!

TZU-HSI: He is a weakling!

THE PEARL CONCUBINE: He is the lawful ruler—!

TZU-HSI: Ah! You are brave! Brave as I was, you beauty! In spite of the fact that we both had nothing here! *(She touches THE PEARL CONCUBINE roughly in the groin.)* Then it's so. You *are* pregnant. My eyes do not deceive me.

WIFE: She doesn't look pregnant—

TZU-HSI: It is a gift old women have—to divine the lump in the belly before it shows. *(She turns to THE PEARL CONCUBINE:)* Whose child is this?

THE PEARL CONCUBINE: The Emperor's.

TZU-HSI: He is as capable of impregnating you as I am! To whom have you opened your treasure?

THE PEARL CONCUBINE: The Emperor.

WIFE: She must have used some kind of magic —

TZU-HSI: There will come a day when all men will be impotent. And we women will procreate ourselves — and rule forevermore... *(She puts her arms around* THE PEARL CONCUBINE.*)* You needn't tell me who he was. I admire your descent into the darkness. You did as I did once. We could be sisters. Brave and young and beautiful. Can you believe that I was once brave and young and beautiful? ... I still have the breasts of a woman young and strong.

I need someone to be the self I was, someone who's more myself than I am. *(She touches* THE PEARL CONCUBINE's *hair.)* You'll come live with me. You'll be my mirror. I'll look at myself — and I'll see you. You'll share my bed, and when I wake at night, instead of seeing the dark, I'll see youth and hope and beauty and salvation...

THE PEARL CONCUBINE: I would rather share my bed with a thousand serpents!

TZU-HSI: Then go. But remember — I offered you life...

*(*THE PEARL CONCUBINE *starts to exit the way she came.)*

TZU-HSI: Not that way.

*(*THE PEARL CONCUBINE *stops.)*

TZU-HSI: Surely you don't think I'll allow you to return to Kuang-Hsu. You are a clear mind. Too much of a luxury in prison. No. Let him dream about you — in your new home — the Garden of Dispossessed Favorites.

*(*THE PEARL CONCUBINE's *face reveals what this separation will cost her, but she doesn't utter a sound.)*

TZU-HSI: You say nothing. ... You do not beg. ... If you weep before me, I will send you back to him.

THE PEARL CONCUBINE: I shall never weep before you.

TZU-HSI: Go!

*(*THE PEARL CONCUBINE *exits.)*

TZU-HSI: She is my young life...

(The WIFE *comes over to comfort her.* TZU-HSI *turns on her.)*

TZU-HSI: Leave me at once! Your face disgusts me!

(The WIFE *exits.* TZU-HSI *turns toward the battle.)*

TZU-HSI: Why does it take so long? It must go faster! Faster! *(We hear the sound of a mosquito. She smacks it dead on her hand. She rubs the bite.)* ...Did we begin the battle on an auspicious day? I forgot to consult the mystic signs...

(Lights change.)

(The Ocean Terrace. KUANG-HSU, *now obviously in failing health, sits cross-legged on the floor surrounded by the dismembered pieces of the clock given to him by the British legation.)*

KUANG-HSU: Time... In pieces... Broken... Not moving... Still, I notice, with time in pieces, the sun still rises, the sun still sets.

(He shakes the mechanical bird which has come off the clock.)

Why don't you sing? Why won't you fly! Speak! Carry messages to her. Bring messages from her! Have you seen her in her garden? Tell me! *(He shakes the bird and breaks it. He screams at the clock face.)* Do not look upon me! Do not speak to me! I do not exist!

(Despondently, KUANG-HSU *sits on the floor amidst the broken pieces. His* WIFE *enters.)*

WIFE: You shouldn't have taken it apart if you couldn't put it back together.

*(*KUANG-HSU *turns away, still not acknowledging his* WIFE's *existence.)*

WIFE: Of all days, today you should be permitted to observe the battle.

*(*KUANG-HSU *concentrates on the pieces of his clock, pretending not to hear.)*

WIFE: Your aunt has ordered our soldiers to set fire to the great library next to the British legation. All of the new books you ordered. All of the old. The wind will fan the flames, destroy the legation, and the siege will come to an end!

*(*KUANG-HSU *stops playing with the clock.)*

WIFE: You hear me! I know you hear me!

*(*KUANG-HSU *is motionless.)*

WIFE: Look at the smoke!

*(*KUANG-HSU *looks up. He rises. He looks across the water, stunned and shaken. We can see the reflection of the flames.)*

KUANG-HSU: Our people set fire to our great library? All the future! All the past! In flames! All the ages! Burning, burning, burning, burning, burning! It is madness! *(He breaks down and sobs helplessly.)*

WIFE: The one who is mad—is you.

(Lights change.)

(The Hall Of Supreme Harmony. Night. Sporadic sounds of gunfire are heard in the distance. TZU-HSI *paces impatiently.)*

TZU-HSI: Who changed the direction of the wind? The flames were supposed to consume the compound. The compound wasn't touched!

*(*LI *enters.)*

LI: This is certainly an inauspicious day—

TZU-HSI: Why don't the legations fall? We have been battering at them for five weeks now! They have no food, no water. They have eaten their cow, their dogs, perhaps their own dead. Still they go on!

LI: Five weeks—

TZU-HSI: I do, I believe, still comprehend the principles of simple logic. And this is what I wish to ask: Why, since they have only one cannon, since they are surrounded, since we have the higher position, more ammunition, more food, more men—*why can we not win!!!*

(LI *takes a jeweled knife out of a sheath at his waist.*)

LI: Do you recognize this knife?

TZU-HSI: It is the knife I gave Jung Lu—

LI: You know it has the power to sing of the brave deeds of its owner—

TZU-HSI: It hasn't been with its owner for some time.

LI: Still, it will sing of his deeds. That is why I asked to keep it.

(LI *holds up the knife. He holds it up for some moments.*)

TZU-HSI: I hear nothing.

(LI *holds up the knife again. Again there is nothing but silence.*)

TZU-HSI: Perhaps it sings too softly—

LI: Perhaps it does not sing at all.

TZU-HSI: What do you mean?

LI: Can it sing of a commander who stops his siege each day at sundown? Can it sing of a commander who orders his soldiers to shoot over his enemy's heads? Can it sing of a commander who sends his starving enemy wagonloads of fruit?

(As LI *speaks,* JUNG LU *slowly enters, his uniform grimy with the dust of battle.*)

TZU-HSI: Is this true?

JUNG LU: I am a soldier, not a butcher. I cannot command my men to fire on helpless women and children—

TZU-HSI: Helpless! They seem to be winning!

JUNG LU: There are laws of humanity—

TZU-HSI: Will you lose the war out of pity?

JUNG LU: You hold pity in such contempt! Our men marched to war with birdcages hung over their bayonets! They are tired of fighting!

TZU-HSI: So you fight a half-way war? Restoring in the evening the gains you made the day before? You are a traitor! ...But what should I expect from a man who was lover to an Empress and chose to go to another's bed?

JUNG LU: Her bed was warm.

TZU-HSI: And mine?

JUNG LU: —is ice. And cruelty. Your greatest pleasure is destruction.

TZU-HSI: Your dying inside of me. Yes, I took pleasure in that.

JUNG LU: And now—in the deaths of thousands?

TZU-HSI: They are dying for a purpose—

JUNG LU: Is that how you justify giving your support secretly to the Boxers?

TZU-HSI: I am not answerable to you—

JUNG LU: *We cannot win!* I told you this before. You can slaughter the legations. Easily. But if you win against the legations, *still* you lose. The wrath of nine global powers will be upon you. You will be subject to retaliation of such force and from so many directions that China as we know it will come to an end.

TZU-HSI: Then let it end! But let it end quickly! Let us not be eaten by them river by river, mind by mind! *(Suddenly her tone changes.)* Leave me! I do not wish to see anyone unless they bring me good news!

(LI *and* JUNG LU *exit.*)

(Once TZU-HSI *is alone, the weariness she has been trying to hide descends upon her. She sits on the throne.*)

TZU-HSI: Can it be that the force of the West is on the ascendancy? Can this hemisphere be moving into darkness? Will the light we held for centuries now illumine the other half of the globe while the dragon goes into eclipse? *(She falls to her knees.)* Great Buddha, what have we done to deserve your anger? Tell me what to do! Smile upon us! *Help us!*

(SHEN TAI *runs in, wildly elated, his clothes torn and bloody, his headband proudly askew on his head, his arms laden with plunder.*)

SHEN TAI: The city is a field of glory!

TZU-HSI: Tell me—!

SHEN TAI: Everything the foreigners have touched will be devoured in flames!

TZU-HSI: At last!

SHEN TAI: The streets are running with blood!

TZU-HSI: *(More to herself than to him.)* I have returned to the glorious days of my Manchu ancestors. They had the courage to ally themselves with darkness.

SHEN TAI: It's not that hard—real killing. I thought of you—of serving you—

TZU-HSI: And you nobly performed your part. You are my hero, Shen Tai. My true hero. One day I will give you your own theatre. In it, you will show the victory of the dragon over the blue-eyed devils!

(JUNG LU *enters, looking more harassed and smoke-blackened than before.*)

JUNG LU: Your Boxers are beyond control! They've set the city aflame! They are attacking not only foreigners—but anyone at all!

TZU-HSI: My Boxers—

JUNG LU: I've sent for a relief force, but it hasn't arrived. You'll be lucky if there *is* a Peking by morning!

TZU-HSI: This is my ecstasy!

JUNG LU: It is not the foreign devils who are dying, it is your own people!

TZU-HSI: Only he who will go to the ends of his being can have a victory. I will dare everything! Burn everything! Even myself! I bless the holocaust— out of which will come a new beginning! (*She turns to* SHEN TAI:) Kill all foreigners. *Kill all foreigners.* I do not want *one* left alive in this land!

(SHEN TAI *bows obediently and runs out.*)

JUNG LU: I no longer recognize you—

TZU-HSI: If the heavens are harsh, I will be harsher. I won't go down without using every weapon that I have.

(JUNG LU *looks at her.* TZU-HSI *continues, deeply:*)

TZU-HSI: You have no idea what it is like to be up here. You think, once you are in power, you can bend events to your will. The splendid joke is—in the seat of power, you are more powerless than ever! It's in the fates, or in the hands of heaven. And there's nothing, nothing you can do! I can endure anything, but I can't endure being helpless!

(TZU-HSI *buries her face in her hands.* JUNG LU *comes to her and gently takes her hands away from her face.*)

TZU-HSI: Can you bear to touch an old lady?

JUNG LU: I can bear it.

TZU-HSI: You are the only one on earth to whom I've ever shown my private face.

JUNG LU: I know. You exist by wearing the mask of cruelty. It's your survival.

TZU-HSI: How did you manage to survive when I stripped you of everything? Why did you not break?

JUNG LU: I bent to the will of heaven, and so rode out the storm.

TZU-HSI: Bending is an undignified posture.

JUNG LU: Sometimes it's the most powerful one there is.

TZU-HSI: *(Suddenly cold)* You're trying to give me hints—

JUNG LU: You never could stand being told anything.

TZU-HSI: It was such a relief when you were banished. There was no one around to think they could tell me what to do.

JUNG LU: Your loss.

TZU-HSI: Brazen bull!

JUNG LU: Stubborn bitch!

TZU-HSI: I could have you executed for that!

JUNG LU: Fine! Then I won't have to watch you lead the country to ruin!

TZU-HSI: *(Icily)* And just what course do you think I should pursue?

JUNG LU: I think you should *talk*! I think you should be in communication with your enemies. I think you should tear down the walls surrounding the Forbidden City and become a part of *life*!

(TZU-HSI *turns away.*)

JUNG LU: Eye-to-eye is the only way this country will be saved. You think they're barbarians. They think *we're* barbarians. We will never understand each other until we can see ourselves through each other's eyes. Meet, in the same room, face to face.

TZU-HSI: I can't seem weak, I can't seem womanly—

JUNG LU: All I'm asking you to do is seem *human*. ... The last time I felt you were human was the night you and I said farewell. You left the next morning to become the Emperor's concubine. Since then—

TZU-HSI: *(Extremely vulnerable)* Since then—I have lived in the fear that all this would be taken from me. There is no moment when I actually believe I have it.

JUNG LU: It cannot be taken from you by people who respect and understand you. ... See the representatives of the legations.

(TZU-HSI *looks at* JUNG LU.)

JUNG LU: It is the only way that will not lead to total mutual disaster.

(TZU-HSI *considers this a long time, then at last says:*)

TZU-HSI: Very well. Tell them I will receive them.

JUNG LU: I doubt very much that they would enter the Forbidden City. They would suspect an ambush. *You* must go to *them*.

TZU-HSI: Me to them! Like a simpering beggar—!

JUNG LU: Like a great woman. The illustrious, all-forgiving, beneficent ruler of five hundred million.

TZU-HSI: *(Simply)* Do you think—outside these walls—without the mystery and grandeur of the throne room—that I can impress those white men?

JUNG LU: I think you can dazzle them.

TZU-HSI: It would surprise them, wouldn't it? An imperial procession—straight through the legations' streets!

JUNG LU: They would be astounded. Six armies couldn't accomplish what could be accomplished by one woman using her mind.

TZU-HSI: *(After considering)* ...Then I'll do it! Single-handedly, I'll end the war! I've always wanted to be a soldier!

JUNG LU: A soldier of reason.

(LI *enters.*)

TZU-HSI: Prepare my traveling chair, Li. I am going on a small journey.

LI: Empress—

TZU-HSI: Bring me my jewels, bring me my imperial robe—

LI: Empress, the relief force has arrived.

TZU-HSI: At last!

LI: Not *our* relief force. *Theirs.*

(*We hear the fife and drum of the Allied armies.*)

LI: Thirty-thousand men. Twice as many as we can muster.

JUNG LU: Then it's over.

TZU-HSI: No! I am going out to talk with them!

JUNG LU: It just became too late for reason.

TZU-HSI: We must try—

JUNG LU: Too late... Too late...

(*Lights change.*)

(*The Gate Of Spiritual Valor. Sounds of invading soldiers, shouting in various languages, are heard in the distance. The Drum of Remonstrance sits silently in the foreground. The* WIFE *runs in, followed by* KUANG-HSU.)

WIFE: The guards have fled! There's no one here! No one to protect us!

(JUNG LU *enters.*)

JUNG LU: I'll protect you.

KUANG-HSU: *(Very formally dressed and coiffed. He speaks in the low Emperor's voice that Shen Tai taught him.)* This is a very fine robe. We must thank our tailor.

JUNG LU: Emperor, I am taking you to the camp of the foreigners. You must not be afraid.

KUANG-HSU: *(He takes out a string of paper soldiers.)* I have the loyal support of my soldiers. I have only to breathe on them to make them come alive.

JUNG LU: You must be the figurehead around whom China can rally. The foreigners are not against all of us. They are against *her*. They will restore you to the throne. They will support you.

KUANG-HSU: *(Holding up the soldiers)* Shall I breathe on them now?

(Seeing the Emperor's madness, JUNG LU makes a gesture of despair.)

(THE PEARL CONCUBINE suddenly appears. Her robes are bedraggled. Her pregnancy is beginning to show. She stares at the Emperor, whom she has not seen in many weeks.)

KUANG-HSU: I was not aware that I was to choose new concubines this morning. Who is this one?

THE PEARL CONCUBINE: *(Sensing his madness and coming toward him with compassion)* My love—

KUANG-HSU: Do not speak to me! Do not hear! Do not look upon the Emperor!

(THE PEARL CONCUBINE moves away, deeply moved and holding back her sorrow. KUANG-HSU observes her coolly.)

KUANG-HSU: She is too fat, that one. Her belly is too round. Rejected! Rejected!

(LI enters, pulling a cart on which are piled old clothes.)

LI: The foreign soldiers are at the southern gate to the Forbidden City. We must escape to the north—to the Summer Palace. We must disguise ourselves as peasants. I have hidden the Great Seal and the imperial jewels. We must hurry—

(LI starts handing out clothing. TZU-HSI enters.)

LI: You must disguise yourself as a peasant.

(LI tries to give TZU-HSI old clothes.)

TZU-HSI: A peasant!—Never! *(She thrusts the clothes away.)* I will not be cheated out of my encounter. If I cannot go to them, I shall address them from the wall. *(She mounts the highest place on the ramparts and cries out:)* Diplomats and soldiers of the allied nations! Listen to me! I am the Dowager Empress! I am the one whose face you've never seen!

In one moment, you will have breached our walls. ... It is too late for talk. But it is not too late for steel. Let this battle be decided one to one! Who will take his sword in hand and meet me blade to blade in single combat? ... Come! Anyone!

JUNG LU: You are mad!

TZU-HSI: Stay away!

(JUNG LU *obeys.* TZU-HSI *stands alone.*)

TZU-HSI: What? No one? ... Then aim your rifles! Aim them to this heart and slay the dragon! *(She stands with arms outstretched, facing us, a willing target. But no shots ring out.)*

JUNG LU: Come down from there—!

TZU-HSI: *(Disappointed)* They will not shoot. *(Reluctantly, she turns and descends.)* They hold me in such contempt that I am not worth killing.

JUNG LU: They would not martyr you. It would arouse the sympathy of the world.

TZU-HSI: Well, what they cannot achieve for me, I can achieve myself... *(She holds a small vial in her hand. She opens the vial and starts to raise it to her lips—but hesitates.)*

(*As* TZU-HSI *stands frozen, undecided, the* THE PEARL CONCUBINE *says, deeply:*)

THE PEARL CONCUBINE: Do not hesitate. Let the country go. You have possessed the land for nearly half a century. It is you who have held her to the past and brought her to this. Release it from your ancient hands, I beg you. Dispatch yourself—and let China live!

TZU-HSI: *(Quietly, after a moment)* ...How lovely it is that the most charming, the most beautiful, the most merciful among you most ardently desires my death. *(She looks slowly from one to another.)* That would be a great solution, wouldn't it? A solution for you. A solution for me. ... And how will China live? Under Kuang-Hsu the weak? *(She looks at* JUNG LU.) So you are going to take him to the foreigners and have them seat him as their puppet on his own throne?...

No! No! I may be ancient, but I will resist with every fiber of my being this humiliating mockery of China's former glory. *(She turns to the* THE PEARL CONCUBINE, *lovingly.)* I thank you, my brave one, my Pearl, for bringing me to life again. You alone see with the eyes of my youth. You see how much I hoped for—and how much I failed. ... I can't bear what you see. ... For knowing me too well, seeing me too clearly, you must die, Pearl. *(She has spoken this sadly.)*

JUNG LU: *(To* THE PEARL CONCUBINE:) Run! There's no one here to carry out her order—

(THE PEARL CONCUBINE *turns to* KUANG-HSU.)

THE PEARL CONCUBINE: My love—

KUANG-HSU: Rejected...

(THE PEARL CONCUBINE *bows to* KUANG-HSU *who, busy with his paper soldiers, hardly even notices her. Slowly, with dignity,* THE PEARL CONCUBINE *walks out.* TZU-HSI *calls:*)

TZU-HSI: If there is anyone within the sound of my voice who is still loyal to me, dispatch this traitor! *(She turns to LI:)* Li, bring me my royal gown. *(She stands as he puts a ragged peasant coat over her imperial robe.)* Now, cut my nails, they only took a lifetime to grow.

(LI removes her nail protectors, kneeling at her feet.)

TZU-HSI: Now, remove my headdress...

(LI performs this task — the ceremonial divesting of the last shred of royalty.)

TZU-HSI: I see a glorious future for China.

JUNG LU: *(Bitterly)* A future under you...

TZU-HSI: It is heaven's will. ... If the Dynasty were to end, the Drum of Remonstrance would be sounded. But see? It is absolutely silent. I still possess the Mandate of Heaven.

(SHEN TAI enters, looking stunned.)

SHEN TAI: The Pearl is at the bottom of the well. I drowned her. I heard you call out to kill and I obeyed. Even when I saw it was the Pearl, I kept on killing. Obeying you...

I shoved her into the well. She resisted at first, but then it seemed she fell into her reflection gladly. ... But what was it? As she disappeared beneath the water, somewhere I thought I heard the crying of a child.

TZU-HSI: Do you not know she was carrying your child?

SHEN TAI: My child! I have killed my child! What have you made me do? What have you made us *all* do? Monster!

(SHEN TAI lurches toward TZU-HSI threateningly, but cannot bring himself to touch her. He cries out in anger and collapses on the ground.)

TZU-HSI: So you, too, desire my death. ... You are many, I am one. Why don't you kill me, all of you? *(She looks each one in the eye. No one moves. She says, deeply, wearily:)* I am, still am, the only one who can hold this country together.

(The walls are breached. The shouts, the gunfire, and the fife and drum of the attacking soldiers are heard, much nearer.)

(TZU-HSI gestures toward LI and JUNG LU.)

TZU-HSI: You. Oxen. Hitch yourselves to my cart.

(On his way to the cart, KUANG-HSU passes TZU-HSI. Holding his paper soldiers, he asks her:)

KUANG-HSU: Shall I breathe on them now?

(TZU-HSI touches his face in pity. She, KUANG-HSU and the WIFE get into the cart. The cart begins to move. As it passes SHEN TAI, he cries out.)

SHEN TAI: I once worshipped you! *(He breaks down, weeping.)*

TZU-HSI: Dry your eyes! Rejoice! As long as I live, China is living! Let no one weep! *I survive!*

(JUNG LU *and* LI *pull out the cart with* TZU-HSI, KUANG-HSU *and the* WIFE *on it.* SHEN TAI *rises. Pulling off his red headband, he cries out:)*

SHEN TAI: I, too, survive! *(He runs over to the Drum of Remonstrance. He starts to pound upon it with his fists. With all the power in his soul, he beats upon the drum in rage and rebellion.)*

(JUNG LU *appears in a light at another part of the stage. As the rhythmic pounding continues in pantomime,* JUNG LU *says:)*

JUNG LU: As the Empress Tzu-Hsi retreated to her summer palace, she saw China for the first time—her subjects and their poverty, as the Tutor and I had described them. The foreign powers, their victory complete, found themselves compelled to look to Tzu-Hsi as the only leader who commanded enough obedience and respect to be restored to the Dragon Throne.

Less than a year after her flight, the Empress was welcomed back to Peking in a magnificent triumphal procession. She ruled for eight more years, gradually instituting many of the reforms which Kuang-Hsu and the Tutor had advocated—even proposing a constitutional monarchy.

But it was all too late. In a bankrupt China, Tzu-Hsi, still ruler of the Empire, died a peaceful death on November 12, 1908, at the age of seventy-three. Her nephew, the Emperor Kuang-Hsu, had died the very day before.

The Empress's appointed heir to the throne was my two-year-old grandson, Prince P'u-i. He sustained the more than four thousand year-old Imperial Throne for three more years until he was deposed by the First Republic. P'u-i was the last Chinese Emperor. He died, a poor government clerk, in the People's Republic of China, in 1967.

(The lights fade on JUNG LU.*)*

*(*SHEN TAI*'s pounding on the Drum increases in pace and loudness. Now wearing a Mao cap, he pounds his fists on the Drum, loudly signalling the end of the Dynasty's Mandate from Heaven.)*

(The pounding of the Drum grows to a tremendous climax.)

(Blackout)

END OF PLAY

PRODUCTION NOTES

EMPRESS OF CHINA may be presented at any one of several levels of production, from the most basic to the most elaborate.

BASIC: The first Pan Asian Repertory Theatre production in New York, directed by Tisa Chang, featured a simple platform similar to a Shakespearean thrust stage. Eight actors performed the play on an almost bare stage without the assistance of any nonspeaking servants or extras. On Bob Phillip's set, changes of place were indicated mainly by changes in lighting.

As written, every scene in the play has at least one physical element or prop—the axe, the clocks, the red headband, etc.—this is the visual and symbolic key to the scene. In this production, these were carried in and removed by the actors. A croquet mallet was substituted for the bicycle. Original background music was on tape.

The second Pan Asian production used a different floor plan but was also at this level.

MODERATE: A second, slightly more elaborate, level of production is reflected in the script herein. A certain amount of scenic elaboration is indicated. The suggestion is for a unit set, with the use of banners or screens to suggest changes of place. These changes may be effected mechanically or by the use of two or more servants whose presence has been suggested within the scenes. Not only do these nonspeaking extras perform tasks that realistically would not be carried out by members of the Imperial Court, their presence adds atmosphere and suggests the stratified ceremonial life within the Forbidden City.

The Australian production, at the Belvoir Theatre in Sydney, took place on a thrust stage. Bench forms, which became containers for props, and on which actors could both stand and sit, were moved into different positions for different scenes.

The production, in Italian, at the Todi Festival in Italy, had a raised central curtained space for the Empress's area. This production used the costumes from the film *The Last Emperor* designed by James Acheson—and these costumes lent a richness and elaboration to a basically simple set.

AUGMENTED: A still more elaborate level of production was reflected in the Cincinnati Playhouse production, directed by Robert Kalfin. Here, Michael

Sharp's set utilized a turntable within a turntable. On the center turntable were two eight-foot square boxes, one on top of the other, which opened and closed to reveal scenes. On its reverse side, the turntable had three broad flights of steps leading up to the elevated Dragon Throne. Some locations moved in on the lower turntable. Projections on scrim were also used to indicate change of place.

This production added a chorus of eight who at various times played Concubines, Eunuchs or Peasants. They not only moved scenery and attended at the court, but appeared in eight "Illusions"—musical and mime numbers which were interpolated into the show.

In this production, three Musicians, seated on stage, played more than thirty instruments, from Chinese gong, cymbal and flute to synthesizer. Their music accompanied much of the action.

The complexity of the production of EMPRESS OF CHINA is at the discretion of the director. But, whatever the level of production, it is to be hoped that the physical elements will not overwhelm the inner life of the characters and play. Although the specific story is Chinese, the ideas, of revolution and reaction, of power and powerlessness, of love of the future vs. love of the past, are universal. Therefore, the slavish reconstruction of a specific time and place in scenery and costumes is to be avoided. The best production will be one that exercises the imagination, using elements of the past creatively to present a vision of a theme that is definitely of the *Now*.

SARAH IN AMERICA

SARAH IN AMERICA premiered at the Kennedy Center's Eisenhower Theater in Washington DC on 11 February 1981.

CHARACTER & SETTING

Sarah Bernhardt

ACT ONE
First American Tour—1880-81
ACT TWO
Sixth American Tour, First Farewell Tour—1905-06
Eighth American Tour, Third Farewell Tour—1913-14
Ninth American Tour, Final Farewell Tour—1916-18

The setting consists of clusters of trunks in varying shapes and sizes. These transform themselves into the spaces and furnishings necessary for the action of the play.

All of the action of the play takes place in America—on docks, on stages, in dressing rooms, in the wings, in hotel rooms and on Bernhardt's special train.

The spaces are created mostly in our imaginations. Place and mood are indicated by changes in lighting.

Bernhardt's costumes consist of one basic dress for each act. Over or under these are fitted the other garments which the scenes suggest.

Simplicity of effect is the aesthetic.

Imagination is the key.

AUTHOR'S NOTE

The only person in Sarah Bernhardt's life and art was Sarah Bernhardt. That is why, in this play, no one else speaks. The hundreds who shared her life, on stage and off, are all present—in our imaginations. They simply have no lines here. To Sarah, they were always just supporting parts.

We all know Sarah Bernhardt, but perhaps we don't realize that the reason she is so famous to us is because she spent a goodly portion of her adult life in this country. From 1880 to 1918 she made nine American tours. She was one of the first great truly international superstars. The new speed of ships and trains suddenly made distant places more accessible. Bernhardt, whose appetite for experience and adventure was insatiable, became an itinerant player on a global scale.

She toured this country from coast to coast, from north to south, in short engagements, one-night stands and longer runs in major cities. What is extraordinary is that she always played in French and, in spite of that, she played, almost always, to sold-out houses. Wherever she went, she was not merely a star, she was a phenomenon. She saw more of this country than most Americans. It is astonishing to discover in how many by-ways, how many forgotten towns, it is still said, "Sarah Bernhardt played here."

In our absorption with the posing, histrionic oddity, we often forget the woman who was driven by creative fire, the indefatigable worker, the human being. A Frenchman once told me, "I think you Americans understood Bernhardt more than we did." It may be true. There was something in her spirit which responded to this country. And the feeling was mutual.

This is the story of Bernhardt against the American landscape. It is the story of Sarah Bernhardt's long love affair with America—and ours with her.

ACT ONE

(Time: First American Tour, 1880)

(At rise:)

(The sky is icy blue. SARAH BERNHARDT, *age thirty-six, appears center stage, as on the deck of a ship. Lively, excited, and hardly aware of the biting wind and cold, She says:)*

BERNHARDT: New York! New York at last!

(She turns to us and says:)

Magnificent! A whole new continent to conquer! I am going to make this country stand up and cheer!

They have never seen anything like what I have to offer! My fire! My genius! My strength! They have seen acting? By God, not like my acting!

I will make them scream in terror, suffer as I suffer, weep as I weep! I will wring their hearts until they shout, "No actress anywhere, in all time, has ever equalled Bernhardt!"

(She looks toward the shore, then turns back to us and asks plaintively:)

What do you think? Have I talked myself into it?

(We hear barking. A small dog jumps into her arms.)

Now, now, Hamlet, don't be afraid. I won't leave you in America.

(She says to her maid, Marianne:)

Look, Marianne! Crowds to greet me! An endless line of dignitaries! A band! Even French flags!

(She picks up a bouquet of red roses.)

Wish me luck! I'm off to conquer the New World! I'm sure we're fated to adore each other!

(The band strikes up The Marseillaise, *the crowd cheers. Roses in her arms, she makes a grand entrance, smiling and waving. The cheers grow louder. She raises her hand for silence.)*

Merci, mes amis. ...A magnificent voyage, thank you. ...Yes, my very first visit to your shores. I know I shall be *enchanted* with America—

(Suddenly a light comes up on a downstage trunk. Her attention is distracted by the appearance of the Customs Officer. She turns and says:)

What are you doing? What are you doing with my trunks? Did my maid give you the keys? ...Marianne, did you give him the keys?

I don't care if you *are* a customs officer, you have no right to go through my luggage!

Where is Mister Jarrett? Where is that man? ...Mister Jarrett is my manager. He's the one who invited me to this country. I'm sure he can explain—

(The Customs Official asks her a question.)

My papers? ...Here.

(French pronunciation, proudly:)

Sarah Bernhardt.

(She repeats, in a flat American accent:)

Sarah Bernhardt.

(To us:)

Mon Dieu, he's never heard of me!

I am an actress. *The* actress.

Hair? ...Red... Eyes? ...Blue.

(Long pause, then quietly:)

Thirty-six.

(He doesn't hear her. She repeats, louder:)

I am thirty-six years old!

(To us:)

No Frenchman would ever ask such a question.

Monsieur, why have you impounded my trunks?

(To us:)

He thinks I'm smuggling!

I don't care if no one ever before has entered the Port of New York with three hundred pieces of baggage. I do!

Are those dresses new?

(To us:)

He thinks I'm going to sell them!

My dear man, I am not in the clothing business! We are a theater company and these are our costumes. Fifty actors. We are going to travel across America, from here to—

(She hears a voice offstage.)

Marianne, what's that man shouting? I think I hear my name. He seems to be handing out pamphlets. ...Oh, here's one.

(She picks up a pamphlet from the ground.)

Ah! It's from a Bishop! Let's see—

(She reads:)

"Our shores must be protected from this Sarah Bernhardt, this female demon sent from modern Babylon to corrupt the New World."

Marianne, take a note. ..."My dear Bishop—" No. "My dear *colleague*: Why attack me so violently? We actors ought not to be too hard on one another. Yours sincerely."

(She turns to us:)

So this is the real reason I've been stopped at your border. They're afraid I'll lead the entire country straight to hell!

(She turns to the Customs Officer, sweet as honey:)

Monsieur le Customs Officer, it hurts me to the quick to think that a Bishop could condemn me. Doesn't he know I was educated in a convent? I never wanted to become an actress. I wanted to become a nun.

Yes, my mother is Jewish. ...Yes, I am a Catholic. ...No, my father was not Pope Pius the Ninth!

(To us:)

What business is it of his if my parents weren't married? He's hinting my mother was a woman of easy virtue. ...She was. ...Not that that's easy, believe me!

(To the Customs Officer:)

Monsieur, everything in this pamphlet is a pack of lies. I do not take milk baths. I do not *always* sleep in a coffin. I am *not* travelling with a fifty-foot long python! He's quite safe at home. ...I am a hard-working woman. A *mother*—

No, not a wife, but, *Monsieur*, one can't take on everything!

(To us:)

He wants to know the identity of my son's father. He was the Prince Henri de Ligne of Belgium—the first man I ever loved. But why should I tell him?

(She turns back to the Customs Man.)

Monsieur, I have no time to waste on this inquisition any longer. If you have grounds to condemn me, place me before a firing squad immediately. Nobody dies as well as I do!

(Jarrett enters.)

Oh, Jarrett—. There you are. Permission for my release?

(To us:)

What a shame, the fun was just beginning.

(To the Customs Officer:)

Monsieur, come see me tonight in *Adrienne Lecouvreur*. You think this was a scene? Wait until you see me on the stage!

(The lights change. She crosses into the hotel suite. She throws off her furs and hat and says:)

Peace! At last! I must rest—

(She is about to collapse on the couch when she hears the babble of dozens of voices.)

Jarrett, who are these people and what are they doing in my hotel suite?

The press! I will not be interviewed now! I am exhausted! I have just crossed an ocean! I am not prepared to be challenged by a crowd of raving hyenas! No! I tell you I am near collapse!

(She throws up her arms and faints dead away on the floor.)

(The door slams shut. The voices cut off.)

(She raises herself up on one elbow and says to us:)

I've been doing this for years. It never fails.

(She gets up and says to us:)

It's so hard on the nerves, coming to a strange city. I must have my own things about me.

(She shows us a pillow with her motto on it.)

My linen—with my motto on it: "*Quand Même.*" "In spite of everything."

(Showing us a framed photograph.)

Maurice. My son. He's fifteen. How I wish I could have brought him with me!

(She shows a stuffed crocodile.)

And my cat—

(She pantomimes its jaws snapping shut.)

Inside.

(She shrugs.)

C'est la vie.

(There is a knock on the door. She calls out:)

Go away!

(She turns to us and says:)

What do you think of this Mister Jarrett? Have I put myself in the hands of a madman? ...Tall. Seventy or more. Silver white hair... I trusted him because he came right out and said, "I've made my way in life with the aid of two weapons: honesty—and a revolver."

Brutal... Daring... Ruthless... Exactly what I need in America!

(More knocking at the door.)

I'm not coming out!

(She continues, to us:)

He walked into my life one day, knowing, somehow, that my life at the Comédie Française, had become, for me, a prison. I was the toast of Paris! But I couldn't live my own life.

I had a wild longing to travel, see something else, breathe another air. If I didn't, I thought I'd do something insane!

So I resigned. My friends said I was mad. I'd walked out on the most prestigious theater in the world. What career could I have? ...But just then, along came Mister Jarrett whispering: "America!"

(The pounding becomes tremendous. She cries out:)

If you break down the door, I'll jump out the window!

(She continues, to us:)

And he whispered something else: "Gold". He said he would pay me in gold. And that's good news for my creditors. I don't know where my money goes, but it goes!

(The knocking becomes overwhelming.)

You can't intimidate *me*, Jarrett! Shoot me and you lose your investment!

(He talks to her from beyond the door.)

I'm *aware* I'm a mere curiosity. ...Of course I want the tour to be a success. Of course I want everyone to get to know me and flock to the theater. But they know me already! Didn't you see the crowds at the dock?

You *what*? You paid them to come? You paid them to cheer! *You* hired the Bishop! ...Oh, I could die!

(She thinks for a moment, then says to herself:)

No. I won't die.

(She calls out:)

I'll see them. ...Give me a moment to prepare myself.

(She gets her black cloak and calls:)

Marianne!

(Marianne enters.)

Marianne, you have to face them for me! Give me a minute to slip out the back way, then get into my cloak and lead them a merry chase. By the time they discover it's you, I'll be barricaded in my dressing room at the theater. I'll talk to no one before the performance. No one!

(She watches Marianne exit then throws her coat over her shoulders and hurries toward the theater, the other way.)

(Moments later, she enters her dressing room. She is beginning to be in a "mood". From the way she throws open her trunk and her make-up case, we can feel it.)

Insanity. Absolute insanity to schedule a performance on the day of my arrival. How on earth can I—

(Someone enters behind her. She whirls suddenly and says:)

Who are you? ...Oh, yes. Yes... Mister Mulcahy. Thank you for coming. ...I'm told you're a good workman and highly experienced. ...You can build one to order quickly? ... Good.

This is what I want: Rosewood. Fine-grained. Highly polished... Not like a box. I want angles. Here.

(She outlines the angles with her hands.)

Mauve satin lining. Mauve. Light purple! ... And very soft on the bottom. Padded. ...The dead don't care? How do you know?

When can you have it ready? I need it immediately.

What size? My size, of course. Or—a little larger. I need room for turning. Sometimes I get restless—

(He runs out, slamming the door behind him. She goes to the door and calls out after him:)

Mister Mulcahy! ...I'll pay you double!

(She re-enters the dressing room.)

He'll do it. ...But until it comes, how shall I survive?

(She starts to make up, becoming more and more depressed.)

I never should have come. It's madness to think I can conquer America.

What's my audience? Those who don't know me. Those who think I'm a sideshow. And those who think I'm a whore!

What am I doing here? I'm going to have to go out and face those barbarians who don't even speak my language! I've crossed an entire ocean to bury my career!

What joy that will give everyone back home. I'll open here, no one will come, the critics will destroy me—and I'll be bankrupt. Splendid!

In France, I have my coffin to comfort me. But here—until Mister Mulcahy brings relief—

(She leans against a trunk in an attitude of prayer.)

Spirits of the dead, help me. Out of darkness, help me face the darkness. Out of death, give me the strength for life.

(There is a knock at the door. She calls out:)

No! I will see nobody!

(Angelo enters. She greets him with joy.)

Oh, Angelo! Angelo, my love! Thank God you're here to see me through this folly! You don't know how much it means to me to know I can count on my leading man.

This trial—it's like going to one's own beheading! But we won't care, will we? No matter how this fails, we'll succeed afterwards in each other's arms, as we always do.

(She kisses him alternately on his cheeks:)

Merde, merde, merde, Chéri. À bientôt.

(He exits.)

(Marianne dashes in.)

Ah, Marianne! Look at you! You must have led them a merry chase! You're a martyr! I'll make it up to you, I promise. I needed to concentrate on *Adrienne*—

(She starts getting into her costume for Adrienne Lecouvreur.*)*

Isn't there a cable from Maurice? You don't think he's ill, do you?

(The warning buzzer sounds.)

Ah! ...Where are my slippers? My lucky slippers!

(She can't find them. She is frantic.)

Marianne, my throat is closing! What's my first line? I can't breathe!

(The orchestra tuning up music begins.)

(She falls on her knees and crosses herself.)

"*Sainte Marie, Mère de Dieu, aide-moi—*"

(*She finds the lucky slippers. Gratefully, she blurts out in Yiddish:*)

Gott tzu danken!

(*She kisses them fervently.*)

(*Three knocks indicate the start of the performance. Her entrance music begins. She cries:*)

I can't go on!

(*The lights change to stage lighting. She moves to the wings, hesitates a moment, then goes on, to slight applause.*)

(*On stage, She begins:*)

"*Ah, mon amour! Vous?! Le comte de Saxe?! Et je vous croyais un simple soldat! Mais non, vous êtes noble! Et moi, je ne suis qu'une pauvre actrice. ...Une grande princesse vous aime. Elle possède tout, et moi, je ne possède qu'un monde imaginaire. Comment est-ce que je peux être sa rivale? ... Qu'est-ce que vous dîtes? Vous voulez m'épouser? Je n'ai jamais osé rêver d'un tel bonheur. Quelle extase! Je me pâme de joie! ...Je vous aime et je serai à vous pour toujours. Rien ne peut jamais nous séparer. Rien! Je vous aimerai jusqu'à la fin de ma vie, jusqu'à la fin du temps. Je vous jure un amour éternel!*"

(*She hurries off into the on-stage wings and gets her shawl. As she puts it on, she says:*)

Good God, Marianne, it's like playing to the dead! Why are they so silent? Is it that they don't understand? But Jarrett gave them the full translation in the program!

Listen. Have a coach waiting at the stage door after the final curtain. We'll run away to Mexico! No! The Amazon! I'll play for the crocodiles! What will they know of my utter disaster on the New York stage!

(*She starts to return to the stage, then remembers:*)

The bouquet!

(*She picks up a bouquet of roses. The stage lights go up. She enters. She begins, in French:*)

"*Des Roses! Ah, je sais qui m'a envoyé ces roses!*"

(*She continues in English:*)

"Roses without thorns. I shall kiss every one."

(*Suddenly she starts.*)

"Oh! That *was* a thorn! He couldn't have sent me these flowers. ...They must be from her, my rival. ...How strange! I feel an icy shiver through my body."

(A sudden realization.)

"Poison! Help! Someone! Save me! ... I do not wish to die! Dear God, let me live a little while longer. I am so young, and life appears to me now so beautiful!"

"My love, come quickly!"

(She falls to the floor.)

"Darkness... Silence... *Adieu*, my love. *Adieu*... "

(She collapses and dies.)

(The stage lights darken as if the curtain has closed. There is some applause and the loud sound of whistles.)

(Exhausted, she rises, listens, then runs to the wings and says:)

Jarrett, they despise me! Don't open the curtains! I'll be pelted in the face with rotten eggs! Listen to that savage sound! Those whistles!

What? Whistles mean *approval* in America? You mean—they like me? ...They like me!

(She goes out onto the stage. The lights come up. The applause and whistles are overwhelming.)

(She puts her hands, palms together, to her lips, then opens her arms wide to embrace their applause.)

(She smiles broadly. She is drenched in admiration. She adores it.)

(She takes off her costume, and as the scene fades to the dressing room, she says to us:)

I am a magnificent success! They love me! The theater is sold out for all five weeks! Jarrett has arranged at my hotel for me to have a room with a balcony, and I appear on it and wave to admirers—as if I were royalty!

(She waves.)

When I left France, they said, "Why bring your work to America? They'd be more entertained by an elephant walking on bottles!"

But they're wrong. They should see my reviews!

(She takes out a series of clippings.)

"She is poetry itself." ... "She is a legend come to life." ... "She glows with the incandescence of a rocket!"

And my brass chest is beginning to glow as well—with the shimmer of gold.

(She shows us her brass chest, opens it and runs her fingers through the coins. Then she says to us:)

According to Harper's Weekly, I am the toast of New York. And I am. But no one will receive me. The Four Hundred of American society are keeping their houses closed to this French actress with the Semitic nose.

The American gentlemen who are such friends of mine when they come to Paris are leaving me strictly alone in their home town. I suspect their wives won't let them see me. I'm too "Frenchy". Ha! When those husbands come to Paris, they are more "Frenchy" than the French!

Snobs! Hypocrites! What do they know about art? They think Racine is a town in Wisconsin!

(She gets up.)

Thank God the New York run is over! The road tour is about to begin. For it, I have a magic vehicle waiting to carry me beyond the horizon. The Sarah Bernhardt Special. My private train.

(The lights change. She crosses, enters the train, and sits in its luxurious red velvet interior.)

It's like a mansion on wheels. It costs a fortune, but that's what I seem to be making in this country!

(The train sound begins. She looks at the countryside with field glasses.)

At last I'm in a land where I can breathe—and no one to tell me what to do, what part to play, or when I have to be at rehearsal. Vast horizons. Higher skies.

I'm free to savor the infinite delights of travel. In Boston, I walked on a whale. Such fun! Like skating on a mound of jelly! ...In Pittsburgh, I visited a steel mill and shouted *Phèdre* into a fiery furnace. ...At Niagara, I dashed out onto a rock in the middle of the torrent—and nearly gave poor Jarrett a heart attack!

I love this country. I love the openness, I love the speed. I love the postal service! No matter where I am, Maurice's letters find me!

(She takes up a letter from a tray, opens it and reads:)

"Dear *Maman*: I love the Christmas presents you sent me from America—especially the tin of beans from Boston. ...How many Indians have you seen?"

"Last week *Monsieur* Sarcey wrote in *Le Figaro* that you are a spoiled exhibitionist who will soon burn up the world and have no place to peddle her overwrought wares. He said the Comédie was well rid of you."

(Aside:)

The old bat!

(She continues reading:)

"I got out your silver sword from *Le Passant,* waited for him behind a tree in the Place Royale and challenged him to a duel. The coward was too afraid to fight, but don't worry, I'll challenge him again and again till he publicly apologizes."

"P S: Can you bring me a tomahawk? Love, Maurice."

(To us:)

Ah, my knight in shining armor! He learned something from all the times I went after my enemies with a whip! Like mother, like son! Isn't he brave!

(But then her mood changes.)

But what if the man he challenged had fought back? Maurice could have been killed! He's trying to frighten me, to get my attention. I know all the tricks. I've played them all myself.

When I was eight, I forced my mother to buy me a coffin. I'd lie in it nightly. The deep fear in her eyes, the fear of losing me, was the only satisfactory love I've ever known.

And now Maurice writes me across an ocean to tell me he is putting himself in jeopardy—for my sake!

(She looks at his photograph.)

How dare you follow me this way—to accuse me of leaving you? I had to!

Having a child is a mistake in my profession. And he knows. He knows no matter how many gifts I lavish on him, there are times I feel he should never have been born. Just as I know my mother felt the same way about me.

A child wants *all* a parent's life. And this I cannot give. So we play these games. He threatens me with self-destruction and I pretend not to know it is his child's voice crying, "Mama, love me!" He will never know I love him beyond anything this world could ever offer. But not, God help me, not beyond this driving necessity of my life.

(She calls to Marianne in the passageway:)

Marianne, tell them to stop the train. I want to buy Maurice a tomahawk.

What, no tomahawks in Cleveland?

(She paces. The train surges on relentlessly.)

Will this chugging monster never stop?

How far it is between things in America!

(To us:)

The schedule is brutal. We catch the train immediately after the performance. We sleep on the train, travel all day, arrive at the new town at six in the evening, go on at eight, come off at eleven and run to catch the train again. I have nightmares that one night we'll arrive in a town just at the time when the performance is supposed to be over!

(The train drives forward at tremendous speed. Marianne enters.)

Marianne, tell the cast to speed things up. We have to do four hundred miles tomorrow. ...And cut the scene before the last. Who will know?

(The train stops.)

Where are we? What play are we doing this evening?

(Crossing to the theater, she sees her Marguerite Gautier costume.)

Ah, *La Dame Aux Caméllias*. Some night I will go out in this costume and start playing Joan of Arc!

(She starts getting into costume.)

Jarrett, what is this "*Camille*" they say we're playing in this theater? The play is *La Dame Aux Caméllias*! The heroine is Marguerite Gautier! Who or what in God's name is "*Camille*"?

Why am I so upset? I'll tell you why. I look down from the stage and they're reading those translations you had printed. I'm playing to the tops of their heads!

But even if they *did* look up, what difference would it make? I could recite the Napoleonic Code in the middle of a love scene and they'd applaud!

(Performance music begins.)

You don't believe me? How much do you want to bet? One week's salary? ...Fine. It's a bet. Just stand there in the wings, Jarrett,—and watch!

(Carrying her Marguerite Gautier handkerchief, she goes out on stage:)

"Oh, Armand... It's true. I've known many men, but I have never known love—until you. Yes, I know what you feel for me, and I know—"

(She glances off stage at Jarrett. Then, in the middle of her love scene with Armand, she passionately begins to recite the Napoleonic Code:)

—"All orphans shall be supported by the state until their eighteenth year, my darling. ...The rights of primogeniture shall be rigidly observed. ...And, my adored one, all widows shall receive all their husband's pigs!"

(She ends as in a passionate embrace. Her performance is greeted with thunderous applause. She bows, comes offstage and says with cynicism:)

I've won my wager, Jarrett. ...Pay... *Merci.*

(The train sound begins. She enters the train and takes off her costume.)

Why in God's name am I wasting my talents? I give of myself every night, Jarrett. I gesture. I shout. And they applaud—just to prove to each other they understand French!

In Europe, I was a legitimate actress. What am I here?

I can't go on. Cancel tomorrow night's performance and let's stay here—wherever "here" is. Can't I have one night where the trees stand still outside my window?

Why can't we cancel? "Net profits?" "Gross?" What do those words mean? I don't understand.

(She notices her brass chest.)

Ah. Money. *That* I understand.

(She runs her fingers through the coins for a moment, then says:)

But it doesn't help. Nothing helps.

(Jarrett exits.)

(There is the yelping of a small dog. She pets him.)

Not even you, Hamlet, my sweet. ...Especially since you've found your Ophelia.

(The yelping of a second, higher pitched, small dog, then two dogs yelping together.)

(Angelo enters.)

Not even you, Angelo, my darling. Though I must admit, there are times when you do, every now and then, help me forget.

(She caresses him.)

How sweet you are. ...Do I love you? ...Well, of course I do! That's what I'm all about—love, love, loving!

(Suddenly, in shock:)

...Will I marry you!?

(She rises.)

Angelo, please, I'm not in the mood for jokes. ...Love and marriage are two different things! One I thrive on, the other makes me want to slit my throat! ... Now don't pout! When did I ever give you the impression that I would submit to being bound and gagged and broken? ... No, I'm not saying let's just be friends. I'm saying let's just be lovers—and not lower ourselves to the disgusting thought of being husband and wife! ...All right, go sleep in another car. See if I care!

(Angelo exits. She says to us:)

He'll be back. The poor thing's absolutely besotted with me. ...A proposal! Did he think I would take a vow to limit myself to just *one*? If you ever see me teetering on the edge of matrimony, shout a warning! Freedom is my watchword. Freedom! ...So why did I sign myself up to living in a box?!

(The train sound rises. She paces.)

Will nothing save me from this endless inescapable incarceration?!

(She notices another letter.)

Ah—another letter from Maurice!

(She opens it eagerly and reads:)

"Dear *Maman: Grandemère* gave me the gold sovereign you left me for my sixteenth birthday. ...I took it to the races. ...But don't worry. I'll return next week and win."

(She lowers the letter in despair, then says to herself:)

Don't think about it. Just keep travelling...

(The lights change. The train chugs on relentlessly. She paces back and forth like a caged animal.)

I am going mad in this confinement! I'm sick of America! Sick of the theaters! Sick of the trains! Sick of the food! Everything comes with beans!

I need room! Space! Air! My God, this is worse than the Comédie Française!

(Desperately, she says:)

I need something to console me in my cage.

(Suddenly there is a loud roar. She caresses her new pet tiger.)

You understand me, don't you, my darling César? You know what it's like to be cooped up behind bars. If only we could roam—you and I—through the jungle—

(He roars again. Marianne enters and scampers to the other side of the space, scared out of her wits.)

What's the matter with you, Marianne? He's only playing. Angelo doesn't mind my sleeping with a tiger under my bed, why should you? Has Angelo returned? Of course he has! Would a little thing like my refusing his *hand* keep us both from savoring all the rest? ...Now, come on, Marianne. Pat César on the head.

(Marianne tries. Suddenly César roars and jumps on Marianne, who runs out in holy terror.)

(She laughs and smacks César on the nose)

Oh, you naughty beast! ...Marianne! Come back! Come back! He was only playing!

(She hugs César, who lets out a satisfied purr.).

(Jarrett enters.)

Oh, Jarrett, what a stormy face! What can be upsetting you? ... So César bit the arm of a reporter. It was only a small bite. It made every paper in the country!

(César lets out a satisfied roar.)

Now don't tell me how to behave. The more I do, the more they love it. The more they love it, the more space we get in the press, the larger the audiences, the more gold!

I can do no wrong here! But if I do wrong, it gets me more benefits than doing right!

My name is plastered from one end of this country to the other—and not just on theater marquees!

(She opens a trunk and takes out one object after another.)

Look! Sarah soap... Sarah perfume... Sarah stockings... Sarah cigars... Sarah whiskey!

There's something about this country that responds to me, and I respond to it. We're one. We understand each other.

(She opens her brass chest and runs her fingers through her gold.)

Excesses? What excesses? If you want someone with the manners of a shop-girl, get a shop-girl. If you want someone who can bring thousands to the theater nightly, you get me. This is what I am! It's what they come to see. My work takes fire because my life does!

(He says something to her. She reacts in shock:)

My work is rotten? ...I beg your pardon—

(To us:)

He says he never expected to be managing a travelling circus—

(To him:)

Me, bizarre? In a country that writes "Carter's Little Liver Pills" on a mountain? ... Corrupted by America! I don't know what you mean! ...I'm betraying my art? Who are you to remind me of my artistic duty?

(To him:)

So what if the most distinguished theater critic in this country calls me "Sarah Barnum?!" ...What! ...You think he's right?!

(To him:)

Out! Get out before I feed you to César!

(César roars. Jarrett leaves and she pushes César out after him.)

(Alone, she says to us:)

I'm making money hand over fist for that man, and he has the temerity to come in here and tell me—

(Angelo enters.)

Oh, Angelo, my darling! Did you see Jarrett? Came in here playing his favorite role: God. He's just spent half an hour shouting at me that I've become a purveyor of cheap tricks, not an actress! If the wildness in me appeals to these Americans, so be it. If they exploit it, so what? That doesn't mean I've abandoned all my standards!

At least *you* understand, my darling. Thank God I have one person who will sympathize and—

(But instead of offering comfort, he chides her.)

You can't agree with him! You traitor! I don't know why I let you share my bed!

Disappointing there as well as on stage? ...You think I've treated you not as a lover but as an audience. ...Well, if so, I've put on some pretty damn good shows for you! ...I see. Not in the recent past. The same as on the stage.

(Icily:)

You may go. You are in my employ, you may remember! ...When I want the truth for my own good, I will ask for it!

(He goes. It is night. It has begun to rain heavily.)

Well, there seems to be a good deal of disapproval for my performances— vertical *and* horizontal.

(She looks into the mirror.)

What do you think, Bernhardt, can Jarrett and Angelo be right?

(She puts the mirror down.)

I am accused of being selfish—in private and in public. ...They say I think the only reason other people exist is to give me applause. ...They say I became an actress not to entertain but to feed my insatiable need for attention. ...I'm not an artist, I'm an exhibitionist. A whore who will do anything for money. A lazy, greedy, lying whore.

(To us:)

No, that's not true! ...I know I lie. But it's only because reality seems so tame to me. There's a wildness inside me—something that drives me till I nearly explode!

I want to seize the deepest secrets of existence and communicate them to others—but they always seem just beyond my grasp. As love is just beyond my grasp. I know the difference between being fawned over and being cherished. I know the difference between being applauded and being loved.

(To the mirror:)

If you loved, you could be loved in return.

(She puts the mirror down.)

Not me. Not Sarah. Never. No matter how many disguises I put on, I'm always there—the bastard Jewess. No matter who I become—Medea, Cleopatra, Iphigenia—they're always only me, the wandering soul without a name.

I think, if I push myself to the limits of existence, I may find me. But no matter how hard I look, all I find is this worthless heap of vanities and deceits.

(Tortured:)

I don't deserve to live!

(She hides her face.)

(There is a knock on the door. She is motionless. The knock is repeated. She cries:)

Go away!

(The knock becomes insistent. At last she cries out:)

All right! All right! One moment—

(She composes herself and opens the door.)

Jarrett—. ...What is it now? ...What emergency?

(Impatient, not really able to concentrate on what he is saying, she repeats by rote what he says:)

Lake Ponchartrain is swollen by the rains. The bridge across it is weakened by the flooding. If we cross it, we may be catapulted into the raging torrent. If we go another way, we'll reach New Orleans safely, but it will take an extra four or five days.

(Suddenly what he's saying hits her:)

Four or five more days in this rolling sardine can? ... Is there a chance the bridge may hold? ...Then for God's sake, take it! Get it over with! Quickly!

(He goes. Alone, she says:)

So we might be hurled into the lake, so be it. Perhaps the best thing I can do for the world is sink without a trace.

(They start over the water. The train begins to pick up speed.)

All my life I've been enamored of death. Now's the time to meet my lover.

(She lies on the train seat. The train sound gets louder, swifter:)

Almost over the water. ...Drown, Bernhardt! It's time!

(They pick up speed. She listens as the train goes faster and faster, it clatters ominously as it goes over the bridge and across the water.)

(The train sound becomes calmer, steadier. But instead of rejoicing, she says flatly:)

We're over. We made it over.

(She gets up and says dully:)

The worthless heap is sentenced to live.

(She sits down, depressed.)

The grand emergency was nothing. Nothing!

(Suddenly a rumbling sound begins. It gets louder and louder. She looks out the window. She hears a horrendous crash and a terrible roar.)

(She is nearly in shock)

My God...

(Slowly, she sits down.)

The bridge—actually—collapsed behind us. Nothing left! ...It never occurred to me we could actually—fall.

(She shakes her head as if coming out of a deep sleep.)

Did I really tell myself I wanted to go to the bottom? And take fifty people with me?

(Soberly, it all becomes clear to her.)

I've been playing at death as I've been playing at life—and at my work...

(She calls out:)

Stop the train! I'm calling a rehearsal!

(The train stops.)

(She puts on a shawl, gets out of the train and walks up and down outside the train calling up at the windows:)

Everybody up! Everybody out! I don't care if you are in your night clothes. Who will see you in this deserted bayou?

(The cast assembles.)

Mes amis, *Monsieur* Jarrett seems to think our work has gone to pieces—mine especially. *Monsieur* Angelo seems to agree. ...The gentlemen are right. We've been cheating our public and cheating ourselves. And this must stop immediately.

Acting isn't play, it's life. Life at the level beyond where anyone can live it. From now on, we must spare ourselves nothing. We must go to the core, to *life*.

Medea went to the very ends of human possibility. To portray her we must feel her torment in our veins, in our bones. We must go as far as she went—even farther.

I will not have anyone say I gave less than all in a performance—ever again! In a theater—or in a swamp!

(So saying, she steps forward and, wrenching a performance from her very sinews, she plays Medea:)

My lover has taken a royal bride.
And after all I did for him—killed for him!
I am to be sent into exile.
I am to be wrenched apart from my dear children!
Dear Gods! Witness my anguish!
For this, the bride will die!

I will send the children with gifts in their hands
To carry to her.
A finely woven dress and a golden diadem
And if she takes them and wears them upon her skin
She and all who touch the girl will die in agony.

I weep to think of what a deed I must do next.
For I must kill my own children.
My babies—for there is none who can give them safety.

Come, my hand, poor wretched hand, and take the sword.
Think of he who has brought you to this terrible deed.
Revenge! Revenge!

(Exhausted, she completes the scene.)

(There is a moment of silence, then, from somewhere off and above, comes the sound of one person applauding.)

(She looks up and off.)

Who's that? I didn't know we had an audience. ...Who's up there?

Is that our engineer?

(She calls up to him:)

That can't be tears, sir. ...From a husky old stoker like you?

You understood the scene? ... You didn't understand the scene. But it moved you without your knowing why it moved you.

Well, if you'd like me to have it—. It's a present I'd be honored to receive.

(She moves toward the wings and reaches upward. When she turns back to us, she is holding a battered blue and white striped trainman's cap. She looks at it and says:)

This gift—means more to me—than the cheers of thousands...

(She contemplates it for a moment, then says to us quietly:)

I thought I might find gold here. I found—myself.

(She raises the hat to her head, tipping it in a salute to the Trainman then says:)

Onward, *mes amis*! On to performances which will not only shake the rafters, but will shake the souls!

(A montage of sound and light in alternating effects as the triumphant tour continues, performances interspersed with train journeys: The train whistle sounds, the train speeds forward. Lights change to stage lighting. Applause rises, she bows. Lights change. Again the train whistle sounds, the train roars on, again the lights change to stage lighting. Applause rises. She bows.)

(Once more the train sound rises and stops. The lights change to bright daylight. Seagulls are heard, and band music playing a march by John Philip Sousa. She stands on the dock and says:)

Merci, *mes Américains!* What a glorious six months! I don't think I ever had a better time.

(She opens her brass chest and runs her fingers through a generous supply of gold coins.)

I could become seriously attached to this country. But for now, I must tear myself away. My homeland calls. Or, let me put it this way, they are *not* calling, so I'd better get back and remind them of my existence. But how splendid it has been to be here—in a place where they truly understand a declaration of independence!

(Hamlet barks.)

What's the matter, Hamlet?

(He barks again.)

Tell Ophelia to wait for you. No doubt about it, we shall return!

(The boat whistle sounds. The band begins to play The Marseillaise. *She picks up an American flag.)*

...Farewell, America!

(She stands with her brass chest in one hand and her American flag in the other. Hamlet barks happily. The Marseillaise rises. She waves her American flag.)

(Blackout)

END ACT ONE

ACT TWO

(Time: Sixth American Tour, First Farewell Tour, 1905)

(At rise:)

(BERNHARDT *makes a grand entrance wearing an extravagant fur coat. Business-like and in control, she is the Woman of Power. She displays the coat, then says to us:)*

BERNHARDT: Yes, it's real. Do you like it? I shot it myself.

Thanks to you, I have a theater of my own and an island of my own. For a year, much to my disbelief, I actually had a husband of my own. A handsome Greek diplomat—well—almost diplomat. An attaché who refused to become attached. He was the only man I'd ever met who wouldn't succumb to my charms, so of course I had to have him. I proposed. I know, I know, I swore no marriage, ever. But at least it was a new experience, though, thank heaven, a short one. After a few months I found I had to sell off all my jewelry to keep him in whiskey, cocaine and other women. So I bought the next best thing—a legal separation.

The French say my greatest love affair is with America. Some Americans say my greatest love affair is with cold cash. I say my greatest love affair is with Americans with cold cash.

This is my final tour. How much I regret it! My first tour was twenty-five years ago. I've been back every five years since then. But at sixty-one, you can't expect me to make another tour five years from now, can you?

What's that? You say I don't look a day over thirty? I know. Duse's not yet fifty and already she's decaying around the edges. But me—I can play every romantic lead I ever did.

(She turns to Marianne.)

Marianne, where's that man who's supposed to meet us? That Mister Shubert. Go and find him, will you? Sometime this century.

(Marianne exits. She says to us:)

She's so slow. ...Aging!

(Shubert enters from the other side.)

Ah, are you Mister Shubert? But you're so young!

(She calls, off:)

Never mind, Marianne! He's here.

(To Shubert:)

So, young Mister Shubert, I'm glad to meet you. ...You're privileged to be managing me this visit? Not at all. I always go with the man who makes the highest offer.

Are the press releases ready? ...And my private train? ...Good. ...Make sure the posters say "Farewell Tour" on top. I want every man, woman and child in America to know it's their last and final chance to see me act.

I think this tour promises to be enormously successful, Mister Shubert. It has to be. I have so many people depending on my largesse. My company. My son. Maurice and his racing! His gambling!

(To us:)

Can you believe I have a forty-two year old son? He manages my theater for me.

The Théâtre Sarah Bernhardt. And he's presented me with two fine granddaughters. *Legitimate.* The first case of that in our family for generations!

Now let me see the itinerary, Mister Shubert. Well, then, go get it. ...Of course I'm not too tired to see it now.

(She takes a step and we see that she is limping. She rubs her knee and says to him:)

This? It's nothing. Go on. I tell you it's nothing.

(Shubert exits.)

(She sits and says to us:)

A ridiculous accident. Happened a few weeks ago, in Rio de Janeiro. The last act of *La Tosca*. I had to jump from the parapet to kill myself—and I nearly did. The stagehands had forgotten to place the mattress on the floor to break my fall and I smashed down on my right knee. It's a mess—but it will soon be better.

(Shubert enters. She picks up a list.)

Ah, thank you, Mister Shubert. Let me see where we'll be going.

(She studies the itinerary.)

Rochester, Des Moines, San Antonio, San Francisco—but, Mister Shubert, in most of these cities you've forgotten to write down the names of the theaters where we'll be playing. ...What do you mean, you don't know yet? Are you telling me the bookings aren't set?

The Shubert Theatres are set? Marvelous! How many Shubert theaters are there? Thirteen. ...Mister Shubert, since we are playing over a hundred cities from here to California, that is not quite sufficient! You were to arrange—

I appreciate that, Mister Shubert. I am aware that most of the theaters in the country are owned by the Klaw-Erlanger Syndicate. I thought you were going to give them a little competition.

You tried. ...Do I understand you've invited me here and can't book me into theaters? ...Oh, you *can* book me into theaters. Thank you. ...Under one condition. ...What condition? ...That I give the Syndicate twenty-five percent of the gross? *My* gross?!

(She paces in fury.)

My dear little man—and I do mean *little* man—you must be joking! They get, for the presence of Bernhardt, full houses, a booking fee, an advertising fee, a percentage of the producer's share—and they want a quarter of my gross?

I don't care if they demand it of all actors, it is illegal! I thought you had a new anti-trust law here. ...I see. Theater is exempt because it is not a necessity of life. Well, theater *is* a necessity of life, Mister Shubert.

No, I will *not* call my friend Teddy Roosevelt. I solve my problems alone. So *do something*, Mister Shubert!

(The lights change. The sound of a train rises then fades. She is seen in a circle of light. She throws a scarf around her neck and says:)

It never occurred to me that at the zenith of my career I would be playing in skating rinks! In stables! I've played in beer halls, in school auditoriums, tabernacles, barns, armories and city halls. At the Poinciana Hotel in Palm Beach, I played *La Tosca* in the dining room!

(She snaps her thumb nail against her upper teeth in a rude gesture.)

Death to the Syndicate!

And now, unable to find a barn or a beer hall in Dallas, Mister Shubert is arranging for me to play in a tent! The French always called my tours a travelling circus. They'll be overjoyed to find they're right!

(The lights change. She calls:)

Marianne! Help me into this costume!

(To us:)

Where is that woman?

(She gets into her Joan of Arc costume herself, saying to us:)

They tell me there's a cowboy out there who rode three hundred miles to see me. As he got his ticket, he asked, "By the way, what does this Bernhardt do—sing or dance?"

...I *act*, God help me. And they've come to see a sideshow.

(She massages her knee. Marianne enters.)

Oh, Marianne, it's one of those nights when my knee is stiff. What am I going to do? I won't be able to kneel. Joan of Arc has to kneel.

(The lights change. She picks up her Joan of Arc banner. She goes on in the tent. She is greeted by wild Texas cheers. When they recede, she falls to her knees and begins:)

"Dear God, in spite of myself I tremble at the destiny which awaits me. Into my hands you have placed the fate of France. Into my woman's soul, infuse the strength of man."

(She rises and stands holding her banner.)

"Oh, Joy! Once more do I behold my banners flying! I see the face of God! I hear His voice from Heaven! While Joan still stands France never shall be conquered! Lead on, my soul! Once more—to victory!"

(She stands in the pose of victory. Suddenly she is overwhelmed by wild hoots and Texas cheers! They go on and on.)

(At last, as the stage lights dim and the applause fades, she comes off into the wings and says to Marianne:)

I knelt, Marianne! Did you see that? I went down on my knees, and it didn't hurt at all!

Oh, Marianne! It's like the second coming! I was Joan's age! Nineteen! And they believed it! This American earth—I swear it has brute strength in it that I can borrow! Especially the earth of Texas!

(She plants her banner in the earth of Texas, stands in front of her tent and says to the press:)

Gentlemen of the press... I love my tent. I would like to roam the world like a gypsy, sleeping in a tent and dining on cornpone and beans!

(They applaud.)

(She returns to her dressing room. As she changes out of her Joan of Arc costume, she says to us:)

People swarm to see me from all over the countryside. Special trains bring thousands directly to my tent. The Syndicate claims it's a grandstand play. That no one can see or hear in my tent, that I'm doing it all for money. Well, what are *they* in business for?

They're jealous because we seat four thousand a night—twice as many as any of their theaters. This is the most successful tour I've ever had!

(She picks up a cowboy hat.)

And I owe it all to the Syndicate! Heartfelt thanks!

(She hears the buzzing of voices outside.)

What is it? What's going on? What's happened?

(She listens a moment then says to us:)

The District Attorney of the State of Texas has declared the Klaw-Erlanger trust illegal and insists they let us play in their theaters for a reasonable fee!

(She throws the cowboy hat into the air.)

Yahoo! Sarah the Trust Buster! Me and Teddy Roosevelt! The tyrants have been vanquished. Theatres are open to me everywhere. And I must say goodbye to my precious tent.

(The lights change. We hear the sound of the train.)

Everywhere I go, I think "This is the last time, the last time I shall see this." ... I return to San Francisco to see, one last time, that lovely city. But it has been shattered by an earthquake. I play a benefit for the earthquake victims—and weep. ...On my way East, everywhere there are new honors, and new and old friends to whom I must say goodbye.

(The lights change. She puts on a pailletted frock. We hear café music. She says to us:)

And now, at the end of the tour—New York. ...Hostesses who would never speak to me before shower me with invitations. And all of them—all the Four Hundred—turn out to honor me at my farewell dinner at the Café des Beaux Arts.

(The music fades. There is applause. She addresses the guests:)

Ladies and gentlemen, do you realize that I've spent nearly one-quarter of my adult life in this country? The French think I'm utterly mad. They still think you are a land of hayseeds and hooligans, where everyone either chews tobacco or totes a gun.

Absurd! No one is more canny than the Innocent American. As a matter of fact, I believe you are destined—no matter what one says, no matter what one does, alas!—to become the first nation of the earth.

(Applause)

Thank you for making this last tour the happiest, the most successful, the most beautiful. ...Although you will never see me here again—remember me.

(She holds out her arms in her characteristic gesture and says:)

Farewell, America!

(There is applause. The café music rises. She exits.)

(The lights change. The music segues into band music.)

(The lights change again. Eighth American Tour, Third Farewell Tour—1913-1914.)

(She enters in a cloth coat with fur collar. She says to us:)

I changed my mind.

(It is seven years later. 1913. She is sixty-nine. She is stooped, immobile. Her face—what we can see of it beneath her shawl—is powdered to hide the ravages of time.)

America is my life blood! And every now and then I need a transfusion.

I don't think three goodbye tours is too much. Do you?

I'll tell you the real reason I'm here. Do you remember my wonderful theater, Le Théàtre Sarah Bernhardt? It hardly supports me anymore. My dear son, Maurice, is bleeding me dry. His losses at roulette, at baccarat—I can't sustain them any longer.

I tried to cure him. But he threatened to kill himself. And so—to keep him alive, I am forced to make tour after tour.

Marianne, where's the press? Surely they knew the hour of my arrival.

(She starts to cross. We see, for the first time, she has great difficulty walking.)

This never could have happened when my dear Jarrett was alive. He died on tour with me some years ago.

(The reporters enter.)

Ah, gentlemen of the press, you almost missed me. I was just about to leave for my hotel. ...Why yet another farewell tour? The last two were just rehearsals. This will definitely be my last. As a matter of fact, I'm traveling with my coffin.

(To us:)

Just a ruse. To fool the eye of heaven. The truth is, I have never felt so young! If you didn't know I was—sixty-nine—and a greatgrandmother, you would take me for thirty! I have been endowed by God with an ageless face. That's what Lou Tellegen says. And when a young man tells you that, one must believe him.

(Lou enters.)

Ah, Lou, come here! Gentlemen, I want you to meet my new leading man. ...How old is he? Thirty-five. What is this American obsession with numbers? All you need to know is he is tall and blond, has eyes of Delft blue, and is a very promising actor. Mister Edson, my advance man, will give you his biography.

Yes, it's true: this time I'm appearing in vaudeville. Mister Martin Beck asked me and I finally said, "Yes, but not between the monkeys!"

Mister Beck is opening his new Palace Theatre here in New York in April. So I will start my tour in California and climax the tour by playing the beautiful new Palace when I return.

(Suddenly, she breaks off the interview, saying:)

Now, gentlemen, why don't you go off with Mister Tellegen—and find out all about him. Go on, go on.

(They go. When they have gone, she cries out:)

Marianne! The ether! Where's the ether? ...Never mind. I've found it.

(She finds the bottle in her bag, applies ether to her knee, and says to Marianne:)

I don't want them to see how badly it pains me. They mustn't know. And Lou mustn't know.

(The lights change. We hear the sound of the train.)

(She limps onto the train. This train is not as lavishly decorated as her earlier one. As it travels relentlessly, she says:)

Edson, why don't they come? Last night the scene was *La Tosca*, the actress was La Bernhardt, and the audience was *Les Misérables*! ...Everybody keeps asking, why don't I do Ibsen? I couldn't act Ibsen. He writes about ordinary people. I am not ordinary. ...They liked my plays before. Why don't they like them now?

(Marianne enters and starts to raise the blind.)

No, Marianne. Don't pull up the blind! Every inch of America looks just like the last!

(She picks up a newspaper.)

Edson, what kind of publicity is this? "Madame Sarah Bernhardt claims her greatest tribute came when she saw two one-armed men banging their remaining hands together to applaud her." That's not funny! ... Who is this Geraldine Farrar? Her picture is twice the size of mine in all the papers. ... An opera singer! ...She's stealing my audiences. Every city we play in, the audience is with her across the street.

(The lights change. She enters her dressing room where she sees a bouquet of camellias.)

Get those out of here! If I see another camellia, I will vomit!

(She says:)

Marianne, how is the house? ... Half full? You mean half empty. Well, maybe people don't want to see Sarah Bernhardt on the same bill with a dancing dog and one Mister McCullough singing, *It's a Long Way to Tipperary*! ... I hear the Palace Theatre has opened and isn't doing well. You watch, when I arrive, I'll finish it off for good!

Where's Lou? Why doesn't he come to see me after each performance any more? Where does he go? Where is he—every afternoon?

(Lou enters.)

Lou, my darling— ...That will be all, Marianne.

(Marianne goes.)

Yes, Lou. I've seen the notices. That's no reason to avoid me—.

So they say you're "worse than mediocre", what does it matter? ...Yesterday's review? No. I haven't looked at it yet.

(She picks up the newspaper and reads.)

"Mme. Bernhardt was wrapped in drapery from head to toe. The young and handsome actor who enveloped her so tenderly in his arms was decidedly incongruous."

That's bad for me, not for you. What does it matter what they say? If I listened to the critics, I would have killed myself long ago.

It's all nonsense! Look at this—it says you and I are going to be married! You see? Rubbish! ...Lou— Lou, darling—

(But he has stormed out, slamming the door. She says to us:)

They have no eyes. Lou and I are perfect as the lovers. We are *perfect*.

(After a moment, she picks up a mirror. She steals a glimpse, then takes a long hard look at herself. Finally, she says:)

I *am* the freak. Sarah Barnum. The oldest woman in the world.

(She looks off toward where Lou exited.)

And him. With his youth...his beauty... Perhaps, because that's what I see when I look at him, I've imagined that's what he sees when he looks at me...

Forty years ago, I played Phèdre—an older woman in love with a younger man. But I didn't know what I was saying. ...I didn't know what she was feeling—until now.

(Still seated, she begins quietly, and full of feeling, the scene from Phèdre:*)*

Fool, where am I, and what have I done?
Where have I let my mind and wishes wander?
I've betrayed the husband to whom faith binds me.
Against all the laws of nature,
I've fallen in love with his son.

(She rises and continues:)

Dear Gods, my passion rages at his beauty.
I shudder and I burn at his dark name.
He passes, and my very soul is troubled.
My eyes see no more. I cannot speak.

(She takes a shawl, a portion of her Phèdre *costume, and puts it over her. The soliloquy in the dressing room becomes a stage performance:)*

I vow to turn away, but I am helpless.
I see him everywhere in his father's face.

I begged to have my beloved enemy banished.
But now he has returned, once more I feel the flame.

Cruel fate, the boy is blind to all my feelings.
I despise my life. My passion is horror.
And the only release, the only peace—is death.

(The end of the performance is greeted with great applause. Serious and moved, she bows, accepting the ovation.)

(The applause fades.)

(She collapses. She falls to the floor and pounds upon it in agony, clawing at her leg in excruciating pain. She cries:)

My God! Ether! Ether!

(She crawls to a corner of the stage where she has hidden an ether bottle and cloth. She applies the ether, then cries:)

It's not enough! Ether isn't enough! ... Sometimes I think I'd rather have it off than endure this agony!

I remember it as if it were yesterday. I remember standing on the parapet as Tosca, seeing there was no mattress below and *making the decision to jump.* I remember—*knowing*— "It will hurt." Then I jumped. ...But I didn't expect the pain to last forever.

(With difficulty, she rises and holds onto the couch. She sits for a moment, then calls:)

Edson!

(He enters.)

Edson, you'll have to cancel my next engagement—my engagement at the Palace. ...Why?

(She rises and demonstrates, with self-horror:)

I cannot walk! I cannot cross a stage!

No, you may *not* say I am ill! I won't give them the satisfaction! ...Tell them anything you like—except the truth.

(He goes. Marianne enters.)

Marianne, where's Lou? Why is he never here when I need him?

(Her eyes follow Marianne.)

Marianne? What have you hidden behind the dressing table? ...Show it to me. ...All right, if you won't, I'll get it myself!

(With great difficulty, she crosses and gets a newspaper. She reads:)

"Was that a purple crutch we glimpsed under Sarah's cloak on stage in *L'Aiglon* last evening? It's bad enough we have to endure her playing a boy of eighteen, but must she attempt to milk our sympathies by parading a host of fake ailments? Are there no depths to which this absurd relic won't sink in her endless attempts to relieve us of our cash?"

(She lowers the paper slowly.)

...Where do they get the license for such cruelty? ...What no human being would ever say to another in private, these strangers, who have no idea who I am or what I am, say to thousands in the press. What makes them think they have the right—? Do they think I am beyond all feeling?

When I first began to raise my head above the crowd, I never knew what venom that would draw. It never occurred to me, just by distinguishing myself, what a tremendous force I was creating in the world—to bring me down.

(She looks down at the paper again, then cries out:)

A purple crutch! ... That was a riding crop, you bastard!

(Another sentence in the paper catches her eye:)

"And why, at sixty-nine, does she insist on playing pants parts? Is it not enough that we have to suffer through this old hag playing *ingénues*? Why does she also think she has the right to usurp the parts that belong to men, particularly young men?"

(She puts down the paper.)

I'll tell you why, you idiot with the brain of a pea! It's because there are emotions which belong to men and to women which women never get a chance to play! Playwrights put into women's mouths only the simpering sentiments they think belong to women. I insist on my right to encompass *all* feelings—including the feelings and emotions of men—especially *young* men!

(She calls out:)

Edson! Get in touch with Mister Wood, the manager of the Palace. We are going to keep our engagement.

What will I play? I will play *Hamlet*. No. Not Gertrude. *Hamlet*! ...My leg? Damn the leg! If I have to play the Prince of Denmark hopping on one leg like a guinea hen, we will play!

(Music. Drums begin.)

(She removes her skirt to reveal black tights. She puts on a black doublet, costuming herself as Hamlet. With great difficulty, she moves to the side of the stage as the lights change to stage performance lights. Holding on to stage furniture to support herself, she begins:)

O what a rogue and peasant slave am I!
Is it not monstrous that this player here,
But in a fiction, in a dream of passion,

Could force his soul so to his own conceit
That from her working all his visage wanned,
Tears in his eyes, distraction in his aspect,
A broken voice, and his whole function suiting
With forms to his conceit? And all for nothing!
For Hecuba!

(Still supporting herself on furniture, she takes a step toward center stage.)

What's Hecuba to him, or he to Hecuba,
That he should weep for her? What would he do
Had he the motive and the cue for passion
That I have? He would drown the stage with tears
And cleave the general ear with horrid speech....

(Again, supporting herself on furniture, she takes another step toward center stage.)

Yet I,
A dull and muddy-mettled rascal, peak
Like John-a-dreams, unpregnant of my cause,
And can say nothing....
Am I a coward?
Who calls me villain? Breaks my pate across?
Plucks off my beard and blows it in my face?...
Bloody, bawdy villain!
Remorseless, treacherous, lecherous, kindless villain!
O, vengeance!

(Forgetting her need to hold onto something for support, she takes center stage.)

Why, what an ass am I!...
I have heard that guilty creatures sitting at a play
Have by the very cunning of the scene
Been struck so to the soul that presently
They have proclaimed their malefactions....
I'll have these players
Play something like the murder of my father
Before mine uncle. If he do blench,
I'll know my course....
The play's the thing
Wherein I'll catch the conscience of the King.

(She finishes with great emotion. She holds her pose. Then, suddenly, there is a great ovation.)

(Assisting herself only slightly, she moves out of the spotlight and comes, as if offstage, to overwhelming applause. Taking off her doublet and putting on her skirt, she says:)

I've saved the Palace Theater! I've assured it a long life. I. Only I. After all these years, no one but I can bring as many people to the theater. What do they come to see? The actress? No. The Legend. *Quand même*. In spite of everything. I go on. And they come. They come...

(As she removes her make-up in the dressing room, she hears someone.)

Lou? Is that you? ...Strange, isn't it, to be going home in triumph after all. ...Still, I'll be happy to be going back to France, won't you?

What do you mean, you're not going back? ...You're going to be *married*—. ...To whom, may I ask? ...Geraldine Farrar. ...Ah, well, why not? After Sarah, you have the best references!

(Bitterly:)

You'll treasure our memories? What's there to treasure? You're a rotten actor, an opportunist, and no marvel as a lover! Out! Get out!

(She throws her hairbrush after him. He goes. She says to us:)

Well, that was a fine comic interlude, I must say.

(As she gets into her cloth coat, she says:)

He's getting married—to an opera singer! Well, she can sing him to sleep!

(We hear sounds of voices outside.)

Who's out there? ...The press?

(As she slowly puts on her scarf, she says:)

They need a final word. How can I sum up this journey?

(Suddenly she covers her face. She is weeping. But it lasts only a moment. She pulls herself together as the press enters. Her tone is tinged with irony as she says:)

Gentlemen, how good of you to come to say goodbye. ...Oh, yes, it's been a triumph, my friends. Every trip to America is like going from strength to strength, from peak to peak.

...Another tour of the States in the future? Out of the question. My coffin's going back empty this time. I don't want to press my luck.

So—for the last time—goodbye. Goodbye. Remember Sarah.

(She starts to leave. Marianne comes to help. She cries:)

No, Marianne! I don't need your assistance!

(With great difficulty, she starts out, stumbles, then, after limping a few steps, turns and says, with a tinge of bitterness:)

Farewell, America.

(The boat whistle sounds. She exits.)

(The lights change. A World War I march begins. Ninth American Tour, Final Farewell

Tour, 1916-18)

(When the lights come on again, she is discovered sitting on a trunk, wearing a short cape. Her legs are covered by a lap robe.)

(She is grand, ancient, sublime, impressive. It is 1916. She is seventy-two. Her right leg has been amputated.)

(There are cheers and applause as she greets people on the dock.)

Good heavens! What a reception! Thank you, my friends, thank you. You used to come to see the strange lady who sleeps in a coffin; now I think you've come to see the strange lady who has only one leg.

Barnum's offered me ten thousand dollars to display the thing—but you know how I hate publicity!

(She laughs.)

You mustn't let this bother you, it doesn't bother me. I'm like a wounded veteran. Some say I had it off to be in fashion. But, believe me, I have seen the war wounded, and that is not an enviable thing to be.

How silent you are! As if I were returning from the grave! I know what you must all have said: "Alas, poor Sarah, she'll never act again!" But here I am, about to begin a tour of ninety-one cities. ...You don't even ask the usual question. About my age. I'm seventy-two.

You remember my son? Maurice? We're now the best of friends. He's stopped gambling.

I beg your pardon? ...No, I'm not travelling with my coffin this time. This time, *mon ami*, death is not a jest.

Someone said, "France has given America two great gifts—the Statue of Liberty and Sarah Bernhardt." Look! There she is—with the torch in her hand. Overacting like me.

I still feel it—the colossal life of this country! The constant hurtling toward tomorrow.

The fast new trains—

(The lights change. The sound of the train begins. She removes her cape.)

(She sits on the train looking out the window at the passing cities:)

Boston, Chicago, Denver, San Francisco—

(As the journey continues, she says to us:)

Ninety-one cities! ...Do you wonder why I bother to go on?

I am in love with the miracle of theater.

The theater is the country of *le mot juste*, where I do not *wish* I had the right word, I always have it.

In the theater, I can be anyone under the sun. I can be man or woman, young or old, Queen or commoner, eternally beautiful. I can live in any time, any place.

In the theater, I can live exquisite moments not once, but a thousand times. I can die and rise again. I can know what's in the future.

In the theater, sorrows are pretend sorrows, erased, impermanent. And love, the most fleeting, the most evanescent of emotions, endures forever, without end.

(Marianne enters.)

No, Marianne, don't pull down the blinds. I want to see every rock, every blade of grass. ...The Pacific... The California hills...

(She picks up a small box and, as she speaks, she takes out of it one by one various props and mementos: the rose from Adrienne Lecouvreur, *a dagger from* Tosca, *a camellia, her Marguerite Gautier handkerchief.)*

Life confuses, but theater illuminates. Life destroys, but theater resurrects. Of all the arts, theater comes closest to creating life, and that makes the gods angry. That's why they make a life on the stage so hard: they're jealous of our power. And yet, in those rare moments on stage when revelation happens, I think the gods look on and secretly applaud us.

(She takes out of the box the trainman's cap.)

Do you wonder, then, that as long as I'm alive, I choose to live within the theater? Can you think of a better life than a life on the stage?

(The lights change and suddenly take on a nightmare quality. The train sound picks up speed.)

What's the matter, Marianne, are we headed East already? Why do you move so fast? You're always speeding! Where are we going in such a hurry?

(Blackout. The train sound increases, screeches and suddenly cuts off. When the lights come on, she has a white sheet over her lap.)

Mount Sinai hospital! That was not on my itinerary. ...An operation for uremia. That was not among the scenes I planned to play. The doctors say I must stay absolutely still or I won't heal correctly.

(She looks around her. She is isolated in a white light, everything is silent.)

This is not the same as when I was practicing in my coffin. Perhaps Time, for an actor, can't really be confounded after all. When a writer dies, he lives. Molière is Molière forever. But what will I be?

I only live—as long as I can act.

(She tries to rise, but falls back.)

I'm supposed to play my farewell performance of *La Dame Aux Camèllias* at the Brooklyn Academy of Music. They're expecting me. I mustn't let them down.

(She says, with deep determination:)

The secret of my life is *will*. You've been with me a long time, Marianne, and you know it. I *will* to do it. I *will* do it!

Quand Même. In spite of everything.

(She throws the white sheet off. She picks up her Marguerite Gautier handkerchief.)

(The music begins. The lights change to stage lighting. She reclines and begins the scene. She is sublimely beautiful:)

"How can I smile, Armand? Because I'm happy. I'm dying, but I'm happy, too. What a strange life this first one is. I wonder what it will be like—the second? ...Speak of me sometimes, won't you? Armand, give me your hand. Believe me, it is not hard to die."

"Ah, it's so strange. I'm not suffering any more. I feel better, so much better than I have ever felt before. ...I'm going to live!"

(She leans back slowly, doing her death scene. Applause begins. But, just before she would expire, she stops. The music and applause fade, the lights change. The scene becomes reality again.)

(She lowers the handkerchief, turns to us and says:)

In the theater, I can die and rise again. In the theater, I am forever young. In the theater, I can know what's in the future...

(The lights change again, to daylight.)

(The Marseillaise begins.)

(She puts a cape over her shoulders.)

(She is once more on the dock, holding her Marguerite Gautier handkerchief.)

(She holds up a hand and the crowd becomes silent to hear her. She says to us:)

Ah, my friends, it's good of you to come to see me off. But don't say such flattering things, you make me feel as if I'm dead!

Don't bury me yet. There's so much I want to do. I would like to climb a mountain, ride a buffalo! Why not?

I'm planning to make a film. ...And on stage I'm planning to play Mephistopheles. I'm going to take a crack at the devil before he takes a crack at me.

The news looks good today. Now that you've joined with us, I'm sure the war will soon be ended. I want not to have to think of U-boats my next time over.

Oh, you don't expect me to come back? Well, you didn't expect it last time and you were mistaken. I could say, "I shall never return!"—but you know how I lie. I'm such a liar. I may even be twenty-one. I may even have two legs!

Or I may be immortal! I am—as long as you remember me.

I'll remember you, my dear friends, wherever I am. Always. I cannot say goodbye to my Yankees. I can only say—*au revoir*. It means—till we meet again. You'll all be here, won't you?

You are—so kind, so youthful, so enthusiastic, so handsome, so generous, so affectionate, so—beloved.

(*She looks at us, knowing it is for the last time. She says, quietly, with great love:*)

Farewell, America.

(*The light fades on* SARAH BERNHARDT.)

(*Blackout*)

END OF PLAY

ELEANOR OF AQUITAINE

ELEANOR OF AQUITAINE, optioned three times for Broadway and London production, was seen in staged readings at the O'Neill Theatre Center in New London, Connecticut and at Playwrights Horizons, New York City.

CHARACTERS & SETTING

Eleanor of Aquitaine
Louis VII of France
Henry II of England

The following roles may be doubled:
Thibault of Champagne
Geoffrey de Rancon
Bernard de Ventadour
Rosamund
Nurse
Abbé
Two Nuns
Young Henry
Richard
Geoffrey
John

Some of the actors in the roles above can be included in the ensemble to play:
Soldiers, Crusaders, Amazons, Attendants, Litter-Bearers, Pages, Messengers, Merchants, Poets, Members of the Court, Citizens of France and England, Servant Girls, Young Bride and Groom.

Cast size: three principals (one female, two male) and a dozen or more ensemble players (a minimum of four females and the others male)

Time: The Twelfth Century.

Place: Europe and the Middle East

Setting: Open. Simple. Suggestions rather than details.

The scenes of the play flow into one another. Changes of time, place or action should be suggested by lighting.

The characters' lands are often in evidence. These should be like pieces of a giant jigsaw puzzle, able to be carried and fitted into place.

ACT ONE

(At rise: An empty stage. Darkness)

(From somewhere upstage, a NUN *of advanced age enters, her clothing in disarray. Two very young* NUNS *follow, impeccably clothed. The ancient* NUN *is* ELEANOR OF AQUITAINE.*)*

ELEANOR: Ties! Panels! Flaps! ...If it takes all this time to get into a nun's habit, when do you have time to pray?

Come, come. Help me into it—even though I know you don't approve. Eleanor of Aquitaine in a nun's suit? I could see you both cringe a little when you had to look at this ancient flesh of mine. It's so unholy! So obviously "trespassed on" by men.

Don't blush. It's the way the generations renew themselves—that unholy trespassing. I renewed the generations ten times. Ah, you approve of that.

What is it then you disapprove of? Oh, you're not allowed to disapprove. You're only concerned with my salvation. Why is it, then, that all you can think of are my sins?

The sins of Eleanor. What was the worst? Her pride? Her gaiety? Her curiosity? Her good looks? Or was the worst of her sins her refusal to live out her life as a lady rabbit, her insistence on being more than just Adam's reproductive rib?

Is that the unholy, uncleansable part of me? Is that the sin I'll be flogged in hell for? Wonderful! Marvelous! Let them flog away!

(With rising emotion) It may be so, that the survival of the world depends on most women being docile—on their bearing children, spinning the flax, boiling the soup, and giving kissing comfort to the men they marry. But the survival of the world also depends on some woman, perhaps one a century, who refuses to believe she is only a carved addendum to Adam, who can't understand why, if her belly is serving her country, she can't throw in her head as well, who can't understand why, if she sees something that desperately needs to be done, she has to swear not to do it, has to confine her hands to plaiting her hair, her tongue to moistening her painted lips, her body to kneeling, reclining and dancing, while all around her the world is crying out for a being who can—

(She breaks off.) Ah, but I mustn't go on. You have an innocence that mustn't be cracked. Not under twenty. I had that innocence, too, at your age.

Impossible, you think? Ah, if only you could have been alive then to see me. I was so pure that my voice could shatter diamonds, so pure that hard truths, spoken in my presence, would dissolve in the air before they reached my ears. I could not hear them. What a spectacle I was! How God must have laughed at me! At the time, long ago, when I was first to meet my future husband, God must have put aside His labors and watched me all that day, laughing, to see a female creature so utterly certain of the promise of His earth.

(The sunlight of Poiters floods in behind her. ELEANOR's *symbol appears: a golden lion on a red ground. Her lands are illuminated.)*

(Simultaneously, the young NUNS *release* ELEANOR *from her nun's habit. It comes away from her in one piece. As it does, she becomes young, wearing the simple but beautiful dress of a girl. The* NUNS *exit.)*

(A sound of trumpets is heard. ELEANOR *runs back and peers off toward the origin of the sound. Her* NURSE *enters.)*

(The trumpets sound again, a little nearer.)

ELEANOR: I have a destiny, Nursey. And it begins today!

NURSE: It's wonderful to be somebody whose destiny is announced by trumpets. But what do you do if the trumpets play off key?

ELEANOR: Those notes are not off key! They are as true as bird song, as true as the truest note of the truest minstrel! The King of France, the Prince of France, and five hundred knights have come all this way to fetch me to Paris!

NURSE: To fetch—or carry, if you won't go willingly.

ELEANOR: Why shouldn't I be willing to marry the son of the King of France?

NURSE: I don't know, dear. I haven't seen him.

ELEANOR: What a grump you are today! Is it because two weeks from now I'll have another confidant? A *husband*?

NURSE: Some husbands don't mind playing confidant. Most prefer to play at something else.

(Trumpets sound again.)

ELEANOR: Nearer! They're coming nearer! Can you see them yet?

NURSE: Not yet.

ELEANOR: A few more minutes—

NURSE: Eleanor, have you any idea why the King of France wants this marriage?

ELEANOR: I think he's heard about my face. That I've never once had a single pimple!

NURSE: Girl child—

ELEANOR: Or perhaps he's a snob, and he knows my blood is one-tenth straight from Charlemagne!

NURSE: My dear—

ELEANOR: Or maybe he'd just like to tie the bond a little tighter between the Kingdom of France and its Duchy of the Aquitaine. And what better way to make the Duchy *really* part of France than to marry the Duchy's Duchess to his son?

NURSE: That's it. That's *all* of it.

ELEANOR: I think I'm quite a bargain. My lands are twice the size of the King's!

NURSE: If I were you, I wouldn't mention it too often in his presence.

ELEANOR: I'll bet the Prince imagines that I'm bald and toothless! Isn't he going to be pleasantly surprised!

NURSE: Eleanor, before he comes, there are some things I must tell you—

ELEANOR: Can you see them yet?

NURSE: Just a bank of dust on the other side of the river.

ELEANOR: The Prince and I are going to be the rage of Paris! Just think of all the things we'll do and see!

NURSE: Things won't be the same on the Île de France as they are here in the south.

ELEANOR: I know. In the north they don't have olive trees, or figs, or sunshine—

NURSE: I mean something more than that. I mean that as a bride, Eleanor, you may have to adapt— ...Oh, why was this premarital talk left to *me*, I wonder? Why didn't your father and grandfather advise you first, and *then* die?

ELEANOR: Are you going to tell me about love, then?

NURSE: Is there something you want to ask?

ELEANOR: No. I know all there is to know about it.

NURSE: Who told you?

ELEANOR: No one. I've been listening for years beneath the stairs.

NURSE: The thing I want to tell you about has nothing to do with what you can pick up by hiding in stairwells. It's a special part of the marriage ceremony. A mystic word. A word that's never been spoken in your presence—

ELEANOR: I can feel the beats of their horses!

NURSE: The word, Eleanor, —is *obey.*

ELEANOR: "*Oh-Bay!*" What a funny word! It's too much like a donkey sound to mean anything!

NURSE: It means doing what's asked of you—no less, no more.

ELEANOR: I have always done what's been asked of me!

NURSE: The first thing you were asked was to be born a boy. You refused. Ever since, you've been going in your own directions!

ELEANOR: Where my father showed me—

NURSE: And he's to blame, too. Bringing you up as if you were the son he was never granted. Giving you the freedom of the fields and the highways—

(The sound of trumpets)

ELEANOR: They're getting very near.

NURSE: It's true. I can see them.

ELEANOR: Can you make out the faces?

NURSE: *(Nods)* They're not far from the gates of the Palace.

ELEANOR: Nurse—

NURSE: Yes?

ELEANOR: Does the Prince look happy?

NURSE: And how in the name of mercy would I know which one is the Prince?

ELEANOR: He must be wearing white, with golden sleeves, and the fleur-de-lis on his breast. He carries a sword, and a shield emblazoned with the figure of a unicorn. On his head is a helmet of silver, with plumes as high as the heavens. But even if he were dressed in rags you could tell the Prince from the others, because no one comes higher than his eyes.

NURSE: He may not be the tallest man in Christendom!

ELEANOR: But then again, he might. ... Oh, the Prince and I are going to be grand together!

NURSE: Your eyes are going bad! You see life with halations!

ELEANOR: Why is it, the older people get, the less they dare speak surely of what's coming? ...There's no one, in all the world, whose future is as promising as mine is.

NURSE: Eleanor—

ELEANOR: It's true! I know it! Why shouldn't I say it right out? I'm not afraid to see my husband and myself, one day, high up on the throne of France, hearing pleas, dispensing justice...

NURSE: It'll be a long time before you get as high as that—

ELEANOR: And I'm not afraid to tell you what the Prince of France will be, because I saw him—in a vision. He'll be taller than my father was, with the broad Capetian shoulders and the handsome Capetian nose. His voice will have command and majesty. He will walk very boldly, with a kingliness already in him. And when I see him for the first time, I will fall on my knees in joy.

(Suddenly, a thin awkward YOUTH *rushes in.)*

LOUIS: Is this the highest turret of the castle?

ELEANOR: Yes, it is.

LOUIS: There isn't any farther I can go?

ELEANOR: No.

LOUIS: I just need a few minutes—to rest—to pray. Dear God... *(He prays fervently to himself for a few seconds, then interrupts himself.)* Is she as perfect as they say she is?

NURSE: Who?

LOUIS: The Duchess. Eleanor.

ELEANOR: *(Coming to stand in front of him)* You may make up your own mind about that, sir.

LOUIS: *(Understanding that this is she)* Oh, God preserve me. ... I am Louis Capet. I'm the one who's going to be—. I'm the person who's supposed to—*(Flustered, he bows. It is half faint, half obeisance.)*

NURSE: *(Sotto voce)* Well, Eleanor, when are you going to fall on your knees?

(The NURSE *exits.)*

ELEANOR: Won't you rise, Louis Capet?

LOUIS: If you promise—for a while—not to look at me

ELEANOR: Whyever can't I look at you?

LOUIS: You can't pretend I'm what you hoped for in a husband! A young man three weeks out of the monastery!

ELEANOR: The monastery?

LOUIS: I was at the altar renewing my vows of chastity when they came in and told me I was engaged!

ELEANOR: I didn't know—. I had no idea—. They didn't tell me—that you planned to go into religious service.

LOUIS: Maybe I never would have been allowed to, really. But since I was a boy they let me spend my hours in the church. It's what I like most—loving God. And now I'm supposed to—

ELEANOR: Now you're supposed to love me. It must be rather a disappointment.

LOUIS: Oh, no. Why, no! You're—very beautiful, now that I see you. Your nose is straighter than the one on my favorite statue of the Virgin Mary.

ELEANOR: Thank you.

LOUIS: But it was my *brother* who was supposed to be the King and ruler. If he hadn't died, you'd be marrying him.

ELEANOR: I'm sure I shall be content with you, Louis.

LOUIS: My father says you will.

ELEANOR: How is your father?

LOUIS: He fell ill on the way here from Paris.

ELEANOR: Oh, I'm sorry.

LOUIS: *(Crossing himself)* May the Lord protect him, body and soul.

(ELEANOR *crosses herself, too.*)

LOUIS: And may He protect you, too, Eleanor.

ELEANOR: Why me?

LOUIS: For what has been wished on you for a husband.

ELEANOR: You've never been a husband, I've never been a wife. I think that makes us excellently suited!

LOUIS: Do you always do that? Make the best of bad things?

ELEANOR: One could do worse than having too good a man for a husband, Louis.

LOUIS: I'm going to do all I can to make you content with me.

ELEANOR: And, Louis, I swear to do all I can to make *you* content with *me*. I swear that to you, and I swear to make it happen.

LOUIS: I was given a gift to give you. But, running up the stairs, I lost it.

ELEANOR: It doesn't matter. I have a gift for you, that no one knows about. It's a private present, from the private me to you. Here it is.

LOUIS: *(Taking it)* A star sapphire—

ELEANOR: It's the stone of young love—and of nighttime. ... It's the symbol of my promise to you—to be everything a wife should be. Companion, friend, advisor, helper—and all the rest. I promise to be very good at—the rest—when I get the hang of it.

LOUIS: Good at what?

ELEANOR: At—at loving.

LOUIS: *(Suddenly agitated, jumping back)* I don't think I should take it! The sapphire! It's vanity! Jewels are vanity! *(He thrusts it back at her.)*

ELEANOR: Very well, if you don't want jewels, you shan't have jewels! I promise to do everything I can to please you!

(Wedding music begins in the distance. The light begins to narrow down.)

ELEANOR: I'll sing to you and play the lute. I know all the songs of the minstrels.

LOUIS: *(Helpless and inadequate)* I only know the tunes of the *Te Deum*.

(ATTENDANTS enter and begin to dress the bride and groom in wedding costume. ELEANOR and LOUIS pay no attention to this, nor to any of the wedding ceremony. It is as if the ritual were happening far above and beyond them.)

ELEANOR: Then challenge me to a game of chess. I'm an excellent player—

LOUIS: I never learned the game.

ELEANOR: Do you play dice or darts?

LOUIS: No.

(ELEANOR and LOUIS are isolated in a shaft of light. The ATTENDANTS are gone. The ABBÉ enters and stands between them.)

(The music strengthens, the ABBÉ begins: "Dear Friends in Christ..." etc. ELEANOR and LOUIS, kneeling, are oblivious to the marriage ceremony going on about them.)

ELEANOR: Then I'll make sure you're entertained without your doing anything. I'll bring my jugglers along, and my acrobats and fiddlers—

LOUIS: Do you know that clowns have always made me sad? I don't know why it is. Their laughter hurts me.

ELEANOR: *(Trying harder and harder to please him)* Then we'll do something gayer. I'll ride with you to the hunt. Even carry your falcon. I can ride like the wind!

LOUIS: *(Becoming more and more agitated)* I don't ride. I don't hunt. Why track down a beast who never did any harm in God's world. Why—

(The music rises, the rings are produced. ELEANOR and LOUIS pay no attention as the ABBÉ continues: "Louis vis achipere Eleanor..." etc.)

ELEANOR: Then we'll do tamer things. We'll walk in the gardens. I'll plant for you the flowers of the Aquitaine. Violets, columbine and marigolds—

LOUIS: Those flowers would never survive on the Île de France—

(The ring is put on ELEANOR, she doesn't notice. The ABBÉ continues: "Eleanor vis achipere Louis..." etc.)

ELEANOR: Well, pheasants grow there. I have a chef who is the master of the world in roasting pheasant. At every ball and party that we give he'll make your guests so envious! His ginger cakes are grand, and his sugared pears, his toasted almonds and his wines—

(LOUIS bursts out, as the ring is put on his finger:)

LOUIS: Oh, Eleanor. I've lived till now *alone*—on bread and cheese!

ELEANOR: Well what would you like? Name anything you'd like of me and you shall have it!

(LOUIS and ELEANOR are made to join hands. LOUIS speaks urgently as the ABBÉ's voice continues the ceremony.)

LOUIS: I would like, more than anything, to go with you to some strange land, where no one knows our names, or ranks, or faces. And I would be a hermit, and you would be a nun and veil your head. And we would spend our days in prayer and good works and live out all our lives as brother and sister—

(The ABBÉ's voice rises strongly:)

ABBÉ: *Ego conjungo vos in matrimonium in nomine Patris et filii et spiritus sancti...* *(He makes the sign of the cross over the kneeling couple.)*

(Absolute silence. The ABBÉ exits. ELEANOR and LOUIS are alone.)

(Slowly, LOUIS rises. He looks at ELEANOR, who remains kneeling, with her face bowed. LOUIS looks inadequate, hesitant. Several times he reaches out to her to touch her, to raise her up. But he cannot bring himself to do it.)

(At last, ELEANOR raises her head and rises by herself. She says, very gently:)

ELEANOR: We shall be the good brother and sister someday, Louis...when we have finished our lives on this earth. ... As for now...don't be afraid. Go slowly. We have all the time in the world.

(He walks to her and takes her hand. He is about to kiss her hand when they become aware of a distant sound, as of the wind, or the voices of the wind. They stop to listen. The chant grows louder.)

(As it does, PEOPLE enter from everywhere and what they have been saying is at last heard clearly:)

MEMBERS OF THE COURT, ATTENDANTS: The King is dead. Long live the King. ... The King is dead. Long live the King...

(The words hardly have a moment to register on LOUIS when a royal litter is carried in. On it is the body of LOUIS THE FAT, his tremendous stomach rising under the blanket. On that stomach are two golden crowns.)

LOUIS: Father! *(He runs to the litter, grieving.)*

LITTER-BEARER: He died, my Lord. We couldn't help it.

LOUIS: Father—

SECOND LITTER-BEARER: He died very humble. On a carpet of ashes and dirt.

(LOUIS sobs.)

LOUIS: I wasn't there. Why wasn't I there? Did he have any last words for me?

LITTER-BEARER: Yes. He said, have many children.

(LOUIS *buries his head and sobs again. The* ABBÉ *takes over, muttering benedictions for the care of the dead King's soul.*)

(*Meanwhile, another scene attracts* ELEANOR's *attention. Some distance from the litter a tall, thin* MAN *is giving commands, while others rush off to do his bidding.*)

THIBAULT: Have horses readied and supplies gathered in for a swift march to Paris. We haven't time to visit every grape in the Aquitaine now. ... Have messengers sent to our allies to tell them what has transpired here, and tell them to have their ambassadors in Paris before a fortnight is out. ... The court will wear mourning for four months. Announce that. ... See that proper arrangements are made...

(THIBAULT *continues to give commands to individuals, privately.*)

ELEANOR: (*Aside, to the* NURSE, *who has joined her*) Who is that man?

NURSE: His name, they tell me, is Thibault of Champagne.

ELEANOR: Can he just take charge? Without *asking*?

NURSE: He brought up Louis from the day he was born. Perhaps he thinks it gives him some privileges.

ELEANOR: But those commands should be given by the *King*!

(ELEANOR *has spoken too loudly.* THIBAULT *has heard her. He turns.*)

THIBAULT: The King is *dead*, Madame.

ELEANOR: Oh, no. He's very much alive! ...I can tell, because he's crying...

(*She goes toward the litter, lifts one crown from the dead King's chest and gives it to* LOUIS. *The other, she takes for herself. Solemnly, the two young people put the crowns on their own heads.*)

COURT & ATTENDANTS: Long live Louis, King of France! ...Long live Louis, King of France! ...

THIBAULT: (*Turning to an* ATTENDANT) Yes, long live Louis, King of France. And make a note: As soon as we reach Paris, I must undertake a few deportment lessons for the Queen.

(*Music, transition. Everyone exits but* ELEANOR. LOUIS *exits with the litter.* THIBAULT *exits with the rest.*)

(*As* ELEANOR *stands watching, the throne room in Paris appears. The Fleur-de-lis is lowered. Two thrones are rolled in, capping a flight of steps.*)

(ATTENDANTS *put in place the lands of France and of the Aquitaine, then exit.*)

(ELEANOR *is alone in the vast throne room. She looks about her in awe. Then she goes, rather timidly, up the steps, and sits gingerly on a throne.)*

ELEANOR: It fits! I've got a Queen's bottom!

(She is sitting there enjoying herself when THIBAULT *enters.)*

THIBAULT: I thought we agreed you were to spend today in your room, practicing needlepoint!

ELEANOR: *(Getting off the throne)* Needlepoint—!

THIBAULT: I told you yesterday that all the other Queens of France have been champion needle-workers.

ELEANOR: I tried, Thibault, but I cannot sew! I can swim, shoot, ride, play the flute, but I can not do decorative stitchery!

THIBAULT: You haven't tried, Madame.

ELEANOR: Yesterday I did, for half an hour. And what a waste of time! It dulls your head, causes your eyes to water, and makes you unfit to do anything but sleep and sew!

THIBAULT: *(Smiling)* Yes...

ELEANOR: And what have you got when you're finished? Nothing but a messy old colored rag!

THIBAULT: Not half as messy as your vocabulary. Your language is scarcely suited to a Queen.

ELEANOR: I've only been Queen eleven months now, Thibault. I expect to improve with time.

THIBAULT: With luck, you may. If you apply yourself to your lessons.

ELEANOR: And what is today's lesson?

THIBAULT: The Art of Silence.

ELEANOR: And how do you practice it?

THIBAULT: Very simple. Like this. You see? *(He points to his lips, sealed.)* This line, this closed straight line, is the most becoming feature of a woman's countenance.

ELEANOR: How odd! I've always been told a woman's smile was her passport to eternity.

THIBAULT: Were you also told, Madame, it was everyone else's passport to hell? No. Her smile has nowhere near the value of her silence. Of all the treasures a woman gives her husband, the one he values most is her closed mouth.

(She displays her mouth, closed.)

THIBAULT: Very good. Very good. It's the only certain way to make a husband happy.

ELEANOR: I'd to anything in the world to make my husband happy!

(LOUIS *enters carrying a small sack.*)

LOUIS: You've already given him as much happiness as any man deserves. It was you, wasn't it, Eleanor, who left this surprise for me?

ELEANOR: Yes, Louis.

LOUIS: I love them! *(Shyly)* I love you.

THIBAULT: What's in the sack, Louis?

LOUIS: Candied apricots.

THIBAULT: Candied apricots! Whatever happened to your bread and cheese?

LOUIS: I think they took the shape of a woman so radiant she makes me love God's richer things.

(LOUIS *and* ELEANOR *exchange a loving look.*)

THIBAULT: Then the present *I* have for you will probably repel you.

LOUIS: A present?

THIBAULT: *(Snapping his fingers for it to be brought in)* It isn't from me, actually. It's from the Pope.

ELEANOR: The Pope! Usually *we* have to give *him* presents!

THIBAULT: Is this how you practice the Art of Silence?

ELEANOR: *(All obedience)* I am silent.

(*A* PAGE *enters, hands* THIBAULT *a box and exits.*)

THIBAULT: Here it is, Louis.

(LOUIS *opens the box.*)

LOUIS: A crown of thorns...

THIBAULT: It's a great and holy honor. He sends it for you to wear, Louis—on Crusade.

ELEANOR: *Crusade!!?*

THIBAULT: How you make such sounds with your lips sealed, I will never know, Madame.

LOUIS: *(Holding the crown before him)* He means to recall me to my father's promise...

THIBAULT: It's a cause more suited to you than to your father.

LOUIS: *(Trying on the crown)* Me...summoned by the Church...to deliver the Holy Land...

THIBAULT: We can have a hundred thousand men armed and equipped by May.

ELEANOR: No, no! It's too soon to go!

THIBAULT: Are you suggesting that you know our capabilities better than I do?

ELEANOR: I mean, it's too soon for Louis to leave France. Too soon for him to risk such a long absence.

LOUIS: There's trouble in Jerusalem...

ELEANOR: Things aren't so very settled here at home. You're new, Louis. Your people don't yet know you.

THIBAULT: And how do you think he should introduce himself? Invite the entire populace to an Apricot Ball?

ELEANOR: I think he should travel through his provinces before he heads for Asia Minor. Show the people who he is—and how he loves them. Let them get the feel of him as King. If they don't have that, and he leaves, there'll be chaos!

THIBAULT: When a King goes away on a pious mission, his country is held to God's truce.

ELEANOR: God's truce isn't man's, and you know it.

THIBAULT: *(To* LOUIS:*)* This lady seems to think she is Prime Minister! *(To* ELEANOR:*)* Are you questioning the wisdom of the Pope?

ELEANOR: I question the wisdom of Crusading at this moment!

THIBAULT: *(Barely controlling his temper)* I thought you failed as far as you could fail on Needlepoint, but you seem to be setting a new kind of record in the Art of Shutting Up!

ELEANOR: I am Queen of France, I can give my point of view if I wish to!

THIBAULT: Only on one condition, Madame. That you're pregnant. Are you?

ELEANOR: *(Stopped)* ...No. I am not pregnant.

THIBAULT: Then you have no right to give your point of view.

ELEANOR: If what's needed to give a point of view is a bulbous belly, then how is it that you are even allowed to speak?

LOUIS: Eleanor—. Thibault—! Please don't quarrel—

THIBAULT: The lady may joke, but it's quite serious. The purpose of this marriage is not to give a means of livelihood to the fruit merchants of Paris, nor to give the King a playmate to while away his leisure hours, nor to give him an adviser who convinces by caress instead of reason. The purpose of this marriage is to ensure the future of the House of Capet, the future of France. It may seem too simple, too biological a task, to appeal to this very clever young lady. Nevertheless, if she has any regard for you, she'll get down to doing it right now.

ELEANOR: I might get down to it if you could leave us alone for a few minutes!

THIBAULT: We'll continue our conversations later, Louis. In private, if possible .... It took a female, didn't it, to introduce hysteria to the throne room of France. *(He goes out.)*

(ELEANOR *and* LOUIS *move downstage—to a more private place, and eventually the thrones disappear. Time passes.)*

ELEANOR: I pledged to do all I could for you—for France. And now, the only thing I'm asked, I can't manage. ... Oh, Louis, I do so want to have a child! I think about him night and day, as if by conjuring him up in my mind, I could create him.

LOUIS: The physicians say you can.

ELEANOR: And the Abbé has prayed, for three years. And you and I have done all we can, I guess, toward making it happen. Oh, Louis—

LOUIS: Yes?

ELEANOR: I wish—I wish sometime you would stay in my bed all through the night—till morning...

LOUIS: Is it—legal?

ELEANOR: I think if I had you with me all night—as a lover—I might be able to do it. Or if I could see you as I imagined you before we met:—tall and broad-shouldered, with white plume waving—

(ATTENDANTS *enter with a heroic battle costume.)*

LOUIS: What's this?

ELEANOR: A surprise. I had it made for you. To help me imagine—the father of my child.

LOUIS: In chain mail? They don't make hero's clothes to fit me.

ELEANOR: Just try them on. Indulge me. ... Here. I'll hold the crown.

(LOUIS *hands over the crown of thorns. The* ATTENDANTS *begin to dress him.)*

LOUIS: I think I'll look very strange in breastplate and helmet.

ELEANOR: Maybe not.

LOUIS: Maybe so. ... I'll put it on to please you, but I'll keep the visor down.

ELEANOR: If you like.

LOUIS: Don't tell me you had a shield made! And a sword, too!

ELEANOR: Solid silver. I always pictured him with a shield of solid silver.

LOUIS: And the sword. A golden handle.

ELEANOR: I always pictured him with a golden handle on his sword.

(The ATTENDANTS *exit.)*

LOUIS: It's lighter than I thought it would be.

ELEANOR: Or else you're stronger than you thought you were.

LOUIS: Well, how do I look?

ELEANOR: Very near. Yes, very near. Almost the way I thought he would...

LOUIS: *(Striding up and down)* It doesn't hurt. It bends right with me. It moves very well, don't you think?

ELEANOR: Why of course. Heroes *move*. It's what they're made for.

LOUIS: I look tall.

ELEANOR: Yes, Louis.

LOUIS: And I have gigantic hands.

ELEANOR: Yes, you do.

LOUIS: I never told a soul—but all those years I knelt in church, I could see, at the corner of the transept, the carved stone statue of a knight. His jaw was very bold and his thighs seemed made of iron. And I used to think—there are men who can wear those costumes, and others who cannot. I used to wonder if just once I could try—

And now I've tried it on, and it isn't so ridiculous. I look as well as any man has looked, wouldn't you say? As tall, as bold, as wide at the shoulder? ...Do you think, Eleanor,—do you think that I might—show myself in this?

ELEANOR: In the palace?

LOUIS: In the streets, on the highways. It isn't just a toy, is it?

ELEANOR: No, it's real. You may wear it where you like.

LOUIS: If I showed myself in this in the provinces, wouldn't that be a vision of their King? In this they might respect me. They might bow, they might cheer!

ELEANOR: Don't you dare to go without it?

LOUIS: ...No. I don't dare.

ELEANOR: Then go in this, and God be with you. ... God bless Louis, hero of France. ... And God bless Louis's child...

*(*LOUIS *exits heroically.)*

(Alone, ELEANOR *prays.)*

ELEANOR: Dear God, France needs a child from me. You mustn't hold back any longer! ...I dressed up Louis in the costume of a man. I had him put into the clothes of the man I always pictured as the father of my children. *(Talking herself into it, eyes closed)* He is the hero of whom I always dreamed. My whole being trembles. If I didn't know him, and he rode by me in the forest, I would throw myself into his power without asking his name or parentage. *(Further into her imagination)* I can feel my whole self yielding, thrilling, surrendering with pleasure in some secret glade. My soul responds! My heart leaps with wonder and creates—creates the future!

(The NURSE enters above her, carrying a bundle trailing white lace.)

(Simultaneously, downstage, LOUIS re-enters.)

(ELEANOR takes the bundle and runs to LOUIS in triumph.)

ELEANOR: Louis! I've done it! I've done it! I spent nine months on my knees in front of the altar, I grew to the size of an elephant, and when I got up, I had this!

LOUIS: How beautiful it is! So beautiful—! *(He takes it, very much moved.)*

ELEANOR: And wise, don't you think? See how it smiles—so wisely, as if it knows things we don't know.

LOUIS: It's very close to God. So are you, to have made it.

ELEANOR: Every inch I grew made me think: I am serving France, I am giving it a Future! Even during the birth-pains, I was *glad*.

LOUIS: Was there very much pain?

ELEANOR: Not enough, if this is the way I can serve you. *(She takes back the child.)* Now, where have you been, Louis? And what have you been doing while you were gone?

LOUIS: Wonderful, wonderful things! I was a hero! I travelled from one end of the country to the other, and everywhere I went, the people cheered! I rode in in this suit, with a hundred knights behind me, we'd wave the flag of France and they would bow! I'd hear reports that there were villages against us, but once they caught a sight of me, they'd bow! I'd charge in at dawn, with my sword raised to the sunlight—

(THIBAULT has entered.)

THIBAULT: And did you tell her that you killed with it?

ELEANOR: Killed with it!

THIBAULT: He charged through the villages expecting everyone to bow before him. And when one person didn't, he ran him through.

LOUIS: No, no—

THIBAULT: And the knights behind you followed your example.

LOUIS: I don't understand you—

THIBAULT: Their swords were raised like yours. Didn't you look behind you? Several hundred are dead. A village—gone.

LOUIS: No, no! It isn't true!

THIBAULT: Then why did God send you a daughter?

ELEANOR: A daughter! *(She unwraps the* BABY.*)* It is...a *daughter*...

THIBAULT: You see? Sometimes even a bulbous belly isn't enough.

ELEANOR: But I thought, by becoming an elephant, I could *serve*...

NURSE: You will. I'll pray for sons. *(She takes the* BABY *and exits.)*

THIBAULT: When a woman fools with affairs of state, she's rewarded with a daughter. When a man of peace fools with a sword, he's rewarded with unnecessary deaths.

ELEANOR: He doesn't remember the deaths you're describing!

LOUIS: *(Coming out of a trance)* I do. ... I do remember now.... It was in a village near the Rhône. ... Everyone everywhere had bowed to me when they saw my armor. But this man just stood as I came charging toward him. I expected him to kneel, and I kept coming. Then suddenly my sword stopped at something— something stopped it—the *man!*

ELEANOR: Oh, merciful God!

THIBAULT: Someone gave you the sword, remember?

LOUIS: A man—stopped the sword! ...I—*killed*—him!

THIBAULT: You have come a great distance from the cloister, Louis. It is a direction I never thought you'd go.

*(*THIBAULT *walks upstage as* LOUIS *talks to* ELEANOR.*)*

LOUIS: There's a beast in man I didn't know existed. He's crouching even in the hearts of cowards like me. So when you disguise yourself as the warrior man, he makes you one. And when you wear a sword for bravado, he strikes.

How can I exorcise the beast? Shake him loose from inside me? He's there, still there, and ready. Ready! ...Is there a penance on God's earth to save me? How can I make certain he never springs again?

(In the background, THIBAULT *raises a great white flag with a crimson cross on it. He waves it back and forth as if he were concerned with nothing else in the world but its motion.)*

*(*LOUIS *sees the flag.)* Yes. ... That's the way. ... At the tomb of Christ, the beast may vanish.

ELEANOR: Crusade. ... I guess you must. ... But who will care for France in your absence?

THIBAULT: *(Coming forward)* Don't worry your woman's head. I will arrange for France to be in good hands while Louis is serving God's purpose. ... And don't worry about the King, either. I'll care for him very well in the lands of the heathen.

ELEANOR: *I will care for Louis in the lands of the heathen!*

THIBAULT: No. ... No women. ... It's the cause of God and Country. Women cannot go.

(*He gives* LOUIS *the crown of thorns which* LOUIS *had discarded*. LOUIS *puts it on and they exit. But their exit is not seen because —)*

(*The Crusade begins!*)

(*There is splendid, stirring, martial music, with a gaiety in its lilt. Magnificently dressed* KNIGHTS *appear, marching eastward, their banners proclaiming their origins in the Aquitaine and in all of France.*)

(*As the* KNIGHTS *stream in, Paris disappears. In the background, flags and gonfalons are blown strongly from the East to give the impression of the great journey eastward.*)

(*The men march and sing with great spirit.*)

CRUSADERS: (*Singing*)
We're marching eastward,
We're on our way.
We're marching eastward,
Sometimes we pray.

We are the best in France,
Our banners now advance,
We'll down the heathen horde
And gather our reward.

We're marching eastward,
To Victory!

(*Just as they finish,* ELEANOR *and a small band of* WOMEN *charge through their lines from behind, dressed as* AMAZONS. *They are plumed, wear gilded buskins, and carry banners.*)

AMAZONS: (*Singing*)
We're marching eastward,
We're on our way.
We're marching eastward,
Sometimes we pray.

We are the best in France,
And though we now wear pants,
We'll fight the heathen horde,
We'll fight without a sword.

We're marching eastward,
To Victory!

(They all laugh.)

(GEOFFREY DE RANCON steps forward. He is a brave, manly knight who wears on his tunic the symbol of the Aquitaine.)

GEOFFREY: Three cheers for the Queen of the Amazons—and for the Amazons—by reason of whose presence there has not been a single case of homesickness in the five months since we left home!

(The MEN cheer.)

ELEANOR: *(In the mock tones of a field general)* Attention!

(The MEN come to instant over-attention. ELEANOR strides about, reviewing her troops.)

ELEANOR: How fare the soldiers of France?

GEOFFREY: Well, my Queen.

ELEANOR: *(To a CRUSADER munching a chicken leg:)* Are there any cases of insubordination?

FIRST CRUSADER: *(Hiding the chicken leg)* There are not.

ELEANOR: *(To a CRUSADER embracing an AMAZON:)* Are there any cases of sadness or melancholy?

SECOND CRUSADER: *(Smiling)* No, my Queen.

ELEANOR: Then you are all loyal and true?

THIRD CRUSADER: With every inch of our beings!

ELEANOR: Then let us cheer for Louis of France!

(She raises her arms to lead them. They all shout, in chorus:)

CRUSADERS: Eleanor!

ELEANOR: A cheer for Louis—!

(ELEANOR raises her arms again. They chorus:)

CRUSADERS: Eleanor Our Queen!

ELEANOR: Will you cheer your King?

FIRST CRUSADER: I will when I see him. I didn't see him when we were crossing the Alps and the Danube. I didn't see him in Byzantium when the Greeks did us out of so much of our gold. I didn't see him in the Levant when we almost got rained out of existence. Why is he always hiding?

SECOND CRUSADER: You don't think he could be *afraid*!

ELEANOR: Louis is as brave and noble as any King was ever!

FIRST CRUSADER: If he's so heroic, why doesn't he ever come out of his tent?

(The CRUSADERS *and* AMAZONS *exit.* GEOFFREY *stays behind with* ELEANOR*.)*

ELEANOR: I thought—if I dressed up like an Amazon, if I spread dazzling smiles here, there, and everywhere—I could keep the men from noticing how little they see of Louis.

GEOFFREY: You dazzle, all right. But nothing could keep them from noticing how little they see of Louis. Men like their leaders to be visible.

ELEANOR: Remember, Geoffrey, how when we were children, we used to play Crusaders, you and I?

GEOFFREY: I remember.

ELEANOR: We were bold. Head-to-toe *bold*. But saints who take the cross are different, aren't they?

GEOFFREY: It can't be easy—being married to a saint.

ELEANOR: It's harder on him than on me. Poor man. He sleeps in the coldest of all tents, wears a hair shirt, fasts, prays—

GEOFFREY: And he still can't cleanse himself from the deaths in that village?

ELEANOR: *(Shakes her head)* No. I'd almost prefer he'd blame *me* for the massacre, the way Thibault does.

GEOFFREY: That Thibault is a pain in the—

ELEANOR: Geoffrey!

GEOFFREY: Such a "godly" man! Forgives God for everything except for making women.

ELEANOR: Does it matter so much?

GEOFFREY: That the King's closest adviser is a woman-hater? If nothing else it's responsible for the disproportion between the time Louis spends on his knees and the time in your bed.

ELEANOR: That's a blasphemous remark!

GEOFFREY: I suppose it is. Still, Thibault's the one who set your husband on the road to chastity. So one can't help wondering where Thibault's chastity was born. Someday I ought to pin him to a wall and discover whether he's continent by choice or by necessity!

(THIBAULT *enters.*)

THIBAULT: So the conversation's pornographic again! It always is, in this section of the line of march. *(To* ELEANOR:*)* Is that why you insisted on coming on Crusade? To see what it would be like to enjoy a dirty joke in Asia Minor?

ELEANOR: Not at all, Thibault, I—

THIBAULT: Your Amazons have turned this holy mission into a Bacchic revel!

GEOFFREY: They've also managed to keep the men from thinking about the meat that went bad, about the fevers that have taken too many of their number, and about the fact that we're nowhere as far along as we should be.

THIBAULT: We'd be farther along if we didn't have to drag the Queen's luggage!

GEOFFREY: You blame the Queen for everything, don't you. Last week you accused her of being personally responsible for six hundred cases of dysentery!

THIBAULT: *(To* ELEANOR:*)* Well, you do have your champions, m'Lady! Maybe that's why you came. To be with your old friends of the Aquitaine.

ELEANOR: I came to keep the King from dying of melancholy. He might, with only you around him.

THIBAULT: If you came to cheer Louis, why are you spreading so much of your sunshine elsewhere?

ELEANOR: Thibault—

THIBAULT: Let's hope there are *some* portions of the lady still reserved exclusively for the King! *(He exits.)*

GEOFFREY: That man is a danger to you.

ELEANOR: What possible danger? Nothing can harm me—so long as I do what I came to do, for the King.

GEOFFREY: And what did you come to do, Queen Eleanor?

ELEANOR: At the moment, to get him to come out of his tent, see his men, and cheer them.

GEOFFREY: I wish you success. ... And while you're at it, please find out why we've been sitting on this desert plateau for two weeks now. Our water supplies are much lower than they should be. Ask King Louis—when will he give the order to move? *(He exits.)*

(For a few moments, ELEANOR *is alone. Color is drained from the sky. The air is gray and barren.)*

*(*LOUIS *appears, dressed as a penitent. He walks slowly, his head buried in a missal. He is dazed, abstracted, as if the greater part of him were somewhere else.)*

ELEANOR: *(Moved at the sight of him)* How are you, my Lord?

LOUIS: *(After a long pause)* ...I haven't been forgiven yet...

ELEANOR: Could there be a God in heaven who could look into such a face—and not forgive?

LOUIS: I've been given no sign, no gesture from heaven—

ELEANOR: If you came out into the camp, and walked among the soldiers, you could feel their love for you, Louis, and that would be a sign—

LOUIS: Why is it that we've had to *fight* our way across the continents? What kind of holy pilgrimage is this? Everywhere they see our flags, they attack us!

ELEANOR: The age is made of strife, it's the only answer. As if things were shaking themselves up, adjusting themselves, getting ready for a better time.

LOUIS: I wish that time were here!

ELEANOR: We're moving toward it. That is, we would be—if we were moving at all. A month is a very long time to sit still in the desert.

LOUIS: It's been very peaceful...

ELEANOR: When are the supplies that we're waiting for coming?

LOUIS: ...They're not.

ELEANOR: They're not?!

LOUIS: The people who swore to be our friends in the desert, are now our enemies. Those same men who swore to show us the way and bring us provisions are out there now—lying in wait.

ELEANOR: How long have you known?

LOUIS: Since the day after we arrived here.

ELEANOR: But why didn't you say something?

LOUIS: ...We've had four weeks of utter peace...

ELEANOR: We are almost out of food, Louis!

LOUIS: God knows.

ELEANOR: We have no water—

LOUIS: He knows all things.

ELEANOR: We have twenty thousand men to feed. We must *do* something. We must send men out, to search, to negotiate—

LOUIS: If we move at all, more blood will be spilled. I won't have it! No more pain! No more blood! No more dying!

ELEANOR: If we stay on this rock, we will starve to death.

LOUIS: It is God's will that we suffer the penance of hunger. When the bones show through the skin, we will be purified.

ELEANOR: When the bones show through the skin, we will be dead.

(THIBAULT *enters.*)

THIBAULT: It is time for your evening prayers, Louis.

(LOUIS *moves toward the altar.*)

ELEANOR: Thibault, tell him we must move from here!

THIBAULT: What's the matter, Madame? Is your faith waning? Don't you believe that God will provide?

(LOUIS *and* THIBAULT *go off.* ELEANOR *watches, disturbed.*)

(*The sky grows dull. A dispirited Crusader's Song is heard in the distance.* GEOFFREY *enters.*)

ELEANOR: *(Quietly)* Geoffrey, I think my husband wants to die.

GEOFFREY: To die?

ELEANOR: To die to be purified. ... Why else would he keep us here for seven weeks?

GEOFFREY: What does Thibault say? Can't Thibault convince him?

ELEANOR: Thibault, for reasons of his own, doesn't try.

(*A weary remnant of* CRUSADERS *and* AMAZONS *stumbles on, singing disjointedly:*)

CRUSADERS & AMAZONS: *(Singing)*
We're marching nowhere,
We're on no way.
We're marching nowhere,
And eating hay...

(*A few continue to hum, under.*)

GEOFFREY: No clearing throats! It's a waste of good spittle! ...Hey, there, green Amazon! It's *her* turn to chew on the bone!

(*A blind* CRUSADER *stumbles on.*)

GEOFFREY: What's the matter with him?

FIRST CRUSADER: He went blind searching the sky for rain.

SECOND CRUSADER: Seven weeks on this filthy rock! I'll trade my boots for water. Does anyone have water? *(He holds up his ragged boots.)*

FIRST CRUSADER: Why should you need water? We came out here to make a hill of human bones. Die and be the hill, Crusader! ...What are you waiting for? Die and be the hill!

(*A few* CRUSADERS *collapse on the ground, despairing.* ELEANOR *watches in pity and disbelief. Then she is moved to speak:*)

ELEANOR: Stand on your feet, you frayed edges of France. Do you think we walked all this way to unravel on the steppes of Asia Minor? If it's possible to stay alive for one minute, it's possible to stay alive for two. And that minute leads to the next — and then to another.

FIRST CRUSADER: The minutes stop somewhere—without water.

ELEANOR: *(After a moment)* ...Stand up. ... Get your packs. ... Prepare to march.

GEOFFREY: What do you mean?

ELEANOR: We're going out—to look for water.

GEOFFREY: Without the permission of the King?

ELEANOR: If I asked, he wouldn't let us.

GEOFFREY: There are rules in an army, Queen Eleanor. The first is: All orders come from the top.

ELEANOR: I've begged him to give some orders—some sensible orders—every time I've seen him. He just looks at me vaguely and goes back to his prayers.

GEOFFREY: But—

ELEANOR: *(To the* CRUSADERS:*)* Leave the banners. It will be better if the others don't discover that we've gone until we're back—with something for them to drink.

GEOFFREY: But the King—

ELEANOR: I want to keep him alive.

GEOFFREY: By finding water?

ELEANOR: As a symbol of God's love.

GEOFFREY: The dangers out there are more than symbolic, you know that! You stay here and let us go for you.

ELEANOR: I'd rather die moving than sitting. I'd rather be cut down in the middle of a battle than perish by wasting away.

(They are moving now, marching out into the desert. Behind her, her TROOPS *sing their crusading song with intensity and spirit.* ELEANOR's *voice rises above their song:)*

ELEANOR: I only know one rule: It's to *do, act, move*—as long as possible. If you're shipwrecked in the middle of the sea, with not one single hope of rescue, you don't take a last look at the sun and let yourself go down. You swim, swim, *swim*, till you sink beyond life and consciousness. And that's your entry into heaven, the fact that you kept swimming till you died.

(The GROUP *seems tired now, weary of the march.)*

ELEANOR: We move, act, *do*—as long as we are able. If the skin comes off the bone, still we move. And when God sees us putting one foot in front of the other, one foot in front of the other, one foot in front of the other, He will cheer, applaud, and shout: These are the creatures for whom I made my Universe! ...He will praise us for putting one foot in front of the other—and He will send us gifts...

(A shaft of light appears.)

CRUSADERS: Water! It's there! My God! Real water!

(They rush toward the light.)

ELEANOR: *(Almost sobbing in gratitude)* He will praise us for putting one foot in front of the other—and He will send us gifts...

CRUSADERS: To water! To Eleanor of France! Water! Water!

ELEANOR: When you've had enough, fill your flasks for Louis and the others— *(She turns to* GEOFFREY:*)* The Lord saw us trying—and He was pleased...

(Suddenly, a great VOICE is heard from nowhere:)

VOICE: *(O S)* Who on this desert has dared to injure the King of France?

(All stop in fear and consternation.)

*(*THIBAULT *enters. It was his voice. He calls back over his shoulder:)*

THIBAULT: They're here! All clean and washed and rested. And not one of them has a single bruise! ...Bring him on!

(The inert form of LOUIS *is carried in on a stretcher borne by two battered* CRUSADERS.*)*

ELEANOR: Louis! ...Louis! ...Dear heaven, is he alive?

LOUIS: *(Stirring)* Eleanor... Why did you leave us?

ELEANOR: He's hurt! He's ill! Bring him water!

(Water is brought. THIBAULT *overturns it with a crash of his hand.)*

THIBAULT: What's water? Can it make a thousand men come alive again?

ELEANOR: Merciful God!

GEOFFREY: What happened?

THIBAULT: Ah, the innocent question! ...The enemy took your place in the dark. And when we woke up yesterday morning, while our swords were still tangled up in our bedclothes, suddenly they—

LOUIS: *(Crying out in delirium)* Why do my men die and die and keep dying? Why is it the more I try to preserve, the more I destroy? More are dead now than if I'd set them all loose by themselves in the desert. ... Dear, sweet Christ— for what am I being punished?

THIBAULT: *(Turning to* ELEANOR*)* For what, indeed!

ELEANOR: Rest, Louis—

THIBAULT: Why did you come out here?

ELEANOR: For water.

THIBAULT: Against orders?

ELEANOR: The men needed water.

THIBAULT: And when you passed our enemies in your search for this water, whatever possessed you to give them your flags?

ELEANOR: We passed no—

THIBAULT: They came toward us waving your banners! That's why we were taken so off guard!

ELEANOR: We left our banners—

THIBAULT: So they could find them!

ELEANOR: ...Are you accusing me of treason?

THIBAULT: Treason? No one said treason. You stole out of camp in the middle of the night, against all the primary rules of civil and military obedience. But no one used the word *treason*. The King was hurt—almost killed—but that's no cause for the word *treason* to be used. By guile, or carelessness, a thousand men died. But why bring up something as unpleasant as *treason*? Of those who have survived this Crusade, the largest number are from the Aquitaine. But why should *treason* come into the question here?

After all, treason requires a motive, doesn't it. A public or a private motive. A desire to gain something—as large as a kingdom, or as tiny as a kiss. And which of these ambitions could possibly move a woman who is already Queen of France?

ELEANOR: Louis, this man is—!

LOUIS: *(Tortured)* Why would you do it, Eleanor? *(He turns his head toward* GEOFFREY.*)* Just because this knight's cloak is softer than mine? And in his tent you find more warmth?

(ELEANOR *is stunned and speechless.*)

(LOUIS *turns his face away in pain and is carried off.*)

(ELEANOR's CRUSADERS *move in to protect her. She shakes her head, indicating she doesn't need protection and dismisses them. They go off.*)

THIBAULT: Geoffrey de Rancon, it is the King's desire that you not be permitted to view the Holy Land. You are to be kept in chains and sent back to France, where judgment will be passed on you.

(SOLDIERS *approach* GEOFFREY *and stand on either side of him.*)

THIBAULT: Queen Eleanor, you will kindly keep to your tent. And if I were you, I'd dispense with the Amazon costume.

(THIBAULT *exits in the direction in which* LOUIS *was taken out.*)

(ELEANOR *and* GEOFFREY *are alone except for* TWO SOLDIERS *who stand ready to remove him.*)

ELEANOR: *(Ripping off the armor)* The Amazon is not this costume; the Amazon is me!

GEOFFREY: Be careful of Thibault. He's more dangerous than I imagined.

ELEANOR: I'll see Louis alone. He'll never believe these accusations.

GEOFFREY: You can't tell. He might. You've hurt him—

ELEANOR: Hurt him!

GEOFFREY: By shining brighter than he does. Just your being the fullness of yourself humiliates him.

ELEANOR: I had to help—

GEOFFREY: The weak never thank you for handing them their crutches. It's a reminder they can't walk on their own.

(The SOLDIERS *move in toward him.)*

GEOFFREY: I'm afraid you're going to be asked to breathe less air than you're used to, to speak more softly, take smaller steps, consume less space. Take care, Queen Eleanor—

(The SOLDIERS *start to drag him off.)*

ELEANOR: Wait! You're handling him too roughly! ...Listen to me! ...I command you to treat him with respect!

(Not listening to her, the SOLDIERS *force* GEOFFREY *out.)*

*(*THIBAULT *has entered behind her.)*

THIBAULT: Apparently your voice is too weak for them to hear you.

ELEANOR: I wish to see the King.

THIBAULT: The King is praying to God in humility and reverence.

ELEANOR: I am afraid for Geoffrey de Rancon. I want the King's assurance that nothing will happen to him.

THIBAULT: Surely you realize, Madame, —that subject is already closed.

(He has spoken with full menace. ELEANOR *looks off in the direction in which* GEOFFREY *was taken.)*

ELEANOR: On the King's instruction?

THIBAULT: The King does not concern himself with the worldly and unclean.

(Lights change. LOUIS *enters, wearing the clothes of the penitent. He seems almost disembodied, his face has an otherworldly air.)*

ELEANOR: Louis..., Louis..., how thin and pale you look. Even thinner than on the day I first saw you. How long ago was it? You look centuries older. And as innocent as a saint.

THIBAULT: Don't touch him. He has just been shriven.

ELEANOR: Are you recovered, Louis?

(LOUIS *doesn't answer. He goes and kneels in prayer and remains there, without moving, through all of the following scene.*)

THIBAULT: He has taken a vow of silence until he reaches the holy sepulchre. He has sworn, by the blood of our Lord, that until he kneels before the tomb of Christ, he will not speak. ... His last act, before beginning this penance, was to decide what is to be done with you.

ELEANOR: (*Looking off in the direction in which* GEOFFREY *disappeared*) What is to be done with me, Thibault?

THIBAULT: For the remainder of the Crusade, you are to stay in your tent. ... When we return to France, you will be given your own quarters. You will remain there, in the company of attendants chosen by the King. You will publish no statements. Your monies will be strictly controlled. You will see the King only when he requests it. You will maintain, at all times, the silence which befits your rank and station. You will act, always and forever, only as given leave to by the King.

ELEANOR: In other words, I am to be put in prison.

THIBAULT: You may think of it any way you like.

ELEANOR: I'm to be put in prison because you choose to blame me for an attack I had nothing to do with.

THIBAULT: If the attack had never happened, you still would be being punished. For disobeying the orders of the King.

ELEANOR: His orders were to stay on the plateau till we rotted.

THIBAULT: That isn't so. Help might have been coming.

ELEANOR: I didn't think so.

THIBAULT: It is not your function to think. It is up to you to let France go its course under Louis the Seventh!

ELEANOR: Even to annihilation?

THIBAULT: If necessary, yes.

ELEANOR: I am his wife! I had to help him!

THIBAULT: You are his wife. You should not have shown an entire kingdom that you do not respect its leader's commands.

ELEANOR: Louis, send this man away. I want to talk with you.

THIBAULT: You know he's under the strictest vows not to speak.

ELEANOR: I wish to see the King alone!

THIBAULT: You no longer have that privilege.

ELEANOR: You mean, I'm to confine myself to my prison—*now*.

THIBAULT: To your *tent*, Madame.

ELEANOR: Into my tent for life—for finding water in the desert.

THIBAULT: You do not seem to understand, you have never understood, it is not your function to find water in the desert!

ELEANOR: Why isn't it?

THIBAULT: Because, Madame, you are not a man! What is this wild, odd blindness of yours? You seem to think it's quite within your realm to be anything that suits your fancy. Prospector, general, prophet—anything!

ELEANOR: Why can't I be anything I want to?

THIBAULT: Because you're a *woman*—and that excludes everything else... Once women start usurping the functions they weren't made for, they lose the one sole function for which they were made. They dry up in their female parts—and the end of the world approaches. ... You can't pretend you're just like a man, and then turn woman just for moments of conjunction! God sees you *all* your hours. He rages! And when you hope for female fruition, He looks the other way.

ELEANOR: You lie, Thibault!

THIBAULT: Then where is the heir to the future of France!

ELEANOR: I am sick to death of hearing of Louis's unborn children!

THIBAULT: I should think you would be, since the reason they are unborn is you. You betray the rules of heaven by taking over functions forbidden to women. You betray the state by acting in defiance of the King. You betray the laws of human decency by lending your hand and your smile to every mercenary and hanger-on, high born or low. You are a voluptuary. Your name and God-knows-what other parts of you are on the lips of every soldier. And the same perfumes and satins that arouse the men, arouse the King—and corrupt him. So when he ought to be tending to the business of the state, he is on his knees begging to be forgiven for being tempted by pleasures of the flesh!

ELEANOR: There is a madness in this place. A topsy-turvy. As if good were masquerading as evil, and evil as good. It is as if, the nearer we get to the Holy City, the farther we get from God.

THIBAULT: You are not qualified to divine our distance from God or any other matter. All you are required to do is go to your tent!

ELEANOR: My prison.

THIBAULT: Your tent!

ELEANOR: How small you must be, Thibault, if *I* can threaten you. ... Why are you doing this,—for power? Consorting with the forces of hell—for power? Letting men die on the desert without water because you knew the more men Louis lost, the more his confidence would be shaken, and the more his confidence is shaken, the more he has to depend on you?...And you will guide him, won't you! Onto his knees, away from the world, into the country of guilt and impotence! I see now why you encourage all this piety! The more he turns inward, the more his dominions are left to you!

THIBAULT: In the name of the cross, be silent!

ELEANOR: I will not. I can not. I was not made for silence. I have been given a life, a heart, a body, a breath which comes and goes. I can't give up using them. *(She approaches her husband.)* If you value your life and your country, Louis, send this man away!

(LOUIS *is motionless.*)

THIBAULT: He's so far into the realms of the soul that voices of libertines can't reach him.

ELEANOR: I don't mind being slandered. I have been slandered before. I don't mind being blamed for the deaths of a thousand, though I know it was not my moving, but your staying, which caused them to die. I don't mind obeying the commands of a husband, if I think they are his commands.

THIBAULT: You will go to your tent, then—

(ELEANOR *goes to* LOUIS *and kneels beside him.*)

ELEANOR: I was ready, when we married, to give you the reins of my life. And as much as I could, I gave them. But it never occurred to me you would lead me where I did not want to go, or, worse, that you would lead me nowhere,— and that one day you would actually expect me to agree to being kept in a stall, muzzled and chained! I am not an animal!

(She rises.) I am me. Eleanor of Aquitaine. I am a person, a living being. I am more than just a womb surrounded by flesh. I have only been given one life. And however short it may be, I must live it. I must do all I can, at every moment. If you wish me to do less, I can't.

If you say that I must—give up all speech, all thought, all action, all power over my own destiny, I will resist it. Though we were sanctified to each other by all the vows of heaven,—I will go my separate way.

Do you wish me to leave you, Louis?

THIBAULT: (To LOUIS:) Don't answer!

ELEANOR: Louis. Do you wish me to stay?

THIBAULT: On pain of anathema, don't speak!

ELEANOR: Make some gesture, some sign, if you wish me to stay, Louis!

THIBAULT: She's tempting you to damn yourself in the eyes of heaven! All France will be sent to damnation if you move!

(LOUIS *looks at no one. He makes no movement.*)

ELEANOR: Dear statue. Dear thin, still statue. Dear relic. Dear husband. ... Goodbye...

(ELEANOR *starts to walk away. She and* THIBAULT *are in light,* LOUIS *in darkness. All setting indications for the Eastern Lands disappear.*)

(THIBAULT *stops* ELEANOR *with:*)

THIBAULT: Dear Lady, you don't imagine that we're going to let you just walk off and take the Aquitaine with you! You and your lands are bound to France forever. We wouldn't be without either of you for the world!

ELEANOR: Surely with all the sins you've called down on me, the Pope will want to release the throne of France from a few!

THIBAULT: Never.

(*The* ABBÉ *enters.* ELEANOR *speaks to him.*)

ELEANOR: Tell the Pope that Eleanor of France is sinful. Tell him I am wild and boisterous and I cannot be curbed. Tell him I gave myself to every soldier from here to Jerusalem. Tell him I caused all the elements of the East to rise up against my husband. I caused drought and famine and bloodshed, and because of me alone, a thousand died.

Tell the Pope that for spite I gave my husband only daughters. Females. Females! Those most disgusting evidences of the Devil's power on earth! Tell the Pope that in the Holy City I would not visit the sepulchre with my head veiled because I am a woman, but went there at night, in secret, with my forehead naked and brazen before my Lord.

Tell the Pope I am addicted to olive trees, and light, and air, and all the basest of God's creations. Tell him I enticed the King of France to love them, too. And under my corrupting spell he once loved ginger sticks, and doves, and fountains, and—

(LOUIS's *voice is heard out of the darkness, calling longingly:*)

LOUIS: *(O S)* Eleanor—

(*Simultaneously, a* MESSENGER *enters, handing a note to the* ABBÉ)

ABBÉ: *(Reading)* By reason of the fact that Louis and Eleanor are found to be related in the fourth degree by blood...

LOUIS: *(O S)* Eleanor—

ABBÉ: ...their marriage is declared null and void. Henceforth, you are no longer man and wife... (*He continues to speak under.*)

(LOUIS *appears dimly in the distance, saying:*)

LOUIS: Eleanor, tell them you'll keep your place. Stay by me. Tell them you won't exert your wishes against us all...

ABBÉ: What was, is declared, by the office of his Holiness the Pope, never to have been...

LOUIS: Eleanor...

(ELEANOR *moves forward, toward her lands, not hearing.*)

ABBÉ: This marriage is dissolved forever. Amen. (*He exits.*)

THIBAULT: Goodbye and good riddance to the baggage of the Aquitaine. I'll find you someone who'll be all a woman need be—a manufacturer of sons.

LOUIS: (*To* THIBAULT:) Get out of my sight. ... Leave me. ... If you are ever seen again, in France or her possessions, I will not answer for your life.

(*The lights go out on* LOUIS *and* THIBAULT. *They exit.* LOUIS's *lands are taken out. All evidences of France disappear.*)

(ELEANOR, *isolated in her own light, has moved downstage, her lands beside her.*)

ELEANOR: Where is the man to whom I can give myself and my lands? The man in whose country I will not be expected to be silent, transparent and invisible? The man who walks the earth without cringing, who is strong and will expect me to be, who moves and acts and orders through his own power and will expect me to also. Where is that man? Where is he?...If such there be, anywhere on the face of this imperfect planet, I will take him.

(*A* MAN *appears downstage opposite her, carrying lands. He is regal in bearing, rough cut and heroic.*)

HENRY: Well, Madame. Take me.

ELEANOR: Who are you?

HENRY: Henry Plantagenet, Duke of Normandy and Pretender to the throne of England.

ELEANOR: Do you know who I am?

HENRY: Anyone who's ever been drunk knows you.

ELEANOR: Have I that little reputation?

HENRY: That *much*. You're what men dream of when they dare to.

ELEANOR: And what do *you* dare, Henry Plantagenet?

HENRY: More than dreaming, Lady. Do you know there are four armed bands out to grab you—for marriage reasons? I'm here to tell them they're all too late.

ELEANOR: I see...

HENRY: I'm the best of the lot, too. You're lucky.

ELEANOR: Am I to get a choice in this?

HENRY: Of course. Here I am. Choose!

(ELEANOR *laughs, then grows serious.*)

ELEANOR: Were you raised in a monastery, Henry Plantagenet?

HENRY: I was raised on the battlefields of Normandy.

ELEANOR: Do you ever wear a hair shirt?

HENRY: Why? I've got enough hair of my own.

ELEANOR: Are you ever closer to God than to living?

HENRY: I've been close to going to the Devil—more than once or twice.

ELEANOR: How many advisers do you have tagging onto your jerkin?

HENRY: None.

ELEANOR: Not one rosy-lipped sage hidden in your pocket?

HENRY: Sorry. None.

ELEANOR: Then to whom do you listen when you have doubts?

HENRY: What are they?

ELEANOR: *(Laughs)* So your rules of life are your own, then, are they?

HENRY: I've only one rule: To jump into bed as much as I can—and to sleep as little as possible. These stories that they tell about you. Is it true that—?

ELEANOR: *(Seriously)* What would it be like for me with you? Would I be expected to keep alone in my own quarters except for the visit of an occasional silk merchant or zither player? Would I have to measure my flame so I wouldn't outdo you in brilliance? Would you expect me to keep my mind sealed tightly in a cosmetic jar and my will in a chamber pot under the stairs?

HENRY: You try it and I'll boot you out of the kingdom. I want as much as you can give me—and more.

ELEANOR: I can give you anything you want. Anything except silence.

HENRY: Who the hell wants your silence? This is the living world, Lady. If you want to be a part of it, you've got to speak up!

ELEANOR: Your answers are too good to be true...

(HENRY *starts toward* ELEANOR.)

ELEANOR: But there's one more question, Henry Plantagenet. ... How old are you?

HENRY: Nineteen. How old are you?

ELEANOR: *(A rueful pause)* ...Thirty.

HENRY: How many men have you known?

ELEANOR: I beg your pardon?

HENRY: Just one, I'll bet—in spite of the stories. Just one, *really*. And what was it like with him? ...Too tame?

ELEANOR: You have a way—

HENRY: I may be younger than you, but I'm twenty times your age in experience. There are things you've never dreamed of, that I have done. Places you don't know about, meats you've never tasted, acts you can't imagine, combats you've never tried. I have. I'll share them with you. Take my hand!

ELEANOR: How can I? It never stays in one place long enough.

HENRY: Here.

(HENRY *thrusts his hand at* ELEANOR *and grasps hers. An audible sound escapes her. She is visibly moved, as if he had communicated to her some wonder.*)

ELEANOR: *(Moved)* Give me the other.

(HENRY *does.* ELEANOR *speaks solemnly, sanctifying the match:*)

ELEANOR: I, Eleanor, give myself to you, Henry Plantagenet, and all my lands and all my soul. I promise to give you aid and succor, to be your ally and protector, till death do us part.

HENRY: And I, also, pledge myself unto you, Eleanor, to love, honor, and protect you, to defend your lands as mine, and to keep your life as sacred as mine, forever.

(ELEANOR *and* HENRY *clasp their hands tighter. Then they move, solemnly, to put their lands together. The lands fit exactly and make a mass several times the size of France.*)

HENRY: Look. They fit! They were made to go together! And up here—across the Channel—when I have England—there'll be that much more. It's got to be ruled by one man. One good, just, strong man.

ELEANOR: Yes. All broken up, it goes nowhere.

HENRY: But with one man's justice and order, this continent will flourish as it never has before.

ELEANOR: We have a lot to do, don't we?

HENRY: Yes. And the first thing to be done is your job. I can only help you slightly with it.

ELEANOR: What is it?

HENRY: Come here, Eleanor.

(ELEANOR *comes to* HENRY.)

HENRY: ... Make me a son.

ELEANOR: *(She hears the command, closes her eyes and turns away in torment.)* ...Again that same request. And all the heavens have to be appealed to! And all the ancient mysteries opened up! And all the humiliations have to be faced for a hope that will never, ever be granted!

(HENRY *stops* ELEANOR *with the most forceful and passionate embrace she has ever experienced.)*

HENRY: What do you mean, won't be granted? That's not the Plantagenet way. I hoped for England and now I have it.

(A PAGE *enters carrying England, with crowns on it. He puts the lands in place and goes out.)*

ELEANOR: England!

(HENRY *takes the crowns and comes toward* ELEANOR.)

HENRY: You said you could keep up with me. Well, come on, Lady! I've promised you all a man can do while he lives. All you have to do is secure it for those who come after. Is it so hard a job? The first thing I ask you? Are you going to start weeping and wailing like a ninny, and telling me you can't come through?

(The symbol of England begins to appear. The lights begin to shine, a golden glow.)

ELEANOR: So that's the way it is, is it? So the world is opening up! So this is the era of Aquitaine and England, of glory and power and love and order! And you think I'll let you produce while I sit in the corner like a weeping willow? Not on your life, Henry!

(A NURSE *enters with a* ROYAL BABY, *trailing lace and blue ribbons.)*

ELEANOR: Here's your son. ... How many more do you want? You'll have them.

(HENRY *gazes at the child.)*

HENRY: I told you it was possible. All things are possible!

ELEANOR: Yes, I believe they are, Henry—with you.

(With the NURSE *and* BABY *following,* ELEANOR *and* HENRY *turn and exit together.)*

(Bells ring, music rises, the lights brighten to a glorious intensity on the symbol of England.)

(Blackout)

END ACT ONE

ACT TWO

(At rise: Early morning in a field in England. In the field are three or four tents.)

(ELEANOR runs gaily out of the central tent and HENRY follows after.)

ELEANOR: I love the mornings! They taste just like you! If you took new-mown hay, fresh milk, a waterfall, a buck, a forest, six wild beavers and the sun, you'd have the taste of Henry.

HENRY: And if you added dawn, grass, dew, bayberries, campion, sparrows and an apple, that would taste exactly like Eleanor.

ELEANOR: Oh, I love this grassy field! I love every inch of England!

HENRY: And England is wild with passion for every inch of you!

(HENRY embraces ELEANOR, then grasps her by the hand.)

HENRY: Back to the tent!

ELEANOR: But it's dawn—!

HENRY: Love's as good in daylight as in darkness—

ELEANOR: We haven't had one minute's sleep!

HENRY: Is "sleep" the thing you crave?

ELEANOR: The crowd will soon be here—

HENRY: Let them come! And let them find us so entwined they can't tell one of us from the other!

ELEANOR: Yes! Let them! ...And let them hear: I love you.

HENRY: That was Henry speaking.

ELEANOR: That was Eleanor!

HENRY: That was her voice, saying what he meant to say.

(ELEANOR and HENRY embrace.)

HENRY: Where did you steal that radiance?

ELEANOR: ...From you.

(ELEANOR and HENRY embrace again.)

HENRY: Do you mind tumbling about the countryside with me? Spending all your days on horseback and half your nights in open fields? Do you mind holding court on a rock, and dispensing justice sitting on a haystack? Do you mind the roughness of our life together?

ELEANOR: Mind it! You're asking me if I mind breathing!

HENRY: Do you mind breathing?

ELEANOR: I was born the day I met you. Tomorrow, I'll be five.

HENRY: Kiss me till your birthday!

(ELEANOR *and* HENRY *embrace passionately. He breaks and cries out:*)

HENRY: To the tent!

ELEANOR: Everyone's coming!

HENRY: Are we or are we not the world's most magnificent couple?

ELEANOR: Oh, modesty!

(*As* PEOPLE *of all ranks enter from everywhere,* HENRY *calls out to them:*)

HENRY: Are we or are we not the world's most magnificent couple?

ELEANOR: The man is shameless—!

HENRY: Are we or are we not—?!

(*The* PEOPLE *cheer them both.*)

PEOPLE: Yes! You are! You are! (*Etc.*)

HENRY: (*Persistently, to* ELEANOR:) Are we or are we not—!

ELEANOR: (*Capitulating*) We are!

(*The* PEOPLE *cheer.*)

HENRY: How this woman here astounds me! That a creature who has so many talents horizontally, can have so many talents vertically as well! She swims, thinks, rides, sings, shoots! She is my best companion! Her pulse is matched to mine, her breath, her blood. She reads my mind without my speaking!

ELEANOR: Perhaps it's that we're one soul in two bodies.

HENRY: Then I thank heaven that I found you. Otherwise, I'd have gone through life in half. May we never be outside each other's sight, outside each other's touch.

(*A* PAGE *brings goblets of wine.* HENRY *takes one.*)

HENRY: Let me never drink in England that my lady doesn't take the first sip from the cup.

(ELEANOR *drinks. Then* HENRY *drinks from the same place. He puts his arm around her.*)

ELEANOR: My lord—there are affairs of state—

HENRY: *(As if wakening)* Oh, yes. I see them. ... Must we?

ELEANOR: Yes. I'm afraid we must.

HENRY: Will you help?

ELEANOR: Of course.

HENRY: *(To* ELEANOR, *as he gestures toward a* FAT CLERGYMAN*)* How shall we keep peace with the Archbishop?

ELEANOR: *(After considering a moment)* Feed him.

(The ARCHBISHOP *laughs. Food is brought. He follows it off.)*

HENRY: And how shall we get this Baron to let me run a highway through his lands?

ELEANOR: Smile.

*(*HENRY *tries it. The* BARON *turns away from him.* ELEANOR *comes down and smiles at the* BARON. *The* BARON *smiles and nods consent.)*

HENRY: And how shall we get this merchant here to pay me his back taxes?

MERCHANT: The air is free and so should be my breathing of it!

HENRY: The air is free so long as I keep it that way. And for me to afford to keep it that way, you must contribute to the cause!

MERCHANT: I swear I haven't got a penny!

HENRY: *(To* ELEANOR:*)* How shall we get this merchant to pay me his back taxes?

ELEANOR: Look inside the lining of his coat.

*(*HENRY *starts to shake the* MERCHANT's *coat.)*

MERCHANT: I swear that I have nothing—!

(Gold coins tumble out of the coat.)

HENRY: *(Picking up the coins)* What exquisite poverty! *(To the* MERCHANT:*)* You see? She's magical! *(*HENRY *takes some of the coins and gives the* MERCHANT *back the rest.)*

MERCHANT: *(Muttering to a bystander)* I see now why they say the King of England is part man, part woman.

HENRY: *(Overhearing)* Who says that?

MERCHANT: Everybody.

HENRY: Which part is which?

MERCHANT: You're the body. She's the head.

HENRY: Oh? Do they say that?

MERCHANT: I've seen drawings of it.

HENRY: I'd like to see one.

MERCHANT: I doubt, my lord, that you would be amused.

(The MERCHANT *goes. There is an awkward silence.)*

HENRY: *(After a moment, suddenly)* Strike the tents!

ELEANOR: But Henry, there are cases to be heard, and judgments to be made. These people have been waiting—

HENRY: The people of Devon have been waiting, too. I've decided to listen to them.

(The tents are being struck. The PEOPLE *are packing and exiting in some confusion.* HENRY *shouts out:)*

HENRY: Follow me west if you need my attention!

ELEANOR: You're leaving here because of that one man?

HENRY: I'm leaving here because I feel like leaving!

ELEANOR: You know that jokes are always made about people in high places. Because commoners are common it's no reason to fly into a rage—

HENRY: I'm not flying into a rage! His words meant nothing to me.

ELEANOR: Then why, if you're going west, are my belongings heading eastward?

HENRY: I need your help.

ELEANOR: Somewhere away from you?

HENRY: In London.

ELEANOR: How can you need my help in London?

HENRY: I want you to civilize the place! Fill it with music, painting, poetry!

ELEANOR: Exiled to the arts!

HENRY: Can't you do it, then?

ELEANOR: My love, if you want a bastion of civility, then you shall have it.

(The scene transforms itself as she describes it.)

ELEANOR: You shall have velvets and candelabra, silver goblets, knives and even forks. You shall have zither players flocking through the windows and poets oozing in from underneath the floor.

*(*POETS *and* MUSICIANS *appear in great numbers and stand, as in tableau.)*

ELEANOR: You shall have painters, sculptors, minstrels, dancers—. Culture to the rafters—! And when it all is done, you'll take one look and— *(She looks around. She can't find* HENRY. *She laughs and searches for him, playfully.)* Henry—? Henry—! *(*ELEANOR *searches for him behind the tapestries, and behind the* POETS *and* MUSICIANS, *who do not move. She searches, but she cannot find him. She murmurs, with a sense of loss:)*

ELEANOR: Henry...

(Suddenly, the MUSICIANS *strike up a chord. The court of London comes to life around her.* DANCERS *and* MUSICIANS *swirl about, with* ELEANOR *at the center. She joins the dance, and is transported to a high, cushioned place. And as she sits, enthroned in pillows,* POETS *make rhymes to her. A* POET *steps forth and sings:)*

FIRST POET:
Oh, golden lady, sitting in the shade,
Why don't you come and sit out in the sun?
Of sun on cheek my poetry is made.
But if you stay in shade, my poem's done.

ELEANOR: *(Ironically)* Superb!

SECOND POET:
Your voice is song,
Your smile is light,
Your eyes are fire,
Your frown is night,
Your breast is grass,
My love is dew,
Oh let the morn
Find dew on you.

ELEANOR: *(Ironically)* Remarkable!

THIRD POET:
If ever there dwelt, in land, sea or air,
A woman of qualities more fair or rare—

(He continues his poem, but ELEANOR *does not hear him.)*

(A thin sensitive YOUTH *with serious dark eyes has come up close and says to her:)*

VENTADOUR: Why do you listen to these songs? You hate them.

ELEANOR: I beg your pardon?

VENTADOUR: It is below you—to look at these creatures and smile!

ELEANOR: *(Amused)* Oh?

VENTADOUR: They aren't worthy of your time!

ELEANOR: And who is?

VENTADOUR: I am.

ELEANOR: And who are you?

VENTADOUR: Bernard de Ventadour. Poet.

ELEANOR: You're brazen, Ventadour.

VENTADOUR: You must be rescued from the company of idiots!

ELEANOR: Ah, now I see! You think your poetry surpasses theirs!

VENTADOUR: I know it does.

ELEANOR: Because it's bold?

VENTADOUR: Because it's honest.

ELEANOR: Can honesty enhance a triolet about an eyebrow?

VENTADOUR: I have no triolet about your eyebrow. That's not your most important part.

ELEANOR: What is?

VENTADOUR: The part inside. The part invisible.

ELEANOR: You cannot write of that. You know nothing about it!

VENTADOUR: I've watched you from the shadows for six months now. I can tell your moods, your thoughts, by the fraction of a glance.

ELEANOR: I doubt that I'm as readable as you imagine.

VENTADOUR: Will you try me? I have a poem about it—

ELEANOR: *(Moving away from him)* I've already given you more time than I should.

(But the others have disappeared and VENTADOUR *persists.)*

VENTADOUR: My poem is about a woman, a woman of great beauty, whose beauty is irrelevant to her fame. My poem is about a proud woman, a great woman, a woman who hates idleness, a woman who loves the pulsing center of the world—but finds somehow that she has been banished from it. She is the queen of poetry and music,—but all the real and serious business happens far outside her realm. Condemned to senseless hours, with fools for her companions, she waits to live the life she loved again. Waits. Expects each moment to be rescued. But somehow has begun to fear—the rescuer may never come...

ELEANOR: Your poetry doesn't scan.

VENTADOUR: Truth doesn't have to.

ELEANOR: If you must make poems, make them on subjects poets know about!

VENTADOUR: Poets know about love.

ELEANOR: And so do women.

VENTADOUR: Poets know about forbidden love.

ELEANOR: And women know about the best love—married love, the love of a woman for the man who is her husband, lover, god and hero.

VENTADOUR: I caught a glimpse of the husband, lover, god and hero months ago, in Normandy. The world exists to be his mirror!

ELEANOR: How handsome, then, the world must be!

VENTADOUR: It looks like this...

(HENRY *strides in.*)

ELEANOR: Henry—!

(ELEANOR *embraces* HENRY.)

HENRY: Madame, I should like to survive your welcome!

ELEANOR: How are you? When did you get here? How strong and firm you are!

HENRY: If all you had for company was this— *(He gestures toward* VENTADOUR.*)*

ELEANOR: Bernard de Ventadour, —poet.

HENRY: Can he think when he's so skinny?

ELEANOR: I got a poem from him for every pinch you were bestowing on the continent.

HENRY: Lady, you must have one hell of a library!

ELEANOR: How good it is to see you! Tell me everything! Tell me all! What kept you away from me so many centuries?

HENRY: Those Barons of your Aquitaine. What a willful lot they are! A contest of wills. But I finally managed to tame them.

ELEANOR: Why didn't you ask me to help you with them?

HENRY: Why? I managed very nicely on my own.

(VENTADOUR *catches* ELEANOR's *eye.*)

VENTADOUR: Excuse me.

HENRY: No, don't leave. I can't stay long.

ELEANOR: Ventadour—

(VENTADOUR *understands she wishes him to go. He exits.*)

HENRY: I only have a minute—

ELEANOR: A minute? After months and months away—

HENRY: The continent is straightened out at last! Heads up and asses in their places. My order, my justice, my law—. And the French and Spanish just stand there blinking. How could Henry Plantagenet get so strong so fast? *(He laughs.)*

ELEANOR: And what do you tell them?

HENRY: Luck! The will of heaven! Why, even the babes who are born are born to my advantage! Last week, your Louis, on his third wife, presented his subjects with another piddling daughter!

ELEANOR: Poor Louis!

HENRY: He made a pilgrimage to Compostella, but only saw his people's backsides. Just as he was passing, all Europe happened to be facing me!

ELEANOR: Is it true, as they say, that you're asked to bathe in wine so your subjects can drink it?

HENRY: On my honor! They pick the grass I walk on to cure dropsy. They slaughter their best calves, so I can eat. Knights offer me their wives, their daughters—

ELEANOR: And do you take them?

HENRY: Only when absolutely necessary.

ELEANOR: I suppose it's a king's prerogative—

HENRY: Do you mind?

ELEANOR: Not as long as I don't know.

HENRY: Oh, Eleanor—you ought to see me as I travel through the country—

ELEANOR: I would like to.

HENRY: The planets are lined up right for me!

ELEANOR: I suspected that some time ago.

HENRY: I have the proof—right here. *(He pats a leather pouch at his waist.)* One night I lay down to sleep in a mossy field in Brittany. The ground was absolutely smooth. But underneath me, I felt something hard. I felt beneath the blanket. There was a rock there. I threw it toward the fire—and it split in half. ... In the morning, when they doused the campfire, both halves of this strange stone were lying there. *(He takes the stone out of the pouch.)* They brought it to me. Would you like to see what was inside? *(He hands it to her.)* Here, on the right half—the outline of all Europe. *All* Europe. And here, on the left half, in the corner, dimly etched but recognizable—an H. You see?

ELEANOR: *(Unable to see it)* It's very—hard—to trace the lines...

HENRY: The skies have chosen me to give a shape to life. To make their manageable, living kingdom. I feel—a certain *will* in nature. As if every stone, every hill, every province were crying out for *me* to give it shape. Make order out of chaos. *I* was picked to do it. It was written in this rock, eons ago. What is written there, will be.

ELEANOR: I pray that you have read its lines correctly. *(She gives him back the stone.)*

HENRY: Oh, God, I am alive—! And for a purpose!

ELEANOR: I envy you...

HENRY: I have to go now. I'm needed in the north. The rock shows lands far more extensive than our borders—

ELEANOR: I'm coming, too!

HENRY: But Eleanor, you can't—

ELEANOR: Why not?

HENRY: You're pregnant.

ELEANOR: I shall be the first to deliver a child on horseback!

HENRY: Don't be reckless with my cubs! I'm making empires for them.

(An adoring CROWD enters and surrounds HENRY.)

ELEANOR: His name will be Richard. He'll look exactly like you. He'll be the favorite of all my sons. And the hour after he is born, I'm setting out to join you!

HENRY: Find me!

(The PEOPLE sweep HENRY out with them.)

(Part of the setting disappears.)

(A NURSE enters, carrying a BOY BABY.)

ELEANOR: Where is the King?

NURSE: No one knows...

(All of the trappings of the court disappear. The NURSE exits with the BABY.)

(ELEANOR is alone in another place, a garden. From a distance, VENTADOUR approaches, singing:)

VENTADOUR: *(Singing:)*
When flowers fade,
And winter comes with snows,
When nothing fragrant grows,
Then there is love,
Love in Idleness.

When eagles rest,
And falcons hide their eyes,
When time no longer flies,
Then there is love,
Love in Idleness.

When winds are still,
When suns no longer rise,
When greyness fills the skies,
When hands that once held oceans
Now are dry and still,

When you're alone,
You hear a distant song,
A singer comes along,
And offers love,
Love in Idleness.

(VENTADOUR *comes toward her. As he talks,* ELEANOR *listens pensively. She does not move away.*)

VENTADOUR: I dare...only because you are so often alone—and so often seen walking in the garden now, doing nothing. Let me walk beside you. This is not the season for women to walk alone.

This is the season when the birds begin to sing. I hear the cries of the stork and the heron. Blue flowers are thrusting their way through the bushes, the streams are clear as they run between their sandy banks, and over there, the white, white petals of the lily—open...

Give me some sign, some token, that says I am allowed to walk beside you—and to speak some of the thoughts that are in my heart...

(*Suddenly the sound of a* SERVANT GIRL'*s laughter is heard off stage. Then the laughter of another* SERVANT GIRL.)

(ELEANOR *turns sharply to listen. As she does, she accidentally drops her gloves.* VENTADOUR *picks them up and holds them.*)

(*Two* SERVANT GIRLS *come running on, laughing. When they see* ELEANOR, *they stop short.*)

FIRST SERVANT GIRL: It was wonderful, having the King again, wasn't it, Madame?

ELEANOR: You mean—having the King home again, don't you?

FIRST SERVANT GIRL: (*Giggling*) Oh, yes, Madame!

SECOND SERVANT GIRL: What a pity he's gone off! The corridors are so full of surprises when he's around!

(*The* SERVANT GIRLS *exit, giggling.*)

VENTADOUR: The pains of married love are sharp. But the pains of forbidden love give pleasure. Be loved by me—in secret. In all these raging empty hours of yours—be loved by me... (*He kisses* ELEANOR'*s gloves and holds them to him.*)

ELEANOR: Your song is lovely. And very tender... But it is meant for some Queen of Love—not for me.

VENTADOUR: You *are* the Queen of Love!

ELEANOR: If I am, it is for one man only.

VENTADOUR: Is that why you lie with him? For love?

ELEANOR: Yes.

VENTADOUR: And why does he lie with you?!

(HENRY's *voice suddenly bellows out:*)

HENRY: *(As he enters)* Here she is! The greatest boy-maker in all of Christendom! Eleanor of England!

(*A bright light picks out* ELEANOR. VENTADOUR *disappears.* HENRY *waves his arm and introduces:*)

HENRY: Louis of France!

(*Louis appears. They are in the throne room of France. The lands of each King are brought in. Henry's lands are extensive, but of a rough texture. Louis's are smaller— but as smooth as satin. Henry says to Eleanor and Louis:*)

HENRY: Kiss, for Christ's sake! You're going to be in-laws!

(ELEANOR *and* LOUIS *approach each other.*)

LOUIS: Eleanor—how are you?

ELEANOR: Louis—how are *you*?

LOUIS: Older. I just get older. But you—you seem to have struck some kind of pact with Time.

ELEANOR: Why, Louis—you've learned about pretty speeches! Tell me, have you lost your taste for candied apricots?

LOUIS: Why, no. I love them more than ever. But my digestive tract is not so tolerant. So all my spiritual conflicts are resolved.

HENRY: *(To* LOUIS:*)* Did you ever think you'd see the day when you'd be matching up her sons to your daughters? What a time we're heading into, eh, Louis? Uniting our children! So one day all of this— *(He gestures to England, then France.)*—all of this—will live under one great banner.

LOUIS: The Plantagenet banner.

HENRY: Can I help it, Louis? I'm the one who's got the sons!

LOUIS: Your sons through Eleanor, the critical portion of your lands through Eleanor...

HENRY: How different things would be this minute, eh, Louis, if, twenty years ago, you'd been half an inch more a man!

ELEANOR: That is a speech which would cast more credit on the speaker if it were left unspoken!

HENRY: *(Aside to her)* There are many speeches which would cast more credit if they were left unspoken. Especially speeches that rhyme!

ELEANOR: Would you be kind enough to clarify that statement?

HENRY: We'll discuss it later. *(He turns from her.)* How does she look to you, Louis? Thrived under me, wouldn't you say? You ought to see her when she's busy boy-making! Oh, God, it must be great to be a woman—and carry the future in your guts!

ELEANOR: Almost as great as being a man—and carrying it in more reasonable parts of you.

HENRY: This is the most triumphant moment of your life, Lady. Smile! Take credit for having made great males to give to history!

ELEANOR: I'm proud of my sons. But I had nothing to do with what sex they were born into.

HENRY: Don't be absurd! We planned it in advance! You know what we should have done, Louis? We should have both married her *together*! You on the left side of the bed and me on the right. Then we could have had our great kingdom in our lifetimes! Or at least a child out of her who'd be heir to us both! Instead, we have to match up our babes and wait and wait—

LOUIS: It will all come to you, —in time... *(He lowers his head despondently.)*

ELEANOR: Are you well? Would you like us to come back another day?

HENRY: No! We're here!

LOUIS: Yes. Let us get it over with. *(He takes up a parchment.)*

ELEANOR: *(Aside to* HENRY:*)* Please be gracious. This is hard for him.

HENRY: It's not my fault. It's destiny. Accept it.

LOUIS: *(Speaking wearily, with great regrets)* I give my little daughter, Marguerite, into your care, to be raised by you, and to be married, when she comes of age, to your son Henry.

HENRY: Her dowry is the Vexin, right?

LOUIS: *(Regretfully)* Yes. The Vexin. ... And for your son Richard, I give you my infant daughter, Alais—

HENRY: She gets the County of Berry. Is that so?

LOUIS: *(More regretfully)* Yes, that is so.

HENRY: The girls come into possession of their lands on the day they marry, don't they? I mean, they don't have to wait to get them till you die?

LOUIS: *(More and more reluctant)* They come into possession on the day they marry. They don't have to wait until I die.

HENRY: Then, when you die, all France goes to our children's children.

(LOUIS *paces. This has become too much for him.*)

ELEANOR: *(Disturbed for* LOUIS*)* Henry—

HENRY: So in the time of my grandsons, all these lands will be under my flag. And that begins the glorious centuries!

(*A* MESSENGER *enters and whispers to* LOUIS *as* HENRY *continues:*)

HENRY: There will be one law, one justice, one King of France and England. He'll sit on a throne in London and—

(*Bells ring—and ring—and ring! The* MESSENGER *exits.* HENRY *and* ELEANOR *look at each other, puzzled.*)

LOUIS: I have just become the father of a son!

(HENRY *and* ELEANOR *are speechless.*)

LOUIS: After twenty-eight years and three marriages—I have managed to produce a son! *(Sobbing for joy)* Oh, God! Dear God! I never thought I'd be granted such a moment!

ELEANOR: *(With mixed emotions)* Louis, this is—wonderful—news—

HENRY: I didn't know you had a wife who was pregnant—

LOUIS: Would you excuse me? Would you excuse me, please? I have to go—

HENRY: Does it still stand? All that we were just discussing?

LOUIS: We'll talk. ... We'll talk tomorrow...

HENRY: You'll want a wife for the boy. Eleanor and I can help you. We have some daughters—*(He turns to* ELEANOR *.)* We do have a daughter or two, don't we, Eleanor?

LOUIS: I think I'll name him Philip. Philip, the gift of God. Forgive me, would you please? I've got to go to church—to give thanks—for my son—my boy baby. I feel, after years and years of wondering, that the heavens are with me after all. *(He goes out.)*

HENRY: Goddam the King of France! Goddam his children!

ELEANOR: And so goes history—on the gender of an egg.

HENRY: I had it all—all—within my hand...

(HENRY *watches, stunned, as the lands are taken out and France is carried away from him. The throne room disappears.*)

(*They are on a dark and windy shore.*)

ELEANOR: How strange, that whole kingdoms can slip away like minnows...

HENRY: The rock said H, not L... *(He reaches for his talisman, takes out one half, then searches wildly.)*

ELEANOR: What's the matter?

HENRY: The right half of the stone—! It's gone—!

ELEANOR: Are you sure?

HENRY: I must have dropped it somewhere, on the road from Paris—

ELEANOR: You couldn't—

HENRY: Only half is here. The left—*(He looks at the rock within his hand. His face grows ashen.)*

ELEANOR: Henry! What is it?

(HENRY hurls the stone away from him.)

HENRY: No—!

ELEANOR: What was on it?

(HENRY, highly disturbed, doesn't answer.)

ELEANOR: What did you see there?

(Agitated, HENRY doesn't respond. ELEANOR crosses to pick up the stone.)

HENRY: Don't touch it! It's cold, *cold*—

(ELEANOR picks up the stone and looks at it.)

HENRY: Do you see—?

ELEANOR: What should I see?

HENRY: ...The death's head...

ELEANOR: Nothing like that is on it. Look for yourself.

HENRY: *(Refusing)* It's there—

ELEANOR: There's no death's-head on this half. There was no map of Europe on the other. Your *eyes* carved out those images—

HENRY: The images were there! Twin prophecies—

ELEANOR: Power or death? ...No, Henry. It's too simple... *(She comes to him.)* You mustn't be afraid...

HENRY: "Afraid—!" *(He suddenly takes the stone from her and hurls it out of sight. His mood changes suddenly to over-elation.)* So heaven has decided to smile on Louis, has it? And decided to show its backside to me? Well, what the hell, I'll manage. If I have to live among enemies, there are ways...

(HENRY is buoyed with defiant strength. Through the following few speeches he moves about, striding purposefully. And in each place he stands, PLANTAGENET SOLDIERS

appear behind him, dimly and silently. HENRY *is arming his borders.* ELEANOR *watches—and each new, silent military presence fills her with alarm.)*

ELEANOR: Louis is not your enemy.

HENRY: Would you say his desires are mine in every particular?

(A few more motionless, unlistening SOLDIERS *appear.)*

ELEANOR: I would say it is perfectly possible for you and Louis to live beside each other in peace and love.

HENRY: Peace and love. Peace and love! You're full to the gills with soppy sentiment, aren't you? Is that why you had to take on a lover? To handle the overflow?

ELEANOR: A lover?

HENRY: You shouldn't have tumbled with a poet, Lady. Poets can't resist immortalizing the experience by telling all. Do you know your breasts are famous from one tip of the continent to the other?

ELEANOR: How do you know they're *my* breasts? Breasts aren't specific.

HENRY: Is this specific? "Were the lands all mine, from Elbe to the Rhine, I'd count that but little pace, if the Queen of England lay in my embrace."

ELEANOR: Poets will sing—

HENRY: And Queens will inspire them

ELEANOR: If there were that much love, there'd be no time for poetry.

HENRY: There won't be time for poetry any more. *(He displays her white gloves, now soiled.)*

ELEANOR: Did you have him killed?

HENRY: Just banished. Farewell Bernard de Ventadour. *(He flings the gloves away.)*

ELEANOR: There was no need for that. He was only entertaining me while I was doing you a service.

HENRY: And pray what service were you doing me?

ELEANOR: What service am I asked to do—again and again—for England.

(A NURSE *comes in bearing a* BOY BABY.*)*

ELEANOR: His name is Geoffrey.

*(*HENRY *takes the* BABY *and looks into its face for a long, long time. Then he starts to hand it back to the* NURSE, *saying:)*

HENRY: Arm him...

ELEANOR: No—!

(ELEANOR *seizes the* BABY *and hands it to the* NURSE *herself.*)

(HENRY *laughs ruefully. A* SECOND NURSE *enters from the opposite side, carrying another* BOY BABY. ELEANOR *stares at her.*)

HENRY: Well, then, I will just have to manufacture armies—without you.

(ELEANOR *stares at the* SECOND BOY BABY, *then at* HENRY. HENRY *leaps to a high place and, as the* FIRST NURSE *exits left with the* FIRST BOY BABY, *he leads his* SOLDIERS *and the* SECOND NURSE *and* SECOND BOY BABY *out in the opposite direction.*)

(ELEANOR *is alone for a moment. Then a* THIRD NURSE *enters. When* ELEANOR *sees her, she shouts:*)

ELEANOR: Show me no more of his bastard children! Not one of them is worth the broken fingernail of one right-born son from the womb of Aquitaine!

NURSE: *(Quietly)* I know...

(ELEANOR *turns—and looks into the face of her* NURSE *from childhood. The landscape has become more peaceful.*)

ELEANOR: Nursey! Nursey! Is it really you?

NURSE: It is.

ELEANOR: How long it's been—!

NURSE: Almost a lifetime.

ELEANOR: Did you come all the way from the Aquitaine?

NURSE: I was considerably younger when I started out.

ELEANOR: Sit. Please, sit with me.

NURSE: Do Queens sit on the grass in England?

ELEANOR: I love to watch the children playing by the brook.

NURSE: I'm surprised to see you here—in a country retreat.

ELEANOR: So far from the court's center?

(*The* NURSE *nods.*)

ELEANOR: There is a certain—rank—in England. I am second.

NURSE: Put there by him?

ELEANOR: By wisdom, Nursey. Henry isn't Louis. Louis left a vacuum. I had to fill it. But Henry—overfills his space. To come within it—is to collide.

NURSE: And so you sit out at the edges.

ELEANOR: Yes.

NURSE: If only all of us could do that, too...

ELEANOR: What do you mean?

NURSE: Do you know how things are in your husband's provinces?

ELEANOR: *(Averting her eyes)* My husband runs his provinces himself.

NURSE: You hear no reports? No rumors?

ELEANOR: I know he runs his lands by law.

NURSE: By law! Oh, God, yes! Law! Laws everywhere! Thou shalt not walk this path or plant this field, thou shalt not catch this fish, thou shalt not sing this song or pick this berry, thou shalt not sell this pot or wear this color on a Tuesday, thou shalt not name this child a name the sovereign does not approve. There are so many laws that one can break them without knowing it! And if you break them, the punishments are six times deadlier than the crimes. Last week a man was hanged for pissing on an oak! It's come to that in your husband's territories. ... His order isn't order—it is tyranny!

ELEANOR: From the moment that the bells rang out for Louis, Henry tightened...

NURSE: It is a country where movements are so regulated that only an ancient messenger like me could get through.

ELEANOR: You were *sent*—?

NURSE: To tell you that your people of the Aquitaine will not put up with this much longer.

ELEANOR: What will they do—?

NURSE: Rebel.

ELEANOR: They are not strong enough—

NURSE: They plan to seek the help of France.

ELEANOR: Louis would not support such a rebellion!

NURSE: Not unless he had some grievances of his own.

ELEANOR: He has no grievances—

NURSE: God grant that it remain that way.

ELEANOR: I must see Henry. Talk with him.

NURSE: Yes. That's what I came to ask you. ... But even as I say it, I know it's won't do any good.

ELEANOR: Why not?

NURSE: They say he is past listening.

ELEANOR: Do they say he is past listening to me?

NURSE: *(Avoiding an answer)* Try what you can...

(*The* NURSE *fades into the shadows.* HENRY *appears and* ELEANOR *approaches him.*)

ELEANOR: Henry—

HENRY: Ssh!

(*Music is heard.* ELEANOR *listens.* HENRY *paces with suppressed excitement.*)

ELEANOR: What is going on?

(HENRY *gestures upstage and a light reveals a wedding scene, now taking place.*)

HENRY: The wedding of Louis's daughter to your eldest son.

ELEANOR: The bride is three years old!

HENRY: Her lands are quite mature.

ELEANOR: She was given into your care. You were to wait—

HENRY: Till Louis changes his mind and revokes her dowry?

ELEANOR: Louis keeps his word—

HENRY: In a few more minutes, he will have no choice.

(ELEANOR *runs toward the ceremony.*)

ELEANOR: Stop the wedding! Stop the wedding!

(*But the ceremony continues.*)

HENRY: The only voice they hear—is mine.

ELEANOR: *You* stop them—

HENRY: Bad luck. Their children would be born two-headed.

ELEANOR: Louis is slow to anger, but this will send him into a rage.

HENRY: What's the matter? Wouldn't it amuse you to see your saint and sinner husbands at each other's throats?

ELEANOR: It would be *you* who had provoked it!

HENRY: Me? I am for peace. All I am doing is witnessing a wedding.

ELEANOR: With this to encourage them, every enemy you have will find refuge in Louis's court. They'll all unite against you—

HENRY: Let them! I'm tired of little brush fires. Tired of diplomacy. Tired of being politic with genteel lies! Let's begin the conflagration! It is killing me to wait!

ELEANOR: You can't take on the world—

HENRY: You thought I could when you and I began—

ELEANOR: Henry, this is madness.

HENRY: How I love your flattery!

ELEANOR: You can't win in such a confrontation!

HENRY: Thank you for your confidence and faith!

ELEANOR: You'll bring it all, all, down upon your head!

HENRY: By God, I married a Cassandra!

ELEANOR: Stop the wedding!

(But the wedding is over. The CHILDREN *are husband and wife.)*

HENRY: Kiss the bride and groom!

*(*ELEANOR *hugs them.)*

ELEANOR: Poor babies. Poor, dear babies.

HENRY: The bride's lands are mine now. If Louis wants them, he will have to fight.

(Two SOLDIERS *appear carrying the bride's lands. They exit with the* WEDDING PARTY.*)*

ELEANOR: I can't believe you know what you're doing...

HENRY: When the world pushes in, you push out in any way that's open to you. I use the weapons that I have. It's only Louis who can depend on weapons made by God.

ELEANOR: But—

HENRY: And don't come at me with your no, no, no's again! I do not have to listen to you! I am the King! The King! That name still has some meaning to it! I take advice from no one. No one at all! *(He strides out.)*

ELEANOR: *(Quietly, after him:)* Not even from the person in the world who cares most what happens to you.

(To a SERVANT *who has entered:)*

ELEANOR: Saddle my horse—

(The SERVANT *exits.)*

(The NURSE *emerges from the shadows)*

NURSE: Where are you going?

ELEANOR: To the Aquitaine.

NURSE: What will you do there?

ELEANOR: End the rebellion before it starts.

NURSE: Are you going without telling the King?

ELEANOR: I can't trust him to deal with them diplomatically. He's spoiling for a fight. If I tell him there's trouble he'll be only too happy to rush in with arms and armies—

NURSE: Please, I beg you, for your own sake—

ELEANOR: Come. No cowardice—

NURSE: I've seen his rage. He's an inferno!

ELEANOR: Of course he is! Do you think that what he has to do can be done by some simpering weakling? He's been charged by God to make an England—and he's making it! The people owe him faith—and time.

NURSE: And you think you can convince your people to give those to him?

ELEANOR: Do they still love me?

NURSE: Of course they love you!

ELEANOR: Then this is their time to show me proof. Hand me my cloak—

NURSE: *(Refusing)* It's dangerous for you! Your husband will be wild—!

ELEANOR: He can't hurt me. But he could hurt my people very badly. *(She takes the cloak herself.)*

NURSE: Forget the hero's role for once—!

ELEANOR: I am not, any longer, the young crusader. I am older, wiser, and I know exactly what I risk. But there's something I can do that no one else can do—to help him. I can go to my people, interpret his laws to them, beg for their patience. I can ask them for their understanding. I can bring him back—their love.

(ELEANOR *throws on her cloak and is instantly enveloped in darkness. The* NURSE *makes one protesting gesture, then goes out.*)

(HENRY *suddenly appears in a pool of light in a great hall of the castle. He speaks in tones that are utterly glacial.*)

HENRY: I understand you've been to the Aquitaine, Lady.

(The light comes up on ELEANOR, *standing in her cloak.)*

ELEANOR: Yes. I've been there.

HENRY: How was the journey?

ELEANOR: I bring you, from my people, their fidelity and love.

HENRY: Did I ask you to go?

ELEANOR: No, Henry. I took permission from the pact we used to have, to help each other.

HENRY: If I wanted your assistance, I'd have sent for you! ...What was the matter? Didn't you trust me to face them? Were you afraid I'd strangle them with my bare hands?

ELEANOR: I wanted them to know you as I know you—

HENRY: *Do* you know me?

ELEANOR: Yes.

HENRY: Do you like what you know?

ELEANOR: I—

(But ELEANOR *has hesitated a beat too long.* HENRY *smiles.)*

HENRY: It doesn't matter. I don't really need your approval, do I?

ELEANOR: No, Henry.

HENRY: You can act without my approval, I can act without yours, isn't that so?

ELEANOR: Yes—. That is so.

HENRY: In fact, neither of us needs the other's approval for anything.

(A SERVANT *enters with goblets on a tray.)*

ELEANOR: True—

HENRY: We're in complete agreement! Blissful harmony! *(He raises a goblet.)* Let me never drink in England, that my lady doesn't take the first sip from the cup!

ELEANOR: Henry, I—

(But ELEANOR *was not the lady that he meant. She turns to see, behind her, the entrance of a golden-haired* YOUNG WOMAN, *and, with her, many* MEMBERS OF THE COURT.*)*

(Well aware of the effect he is creating, HENRY *walks past* ELEANOR *and offers his goblet to the* YOUNG WOMAN. *The* YOUNG WOMAN *drinks. Then* HENRY *drinks.)*

(Then, with the YOUNG WOMAN *on his arm,* HENRY *sweeps upstage, where there is wine and gaiety.)*

(Far outside the circle of merriment, ELEANOR *watches. Then, stealthily,* VENTADOUR *appears beside her. And as* HENRY *flaunts the* YOUNG WOMAN *before the court,* VENTADOUR, *accompanying himself, sings so only* ELEANOR *can hear:)*

VENTADOUR: *(Singing:)*
Who is the woman
Who holds the King,
Who salves the King,
Who loves the King?
Who is the woman who enfolds the King?
Is it not the Queen?

Who is the woman
Who is always there,
Who plaits his hair,

Who chases care?
Who is the woman who removes despair?
Is it not the Queen?

Who is there in the evening and the morning?
Who is ever at his beck and call?
Whom does he seek when his heart with love is calling?
Whom does he cherish above one and all?

Who is the woman
With blue eyes bold,
With hair of gold,
Whose breasts unfold
All of the comforts that a king can hold?
Her name is Rosamund...

ELEANOR: *(Repeating the name in a whisper)* Rosamund...

VENTADOUR: *(Singing:)* Eleanor—is Queen.

(HENRY *lifts* ROSAMUND *in his arms and shouts:*)

HENRY: This is what women are for, you see? To be carried from the bed to the embroidery frame and back to bed again! My lovely lady never speaks, she never scolds, she never meddles. She never thinks she can do my work better than I. She does her needlepoint by day—and by night, she makes me happy. Here she is, the healer, mender, lover—Rosamund! I give you Rosamund! She's everything that ever a woman should be!

(HENRY *starts to take* ROSAMUND *off. The* COURT *starts to follow. But* HENRY *shakes his head. The members of the* COURT *laugh knowingly and exit in the opposite direction.* HENRY *carries* ROSAMUND *out.*)

(*When they have gone,* ELEANOR *hears* HENRY's *bawdy laughter,* ROSAMUND's *responding laughter, and* HENRY's *manfully erotic response.*)

(*Unable to bear the look on her face,* VENTADOUR *comes to* ELEANOR *and covers her ears with his hands. Quietly,* ELEANOR *says:*)

ELEANOR: You and I may be the only two in England who remember what it is to be tender. All gentleness has gone out of the world, except for this little glow right here. It is only the smallest spark—

VENTADOUR: With me, it is a raging fire!

ELEANOR: *(Smiling gently)* It is only the smallest spark,—but we must keep it burning. *(She turns toward him.)* You and I must keep love alive in the world. When this spark goes out, there is only—

NURSE: Death.

(*The* NURSE *is assisted in, barely conscious.* ELEANOR *runs over to her.*)

ELEANOR: Dear God, what has happened!

NURSE: I got in the way of an arrow...

ELEANOR: An arrow—!

NURSE: There is too much order in England. ... I walked into a field—where people of my rank—are not allowed to go... *(Her eyes close.)*

ELEANOR: No... No... Die of plague, die of leprosy, die of old age, but do not die of an arrow! ...Nurse! Nurse! Wait! Do not die in England of an arrow!

(The NURSE opens her eyes once more—then dies. ELEANOR cries out:)

ELEANOR: I commanded you! I told you you must *not*—!

(The NURSE's body is carried upstage into the shadows, where PEOPLE who carried her in minister to it.)

(VENTADOUR remains where he was standing. Slowly, ELEANOR gets his instrument and hands it to him. A long look passes between them. He goes.)

(From the distance, HENRY enters noisily, carousing with some DRINKING COMPANIONS. ELEANOR goes over to him. Her tone is strained, ironic.)

ELEANOR: My lord, I would like to ask a favor.

HENRY: The old crone wants to ask a favor! She usually manages everything by herself. She must be weakening. Today she comes to me to ask a favor. Yes? What is it?

ELEANOR: *(Steadily)* I should like you to give me back my nurse.

HENRY: She wants her old nurse! She has reached her second childhood! Got to have her nursey!

ELEANOR: It is a simple request. Give me back my nurse!

(At that moment, the PEOPLE raise the NURSE's body and start to cross in a funeral cortege.)

(Suddenly silent, HENRY stops them with a gesture as they pass before him. He looks into the lifeless face, then allows them to pass on. All exit but ELEANOR and HENRY.)

ELEANOR: What a perfect, ordered world you have created, Henry. You are just, you are guiltless, but all around you bloodshed happens. What could be the cause?

(HENRY is silent.)

ELEANOR: Do you think her death is one of few? It's one of many! What are you doing to your country? Your "order" has become abomination. Your "law" is wanton permission for inflicting death. It's Satan's law! It's anti-life! And you—you are the murderer! ...Where is the glorious kingdom of Henry the Second? Bring on the great just kingdom that you promised me so long ago!

HENRY: It's not as easy as it seemed in the beginning! Things slip this way and that! They will not stay in line!

ELEANOR: So you destroy whatever wanders?

HENRY: I could have managed it if luck had stayed on my side!

ELEANOR: It isn't luck you need, it's *sense*. Look at what is happening and deal with it. Your enemies grow daily. Men who swore to be faithful to you can no longer tolerate the life you offer. They're scurrying to Louis. And Louis waits—

HENRY: Why does he wait?

ELEANOR: God knows. He already has more than enough provocation. Perhaps he hopes for some sign from you. Some personal assurance—. Go to him—

HENRY: Go crawling on my knees to his palace on the Seine?

ELEANOR: Meet him beneath an oak, in neutral territory. Give him the kiss of peace.

HENRY: The kiss of ass! You want me to capitulate!

ELEANOR: Show him you're his friend.

HENRY: You want me to give in!

ELEANOR: Only a bit.

HENRY: I won't!

ELEANOR: Then you're a madman, not a king.

HENRY: *(Sarcastically)* I knew I could depend on you for support in all corners!

ELEANOR: You know you can depend on me to tell you what no one else would dare to say: You have no reasons for what you do any more. You do them because you do them. You stride about like a giant, but do not have the greatness to make a single, soft conciliating gesture, the gesture that would help you to—

HENRY: Nasal! All so nasal! Do female voices all go hard like that when they reach the decade you have got to?

ELEANOR: The order that you hope for will never come through force. You've got to make men *want* your order. And arms and swords and running to and fro, and blood and the making of countless new enemies daily will never in a million years assist you in—

HENRY: Women should be killed, I tell you, just before their tubes dry up! Before they turn into these screaming, cackling furies—!

ELEANOR: I hate my voice! I cannot bear the sound of it! I can't believe these strange, shrill noises are coming from my throat. But listen, if you can—

HENRY: Shrew! Harpy!

ELEANOR: *(Deeply)* There is no way to warn but to warn. And no way to warn quietly one who is all but deaf to you. It is not a side of beef which is at stake, it is a kingdom. If words of mine, however shrill, can save it, I will shout. If I am within your hearing because I have been, until very recently, within your bed, then I will speak.

HENRY: Then speak, but do not criticize. I did not share my mattress with a judge!

ELEANOR: I love and want to help you—

HENRY: Help me what?

ELEANOR: Bring *love* alive again! Bring *mercy* alive again!

HENRY: Then come! Come help me! Serve up the breast and thigh meat, Lady! Come on! Let's go to bed! We can cuddle up. You can take my hoary head upon your bosom and say, "There now, there, there, now, Henry. Everything you say and do is right."

ELEANOR: There's nothing in the world I want to give you more than my praise and full support—

HENRY: Then do it!

ELEANOR: God! If I only could—

HENRY: Do it! It's the duty of a wife—

ELEANOR: To let her husband take any terrible course, without opposition? To approve of all he does even if she foresees disaster in its wake?

HENRY: Act like a woman!

ELEANOR: You have women enough. Or—one woman. There is all about you the odor of love fulfilled. The perfume of secret trysts, of being folded too long and pressed too hard within the clasp of some secret woman. Where is she? What does she give you that I can't supply in even greater measure?

HENRY: SHE—GIVES—ME—SILENCE! *(He shouts it at her—and then goes out.)*

(ELEANOR *is alone.*)

ELEANOR: So she gives him silence. Silence and comfort. Is that what I should give him? Dear God, if that is all he wants of me, is that what I should give?

(*As* ELEANOR *stands, the setting disappears and she moves toward a room in a country castle.*)

(ROSAMUND *enters, doing embroidery. She hums peacefully as she works.*)

(*Slowly,* ELEANOR *walks toward her, watching the* GIRL *for a long time without speaking. Then she stoops and picks up a thread, saying:*)

ELEANOR: I believe, somehow, you came unraveled.

ROSAMUND: *(Starting suddenly, then falling on her knees)* Madame!

ELEANOR: You have seen me before?

ROSAMUND: Yes.

ELEANOR: From a distance?

ROSAMUND: A great distance.

ELEANOR: *(Steadily)* You lie. You cannot see the King without seeing me. I am the shadow, the substance, the helpmeet, the partner, the tears, the cloak, the halo of the King. And you have seen the King — very closely — have you not?

ROSAMUND: Yes, Madame...

ELEANOR: More closely, even than the Queen has been privileged to see him lately. And therefore, in all justice, you should be the Queen. You must be the Queen — or you must go live in a nunnery. But you shall have the choice yourself.

ROSAMUND: Me, the Queen! And my father was only a simple knight from Wales!

ELEANOR: Ah, Fate, that works so strangely, and thrusts itself even upon the daughters of Welshmen!

(All through the following scene, ELEANOR keeps taking off items of her own clothing and putting them on the girl, so that at the end of the scene, ROSAMUND is almost completely dressed in the Queen's costume.)

ELEANOR: Come now, let's see how you'll do as Queen. Do you have table manners? Can you use a knife and napkin?

ROSAMUND: Oh, yes. And I can keep down three goblets of mead as well!

ELEANOR: You see? You surpass me already! Now let's try another test. ... The Ambassador from the Holy Roman Emperor arrives and looks just like the roast boar you are serving for dinner. The resemblance is unmistakable. What do you do?

ROSAMUND: Roast boar! I think I should love that! Is it anything like mutton?

ELEANOR: Or, what about this? One day, at dawn, a messenger arrives, having found out one of your misdeeds, and offers to be bought into silence. Do you pay him — he is young — or have him killed?

ROSAMUND: At dawn, you say? I never get up until noon. I'm sure by the time I get up, it will all be taken care of.

ELEANOR: Well, you wake up at last. Your husband wants to take you hunting, your children want to take you fishing. What do you do?

ROSAMUND: I have no children, Madame.

ELEANOR: What about this? Your husband says you have the right to certain lands, your Bishop says you'll be damned if you claim them.

ROSAMUND: I have no right to any lands.

ELEANOR: Imagine this, then. Your husband is about to lock himself into a life and death struggle with a man who should be his friend. What do you do?

ROSAMUND: Oh, I know. I tell them to shake hands and kiss each other on both cheeks.

ELEANOR: And if your husband won't?

ROSAMUND: I rub his temples.

ELEANOR: And if it doesn't help?

ROSAMUND: I rub his back.

ELEANOR: And if that doesn't help?

ROSAMUND: I hold him in my arms all night, and sing his favorite songs to him.

ELEANOR: And in the morning?

ROSAMUND: He'll give me a ruby—or an emerald—he always does.

ELEANOR: And what about the friend?

ROSAMUND: What friend?

ELEANOR: The friend who wants the kiss of peace!

ROSAMUND: Oh, him! I've forgotten all about him.

ELEANOR: The kingdom may fall apart if you forget about him.

ROSAMUND: Well, if it does, I'll have my lover all to myself then. And that would be the grandest thing in the world!

ELEANOR: Rosamund—you are forgetful, silent, indolent, stupid—everything the King seems to want in a wife.

ROSAMUND: Am I the Queen yet?

ELEANOR: One moment. One more test and then you'll have the crown. Picture yourself getting up one morning—

ROSAMUND: But I never—

ELEANOR: Picture it as early morning. And picture yourself getting up. Your room is surrounded by doors, and behind each one, someone is waiting.

Behind this one is the King, who orders you to ignore your hereditary lands. Behind this is a baron from your lands, asking why the King is bleeding him dry of money and power.

Behind this great door are your sons, who want you to get favors for them from their father. You want to keep their faith in their father, so you don't dare tell them that what they're asking is more than their father has. ... Behind this door are the merchants.

(ROSAMUND *smiles.*)

ELEANOR: If you buy from them, you will drain the treasury. If you don't, you will cast doubt on the power of the crown. Behind this door is a soldier making threats. Behind this is your husband, refusing to see him. Behind this door is a poet, promising you love. Behind this is your husband, daring you to take it. *(She holds forth the crown.)*

Wake up, my dear, the King is waiting, your sons are waiting, the merchants are waiting, the barons are waiting, the soldiers are waiting, the poets are waiting. Face them, address them, juggle them! Start with which, which one? Where will you start? What will you say to them?

(ROSAMUND, *confused, doesn't know which way to turn.*)

ELEANOR: But wait—but wait—. Before you see anyone, you must bring forth in pain, from your own loins, one healthy, screaming, royal-blooded son—to save them all if nothing that you say can help them.

ROSAMUND: A son?

ELEANOR: And more. More sons, more daughters, more sons and more and more and more, because they die and rebel and get lost and go wild—. Bring him forth, dry your sweat, because the doors are opening and they're all rushing in on you—!

ROSAMUND: *(Thrusting back the crown)* No! No! Take it back! Take it back! I want to live in a nunnery! I want to live in a nunnery! Oh, please!

(HENRY *enters suddenly.*)

HENRY: No! Not to a nunnery! If you want protection, you will always find it in my bed! Go there. Now. And stay. Never leave it.

(ROSAMUND *exits.*)

(*The castle room disappears. There is silence. Then* ELEANOR *speaks softly, with deep emotion:*)

ELEANOR: I would have thought that the heart of a Queen would be large enough to bear anything. But in spite of all your suspicions to the contrary, I find that I am only a woman after all.

I cannot bear to see this stupid girl in my country castle. I cannot bear to see you overcome by demons and unable to let me help you shake yourself free. I cannot bear to find that I am nothing but a thorn to you, and every time you move, I cause you pain.

I came—to view this girl—and to see if, after all, her way was right. Could it be that Eve was put onto the earth to blindly comfort? Was she given gentle hands, compliant breasts, so that man might rest on her in pleasurable, unchallenged sleep?

If all man craves of Eve is that she give solace without question, shouldn't she give it? Should she not, no matter what he does, eternally be there? In a terrifying and chaotic world, shouldn't she be for him still waters, green fields, untroubled earth and sky, his perfect haven?

I listened to this girl—and I answer: ...No. *No!*

The woman who smiles gently as her lover races down the road to his destruction is a monster! A *monster!* Whether she is acting out of ignorance or out of guile. She must cry out against his danger. Cry out to the utmost power of her lungs

But what if he's forbidden her to speak? What if, through some wild and foolish turn of fate, her voice has become an instrument of torture to him, and every word she utters is like a fatal wound?

Shouldn't she *then* shut up? Shouldn't she, for the love they used to bear each other, stop her ears, bind her lips, and seal her eyes, if this is what he wants of her? If all he asks of her is silence, can't she give it?

I answer you with every atom of my being: ...*No!*

Oh, why didn't God make Eve an eyeless, voiceless, brainless creature, a featureless mass of flesh, a throbbing womb for copulation, procreation and death? Why did He have to fashion her with all the senses that He gave her husband? Why did He have to give her the power to see and think and feel in every way the same? If we were to be put on earth to accept self-mutilation and living death, why couldn't we have been made unfeeling and unseeing?

But no. We feel. We see. We overflow with all the gifts of being—and have, with these gifts, just one minuscule restriction: Only by giving them up can our world remain serene...

You have no idea how strongly I've been tempted. I've watched you pacing in the night and screamed out soundlessly to myself: "Good God, he is in *torment!* Give him what he *wants!* What he *needs!*" For I know what you want, what you need, poor husband...

You want me to be your grace, your blessed virgin. You want, from my hand, or some lady's, divine communion, solace, peace. The grace that only God can give, you'd like to have administered by woman.

Don't look at me that way. I know what you are asking. That I, for God, bless you and forgive—no matter what you do, what terrible acts, what great transgressions.

If I could save your soul by that counterfeit grace, then I would give it. But I know, with the force of revelation, that in that touch, erotic and benumbing, would be your soul's death.

I cannot be your grace, Henry. But neither can I be your hell... All I can do, in memory of the love we used to bear each other, is give you presents.

(The light begins to change)

ELEANOR: This cloak. Rosamund's. Empty for the moment. In the hope it may recall you to yourself.

(A NURSE *enters with a* BOY BABY.)

ELEANOR: This child. John. The last that Nature will grant me.

(ELEANOR *takes the child and gives it to* HENRY.)

(HENRY *opens the blanket and gives a sudden intake of breath, in shock.*)

ELEANOR: Yes. He's carrying a knife. He was born with it. You wanted to arm your infants. You have your wish.

(*She gives the* BABY *back to the* NURSE, *who exits*)

ELEANOR: And now the gift you want most in the world: ...My silence. I would never have believed that I could offer you that. It must be some measure of my feeling for you.

I'm going back to the Aquitaine, Henry. To stay. ...I'm going to raise the children there. When I speak, you will not hear me. When I disagree with you, it will not matter, I'll be so far away.

But if ever you should need me—

HENRY: On the day I'd suck the mouth of Hell, I'll need you!

ELEANOR: Goodbye..., husband...

HENRY: Bravo! Bravo! This is the greatest moment of my life! My wife withdraws to head the forces of those who are against me!

ELEANOR: I am not against you. I shall never be against you. Your sons and I are your greatest allies and protectors. We are your supporters. We are, and will always be, your friends.

(HENRY *laughs, long and loud and cynically. The light on him begins to fade—and eventually goes out.*)

ELEANOR: I am going to establish, in the south, a court of peace and love...

(*As* ELEANOR *speaks, the banners of the Aquitaine descend around her. Everything glows in the warmth of a brilliant sun.*)

ELEANOR: ...a court where all will be serene and quiet, where cities can be built, and vineyards tended, where all living beings can walk together in friendship and in trust.

(*As* ELEANOR *continues to speak, each of her* SONS, *now fully grown, appears in turn behind her. Each one, deliberately and quietly, is dressing himself for war.*)

ELEANOR: Illusions, lies and threats we'll leave to the magicians. While we, with finer magic, devote ourselves entirely to love. If there are tears, they will be mock tears, shed by jesters. And if there are battles, they will be sham battles, where the whole reward of victory is a kiss. Weapons will be absolutely outlawed. Armor will be banished—even for child's play. And if anyone is found dressed up in soldier's costumes —

(ELEANOR *turns and sees her* SONS, *dressed up in soldier's costumes. The drums of war begin, in the distance, a slow, insistent beat.*)

ELEANOR: Henry — Richard — Geoffrey — John — ...You know the penalties for playing soldier —!

YOUNG HENRY: *(Who is serious and sensitive)* We're not playing, Mother.

ELEANOR: Why are you all dressed this way, then?

JOHN: *(Playing with a knife. He is immature, incipiently evil.)* For war.

GEOFFREY: *(Who is rather simple)* We have to arm, to face the enemy.

ELEANOR: Who is the enemy?

RICHARD: *(Who is manly)* Henry. The King.

ELEANOR: You're planning war against the King of England —

RICHARD: *(Seriously)* Yes, Mother.

ELEANOR: You're planning war against your father —

YOUNG HENRY: He doesn't know what "father" means!

GEOFFREY: He hates us all —

YOUNG HENRY: For being younger.

ELEANOR: All sons are younger than their fathers.

RICHARD: He doesn't seem to think that that's the proper way. He deals with us as if we were his rivals.

YOUNG HENRY: He gives us provinces to govern and then, for no reason, takes them away. He sends us boon companions — who turn out to be spies.

JOHN: He keeps us poor, so that every coin we need we have to beg him for!

YOUNG HENRY: One minute he shows us off like his fine young bucks, the next he turns on us in a rage.

RICHARD: Some say he's mad. He changes his mind every half second. He's hot, he's cold. He's sated, he's famished. He's laughing, he's furious —

ELEANOR: So, for inconsistency, you begin an insurrection!

GEOFFREY: No, not for that —

ELEANOR: During all the years of your youth, there was a great struggle going on between your father and the King of France. It looked, every minute, as if the great ravaging war were going to break out. But Louis held. Louis did not attack, though he had every reason. We had something like armed peace —

YOUNG HENRY: But Louis did not risk losing everything by not attacking.

ELEANOR: Do you risk losing everything by not attacking?

RICHARD: There is a rumor—that our father is planning to leave his kingdom to one of his bastard sons.

ELEANOR: When did you hear this?

RICHARD: I've been hearing it for weeks now.

ELEANOR: Who told you?

RICHARD: I hear it everywhere I go.

ELEANOR: Do you think it's true?

YOUNG HENRY: God knows—perhaps. I'll bet my father doesn't. He doesn't know his mind from one half second to the next!

ELEANOR: He swore the lands would be yours. He believes in oaths.

RICHARD: Everyone else's. His own, he annuls with a gesture of his thumb. He shoves his destiny down people's throats as if they had no private destinies. And if they choke and die in the process, what's that to him?

GEOFFREY: He has so many enemies, he can only ride through his kingdom after dark, unrecognized.

JOHN: He has more enemies than he has friends!

ELEANOR: And so you're going to lie in wait for him, like marauders. He said we'd rise against him. Is this the day? Is this the day I kiss my sons and wish them luck as they go off to war against their father?

YOUNG HENRY: What else can we do?

ELEANOR: You can be on his side.

YOUNG HENRY: He doesn't want us.

ELEANOR: Then stay out of his battles.

RICHARD: That's a funny phrase—from you—who fought so often at his side.

ELEANOR: There must be some way for you to live in peace beside your father!

RICHARD: You couldn't find one.

ELEANOR: My case is different!

RICHARD: No, Mother. It's just that you were first.

YOUNG HENRY: The land is seething. Everyone is rising up against him for their own hurts.

RICHARD: They've come to us—to ask us to lead them against him.

ELEANOR: God in heaven—!

YOUNG HENRY: If we don't, they'll go ahead on their own.

RICHARD: And then what will become of England? Plantagenet England? If England doesn't come to us, why did you give us life?

YOUNG HENRY: We want your blessing...

ELEANOR: My blessing! You mean, you want my strength!

YOUNG HENRY: ...Yes.

ELEANOR: Oh, God, if ever I wished I were a seamstress, I wish I were a seamstress now. Then no one would ask me to send my banners into battle. And no one would ask me to secure the future by striking at my husband through his own seed.

(The drums of war grow more insistent.)

GEOFFREY: We'll fight for *your* banner, Mother!

(GEOFFREY grabs ELEANOR's banner. He and JOHN dash out.)

ELEANOR: We will not fight! We are not barbarians! We can reason with him! We can *talk*!

(The noises of war grow louder and louder.)

ELEANOR: What's that?

YOUNG HENRY: Conversation!

RICHARD: For your banner, Mother!

(RICHARD grabs another banner. He and YOUNG HENRY dash out.)

ELEANOR: No! No—!

(The sounds of battle rise to a tremendous pitch—then break off suddenly.)

(Iron bars descend around ELEANOR.)

(HENRY enters.)

HENRY: And so begins the Golden Age of Henry the Second. And the Golden Silence of his good Queen Eleanor. ... Did you think you and your cubs could win against me? It's surprising how the universe has fallen into place now. Even my sons, those puking traitors, tow the line. Everything in place. Everything silent. What a blessed peace I have now that I've decreed that Eleanor of Aquitaine shall spend the rest of her life in prison! *(He turns and starts to go. Then he turns back.)* What did you say?

ELEANOR: *(Serenely)* Nothing.

(HENRY starts to go, then turns again.)

HENRY: What did you say?!

ELEANOR: Nothing at all...

HENRY: I cannot stand your voice!

ELEANOR: *(Smiling)* I have been in prison fifteen years now. I have no voice.

HENRY: *(Tortured)* You do.... You *do*.... I have heard you night and day, year in, year out, no matter where I've been, awake, asleep, I've heard you! You've sewn your voice inside me. You're in there, shouting endlessly! Damn you! Give up!

ELEANOR: We are the perfect couple, you and I. I ride you like some haggard insect clawing on an ass's haunch, warning him about pits in the road and bowmen in the bushes, warning him about his soul's defeats and plagues that fester up his conscience. I won't let go! I am fastened to your rump for life!

HENRY: You are almost three quarters of a century old. Why don't you die?

ELEANOR: Why don't you kill me?

HENRY: *(Inwardly)* I think of it, very often, when I'm lying in bed at night. When I'm lying in bed—and I hear your voice from the tower. I think—if I could snuff her out...if I could stop her breathing. ... I think of it—and it's a great temptation. I would do it. But I am afraid, that if I killed you, your voice would still go on.

ELEANOR: And what would it say, Henry?

HENRY: I will not listen to it!

ELEANOR: What does it say, Henry?

HENRY: ...Make peace with my sons. ... I won't!

ELEANOR: You must be the only man on earth who really believes he is going to live forever...

HENRY: I shall live forever because this country will live forever!

ELEANOR: This country? Under one of your bastard children?...Or under one of the "puking traitors" you have nourished so tenderly with your love? ...

(HENRY *is moved, pensive. At last he makes a gesture, and a* MESSENGER *enters.*)

HENRY: Take this ring to my eldest son. Young Henry. Tell him—I am his blood,—his—father, and I—love him. Tell him I will forgive—may he forgive. Tell him—to come...

(*The* MESSENGER *takes the ring and starts to exit.* HENRY *says to* ELEANOR:)

HENRY: You'll see. My lovely son will sell the ring for arms against me—or for a girl.

(*Before the* MESSENGER *can leave,* YOUNG HENRY *is brought in, dead, on a stretcher borne by* LITTER-BEARERS. *The* MESSENGER *goes over and tries to fit the ring onto his finger.* HENRY *watches, frozen in disbelief.*)

MESSENGER: *(After a long time of trying)* I'm sorry, your majesty. The ring—will not go on.

(HENRY *cannot speak. He only watches. The litter moves by him and starts out the other way.* HENRY *shouts out:*)

HENRY: But he's to be King, don't you understand? He's to have all this—after me!!!

(*The* LITTER-BEARERS *exit with their burden.*)

(*Numbly,* HENRY *extends a hand toward* ELEANOR. *The bars around her disappear. She comes toward him.*)

HENRY: He's dead.... And I'm alive. I never thought of that...
   You see? You see? It isn't possible. Nothing—is possible—on this earth. How can I put the world in order, when the world's first law is Chaos? How can I keep on trying, when I know what I know?
   Lucky the man who dies young, who never discovers that the world he hoped to benefit is a world of paradox and illusion, where what nourishes the future kills the present, what nourishes a man's sons, kills the man, where what seems, in youth, the beautiful life plan, years later is a plan for horror—and it is the *same plan*, faithfully kept and nurtured!—and still seems to him as worthy as ever it was.
   ...Now's the time to be a woman.

ELEANOR: Being a woman doesn't save you—

HENRY: Doesn't it? Woman is the creature who has someone else to blame. When things go wrong she shouts: "*He* did it to me! My son, my lover, my father, my husband! It's his fault! I am not responsible!"...The only one responsible—is man.
   I see in your eyes rage, accusation, disappointment—for all the things I couldn't give you—or England. If I could put out your eyes to be rid of them, I would. But it is part of the joke of life, that putting out your rage would only add to God's rages against me. And that pile of failings I have spent my life in adding to, would grow, even higher, into the air. (*He buries his head, despairing.*)

ELEANOR: Henry. ...Let us try...even if there are only minutes left to us...to build the world we thought we could. ... We have other sons...

HENRY: Geoffrey died last month. His death was like his life—invisible.

ELEANOR: There's Richard—

HENRY: Your boy. He's insolent to me.

ELEANOR: And noble. But if you won't have him, there's John—

HENRY: John, little John, sweet John...the baby... (*He takes from his pocket a cloth in which something is wrapped and hands it to her.*) We captured the leader of the French this morning. Do you know who he was?

(ELEANOR *opens the cloth. In it is a jewelled knife.*)

ELEANOR: John...

HENRY: *(Wearily)* It's very strange... Today is strange... This knife—did not surprise me. I knew my boys were all my enemies. I wonder why that bothers me today. ... It's odd, so odd, but blows I could stand up to yesterday, today I just can't take. ... I feel—exposed—today. The slightest touch—is agony. Today—for some strange reason—I just cannot endure.

(Wearily, HENRY goes and lies, face down, on a bench.)

(Four MEN enter, carrying the hollow case of a sepulchre. ELEANOR watches, her hand moving out to stop them.)

(But they continue, slowly, unrelentingly, as in a dream. They lower the case over HENRY. On its top is HENRY's likeness, carved in stone.)

ELEANOR: Turn him face up, the way he lived. And if his eyes are open, leave them that way.

(The MEN raise the case and turn HENRY's body face up. As they do, he makes one last spasmodic gesture, of covering his head with his arms in shame, and sobbing one last cry. Then, suddenly he is still, dying with his mouth open, the scream still on his face.)

ELEANOR: *(Much moved:)* Why am I still alive—to see this. ... This—should not be seen...

(The MEN lower the case, secure it, then raise it on their shoulders, carrying HENRY and his image out.)

(Dimly, the lands appear behind her. The lights on them gradually grow in intensity. Then, suddenly RICHARD jumps out from behind them.):

RICHARD: Say, Mother! How do I look as King?

(All is bright and gay again. The lights are brilliant. RICHARD is a wonder in his shining costume and crown.)

ELEANOR: Oh, but you're handsome, Richard!

RICHARD: I am going to be the bravest King who ever lived!

ELEANOR: Yes. You are. Beautiful and brave. My Richard!

RICHARD: And a *good* King, Mother.

ELEANOR: All that your father could have been.

RICHARD: It's strange, this crown. It has a power. It makes me want—only what's good.

(A spirited song is heard being sung somewhere beyond them.)

ELEANOR: I've loved you the most—of all my children.

RICHARD: And every dream you ever had for me—I heard. I'm going to be the greatest King of all time for you! I'm starting right now on a new age of heroes!

...I'm going to go on Crusade!

ELEANOR: *(In protest)* Richard—!

(The crusading song outside grows more intense. YOUNG MEN, *singing, march by in the background, their glorious white-crossed flags unfurling.)*

RICHARD: The people see me marching in the street. They fall in behind me! They love my flag, my costume, my face! The girls throw flowers, and the men all shout: "For God and Richard!" And everybody shouts together, hear them? The *same* shout!

(The men's voices rise: "For God and Richard! For Richard! For Richard!" The YOUNG MEN *march off, shouting his name.)*

RICHARD: I'm coming! I'm coming!

(He embraces ELEANOR *roughly.)*

RICHARD: Think of me, Mother, will you, while I'm gone?

(Heroically, flags waving, RICHARD *dashes out.)*

ELEANOR: But Richard—! The country—!

(But he is gone. ELEANOR *is stunned, alone. She takes a few steps after him. They are the steps of an ancient woman. The sky is threatening. The lights on the lands grow harsh.)*

(Stealthily, and then with increasing openness, PEOPLE *of all sorts come in from all sides and begin to pillage the lands.* ELEANOR *watches as the ravaging grows around her, then calls out:)*

ELEANOR: Stop! Stop! Barbarians! Thieves! Traitors! ...Out of my way, you snarling horde of scavengers. Take your claws and dig them into something else. The thing within your hands is England. England! And England is inviolate while I am still alive.

Ah, that I still breathe surprises you. You see my weary eyes, my skin that's hanging off the bone. What? Is she still moving? Does she still dare to walk the earth?

Yes. I dare. With my wizened hands, I stroke the living heart of England. I breathe into her mouth. I hold her fast. I will protect her, succor her, shield her with my body. If you want to claw your way into her sacred vitals, you must, first, claw your way through mine. *(She stands before the lands.)* Well? Come! I won't cry out. Set to it!

(No one moves.)

ELEANOR: I see. You prefer to wait. You think: "She can't hold up the world for long on those frail shoulders. She will collapse beneath the load and then—."... All right...wait. But I warn you, I can manage. For this year...and for this year... and for this year...and for this year... *(Etc.)*

(For ten long years she stands, her back against the lands, like some ancient, haggard female Hercules. The task becomes harder and harder. And as she stands, struggling beneath the burden, the PEOPLE *fall, one by one, upon their knees in awe.)*

(At last, in the tenth year, when it seems that she could not carry the weight another moment, heroic music is heard approaching from the distance.)

ELEANOR: Listen—! Music—! Coming from the East—! Marchers' music, coming from the East!

(Cheers are heard.)

ELEANOR: At last he's here! He's King! My Richard!

(He is borne toward her. A triumphant, heroic vision, arms outstretched. Just before he reaches her, his smile grows stiff and his eyes glassy. He is still heroic—but like a statue. ELEANOR *stares at him.)*

ELEANOR: Richard—! *(Then, in horror:)* He is dead!

(The statue falls into the arms of its BEARERS. *In silence, all the* PEOPLE *follow it out.* ELEANOR *watches it go. She stands, stunned and alone. Then, from behind her, she hears a strange sound.)*

*(*JOHN *appears from behind the lands. Irreverently, he is chipping away at them with his jeweled knife. He is wearing a crown.)*

JOHN: I knew I'd be the oldest some day. These things take care of themselves. Here I am on the high seat. Now what will I do with it? I'll have to think that out...

*(*JOHN *aims at the lands with his knife, using them as a dart board.)*

*(*ELEANOR *turns to him in horror.)*

ELEANOR: John... Baby John...

*(*JOHN *aims again at the lands.)*

ELEANOR: John!

(She starts toward him. But before she can reach him, two NUNS *enter and come toward her, bearing the habit of a nun.)*

ELEANOR: What's this?

FIRST NUN: You always said, Madame, you wanted to be buried in the habit of a nun.

ELEANOR: What? So soon?

(The NUNS *start outfitting* ELEANOR *in the nun's habit.)*

*(*JOHN *continues to go at the kingdom with his knife.)*

ELEANOR: Is he to get it all? Is this what we worked so many years for? John! John!

(JOHN *continues, heedlessly.*)

ELEANOR: He doesn't seem to hear me! *(To the* NUNS:*)* You do this so quickly. Why must you do it so quickly? John!!

(ELEANOR *is nearly frantic trying to reach him, but the* NUNS *do not seem to notice, and* JOHN *does not seem to hear. As they continue to dress her, the young* NUNS *talk as if* ELEANOR *could not hear them.*)

SECOND NUN: How old is she?

FIRST NUN: Oh, older than anyone. Eighty-two, they say. She's lived enough life for three women.

SECOND NUN: Weren't there some awful scandals about her?

FIRST NUN: Oh, yes! Haven't you heard the things they say?

(They continue to dress her.)

ELEANOR: John. John, please. You are the King. Remember everything your father told you. Your father put order into the world. Now people expect it. They'll never put up with a King who—

(*But* JOHN, *unheeding, and balancing a knife on one finger, goes out.* ELEANOR *shouts after him:*)

ELEANOR: Order and Love, John! *(She turns to the* NUNS:*)* Tell him Order and Love. Love and Order. Will you tell him?

FIRST NUN: Yes, we'll tell him.

ELEANOR: Will I know if England turns out all right?

FIRST NUN: Hurry, please—

ELEANOR: Will I know? *(Silence... She turns to heaven and demands:)* Will I know!

(A pause. A silence. She seems to hear an answer. She smiles, she looks relieved.)

FIRST NUN: Hurry, please.

ELEANOR: Why should I hurry?

FIRST NUN: You've got to say your final confession.

SECOND NUN: There are five priests waiting to hear you—

ELEANOR: Five priests! They couldn't think I need that much absolution!

FIRST NUN: You have a great deal to repent of, Madame.

SECOND NUN: You married twice—

FIRST NUN: Some say there were more men—

SECOND NUN: Poets and lovers—

FIRST NUN: Some say that you were willful, that you never followed orders—

SECOND NUN: Some say that you went far beyond the bounds of women—

ELEANOR: I was given a life and I lived it! If I were given eons on this planet, I wouldn't for one solitary second, do less than that!

FIRST NUN: But you must confess—

ELEANOR: I have nothing to confess.

SECOND NUN: Be remorseful, contrite—

ELEANOR: I have no reason.

FIRST NUN: Atone and repent—

ELEANOR: I repent of nothing. I am sorry for nothing.

(ELEANOR *is completely dressed in the nun's habit. The light seems to be changing.*)

SECOND NUN: Repent! It's the next to last thing you must do before entering heaven.

ELEANOR: And what is the last, the very last? Tell me.

FIRST NUN: *(Gently)* Why, Madame, the last thing you must do before entering heaven—is die.

ELEANOR: To die? To stop up all my senses? Go silent, blind and dumb? And they call that *heaven*? I don't accept it! If *dying's* what they want, to hell with heaven!

(*She pulls off her headdress. She takes the only light, bareheaded, facing upward.*)

ELEANOR: Come! Make way for Eleanor—alive!

(*The light glows brilliantly upon* ELEANOR's *upturned face. Then suddenly it goes out.*)

(*Silence*)

(*Blackout*)

END OF PLAY

GEORGE AND FREDERIC
A Play with the Music of Frederic Chopin

GEORGE AND FREDERIC premiered April 29th, 1982 at the University of Utah, Salt Lake City, Utah. Staged readings include those at Bard College, at the Yale Club of New York and at the Williamstown Theater.

CHARACTERS & SETTING:

MAURICE DUDEVANT
GEORGE SAND
FREDERIC CHOPIN
SOLANGE DUDEVANT
FRANÇOIS BULOZ
AUGUSTE CLESINGER

Time and place: The action takes place in France and Spain between 1837 and 1849.

Setting: The setting begins with almost empty space. Upstage right is a grand piano. Downstage left is a small writing desk and a chair.

The different locations should be created simply, by changes of light or sound, or by projections, or by the addition of a few pieces of furniture or hand props. Only the essence of each place should be suggested, with elements appearing and disappearing fluidly, creating a sense of place by suggestion rather than by literal detail.

MAURICE *should be able to perch (on a stool, box, ledge, etc.) at the extreme downstage left and right edges of the space and be quite out of the light when he is less visibly observing. Accommodation should be made for him to both store and display his puppets in these areas. The puppets should be of a large enough scale so that the character each represents can be readily seen from the last row of the theatre.*

The piano is always present. When it "disappears" it simply retreats temporarily into the shadows. The music can be produced live or on tape. The actor who portrays Chopin is not expected to always pretend to play it. As with the entire production, imaginative use of elements is the key.

Music: compositions of Frederic Chopin selected by Laurence Rosenthal

Solange's Songs: lyrics by Ruth Wolff, music by Laurence Rosenthal

ACT ONE

(At rise: The space is empty.)

(MAURICE, George Sand's son—not a boy and not quite a man—enters carrying a couple of hand puppets. He says to us in a sardonic tone:)

MAURICE: They blazed across the sky of France for nine years—my mother and her pale composer. Nine years. While I was growing from a boy into a man and my little sister was growing from a baby into—I suppose you'd call it young woman—though, when it comes to Solange, "woman" isn't quite the word. All that time, my mother— "George" —and her lover were having the kind of love affair that is the stuff of legends. And I? I was busy trying—with very little success—not to watch... *(He fixes a top hat onto his GEORGE PUPPET, which is dressed in pants, formal black jacket and flowing black tie.)*

I know a lot about my mother's life—even scenes I never witnessed—because she wrote about it. She used her life to feed her writings—fiction, fact, and some hazy area in between. But she never really told the whole truth about herself and the skinny pale composer. I want to try to. She never got over that episode. And, in some sense, neither did Solange and I. *(He fixes a flowing black tie onto his FREDERIC PUPPET, which is dressed, like the GEORGE PUPPET, in pants and formal black jacket)*

It wasn't easy, sewing up this puppet of my mother's lover. Frederic was thin as a stick, all shades of grey, like a walking daguerreotype. He had the most gigantic hands! With long slender fingers. And their spread! Incredible! Like no one else! That's why so few of us can play his compositions! *(He shows us the hands of his FREDERIC PUPPET.)* My mother's hands were tiny, but, oddly enough, had more life force in them than Frederic's. *(He shows us the hands of his GEORGE PUPPET.)* ...The first time they met was at a salon musicale in Paris.

(FREDERIC enters, dressed exactly like the FREDERIC PUPPET, sits at the piano, and begins to play.)

(Music begins: **Nocturne Op. 27, No. 2, D Flat Major***)*

MAURICE: My mother walked in, took one look at the skinny fellow seated at the piano and thought:

(GEORGE enters, dressed exactly like the GEORGE PUPPET, and says to us:)

GEORGE: Shall I take this little Chopin as my lover?

MAURICE: *(To us:)* She was very direct, my mother. When she wanted a man she went after him and—whether he wanted it or not—the poor fellow was caught!

GEORGE: *(To us:)* How thin and pale he is, this little emigré from Poland. He's only twenty-six and all Paris adores him. Women especially. But in this crowded drawing room, how lonely he looks, how withdrawn...

MAURICE: My mother, of course, set out to effect a cure! Her friend and publisher, François Buloz, tried to talk her out of it.

(MAURICE *takes out a puppet of the paunchy effete* BULOZ *just as* BULOZ, *dressed exactly like* GEORGE, *enters and says to her:)*

BULOZ: I suppose you realize he hates women writers—

GEORGE: I'll convert him.

BULOZ: That music is his life—

GEORGE: I'll make it mine.

BULOZ: That you're six years older than he is—

GEORGE: He needs a woman of experience.

MAURICE: *(To us:)* Nothing anyone could say could talk her out of it.

GEORGE: I must have him!

BULOZ: George, *think*—!

GEORGE: Listen to that melody, Buloz. Its sadness, its melancholy—

BULOZ: And that attracts you?

GEORGE: He looks so lost! So helpless! He needs someone to take him in hand, show him the way.

BULOZ: George, forget love. Write another novel. I'll publish it in the Spring and you can—

GEORGE: He needs me, Buloz. He needs me!

BULOZ: Then God help him... *(He exits)*

MAURICE: *(To us:)* She stood across the room just gazing at him. Gazing. Wooing him by a technique she had never used before—silence.

(He *holds the* GEORGE *and* FREDERIC PUPPETS *absolutely still, facing each other at a distance.* FREDERIC *turns to us and says:)*

FREDERIC: Why does she stare at me with those dark eyes of hers? Why does she stare? Why doesn't she go? Why does she never speak? What is she thinking? What does she want of me? The answer will be no!

MAURICE: *(To us:)* She knew the power of her eyes, my mother. She made her way to him across the room.

(As MAURICE *moves the puppets toward each other,* GEORGE *walks over to* FREDERIC *at the piano.)*

MAURICE: And what did she say? What were her first words to this man she'd never met before?

GEORGE: I adore you!

MAURICE: *(To us:)* And what does the pianist reply?

FREDERIC: I have to go.

GEORGE: Are you afraid of me?

FREDERIC: I have an engagement.

GEORGE: At three A M?

FREDERIC: You must excuse me, Madame Sand—

GEORGE: You know me—

FREDERIC: All Paris knows you.

GEORGE: You've thought about me—

FREDERIC: I've thought about your cigars.

GEORGE: What did you think?

FREDERIC: I thought—if she lights her cigar while I am playing I will slam the piano shut and run from the room.

GEORGE: It never occurred to me! I stood there, thunderstruck by your genius—

FREDERIC: *(To us:)* If she says the word "Poland" in the next five minutes, I will love her forever!

GEORGE: How old were you when they first called you a genius?

FREDERIC: Six.

GEORGE: Did you run to the piano one night and suddenly play—your legs dangling from the bench like the little Mozart?

FREDERIC: Yes—

GEORGE: Oh, I would have loved to have known you as a child in Poland!

(GEORGE *has said it.* FREDERIC *is stunned, overwhelmed!* MAURICE *turns to us and says:)*

MAURICE: He was lost—completely lost—that very first night!

(GEORGE *and* FREDERIC *embrace and exit, their arms around each other.)*

(*Music rises:* **Ballade Op. 23, No. 1, Meas. 68-93***)*

MAURICE: One kiss—and he was conquered. *(He has his* GEORGE *and* FREDERIC PUPPETS *kiss, then has the* FREDERIC PUPPET *swoon with love and embarrassment.)* Solange and I always knew when there was a new man in mother's life. For one thing, the food got better. For another, we had more freedom. She had someone to think about. It wasn't us. And there was joy in the house. An overflow from her new pleasure.

(GEORGE *enters wrapped in a robe and says to us:*)

GEORGE: He is a lovely lover! Everything you might expect! Boyish, tender, elegant, shy—with sudden surges of overwhelming passion! Oh, I will love loving him!

(FREDERIC *enters, in shirtsleeves, carrying his jacket.*)

FREDERIC: I have to go—

GEORGE: Escape? Again?

MAURICE: *(To us:)* Most of her lovers couldn't wait to be asked to stay.

GEORGE: Are you afraid of me?

FREDERIC: Please—I must—

GEORGE: Tell me about the women you have loved—

FREDERIC: How can you ask these things?!

MAURICE: *(To us:)* She could use his answers in a future novel—

GEORGE: They say you have a recent wound.

FREDERIC: ...Marie... *(He sighs.)* She was just sixteen...

GEORGE: What happened?

FREDERIC: Her parents thought I was too—thin—to be a husband.

GEORGE: Poor Frederic—

FREDERIC: For months she wrote me love letters—and then she started writing me about her dog!

GEORGE: And that's all? Marie is all?

MAURICE: *(Aside to us:)* She's sure the number of his conquests couldn't possibly equal hers!

FREDERIC: There was Constanza. We were music students together in Warsaw. I adored her vibrato.

GEORGE: Your loves sound—very ascetic.

FREDERIC: Unlike yours.

GEORGE: Would you like to hear about mine?

MAURICE: *(Aside to us:)* I've never understood why anyone thinks a new lover would find a list of one's old lovers appealing.

FREDERIC: I really must leave—

GEORGE: Do you always run off immediately the next morning?

FREDERIC: I can't—I can't love a woman named *George*!

GEORGE: Call me "Aurore", then. I was born Aurore.

FREDERIC: Why did you take a man's name?

GEORGE: I decided to *live* this time around. And I notice that all who live are men.

FREDERIC: But do you have to wear men's clothes?

GEORGE: When I dress as a man, how firm my step is! I have power, force, speed! I can seduce anyone I want!

FREDERIC: I will not join the ranks of your infinite number of conquests!

GEORGE: There weren't *that* many—

FREDERIC: There was that starving writer you ran off to live with in Paris—

GEORGE: Julian Sandeau. He gave me my name—and helped me write my first novel.

FREDERIC: There was that opium eater—

GEORGE: Alfred de Musset was a poet of brilliance and grace!

FREDERIC: You ran off with him to Venice and made love to his doctor at his bedside!

GEORGE: It's the atmosphere of a bedroom. I never can resist.

FREDERIC: Then there was that ugly lawyer—

MAURICE: He's well-informed, this fellow. Even *I* forgot about the lawyer.

GEORGE: I'd have given *anything* to the man who won me my separation from my husband.

FREDERIC: Your husband! I didn't even *think* about your husband!

MAURICE: *(To us:)* My father.

GEORGE: *(To FREDERIC:)* You must be grateful to the Baron Dudevant. *I* am. Just think of all I'd have missed if he hadn't been such a bastard! Never underestimate the value of your disadvantages.

FREDERIC: So many lovers!

GEORGE: Granted. But I have one rule of love that never wavers.

FREDERIC: What is that?

GEORGE: Fidelity.

FREDERIC: "Fidelity!"

GEORGE: Only one man at a time. ... I have one now.

FREDERIC: Who?

GEORGE: ...You.

MAURICE: *(To us:)* Who could resist such a declaration?

FREDERIC: George,—I'm afraid I'm going to love you!

GEORGE: Oh, you magnificent, astonishing boy!

FREDERIC: I'm being foolish—

GEORGE: No. Never be ashamed of loving.

FREDERIC: But what will Paris say? I don't want us being fodder for a million gossips.

GEORGE: In that case, we'll have to remove ourselves from their sight.

FREDERIC: You mean—go away? Together?

GEORGE: We can't very well be lovers if we go away separately...

FREDERIC: Where could we go?

GEORGE: I've been thinking about—Majorca.

FREDERIC: An island in the south—

GEORGE: Where we'll have sun and warmth and privacy and love—

FREDERIC: Yes. Oh, yes! Let's go!

GEORGE: We'll leave next week. I'll pack up the children—

FREDERIC: The children!

MAURICE: *(To us:)* The fly in every mother's ointment.

(He brings out the MAURICE *and* SOLANGE PUPPETS *and during the following finishes braiding the* SOLANGE PUPPET's *hair and putting on the* MAURICE PUPPET's *vest.)*

FREDERIC: I suppose you'll bring along your husband, too!

GEORGE: *(Teasing)* Well, we *could* invite him—

FREDERIC: George, —you and I—and your *children*?!

GEORGE: Frederic, I'm not ashamed of what I do. I'm proud to have my children know it. The laws by which I live are higher than the laws of scandal. I won't be held back by rules which make it impossible to live! The only way to live is to be free! *(She exits.)*

MAURICE: *(To us:)* Her creed. It only works if the whole world doesn't live by it.

FREDERIC: *(To us:)* She must have been teasing, don't you think? About the children?

(He begins to play a series of wild arpeggios which continue, under:) Children whine—

(Imitating their voices, MAURICE *animates the* SOLANGE *and* MAURICE PUPPETS *as, with the arpeggios as a raucous background, he and* FREDERIC, *with ever-quickening pace, shout out, one after the other:)*

MAURICE: *(As his own* PUPPET*)* Children giggle—

FREDERIC: Children fight—

MAURICE: *(As* SOLANGE PUPPET*)* Children stamp—

FREDERIC: Children cry—

MAURICE: *(As his own* PUPPET*)* Children quibble—

FREDERIC: Children kick—

MAURICE: *(As* SOLANGE PUPPET*)* Children slap—

FREDERIC: Children spy—

MAURICE: *(As his own* PUPPET*)* Lie—

FREDERIC: Scream—

MAURICE: *(As* SOLANGE PUPPET*)* Chatter—

FREDERIC: Break—

MAURICE: *(As his own* PUPPET*)* Batter—

FREDERIC: Soil—

MAURICE: *(As* SOLANGE PUPPET*)* Sully—

FREDERIC: Filthify—

MAURICE: *(As his own* PUPPET*)* —and pollute!

FREDERIC: Children stick their fingers in—

MAURICE: *(As* SOLANGE PUPPET*)* Are always underfoot of—

FREDERIC: Inhibit the performance of—

MAURICE: *(As his own* PUPPET*)* Throw up all over the—

*(*FREDERIC *turns to us:)*

FREDERIC: She couldn't have been serious!

(The loud sound of tapping heels is heard and SOLANGE, *age twelve, dances in, clacking castanets, sporting a mantilla and singing and dancing a flamenco.)*

(Music rises: A flamenco.)

*(*FREDERIC *stares at* SOLANGE *for a moment, then turns to us and says:)*

FREDERIC: My God, she *was*—!

(He exits in haste.)

(Suddenly the place is flooded with light! Sun! Air! MAURICE *says to us:)*

MAURICE: Majorca!

SOLANGE: *(Continuing her flamenco)* I'm going to be a Spanish dancer!

MAURICE: Mother said no noise, Monsieur Chopin is resting.

SOLANGE: He looked positively *green* coming up the mountain!

MAURICE: When you're so bony, riding a donkey is hard on your behind.

SOLANGE: You almost fell off yours.

MAURICE: *You* had to be tied on!

SOLANGE: Only because my legs aren't long enough to reach the stirrups! *You* were scared! You were an ass on assback!

MAURICE: You be quiet—!

SOLANGE: An ass on assback!

MAURICE: Stop it, Solange!

SOLANGE: Ass! Ass!

(FREDERIC *enters looking lost and disconcerted, as if he had just been wakened.*)

MAURICE: *(To* SOLANGE:*)* I *told* you you'd wake him—! *(He says to* FREDERIC:*)* Good afternoon, Monsieur.

FREDERIC: *(Ill-at-ease)* Good afternoon, Maurice.

SOLANGE: Good afternoon, Monsieur.

FREDERIC: Good afternoon, Solange—

(SOLANGE *whispers, aside, to* MAURICE:*)*

SOLANGE: He's handsomer than Monsieur de Bourges.

MAURICE: But not as handsome as Monsieur de Musset.

SOLANGE: He's twice as handsome as Monsieur Sandeau!

MAURICE: He's handsomer than Monsieur Sandeau but *not* as handsome as Monsieur de Musset!

SOLANGE: Handsomer!

MAURICE: Less handsome!

SOLANGE: Handsomer!

MAURICE: Less handsome!

(*Upset by the noise,* FREDERIC *turns to them in helpless remonstrance. They become silent. Suddenly* SOLANGE *says:)*

SOLANGE: I have a present for you, Monsieur!

FREDERIC: How nice of you, Solange. Thank you.

(SOLANGE *puts something into* FREDERIC's *hand. He cries out:*)

FREDERIC: Oh—! (*He opens his hand and lets the thing drop.*) What was it?

MAURICE: A cockroach.

SOLANGE: Oh! You lost it!

MAURICE: Here it is. (MAURICE *crushes it beneath his foot.*)

FREDERIC: Thank you, Maurice.

(SOLANGE *kneels over the remains of the cockroach.*)

SOLANGE: How beautifully he dies! His little feet are still kicking! ... They've stopped now...

(FREDERIC *turns away.*)

SOLANGE: Don't be sad, Monsieur. I'll get you another!

(*She runs wildly around the room, trying to capture another cockroach.*)

(GEORGE *enters, her arms full of laundry.*)

GEORGE: Maurice! Take your sister outside.

MAURICE: Yes, Mother. Would you like me to fold those for you?

GEORGE: Thank you, Maurice.

MAURICE: (*To us as he takes the laundry:*) What a mama's boy I was! It's a wonder anyone could stand me!

(GEORGE *kisses* MAURICE *on the forehead.* SOLANGE *looks on jealously. Noticing this,* FREDERIC *says to her:*)

FREDERIC: Thank you for the present, Solange. Next time, I'll be more prepared for it.

SOLANGE: (*Brightening*) Maybe next time I can catch you a rat!

(*She runs out happily.* GEORGE *gestures for* MAURICE *to keep an eye on her.* MAURICE *moves to the side and folds the laundry.*)

GEORGE: You are the man in the world least suited to domesticity!

FREDERIC: I thought there'd be someone to do these things—

GEORGE: Unfortunately, no one wants to come and live with us on our mountain top.

FREDERIC: You had to choose a deserted monastery—

GEORGE: I chose it for the isolation—and the view. And then, I thought of all those poor devoted souls who used to lie in those twenty separate cells at night, making love to no one. You and I shall have to consecrate each room! Make love for all of them!

FREDERIC: Yes, it is our duty!

GEORGE: We have six more cells to go—

FREDERIC: Come *now*—!

GEORGE: And to think, two months ago, when I first met you, I had to *beg* you to come to my bed!

(GEORGE *and* FREDERIC *embrace each other and start to make love.*)

(*The lights go down on them and come up on* MAURICE. *He finishes folding the laundry and takes out a sack with unfinished puppets. As he works to imitate the effect of* FREDERIC's *wild black hair, he says to us:*)

MAURICE: Mother used to help me with the sewing, but now she has no time. She's always running her fingers through Frederic's shocks of black hair. That hair, hard to capture in a puppet. And it's hard to do his face. He's always changing! At the moment, his main expression is utter rapture—

(*The lights come up on* FREDERIC. *After the love-making, he says to us:*)

FREDERIC: She is insatiable! She is—universes—of desire! She makes me so delirious with joy, I want to stay within her arms forever. I want to lie on her breast, exhausted, spent, at peace...

GEORGE: You look pale—

FREDERIC: It's this monastic life!

GEORGE: (*She laughs.*) Well, you won't be pale for long... The Spanish sun will fill the marrow of your bones with energy! I will feed you magic herbs and ripe fresh fruit. You will lie beneath the sun all day— ...This is Eden...

(FREDERIC *says nothing.*)

GEORGE: Isn't it Eden?

FREDERIC: Possibly.

GEORGE: Possibly! What does it lack?

FREDERIC: A piano.

GEORGE: Oh? Does Eden need a piano?

FREDERIC: Do you think there's an old one in the village I could go down and use?

GEORGE: Why not have one up here?

FREDERIC: On this mountain top? How would we get it up here? On the back of a donkey?

(GEORGE *smiles.*)

(*Outside is heard the sound of aimless banging on a piano keyboard.* FREDERIC *looks at*

GEORGE.)

FREDERIC: You can't have—! You can't have—!

GEORGE: How little you know me.

FREDERIC: *(Looking out at the piano)* It's beautiful!

GEORGE: I had it shipped from Paris.

FREDERIC: From Paris! And I would have settled for *anything*.

GEORGE: I wouldn't. Not for you.

FREDERIC: *(Looking at her, deeply moved)* I love you, you know.

GEORGE: *(With love)* You'd better rescue your piano.

(The piano appears. SOLANGE is banging on the keys. MAURICE says to us:)

MAURICE: Now they are joined—the man and his piano—

(FREDERIC goes toward the piano. SOLANGE relinquishes her place. FREDERIC tries a few notes, then begins to play in earnest, the **Polonaise Op. 53, A Flat**.*)*

(GEORGE and the CHILDREN listen. As FREDERIC plays with amazing speed and strength and virtuosity, GEORGE says to us:)

GEORGE: How such powerful music can come from such a frail body, I can't comprehend! His music is beyond himself! Such genius! Such majesty! ...I am in awe of this man who makes love so gently, so politely—and then steals thunder from the gods like this.

(The lights change. FREDERIC continues to play.)

(GEORGE sits writing. MAURICE sits sewing on puppets. SOLANGE amuses herself with them. MAURICE says to us:)

MAURICE: Here we are—my mother, her lover, my sister, myself. An idyllic little family on an idyllic Majorcan mountain top.

(FREDERIC is playing. As GEORGE continues writing, she says to him:)

GEORGE: That is perfection, Frederic—

FREDERIC: No...not yet... *(He continues to work on the composition.)*

GEORGE: *(To us:)* He revises a thousand times!

FREDERIC: *(To us:)* She never revises anything!

GEORGE: He polishes and polishes!

FREDERIC: Each morning she sends off what she wrote the night before without changing a line.

GEORGE: Music is his life!

FREDERIC: She does *everything*!

GEORGE: We are a union of opposites!

FREDERIC: We never quarrel.

GEORGE: Except when I have to go out of his sight.

(GEORGE *is putting on her cape. The music stops.*)

FREDERIC: Where are you going?

GEORGE: Down to the village for a few supplies. I won't be long.

FREDERIC: Do you have to go?

GEORGE: Even *you* have to eat, my darling.

FREDERIC: Come back quickly.

GEORGE: *(Indicating the puppets)* Maurice will entertain you while I'm gone...

(GEORGE *exits.*)

(MAURICE *picks up some puppets to do a show, but before he can speak* SOLANGE *says to* FREDERIC:)

SOLANGE: I'll entertain you! I'll entertain you, Monsieur! You're not the only one who can make music! *(She announces:)* A Winter Song, by Solange Dudevant! *(She sings her* **Winter Song**:*)*

December is a chilly month
With snow and cold and ice,
And in the northern countries
It isn't very nice.

But in the south we're happy,
We're cozy and we're warm—
The sun shines very brightly—
We never have a storm.

(*Suddenly the heavens open with a deluge. The thunder roars, the lightening flashes, the winds howl.* MAURICE *finds it dramatic.* SOLANGE *loves it.* FREDERIC *listens in terror then cries out:*)

FREDERIC: *Where is your mother?!*

MAURICE: She went down to the village, Monsieur—to get the herbs to brew the tea you like so much. *(To us:)* You should see how wild he gets when we run out of his chamomile!

FREDERIC: She should have been back hours ago!

SOLANGE: *(Ecstatic)* The rain is coming through the roof! *(Joyously, she opens her mouth to catch the raindrops in it.)*

FREDERIC: I thought we came here for the sun!

MAURICE: The natives say this is the coldest winter they can remember.

FREDERIC: Where can she be?

SOLANGE: The sea is higher than the tallest rocks! The roads must be washed away!

FREDERIC: Stop it! Stop it! We won't think about the storm. We will do what we usually do. Go back to doing what you were doing—

MAURICE: I'm sure she's all right—

FREDERIC: We won't think about it!

(The CHILDREN go back to the puppets. FREDERIC goes to the piano and is about to begin to work, but something is wrong.)

FREDERIC: Did one of you use my pen?

MAURICE: Yes, Monsieur. I borrowed it for a second.

FREDERIC: You didn't put it back the way you found it.

MAURICE: Yes, Monsieur. I did. It's right there. *(He indicates the music stand of the piano.)*

FREDERIC: It was pointing in the opposite direction!

MAURICE: The opposite—? *(He looks at FREDERIC strangely.)* Well, Monsieur. I'll turn it. *(He comes over to the piano to turn the pen.)*

FREDERIC: No! It's too late!

MAURICE: I don't understand—

FREDERIC: How long has it been lying that way?

MAURICE: I don't know. A couple of hours—

FREDERIC: Hours! My God, my God... She's lying dead somewhere, I know it. She lost her footing in the torrent! She's been washed into the sea! What will become of us? *(He turns to MAURICE:)* Never touch anything of mine! I have special ways of putting things! If they're moved you never know what it will bring down upon us!

(Privately, seditiously, MAURICE has the FREDERIC PUPPET say to us:)

MAURICE: *(As FREDERIC PUPPET)* You put a pen out of place! You'll be struck by lightening!

MAURICE: *(As himself:)* I'm really sorry, Monsieur—

FREDERIC: It's too late!

(GEORGE dashes in out of the rain. FREDERIC stares at her as if she were a ghost.)

SOLANGE: Mother, isn't the storm wonderful!

GEORGE: Wonderful! *(She hands SOLANGE her soaking wet cloak and bundles.)* I could hear your voices halfway up the mountain! What was the shouting about?

MAURICE: I moved his pen.

(GEORGE *looks at* FREDERIC. *He doesn't speak.*)

GEORGE: The bridge was out. I had to take the long way up the mountain.

FREDERIC: *(Suddenly, emotionally)* You should never have gone on a Friday!

(*Privately, seditiously,* MAURICE *has the* FREDERIC PUPPET *say to us:*)

MAURICE: *(As* FREDERIC PUPPET*)* Fridays are bad luck! Never move from the house on Fridays!

(GEORGE *says to* SOLANGE *and* MAURICE:)

GEORGE: Go to bed, children.

(SOLANGE *kisses* FREDERIC *goodnight.* MAURICE *exchanges a goodnight nod with him, then takes* SOLANGE *downstage left.* MAURICE *says to us:*)

MAURICE: When the children are told to go to bed is when the secret things happen—the deep discussions, the battles, the speaking of the truths, the formation of the lies...

(MAURICE *gives* SOLANGE *the* SOLANGE PUPPET *and tucks her in with it. He puts his* MAURICE PUPPET *to sleep. Then he stands in the downstage shadows observing* GEORGE *and* FREDERIC.)

FREDERIC: I thought you were dead.

GEORGE: I knew you would worry. I hurried.

FREDERIC: I saw you dead.

GEORGE: Well, now you see me alive—

FREDERIC: I saw you dead, George! I thought of killing myself!

GEORGE: Frederic, —*nothing* happened. What happened happened only in your imagination!

FREDERIC: What happens in my imagination *happens*. What I conjure up in here is *real*! That's how I compose!

GEORGE: Frederic—

FREDERIC: You were dead! Because you're not dead now doesn't mean it didn't happen!

GEORGE: Play me what you wrote today.

(FREDERIC *looks at* GEORGE. *She knows that playing will calm him.*)

GEORGE: Play...

(*He sits at the piano. He begins to play* **Prelude Op. 28, No. 15, Raindrop**

Prelude.)

GEORGE: Lovely... So lovely...

(FREDERIC *continues to play,* GEORGE *listens.*)

GEORGE: It's beautiful, Frederic. It sounds like the rain falling on the roof tiles.

(*Suddenly* FREDERIC *pounds the piano keys and lashes out:*)

FREDERIC: I do not write *weather* music! I do not write water music! I do not write moonlit sonatas or concertos to imitate the quacking of geese! I write *notes*! Notes and chords and arpeggios and cadenzas! I write— (*He breaks off, coughing.*)

(GEORGE *comes to him and touches his forehead.*)

GEORGE: You're feverish!

FREDERIC: Rain on the roof! My God!

GEORGE: It's freezing in here! Why didn't you get Maurice to light a fire?

MAURICE: (*To us:*) If I'd lit a fire he'd have complained the heat was curling his music.

GEORGE: (*As* FREDERIC *continues coughing:*) Why didn't you throw a blanket around your shoulders? Even a child would know enough to keep warm!

(FREDERIC *looks at* GEORGE *once, as if surprised at her chastising him. Then he collapses onto the floor.*)

GEORGE: Maurice! Solange! Bring blankets!

(*She leans over* FREDERIC. MAURICE *gets blankets. They cover* FREDERIC.)

GEORGE: Light the fire! Boil water! Put boards against the windows to keep out the wind.

(MAURICE *and* SOLANGE *go about these things.*)

(*The lights change. The piano disappears.* GEORGE *tends* FREDERIC *in his delirium. As she does, she says to us:*)

GEORGE: The fever has been raging for days. Nothing can assuage it. Sometimes his breathing is shallow and fast. Sometimes horrendously deep and irregular. He alternates between coma and delirium. His tongue is swollen. His lips are cracked and dry.

(FREDERIC *awakens, racked with coughing.* GEORGE *holds her handkerchief over his mouth as he coughs. Then, in horror, she looks at the dark stain on the cloth. One word escapes her:*)

GEORGE: Blood—!

FREDERIC: What—?

GEORGE: *(Hiding the handkerchief)* Rest. Rest, my love...

(FREDERIC *tries, but is racked by a fit of coughing. He begins to choke and falls back, unconscious.* GEORGE *calls out:*)

GEORGE: Maurice!

(MAURICE *comes to her.*)

GEORGE: We must get him back to France, to doctors we can trust, before it's too late! Go down to the village. Hire a cart so we can move him to a ship—

MAURICE: No one will hire us a cart. They're all afraid of his illness—

GEORGE: Then we'll carry him. We have to get him to a ship.

(GEORGE *and* MAURICE *wrap* FREDERIC *in a blanket and start to move him.*)

GEORGE: It was insane of me to bring him here! What did I think we would find, eternal summer? If anything happens to him, it's my fault. *My fault!*

(SOLANGE *hands* GEORGE *a cloak.* MAURICE *gathers up the puppets he's been working on. As he puts them in a sack, he says to us:*)

MAURICE: So this is what it's going to be like—living with an invalid who depends on us to keep him alive.

(*The lights change. The room in Majorca disappears.*)

(*It is a dark and windy night on the water.* SOLANGE *and* MAURICE *stand on the deck of a ship.* GEORGE *says to us:*)

GEORGE: They wanted to put him in the hold with the pigs! My lover! I shall keep him here on deck, where he can *breathe!* (*Agitated, helpless, she stands looking out to sea.*)

(*Isolated in his own light,* FREDERIC *lies on the deck. Noticing the* FREDERIC PUPPET *sticking out of* MAURICE's *sack, he picks it up, puts it on his hand and says to it, while his* **Nocturne Op. 48, No. 1, C Minor** *plays under:*)

FREDERIC: Die, Chopin, why do you hesitate about it? Now that you've found true love at last, it must be time to go. Think of your mistress, who will no longer have to cater to your whims and fancies. Think of your mother, who will no longer have to wonder how long her little Freycek will survive. Think of your students, who will not have to struggle through your horrid polonaises. Think of your public, who will escape your endless musicales for food and sleep. Who will miss another twenty-seven etudes? By now haven't you used up all the notes? Die, Chopin, you're taking much too long about it. Die, Chopin, isn't death your constant friend? (*He makes the puppet die, then he falls back, unconscious.*)

(GEORGE *runs over to* FREDERIC *and cries out:*)

GEORGE: Maurice, I think we're going to lose him! He's slipping away! I can't hold him to life! Frederic! Frederic! Live! Live! *(She shakes his lifeless form violently.)*

MAURICE: *(Stopping her)* Mother! What are you doing?!

GEORGE: *(Wildly)* I want to give him my life!

MAURICE: Mother—

GEORGE: *Help!* My God, can't somebody help him!

MAURICE: Mother! We're back!

GEORGE: What?

MAURICE: We're home! In Nohant! In our place in the country!

(The darkness disappears. The sun breaks through. They are in the green leafy cool of the country. GEORGE *looks around. She can hardly believe it.)*

GEORGE: Is he still breathing?

MAURICE: Yes.

GEORGE: Thank God. Thank God...

*(*FREDERIC *looks up at her.* GEORGE *and* SOLANGE *help him up and take him out. As they exit,* MAURICE *picks up the* FREDERIC PUPPET. *Looking at it, he says to us:)*

MAURICE: They say: When you save a person's life, you are responsible for him forever...

(The lights change.)

*(*MAURICE *takes the puppets out of the sack and, as he speaks, starts putting them up in this order:* GEORGE, MAURICE, SOLANGE.*)*

MAURICE: So the little family in its lovely country home—which used to consist of my mother, myself and my sister—now became my mother, *her lover*, my sister and me.

(He inserts the FREDERIC PUPPET *next to the* GEORGE PUPPET, *moving the* MAURICE *and* SOLANGE PUPPETS *farther from* GEORGE.*)*

(Time has passed. SOLANGE *runs in saying:)*

SOLANGE: Monsieur Chopin is well! He's going to give me piano lessons!

(A piano appears beneath an elm tree. SOLANGE *dances around it.* MAURICE *says to us:)*

MAURICE: The domestication of genius.

*(*FREDERIC *enters. He is thin, but well. A hint of color has returned to his cheeks.)*

FREDERIC: *(To* SOLANGE:*)* Before we start, there's something you must learn to do.

SOLANGE: What's that?

FREDERIC: Sit down.

(SOLANGE *sits*.)

SOLANGE: My feet don't reach the pedals.

FREDERIC: Forget the pedals. *(He plays a note.)* This is middle C. *(He plays middle C.)*

(SOLANGE *plays it several times.*)

SOLANGE: I like it!

FREDERIC: That bodes well for the enterprise.

SOLANGE: Will you write me a waltz?

FREDERIC: I'll write you a waltz when you can play it.

FREDERIC: Maurice, would you like to join us?

MAURICE: No, thank you. *(To us:)* He has his music, I have my pencil and sketch pad and pen. *(He takes out an artist's pad and begins sketching.)*

(SOLANGE *and* FREDERIC *continue practicing five finger exercises.*)

(GEORGE *enters. Aside,* MAURICE *says to her:*)

MAURICE: Did you have to give Monsieur Chopin *my* bedroom?

GEORGE: I want to be nearby to hear him if he needs me.

MAURICE: There are other rooms—

GEORGE: I don't want him to have to climb any stairs.

MAURICE: How long is *this* one going to stay?

GEORGE: Oh, Maurice—

MAURICE: *(To us:)* I was still under the illusion that, like all the others, Chopin was just a passing fancy.

GEORGE: Maurice, you must draw me a portrait of Frederic!

FREDERIC: Oh, no!

(MAURICE *looks insulted.* FREDERIC *tries to make light of it.*)

FREDERIC: I'm afraid of what he'll do to my nose!

MAURICE: Yes! He's afraid I might get it right!

(Not wanting a quarrel, and wanting to show he's a good sport, FREDERIC *takes up the* FREDERIC PUPPET *and says to it:)*

FREDERIC: Poor Chopin! Your nose is like a Polish sausage! Or like a flute! You can blow in any key. How can you play? Your nose must get between the octaves! How can you write such complicated music? *(To his own puppet)* I write for two hands and a nose!

(GEORGE *laughs and kisses* FREDERIC's *nose, then kisses his mouth directly beneath it. It becomes a passionate kiss—which excludes the watching children.* FREDERIC *rids his hands of the puppet to embrace* GEORGE.)

(MAURICE *says dryly:*)

MAURICE: I think I'll go draw a tree.

SOLANGE: I think I'll go climb one.

(SOLANGE *runs off.* MAURICE *picks up the discarded puppet and, deliberately turning his back on* GEORGE *and* FREDERIC, *sits at the side of the stage, sketching.*)

(*The lights go down on* MAURICE *and up on* GEORGE *and* FREDERIC, *who are wrapped in each other's arms. Behind their exchanges is heard* **Sonata B Flat minor, 1st Movement, 2nd theme**.)

FREDERIC: You haven't held me like this—for longer than I can remember.

GEORGE: How have I been holding you?

FREDERIC: Like a nurse.

GEORGE: Thank God you're not my patient any longer!

FREDERIC: There's something else I'd like to be.

GEORGE: What's that?

FREDERIC: Your lover once again...

GEORGE: Oh, Frederic! How long I've been waiting to hear you say that!

FREDERIC: Let's do it. Here! On the grass! With every sparrow watching!

GEORGE: And you were the man who wouldn't make love by daylight!

(*They tumble onto the grass. The sonata music rises.*)

(*The lights dim on them. At the side of the stage,* MAURICE *says to us:*)

MAURICE: Avoiding their amorous displays takes some effort. They can be on any patch of grass, or in any room. I cough as I approach any space where a tryst might be occurring. I don't always succeed in not surprising them. But at least I try.

(*The lights come up on* GEORGE *and* FREDERIC. *It is a little while later. His head is in her lap. They are both content.*)

GEORGE: *(Caressing him)* Where did you learn to make love like that?

FREDERIC: You taught me.

GEORGE: Your hands...Your beautiful hands...They know things on their own. (*She kisses his hands*) Oh, Frederic, we will have such times together! We'll get a place in Paris—

(FREDERIC *looks at* GEORGE.)

GEORGE: Ah, well, *two* places separated from each other by a courtyard, if you insist! We'll entertain the world, you and I! You won't mind our being known as a *couple*, will you?

(FREDERIC's *face is in* GEORGE's *lap. He doesn't answer.*)

GEORGE: Will you?

(FREDERIC's *face buried in* GEORGE's *skirt, he has a fit of coughing.*)

GEORGE: Frederic—! (*She rises. She looks down at her skirt. It is stained with blood.*) Oh, my God—! We shouldn't have—! I shouldn't have let us—!

FREDERIC: (*Choking out the words*) I—am—fine—. (*He gets up.*) See? *Fine*!

(FREDERIC *smiles, making a gesture of complete health. Deeply concerned,* GEORGE *looks at him. Then she touches the stain on her dress and goes into the house.*)

(FREDERIC *turns to us and, choking out the words, says:*)

FREDERIC: She shouldn't be afraid of a little coughing. And as for the blood, it's only what we all have, gushing around us, always, inside. Adversity is a treasure to an artist. It's the sand in the oyster, the burden against which we can create.

(*The lights begin to change. Sounds of male voices and clinking glasses begin to be heard, off left.*)

(MAURICE *says to us:*)

MAURICE: Here we are in the glorious city of Paris where, separated by a discreet courtyard, the composer and his piano have *his* apartment and my mother—and her children—and her friends—have *hers*.

(*The sounds of male laughter and clinking glasses grow louder. In his apartment up stage right,* FREDERIC *says to us:*)

FREDERIC: I can create against disease, and plague, and pestilence, against roaches, floods, and tidal waves, and earthquakes, and avalanches. The only thing I can't create against—is *noise*!

(FREDERIC *sits at his piano, trying to play, but is disturbed by the raucous laughter. Off-stage left a* MALE VOICE *cries:*)

MALE VOICE: (*O S*) George, you beauty!

FREDERIC: (*Playing a chord and imitating in mocking tones:*) "George, you beauty!" (*Another chord*) "George, let me worship at your feet! Let me polish your boots!" (*Another chord*) "I shall throw myself into the Seine, George, if I'm not in your next novel!" (*Another chord*) "I swore off women forever. But for you, George, I make an exception. After all, aren't you one of the boys?"

(Laughing, GEORGE and BULOZ enter her apartment downstage left carrying glasses of champagne. They both wear opera capes. Beneath hers, GEORGE is dressed as a dandy, in trousers and top hat. BULOZ is identically dressed. She calls back over her shoulder toward the roomful of male laughter:)

GEORGE: Help yourselves to the wine, my friends—!

MAURICE: *(To us:)* My mother and her publisher both patronize the same tailor.

(He takes out the GEORGE and BULOZ PUPPETS, identically dressed:)

BULOZ: My God, the Comédie Française creaks! You looked more like El Cid than El Cid did!

GEORGE: That must be why they dragged me onto the stage!

(In his apartment, FREDERIC plays a chord. He says to us:)

FREDERIC: She associates with Bohemians! *(Another chord)*

MAURICE: *(To us:)* Gypsies!

(Another chord)

FREDERIC: Socialists! *(Another chord)*

MAURICE: She's the darling of Paris!

(Another chord)

FREDERIC: Their pet! *(Another chord)*

BULOZ: That was a marvelous moment—when you kissed the leading lady on the mouth!

GEORGE: I felt it was expected of me!

(Another chord)

FREDERIC: She will do anything to shock!

GEORGE: Most people are dead, Buloz. I live for them!

BULOZ: There's not a woman in Paris who wouldn't give her soul to live your life!

FREDERIC: Total freedom!*(A chord)*

MAURICE: Two children!

(Another chord)

FREDERIC: A genius lover! *(Another chord)*

MAURICE: A new and magnificent novel!

(Another chord)

FREDERIC: Rooms full of men!

(To drown his feelings, FREDERIC *plays a rampant revolutionary etude.* **Etude Op. 10, No. 12.** *He continues to play furiously, under:)*

BULOZ: There are so many ladies emulating you I can hardly fight my way into my tobacconist.

*(*SOLANGE *enters, smoking a cigar.)*

GEORGE: Solange! Put that thing out at once! I won't have you smoking!

SOLANGE: *You* do it!

BULOZ: Yes, but she does it with flair.

SOLANGE: There's a man outside with a naked lady.

GEORGE: You and your stories—!

SOLANGE: It's true!

CLESINGER: *(O S)* Let me in! Let me in!

MAURICE: *(To us:)* I should have locked the door. I should never have let him enter!

(He brings out a young burly MALE PUPPET *in an artist's smock and beret.)*

BULOZ: It must be that young sculptor I sent away last night. He's done you in marble. He wants to give you the thing.

CLESINGER: *(O S)* I insist on being admitted!

GEORGE: Well, why not? It's better than losing the door. ... Let him in, Solange—and then, go to bed—without the cigar!

*(*SOLANGE *exits to let the visitor in.* GEORGE *calls out:)*

GEORGE: Frederic! Come see me immortalized in stone!

*(*FREDERIC *plays one loud chord and says to us:)*

FREDERIC: She's about to add another member to her harem!

(A YOUNG BURLY SCULPTOR *enters* GEORGE*'s apartment, a wrapped form under his arm.)*

CLESINGER: You have no right to keep me out. I am a fellow artist!

GEORGE: What is your name, fellow artist?

CLESINGER: Auguste Clesinger.

GEORGE: Do I understand you've done me in stone?

CLESINGER: I have.

GEORGE: Without meeting me?

CLESINGER: I did you from my mind's eye.

GEORGE: And how do you see me?

CLESINGER: As the Goddess of Love.

(*With a flourish,* CLESINGER *unwraps his bundle and presents a fully nude figure carved in stone.* GEORGE *studies it. He studies her.*)

CLESINGER: You *are* the Goddess Venus. I was right about you. Oh, let me do you from life! It would be a masterpiece.

BULOZ: *(Aside to George:)* It would also make his reputation.

CLESINGER: Why not? Why shouldn't I do something that will make my reputation?

GEORGE: At least you're honest.

(FREDERIC *enters.*)

GEORGE: Well, Frederic. How do you like me as the Goddess of Love?

FREDERIC: Did you pose for this?

GEORGE: He's been worshipping me from afar.

FREDERIC: *(Dryly)* Haven't we all.

GEORGE: Come, Frederic. Your artistic judgment. How do you like it?

FREDERIC: I think it should be draped.

GEORGE: *(Draping the cloth up to the statue's knees, but leaving from there upwards bare)* Frederic hates knees. He thinks them the most obscene part of the body. No one has ever seen his.

FREDERIC: *Everyone* has seen yours!

GEORGE: You must forgive Monsieur Chopin. Monsieur Chopin is very grouchy. After four years, he's finally consented to appear before the world once more in concert. In the agony of his preparation for it, the entire household must suffer dozens of his insults every day.

CLESINGER: No matter how distraught he gets, I'm sure that you can soothe him.

GEORGE: *(To* CLESINGER*:)* How well you know me... Come, let's show your masterpiece to my friends.

(GEORGE *takes* CLESINGER *out stage left.*)

MAURICE: *(To us:)* Who would have thought that the arrival of this lout would have such consequences? *(Bringing out and holding the* CLESINGER PUPPET, *he stays outside the scene, observing* BULOZ *and* FREDERIC.*)*

FREDERIC: Why does she associate with such rabble?

BULOZ: They flock to her—

FREDERIC: One is more idiotic than the next.

BULOZ: I understand your concert is sold out two months in advance.

FREDERIC: I'm probably the only person in Paris who isn't looking forward to it.

BULOZ: It will be the event of the season.

FREDERIC: Oh, those glorious moments of triumph! Thousands of eyes upon you. Ladies staring at your bony fingers. Husbands snoring. Dandies flirting. Critics ready to pounce on your innovations—or blame you for your lack of innovations. Everyone more interested in each other than the music. Everyone more interested in your love-life than in you. Everyone hoping for one false note! ...And not a music-lover in the lot!

BULOZ: No?

FREDERIC: Don't you think I know they come out of curiosity? To catch an inside glimpse of George and me?

MAURICE: *(Aside to us:)* The awful price of fame—having people pay attention to you.

FREDERIC: *(Mocking the dilettante ladies)* "That passionate cadence. Isn't that George Sand's heavy breathing? ...That furious contrapuntal bass. It's a lover's quarrel, I'm sure!"

BULOZ: You can't blame people for wanting to see the world's most famous lovers.

FREDERIC: What would they say if they knew the world's most famous lovers never meet in bed?

(BULOZ *looks at* FREDERIC *in silence.* MAURICE *says to us:*)

MAURICE: This is no surprise to me. I'm well aware there is no traffic between my mother and her lover's separate bedrooms.

FREDERIC: Does our asceticism shock you?

BULOZ: A little.

FREDERIC: It's the lady's idea. She thinks my art should be my only mistress.

BULOZ: She must have a reason.

FREDERIC: She thinks that making love will kill me.

BULOZ: And she doesn't want to be responsible—

FREDERIC: I tell you the *deprivation* will kill me.

BULOZ: How long has this been going on?

FREDERIC: Two years.

BULOZ: Two years of total, absolute, unwavering abstention?

(GEORGE *enters.*)

GEORGE: Two years of glorious, magnificent, unmatchable *work*!

FREDERIC: Ah, the uses of frustration!

GEORGE: I want him to live a long life, composing all he has to compose. I don't want to rob the world of a single composition. I want to preserve, protect and nurture him—

FREDERIC: But not sleep with him—

GEORGE: My saying no is a measure of my love for you.

FREDERIC: Couldn't you love me a little less?

(*As* GEORGE *sees* BULOZ *to the exit, he says to her:*)

BULOZ: Are you really insisting you and Frederic live like two nuns in a nunnery?

GEORGE: I didn't make the rule, his doctors did. But I don't want to tell him that.

BULOZ: So you take the blame—?

GEORGE: It's best for Frederic to think himself totally well.

BULOZ: Careful, George. He's a young man. This is unnatural.

GEORGE: Frederic and I are above nature.

BULOZ: No one can be above nature. Nature burrows from within.

GEORGE: We are immune.

(GEORGE *accompanies* BULOZ *out.*)

(*Coughing slightly,* FREDERIC *sits at the piano and starts to play the* **Minute Waltz, Waltz Op. 64, No.1, D Flat***, furiously, as if to finish it in half a minute.*)

(*Over it,* MAURICE *says to us:*)

MAURICE: Which is worse—telling people things for their own good, or *not* telling people things for their own good? Sometimes the results can be the same one way or the other.

(MAURICE *retreats into the shadows downstage.* FREDERIC *breaks off playing and says to us:*)

FREDERIC: If love can be devastated by the proverbial headache, just think what a little chronic bronchitis can do! Are art and love mutually exclusive? Does the heat that fires the imagination fire the loins? If so, think of all the great creations thrust upon the world by virgins! Oh, the infinite imaginations of the pure! What else have they to do?

(GEORGE *returns.*)

GEORGE: You're a beast when you're working.

FREDERIC: So you've added another to your coterie of hangers-on!

GEORGE: They're my friends.

FREDERIC: All *men*!

GEORGE: Can I help it if only *men* manage to preserve their minds?

FREDERIC: It's a menagerie! A circus! A goddam florist shop! *(He rips some flowers from a vase and throws them across the room.)*

GEORGE: *(Looking at him steadily)* So you're that nervous about the concert—

FREDERIC: *(Deeply)* It's been years since I've played in public. My work has changed. My playing's changed.

GEORGE: They will adore you.

FREDERIC: They ask too much! If I compose, why must I play? If I play, why must it be what I write?

GEORGE: You do both beautifully.

FREDERIC: It's like facing an army—alone—every time.

GEORGE: You have weeks to prepare—

FREDERIC: George—I'm afraid—I won't have the strength for it.

GEORGE: What do you want me to do?

FREDERIC: Put the world in order for me!

(He stands helplessly, in panic. She takes his hands in hers.)

GEORGE: Yes. I will.

(Her grasp infuses him with strength. Strengthened and encouraged, he returns to his piano.)

MAURICE: *(To us:)* This putting the world in order for him—we're all enlisted. The house is now devoted to one cause and one cause only: getting Frederic ready for the crucial night.

(Lights change. FREDERIC *is heard practicing in the background. Music,* **Waltz Op. 42, A Flat Major**, *continues under all the following as* GEORGE, *writing at her desk, says to us:)*

GEORGE: My tasks are humble. All I have to do is bring him chocolate in the morning, tea in the afternoon, and bouillon at night. I must make sure that no one ever comes to see him at exactly twenty of or twenty past the hour. I must make certain nothing in his presence ever adds up to thirteen. I must also get my next chapter to the printers— *(She tries to write.)*

FREDERIC: My hands are cold!

GEORGE: *(To us:)* I have to provide a correctly heated hot water bottle—

(FREDERIC *calls again from a distance.*)

FREDERIC: I can't find my fresh shirt—

GEORGE: Wear one of mine.

(*Downstage, bored,* MAURICE *bounces a ball.*)

FREDERIC: His ball isn't bouncing in time to the music!

GEORGE: Throw it *up*, Maurice—

(MAURICE *bounces the ball downward once, defiantly, then throws it up into the air, saying to us:*)

MAURICE: We have to keep the thunder from crashing too loudly. We have to be certain the wind doesn't howl off key.

(SOLANGE *runs in.*)

SOLANGE: I've found it!

GEORGE: What?

SOLANGE: The rat I promised Monsieur Chopin in Spain! (*She holds it up, swinging it by the tail.*) I'm going to give it to him for luck!

GEORGE: Solange, if you please—

SOLANGE: He'll love it! I know he will!

GEORGE: Another time, Solange!

(*Disappointed,* SOLANGE *exits. Exhausted,* GEORGE *tries to return to work.*)

MAURICE: *(To us:)* We have to keep the rain from pattering against his windows. We have to keep bad dreams from robbing him of sleep. We have to let in the spirits of Bach and Mozart, but keep the ghost of Beethoven out.

(FREDERIC *calls out:*)

FREDERIC: I dreamt of Beethoven last night!

GEORGE: I'm sorry!

FREDERIC: My lucky talisman is missing—

GEORGE: It's in your left breast pocket, under your watch. (*She tries to write.*)

FREDERIC: There are thirteen brussels sprouts on this plate!

GEORGE: *(Exasperated)* Eat one!

(*From outside on the street come sounds of crowds, voices vibrant with excitement. Writing,* GEORGE *pays no attention.* FREDERIC *cries:*)

FREDERIC: Stop that noise!

GEORGE: I think it's a revolution.

FREDERIC: Stop it!

(GEORGE *throws up her hands. With two sticks,* MAURICE *starts to bang loudly on a washbasin.* SOLANGE *runs in waving a red, white and blue revolutionary banner.*)

SOLANGE: They're marching in the streets! They're waving flags! They're singing!

MAURICE: They're crying out for bread and wages! For liberty! For justice! They want it now!

FREDERIC: George! Make it stop!

(GEORGE *has had enough. She grabs the sticks from* MAURICE *and beats furiously on the washbasin.*)

GEORGE: Long live Louis Philippe! Feed the poor! Free the women! (*She adds another loud volley on the washbasin.*)

(*Breaking off his playing,* FREDERIC *cries out:*)

FREDERIC: *Stop!*

(*The sounds stop. There is silence.* SOLANGE *exits.*)

(*The lights change. The rooms disappear.*)

(MAURICE *stays down right, out of the light, observing.*)

(*In total stillness,* FREDERIC *comes forward, thin, pale and in terror.* GEORGE *and* FREDERIC *are alone in the dressing room of the concert hall. She helps him into his formal jacket.*)

FREDERIC: ...It's almost time...

GEORGE: ...You have a quarter of an hour.

FREDERIC: ...I think death must be like this. Suspended. Numb.

GEORGE: I wouldn't be surprised.

FREDERIC: The action of the keyboard is hard.

GEORGE: It won't seem so once you begin.

FREDERIC: They'll say I play too softly—

GEORGE: They will *listen*, Frederic—

(*He paces nervously.*)

FREDERIC: Where are you sitting tonight?

GEORGE: Here.

FREDERIC: In my dressing room?

GEORGE: I want all eyes to focus on you. Maurice and Solange will be out front, with Buloz.

FREDERIC: And who'll be in here with you?

GEORGE: No one.

FREDERIC: Don't lie to me! Who is it!

GEORGE: The entire Imperial Army!

FREDERIC: I'm sorry. Forgive me. I'm in a state of insanity and terror. *(He listens. He hears the sounds of the audience.)* They're waiting for me— *(In sudden panic:)* George, I can't—!

GEORGE: Come here. *(She takes a small vial out of her pocket.)*

FREDERIC: What's this?

GEORGE: Once you told me that when you were a boy, before each concert, your mother would draw a star—in rosewater—on your forehead. *(She opens the vial.)* This is real Polish rosewater. ...I had it sent...from Warsaw.

(Like a child, he lowers his head. With her index finger, GEORGE slowly draws a star, in rosewater. Then she kisses his forehead. ... FREDERIC is deeply moved. Now calm, he removes his gloves and hands them to her. Then he goes toward the stage door. Just as he reaches it, he turns to her and says:)

FREDERIC: Why do I do this?

GEORGE: *God* knows.

(FREDERIC exits.)

(Applause is heard, off. The concert begins.)

(FREDERIC is seen at the piano in silhouette, playing his **Scherzo Op. 3, B Minor** *passionately.)*

(In her own light, GEORGE sits listening in the dressing room, holding FREDERIC's white gloves. As he continues to play, she says to us:)

GEORGE: He plays—beyond the capacity of any mortal. He plays—as if possessed by the spirit of a god. ... The audience is stunned, silent, as at the morning of the Revelation. And I, who know every aspect of the man—his spirit, his mind, his body—I am the most stunned of all. *(Worshipfully, she holds his gloves to her lips as the music continues.)*

MAURICE: *(Aside to us as he looks from the FREDERIC PUPPET to FREDERIC at the piano:)* Before this, he was only a man in my house who played the piano. Tonight I've seen him hypnotize a room. Strangers. Friends. What sounded—interesting—at home here sounds transcendent. It is very odd to realize you have been sitting at breakfast, lunch and dinner with the transcendent. Beside him—and remember I'm used to living with my genius mother—beside him, everyone else seems less.

(The music climaxes and ends. The concert is over. FREDERIC *rises and bows again and again to waves of applause.)*

(Then FREDERIC *leaves the concert stage and enters to* GEORGE *in the dressing room.)*

FREDERIC: They liked my music! Listen!

GEORGE: You are a miracle.

FREDERIC: No. The miracle is you. Thank you for getting me to it and through it.

GEORGE: I am in awe of you.

FREDERIC: Awe? That means you hold me at a distance.

GEORGE: I don't hold you at a distance.

(She holds out her arms. He comes to her. They hold each other in a tight embrace.)

FREDERIC: This is as far away from each other as we should ever be. *(He kisses her.)*

GEORGE: *(Disengaging herself gently)* Come. Buloz and the children are waiting.

MAURICE: *(To us, with an edge:)* I'm nearly twenty and she still refers to me as one of her children!

FREDERIC: George, I ordered us a separate carriage.

GEORGE: But we're all to go to dinner—

FREDERIC: No. You and I are going somewhere else.

GEORGE: Where?

FREDERIC: To a room at an inn.

GEORGE: What a splendid idea!

FREDERIC: To hold you in my arms all night—

GEORGE: How lovely—

FREDERIC: To make love to you again.

(This changes her mood.)

GEORGE: Frederic—

FREDERIC: I've been planning it for weeks. It's the heaven I promised myself after this horrendous ordeal was over.

GEORGE: Frederic—

MAURICE: *(To us:)* At a loss for words, all the novelist can say is "Frederic".

FREDERIC: The thought of having you once more was my only strength.

GEORGE: Please—

MAURICE: *(To us:)* Having run out of "Frederics", all the novelist can say is "please".

FREDERIC: You can't say no—

MAURICE: *(To us:)* She can.

FREDERIC: There's not a woman in Paris who would deny me anything tonight—except my mistress!

GEORGE: It does no good going over this, over and over—

FREDERIC: Why won't you give yourself to me?

GEORGE: My God, don't you think I want to?

FREDERIC: I wonder—

GEORGE: It's not me—it's your doctors who've said—

FREDERIC: Why are you quoting doctors?

GEORGE: Because I'm the one who has to carry out their prescription!

(BULOZ *enters, his arms filled with bouquets.*)

BULOZ: Paris is yours tonight, Frederic!

FREDERIC: Not all of it.

BULOZ: There are a thousand ladies out there who would kill to touch one finger of your glove!

(*In the mass of bouquets,* FREDERIC *sees a small bouquet of violets. He takes it up and looks at the card. He smiles.*)

GEORGE: From someone you know?

FREDERIC: The Countess Delphine Potocka.

(FREDERIC *hands* GEORGE *the card.*)

GEORGE: A woman of quality.

FREDERIC: An old friend.

GEORGE: You told me about little Marie and little Constanza, but this lady is in a different category.

FREDERIC: Delphine was my first mistress.

GEORGE: She writes nothing.

FREDERIC: Delphine and I never needed words.

(GEORGE *and* FREDERIC *exchange a look.* FREDERIC *says:*)

FREDERIC: It's an invitation...

(MAURICE *takes out an elegantly dressed* COUNTESS PUPPET *and, in aristocratic*

Polish accent, has her say:)

MAURICE: *(As* COUNTESS PUPPET*)* "Come to me, my little Polish pumpkin. I will wait at my palace for you to arrive. We shall rekindle our love over plump fresh peaches and ambrosia. I will cover you with kisses, Frederushka. Come, my little Polish pumpkin, come..."

(SOLANGE *runs in. As though transformed, she runs up to* FREDERIC, *ecstatic.*)

SOLANGE: You were wonderful! I had no idea! You were like someone else! Like an angel! I didn't know you could be like that! I didn't know—! I didn't know—!

(SOLANGE *throws her arms around* FREDERIC. GEORGE *extricates her and says to* BULOZ:)

GEORGE: You and the children wait for us in the carriage, will you? We won't be long. Where's Maurice?

BULOZ: He said he would congratulate Frederic later, in private.

MAURICE: *(To us:)* When I'm no longer speechless with envy...

(BULOZ *takes a reluctant* SOLANGE *out with him.* GEORGE *says to* FREDERIC:)

GEORGE: You see? After all your worry, it's a triumph.

FREDERIC: Why is it that triumph is always mixed with pain?

GEORGE: So the great debate continues.

FREDERIC: Not at all. I wouldn't dream of forcing myself on you.

GEORGE: Now there's an image—

FREDERIC: Don't you think I could do it?

GEORGE: Rape me? No.

FREDERIC: Delphine never had to be raped. Delphine made love like a woman.

GEORGE: And how do I make love?

FREDERIC: Like a man.

(MAURICE *attaches a dress to the* FREDERIC PUPPET *and a man's formal suit to the* GEORGE PUPPET.)

GEORGE: I'm sure you would know!

FREDERIC: And what does that mean?

GEORGE: Nothing. Let's go—

FREDERIC: Someone sent me a copy of a cartoon that was in last week's Figaro—

GEORGE: I saw it.

FREDERIC: You in trousers, me in a ruffled dress—

(MAURICE *animates the* GEORGE *and* FREDERIC PUPPETS *in their trans-sexed clothes.*)

GEORGE: I was amused—

FREDERIC: I don't like what they think!

GEORGE: I don't *care!*

FREDERIC: Come to the inn, George—

GEORGE: You don't have to prove your manhood to me.

FREDERIC: You don't have to prove *yours!*

GEORGE: Your life depends on my remaining strong!

FREDERIC: Monsieur Sand, Madame Chopin?

(MAURICE *makes the gender-transposed puppets bow to each other.*)

GEORGE: Oh, Frederic, we are beyond all that! ...We are *monsters*, you and I. That is our secret. We hold within ourselves every sex and every shape. We are tree, rock, jackal, hunchback, snake! We are god and we are demon! We would steal, ravage, plunder, pervert all life for one perfect word, one perfect note! We can *create*, you and I. That is our triumph! Accept it! We can't ask, also, for the common pleasures.

FREDERIC: We *can!*

GEORGE: The last time we made love—

FREDERIC: Two years ago—

GEORGE: —I had a vision. I saw us, not as two beings, but as one. One giant, winged, hermaphrodite creature. Striving, striving—

(MAURICE *works the puppets locked in passionate embrace.*)

GEORGE: And when we wrenched ourselves apart—I saw you dead.

(MAURICE *makes the* FREDERIC PUPPET *die.* GEORGE *continues, deeply serious:*)

GEORGE: I'm unlike you. I have no superstitions. I've had no visions but this one—in which I was your death.

(*Contemplatively,* MAURICE *returns the* GEORGE *and* FREDERIC PUPPETS *to their appropriate clothing and puts them on stands beside each other.*)

GEORGE: I died once, in your mind, do you remember? And now you've died in mine, in my arms, in my bed. Love is so close to death. In it we know so much, give so much, take so much—we could destroy each other. And Frederic, Frederic—I *can't*—

FREDERIC: Why not? ...I'm not afraid of death... Sometimes I want it.

GEORGE: Is that what you want of me?

(FREDERIC *is silent. She stares at him then cries out:*)

GEORGE: I won't! I won't—!

(FREDERIC *moves away, then turns and says to* GEORGE, *quietly, steadily:*)

FREDERIC: George, I have been working—to the ends of my strength—for longer than I can remember. Tonight I *want* the common pleasures. Please. Come to the inn...

(SOLANGE *runs in.*)

SOLANGE: We've been waiting and waiting! Come on—!

(FREDERIC *puts on his cape, then turns to* GEORGE *and asks:*)

FREDERIC: George—?

(GEORGE *hears the unasked question. She answers firmly, quietly:*)

GEORGE: ...No, Frederic...

(*He takes up Delphine's card.*)

FREDERIC: Then you won't mind if I spend the evening elsewhere—

GEORGE: This is your night, enjoy it! There's no earthly reason why we should limit each other. Have a wonderful time!

(FREDERIC *puts on his top hat and exits stage right.*)

(GEORGE *looks after him for a moment, then exits stage left.*)

(*Alone in the dressing room,* SOLANGE *sees that, in his haste,* FREDERIC *left his gloves behind. She picks them up, thinks briefly of running after him to give them to him, but then stops. Instead,* SOLANGE *raises the gloves to her lips and kisses them— exactly as* GEORGE *had done earlier.*)

(MAURICE *places the* SOLANGE PUPPET *in between the* GEORGE *and* FREDERIC PUPPETS. *He turns to us and says:*)

MAURICE: And so begins another part of the story...

(*Music is heard,* **Ballade Op. 47, A Flat Major.**)

(*As* MAURICE *exits stage left, the lights iris in on the* SOLANGE PUPPET *between the* GEORGE *and* FREDERIC PUPPETS—*and on* SOLANGE *with* FREDERIC's *gloves pressed rapturously to her lips.*)

(*Blackout*)

END ACT ONE

ACT TWO

(At rise: Several years later. It is morning in the Music Room at Nohant.)

(SOLANGE, now older, precocious, nubile, runs in, carrying music. Putting down the music, and knowing she is doing something forbidden, she scurries over to the row of MAURICE's puppets, takes up the FREDERIC PUPPET tenderly and sings to us a song she has thought up herself: **When Mornings Come**.*)*

SOLANGE: *(Singing:)*
When mornings come
I hear his music
From his heart
It wafts itself to me

Curling softly
Swirling lovely music
Touching every rock
And every tree

(Unseen by SOLANGE, MAURICE enters, is surprised to see what she is doing, and, bemused, watches from the shadows.)

And Oh I hear his heart
I hear it calling
Oh I feel him beg
On bended knee

Oh I know his heart
Yearns for a flower
Oh I know his heart—
It yearns for me.

(MAURICE makes his presence known. Guiltily, SOLANGE puts the FREDERIC PUPPET back where she found it and, picking up her music, hurries over to the piano.)

(Downstage, in his own light, MAURICE says to us:)

MAURICE: What a scamp she is, my sister! Years after the concert, she still keeps those gloves she stole from Frederic, like holy relics, in her room. He, so used to being worshipped, wouldn't find such a thing unusual—if he knew about it. But believe me, for Solange—unsentimental rebellious Solange—it is *very* unusual. It's quite amusing, actually; she's become a little acolyte. At least it keeps her out of Mother's and my hair!

(As MAURICE retreats, out of the light, to his own space with his puppets, FREDERIC enters the music room. SOLANGE hands him the sheets of music.)

FREDERIC: Thank you, Solange. I couldn't manage without you.

SOLANGE: I like to help you, Frederic.

FREDERIC: No one draws a better G clef.

SOLANGE: *(To FREDERIC:)* Why do you always dedicate your pieces to princes and princesses?

FREDERIC: They're the tastemakers. They're the ones who clap their hands at musicians and command, "Play Bach! Play Handel!"

SOLANGE: *(Clapping her hands imperiously)* "Play Chopin! Play Chopin!"

FREDERIC: That's it exactly.

SOLANGE: You've never dedicated a piece to Mother, have you?

FREDERIC: No.

SOLANGE: Why not?

FREDERIC: I suppose—propriety.

SOLANGE: Would it be proper for you to dedicate a piece to me?

(FREDERIC looks at SOLANGE.)

SOLANGE: You promised me a waltz once, don't you remember? When I was little. You said you'd write me one when I could play it. I could play it now, Frederic. I could play it very well.

FREDERIC: So you could.

SOLANGE: Then shall I have one?

FREDERIC: Yes, Solange. The very next I write!

(SOLANGE runs out. FREDERIC continues working at the piano.)

(The lights on FREDERIC fade and come up on GEORGE and BULOZ walking in the garden.)

(Observing them from a distance, MAURICE says to us:)

MAURICE: A hotbed of creativity—that's what it is—our country establishment at Nohant. Frederic churning out reams of music from morning until evening. Mother churning out reams of words from after dinner till dawn. You have only to turn around and one or the other of them has spewed out some new composition! *(He puts aside his puppets and takes up sketchpad and pencil.)* And I'm drawing—well enough to feel I might have a possible career in illustration. Mother says she'll talk to Buloz about it. He's come to the country to ask her to come to Paris and write for a new political journal he's putting together.

GEORGE: A new review is exactly what the movement needs!

BULOZ: What the movement needs is you, George. You attract attention.

GEORGE: So that's what I am! Your freak! Your dancing bear!

BULOZ: The cause needs one.

GEORGE: Yes. I know it does. But it's going to take some doing to convince Frederic to desert the country for the city. He prefers working here. And he likes me to be here with him.

BULOZ: Seven years, you two. Isn't this fidelity a bit excessive?

GEORGE: Frederic is *the* connection of my life.

BULOZ: No brief subsidiary excursions?

GEORGE: None on my part. And as for Frederic, none since the Countess, a few years ago. He spent a week with her and accomplished nothing but a minor tarantella and a cold.

BULOZ: Which he brought to you to cure, no doubt.

GEORGE: Why not? We are the perfect pair.

BULOZ: And still just platonic?

GEORGE: Just platonic.

BULOZ: If chastity is this idyllic, I must recommend it to my friends.

(FREDERIC *enters to them.*)

FREDERIC: George, have you seen my sweater?

GEORGE: *(Handing it to him)* Here. You left it by the fountain.

(FREDERIC *takes it and starts putting it on.*)

GEORGE: Frederic, I'm thinking of going to Paris for a few weeks—

FREDERIC: *(Coolly)* Oh?

GEORGE: Would you like to come with me?

FREDERIC: No, thank you.

BULOZ: The revolution needs her.

FREDERIC: "Revolution—!"

GEORGE: *(To* BULOZ:*)* Frederic is partial to *Polish* revolutions. Ours, he finds, aren't serious.

FREDERIC: The French think they're being oppressed when all they're being is inconvenienced.

GEORGE: Our farmers are being taxed beyond endurance. Our factory workers are being worked to the bone. I must speak out—

BULOZ: No one's as eloquent as George on the subjects of bread and freedom.

FREDERIC: In Poland, we rebel with blood; in France, you rebel with slogans! It's not a cry from the soul, it's a cry from the dictionary!

GEORGE: ...So you're that much against my going to Paris.

FREDERIC: *(In strained tones)* Do what you like. We'll be fine here.

GEORGE: You're sure you'll be all right?

FREDERIC: Of course. Go right ahead.

GEORGE: You're positive?

FREDERIC: You could always be back in a day if we needed you. *(He leaves them, returning to his piano.)*

GEORGE: *(To* BULOZ:*)* You go back to Paris. I'll come in a few days.

BULOZ: If he lets you.

GEORGE: I'll come, I said.

BULOZ: You are his nursemaid.

GEORGE: No.

BULOZ: His prisoner.

GEORGE: No.

BULOZ: His slave.

GEORGE: I am not, Buloz.

BULOZ: Then why do you work in the gardener's cottage while he works in the house?

(GEORGE *says nothing. From the house, they hear* FREDERIC *playing his* **Impromptu Op. 29, No. 1, A Flat**.*)*

BULOZ: If you're ever released from prison, let me know. *(He leaves.)*

(MAURICE *enters to* GEORGE.*)*

MAURICE: Well, what did Buloz say when you told him you want me to illustrate your new novel?

GEORGE: Oh, Maurice! I didn't get a chance to ask him! I'm sorry. I got so carried away thinking about going to Paris—

(CLESINGER *calls from off:)*

CLESINGER: *(O S)* Why go to Paris? Paris has come to you!

MAURICE: *(To us:)* Now *there's* a voice I thought I'd never have to hear again—!

(CLESINGER *enters.)*

MAURICE: You can't just break in—

CLESINGER: I'm not breaking in. I'm arriving. *(To* GEORGE:*)* I've come to sculpt you.

GEORGE: You sculpted me already—

CLESINGER: True. But not from life.

MAURICE: She doesn't have time—

CLESINGER: She'll have to make time. *(To* GEORGE:*)* I have a commission from the Academy to do your portrait.

MAURICE: If you start hammering away at stone, Monsieur Chopin will have your hide.

CLESINGER: I don't plan to do your mother in stone, I plan to do her in clay. Then I'll cast her in bronze. I can sell a hundred copies!

MAURICE: You can't line your pockets by selling copies of the image of my mother—

CLESINGER: Why don't you go back to your puppets and leave your mother and me to discuss—

MAURICE: Mother, are you going to consent to sit for this intruder?

GEORGE: Since he has a commission from the Academy, I guess I must.

(Upset, MAURICE *leaves them and goes downstage and says to us:)*

MAURICE: The snake has appeared in our Garden of Eden!

CLESINGER: *(To* GEORGE:*)* How do you intend to pose?

GEORGE: I don't pose. I write. You'll get what you can get.

(The lights change. GEORGE *sits, writing.* CLESINGER *begins to model her head in clay.)*

(In rebellious mood, MAURICE *takes out his* CLESINGER PUPPET *and starts to redesign the face.)*

MAURICE: He comes prancing in playing the artist! I'm an artist, too! *(As he works on the* CLESINGER PUPPET:*)* There's a dishonest look in his eye. And a mouth that curves up on one side and down on the other. It's a hypocrite's face—a face of evil. Evil! I know exactly what he's thinking: *(He puts the* CLESINGER PUPPET *on his hand and, in its voice, says:)* There's something here. Rich pickings. I'm not fooled by civil surfaces. I can see beneath. The rot's already infecting the garden. All I have to do is wait—and pick the fruit that falls from the trees! *(He pulls the puppet from his hand.)* That's him! Exactly! Why am I the only one who sees it? *(He retreats and, in his mind's eye, observes the scene in the gardener's cottage.)*

(As CLESINGER works on GEORGE's head in clay, he says to her:)

CLESINGER: You're amazing.

GEORGE: Why amazing?

CLESINGER: Your troubles never show in your face.

GEORGE: Perhaps it's because I have no troubles.

CLESINGER: You can't be taking it as well as you seem.

GEORGE: Taking what?

CLESINGER: Chopin's coming marriage.

GEORGE: His coming marriage—!

CLESINGER: You don't have to act surprised with me. I know everything.

GEORGE: Then perhaps you know the identity of the bride?

CLESINGER: Of course I do. Everybody does. Your daughter.

GEORGE: My daughter! My little daughter! *(She laughs a tremendous laugh.)*

CLESINGER: They say he asked you for her hand and they're so in love you had to consent.

GEORGE: *(Highly amused)* Paris has outdone itself this time!

CLESINGER: You mean you know nothing about it?

GEORGE: On what do they base this fantastic news?

CLESINGER: On the locket.

GEORGE: What locket?

CLESINGER: The one he ordered from the jeweler for her. The one inscribed: "To Solange: My tenderest thoughts, Frederic."

GEORGE: My God, that city can make a scandal out of nothing!

CLESINGER: I usually find, when there's scandal, that they're basing it on something—

(A pause. GEORGE looks at CLESINGER.)

GEORGE: Excuse me. It's time for me to bring Frederic his tea... *(She exits.)*

(MAURICE says to us:)

MAURICE: Bringing Frederic his tea is a ritual, an act of tribute. In our house, the world of tea, for the giver and the receiver, has infinite meanings beyond the simple offering of the cup.

*(The lights come up on the music room where FREDERIC is playing his **Waltz Op. 64, No. 3**. GEORGE enters with his tea on a tray. At the exact same moment, SOLANGE enters from the other side, with another tray, also bringing him tea.)*

GEORGE: I didn't know you knew how to brew Frederic's tea...

SOLANGE: I learned last time you were in Paris.

GEORGE: It's good to know Frederic isn't neglected in my absence.

FREDERIC: *(Drinking from the cup* SOLANGE *offers him)* She's a magnificent little tea-maker.

SOLANGE: I'm glad I please you, Frederic.

GEORGE: *(Holding out her tray to* SOLANGE:*)* Perhaps you won't mind taking this back to the kitchen for me.

SOLANGE: *(The perfect superior angel)* Not at all, Mother.

(SOLANGE *comes over to take the tray. As she takes it,* GEORGE *says to her:)*

GEORGE: What a pretty locket—

SOLANGE: Frederic gave it to me. It's an exact copy of a locket worn by the Grand Duchess.

(SOLANGE *sails out with the tea tray.)*

GEORGE: Don't you think she's a little young to play the Grand Duchess?

FREDERIC: She enjoys it.

GEORGE: You spoil her.

FREDERIC: Why shouldn't I? She's a great help to me.

GEORGE: Brews tea. Copies music. Provides the necessary daily dose of worship—

FREDERIC: Why not? Maurice provides you with yours.

MAURICE: *(To us:)* At least he notices I exist!

GEORGE: He's my son, she's not your daughter.

FREDERIC: I don't see that that makes any difference.

GEORGE: Are you aware all Paris says you've asked me for her hand?

FREDERIC: What?!

GEORGE: The locket—

FREDERIC: I gave it to her in appreciation of the work she does for me—

GEORGE: You know the connotation people put on gifts of jewelry!

FREDERIC: They see me as her suitor? Well, why not? I'm young, eligible, a bachelor with a reluctant mistress. I think I'm perfectly suited to marriage!

GEORGE: You wouldn't survive your wedding night.

FREDERIC: I'm not so sure about that. You know, I sometimes wonder if all this abstinence isn't more for your sake than for mine.

GEORGE: What do you mean?

FREDERIC: Did you really like it, George? Making love?

GEORGE: I should think the answer to that would be self-evident.

FREDERIC: Really? I often felt you were resisting being taken, that you didn't want to be possessed by a man.

GEORGE: Perhaps not by one who felt, while he was making love, that he was pure and I wasn't. You wanted to sleep with me and simultaneously condemn me for it!

MAURICE: *(To us:)* The sex life of the holier-than-thou.

FREDERIC: Why did all your men leave *you*—?

GEORGE: We are not discussing me, we are discussing you and Solange! ...Are you aware this story about you and her could ruin her reputation?

FREDERIC: Since when have you cared about reputation?

GEORGE: It could destroy her chances for a proper marriage.

FREDERIC: Marriage! She's only sixteen!

GEORGE: And has that look in her eye that says she needs a husband.

FREDERIC: You said an early marriage ruined your life—

GEORGE: Because I married the wrong man. The right one can make all the difference.

FREDERIC: She's too young to know one from the other.

GEORGE: I'm not. I'll pick him for her.

FREDERIC: I can't believe my ears! George Sand! Ready to sell her daughter into bondage!

GEORGE: Solange needs a man to steady her—

FREDERIC: If only all those ladies who dashed off to copy your Bohemian life could hear you now!

GEORGE: The free life isn't for everyone—

FREDERIC: No. Only for you!

GEORGE: You benefited from it—

FREDERIC: And perhaps Solange would, too!

GEORGE: I wonder if Paris is right. That you *do* want her after all—

FREDERIC: And I wonder if you want to marry her off to get rid of a potential rival!

GEORGE: Is that what you think?

FREDERIC: I want her to have some chance at a life! I say—

GEORGE: You say! You say! She is not your daughter! May I point out, most humbly, that the only one to decide what to do about her is *me*! You have no right, no right at all, even to give your opinion!

FREDERIC: I care about her welfare!

GEORGE: If you care about her welfare, you will try, in the future, to behave with more prudence! You will see that she is an impressionable child on whom you have been playing some game—to get even with me!

FREDERIC: You're *mad*!

GEORGE: I warn you, stop encouraging her in her adolescent fantasies!

FREDERIC: I will treat her any way I like!

GEORGE: You will treat her as *I* like! You are my *guest*!

MAURICE: *(To us:)* I always wondered what to call him.

(GEORGE *turns and goes*).

(FREDERIC *plays* **Etude Op. 25, No. 10, B Minor** *wildly as he says to us:*)

FREDERIC: Guest! So it has come to that, has it? "Guest!" I've been called child, lover, husband, god—and now *guest*! ... What could she mean? What place has *guest* within a household? ...Guest—must be polite at all times. Guest—has no say in anything. Guest—is less than friend...

(The lights change. FREDERIC *sits at the piano.)*

(SOLANGE *enters, humming and waltzing around with a piece of music she has just copied*—**Waltz Op. 70, No. 2**.*)*

SOLANGE: Oh, Frederic! It's a waltz! The new piece is a waltz! It's beautiful! *(She dances, humming the music.)* I hummed it as I copied it! It made me dance! And you wrote it for me!

FREDERIC: Solange—

SOLANGE: Here. Inscribe it yourself. "To Solange Dudevant—who adores me!"

FREDERIC: Solange—I'm sorry that I have to disappoint you. But I just remembered—it's already promised. I told the Duke of—

SOLANGE: No, no! It's mine! You were thinking of me when you wrote it!

FREDERIC: Another time, Solange—

SOLANGE: You promised!

FREDERIC: Another time.

SOLANGE: ...It was Mother who made you change your mind—

FREDERIC: I told you—

SOLANGE: What power does she have over you?

FREDERIC: I can do anything I want!

SOLANGE: And this is what you want?

(FREDERIC *is silent.*)

SOLANGE: She doesn't want me to have something *she* doesn't have.

FREDERIC: That's not it.

SOLANGE: She hates me!

FREDERIC: That isn't true, Solange.

SOLANGE: Then write here, Frederic. Frederic, my dear, dear Frederic... Write my name...

(FREDERIC *looks at* SOLANGE, *then, after a long pause:*)

FREDERIC: ...I can't....

(SOLANGE *throws the sheet of music onto the piano and runs out.* FREDERIC *picks up the music and straightens it automatically. He puts up the music in front of him and aimlessly begins to pick out the melody of the waltz...***Waltz Op. 70, No. 2**.)

(*The lights on* FREDERIC *fade.*)

(*In the gardener's cottage,* CLESINGER *is completing* GEORGE'*s head in clay while she concentrates on her writing.*)

(MAURICE, *holding the* CLESINGER *and* GEORGE PUPPETS, *says to us:*)

MAURICE: This was the beginning, when, one after the other, the force of each of us began smashing up against the next—with consequences none of us could foresee...

(MAURICE *makes the* CLESINGER PUPPET *knock against the* GEORGE PUPPET. *Then he moves into the shadows and in his mind's eye observes the scene in the gardener's cottage, as the music of* FREDERIC'*s playing of his* **Waltz Op. 70, No. 2** *rises from inside the house.*)

CLESINGER: Why do you keep him? They say you haven't slept with him in years.

GEORGE: You have a small mind, Clesinger.

CLESINGER: What a terrible waste for you—

GEORGE: Not at all. There comes a time when the blood cools.

CLESINGER: And has yours cooled, George?

GEORGE: Mercifully.

CLESINGER: You could be touched and you'd feel nothing?

GEORGE: Nothing.

CLESINGER: You could be caressed and you wouldn't be aroused?

GEORGE: Not at all.

(CLESINGER *touches* GEORGE *with his hands as if she were clay.*)

CLESINGER: I can mold stone with my bare hands, George. I could mold you—

(GEORGE *shoves* CLESINGER's *hands away.*)

GEORGE: Save your advances for the fillies in the village!

CLESINGER: You felt a spark, didn't you! A glimmer of the old desire!

GEORGE: You flatter yourself!

CLESINGER: Do I?

(CLESINGER *grabs* GEORGE *and kisses her forcibly. She fights him off but is aroused—and he knows it. He laughs at her.*)

CLESINGER: So your blood has cooled—!

(GEORGE *tries to pull away.* CLESINGER *holds her fast.*)

CLESINGER: For effete piano players, maybe. But when were you last touched by a *man*?

(CLESINGER *kisses* GEORGE *again. After a moment, she finds herself responding.*)

(*While they are in this embrace,* SOLANGE *enters, wrapped in* GEORGE's *dressing gown.* SOLANGE *watches silently. After a moment* GEORGE *sees her and breaks away from the embrace.*)

(MAURICE *moves the* GEORGE PUPPET *to bump against the* SOLANGE PUPPET.)

SOLANGE: (*Totally self-possessed, to* CLESINGER:) It's right that you find my mother attractive. She has a way with men that's really quite exceptional. Everybody says so.

GEORGE: Solange—

SOLANGE: Is it nice kissing a man, Mother? Someday soon I'll have to try it.

GEORGE: What are you doing here?

SOLANGE: Same as you. I came to pose for Monsieur Clesinger.

CLESINGER: I already have a model.

SOLANGE: I thought you might like a firm *young* body for a change.

(SOLANGE *opens her gown facing him and shows* CLESINGER *that, beneath it, she is naked.*)

GEORGE: Cover yourself!

CLESINGER: The trick isn't to be young, the trick is to *be* somebody!

SOLANGE: I am Solange Dudevant Grandsagne Sandeau Musset Pagello de Bourges Leroux Chopin Sand! *(She whispers to* CLESINGER:*)* Some day my mother's going to tell me my true name.

GEORGE: You are Solange Dudevant!

(GEORGE *closes the robe around* SOLANGE. SOLANGE *moves closer to* CLESINGER *and says mockingly:)*

SOLANGE: I am Solange Dudevant. I inspired Frederic Chopin. I can inspire you. *(Again, she opens her robe.)*

GEORGE: Go get dressed! Go get dressed, do you hear me?!

SOLANGE: I hear. I obey, wise Mother.

(GEORGE *pushes* SOLANGE *out.*)

GEORGE: *(To* CLESINGER:*)* Don't touch her. Don't go anywhere near her. I warn you...

CLESINGER: *(Smiling)* Did I say anything about going anywhere near her?

(CLESINGER *goes out in the opposite direction from which* SOLANGE *exited.)*

(GEORGE *is alone in the cottage. She stares at the clay portrait of herself. Touching the clay sculpture of herself she says to us:)*

GEORGE: Why did I make her cover herself so quickly? When I was young, I romped about in the nude. ...Can it be I'm jealous of her smooth young body? That her first taste of love is yet to come? ...I see her, wild as I was, and I want to tame her. Why should I want to tame her? ...When I look at her, so much like myself at her age, what do I see I do not wish to know? *(She releases her hands from the clay head. Unconsciously, as she was speaking, her thumbs slowly pressed down deeply upon the eyes. She looks at the dark cavities made in the head, then turns and slowly exits.)*

(For a moment the head stares at us from deep hollow eyeless sockets.)

(The lights on the head go out. MAURICE *moves the* SOLANGE PUPPET *to knock against the* FREDERIC PUPPET.*)*

(We begin to hear the music of **Ballade Op. 23, G Minor.***)*

(The scene changes to the music room where SOLANGE, *with feverish intensity, enters and begins pouring out her story to* FREDERIC:*)*

SOLANGE: When I was two, my mother left my father and ran away to Paris with a lawyer. She took me with her. I slept behind a screen. I used to hear them on the other side—making sounds—when they thought I was sleeping. Funny sounds. They made me shivery. Sometimes I used to get up. I used to peek. ...How many men I have seen silhouetted in her embrace, Frederic!

Sometimes a different silhouette every night! ...You think she is your nurse, your friend, your dear pure comrade? How innocent you are. Sometimes, I think, more innocent than me. ...Why do you think she keeps a gardener's cottage, but no gardener? What do you think she does all day there? ...My mother is unfaithful to you with every rock, every tree, every passing tradesman! You think she's sitting chastely to be sculpted? Did it never occur to you, you not only can *sit* for your portrait, you can *lie*?! *(She runs out.)*

(FREDERIC, in a rage, plays one loud chord then says to us:)

FREDERIC: Such an honor to live in the house of a lady of virtue! Such a tribute to be in the glorious presence of such celibacy! "I've been chaste and pure for years, only for your sake," says the lady. Wears a cast-iron chastity belt—to which everyone has the key but me!

(He sits at the piano and begins to play the same wild passage over and over. **Etude Op. 10, No. 4, C Sharp Minor.***)*

(The lights fade on FREDERIC. The music continues to be heard, angry, loud, monotonous, filling the world, indoors and out. Unable to bear the raging fortissimo, MAURICE says to us:)

MAURICE: And finally, the force which made each of us crash against each other crashed against me!

(MAURICE makes the FREDERIC PUPPET crash against the MAURICE puppet, which causes the MAURICE PUPPET to crash against the GEORGE PUPPET.)

(Then, throwing the puppets to the ground, he runs over to GEORGE who is on her hands and knees in the garden.)

MAURICE: He's been playing the same measure for days! He's driving me insane!

GEORGE: You know how he is when he gets in one of his moods—

MAURICE: Look at you! On your hands and knees!

GEORGE: He hasn't eaten for days. I thought if I could tempt him with some wild mushrooms—

MAURICE: If it's not the food he's complaining about, it's the linen. If it's not the linen, it's the dogs. If it's not the dogs—

GEORGE: Now Maurice—

MAURICE: I'm trying to draw the illustrations for your book. I can't concentrate! Everything I draw comes out badly!

GEORGE: Why don't you go sketch in the field?

MAURICE: I want to work *here*! Why should I be exiled from my own house?

(As the same crescendo is repeated furiously again and again on the piano, MAURICE

shouts:)

MAURICE: I'm tired of timing my life to his music! Tired of stifling my every breath! I am twenty-one! I'm the man of the house! I can have silence if I want it!

(MAURICE *dashes into the music room where* FREDERIC *is playing his furious crescendos. In a rage,* MAURICE *cries:)*

MAURICE: I want—one hour—of silence!

(MAURICE *slams his hand on the top of the piano.* FREDERIC *cuts off playing and stares at him.)*

MAURICE: My mother is pawing the ground for you! And you won't even speak to her civilly! My mother is a great woman! And you humiliate her! She is afraid to speak! Well, I'm not!

(GEORGE *enters.*)

GEORGE: Maurice! Maurice! Stop this!

MAURICE: Ever since we were small we've had to go on tiptoe and in whispers. I'm silenced if I cough in the wrong key! If I belch, it has to be in time to the music! If I want to gnaw on a chicken bone, I have to wait till the fortissimo begins!

FREDERIC: The little Napoleon has drawn up all his cannon!

MAURICE: Who do you think you are? Somebody has to speak out to you!

FREDERIC: Your manners leave much to be desired.

MAURICE: You can't talk to me that way! You are not my father!

GEORGE: Maurice! *(She turns to* FREDERIC.*)* I'm sorry, Frederic. His work isn't going well.

FREDERIC: Did it ever occur to you it may be because he has no talent?

MAURICE: Now I have to listen to insults!

GEORGE: Frederic, that's not fair—

FREDERIC: I detest people who *play* at the arts.

MAURICE: None of *us* can prove how hard we work by getting consumption!

(There is a shocked silence.)

FREDERIC: "Consumption." Now there's a word that's never said in my presence. "Bad cold," "bronchitis," "hypochondria," maybe. But never *consumption.*

GEORGE: Maurice, that was cruel—

MAURICE: *(Deeply, to her:)* You protect him too much. And he thanks you by hurting you. I can't stand to see him hurting you! It's more than I can bear! *(He escapes from the scene and, contemplating the puppet of himself, says to us:)* I don't know what gave me the courage, for once in my life, to say aloud what I was really thinking—

(Pensively, one by one, he picks up the puppets which he had thrown down. He puts the others aside and holds the GEORGE *and* FREDERIC PUPPETS.*)*

(Meanwhile, in the music room:)

GEORGE: Forgive Maurice, Frederic—

FREDERIC: There was a time when *I* was your defender. Now you have your son...

GEORGE: You've been playing, for days, like a madman. Why have you been playing that way?

FREDERIC: To keep myself from speaking.

GEORGE: And what could you have to say that would call up such fury?

FREDERIC: Don't you know?

GEORGE: No.

FREDERIC: You're in the gardener's cottage all day every day. What do you do there?

GEORGE: I write.

FREDERIC: That's all?

GEORGE: And I pose.

FREDERIC: So that's what you call it!

GEORGE: What do you think goes on there?

FREDERIC: Things that have precious little to do with art! ...I've always known you've had other men. But never before have you been so bold as to cavort with them beneath my very window!

GEORGE: Is that what you believe I have been doing?

FREDERIC: Solange told me everything.

GEORGE: Solange has a lively imagination!

FREDERIC: Did she imagine the orgies you used to have with your little lawyer? Did she invent the odor of opium, the sound of whips? How could you do these things in front of your own daughter? All your men—!

MAURICE: *(To us:)* The thought of those always haunted all of us.

GEORGE: You knew about them all before you met me. You know that for your sake I have lived as a virgin for seven years!

FREDERIC: What is a virgin? Someone who forgets in the morning what she's done the night before?

GEORGE: You are incredible—

FREDERIC: Every man you've ever had still surrounds you—

GEORGE: This is madness—

MAURICE: *(To us:)* The images, of all of them, are always there -- in the backs of our minds!

FREDERIC: They cling to you, possess you still—

GEORGE: You can't accuse me of my past!

FREDERIC: I can!

GEORGE: You can't throw time at me!

FREDERIC: I can use anything that's in my arsenal!

GEORGE: Then I'll throw time at you!

FREDERIC: How!

GEORGE: Your early death!

(Silence. A sudden, long silence. The words came tumbling out so quickly! Downstage, MAURICE is holding the GEORGE and FREDERIC PUPPETS absolutely still, confronting each other. FREDERIC looks at GEORGE in shock. It was something she never meant to say.)

GEORGE: I'm sorry...I'm sorry...

FREDERIC: *(Quietly)* So you think I will die young...

GEORGE: No. No, Frederic—

FREDERIC: One never faces these things. One should.

GEORGE: Please—

FREDERIC: I thank you for the truth. It's a gift—

GEORGE: Frederic, don't—

FREDERIC: I never really thought I was immortal...

GEORGE: Oh, Frederic—

FREDERIC: If my time is limited, I mustn't waste it, must I? I must—work—as much as possible. Preserve myself—as much as possible. Get as much done in whatever time I have left.

GEORGE: You have acres of time!

FREDERIC: Perhaps. But none to squander. You know, I think I can survive consumption—but I can't survive bickering. *(He starts to pick up his music.)*

GEORGE: What are you doing?

FREDERIC: I think I can work better in my apartment in Paris—

GEORGE: I'll come with you.

FREDERIC: I can work better alone.

GEORGE: Frederic, don't go like this—

FREDERIC: I realize you cherish the illusion that I can't take care of myself. Actually, I can survive without you very well... *(He turns and goes.)*

(Stung by his departure, GEORGE *turns to us and says:)*

GEORGE: He'll be back. Just wait until the first time he can't find his sweater. *(She puts a positive view on things:)* Perhaps a brief separation is exactly what we need. *(She goes to her writing desk and begins writing.)*

*(*MAURICE *places the* GEORGE PUPPET *at one side of the stage and the* FREDERIC PUPPET *at the other.)*

(The lights change. Two separate pools of light now divide their spaces. Music that FREDERIC *is playing—his* **Scherzo Op. 31**—*is heard at a great distance and continues throughout the following scene.)*

MAURICE: *(To us:)* With Frederic gone, peace, has settled on the household... But then, in this life, peace is not the natural state of things, is it?

*(*SOLANGE's *voice is heard, off, calling:)*

SOLANGE: *(O S)* Mother—!

*(*SOLANGE *enters, stands before* GEORGE *and says:)*

SOLANGE: Mother...I have something to tell you. ... I know about it. I know what you've been living—and what you've been writing about in your books.

GEORGE: Solange—

SOLANGE: I thought it was time that *I* explore it, too, Mother.

GEORGE: You didn't—

SOLANGE: I went to Clesinger. I offered once again to pose for him. I brought him my firm young body. He liked it. I could see he liked it. And he wanted it. I made him want it! And I made him take me—on the couch next to where you pose.

GEORGE: Oh, Solange—

SOLANGE: I wanted to know what it was all about—

GEORGE: And now that you know?

SOLANGE: I love it! I want it all the time! I want more! More!

GEORGE: I must warn you—

SOLANGE: What's the matter, Mother? Are you jealous? Are you afraid I might have found what all your life you have been seeking? Are you afraid I might know all the world's dark secrets—?

GEORGE: Why do women always feel that in the act of love they will find the answer to everything? There are no revelations in the bedchamber!

SOLANGE: There are! There are! When I cried out with joy at the last, I felt I was you! I *knew* you!

GEORGE: You know nothing!

SOLANGE: I know now how you felt in the moment that I was conceived. So wild a moment! So illicit a moment!

GEORGE: Solange—

SOLANGE: Don't you think I know I am the product of some passing cock? You never could resist one, could you!

GEORGE: How can you talk this way?

SOLANGE: The shock isn't in the *word*, Mother. It's in the *deed*! I didn't ask to be your bastard daughter—

GEORGE: Love-children can be blessed above all others.

SOLANGE: Then bless me, Mother. I'm going to be married.

GEORGE: Married!

SOLANGE: I want to make Clesinger mine completely.

GEORGE: A marriage contract has never been the way to accomplish that.

SOLANGE: I'm going to be his wife.

GEORGE: Solange, listen to me: Choosing the man you marry is the most important decision you will ever make in your life. It will affect every moment of your existence.

SOLANGE: I love him.

GEORGE: He's nothing but a callous fortune-hunter! He'll never stay with you—

SOLANGE: I will keep him as long as I can.

GEORGE: Solange, it is your *life*—

SOLANGE: I have to have him!

GEORGE: Why? Because he wanted *me*?

SOLANGE: Do you think everything in my life revolves around you! You have nothing to do with it!

GEORGE: I want to save you from my mistakes—

SOLANGE: "Save me from your mistakes!" I *am* them! You took my breath from me! You stole my fire! You lived so many lives you used mine up! There isn't spirit enough left for me to live any!

GEORGE: I lived the way I lived so I could write about it! Pushed myself to the limits of experience—for my *books*!

SOLANGE: That's what you've always said. How you've justified everything. Had to taste it all to put into your books. Well, I've read your books. I know the value of them. And you know what, Mother? I think, in the future, no one's going to read them! You're going to go down in history—if anyone remembers you—not as a writer, but as a *whore*!

(*The music stops.* GEORGE *is stunned. She says, at last, in deep pain:*)

GEORGE: You have understood *nothing*—

SOLANGE: I'm going to be married—

GEORGE: Not to this man.

SOLANGE: I am!

GEORGE: I will not permit it!

SOLANGE: Yes, you will. You will permit it. You will give us your blessing. And you will make us a lovely wedding—right away! You see, Mama, you're going to be a *grandmother*!

(SOLANGE *runs out.* GEORGE *stares after her daughter, saying nothing. Events have taken over, beyond her control. She is stunned, helpless.*)

(*The lights change. Music is heard.* **Berceuse Op. 57, D Flat.**)

(MAURICE *dresses the* SOLANGE *and* CLESINGER PUPPETS *in wedding clothes—veil and top hat—and stands them side by side. Then he says to us:*)

MAURICE: Mother and I were numb throughout the ceremony. It seemed to be happening as in some fiction. But it was all too real.

(CLESINGER *runs in taking off his top hat.* SOLANGE *runs in, throwing off her veil.* GEORGE *stands numbly, as if she can hardly believe what's happening*)

SOLANGE: Thank you for the lovely wedding, Mother!

CLESINGER: A little hasty—but very nice hors d'oeuvres!

(CLESINGER *walks around the room, as if taking possession.* GEORGE *is speechless.*)

SOLANGE: Now that we're going to live with you, we must make a few arrangements.

(*When* GEORGE *doesn't respond,* MAURICE *asks:*)

MAURICE: What arrangements?

SOLANGE: You must pay up my husband's gambling debts, Mother.

CLESINGER: You must pay off the two young ladies who claim I got them with child.

SOLANGE: You must let Auguste have the cottage for his workroom—

CLESINGER: I want a whole new studio!

GEORGE: *(Finding her voice:)* I'll do none of these things!

CLESINGER: You will. There's something that you need from me.

GEORGE: What?

CLESINGER: My silence. ... You wouldn't want all Paris to know of the secret wedding of your daughter, rushed to the altar with a bun already in the oven. You wouldn't want them to know that George Sand, the woman who believes in freedom, had raced to marry off her pregnant daughter—and to a drinking, whoring, gambling wretch!

GEORGE: I could survive it.

CLESINGER: Then you won't mind if I accept the offer from a certain Paris journal. They say they'll pay me handsomely for telling the inside story of you and Monsieur Chopin.

GEORGE: You don't know the inside story!

CLESINGER: I can invent it!

GEORGE: This is blackmail! I won't stand for it!

CLESINGER: You will. Or George the Great, Monsieur George, will find herself the laughing-stock of Paris, with all the ideals she struggled for exposed as so much rot!

MAURICE: You can't talk to my mother that way!

GEORGE: Maurice, don't listen to him—

MAURICE: *(To* CLESINGER:*)* Apologize to her!

CLESINGER: She knows I'm speaking the truth—

MAURICE: *(Threateningly) Apologize!*

CLESINGER: Is the mama's boy going to make me?!

(MAURICE *takes a swing at* CLESINGER *but misses.)*

GEORGE: Maurice! Stop—!

(CLESINGER *swings back. He connects. A fight breaks out.* GEORGE *dashes between them, trying to separate them.* CLESINGER *swings at* MAURICE *but hits* GEORGE *instead. She falls to the floor.)*

(*For a moment there is silence, utter shocked silence.* SOLANGE *stares at her* MOTHER, *who is on the floor. Then* SOLANGE *starts to laugh—a horrible, triumphant, wicked laugh.* GEORGE, *more wounded by the laugh than by the blow chokes out:)*

GEORGE: Get out! Get out! Both of you!

SOLANGE: *(Laughing)* You don't mind if we take a few things, Mother—

CLESINGER: Those candelabras look like they will fetch a pretty penny—

SOLANGE: Those crystal goblets. I've always been fond of those—

CLESINGER: Don't get too fond, dear, because we're going to be selling them—

(SOLANGE *and* CLESINGER *exit, gathering up valuables as they go.* MAURICE *cries out after them:)*

MAURICE: Give those back—!

GEORGE: Let them go, Maurice. It's only *things*. That's not what we value...

(The lights change. MAURICE, *weary and nursing his wounds, returns to his puppets. Removing the veil and top hat from the wedding couple, he says to us:)*

MAURICE: Mother and I were alone, now, in the country. But the peace we used to find there was now gone.

(In the distance, FREDERIC *is heard playing.* **Etude F Minor.***)*

(GEORGE, *in her own light, at the lowest point in her life, says to us:)*

GEORGE: I know what all Paris is saying: "George Sand got what she deserved." All those who envied that I *lived* while they vegetated are now smiling self-satisfied smiles. "After all her wild behavior, what did she expect? Now she has reaped what she sewed." ...If I'd married and stayed with one man, if I'd had no career, if I'd stayed by the hearth all my life, cooking and crocheting, would Solange have turned out differently? Maurice was brought up exactly like Solange and he turned out just fine. ...How much does one owe to a child? Must we give them birth and then, for their sakes, stop living?

(The lights come up on FREDERIC *in his Paris apartment.* GEORGE *and* FREDERIC *are each isolated in their separate spaces.)*

FREDERIC: *(To us:)* How could she have let Solange marry such a person! She didn't even tell me of the wedding! *(He sits down and starts to write a letter.)* "Dear George: You should have stopped her— "

(In her own light, GEORGE *reads his letter and sits down to write her own:)*

GEORGE: I should have stopped her! What right do you have to judge me? What can you, who have saved yourself so painstakingly, know about anything? You, who never committed yourself to marriage, or to the ties of blood. ... The act of entering the womb is nothing compared to the incomparable daring of bringing something out. Some being to whom you are forever tied—and who knows, like none other, where you can be injured. You can be injured—through them.

MAURICE: *(To us:)* Then came the ultimate betrayal—

(SOLANGE, *pregnant, enters* FREDERIC's *apartment with* CLESINGER.)

(MAURICE *moves their puppets to Frederic's side of the stage.*)

(SOLANGE *kneels before* FREDERIC.)

SOLANGE: How kind you are, dear Frederic.

FREDERIC: You know I'll always do all I can for you, Solange.

SOLANGE: It was good of you to take us in.

FREDERIC: Well, aren't you almost my child?

SOLANGE: I'll make your tea...

(SOLANGE *touches* FREDERIC *tenderly.* SOLANGE *and* CLESINGER *go out.*)

(*In her own light,* GEORGE *says to us:*)

GEORGE: He's taken them into his apartment! He's sheltering, beneath his roof, the people who hate and despise me! ...I cared for him—and for thanks he stole my daughter!

(*In* FREDERIC's *space,* SOLANGE *enters with his tea.*)

GEORGE: My God, my God... He came into my life and got between me and my children! He took the love I should have been giving them! He is the cause, the cause, of all my troubles! He drained my life! He drained my strength! For seven years, while I could have been living a life, I was chained to him, thinking, "If I say a single word that upsets him he will die and *I* will have killed him!" And now, instead, it's *he* who's killing *me*!

(SOLANGE *puts her arm around* FREDERIC's *shoulder.*)

GEORGE: *(Seeing this in her mind's eye, she cries out:)* Assassins! *(She laughs ironically.)* Some lovers are parted by fate, others by war or circumstance. But none that I know of have been ripped apart because of children. Of all the reasons I might have imagined, I never would have thought of that.

(SOLANGE *whispers something into* FREDERIC's *ear.*)

GEORGE: Do they sit gossiping about me in the evenings? Do they tick off all my faults and tell each other how, for everything, I was to blame?

MAURICE: *(To us:)* To exorcise his ghost, Mother did what she knew how to do. She wrote about it.

(MAURICE *picks up a book and shows it to us*).

(*In* FREDERIC's *apartment,* SOLANGE *says to him:*)

SOLANGE: You know, Frederic, you should read mother's new book. You're in it.

(SOLANGE *hands* FREDERIC *a book and exits.*)

(The lights fade on GEORGE.*)*

*(*FREDERIC *opens the book, reads some passages here and there, then slams it shut.* BULOZ *enters to him.)*

FREDERIC: Have you read this?

BULOZ: I published it.

FREDERIC: How could you—?

BULOZ: It's one of her best.

FREDERIC: All Paris is saying this arrogant self-centered prig she writes about is me!

BULOZ: Surely you're beyond believing what all Paris says.

FREDERIC: How can she ridicule me like this in public! It's unforgivable!

BULOZ: Have you read the entire book, Frederic?

FREDERIC: Why should I subject myself to such derision?

BULOZ: Read it. Read *all* of it.

*(*FREDERIC *coughs and turns away.)*

FREDERIC: Have you seen my sweater? *(Unable to find it, he removes the shawl from the piano and puts it over his shoulders.)*

BULOZ: It's not *you* she's laid bare. It's herself. Listen to what she says—

FREDERIC: No! I don't want to hear it!

*(*BULOZ *finds a paragraph and holds it open to* FREDERIC, *but* FREDERIC, *pale and withdrawn, refuses to look at it.)*

*(*BULOZ *starts to read it out loud. His voice segues into* GEORGE's *voice:)*

BULOZ: "One day Lucrezia Floriani turned forty. She wasn't beautiful any more. She had to work every moment in order to live—"

GEORGE: *(In her own light, quoting the book by rote)* "—She was exhausted at having reached the sufferings of premature age without gathering its rewards, without having won back the esteem of her lover. If she could have seen him she would have said, 'You are everything to me—'"

BULOZ: *(Continuing the same passage:)* "— and if I wish to go on living, it is only for you."

FREDERIC: That love for her former lover is fiction, Buloz. Total fiction. *(He retreats beneath his shawl into the armchair.)*

(The lights go out on FREDERIC.*)*

(The lights come up on GEORGE *at her desk.* MAURICE *says to us:)*

MAURICE: Buloz tried to play Cupid.

(BULOZ *crosses to* GEORGE. *He says:*)

BULOZ: George, this separation is absurd. You two should somehow reconcile—

GEORGE: He hasn't answered a single one of my letters.

BULOZ: He isn't well. You should go see him.

GEORGE: And have the door slammed in my face? No. His failure to respond means he wants to be rid of me. Well, I've arranged that for him. I've sent Maurice to close my Paris apartment.

(BULOZ *exits.*)

(*The lights change.* MAURICE *says to us:*)

MAURICE: I could do that. Help her make the break. I thought I'd find it easy, but it wasn't. ...I never would have thought that, while I was removing things, I'd have so many complicated thoughts. ...Every object I moved out had a memory of the life my mother and her friend had lived together, a life that, now it was dissolving, seemed to me to have been extraordinary. (*He picks up his* FREDERIC PUPPET *and looks at it with great affection while—*)

(FREDERIC, *alone, looks out the window of his apartment and says to us:*)

FREDERIC: There go her silks, her coffee cups of pale blue china, her writing desk, ...her cigars. Where is she today, while all her things go pirouetting out the doorway? Not coming, I imagine. She wouldn't dare! If she does come, I won't let her in!...

(MAURICE *tries to effect a reconciliation between the* GEORGE PUPPET *and the* FREDERIC PUPPET—*but the* GEORGE PUPPET *proudly turns her back on the* FREDERIC PUPPET.)

FREDERIC: Sand, you Jezebel! You Lorelie! You Medusa! ...You won't come, will you! ...Shrew! Virago!... (*To us:*) Love mocks us with incredible accommodations, stuffs geniuses and simpletons into the same sack—the sack of fools! ...

(*He sits at the piano and begins to play, sadly, overwhelmed with melancholy:* **Etude Op. 10, No. 3, E Major**.)

(*The lights change. As* FREDERIC's *music continues, under,* MAURICE *returns to* GEORGE.)

GEORGE: Have you managed it?

MAURICE: Yes, Mother.

GEORGE: Did you see him?

MAURICE: Briefly. Through a half-opened door.

GEORGE: What did he say?

MAURICE: He said—you may keep his piano.

GEORGE: I have no desire that Frederic should make me a gift of his piano!

MAURICE: Mother, Frederic needs you. You two shouldn't be apart.

GEORGE: Oh, we're not apart. He's everywhere I go. Every time I enter a room, someone is playing a Chopin composition. Other people are moved. I am devastated. To them, it's music; to me, it's the ruins of my life.

MAURICE: Go to him, for God's sake!

GEORGE: I don't want him to see how much I have failed. I began with such expectations. I've succeeded at nothing.

MAURICE: That isn't true.

GEORGE: I believed in freedom. I found—freedom isn't possible. Dear God, is anything possible on this earth.

MAURICE: Make it up with Frederic.

GEORGE: I can't begin again. I couldn't survive it.

MAURICE: *He* isn't surviving.

GEORGE: He doesn't want me in his life...

(MAURICE *returns downstage. With a sense of compassion, he wraps a shawl around the shoulders of the* FREDERIC PUPPET, *then keeps it with him.*)

(*The lights hold on* GEORGE *in her space and* FREDERIC *in his.*)

(*A lullaby is heard—***Berceuse Op. 57, D Flat.***)

(MAURICE *says to us:*)

MAURICE: Months passed, and one day Mother received a letter from her former lover...

(FREDERIC *is seen sealing a letter.*)

FREDERIC: "Dear Madame Sand. I am happy to inform you that your daughter has been safely delivered of a daughter."

(*In her own space,* GEORGE *reads the letter and thrusts it away angrily.*)

GEORGE: *He* tells *me* that my daughter has a daughter! *He* tells *me* that my child has a child!

(MAURICE *displays his* SOLANGE PUPPET *cradling a* BABY PUPPET.)

MAURICE: (*To us:*) Yes, there was a baby. And soon its daddy left forever— which was no surprise.

(*The lights brighten on* GEORGE, *writing, but, for the first time, having difficulty.*

MAURICE *says to us:)*

MAURICE: The new grandmother kept sane by writing. Writing was all she knew...

(In her own space, GEORGE *continues writing.)*

*(Music—***Berceuse Op. 57, D Flat***—rises and fades.)*

(The lights brighten on FREDERIC *in his Paris apartment, huddled in the shawl in his armchair. He murmurs:)*

FREDERIC: They're taking out her lamp... There goes her writing desk...

(SOLANGE *appears behind his chair.)*

SOLANGE: That was two years ago, Frederic.

FREDERIC: George! How good of you to come!

(SOLANGE *stands upstage of him, her face full of pity.)*

FREDERIC: You always said I should write you an opera, George. So I've done it! Would you like to hear it?

SOLANGE: Very much, Frederic—

(The lights come up on GEORGE. MAURICE, *holding the* FREDERIC PUPPET, *enters to her:)*

MAURICE: Mother, I've had a premonition. You should go to him! You should go to him now!

GEORGE: *(After a moment)* Yes. No more pride. All that matters is that he live to go on composing. I can help him do that. Love can repair anything—

MAURICE: Hurry!

(GEORGE *hurries out.)*

*(Music begins—***Mazurka Op. 68, No. 4***)*

(FREDERIC, *in his chair, performs his opera, half singing, half speaking to the music, his voice failing.)*

FREDERIC: *(Singing and speaking:)*
George and Frederic
George and Frederic
What a loving couple
How could they part?

She was proud
He as proud as she was
They had a child
Two children:
Their arts.

She for silly books
Sacrificed her babies
He for silly music
Sacrificed his life

Fools, these two,
Hideous, unlovely,
Can those who snatch
At immortality,
Also snatch
At life?

FREDERIC: *(A pause, then:)* Do you like my opera, George?

SOLANGE: Yes, I like it very much, Frederic.

FREDERIC: I'm dedicating it to you.

SOLANGE: *(Deeply moved)* I'm very—honored—

FREDERIC: Come here—

(SOLANGE *comes over to* FREDERIC.)

FREDERIC: ...I know you're not George. I'm just pretending.

(SOLANGE *takes his hand.*)

FREDERIC: George promised—I would die—in no other arms but hers... I didn't want her to have lied.

(FREDERIC *dies.*)

(*Silence. Then, from outside,* GEORGE's *voice cries:*)

GEORGE: *(O S)* Frederic, I'm here! I've come to take care of you—

(SOLANGE *admits* GEORGE. *From a distance* GEORGE *sees* FREDERIC. *She stops. She knows. She says to* SOLANGE:)

GEORGE: He is dead?

(SOLANGE *nods. A pause, then* GEORGE *says:*)

GEORGE: ...I should have been here.

SOLANGE: *(A very long pause, then:)* ...You were.

(SOLANGE *comes and puts her arms around her mother.* GEORGE, *very much moved, wraps her daughter in an embrace of reconciliation and love.*)

(*Then* GEORGE, *overwhelmed with love and loss, goes toward* FREDERIC *and pulls the shawl closer around him.*)

(*As* GEORGE *stands touching her lover's shoulders in a gesture of protection and infinite love.* MAURICE *says to us:*)

MAURICE: And that was the end of their story. Mother went on to other men, but this, as she once said, was *the* connection of her life. I wish I'd understood how special it was while it was happening. I would have treasured it while we were living it. ...But how many of us only recognize the splendor in our lives when it is too late?

(MAURICE *puts the* GEORGE *and* FREDERIC PUPPETS *side by side on adjacent stands.*)

(*A snatch of melody is heard, as though picked out slowly, with one hand, at the piano—***Fantasie Impromptu, Op. 66.***)

(*The lights iris in on the* GEORGE *and* FREDERIC PUPPETS. *The music ends.*)

(*Blackout*)

END OF PLAY

JOSHUA SLOCUM
SAILING ALONE
AROUND THE WORLD

JOSHUA SLOCUM SAILING ALONE AROUND THE WORLD premiered at the Rhode Island Shakespeare Theatre, in Newport, RI, 16 July 1992.

CHARACTER & SETTING

Joshua Slocum, *sixty-four years old*

Time: November 1909
Place: Slocum's boathouse in Menemsha on the island of Martha's Vineyard in Massachusetts
Setting: In this boathouse Slocum keeps all his sailing gear and the mementos of his life and past voyages.

Ancient timbers suggest the limits of the space, a space which protects and shelters. A private space impervious to storms.

Center stage is a battered kitchen chair. Trunks on the floor provide not only storage but seating. There are shelves along the walls and a small wooden barrel downstage.

Here and there about the room are his log books, pens and pencils, spectacles, a pipe, a brass lantern, a tin clock, a model or photo of the Spray, *books, papers, charts, photos, articles of clothing, pots and pans, cans of food, coils of rope, a sack of potatoes, a tin of carpet tacks, a box of matches, a rifle, a primitive slide projector, a seahorse preserved in a jar, a large piece of coral, a tropical straw hat with a bite taken out of its brim and a large seabag into which everything he wishes to take on his voyage can be packed.*

Upstage center is a large map of the world. A detailed map of Tierra del Fuego leans against a trunk.

Slocum is at home in this space. It is his private domain. He is as solitary here as he is on the Spray. *In fact, the space has the atmosphere of a seaworthy craft—compact, water-tight, and secure.*

This play is based on Joshua Slocum's experiences as recounted in his book Sailing Alone Around the World.

ACT ONE

(JOSHUA SLOCUM, *sixty-four, weather-beaten, balding, with a thin grey beard, enters the boathouse carrying articles of clothing. He turns to us and says:*)

JOSHUA SLOCUM: She doesn't want me to go. ... I'm going.

(*He shoves the clothing into an empty sea-bag.*)

My first wife was a sea wife. This one *looked* like a sea wife at first, *pretended* to be a sea wife—but she turned out to be not a bark but a goddam *tree*! Firmly rooted on land. ... Wants to root me, too.

(*He looks toward the house.*)

Can't be done, woman! ...We're going. The *Spray* and I are going. It was in the *Spray* that I went on the greatest journey I've ever taken. That was eleven years ago. Did you hear about it? It was in all the papers. Matter of fact, after it, Teddy Roosevelt had me in for a little pow-wow at the White House. Wanted to meet the man who was the very first to sail alone around the globe. Well, I wasn't exactly alone. The *Spray* was with me. She and I did it together.

She's out there now, lying at anchor in Menemsha harbor. I could feel her fairly jumping at her cables this morning, when she realized I was starting to fill her hold with stores for a brand new trip. She's like me—can hardly wait to head out over the water—prow into the wind and sails unfurled.

If Virginia were here, she'd be rushing back and forth from the house to the shed, her black hair flying out behind her. She'd be darning the holes in my sea duds. She'd be baking me breads and wrapping them in waxed cloth so they'd last as long as they can on the journey. She'd be hiding little gifts about the boat, a pressed flower, a bit of rock candy, for me to find when I was far away at sea, to remind me—as if I needed reminding—how much I care about her.

But Hettie—who doesn't even like my company!—Hettie's up there weeping and wailing and sobbing I mustn't go. She doesn't understand: I was born in the breezes. ... The sea cast its spell on me from the beginning. I first saw the light of day in a cold spot overlooking the Bay of Fundy, Nova Scotia. On both sides, my family were sailors. When I was a lad, I filled the important post of cook on a fishing schooner. But I didn't stay long in the galley. The crew mutinied at the appearance of my first grub!

I soon found myself before the mast in a full-rigged schooner bound on a foreign voyage. I took to it well enough and by the time I was twenty-five, I was given command of a ship. I sailed the Atlantic and Pacific hauling cargo of every sort—coal, lumber, fish, ice, gunpowder, tea. So long as I could have a full hold out and a full hold back, I was happy. One day, in Sydney, Australia, I saw and fell in love with a New York-born beauty named Virginia Albertina Walker.

(He takes her photograph out of his pocket and shows it to us.)

A few weeks later, we married. For thirteen years she sailed everywhere with me. With my cargo and my family aboard, I sailed all over the world—China, Alaska, Australia, Japan, and up and down the coast of South America. On my ships Virginia gave birth to our seven children. The twins died when they were babies. But our two daughters and three fine sons have survived.

(He shows us photographs of his children.)

It was a splendid life, Virginia and I and the children—sailing everywhere together. The ship was our home. The captain's cabin was our cottage and the deck was our front yard. On the boat, Virginia nursed the children and taught them their letters and their numbers. She taught them their music on a piano bolted to the deck. And I—I taught them the meanings of the waves and the winds and how to read the sky.

My best command was of the magnificent ship, *Northern Light*. I was part owner. In the eighties, she was the finest American sailing-vessel afloat.

(He shows us a drawing of a large square-rigged sailing ship.)

After the *Northern Light*, I owned and sailed the *Aquidneck*, a little bark which to me was the perfection of beauty.

(He shows us a model of the single-deck sailing ship, the Aquidneck.*)*

I had been nearly twenty years a shipmaster when I wrecked her on the coast of Brazil. I am a careful man at sea, but I'd gone crazy, I think. You see, I'd just buried my beloved Virginia in the English Cemetery in Buenos Aires.

The plague took her. The ports were full of it. We'd stayed in quarantine. But it hopped aboard with some foreign sailors—and it took my wife.

I salvaged the *Aquidneck* that time. I continued sailing her. But the bachelor's life didn't suit me. So a few years after Virginia died, I took a second wife, Henrietta Elliott, a cousin of mine from Massachusetts. She was twenty years my junior. A square-rigged capable vessel—and I needed a mother for my five children. I sailed on the *Aquidneck* with her and my two sons, Victor and Garfield. I thought it would be the same as it had been with Virginia.

But Hettie never really took to the life. Don't know exactly why. May have something to do with the fact she was aboard when the *Aquidneck* got permanently wrecked off the coast of South America. I made us a canoe from the ruins and sailed my little family up the Atlantic. I thought it a splendid adventure. But Hettie swore she'd never go to sea again! You know what she wanted me to do? She wanted me to take up farming!

But mine wasn't the sort of life to make one able to coil up one's ropes on land, whose customs and ways I had almost forgotten. When times for freighters got bad, and great sailing ships gave way to steamers, I tried to quit the sea. But what was there for an old sailor to do?

I had studied the sea as perhaps few men have studied it, neglecting all else. I could not obtain work in the shipyard without first paying fifty dollars to a society. And as for a ship to command, there were not enough ships to go round. I was at loose ends and looking for a ship when a friend of mine said he had one.

First time I looked at her, I thought he was having a joke! She was lying high and dry in a pasture in Fairhaven on the eastern shore of New Bedford harbor. She looked less like a boat, more like a pile of lumber. But I set to, and for more than a year I worked on making her a seaworthy craft.

The *Spray* changed her being so gradually that it was hard to say at what point the old died or the new took birth. I made her planks from Georgia pine an inch and a half thick. I steamed the timbers for ribs till they were supple, then bent them over a log till they were set.

(He shows a drawing of the deck plan of the Spray.*)*

I built two deck enclosures—one, six by six, over the main hatch for a cooking galley, and another slightly larger one for a cabin farther aft, about ten feet by twelve.

In the spaces along the sides of the cabin I arranged a berth to sleep in and shelves for small storage, including a medicine chest. In the midship hold was room for storage of water, salt beef, and other supplies, ample for many months.

(He shows a drawing of the elevation of the Spray, *with its sail plan.)*

I caulked her, painted her, fitted her mast and raised her sails—and early in 1895 the *Spray* was ready. She was thirty-six feet long, fourteen feet wide, four feet two inches deep in the hold, her tonnage was nine tons net. All told, she cost $553.62 for materials and thirteen months of my own labor. I launched her. As she rode at her ancient, rust-eaten anchor, she sat on the water like a swan.

(He proudly shows us a large model of the Spray.*)*

First I thought I'd use her as a fishing craft and take that up as a new profession. But I found out soon enough I didn't have the cunning to properly bait a hook. I didn't know what to do with myself. I had an overwhelming urge to get to sea again. And suddenly it came to me—this idea: I would sail around the world in the *Spray*—and I would sail alone.

There seemed nothing on land to hold me. I wanted to test my skills to the limit on a voyage no one else had ever attempted. I had nothing to lose—and I couldn't—not one moment longer—bear being anchored to the land.

So I stocked my ship, said goodbye to my wife, and on the morning of April 24, 1895, two months after my fifty-first birthday, the *Spray* and I weighed anchor and set sail from Boston. The twelve-o'clock whistles were blowing as the sloop shot ahead under full sail. A thrilling pulse beat high in me. My step was light on deck in the crisp air. I felt that there could be no turning back, and that I was engaging in an adventure the meaning of which I did not yet thoroughly understand.

The wind freshened. The *Spray* rounded Deer Island light and squared away direct for Gloucester, to procure some fishermen's stores. The day was perfect, the sunlight clear and strong. Every particle of water thrown into the air became a gem. The *Spray* made good her name as she dashed ahead, snatching necklace after necklace from the sea, and as often throwing them away. We have all seen miniature rainbows about a ship's prow, but the *Spray* flung out a bow of her own that day, such as I had never seen before. Her good angel had embarked on the voyage—or so I read it in the sea.

Nahant was soon abeam, then Marblehead was put astern. Other vessels were outward bound, but none of them passed the *Spray* flying along on her course. I heard the clanking of the dismal bell on Norman's Woe as we went by. And as I passed close to the reef where the schooner *Hesperus* struck, I saw the bones of a wreck, tossed up and lying bleaching on the shore.

I made for Gloucester cove, again to look the *Spray* over and again to weigh the voyage and my feelings. The owners of the wharf were old skippers themselves and took a great interest in the voyage. They also made the *Spray* a present of a fisherman's lantern, which I found would throw a light a great distance round. A ship that would run down a boat that had such a good light aboard would be capable of running into a lightship!

(He shows us the lantern, then takes a pencil out of his pocket and snaps it in half.)

For a boat to take along, I cut in two a castaway dory, boarding up the end where it was cut. There wasn't room on deck for more than half of a boat. And the thing could be used for a washtub and a bathtub.

All that worried me now was the want of a chronometer. Landlubbers are always asking sailors: "When you're on the ocean, how do you know where you are?" I always answer: "If you know what time it is, and where the stars are, you know where *you* are. It's that simple." But with our newfangled notions of navigation, it is supposed that a mariner cannot find his way without this exact timepiece, impervious to pitch and weather. I myself had drifted into this way of thinking. My old chronometer, a good one, had been long in disuse. It would cost fifteen dollars to clean it. Fifteen dollars! For sufficient reasons, I left that timepiece at home.

(He gets out his old logbook and puts it on a downstage trunk.)

I packed my new logbook and plenty of pens and pencils. Why pens and pencils, you ask? We all need to leave a record, don't we. There are no footprints on the sea. And yet, if we pass this way but once, we do like to think that others may note, and may remember. Wherever I sailed, it wasn't only for myself—it was to share.

(He gets out and waves his handkerchief.)

On May 7th I sailed. As the *Spray* stood out from Gloucester cove, a tall factory was a flutter of handkerchiefs. Pretty faces peered out of the windows, all smiling *Bon Voyage*. Some hailed me to know where away and why alone. Why? As the *Spray* skipped along I asked myself once more whether I ought to sail beyond the ledge and rocks at all. But my charter with myself seemed to bind me, and so I sailed on.

(On the map, he begins to indicate his voyage.)

I passed the Island of Frogs, where the *Spray* was charmed by a million voices. From there we made for the Island of Birds. Then the *Spray* sailed directly through the worst tide-race in the Bay of Fundy and got into Westport harbor in Nova Scotia, where I had spent eight years as a lad.

To find myself among old schoolmates now was charming. I took in some butter, a barrel of potatoes, and filled six barrels of water. Then, at Yarmouth, I got my famous tin clock, the only timepiece I carried on the whole voyage. The price of it was a dollar and a half, but because the face was smashed, the merchant let me have it for a dollar. On my trip around the world it did more than a dollar's worth of duty, believe me!

(He shows us his old tin clock.)

Since the boisterous Atlantic was before me, I now stowed all my goods securely. On July 1, 1895 I sailed from Yarmouth and let go my last hold on America. Before the sun went down I was taking my supper of strawberries and tea in smooth water under the lee of the east coast land.

(He shows us his point of departure then sits and relaxes on his chair.)

I watched light after light sink astern as I sailed into the unbounded sea till the last of them all was below the horizon. The *Spray* was then alone, and sailing on. The fog, which till this moment had held off, now lowered over the sea like a pall. I was shut off from the universe.

But at dusk on July 5th the fog lifted and I got a look at the sun just as it was touching the sea. I watched it go down and out of sight. Then I turned my face eastward and there, seemingly at the very end of the bowsprit, was the smiling full moon, rising out of the sea. "Good evening, sir," I cried, "I'm glad to see you." Many a long talk have I had since then with the man in the moon. He had my confidence on the voyage.

About midnight the fog shut down again, denser than ever before. One could almost stand on it. It continued that way for a number of days, while the wind increased to a gale. The waves rose high, but I had a good ship. Still, in the dismal fog I felt myself drifting into loneliness, an insect on a straw in the midst of the elements.

During these days a feeling of awe crept over me. My memory worked with startling power. I heard all the voices of my past laughing, crying, telling what I had heard them tell in many corners of the earth.

The loneliness of my state wore off when the gale was high and I found much work to do. But when fine weather returned, then came the sense of solitude, which I could not shake off. I'd been told I'd lose my speech from disuse, so I used my voice often. At first I gave some order about the affairs of the ship. I called aloud: "Eight bells!" Or from my cabin I called out to an imaginary man at the helm: "How does she head, there? Is she on her course?" But since I got no reply, I was reminded more strongly of my condition. My voice sounded hollow on the empty air, and I dropped the practice.

However, it was not long before I remembered that when I was a lad I used to sing. Why not try that now, where it would disturb no one? My musical talent had never bred envy in others. But out on the Atlantic, you should have heard me croon!

(He sings:)

It's a Yankee ship with a Yankee crew
John Kanaka-naka tulai-e,
And we're the bucko's to kick 'em through
John Kanaka-naka tulai-e,
Tulai-e, O-oh—, tulai-e,
John Kanaka-naka tulai-e!

You should have seen the porpoises leap when I pitched my voice to the waves! Old turtles with large eyes poked their heads up out of the sea. On the whole, the porpoises were vastly more appreciative than the turtles. One day when I was humming *Babylon's a-Fallin'*, a porpoise jumped higher than the bowsprit. Had the *Spray* been going a little faster, she would have scooped him in!

July 10th, eight days at sea, the *Spray* was twelve hundred miles east of Cape Sable. We were making one hundred and fifty miles a day, and that, for so small a vessel, must be considered good sailing. It was the greatest run the *Spray* ever made before or since in so few days.

Early in the morning of the 15th the *Spray* was close aboard a barkentine, *La Vaguisa*. When I came near enough, the captain threw a line to me and sent a bottle of wine across, slung by the neck, —and very good wine it was. I asked him to report me "all well" —but when he found I was alone, he crossed himself and made for his cabin.

There was now less and less monotony. My little sloop passed great ships. The wind was light so the large barks made poor headway. But the *Spray*, with a great mainsail bellying even to light winds, was skipping along as nimbly as one could wish.

The acute pain of solitude experienced at first never returned. I had penetrated a mystery. I had met Neptune in his majesty, but he found that I had treated him with respect, and so he suffered me to go on and explore.

Early on the morning of July 20th—land ho! I saw the Azores looming over the clouds on the starboard bow. As I approached nearer, cultivated fields appeared. And oh, how green the corn!

(He points out the Azores on the map.)

At 4:30 PM, exactly eighteen days from Nova Scotia, I cast anchor at Fayal. Soon the deck of the *Spray* was crowded with men, women and children from morning till night. It was the season for fruit when I arrived at the Azores and when I set sail again I found that more kinds of it had been put on board than I knew what to do with.

Plums seemed the most plentiful on the *Spray* and these I ate without stint. I also had a white cheese that the American consul-general had given me. And this I ate with the plums.

Alas! By night time I was doubled up with cramps. The wind was increasing. There was a heavy sky to the sou'west. In the coming storm, I should have made all snug and gone down at once to my cabin. In a word, I should have laid to—but I did not. Instead, I gave her the double-reef mainsail and whole jib and set her on her course.

Then I went below and threw myself on the cabin floor in great pain. How long I lay there I couldn't tell, because I became delirious. When I came to, as I thought, from my swoon, I realized that the sloop was plunging into a heavy sea. I looked out of the companionway and to my amazement I saw a tall man at the helm!

His rig was that of a foreign sailor. He had shaggy black whiskers, and a large red cap was cocked over his left ear. He looked for all the world like a pirate! I wondered if he had come to cut my throat. This he seemed to divine. "Señor," said he, doffing his cap, "I have come to do you no harm." And a faint smile played on his face. "I am one of Columbus's crew. I am the pilot of the *Pinta* come to aid you. Lie quiet, *señor* captain. I will guide your ship tonight. You did wrong, captain, to mix cheese and plums. White cheese is never safe unless you know whence it comes."

"Avast, there!" I cried. "I have no mind for moralizing!" Whereupon he bit off a large quid of black twist and cried, "Yonder is the *Pinta*. We must overtake her. Give her sail! Give her sail!" And that he did, chuckling and chanting a wild song. "I detest your jingle," I cried—and begged he would tie a rope on the rest of the song.

I was still in agony. Great seas were boarding the *Spray* but in my fevered brain I thought they were boats falling on deck. "You'll smash your boats!" I called. ... But I found, when my pains had gone, that the deck, now as white as a shark's tooth, had been swept of everything movable. At broad day, I saw, to my astonishment, that the *Spray* was still heading as I had left her and was going like a race-horse. Columbus himself could not have held her more exactly on her course. I felt grateful to the old pilot, ...but I marveled some that he had not taken in the jib.

I was getting much better now, but was very weak. I put my wet clothes out in the sun, then lay down there myself and fell asleep. I awoke completely refreshed, and with the feeling that I had been in the presence of a friend and seaman of vast experience. I gathered up my clothes, which by this time were dry. Then, by inspiration, I threw all the plums overboard.

(He refers to the log.)

July 28 was exceptionally fine. To get the salt out of my clothes, I did some washing in my dory. After it all I was hungry, so I made a fire and very cautiously stewed a dish of pears and set them carefully aside till I had made a pot of delicious coffee, for both of which I could afford sugar and cream. But the crowning dish of all was a fish-hash. I was in good health again, and my appetite was ravenous. While I was dining I had a large onion stewing over the double lamp for luncheon later in the day. And later in the afternoon I baked a loaf of bread. High living!

(He packs some old pots and pans in his seabag.)

One great feature about ship's cooking is that one's appetite on the sea is always good. After dinner, I sat for hours reading the life of Columbus. ... As the day wore on I watched the birds all flying in one direction. I said to myself, "Land lies there." ... Early the next morning I discovered Spain.

(He shows us the Atlantic transit.)

The *Spray* continued on her course till she passed through the Strait of Gibraltar where she cast anchor.

It was now twenty-nine days from Nova Scotia. I found myself in excellent health—though thin as a reef. Next day the Governor of Gibraltar, with other high officers of the garrison, came on board and signed their names in the *Spray*'s log book.

(He shows us the names in his logbook.)

The night before I was to sail, I had dinner with the admiral at his palace.

(He indicates the eastward and westward passages.)

Now, my intention had been to sail around the world eastward, reaching the Indian Ocean through the Suez Canal. But the Admiral and his men, officers of great experience in these waters, warned me that, sailing alone in the Mediterranean, I'd have no chance against the pirates who prey on every ship that passes through.

I am a man of some little courage,—but I'm not a fool. I decided to take their advice, reverse my course, and sail around the world to westward, not only to avoid the pirates, but to take advantage of the currents and the trades. It meant re-crossing the Atlantic—but no matter! I'd just done it once, I could do it again!

So on Monday, August 25th, 1895, the *Spray* sailed from Gibraltar and headed once more into the Atlantic. There the wind rose rapidly to a furious gale. My plan now was to head south, hauling offshore of the northwest African coast, well clear of the land, in order to avoid any possible encounter with pirates.

(On the map, he shows us his course off the northwest African coast.)

But hardly had I reached the open water when I caught sight of an evil-looking felucca making out of the nearest port and following in the wake of the *Spray*. I changed my course; the felucca did the same. Both vessels were sailing very fast, but the distance was growing less and less between us. The *Spray* was doing nobly, but in spite of all I could do, she would broach now and then. She was carrying too much sail. I must reef or be dismasted and lose all—even if I had to grapple with the pirates!

I wasn't long in reefing the mainsail but in the meantime the felucca had so shortened the distance between us that I now saw the tufts of hair on the heads of the crew. They were coming on like the wind and I saw by their movements that they were preparing to strike a blow. I reached for my rifle.

(He takes out his rifle.)

But suddenly, their craft, with too much sail on, broached to on the crest of a great wave. In one instant, the exultation on the pirates' faces was changed to a look of terror. This one great sea changed the aspect of affairs completely.

The felucca was dismasted. As I left them behind, I looked back and saw the thieving crew struggling to recover their rigging from the sea.

Free and unaccompanied, I set my course southwestward across the Atlantic toward the coast of Brazil. Sailing these seas more than four hundred years earlier, Columbus, in the Santa Maria, was not so happy as I. There was dissension on the Santa Maria—something that was unknown on the *Spray*.

(On the map, he shows us his course and the directions of the trade winds.)

As we passed through the channel between Africa and the Canary Islands, the *Spray* settled down to the trade-winds and to the business of her voyage. Her mast now bent under a strong, steady pressure and the rolling waves thrilled me as they tossed my ship, passing quickly under her keel. This was grand sailing!

Late one day a droger hove in sight, plunging into the head sea and rolling like a wild steer. The poor cattle in her hold, how they bellowed! Time was when ships passing one another at sea backed their topsails and had a gam, and on parting, fired guns. But those good old days have gone. People hardly have time nowadays to speak, even on the broad ocean, where news is news. And as for a salute of guns, they cannot afford the powder. It is a prosy life when we have no time to bid one another good morning.

(He sits.)

Passing the Cape Verde Islands, I found myself once more sailing a lonely sea in solitude supreme. I lashed the helm and my vessel held her course. And while she sailed, I slept. When I slept I dreamed that I was alone. This feeling never left me; but, sleeping or waking, I seemed always to know the position of the sloop, and I saw my vessel moving across the chart, which became a picture before me.

(Quietly, he says:)

One night while I sat in the cabin under this spell, the profound stillness was broken by human voices alongside! Startled, I sprang instantly to the deck. Passing close under the lee, like an apparition, was a bark under full sail. Sailors on board her were hauling on sheets to brace the yards, which just cleared the *Spray*'s mast as she swept by. No one hailed from the white-winged flier, but I heard someone on board say he saw lights on my sloop and he made her out to be a fisherman. ... I sat long on the starlit deck that night, thinking of ships, and watching the constellations on their voyage.

(He shows us the chart of the currents.)

The sloop was now rapidly drawing toward the region of the doldrums and the force of the trade-winds was lessening. I could see by the ripples that a counter-current had set in. On the 16th the *Spray* entered this gloomy region, to battle with squalls and be harassed by fitful calms.

The sea was tossed into confusing cross-lumps and eddying currents. And as if something more were needed to try one's nerves and patience, the rain poured down in torrents day and night. The *Spray* struggled and tossed for ten days — making only three hundred miles on her course in all that time. I didn't say anything!

On September 23rd the fine schooner *Nantasket* of Boston, laden with lumber, came up with the *Spray* and her captain passed a few words before she sailed on. Since she was much fouled on the bottom by shell-fish, she drew along with her fishes which had been following the *Spray*—which was less provided with that sort of food.

(He sits on a downstage trunk.)

Fishes will always follow a foul ship. One of those who deserted was a dolphin that had been following the *Spray* for about a thousand miles, content to eat scraps of food thrown overboard from my table. I had become accustomed to seeing the dolphin, which I knew by its scars, and missed it whenever it took occasional excursions away from the sloop.

One day, after it had been off some hours, it returned in company with three yellowtails, a sort of cousin to the dolphin. This little school kept together, except when in danger and when foraging about the sea. Their lives were often threatened by hungry sharks that came round the vessel and more than once they had narrow escapes.

Once threatened, they would dart away, each in a different direction, so that the wolf of the sea, the shark, pursuing one, would be led away from the others. Then after a while they would all return and rendezvous under one side or the other of the sloop.

Their precarious life seemed to concern the yellowtails very little. All living beings, without doubt, are afraid of death. Nevertheless, some of the species I saw huddled together as though they knew they were created for the larger fishes and wished to give the least possible trouble to their captors.

I have seen whales swimming in a circle around a school of herrings, bunching them together in a whirlpool set in motion by their flukes. And when the small fry were all whirled nicely together, one or the other of the leviathans, lunging through the center with open jaws, would take in a boat-load or so at a single mouthful! The little fish didn't try to escape. They just swam right in!

(Making "jaws" with his hands, he claps them shut.)

September 30th, at half-past eleven in the morning, the *Spray* crossed the equator in longitude 29 degrees 30 west. The southwest trades now gave her sails a stiff full breeze sending her handsomely over the sea toward the coast of Brazil. On October 5th, without further incident, she made the land, casting anchor in Pernambuco harbor forty days from Gibraltar and all well on board.

(He shows us the trans-Atlantic route from Gibraltar to Pernambuco.)

Did I tire of the voyage in all that time? Not a bit of it! I was never in better trim in all my life, and was eager for the more perilous experience of tackling the Strait of Magellan.

(He shows us his route along the Brazilian coast to Rio de Janeiro.)

My next port of call was Rio de Janeiro where I arrived November 5th. I had decided to give the *Spray* a yawl rig to give her balance in the tempestuous waters off Patagonia. So here I placed on the stern a semicircular brace to support a jigger mast. Then, on November 28th, the *Spray* sailed from Rio de Janeiro, headed southward along the coast of Brazil toward Uruguay.

Along this part of the coast there was a strong current running north, making it necessary to hug the shore. Actually, I confess, I hugged the shore entirely too closely. In a word, at daybreak on the morning of December 11, the *Spray* ran hard and fast on the beach.

I managed to launch my little sawed-off dory from the deck. I felt if I could sink the anchor in deeper water I could haul on the anchor line from the dory and free the *Spray* from the beach. But the weight of the anchor was too much for the frail dory and she was leaking fast. By the time I had rowed out far enough to drop the anchor, the dory was sinking.

There was not a moment to spare. If I failed now all might be lost. I jumped up, lifted the anchor above my head, and threw it clear just as the dory started turning over. I grasped her gunwale and held on as she turned bottom up—for I suddenly remembered that I could not swim!

I tried to right her, but she kept rolling over. I hung on to her gunwale. Then I realized the current was carrying me out to sea. Something would have to be done or this was the end! Thrashing about in the water, I thought of all those prophets of evil who had predicted I'd fail saying "I told you so!" I was seized by a determination to succeed. By the utmost care I finally succeeded in turning the dory upright and hauling myself into her. And with one of the oars, which I had managed to recover, I paddled to the shore, full of salt water and somewhat the worse for wear.

I flung myself on the sand to rest. I was on the wild coast of Uruguay, but there was nothing to do but wait for high water. I was dozing off when I heard the patter of many feet approaching along the hard beach. For a moment, I thought I was a goner. ... But fortunately, the natives were friendly.

With their help I managed to float the sloop and again set sail. The *Spray* had lost part of her false keel and received other damage which would have to be mended in dock. But we were both still seaworthy!

(On the map, he shows us Montevideo, Uruguay.)

Just before Christmas 1895 the *Spray* arrived in Montevideo. It is not at all strange in a sailor's life that, half-way from Boston to the Horn, I should still find myself among friends.

The *Spray* had barely come to anchor when some old acquaintances at the Royal Mail Steamship Company sent word that they would dock and repair her free of expense. They also refitted the *Spray* with a wonderful makeshift stove contrived from a large iron drum punched full of holes to give it a draft.

Its one door swung on copper hinges, polished like a luxury steamer's brass.

(He shows us Buenos Aires and the River de la Plata on the map.)

The *Spray* was now ready for sea, but instead of proceeding at once on her voyage, she made an excursion up the River de la Plata to visit Virginia in the English Cemetery where she had lain so long without me. I had not been in Buenos Aires for many years. The old lemonade-seller who used to get a barrel of drink from the juice of one limp lemon was still at his stand, but otherwise the city was much changed. And since I had last walked her streets with Virginia beside me I was eager to be away.

(On the map, he traces his journey southward.)

On January 26, 1896, with the *Spray* refitted and well-provisioned, I sailed from Buenos Aires. I can't say that I expected all fine sailing on the course for Cape Horn, but I thought only of onward and forward. It was when I anchored in the lonely places that a feeling of awe crept over me. And at the last anchorage, weak as it may seem, I gave way to my feelings. Memories of earlier trips along these shores with my beloved Virginia were too much for me. I resolved then that I would anchor no more north of the Strait of Magellan.

As I headed south, I gave all the capes a berth of about fifty miles, hoping the *Spray* might go clear of the destructive seas. But one day, well off the Patagonian coast, a tremendous tidal wave rolled down upon her in a storm, roaring as it came. I had only a moment to get all sail down and scramble up on the peak halyards when the mountain of water submerged my vessel.

We were under water for perhaps less than a minute, but it seemed a long while, for under great excitement one lives fast. The past, with electric speed, flashed before me, and I had time to make resolutions it would take a lifetime to fulfill. However, the incident, which filled me with fear, was only one more test of the *Spray*'s seaworthiness.

After the great wave, the weather became fine, the sea smooth, and life tranquil. Then the phenomenon of mirage frequently occurred. An albatross sitting on the water one day loomed up like a large ship. Two fur seals appeared to be great whales to me. And a bank of haze I could have sworn was a high island peopled by dwarfs.

(Outside the boathouse it begins to rain. He puts up the detailed map of the Strait of Magellan. As the storm rages outside, he tells us:)

On February 11, 1896 the *Spray* rounded Cape Virgins and entered the Strait of Magellan. The scene was real and gloomy. The wind began blowing a gale. For thirty hours it kept on blowing hard. But the *Spray* held on stoutly. She was not to be blown out of the Strait at the very start of the transit!

At last the weather moderated. Moving through the Strait, the *Spray* passed great piles of granite mountains of bleak and lifeless aspect.

Not knowing what I would find, I threw out my anchor, launched my skiff, and, with ax and gun, landed at the head of the cove and filled a barrel of water from a stream. The fine weather seemed to add loneliness to the place. And when I came upon a spot where some graves were marked, I went no farther.

(He shows us a drawing of crosses in his sketchbook.)

Men from vessels which had anchored here from time to time had nailed boards on the trees with name and date of their harboring carved or painted. Some of the names were illegible. On the graves, many of the crosses had decayed and fallen, and many a hand that put them there I had known, many a hand now still. The air of depression was about the place and I hurried back to the sloop to forget myself again in the voyage.

During this passage, I saw no living thing except a small spider, which I discovered nesting in a dry log that I boated to the sloop. The conduct of this insect interested me intensely. In my cabin it met a spider of its own size and species that had come all the way from Boston—a very civil little chap, too, but mighty spry. Well, the Fuegian threw up its antennae for a fight; but my little Bostonian downed it at once, then broke its legs, and pulled them off, one by one, so dexterously that in less than three minutes the Fuegian spider didn't know itself from a fly!

The *Spray* passed through the narrows without mishap and cast anchor at Sandy Point, a Chilean coaling-station. Because of the danger of attack by Indians in the Strait, the port captain advised me either to take on hands to fight them or to allow the *Spray* to be towed through by a gunboat. Neither course appealed to me.

(He shows us a box of carpet tacks.)

At this point an Austrian Captain came along and gave me a box of carpet-tacks. I protested that I had no use for them. But the Captain smiled at my lack of experience and said, "You must use them with discretion. That is, don't step on them yourself." With this remote hint, I saw the way to maintain clear decks at night without having to stay awake watching.

With thoughts of a strange and stirring adventure beyond anything I had yet encountered, I now braced the *Spray* against storms and sailed into the very core of the savage Fuegians.

(He lights a match and blows it out.)

February 20th was my 52nd birthday and I found myself alone, with hardly so much as a bird in sight, off Cape Froward, the southernmost point of the continent of South America.

(He packs the matches and shows us Cape Froward on the map.)

Hard beating in the heavy squalls and against the current had told on my strength. At midnight, I anchored in the lee of a little island in Fortesque Bay, for to tell the truth, I was sorely in need of a cup of coffee.

Natives' signal fires blazed up on all sides. While the storm raged, no one came near me. But as soon as fair weather came and I again sailed out on the Strait, canoes manned by savages immediately came in pursuit. They gained on me rapidly, calling out "Yammerschooner! Yammerschooner!" which is their begging term. I shouted back, "No!"

Now, I was not for letting on that I was alone. So I stepped into the cabin and came out the fore-scuttle in different clothes.

(He holds up a sweater then packs it.)

That made two men. Then I dressed up the bowsprit to look like a seaman.

(He holds up another sweater then packs that, too.)

That made three of us. And none of us wanted to "yammerschooner". But the savages came on faster than before.

(He gets out his rifle.)

At twenty yards I fired a shot across the bow of the nearest canoe. The chap who wanted to "yammerschooner" bellowed with fear and turned tail. I found out later it was none other than "Black Pedro", a leader in several bloody massacres and the worst murderer in Tierra del Fuego. He made for the island and the others followed him.

But that night, about twelve o'clock, as I was asleep in my cabin, the savages paddled quietly toward me. They stepped on deck—then suddenly their minds changed.

(He picks up and rattles the tack box.)

You see, before I'd gone to sleep, I'd scattered my carpet tacks, business-side up, on the deck! Crying out in pain, they jumped pell-mell, some into their canoes, some into the sea. That night, they bothered me no more!

(He packs the box of tacks.)

At daybreak, I swept the deck of tacks and sailed on.

Now I began to understand what would become the character of my sail through the Strait of Magellan. There would be constant danger from the heavy weather. But any time the weather abated, there would be savages to face.

(He shows us Port Tamar and Cape Pillar.)

For many days the *Spray* and I battled against "Magellan weather", but at last we finally gained anchorage at Port Tamar. There was Cape Pillar, the gateway to the Pacific, in sight to the west. Here, though it was still a day's sail away, I began to feel the throb of the great ocean that lay before me.

(On the map, he shows us his route to the Pacific Ocean.)

On the third of March, the *Spray* sailed from Port Tamar direct for Cape Pillar and the Pacific. It soon began to rain and thicken in the northwest, boding no good. The *Spray* neared Cape Pillar rapidly and plunged into the Pacific Ocean at once, taking her first bath of it in the gathering storm. There was no turning back even had I wished to do so, for the land was now shut out by the darkness of night.

(Outside the boathouse, the lightening flashes and the thunder roars. He shows us the southeast course of the Spray.*)*

But the sea was confused and treacherous. The wind blew with terrific force from the northwest. The *Spray*, under bare poles, was being beaten back toward the east—heading back toward the Atlantic! There was nothing I could do but keep her before the wind.

No ship in the world could have stood up against so violent a gale. The *Spray* rode, now like a bird on the crest of a wave, now like a waif, deep down in the hollow between seas. But even while the storm raged at its worst, my ship was wholesome and noble.

When I had done all I could do for the safety of the vessel, I prepared a pot of coffee and made a good Irish stew, for I insisted on warm meals. But the sea was so uneven and crooked, my appetite was slim. ... Confidentially, I was seasick!

In no part of the world could a rougher sea be found. The sea was majestic. Whole days passed, counted as other days, but with a thrill—yes, of delight.

By the fourth day of the gale I had been blown far off course to the southeast and I was rapidly nearing the point of Cape Horn—a passage I had never intended! The mainsail was torn to rags. Night closed in. I heard the tremendous roaring of breakers ahead and on the lee bow. Broken water all about me. Rocks!

This puzzled me, for there should have been none where I supposed myself to be. Hail and sleet in the fierce squalls cut my flesh till the blood trickled over my face, but what of that? At last it was daylight and I found to my horror that the sloop was in the midst of the Milky Way of the sea, northwest of Cape Horn.

What could I do but fill away among the breakers till I could find a channel between them? This was the greatest sea adventure of my life. God knows how my vessel escaped. When Darwin looked over this wild seascape from the deck of the Beagle he wrote in his journal, "Any landsman seeing the Milky Way would have nightmares for a week." Any seaman would, too!

(He shows us Cockburn Channel on the map.)

When I found a moment to look at my charts, I realized we were in the Cockburn Channel, which leads eastward into the Strait of Magellan. I tried to head the ship westward, but suddenly a fierce wind came down with such terrific force that it carried the *Spray*, with two anchors down, like a feather out of the cove and toward the northeast.

This was my first experience with the terrific squalls called williwaws— compressed gales of wind that come over the hills in chunks. A full-blown williwaw can throw a ship over on her beam ends.

I had no choice but to go on, heading toward Cape Froward, where I had cast anchor February 19th. It was now the 10th of March! I was headed back to where I started almost a month earlier!

(On the map, he shows us how his route has come full circle.)

I had circumnavigated the wildest part of desolate Tierra del Fuego. And the place wasn't through with me. For suddenly I saw a dark cliff ahead and breakers so close under the bow that I felt surely I was lost. In my thoughts, I cried, "Is the hand of fate against me, after all, leading me in the end to this dark spot?"

I sprang aft and threw the wheel over, expecting, as the sloop came down into the hollow of a wave, to feel her timbers smash under me on the rocks. But at the touch of her helm, she swung clear of the danger.

I thought I would anchor and rest till morning, but just as I let go the anchor another williwaw struck down from the mountain, whirled the sloop around like a top and carried her off faster than I could pay out cable.

Instead of resting, I had to man the windlass and heave up the anchor plus fifty fathoms of cable hanging down in deep water. On that little crab-windlass I worked the rest of the night.

(He demonstrates cranking the windlass.)

Blood started from my fingers. I thought how much easier it was for me when I could say "Weigh anchor!" rather than have to do it myself! But I hove away on the windlass singing—

My old mother said to me
Go down, you blood red roses, go down.
Son o' son come home from sea
Go down, you blood red roses, go down.
Go down, you pinks and posies,
Go down, you blood red roses, go down.

(Exhausted, he finishes the task.)

At last it was daybreak and the anchor was in the hawse.

For a few days the *Spray* and I enjoyed fine weather. But because this meant danger from savages, I now enjoyed the gales of wind as never before. I became in a measure inured to the life and began to think that one more trip through the Strait would make me the aggressor and put the place, the weather and every damn savage entirely on the defensive.

(He picks up his rifle.)

I repaired the windlass and made a landing for fuel—taking my rifle along. I discovered wreckage and goods washed up from the sea. I worked all day boating off a cargo to the sloop. The bulk of the goods was tallow in casks, some weighing over eight hundred pounds. And embedded in the seaweed was a barrel of wine, which I also hoisted aboard.

The habits of an old trader would come to the surface and I was happy in the prospect of doing a good business farther along on the voyage.

(He shows us his route on the map.)

Then, since the wind was coming from the northeast, I turned the prow of the *Spray* westward once more for the Pacific—to cross a second time the second half of my first course through the Strait. To reach the Pacific again there were two hundred miles to go.

(Using his handkerchief, he shows us the expanding squaresail.)

I was determined to rely on my own small resources to repair the damages of the great williwaws. I set to work with my palm and needle. It was slow work, but little by little the square-sail expanded to the dimensions of a serviceable mainsail. If it was not the best-looking sail afloat, it was at least very strongly made and would stand a hard blow. A ship, meeting the *Spray* long afterward, reported her as wearing "a mainsail of some improved design"! But that was not the case.

The *Spray* once more reached away for Fortescue Bay. The loneliness of the place was broken by the appearance of a great steamship. I threw out my flag and immediately saw the Stars and Stripes flung to the breeze from the great ship. That night I went to the steamer, which I found to be the *Columbia*. Its chief mate, Mister Hannibal, was an old friend.

The *Columbia* had an abundance of fresh stores on board and the steward asked if I would like a few cans of milk—and cheese. When I offered a bit of gold for these supplies the captain roared like a lion and told me to put away my money.

(He takes tins from shelves and puts them in the seabag.)

That night an impromptu entertainment was gotten up by one Midshipman singing songs in five languages. They asked me to sing, but I replied, "I only sing for porpoises!" Altogether, it was a very merry time.

Returning to the *Spray*, I found all secure. I watched the steamer, on and off, through the night for the pleasure of seeing her electric lights. In the morning, the *Spray* was the first under way. But the *Columbia*, soon following, passed and gave me three long blasts of her steam whistle. ... I read afterward that she was wrecked on the rocks off the California coast.

Another gale sprang up. The wind was cold but still fair and I had only twenty-six miles to run for Port Tamar and the gateway to the Pacific. The *Spray* fairly flew along, all covered with snow, which fell thick and fast, till she looked like a white winter bird.

I remained at Port Tamar some days, arranging my cabin in better order and taking in a good supply of wood and water. When all was ready, I set sail. I made six attempts to launch myself into the Pacific from Port Tamar, but each time was driven back!

(The weather outside the boathouse is abating. The sunlight reappears.)

At last, on the 13th of April, for the seventh and last time, the *Spray* weighed anchor and sailed from Port Tamar. Although thirteen is my lucky number, I had a superstitious fear that I shouldn't persist in sailing on a 13th day.

When I found myself disentangling the sloop's mast from the branches of a tree after she had drifted three times around a small island against my will, it seemed more than one's nerves could bear.

I shouted at the *Spray*, "Don't you know you can't climb a tree?!" But my heart softened when I thought of what she had gone through. And now, at last, the *Spray* carried me free of Tierra del Fuego.

The waves doffed their white caps to her in the Strait that day before the southeast wind, the first true winter breeze of the season from that quarter. She cleared the great tide-race off Cape Pillar and the Evangelistas, the outermost rocks of all.

The next morning only the tops of the highest mountains were in sight and the *Spray*, making good headway on a northwest course, soon sank these out of sight. She had come, thus far, 9,600 miles and at last we were truly on our way across the Pacific!

"Hurrah for the *Spray*!", I shouted to seals, sea-gulls and penguins. I shook out a reef, and set the whole jib, for she was the wholesomer under a press of sail.

In the evening, one wave broke over the sloop fore and aft. It washed over me at the helm. It seemed to wash away old regrets. All my troubles were now astern; summer was ahead; all the world was again before me. I had stood at the helm since eleven o'clock the morning before. Thirty hours. Then was the time to uncover my head, for I sailed alone with God.

(A bell is heard clanging outside.)

...Which is a damn sight better than having to answer a lunch bell!

(He exits.)

(Blackout)

END ACT ONE

ACT TWO

(JOSHUA SLOCUM *enters carrying a covered wicker basket. He says to us:*)

JOSHUA SLOCUM: It never stopped, all through lunch, the jabber-jabber. You'd think, if she wanted me not to weigh anchor, she'd make it more pleasant for me to stay at home! But no! She goes on and on with every fear in the book: death by drowning, death by having a savage spear me through the heart, death by being eaten by a fish, death by *eating* a fish—

"You have to cast out fear," I tell her. So she answers, "It's fear that will save you." "It only works against you," I tell her. "Go and good riddance to you!" she shouts. And she hands me this—

(*He opens the basket and takes out a parcel wrapped in cloth. He unties the parcel. Inside is a very sorry-looking cake.*)

Baked it herself. Said if Virginia could do it, she could do it...

(*Tying up the cake, he unceremoniously dumps it into a garbage barrel, saying:*)

Death by indigestion.

Hettie doesn't realize it wasn't with *cake* that Virginia fed me. She fed me with the spirit of going forward. That's what I need now. I had it stronger in the past...

(*He returns to the map and shows us the Horn and the Pacific.*)

On that journey alone around the world how splendid it was—after the trials of the Horn—to see the wide Pacific stretching out before me! In every direction, the horizon was unbroken by land. The roaring seas turned to gossiping waves that rippled and pattered against the *Spray*'s sides as she rolled among them with delight.

Rapid changes went on, those days, while she headed for the tropics. New species of birds came around. Albatrosses fell back and became scarcer and scarcer. Lighter gulls came in their stead, and pecked for crumbs in the sloop's wake.

(*He shows us Juan Fernandez.*)

I steered for Juan Fernandez, three hundred and forty miles from Chile. Fifteen days out, I caught sight of its blue hills, thirty miles off. Soon after daylight I saw a boat with six rowers in her putting out toward me. Since they pulled with oars in oarlocks, in the manner of trained seamen, I knew they belonged to a civilized race—so I put away my gun.

They took me in tow to port. There I prepared a pot of coffee and a plate of doughnuts fried in tallow.

(He picks up a large pot.)

The islanders had never seen anything like these round buns with the hole in the middle. I could hardly make them fast enough before they hollered, "More!" I didn't charge a high price for what I sold. But since I was paid in coins salvaged from the wreck of an ancient galleon, I sold the coins afterward for far more than face value.

(He shows us a gold coin.)

The children, who were all healthy and beautiful, had never heard a word in their lives except Spanish. When I told them that the *cabra* they pointed out was only a goat, they rolled on the grass in wild delight! To think that a man had come to their island who would call a *cabra* a goat!

(He shows us a worn copy of Robinson Crusoe *with its illustrations.)*

Juan Fernandez is the island where Alexander Selkirk was marooned. It was his adventure which inspired Daniel Defoe to write *Robinson Crusoe*. I made a pilgrimage to the cave at the top of the mountain where Selkirk spent four years in complete solitude peering into the distance for the ship which seemed never to come. He was finally taken off the island in 1709 when he managed to catch the attention of a passing privateer.

(He packs several books, then shows us his route across the Pacific.)

On the morning of May 5, 1896 I sailed from Juan Fernandez, and headed out across the Pacific on what I knew would be the longest part of the journey with no land in sight. I bore away to the north, where I at last reached the trade-winds, which seemed slow in reaching their limits. When they did come they came with a bang, however, and the *Spray* flew before a gale for a great many days as she headed toward the Marquesas in the west, forty-three days away.

My time was all taken up those days, not by standing at the helm; no man could stand or sit and steer a vessel round the world. With the wheel lashed, I sat and read my books, mended my clothes or cooked my meals and ate them in peace.

(Pointedly, he looks back at the house.)

I made companionship with what there was around me. Sometimes with the universe and sometimes with my own insignificant self. But my books were always my friends, let fail all else.

(He selects charts to take on his journey.)

I sailed with a free wind day after day, marking the position of my ship on the chart with considerable precision. For one whole month my vessel held her course true. In that time I did not see the lights of one single ship on the horizon. I saw the Southern Cross every night abeam. Every morning the sun came up astern; every evening it went down ahead. I wished for no other compass to guide me.

There was no denying the comical side of the strange life. Sometimes I awoke to hear the water rushing by with only a thin plank between me and the depths and I said, "How is this?" But it was all right; it was my ship on her course, sailing as no other ship had ever sailed before.

To cross the Pacific Ocean brings you close to nature and you realize the vastness of the sea. On the forty-third day from land—a long time to be at sea alone—I threw up my sextant for sights and felt confident that in a few hours more I should see land. And so it happened, for then I saw the island of Nukahiva, the southernmost of the Marquesas.

(He shows us the Marquesas on the map.)

The fact that I had reached this point by intuition and by dead reckoning tickled my vanity. I was proud of the little achievement alone on the sloop. To be alone forty-three days might seem a long time, but in reality, winged moments flew lightly by. I had become used to the silence of my own company, so instead of hauling in for Nukahiva, which I could have made as well as not, I kept on for Samoa, twenty-nine days away.

(He shows us the distance to Samoa.)

I was not distressed in any way during that time. The coral reefs kept me busy. I was threatened now and then by hungry sharks. I had a narrow escape from collision with a great whale. But by and large it was a pretty tame passage.

(He takes out a tub of potatoes and examines each before putting it in a sack to take along.)

My diet on these long stretches usually consisted of potatoes and salt cod and biscuits, which I made two or three times a week. I usually carried a good supply of potatoes, but through meeting a Portuguese trader at Juan Fernandez who nearly traded me out of my boots, I ran out of potatoes in mid-ocean and was wretched thereafter.

I pride myself on being something of a trader, and I thought I'd made a fine bargain when this fellow gave me new potatoes for the older ones I'd gotten in the Strait of Magellan. I tied up the sack and took it aboard. But when I opened it three weeks later on the ocean, out flew millions of winged insects! His potatoes had all turned to moths! I tied them up quickly and threw all into the sea.

But taking things by and large, I got on fairly well in the matter of provisions.

What I lacked of fresh meat was made up in fresh fish. Flying fish would leap onto the deck in such abundance one had to be careful in the dark lest one get a black eye! They would hit the sails and fall on the deck. I would cook the one which fell closest to the frying pan!

(He takes his straw hat with a bite out of its brim off a hook and puts it on, relaxing in a chair with his feet up on a trunk.)

On the 16th of July, 1896, seventy-two days after last setting foot on land, I cast anchor at Samoa. Once the vessel was moored, I spread an awning, and instead of going on shore at once, I sat under it till late in the evening, listening to the musical voices of the Samoan men and women.

A canoe came down the harbor with three young women paddling it. One hailed me with the native salutation: *"Talofa lee"* — "Love to you, Chief." "Love to you," I answered. "You come 'lone?" I answered yes. "Don't believe that. You had nother mans, you eat 'em." The others laughed. "What for you come long way?" they asked. "To hear you ladies sing." "Oh, talofa lee!" they cried — and paddled on.

(He shows us a photograph of the king.)

At Samoa I had the pleasure of hobnobbing with the king himself. King Malietoa was a great ruler. He never got less than forty-five dollars a month for the job and this amount had lately been raised, so graceless beachcombers would no longer be able to call him "tin of salmon Malietoa". His daughter, the princess, gave me a bottle of coconut-oil for my hair. I'm not certain it did anything to enhance my looks, but I swabbed some on out of courtesy.

As I sailed farther from the center of civilization I heard less and less about what would and what would not pay. When I came to a Samoan village, the chief did not ask "How much will you pay for roast pig?" Instead, he said, "Dollar, dollar. White man know only dollar. Never mind dollar. Let us drink and rejoice. On the tree there is fruit; let us eat. Let the day go by; why should we mourn over that? There are millions of days coming. Our house, which is good, cost but the labor of building it, and there is no lock on the door." While the days go this way in these Southern islands, we in the North are struggling for the bare necessities of life.

(He shows us a photograph of Mrs Robert Louis Stevenson.)

On my last morning, bright and early, Mrs Robert Louis Stevenson came to the *Spray* and invited me to Vailima, the estate she used to share with her late husband.

Of course I was thrilled when I found myself face to face with this bright woman, for so long the companion of the author who had delighted me on the voyage. The teller of tales is buried on Samoa, high on a mountain under the "wide and stormy sky" of which he wrote. With Mrs Stevenson in her Panama hat, we walked over the whole estate. She ordered some men to cut a couple of bamboo trees for the *Spray*. I used them for spare spars.

(He takes off the straw hat and hangs it back on the hook.)

Then I took ava with the family and was ready for the sea. I said "Tofa!" to my good friends of Samoa and the *Spray* stood out of the harbor August 20, 1896 and continued on her course.

A sense of loneliness seized me as the islands faded astern, and as a remedy I crowded on sail for Australia.

(On the globe, he traces his course toward Newcastle.)

After a passage of forty-two days, mostly of storms and gales, I put into port at Newcastle, in New South Wales. There I found that a French mail steamer had sighted me during the passage and, losing me in a storm, had reported me missing! The *Spray* was all right, but the passengers on the steamer were up to their knees in water in the saloon!

(On the map, he traces his course to Sydney.)

After a few days rest, a port pilot with a tug carried the *Spray* to sea again and she made along the coast toward the harbor of Sydney, where she arrived on the following day.

Summer was approaching. The harbor of Sydney was blooming with yachts. I saw all manner of craft, from the smart steam launch and sailing-cutter to the smaller sloop and canoe, pleasuring on the bay.

In Sydney, the *Spray* shed her Fuego mainsail, and, wearing a new set of sails given her by the head of an Australian department store, was flagship of the Johnstone's Bay Flying Squadron when the circumnavigators of Sydney harbor sailed in their annual regatta.

(He shows the pennant of the regatta.)

One day when the rain was coming down in a deluge, the commander of the H M S Orlando came aboard with a party of gentlemen and young ladies from the city. As luck would have it, one of the young gentlemen, in the full uniform of a very great yacht club, with brass buttons enough to sink him, slipped on the rain-slicked deck and tumbled holus-bolus, head over heels, into a barrel of water I had been coopering and, being a short man, was soon out of sight! He nearly drowned before he was rescued! It was the nearest to a casualty on the *Spray* in her whole course!

Time flew fast those days in Australia and it was December 6th when the *Spray* sailed from Sydney. My intention was now to sail south around Australia on my way home.

(On the map, he shows us this southerly direction.)

Passing the lighthouse on Cape Bundooro, I saw festoons of evergreen in token of Christmas. I called "A Merry Christmas" to some children waving handkerchiefs on the balcony of a cottage near the shore—and could hear them call in reply: "Merry Christmas!"

(His voice breaks when he speaks this last and he shakes off the mood.)

The *Spray* paid no port charges in Australia till she poked her nose into Melbourne harbor. There the customs officer demanded tonnage dues. I squared the matter by charging people sixpence each for coming on board, and when this business got dull I caught a shark and charged them sixpence each to look at that.

(He shows us a shark's jaws.)

I now realized that in these summer months—that is, December, January and February—there was bad weather and vast amounts of ice drifting up from the Antarctic. I considered it impractical to continue southward and decided to sail from port to port in Tasmania waiting for the season of favorable winds.

(He gets out his primitive slide projector and shows us a series of glass slides from places visited thus far on his trip: Gibraltar, Rio, the mountains in the Strait of Magellan, the women of Samoa, etc.)

Since I had seen something of the world, and since I found people here were interested in adventure, I talked the matter over before my first audience in a little hall by a country road. A piano was brought in from a neighbor's. I was helped out by the severe thumping it got, and by a song from a strolling comedian. People came from a great distance and attendance all told netted the house about three pounds sterling. A great success. So I continued on the trip to do this often.

I must say, however, that before getting up to speak I always suffered an attack of nerves. I mentioned this to a doctor. He said, "Man, man,—great nervousness is only a sign of brain. The more brain a man has the longer it takes him to get over the affliction." ...I make no claim to great brain, but I confess I am not yet entirely cured.

It was with regret that I thought of sailing from a country of so many pleasant associations. But after a six months stay in Tasmania—the longest stop on my journey—I weighed anchor April 16, 1897 and again put to sea.

(On the map, he retraces his route to the north.)

Summer was then over. Since winter was rolling up from the south, I decided the *Spray* should retrace her course northward. This route would afford me the pleasures and challenges of sailing through the Coral Sea.

(He shows us charts of the Great Barrier Reef.)

Lady Elliott Light stands on an island as a sentinel at the gateway of the Great

Barrier Reef. The reef extends for over a thousand miles along the northeast coast of Australia, forming a natural breakwater. Made of undersea mountains of coral, the reef forms a channel, sometimes as narrow as ten miles, sometimes as wide as a hundred. Its waters are of many colors, reflecting the coral beneath the surface, and every now and then the coral rises above the water creating an enchanted isle.

(He shows us a large piece of sharp coral.)

As she entered the channel, the *Spray* was now in a protected sea and smooth water, the first she had dipped her keel into since leaving Gibraltar. The sea itself might be called smooth, but coral rocks are always rough, sharp and dangerous. Armed with a good set of admiralty charts, I kept a good lookout for perils on every hand. Suspecting jagged coral everywhere, the *Spray* sailed for hours in suspense, stemming a current. Almost mad with doubt, I grasped the helm to throw her head off shore.

The *Spray*, going at full speed, with sheets off, hit a reef. She swung off quickly on her heel, however, and with one more bound cut across the shoal so quickly that I hardly knew how it was done.

Now the sloop ran before the constant trade-wind and made no stop at all, night or day, till May 31, 1897 when she reached Cooktown on the northeast coast of Australia. I moored the *Spray* at sunset near the Captain Cook monument. Next morning I went ashore to feast my eyes on the very stones the great navigator had seen, for I was now on a seaman's consecrated ground.

(He shows us a photo of Cook Monument.)

From Cooktown, the *Spray* weighed anchor for Thursday Island. In the dark of night I arrived to find some four hundred naked aborigine warriors and their wives and children—fantastically painted like birds and beasts and human skeletons—dancing and leaping about before a blazing fire.

(He shows us photos of the natives in fantastic costumes.)

All kept time to music, vocal and instrumental. The instruments were bits of wood and bone which they beat against each other in the palms of their hands. They danced all night. I didn't find out till morning that this native shebang was all in honor of the Jubilee—the fiftieth year of the reign of Queen Victoria.

(He shows us on the map the route down the Indian Ocean.)

On June 24th the *Spray* passed the outer limits of the Great Barrier Reef and, released from its dangers, sailed for the long voyage ahead, down the Indian Ocean. I shaped course now for Keeling Cocos, a tiny atoll, twenty-seven hundred miles distant. It was so small it would require great skill to find. But I turned my prow in its direction and prayed my reckoning would lead me, without error, to its shores.

(He shows us the route to Keeling Cocos on the map.)

I passed Booby Island, where, in earlier days, passing ships landed stores in a cave for shipwrecked wayfarers. There had been a sort of improvised post office, where whalemen left letters with the request that the first homeward-bound ship carry them along and see to their mailing.

Sailing on, the sloop found herself in the Arafura Sea. There, for days, she sailed in water milky white and green and purple. On dark nights I witnessed the phosphorescent light effect. The sea, where the sloop disturbed it, seemed all ablaze, so that by its light I could see the smallest articles on deck, and her wake was a path of fire.

Now was the time to crowd on sail. I got out the flying-jib made at Juan Fernandez and set it as a spinnaker on the stout bamboo that Mrs Stevenson had given me at Samoa. The *Spray* picked up speed. For several days she sailed west as true as a hair. If she deviated at all from her course, she was back, strangely enough, at noon, at the correct latitude. My tin clock and only timepiece had by this time lost its minute-hand and was acting sluggish, so I boiled her. After that, she told the hours, and that was near enough on a long stretch.

(He packs the tin clock.)

To the Keeling Cocos Islands was now only five hundred and fifty miles. But even in this short run it was necessary to be extremely careful in keeping a true course or I would miss the atoll.

The first unmistakable sign of land was a visit one morning from a white tern that fluttered very knowingly about the vessel and then took itself off westward with a businesslike air.

My reckoning was about to prove itself. Springing aloft, I saw from half-way up the mast coconut-trees standing out of the water ahead. I expected to see this; still, it thrilled me as an electric shock might have done. I slid down the mast, trembling under the strangest sensations; and, not able to resist the impulse, I sat on deck and gave way to my emotions. To folks in a parlor on shore this may seem weak, but for a voyage alone, this had been an accomplishment indeed.

I didn't touch the helm. With the current and heave of the sea the sloop found herself at the end of the run absolutely in the fairway of the channel. You couldn't have beaten it in the navy!

Now there might be those who couldn't believe one could lash the helm and let the boat steer herself. But the point is, a boat on an ocean is not a horse and buggy. You can't tie her to a post and tell her to hold still to spend the night. She will always be sailing—and some of that time the navigator will have to be sleeping. But the *Spray* and I were partners, and sometimes it seemed she knew where to go on her own.

(He gets out a coil of rope and starts to inspect it, illustrating the story.)

For a long time after I arrived on Keeling Cocos the children regarded my one-man ship with suspicion and fear. One day when I tried to haul the sloop I found her fast in the sand. The children all clapped their hands and cried that a *kpeting*—a crab—was holding her by the keel. It was decided that if I should give the priest a pot of jam, he would ask Mohammed to make the crab let go the ship's keel. I gave the priest the jam, the *kpeting* let go, and the ship floated on the very next tide.

(With one final yank, the rope releases itself. He coils it and puts the length in his sea-bag.)

Now I headed toward the island of Rodriguez across the Indian Ocean.

The sea was rugged and we ran under reefed sails. I got tired of the never-ending motion of the sea, and, above all, of the wetting I got whenever I showed myself on deck.

(He looks at himself in a mirror.)

My first night on Rodriguez I was invited to a formal dinner. In the land of napkins and cut glass, I saw before me the ghosts of hempen towels and of mugs with handles knocked off. Instead of tossing on the sea, however, here I was in a bright hall, surrounded by sparkling wit and dining with the governor of the island!

Officers of experience now reckoned that the hardships of the voyage were now nine-tenths finished, and yet, somehow, I could not forget that the United States was still a long way off.

(He shows the Cape of Good Hope.)

The Cape of Good Hope was now the most prominent point to pass. Fierce gales sweeping round the Cape were frequent, one occurring, on an average, every thirty-six hours. On Christmas, 1897, my third Christmas at sea, I came to the pitch of the Cape. On this day the *Spray* was trying to stand on her head! She began to toss about in a most unusual manner, and I have to say that, while I was at the end of the bowsprit reefing the jib, she ducked me under water three times for a Christmas present. I got wet and did not like it a bit!

Two days later, the *Spray* finally beat around the Cape of Good Hope, and that evening the steam-tug *Alert*, then out looking for ships, came to the *Spray* and towed her to anchor in the bay off the city of Cape Town. There I remained for one day alone, in the quiet of a smooth sea, enjoying the retrospect of the passage of the two great capes. On the following morning the *Spray* sailed into Alfred Dry-docks, where she remained for about three months, while I traveled over the country.

I enjoyed my visits to Kimberley and Johannesburg and at Pretoria I met Mr Kruger, the Transvaal president. This gentleman firmly believed the world was flat. When it was mentioned to him that I was on a voyage around the world, he cried, "You don't mean *round* the world. It is impossible! You mean *across* the world!" I got out my map and tried to show him how my journey, going in one direction, would end at the place it started. But this proved nothing to him because, of course, the map was flat!

(He begins to sort out tools, some to take and some to leave behind.)

On the plains of Africa I passed through hundreds of miles of rich but still barren earth and I found myself seized by a longing for a foothold on land. But instead of remaining to plant forests and reclaim vegetation, I returned again to the *Spray*, where I found her waiting for me, with everything in order, exactly as I had left her.

On March 26, 1898, the *Spray* sailed from South Africa and the high peaks of the Cape of Good Hope. Now the world changed from a mere panoramic view to the light of a homeward-bound voyage.

(On the map, he shows us his direction up the Atlantic.)

I was once again in the Atlantic. Porpoises and dolphins and such other fishes as did not mind making a hundred and fifty miles a day, were her companions now for several days.

And so the *Spray* reeled off the miles till April 11th, when we arrived at Saint Helena, the last exile of the Emperor Napoleon.

(On the map, he shows us the location of Saint Helena.)

There I visited the home where Napoleon lived. I even slept in a room he supposedly haunts. I hoped the Emperor would come by and have a gam, but the great Napoleon obviously had nothing to say to a mere single-handed sailor.

(He shows us a portrait of Napoleon in his scrapbook.)

On the 20th of April I set sail, taking with me a gift from the Governor's lady, a large, delectable fruit-cake. I ate sparingly of it, intending it to last to the end of the voyage. But it only lasted forty-two days.

A friend of the Governor's, in a luckless moment, had put a goat on board. He said that the animal would be as companionable as a dog.

From the moment this dog with horns came on board I had no peace of mind. This incarnation of evil threatened to devour everything! He began by eating my chart of the West Indies. Next he started chomping on my favorite straw hat.

(He points to his straw hat with the piece chewed out of it.)

This last unkind stroke decided his fate. On the 27th of April the *Spray* arrived at Ascension, which is garrisoned by a man-of-war crew. I hired them to land the wretch at once and that was the end of our association.

Now some might say, "Why didn't you slaughter the beast and dine on goat stew?" I couldn't. In the loneliness of the journey I found myself in no mood to make one life less in the world, except in self-defense. However well I may have enjoyed a chicken stew at Samoa, a new self rebelled at the thought of carrying chickens on the voyage to be slain for my table. To kill the companions of my voyage and eat them would be next to cannibalism.

As to pets, there was no room for a noble large dog on the *Spray* on so long a voyage. A cat would have been harmless, but puss is an unsociable animal. True a rat got into my vessel at Keeling Cocos and at first I had a mind to keep him, but a breach of discipline decided the matter against him. While I slept one night, he undertook to walk over me, beginning at the crown of my head, concerning which I am always sensitive. Before his impertinence had gotten him even to my nose I cried "Rat!", grabbed him by the tail, and threw him into the sea.

On the last day of April the *Spray* filled away clear of the sea-beaten rocks, and the trade-winds, cool and bracing, sent her flying along on her course. On May 8, 1898, off the northeast coast of Brazil, she crossed the track that she had made October 2, 1895 on the voyage out. The *Spray* had circumnavigated the globe.

(On the map he shows the two tracks crossing in the Atlantic.)

I felt a glow of contentment and I was in no way discouraged as to the journey's utility. I said to myself, "Let what will happen, the voyage is now on record." But I was still thirty-five hundred miles from home.

There could still be some mishap. What if something happened on the last leg of the journey — and the fact that I'd done what I set out to do remained a secret between myself, the *Spray* and the sea?

So many things, almost achieved, have been snatched from the jaws of victory. What if some jealous God did not, after all this, wish me to make it to my final destination?

He had tested me before, and on these very waves, when, after the wreckage of the *Aquidneck*, I transported Hettie and the boys home in our makeshift canoe. And now, in the *Spray*, I was sailing back to Hettie. My land wife. How had things gone with her in my time at sea? I tried to keep my mind on the voyage, tried not to think of what I would find once I was on shore.

(He consults his log.)

On May 10 there was a great change in the sea. Long-forgotten current ripples pattered against the sloop's sides and on the 14th of May, just north of the equator, near the longitude of the river Amazon, I saw a mast, with the Stars and Stripes floating from it, rising astern as if poked up out of the sea. Then, like a citadel, the battleship *Oregon* appeared!

(He shows us a sketch of the warship.)

As she came near I saw that the great ship was flying the signals "C B T"—which means, "Are there any men-of-war about?" I had not heard anything about the Spanish-American war which was then raging! I hoisted the signal "No," and sent a signal: "Let us keep together for mutual protection"—but the Oregon steamed on, doubtless not needing me.

(He turns a page in his log.)

On May 18, 1898—in large letters, I wrote in the *Spray*'s log book—"Tonight, in latitude 7 degrees 13 minutes north, for the first time in nearly three years I see the north star." The *Spray* was drawing rapidly toward her home destination and every mile that passed I felt more assured that we would make it.

But later that night, sailing in what I thought should be clear waters, I was startled by the sudden flash of breakers on the port bow. It was evidently a coral reef—and a bad reef at that. Worse still, there might be other reefs ahead into which the current would sweep me.

I had not sailed these waters for many years and I cursed the day I had allowed on board the goat that ate my chart. I taxed my memory of sea lore, or wrecks on sunken reefs, but nothing gave me any information. Suddenly a wave greater than the rest threw the *Spray* higher than before and behold, from the crest of it, I realized what made the flashes on the water.

It was the great revolving light on the island of Trinidad, thirty miles away! The orb of the light throwing flashes over the waves had deceived me! But, dear Father Neptune, I would have sworn those reefs existed! All the rest of the night I saw imaginary reefs. I tacked on and off until daylight, not knowing what moment the sloop might crack up on a reef that was real.

But when morning came, and I was past the imaginary danger, I wondered why, so near my destination, I had suddenly begun to misinterpret the language of the sea.

(He takes out a bible, looks at it, then packs it.)

On the fourth of June, 1898, the *Spray* cleared from the United States consulate at Antigua and her license to sail was returned to her for the last time.

(He packs his new sailing papers.)

A few days later the *Spray* was booming joyously along, making her usual good time, when of a sudden she struck the horse latitudes. The *Spray*'s sail flapped limp. Her keel sat still in the water. I had to adopt a philosophical frame of mind or my patience would have given out almost at the harbor entrance!

(He paces in a confined space.)

The term of our probation was eight days. Evening after evening I read by the light of a candle on deck. There was no wind at all, and the sea became smooth and monotonous. For three days I saw a full-rigged ship on the horizon, also becalmed. Sargasso weed scattered over the sea in great fields. Gathered together in it were strange sea-animals, little and big, swimming in and out. The most curious was a tiny seahorse, which I captured and brought home in a bottle.

(He shows us the seahorse.)

But on the 18th of June a gale began to blow from the southwest and soon there was wind enough to spare. Suddenly the *Spray* was jumping like a porpoise over the uneasy waves. Cross seas tumbled about and shook things up with great confusion.

Just as I was thinking about taking in sail, the jib-stay broke at the masthead and fell, jib and all, into the sea. It gave me the strangest sensation to see the bellying sail fall—and where it had been, suddenly to see only space. However, I had the presence of mind to gather it in on the first wave before it was torn to shreds by trailing under the sloop's bottom.

I had to do the work in three minutes or less, and found I had by no means grown stiff-jointed on the voyage. Yes, my health was still good, and I could skip about the decks in a lively manner—but could I climb up the mast to refasten the jib?

King Neptune tested me severely this time, for with the stay gone, the mast itself swayed about like a reed and was not easy to climb. But I managed it. However, had the *Spray*'s mast not been well stepped, it would have been the end for sure.

By the 23rd of June I was at last tired, tired, tired of battling squalls and fretful seas. I had not seen a vessel for days and days, where I had expected the company of at least a schooner now and then. As to the whistling of the wind through the rigging and the slopping of the sea against the sloop's sides, that was well enough in its way, but there was so much of it now, and it lasted so long!

(He looks around the room and stows in cabinets and shelves anything he is not taking on the voyage.)

I was impatient to be home and wished only for a stiff breeze and clear sailing weather. But at noon of that day, suddenly a winterish storm came upon us from the northwest. In the Gulf Stream, late in June, hailstones were pelting the *Spray*! Lightening poured down from the clouds, not in flashes, but in almost continuous streams! Off Fire Island, we were in the midst of a tornado!

It was the climax storm of the voyage, but I saw its character in time to have all snug aboard and receive it under bare poles. Even so, the sloop shivered when it struck her, and she heeled over unwillingly on her beam ends. But, rounding to, she righted and faced out the storm. In the midst of the gale I could do no more than look on—for what is man in a storm like this?

When all was over, I rose and made for a quiet harbor to think things over. Under short sail, the *Spray* reached in for the coast of Long Island, while I sat thinking and watching the lights of coasting-vessels which now began to appear in sight. Reflections of the voyage so nearly finished stole in upon me. Many tunes I had hummed again and again came back to me, and I pondered on the experiences of the voyage of the *Spray*, reaching over three years.

When daylight came, I saw that the sea had changed color from dark green to light. Passing Montauk and Point Judith, I made for Newport. But the *Spray* had one more danger to pass: Newport harbor was mined. The *Spray* hugged the rocks where neither friend nor foe could come if drawing much water. It was close work, but was safe enough, so long as it was the rocks she hugged close, and not the mines.

At last she reached port in safety and there, at 1 A M on June 27, 1898, cast anchor, after a cruise of more than forty-six thousand miles.

(He looks around the room. Everything except what he will take with him is neatly stowed.)

Was the crew well? Was I! I had profited in many ways by the voyage. I had even gained flesh. I actually weighed a pound more than when I sailed from Boston. As for aging, why, the dial of my life was turned back! All my friends said, "Slocum is young again." And so I was.

My ship also was in better condition. She was still sound as a nut and as tight as the best ship afloat. She did not leak a drop—not one drop!

The *Spray* was not quite satisfied till I sailed her around to her birthplace in Fairhaven, Massachusetts. So on July 3rd, with a fair wind, she waltzed beautifully round the coast and up the Acushnet River, where I secured her to the same cedar pile driven in the bank to hold her when she was launched. I could bring her no nearer home.

(He packs his new logbook and closes his sea-bag.)

If the *Spray* discovered no continents on her voyage, it may be there were no more continents to be discovered. She did not seek new worlds, or sail to powwow about the dangers of the seas. The sea has been much maligned.

The *Spray* accomplished all she undertook to do and discovered that even the worst sea is not so terrible to a reasonably well-appointed ship—and to a crew who has had some years of schooling in the laws of Neptune.

(He puts his spectacles in his pocket.)

And now, having endeavored to tell the story of the adventure, I loosen cables, weigh anchor, and set out for new horizons.

(He shows us his proposed journey on the map.)

My destination? Venezuela. Then Brazil. I'm planning to sail down the Orinoco River into the Rio Negro, then down the Amazon into the sea. There will be rapids to shoot, alligators to escape and savages to outrun, but the *Spray* and I are eager to test ourselves on a journey which no one before has ever accomplished.

It will be summer there. I won't need my heavy duds. But my lucky hat, I'll take that with me. It floats better than I do!

(He takes his chewed straw hat off its hook, then looks toward the house.)

Must go.

(He takes some paper money out of a box and puts it in his pocket. Then he takes it out again. He pockets a few dollars, then, with a glance toward the house, leaves the rest of it sticking out of his old log, which he now closes.)

Hettie says she won't come down to the dock to bid me goodbye. So be it. She doesn't realize she's happiest when I'm not at home. So partly I leave—as a present for her. In any journey, there's as much pushing you from behind as beckoning you forward.

(He puts on his straw hat and checks the room once more with his eyes. His gaze lights on the garbage barrel. He considers a moment, then fishes Hettie's cake out and stands looking at it.)

(The lights change. He is frozen in time. These words are projected on the map:)

"Joshua Slocum sailed from Martha's Vineyard on 14 November 1909. He and the *Spray* disappeared at sea and were never seen again."

(The lights come up again on JOSHUA SLOCUM. *He gives one last, not un-fond, look toward the house, puts the cake into his seabag, then says to us:)*

It has been good remembering the voyage alone around the world. Of course, the moment I docked I knew I could never surpass it. But where can you go after you've had your great journey—except sail on?

(He hoists his sack over his shoulder and exits.)

(Blackout)

END OF PLAY

THE SECOND MRS WILSON

THE SECOND MRS WILSON premiered at the Barter Theatre, the State Theatre of Virginia, on 15 September 2001.

CHARACTERS & SETTING

EDITH BOLLING GALT WILSON
IRWIN HOOD "IKE" HOOVER, *Chief Usher*
MARGARET WILSON
WOODROW WILSON
DR CARY GRAYSON
JOSEPH TUMULTY, *President's Secretary*
SENATOR GILBERT M HITCHCOCK, *Nebraska, Democrat*
SENATOR HENRY CABOT LODGE, *Massachusetts, Republican*

Time & Place: The action takes place in the living room and bedroom of the private quarters of the White House in Washington, D C from 28 September 1919 to 4 March 1921.

Setting: the private upstairs living quarters of the White House.

We see the living room and, occupying a smaller space up stage right, the bedroom.

In the living room, double doors leading to the corridor are up left of center. Stage left is a fireplace. Above the mantel is a tall mirror. Upstage right of center, in front of tall arched windows, is a large work desk. On one side of it is an important-looking box called "The Drawer". The center of the room is furnished with a sofa and several chairs.

The bedroom is dominated by the Lincoln bed. Upstage is a heavily draped window. Downstage right is the door to the bathroom.

There is a telephone on the table beside the bed and another downstage left in the living room.

The rooms are pleasant and tastefully decorated with potted palms and lamps (with electric lights) and China vases. Carved moldings define the doors and windows. The colors are harmonious and appealing. This is an informal at-home space for America's head of state, and while the Lincoln Bed is imposing, the rest of the furnishings are of a very human dimension.

These rooms are bright and cheerful when their doors and windows are open to light. When all doors are closed, and the draperies pulled shut, this is an area totally isolated from the outside world.

ACT ONE

(At rise:)

(The stage is dark. The sound of a speeding train is heard. It fades and holds under as a spotlight reveals EDITH BOLLING GALT WILSON, *stage center. A handsome and vivacious woman in her late forties, she says to us:)*

EDITH: I can not imagine why anyone would want to be President! It's a killer job, draining on the mind, the spirit and the body. One gets elected to be the *leader*, and instead finds one's been elected to be the target. ... Being First Lady means you're a target, too. You have to learn to take it—and even, sometimes, to deliberately attract the assaults—so fewer blows will fall upon your husband.

    What a place—the White House. Mansion, monument, fortress—and jail. But for me, speeding back on the train with Woodrow that desperate autumn of 1919, to get him to that place was all I wanted. To get him *home*.

(The sound of the train rises and fades to silence.)

(The lights come up to reveal that EDITH *is in the living quarters of the White House, Sunday morning, September 28, 1919.)*

*(*IRWIN HOOD "IKE" HOOVER, *the Head Usher for the White House, a lean, direct, business-like man in his middle years, enters carrying her suitcases.)*

EDITH: Thank you, Ike.

IKE: Forgive me, Mrs Wilson, but we're all very worried. The President's suddenly breaking off his trip to come back to Washington—that's not like him, not like him at all.

EDITH: I know that, Ike. Believe me, it was almost impossible for Doctor Grayson and me to convince him to do it.

*(*IKE *enters the bedroom and starts turning down the bed.)*

EDITH: *(At the bedroom doorway, she says:)* Oh, don't do that! The President would have a fit if he thought we expected him to get into bed in the middle of the morning.

IKE: I pray he's going to be all right—

EDITH: Of course he will be. Now that we're back home.

IKE: *(Taking an old grey sweater out of a drawer)* Maybe all he'll need will be to relax in his lucky sweater.

(MARGARET WILSON, *the President's daughter, enters just in time to see this. A plain but intelligent woman of thirty-three, she is wearing a hat and coat.*)

MARGARET: You mean he didn't take it with him? (*The thought, to her, is alarming.*)

EDITH: Margaret—

(MARGARET *takes the sweater from* IKE *and holds it.*)

EDITH: Ike, perhaps you could go down to help Doctor Grayson with the President when they arrive.

IKE: Yes, Mrs Wilson. (*He exits.*)

MARGARET: He's not with you?

EDITH: He'll be here in a few minutes. There were some veterans at the station to greet him and he wanted to say a few words to them. I came on ahead—

MARGARET: You never should have let him go on this trip!

EDITH: Have you ever known anyone to say no to your father?

MARGARET: My mother never would have allowed it.

EDITH: I think even your mother would have found it impossible to talk him out of *this* one.

MARGARET: The idea of his going coast to coast trying to get millions of people to write their Senators to vote for our entering the League of Nations—it was a fool's errand!

EDITH: Well, Margaret. Your father is just that kind of idealistic fool.

MARGARET: I don't mean to insult him, but he makes me so angry sometimes!

EDITH: I know what you mean.

MARGARET: Edith, what happened?

EDITH: As usual, your father was driving himself beyond endurance. Speech after speech. Day after day.

MARGARET: From the back of the train?

EDITH: Most of the time. By Seattle, he was exhausted. At Denver, he stumbled going out onto the platform. When he started to speak, he swayed. Then, in the middle of his speech, he stopped, as if he couldn't remember what he was going to say—he, who always knows precisely—. It was awful—.

MARGARET: And no one could make him quit?

EDITH: Doctor Grayson and I both tried. But even in the middle of the worst— two nights ago—he was insisting he wanted to continue.

MARGARET: There was some crisis?

EDITH: Well,—I think you should be told. But this is not to be talked of outside the family—

MARGARET: Don't you think I can keep a confidence?

EDITH: Yes, of course—*(She looks to see if* WILSON *is coming. A pause, then:)* We were crossing the plains, somewhere west of Kansas City. Around three AM your father knocked on the door of my compartment. He looked ill, very ill. He said he had a headache. I went to summon Doctor Grayson. When we returned, your father was sitting with his forehead pressed against the back of a chair, in pain so intense that Cary could do nothing to relieve it. His face was ashen. The whole left side of his body seemed to droop a little—

MARGARET: Oh, no—

EDITH: I only say it to prepare you. When he comes in, you mustn't seem to be shocked by his appearance.

MARGARET: I know how to act—

EDITH: Around dawn, he fell asleep. And then, believe it or not, when I went in a few hours later, he'd gotten up, and dressed, and shaved himself— and intended to speak as planned—though he could hardly stand without collapsing! ...Cary had to tell him, gently, he couldn't allow himself to be seen like that. He told him—he was a very sick man, he would have to return to Washington. ... Your father looked—like a lost little boy when he heard that. *(She breaks out angrily:)* Damn Senator Henry Cabot Lodge and that gang of contrary hyenas in the U S Senate—! Damn them for making it necessary for Woodrow to go on this trip!

MARGARET: I knew it would be an exercise in futility! Soon, when the Senate majority is made up of *women*—which it will be once we get the vote—

EDITH: So you're still campaigning with the Suffragettes—

MARGARET: We're planning to picket the White House.

EDITH: Not if your father has anything to say about it.

MARGARET: He doesn't.

EDITH: Such tactics are unlady-like.

MARGARET: It's not a question of being lady-like or unlady-like. It's a question of fighting for something we women deserve. Just because you've never had to fight for anything—

EDITH: I *am* fighting for something, Margaret. I am fighting—with every ounce of my strength—for your father's health.

(They hear WILSON's *voice as he approaches:)*

WILSON: *(Off)* I see no one took advantage of my absence to change that hideous wallpaper—

(WOODROW WILSON *enters, supported on one side by* IKE, *and on the other by* ADMIRAL CARY GRAYSON, *a slender attractive man in his forties, the President's physician and personal friend.*)

(WILSON *is sixty-four, thin, gaunt, with a long narrow face, strict mouth and piercing eyes. His manner is direct and serious, with a dry intellectual humor which, at the moment, he is attempting to use to minimize his obviously weakened physical state. He seems immensely weary, his left arm and leg seem slightly weak and sometimes his tongue seems to stumble over words.*)

(*As soon as* WILSON *enters,* EDITH *hurries over and helps him off with his coat. They kiss lightly.*)

MARGARET: Father—

WILSON: Margaret. Don't tell me you skipped choir just to greet your old father.

MARGARET: There's no such thing as an indispensable soprano.

WILSON: *(Seeing the sweater)* Ah, there it is! That's the only reason I came back: Forgot my old grey sweater.

(MARGARET *hands him the sweater. He holds it.*)

MARGARET: How is he, Doctor Grayson?

GRAYSON: He's as strong as a horse—a horse who's tried to run the Belmont, the Preakness and the Kentucky Derby in one day.

EDITH: We could do with some tea, I think, Ike.

IKE: Right away, Mrs Wilson. *(To* WILSON*)* Good to have you back, Mister President.

WILSON: Don't worry, Ike. You won't have me around here for very long. This is just a whistle stop before I hit the road again.

(EDITH *and* GRAYSON *exchange a glance.*)

(IKE *begins to exit,* WILSON *looks toward the desk.*)

WILSON: Anything for me in The Drawer—?

IKE: Quite a few things have arrived, sir. *(He exits.)*

(WILSON *starts over to the desk.*)

EDITH: Surely anything in there can wait—!

(WILSON *starts to open a mahogany box with drawers in it which sits on the top of the desk.*)

WILSON: There might be something urgent—*(He sways, seems to lose his balance and has to sit down.)*

MARGARET: Doctor Grayson, is he all right?

WILSON: I'm fine. Only cut short the trip because these two ganged up on me. *(He indicates* EDITH *and* GRAYSON.*)* Problem with having a personal physician is he thinks he can dictate to you. What are you going to do now, Grayson, bleed me?

GRAYSON: I'm going to get you into bed.

WILSON: After church.

EDITH: You are not going to church!

WILSON: I married a heathen!

EDITH: And I married the son of a preacher! You are going to skip one Sunday!

WILSON: Can't. I'm Presbyterian.

MARGARET: *(Rising to leave)* I'll go pray for us all. Right now, you follow Doctor Grayson's orders and rest. Nellie and Jessie told me to tell you—

WILSON: Don't let your sisters come racing down here—

MARGARET: All right. But you telephone them later and let them hear how well you are.

WILSON: *(His voice weak)* I'll do that.

(MARGARET *picks up the sweater which he'd left over the sofa.)*

MARGARET: And if this is what you came back for, at least put it on! *(She hands it to him.)*

WILSON: *(Formally)* Thank you, Margaret.

(WILSON *starts to put it on, but fumbles.* EDITH *moves immediately to help him.* MARGARET *watches* EDITH *help him. Then she goes.)*

EDITH: Now, you are going to rest—

(JOE TUMULTY, WILSON's *devoted secretary, a man in his forties, ebullient, Irish, rushes in, carrying newspapers.)*

TUMULTY: Couldn't stand being away from me, eh, Guv'nor? That's why you came back early!

WILSON: That's it, Tumulty. Couldn't handle the Fourth Estate without your special touch.

TUMULTY: I knew you should have taken me along—*(He gives* EDITH *a remonstrating glance.)*

WILSON: I will, next time.

TUMULTY: Still, you know, Guv'nor, this little setback might just work *for* us! The papers are very sympathetic! Listen: *(He reads:)* "President Wilson, worn out from his efforts in the war, has shown he is willing to sacrifice his health to bring about a just peace." ... Isn't that swell?

EDITH: *(Ironically)* "Swell."

WILSON: Lodge will call me a quitter.

EDITH: Forget Lodge!

TUMULTY: Senator Hitchcock's on his way over—

GRAYSON: You will not see Senator Hitchcock!

WILSON: Not see my minority leader? As Tumulty would say, don't be daft! I need to have Hitchcock fill me in on what's been happening with the Treaty in the Foreign Relations Committee. If I don't know that, I most certainly cannot rest.

GRAYSON: All right, but no one else! ... Mister Tumulty, from now until further notice, the President is cancelling all engagements.

WILSON: Wait a minute! Who's boss here?

GRAYSON: I am. And I say all appointments, from now until further notice, are off.

TUMULTY: But Doc, next week the President is supposed to address the conference of employers and laborers—

GRAYSON: His appearance is cancelled.

TUMULTY: The King and Queen of the Belgians are coming for a State visit—. They're already on the water—

GRAYSON: Tell them to turn around and go home.

TUMULTY: *(To* WILSON*)* But you'll see Mister Lansing won't you? He's bothered about the troubles with Mexico—

WILSON: I have a Secretary of State who's looking for an opportunity to declare war on Mexico! Lansing was born with a sword in his hand. I spent six months in Paris trying to hammer out a peace treaty for Europe. Every time Lansing came up with a suggestion, it sounded like a treaty for war! *(He puts his hand to his throbbing head.)*

EDITH: Mister Wilson will definitely not see Mister Lansing, Tumulty! I am planning to take Mister Wilson somewhere out of the city for a rest—

TUMULTY: But things are piling up—

EDITH: Let them.

TUMULTY: "Let them!" You wouldn't say that if you'd been with the Guv as long as I have—

WILSON: All right, Tumulty!

TUMULTY: Sorry, Guv'nor. ... But what am I going to tell the reporters at the gate?

WILSON: Are there reporters at the gate?

EDITH: When are there not reporters at the gate? Tell them to go away.

TUMULTY: They want to know what you're going to do about the coal miners who're threatening to strike.

EDITH: I thought it was the *steel workers* who were threatening to strike.

TUMULTY: Them, too.

EDITH: We should have turned that train south and headed straight for Peru!

(IKE *enters with tea on a tray. He announces:*)

IKE: Senator Hitchcock is here, Mister President.

WILSON: Send him in, Ike. (*He suddenly puts his hand to his head, racked by a tremendous headache.*)

EDITH: You're trying to kill yourself!

(GRAYSON *comes over and takes* WILSON's *pulse.*)

GRAYSON: Five minutes, Woodrow. That's all. Then I don't care if you're the President of the earth and all the planets—you're going to bed!

(SENATOR GILBERT M HITCHCOCK, *Democrat of Nebraska, tall and capable, enters.*)

HITCHCOCK: How are you, Mister President?

WILSON: Well, my Constitution may be a little weak, but I'm still managing to assert a few Declarations of Independence.

GRAYSON: *(To* HITCHCOCK*)* Five minutes, Senator. Then a medical veto goes into effect.

(EDITH *serves tea to* WILSON *and* HITCHCOCK. *Then she and* GRAYSON *move to the side and confer privately, their eyes always on the President.*)

(TUMULTY *sits at the desk going through newspapers, and marking items.*)

WILSON: So, my friend, how goes the fight? How soon are we going to sign the Treaty and get ourselves into the League?

HITCHCOCK: Wish I had better news, Woodrow.

WILSON: God damn it, it's still Sir Henry Cabot Lodge of Massachusetts, isn't it!

HITCHCOCK: I swear if he says "We must preserve the isolationist ideals of the Monroe Doctrine" one more time, I'm going to punch him in the nose!

WILSON: His Brahmin proboscis is so high in the air you may not be able to reach it.

HITCHCOCK: I hate to say it, but he and his cronies have come up with several more amendments to the League charter.

WILSON: How many does that make?

HITCHCOCK: Fifty.

WILSON: Fifty!

HITCHCOCK: He still insists all he's doing is trying to "improve" it.

WILSON: The hell he is! When are we going to get this thing out of Committee and onto the Senate floor for a vote?

HITCHCOCK: I don't think we're in good enough position for a vote yet.

WILSON: It should be illegal for a Democratic President to be saddled with a Republican Senate!

HITCHCOCK: I agree. Nevertheless, we still have to convert a few more of those elephants across the aisle or we won't make the two-thirds we need to ratify—

WILSON: So nothing has changed since I left—*(He clutches and unclutches his hands, obviously in pain.)* After the carnage we've just been through, how can anyone in his right mind possibly be against creating a world body where all nations can talk to resolve differences rather than having to resort to war?

HITCHCOCK: I honestly don't know. But Woodrow, look. Why don't we let the Senate vote first for accepting the conditions of the peace, and after that take a separate vote on our entering the League of Nations?

WILSON: But there *is* no peace without the League of Nations! What do you want to do, grab any old peace now and the future be damned? If we separate one vote from the other, all hope for our joining the League is lost! Without us in, the League will have no strength, it will collapse—and soon the world will be at war again!

(WILSON's *head is pounding.* EDITH *pours him another cup of tea, but he doesn't touch it.)*

HITCHCOCK: Then, sir, if we could just accept a few of the Republicans' more innocuous amendments—

WILSON: *(At the end of his strength)* How many times do I have to say it? The Senate has to agree to exactly what I signed at Versailles! *(He is pacing back and forth like a caged animal, in pain and trying to hide it.)* Each country can't just pick out the parts of the peace it wishes to agree to and change all the others! If the Senate does not accept the Treaty *exactly as written*, then it has rejected it! I will have to go back to Paris, convene all the other nations, begin again—! It will be chaos! Chaos! *(He seems about to pass out from exhaustion.)*

EDITH: Cary, do something!

GRAYSON: *(Interrupting)* Gentlemen, this meeting is adjourned until further notice.

WILSON: Lodge and his gang are counting on my not having the strength to finish the fight. But I have! I'm going to show them. I—*(His eye catches an item in the newspaper.)* What's this? "President returning to Washington. Complains of abdominal distress. Nervous reaction in his digestive organ." *(In a rage)* Who told them this?!

TUMULTY: I did, Guv'nor. Doctor Grayson's wire said that's what it was, and the reporters kept asking and asking—

WILSON: Which doesn't mean you have to keep telling and telling! Does the whole country have to know the state of affairs in my belly? Don't you know Lodge and his Henchmen are all out there waiting to find my Achilles heel? It's nobody's business how I—*(He begins to choke. He reaches for a teacup. He picks it up in his left hand and tries to raise it to his mouth. It trembles noisily, then suddenly clatters out of his hand onto the floor.)*

(EDITH rushes over.)

EDITH: Enough! You refuse to take orders? You're going to take orders. ... If you'll excuse us, Senator Hitchcock—

HITCHCOCK: I deeply regret if anything I said—

EDITH: No, no. It's Woodrow. He doesn't know when to stop.

HITCHCOCK: *(To WILSON)* Don't worry. You save your strength. We'll carry on for you.

WILSON: Never underestimate the dadblame ornery stubbornness of the opposition!

HITCHCOCK: They certainly don't underestimate yours.

(WILSON has the grace to laugh.)

HITCHCOCK: Take care of yourself, Woodrow. ... As for us, we'll do everything we humanly can. *(He exits.)*

(EDITH and GRAYSON help WILSON to his feet and begin to lead him to the bedroom. TUMULTY rushes over.)

TUMULTY: I apologize for that rot in the papers, Guv'nor. You know I'd never say anything you don't want me to say. It's my big Irish mouth—

WILSON: *(Affectionately)* Just don't put my foot in it.

(EDITH and GRAYSON guide WILSON into the bedroom. In the living room, TUMULTY gathers up the newspapers and goes out.)

(In the bedroom, WILSON starts to lie down, fully clothed.)

GRAYSON: Not *on* the bed, *in* it.

(Even EDITH *looks at* GRAYSON.*)*

GRAYSON: I'm serious.

*(*EDITH *gets out* WILSON's *pajamas.)*

WILSON: I am not going to get into pajamas in the middle of the day!

EDITH: Fine. Get under the covers in your clothes—and when you wake up I'll have them sent to the Salvation Army.

(Reluctantly, WILSON *starts unbuttoning his shirt. Suddenly he sways and holds onto one of the posts of the bed.)*

GRAYSON: Hurts a great deal, does it?

WILSON: *(Lying)* Not at all. You medical men think you possess the wisdom of the ages.

GRAYSON: *(Handing him two pills)* Take these.

WILSON: The wisdom of the ages in two pills. ... Have you anything to cure the Senate?

GRAYSON: These don't work in cases of insanity.

*(*WILSON *takes the pills and the pajamas and exits into the bathroom.)*

*(*EDITH *accompanies* GRAYSON *to the hall door. Quietly, he says to her:)*

GRAYSON: I'll be at the house. Call if you need me.

EDITH: Give my love to Altrude. With the baby due soon, I'm sure she'll be glad to have you back home.

GRAYSON: ...It seems like only yesterday that I invited Altrude to the White House for tea—and suggested that she bring along her guardian.

EDITH: ...And Woodrow got rained out of his golf game...so you insisted that he join us.

GRAYSON: How you cheered him up! I hadn't seen him laugh like that since before he lost Ellen.

EDITH: Wish I knew now how to keep him smiling.

GRAYSON: That Woodrow will come back, you'll see.

(A cloud crosses EDITH's *face.* GRAYSON *pats her shoulder.)*

GRAYSON: If anything happens, I can be here in five minutes.

(She nods. GRAYSON *exits.)*

*(*EDITH *returns to the bedroom and pulls back the covers of the bed.* WILSON *comes out of the bathroom in his pajamas.)*

WILSON: I guess I'm all in....

EDITH: You're going to be fine. All you need is rest, a really good rest.

(WILSON *lies back on the bed.* EDITH *starts to cover him. He suddenly rises.*)

EDITH: What is it?

WILSON: I was just thinking about that young soldier in the hospital at Verdun, the one with the red hair. Remember him?

EDITH: Yes.

WILSON: I wonder if he survived the amputation.

EDITH: I don't know. I hope—

WILSON: I promised him I'd read every day from his Bible. Where is it?

EDITH: I'll find it. I'll read something for you.

(WILSON *lies down again.*)

EDITH: Any particular passage?

WILSON: *(Wearily)* ..."Leadeth me beside the still waters. Restoreth my soul..."

EDITH: I'll mention to God that I'm reading it on your behalf.

(EDITH *covers* WILSON *with the coverlet.*)

WILSON: Thank you, Ellen. *(Then, quickly realizing his mistake)* Edith! ... Thank you, *Edith!*

EDITH: Sleep well, my darling. *(She kisses his throbbing head then goes quietly into the living room. Once there, she turns to us and says:)* All right, he called me by his first wife's name. I don't mind. You can't erase a twenty-nine year marriage with a fledgling one of less than four. *(She picks up a photo of Ellen.)* Ellen died, suddenly, early in Woodrow's first term in the White House. But she's the one who saw him through being President of Princeton and Governor of New Jersey. She's the one who bore him three daughters. I've had no children—with Woodrow or with my first husband. I looked forward to being a mother to Woodrow's girls, but they're so grown up, two of them married, and all three with lives of their own— *(Looking for the bible, she picks up a pile of official papers on* WILSON's *desk.)* Oh, the people really want their money's worth from their President! That's why they make him have his office in his home! ...I'll have to get him away to rest. Perhaps we can go back to the place where we spent our honeymoon, the Homestead Hotel, in Virginia—the state where both of us were born.

Can you imagine what it's like to be on a honeymoon with the President of the United States? Guests winking and smiling at you in the lobby. Reporters stalking you from behind potted palms. Waiters coming up to serve you breakfast wearing silly grins. Secret Servicemen in every corner. Woodrow was so demonstrative the morning after our wedding night that it was two weeks before I could look the Secret Servicemen in the eye!

(IKE *enters with luggage, puts the pieces down and starts to open them.* EDITH *says quietly:*)

EDITH: I'll take care of those.

(IKE *exits.* EDITH *opens the suitcases and continues searching. She comes upon a packet of letters tied with a lavender ribbon.*)

EDITH: If you could hear the things Woodrow wrote me before we were married! You wouldn't think it to look at him, but he is a tremendously passionate man! And so decisive! I'd hardly ever been alone in a room with him when, two months after we met, he suddenly proposed!

I didn't know what to say! I wasn't ready for—that kind—of a relationship. Twelve years of marriage to a jewelry store owner had made me delighted with my seven years of independent widowhood! But Woodrow wanted—and soon *I* wanted—and so, finally, I said yes.

There was hell to pay, of course, when the President of the United States said he wanted to remarry—with his wife not dead eighteen months and the bride-to-be sixteen years younger than the groom. I'm not sure anyone would have minded if the President took a *mistress*. But a new *wife*! ...The Democratic Party nearly had a fit! There was an election coming up. How would the people take it?

Well, the people took it just fine! They re-elected him—in spite of his new First Lady. And they understood when the President who had promised to keep them out of the war had to take us in. Night after night we'd sit here. I'd decode the messages from the front and read them to him. How we rejoiced at the cables which told about our victories! ... Until the casualty figures came in. (*Searching in a suitcase, she comes up with the battered khaki-covered bible.*) Then, at last, the war was over! The Europeans cheered him as a messiah when he went over to hammer out the peace! The Americans cheered him when he returned with the Treaty and his vision of a federation of nations which could end wars forever. But the American Senate—! Selfish, myopic, unprincipled men! They're the ones who forced him to go on this trip! And look what I've brought back with me. A man on the brink of—. No. No. He's going to get well.

(*Lights change. Time passes.*)

EDITH: We've been back four days now, and each day he seems a little stronger. Tomorrow morning I'll talk him into going on vacation. ... I shall lead him beside the still waters... Wherever those might be—

(EDITH *hears a sound from* WILSON's *room. As she starts to go quickly toward it, she hears him weakly but urgently call her name:*)

WILSON: Edith—

(EDITH *enters the bedroom. She finds* WILSON *sitting on the side of the bed in pajamas. He is in great pain. He is massaging the back of his head.*)

WILSON: Didn't mean to wake you—

EDITH: I wasn't asleep. What is it?

WILSON: Pain. Oh, my God. The pain—

EDITH: Where?

WILSON: Head. Whole Head. ...Feel—bad. All over. Nauseous...

EDITH: I'll call Cary—

(EDITH *picks up the telephone at* WILSON's *bedside. He stops her.*)

WILSON: No. The other. Don't go through the White House operator.

EDITH: Sit there. (*She starts toward the living room.*)

WILSON: To tell the truth, I've never felt so awful in my life.

(EDITH *hurries into the living room and, stopping only to lock the corridor door, picks up the telephone on the downstage left table.*)

EDITH: Two seven four six.

(EDITH *waits impatiently for a response.*)

(*Meanwhile, in the bedroom,* WILSON *begins to feel more nauseous. He rises unsteadily and tries to put on his slippers, but feels too dizzy.*)

(*Steadying himself by holding onto pieces of furniture,* WILSON *tries to make his way toward the bathroom.*)

(*In the living room,* EDITH *says urgently into the telephone:*)

EDITH: Cary? Please. Hurry over.

(WILSON *enters the bathroom and puts on the light, leaving the door open.*)

EDITH: His head hurts very badly. He feels dizzy. Nauseous—

(*Suddenly,* EDITH *hears a crash.* WILSON *has collapsed across the bathroom threshold, hitting his head on the door jamb. She cries into the telephone:*)

EDITH: Hurry—!

(EDITH *hangs up the receiver and rushes back into the bedroom.*)

(EDITH *sees* WILSON *lying on the floor. She calls:*)

EDITH: Woodrow—! Woodrow—!

(WILSON *doesn't respond. He is unconscious.* EDITH *doesn't know what to do. She touches his face. She sees he is still breathing. She sees there is a gash above his eye where he has hit his head. She tries to lift him up to get him to the bed, but he is too heavy.*)

(EDITH *runs to the bedside telephone and picks up the receiver. She paces nervously, but when the White House Operator comes on the line, she controls herself and says in a calm voice:)*

EDITH: Ike Hoover, please.

(A moment. EDITH looks concernedly toward WILSON. He has not moved.)

EDITH: Ike? *(Forcing herself to keep control)* Would you kindly come to the President's room? ...Yes. At once, please. ... Thank you.

(EDITH replaces the receiver then rushes back to WILSON. Not quite knowing what to do, she gets a cloth, wets it and starts to wash the blood from the gash on his face.)

(There is a knock on the outer door. She rushes to it and asks, through the door:)

EDITH: Yes?

IKE: *(O S)* It's Ike Hoover, Mrs Wilson.

(EDITH opens the door, admits him, and locks the door behind him.)

EDITH: I need your help, Ike. The President has had an accident.

(IKE follows EDITH into the bedroom. He is shocked to see the President lying motionless on the floor.)

IKE: What happened—?

EDITH: *(Not answering)* We have to get him onto the bed—

(Together they drag and lift WILSON onto the bed. He is still unconscious. EDITH straightens the covers.)

EDITH: Ike, I need your promise that you will say nothing about this—nothing—to anyone.

IKE: I swear, Mrs Wilson.

EDITH: We don't want to alarm everyone unnecessarily.

(There is a knock at the corridor door. IKE starts toward it.)

EDITH: Only open it if it's Doctor Grayson.

(IKE nods. As he goes to the door, EDITH looks toward the nightstand and says, partly to herself, partly to us:)

EDITH: I should have known there was something wrong. He forgot to wind his watch. He never forgets to wind his watch...

(IKE admits GRAYSON.)

(GRAYSON hurries into the bedroom carrying his black bag. EDITH indicates that IKE may go. He exits.)

(GRAYSON checks WILSON's vital signs.)

GRAYSON: What happened?

EDITH: He was in the bathroom. He fell and hit his head.

(GRAYSON *checks the wound.*)

GRAYSON: Not deep.

(GRAYSON *continues to examine* WILSON.)

EDITH: But it must have knocked him out—

(GRAYSON *raises* WILSON's *right arm and drops it. He does the same with the left. He murmurs.*)

GRAYSON: No. No, I don't think so. (*He raises the lids and looks into* WILSON's *eyes.*) This is exactly what I was afraid of. Exactly what I've been trying to prevent for months... (*He says, trying to conceal his own emotion:*) I'm almost certain, Edith, that he's had a stroke.

EDITH: Dear God, no—!

GRAYSON: I'm afraid it looks more severe than the others.

EDITH: There were others?

GRAYSON: It's what was beginning to happen in Kansas. And there were a few, minor ones, every now and then,—over the past thirty years.

EDITH: I didn't know—

GRAYSON: He didn't want to worry you.

EDITH: The left side of his face looks all sunken!

GRAYSON: It affects the facial muscles.

EDITH: What are you going to do?

GRAYSON: I'm afraid there's nothing we can do except wait till he regains consciousness.

EDITH: Wait—! How long—?

GRAYSON: There's no way of knowing.

EDITH: You mean—there's no way of knowing if he'll ever regain consciousness at all?

GRAYSON: Let's not imagine the worst.

EDITH: If he *does* come to—will he be—impaired?

GRAYSON: Can't tell, Edith. (*He tests* WILSON's *limbs again.*) I think it likely that there's some paralysis.

EDITH: Oh, no—. Cary, no—

(*There is a knock at the hall door.* EDITH *goes into the living room and asks:*)

EDITH: Who is it?

TUMULTY: (*Through the door*) Tumulty.

EDITH: *(Through the door)* What is it, Tumulty?

TUMULTY: *(Through the door)* Some press boys and I were just going home when we saw Doctor Grayson's car in the drive. Is everything all right?

(GRAYSON *comes into the living room, closing the bedroom door behind him.* EDITH *opens the door to the corridor.* TUMULTY *enters.*)

TUMULTY: Is anything wrong?

GRAYSON: No, no. The President's had another one of his spells, that's all.

TUMULTY: Is it serious?

GRAYSON: Just—just a little setback, that's all.

TUMULTY: I'll go in and ask him if there's anything I can do for him—

EDITH: No—!

(TUMULTY *gives her a look.* GRAYSON *covers for her.*)

GRAYSON: He's asleep. We don't want to wake him.

TUMULTY: Right. I know how the boss is when somebody wakes him. You tell him I'll be saying some Hail Marys for him.

EDITH: We will, Tumulty. Thank you.

(TUMULTY *goes out.* EDITH *locks the door behind him.*)

EDITH: Thank you, Cary.

GRAYSON: The last thing we need is to have the President's condition diagnosed in the press before we know what's going on.

(EDITH *and* GRAYSON *go back into the bedroom.* WILSON *has not moved.*)

GRAYSON: Edith, I'm going to call in a couple of specialists—

EDITH: Can't you treat him yourself?

GRAYSON: I'm a general practitioner. He has to be seen by the best doctors in this field.

EDITH: But—

GRAYSON: Don't worry. I'll get men who'll be absolutely discreet.

(GRAYSON *picks up the bedside telephone.* EDITH *stops him.*)

EDITH: No. Use the outside line.

(GRAYSON *starts toward the door which leads to the living room.*)

EDITH: Oh, Cary—are we going to lose him?

GRAYSON: We'll do everything we can—

(*He enters the living room, turning back to say, more to himself than to anyone else:*)

GRAYSON: Goddam you, Woodrow! I should never have let you set off on that blasted journey! *(He picks up the downstage telephone and starts making calls.)*

(EDITH *stands at the bed looking at her husband. She picks up his watch and clutches it in her hands).*

(WILSON, *his face pale and sunken, lies on the bed, absolutely still.)*

(There is a knock on the door. GRAYSON *opens it.* IKE *enters and wheels a tank of oxygen into the bedroom. Then he and* GRAYSON *exit.)*

(Lights change. Time passes.)

(EDITH *returns to the living room and paces, continually looking in at the bedroom. Numbly, she says to us:)*

EDITH: Three days! And no movement, no reactions, nothing. Cary has moved in down the hall, but neither of us has slept since this began. There's this awful stillness. This awful, awful stillness. I keep waiting for Woodrow to wake up and tell us what to do. But he just lies there! ...The only one we're allowing to see him is Margaret.

(MARGARET *enters through the living room and goes into the bedroom.)*

EDITH: Tumulty comes by once an hour wanting a bulletin on the President's health for the latest editions. Cary keeps saying, "It's nervous exhaustion"—but the newspapers say that Lodge believes nothing's wrong at all, that Woodrow's in here sulking! ... Meanwhile, Secretary of State Lansing has summoned Grayson to come see him in his office. He's there now. He's been there for two hours! What's going on there?

(MARGARET *comes out of the bedroom and into the living room, deeply disturbed.)*

MARGARET: The morning papers say my father's so anxious to work you can hardly keep him in bed—and he isn't even conscious!

EDITH: Margaret, listen. To say the President is comatose would put the nation in a panic. All sorts of things would begin to happen that may not need to happen at all! Suppose we let it be known that he's in this state,—then in a few hours he wakens and totally recovers. We'd have done him irreparable political damage. We must protect him when he can't protect himself. Do you understand?

MARGARET: This isn't what my mother would have done.

EDITH: Fortunately for her, she never had to make such a decision.

MARGARET: He ought to be in a hospital!

EDITH: Doctor Grayson feels he can be just as well cared for here.

MARGARET: This house killed my mother, and now it's killing my father.

(There is a knock on the corridor door. EDITH *opens it and* TUMULTY *enters.)*

TUMULTY: The papers want some word for the afternoon editions.

EDITH: *(With a glance at* MARGARET:*)* The word is—no change.

(MARGARET *makes a gesture of frustration, then exits.)*

(TUMULTY *holds out some documents and asks:)*

TUMULTY: What am I going to do with these?

EDITH: What are they?

TUMULTY: Appropriations. Two dams, three bridges. The President has to sign them by midnight tonight.

EDITH: *(For a moment,* EDITH *looks at him helplessly, then:)* ...What happens if he doesn't sign them?

TUMULTY: They become law without his signature.

EDITH: *(After a moment:)* ...Was he in favor of them?

TUMULTY: Yes.

EDITH: ...Then I guess they'll become law without his signature.

TUMULTY: That's not the way he works!

EDITH: Well, that's the way he's working this time.

TUMULTY: If I could only see him for a second—

(GRAYSON *enters, agitated.)*

TUMULTY: Just for a second!

GRAYSON: No, Tumulty. And tell those ravenous hounds at the gate I'm not going to be giving them new bulletins on the President's health every five minutes!

(Upset, TUMULTY *exits.* EDITH *locks the door after him.)*

EDITH: Cary! What happened?

GRAYSON: I got over to Lansing's office. Vice President Marshall and the entire Cabinet was with him.

EDITH: The entire Cabinet—!

GRAYSON: Every blessed one of them. Sitting around a table—and me standing before them, on the carpet.

EDITH: What did they want?

GRAYSON: Lansing said that, since the Vice President was reluctant to do it, as Secretary of State it was his duty to get everyone together to make sure they were clear on what the Constitution says about Presidential disability.

EDITH: So the wolves are already at the door—! And from Woodrow's own party!

GRAYSON: I told them I thought such a meeting was premature—and in the worst possible taste.

EDITH: Good taste was never one of Lansing's strong suits.

GRAYSON: He insisted on reading the damned thing aloud—the part where it says if the President is unable to discharge his duties the office shall be assumed by the Vice President.

EDITH: By Marshall—!

GRAYSON: Don't worry, Marshall knows he couldn't handle it. He said so.

EDITH: Thank heaven for the meek who do not seek to inherit the earth.

GRAYSON: If it weren't for the Vice President's reluctance, I think Lansing would make some move. He senses there's an emergency.

EDITH: He's always hoping.

GRAYSON: They asked me point blank if Woodrow was incapacitated.

EDITH: What did you tell them?

GRAYSON: *(Agitated, with guilt)* I tried to avoid the question. They asked me if he was capable of carrying out his duties. I said he was extremely run down. I found myself babbling on about how many leaders in the past have sustained great physical impairment without it in the least impairing their mental processes. So, of course, they asked me if he was impaired!

EDITH: What did you answer?

GRAYSON: God help me—I said his mind was clear as a bell! *(He puts his head in his hands.)*

EDITH: They must have backed you into it.

GRAYSON: Lansing said, in that case, he would like to come by at once to consult Woodrow on the Mexican crisis!

EDITH: If only the world would hold still for a moment!

GRAYSON: What was I to say? "Gentlemen: For three days now you've had no President?" ... I don't know how much longer we can keep the country from knowing, Edith. The Cabinet isn't prying. They are absolutely right! But suppose we let them know how things are and they put that incompetent Marshall in Woodrow's chair and then moments later Woodrow wakens to find out he's been removed from office?

EDITH: Don't you think, in such a case, that Marshall would step aside and Woodrow would be reinstated?

GRAYSON: I very much doubt it. There's something about physical disability—

the impression of it seems to stick. People feel, if it happened once, it can happen again. In a public servant, bad health is the one unforgivable sin.

EDITH: *(Sitting down, dejected)* Then it looks like we're going to have to let people know, and if they remove him, they remove him. Maybe it's all for the best. Maybe, if he comes to, and he doesn't have all these burdens on him, he'll have some chance at life!

GRAYSON: Do you think that's what he would call living?

(EDITH *knows he's right. She looks discouraged, extremely depressed.*)

EDITH: But, Cary, how much longer can we hold them off!

(Suddenly, in the bedroom, WILSON *makes a sound and stirs.)*

*(*EDITH *and* GRAYSON *rush into the bedroom.* WILSON *is making a sound in his throat, as if coming out of a deep sleep.)*

EDITH: Woodrow! Woodrow—!

GRAYSON: Woodrow, can you hear me?

WILSON: *(With muffled speech)* I'm—not—deaf—

GRAYSON: What?

EDITH: *(Joyously)* He says he's not deaf!

(EDITH *and* GRAYSON *both grin with relief.*)

GRAYSON: Well, at least you haven't lost your sense of humor!

WILSON: How long have I—?

GRAYSON: Long enough to give Edith and me a few minutes peace.

EDITH: Are you in any pain?

(WILSON *grunts in the negative and croaks out:*)

WILSON: Wa—ter—

EDITH: *(Bending down to hear him)* He'd like a drink of water.

GRAYSON: That's a good sign.

(EDITH *brings* WILSON *a glass of water with a straw, raises his head and helps him drink. Some water spills down the side of his face. She wipes it.)*

WILSON: *(His speech slurred, his voice barely audible)* What—happ—?

GRAYSON: ...You've had a—a seizure, Woodrow. You know. You've had this sort of thing before.

WILSON: My arm. Can't—seem to move—my left arm—

GRAYSON: It's been affected—

WILSON: And my left leg—

GRAYSON: For the time being, we're going to have to cancel your appearance in the Boston Marathon.

(EDITH *is standing on the left side of his bed. Suddenly* WILSON *seems agitated and calls:*)

WILSON: E—dith! Where's E—dith!

EDITH: I'm here, my darling.

(*Impatiently he slaps the bed with his right hand. She comes around to that side and bends down to hear him say:*)

WILSON: Don't...let...them...take...it...away... (*The effort is too much. His eyes close. He is exhausted.*)

(*Aside,* EDITH *whispers to* GRAYSON)

EDITH: "Don't let them take it away." ... What is he talking about?

GRAYSON: (*After a pause*) ...The Presidency.

(EDITH *and* GRAYSON *exchange a glance.*)

(*There's a knock on the corridor door*)

WILSON: Who's that?

EDITH: I don't know—

WILSON: Don't let anyone see me like this—!

GRAYSON: I'll go.

EDITH: I'll stay with Woodrow.

GRAYSON: (*Aside to* EDITH, *quietly*) Stand on his right side, Edith. ... I think he's blind in his left eye. (*Closing the bedroom door behind him, he goes into the living room.*)

(*Speaking with difficulty,* WILSON *says to* EDITH:)

WILSON: Guess you made a mistake. Should have chosen a younger man for a second husband.

EDITH: When I want your advice on my marital affairs, Mister President, I will ask for it. ... I happen to think I showed very good taste.

WILSON: Not as good as mine...

(*She clutches his right hand. He falls asleep.*)

(*Closing the bedroom door behind her,* EDITH *goes into the living room where* GRAYSON *has admitted* TUMULTY *who is carrying official documents and a bunch of yellow roses.*)

TUMULTY: (*To* EDITH:) Doc Grayson says I can tell the papers there's some improvement.

EDITH: There is, thank heaven.

TUMULTY: Then my Hail Marys worked! Been to hell and gone looking for his favorite kind of posies—*(He starts toward the bedroom.)*

GRAYSON: *(Barring the way)* Sorry, Joe. Have to keep strictly to my rule of no visitors.

TUMULTY: But I promised I'd tell the boys at the gate how he looks!

GRAYSON: I'll keep you informed on how he looks.

TUMULTY: Margaret saw him—

GRAYSON: She's family.

TUMULTY: I'm like family!

GRAYSON: I understand. But for the moment the President is going to be seeing no one.

TUMULTY: If he doesn't see my mug, he'll think I don't care!

EDITH: Don't worry. I'll tell him.

(Reluctantly, TUMULTY *hands* EDITH *the roses.)*

TUMULTY: But I have to find out if he wants the budget brought to Congress now or wait till after the Christmas recess.

EDITH: I'll ask him.

TUMULTY: And is he still planning to veto prohibition?

EDITH: I'll find that out, too, and let you know. *(She gets a notepad and begins to write things down.)*

TUMULTY: But I always go through these things with the Guv'nor!

GRAYSON: Well, for now, it looks like you're going to be going through them with the Guv'nor's wife.

TUMULTY: With the Missus!

EDITH: It seems the only thing to do.

GRAYSON: Yes, I think that's the best plan. You go over things with Mrs Wilson, she'll take them in to the President, then tell you his decisions.

TUMULTY: Holy Jeezus! *(To* EDITH:*)* You think you can get the drift of all this stuff?

EDITH: After my first husband died, I did co-manage his jewelry store.

TUMULTY: The country's not a jewelry store!

*(*EDITH *holds out her hand for* TUMULTY *to give her the papers. He asks:)*

TUMULTY: Do you want me to explain these things to you?

EDITH: Thanks. I think I can manage.

(GRAYSON *and* TUMULTY *start to exit. On the way out,* TUMULTY *says to* GRAYSON:)

TUMULTY: Never thought I'd see the day when I'd be handing Presidential papers over to a dame!

(GRAYSON *and* TUMULTY *exit.*)

(EDITH *looks at the official documents* TUMULTY *gave her. She reads off some titles:*)

EDITH: "Report of the ad-hoc committees on non-navigational uses of international waterways." ... "Intermediate pro forma propositions regarding litigable confutations." ... "Conclusions preceding a judicatory concurrence on pending legislatory policies of *laissez-faire*." ...Good God! At least in the jewelry business they wrote in English!

(*She continues to read. Night falls.*)

(*Lights change. Time passes.*)

(WILSON *calls from the bedroom:*)

WILSON: Edith—! Edith—!

(EDITH *hurries into the bedroom.*)

WILSON: Get them out of here! Get them out!

EDITH: Who, dear?

WILSON: Those people in the corner!

(WILSON *gestures.* EDITH *inspects.*)

EDITH: There's no one here, Woodrow.

WILSON: Lodge sent them! They're spying on me! They want to know everything about me!

EDITH: Ssh...ssh... I'll get them out. I'll see they don't come back. You're safe, my love. Sleep now...

(EDITH *calms* WILSON *and returns to the living room.*)

(*The lights change. Time passes.*)

(EDITH *says to us:*)

EDITH: His mind plays tricks. It's frightening. Sometimes he's perfectly lucid, sometimes he's not rational at all. He makes mistakes on words. Has memory lapses. His thoughts get muddled. And the worst thing is, I have to keep everyone from knowing!

(*Lights change. Another day dawns.*)

(TUMULTY *enters.* EDITH *says:*)

EDITH: What's on the docket for today?

TUMULTY: *(Aside)* She has a docket! *(To* EDITH:*)* We need to get the President's approval on immigration quotas.

EDITH: I'll go over it with him.

TUMULTY: Lloyd George needs an answer on his letter about Great Britain's entry into the League.

EDITH: You draft a reply, I'll get the President to approve.

TUMULTY: And this is right up your alley: Is the President going to reiterate his support for Woman Suffrage?

EDITH: He won't if those women don't stop marching up and down in front of the White House!

(MARGARET *enters, wearing a bright red "Votes for Women" sash across her bodice.*)

EDITH: Are you marching with those women?!

MARGARET: I'm their leader.

(TUMULTY *shakes his head and exits.*)

EDITH: Good heavens!

MARGARET: I believe so much in this cause! We would like a statement—

EDITH: I already told you! Your father is in favor of your ideals, but not of your methods! He has nothing more to add on the subject.

MARGARET: We're not asking for a statement from father. We want one from you.

EDITH: From me!

MARGARET: You're an independent woman. Don't you want independence for all of us?

EDITH: I want independence for those who know how to use it.

MARGARET: We only have three more states to go! A word from you could help get ratification of the Amendment!

EDITH: I don't take public positions! I do my best to serve your father, nothing more.

MARGARET: *(Giving up, gracefully)* Well, even if you won't speak out, I have something for you.

(MARGARET *takes out a red "Votes for Women" sash.* EDITH *doesn't move to take it.*)

MARGARET: You don't have to put it on, Edith. Just wear it in your mind. *(She drapes the sash over the mantel and leaves.)*

(EDITH *looks at the sash, then turns to us and says:*)

EDITH: All I need is to involve Woodrow in another controversy! I feel as though I'm walking on a tightrope. And everyone's waiting for me—hoping for me—to fall! I just keep praying that no emergencies come up which need Woodrow's reason and wisdom!

(EDITH *returns to work.*)

(*Lights change. Time passes.*)

(TUMULTY *enters hurriedly.*)

TUMULTY: Mrs Wilson—

EDITH: *(Startled)* Yes—?

TUMULTY: The miners went on strike just before dawn this morning. The Attorney General needs the Guv'nor's permission to call out the National Guard to work the mines.

EDITH: The National Guard! But there could be confrontations! Riots—!

TUMULTY: There'll be riots if folks are freezing. To mobilize the Guard we need the President's signature—

EDITH: His signature—*(This poses problems.)*

TUMULTY: Something wrong?

EDITH: No, no. I'll get it for you.

TUMULTY: Can't I—?

EDITH: Tumulty, how many times must I say it? The President still has great affection for you but he's not allowed to see you! Can't you understand—?

TUMULTY: "Understand!" I'm not some mick from the Old Country! I was born in New Jersey!

EDITH: What does that have to do with anything?

TUMULTY: I trained as a lawyer, Mrs Wilson! You treat me like some Irish pol!

EDITH: And you treat me as if I were a three year old!

(*She is about to go into the bedroom when* IKE *enters.*)

IKE: Excuse me, Mrs Wilson. Senator Hitchcock would like to see you.

EDITH: Send him in, Ike.

(IKE *exits.* HITCHCOCK *enters.*)

HITCHCOCK: Sorry to bother you, Mrs Wilson—

EDITH: Another crisis?

HITCHCOCK: Senator Lodge has come up with a new list of reservations to the League Charter.

EDITH: *(She looks at the list he hands her.)* All these?!

HITCHCOCK: See, will you, if you can get Woodrow to accept a few of them? There has to be some give and take or we'll get no place.

EDITH: I'll do my best. *(She goes into the bedroom.)*

(In the living room, TUMULTY *looks out the window and says to* HITCHCOCK:*)*

TUMULTY: It's a wonder Mrs Wilson isn't out there marching with those ladies.

HITCHCOCK: She's not a Suffragette.

TUMULTY: Yeah, that's right. She doesn't have to *vote* for President, she *is* one.

(Inside the bedroom, EDITH *guides* WILSON's *hand as he starts to sign the executive order.)*

WILSON: I don't like calling out the Guard. Make sure they don't use force except as a last resort.

EDITH: I'll tell the Attorney General. ... Now just dot the "i."

WILSON: It looks like noodles! It looks as though I'm *non compos mentis*!

EDITH: Anyone who can say *non compos mentis* isn't.

*(*WILSON *hands* EDITH *the document.)*

WILSON: There. That's it.

EDITH: Not quite.

WILSON: There's more?

EDITH: *(Taking out the pages* HITCHCOCK *gave her)* Woodrow,—the Republicans are proposing a few reservations to the League charter.

WILSON: "The Republicans." You mean Lodge! Say so! What does the old buzzard want now?

EDITH: Some deletions.

WILSON: De-le—?

EDITH: You know. Not things to add. Things to cut out.

WILSON: We mustn't have holes in the paper! Don't let him make holes in the paper! No holes! No holes!

*(*WILSON *is immensely upset. In the living room,* HITCHCOCK *and* TUMULTY *can hear the sounds and exchange a concerned look.)*

EDITH: Woodrow, please! Hitchcock and Tumulty will hear you!

WILSON: No holes in my League! No holes!

EDITH: If you don't behave, I swear I'll go out and start marching with those women!

(Leaving WILSON *tremendously upset,* EDITH *returns to the living room.* WILSON *can still be heard crying "No holes!"* EDITH *hands the signed executive order to* TUMULTY:*)*

EDITH: Here's the authorization to call out the National Guard. But make sure they use restraint.

TUMULTY: Is that your say so or the Guv'nor's?

EDITH: The President's. *(She turns to* HITCHCOCK:*)* I'm sorry, Senator Hitchcock. The President will not accept any of Lodge's deletions.

HITCHCOCK: *(Disappointed)* We'll make every attempt to follow his instruction. *(He can hear* WILSON *still crying: "No holes!")* How is he feeling?

EDITH: Never better! He'll be back in fighting shape in no time.

HITCHCOCK: *(Concerned)* For all our sakes, I hope so.

(On their way out, TUMULTY, *looking at the executive order, says to* HITCHCOCK:*)*

TUMULTY: Holy gee! It looks like noodles!

*(*HITCHCOCK *and* TUMULTY *exit.)*

(Lights change. EDITH *goes back into the bedroom and confronts* WILSON:*)*

EDITH: How can I help you if you don't help me!

WILSON: I don't want you helping me! I want to do things on my own.

EDITH: In that case, take this. *(She holds out a small rubber ball.)*

WILSON: No.

EDITH: You won't improve if you don't do your exercises. *(She puts the ball into his left hand.)* Now—open, close, open, close—

WILSON: The League I want to join is not the Major League!

*(*WILSON *throws the ball across the floor.* EDITH *retrieves it, hands it to him and says:)*

EDITH: Mister President, play ball!

(Upset, WILSON *sullenly practices opening and closing his hand around the ball as* EDITH *returns to the living room.)*

(Lights change. Time passes.)

(As IKE *wheels an armless wheelchair into the bedroom, then exits,* EDITH *says to us:)*

EDITH: I have to be so careful choosing what to say to Woodrow and what not to. His emotions are always bubbling just below the surface, ready to burst out. If I say the wrong thing, I risk his having a relapse. He begins to tremble, his blood pressure begins to rise. I'm so afraid he'll have another stroke!

(Suddenly, very close, there is the loud boom of a cannon.)

(In the bedroom, WILSON *cries out:)*

WILSON: War—! *(Very upset, he begins to beat the bed with his hand.)* War! War!

*(*EDITH *rushes into the bedroom and tries to calm him.)*

WILSON: I told them what would happen if they didn't ratify the Treaty! I told them America was no longer safe from attack!

(The cannon booms again.)

EDITH: I'll get Cary. He'll give you something to calm you.

WILSON: I don't want something to calm me!

*(*EDITH *hurries to the living room phone and says into it:)*

EDITH: Please ring Doctor Grayson. ... Cary? Please come—

*(*TUMULTY *enters.* EDITH *puts down the receiver.)*

TUMULTY: How does the Guv'nor like it? I arranged for them to celebrate the first anniversary of the signing of the Armistice across the way in Lafayette Park so he could hear!

EDITH: You arranged—!

(The cannon continues to boom slowly through the following scene, eventually reaching the count of eleven.)

TUMULTY: I know he'll want to say something on this occasion. I've told the papers he'll have a statement.

EDITH: The President will have no statement.

TUMULTY: Well, just in case—. I've prepared a little something—*(He takes a paper out of his pocket.)*

EDITH: The President will have nothing to say.

TUMULTY: He needs to show that he's still in charge of things. He needs more public presence! The way you keep him holed up here—!

EDITH: That is quite enough!

TUMULTY: On this day of all days!

EDITH: He doesn't even know what day it is!

TUMULTY: You don't even tell him what day it is?! What is he in there, a prisoner?

EDITH: *(Indicating he should leave)* If that is all—

TUMULTY: How much else are you not telling him?

EDITH: He knows everything he needs to know.

TUMULTY: I can't promise the papers a statement and then not come out with a statement. It won't look good.

EDITH: That's your problem, isn't it. You have no right to speak on his behalf!

TUMULTY: And what about you?

EDITH: Mister Tumulty, that is quite enough!

(Outside, a Chorus begins to sing "Over There". It is moving, stirring. EDITH fears for WILSON's reaction.)

(EDITH turns and exits into the bedroom.)

(Under his breath, TUMULTY hurls after EDITH.)

TUMULTY: Bitch! *(He exits.)*

(In the bedroom, WILSON asks:)

WILSON: Edith—! What were those guns?

EDITH: A salute—to a special occasion.

WILSON: What occasion?

EDITH: ...It's the anniversary of the signing of the Armistice.

WILSON: *(With great emotion)* One year since the Armistice was signed and we're still tech-ni-cal-ly—we're still at war! ...The peace—I'm never going to manage it...

EDITH: You are, my darling....

(The Chorus continues singing.)

WILSON: It's slipping away. Everything. Everything. Slipping away—! *(He breaks down and weeps helplessly in her arms.)*

(GRAYSON enters and gives him a shot. GRAYSON comforts EDITH as WILSON falls asleep. EDITH closes the curtains and lies down on the couch at the foot of Wilson's bed as the bedroom darkens.)

(The lights change.)

(GRAYSON goes into the living room. After a moment, HITCHCOCK enters.)

HITCHCOCK: Ah, Doctor Grayson. ... How is the President?

GRAYSON: He's progressing very favorably.

HITCHCOCK: I mean—how is he *really*? Everyone noticed when he didn't take the opportunity of the anniversary of Armistice Day to issue a statement of some kind.

GRAYSON: Perhaps he felt none was necessary.

(EDITH wakens and hears the conversation in the next room. She sits up and listens.)

HITCHCOCK: Doctor Grayson,—no one has seen the President since the last week of September. There are rumors afloat that he's lost his mind. The signatures he's signed for the past six weeks look like the scribbles of a chimpanzee.

GRAYSON: That's not unusual for a man in his condition.

HITCHCOCK: Is it his own hand?

GRAYSON: Of course!

HITCHCOCK: Without Mrs Wilson guiding it?

(EDITH *enters.*)

EDITH: If I help a bit, so what?

HITCHCOCK: Is that the only way you help? "A bit?"

EDITH: What do you mean?

HITCHCOCK: I feel it's my duty to tell you there's a suspicion that many matters put before the President never reach him.

EDITH: I can assure you that what is important to reach him does reach him.

HITCHCOCK: Just this morning the Secretary of State asked me: When Mrs Wilson comes out of that room saying what Wilson has said, how do we know it's what he's said?

EDITH: Leave it to Lansing to think I would lie—

HITCHCOCK: The Republicans are saying we're living in the reign of the first woman President! They say you are making many major decisions—

EDITH: The only decision I make is what to bring to the President's attention and what not to.

HITCHCOCK: That's a rather large decision! ... Forgive me, Mrs Wilson, but many are saying that this is too much of a responsibility for a—

EDITH: —for a woman?

HITCHCOCK: —for a person who's had only two years of formal schooling.

EDITH: They insult the President to assume he'd marry an idiot!

HITCHCOCK: No one suggested—

EDITH: They discount the fact that during and after the war it was I who was closest to the President, that he constantly relied on me to talk things out.

HITCHCOCK: I didn't mean to infer—

GRAYSON: The charge that Edith is running the country is ridiculous!

HITCHCOCK: And the charge of Presidential disability. Is that ridiculous, too? If Wilson really *is* unfit, and we know, and the Cabinet allows it to go on, we'll all be charged with gross conspiracy, do you realize that?

GRAYSON: You have my word: The President is fit to govern.

HITCHCOCK: ...I'm afraid we need proof.

EDITH: What proof?

HITCHCOCK: We have to see him. ... A bi-partisan committee has been appointed to come to the White House to pay its respects to the President.

EDITH: But—

HITCHCOCK: I fear, if this is not acceptable, the Republicans may start proceedings for removing him from office.

(A moment, then:)

EDITH: I see. ... When will this—visit—take place?

HITCHCOCK: Tomorrow morning.

EDITH: And who will make up the visiting committee?

HITCHCOCK: I will represent the Democrats. The Republicans will be represented by—

EDITH: Don't tell me. ... Senator Henry Cabot Lodge.

(HITCHCOCK nods, then goes.)

(EDITH turns to GRAYSON and says:)

EDITH: Well, if anything can kill Woodrow, that will! Maybe that's what Lodge has in mind—assassination by exposure to his face!

(The lights change. GRAYSON goes into the bedroom.)

(Upset, EDITH comes upon the Suffragette sash on the mantel. She touches it and says to us:)

EDITH: Damn it! If I were a man—a Lieutenant faithfully serving his injured Commander on the field of battle, I'd get praise for what I'm doing, instead of all this blame. *(She puts the sash in a drawer.)*

(The lights change.)

(While EDITH straightens the living room and prepares herself for the visit, IKE enters and goes into the bedroom to assist GRAYSON.)

(They turn the bed so WILSON's right side is the one most illuminated. GRAYSON removes the bottles of pills from the night-table, hides them in a drawer and goes into the living room.)

(IKE puts an overturned chair behind WILSON. He props him up to an almost sitting position and begins to plump up pillows behind him.)

WILSON: For God's sake, Ike, it's not a beauty contest!

IKE: Don't you worry, Mister President. You'll do fine.

(EDITH *enters the bedroom and checks to see that everything's in order. She sees the oxygen tank and gestures to* IKE, *who wheels it out into the hall.*)

WILSON: I knew it would only be a matter of time before they'd send a sniffing committee.

EDITH: They just want to pay their respects.

WILSON: They're coming to test me, to see if I'm fit to continue in office.

EDITH: No matter what they say, don't let them get your goat.

WILSON: Do I ever let anyone get my goat? (*A look. He knows he does.*) Well, I wouldn't give that scoundrel Lodge the satisfaction. Think of it—after all this time—face to face—

EDITH: Senator Hitchcock will be here, and he's your ally.

WILSON: Ally or not, he'll have to be honest. And as for the distinguished Senator from Massachusetts—

EDITH: I'll make certain he hasn't brought a pistol.

WILSON: Lodge doesn't need a pistol. Lodge's weapon is words. That weapon used to be mine...

(IKE *enters the living room and announces to* GRAYSON:)

IKE: Senator Hitchcock and Senator Henry Cabot Lodge.

(*In the bedroom,* EDITH *puts* WILSON's *left arm under the covers.*)

(HITCHCOCK *and* LODGE *enter the living room.* LODGE *is a proud aristocratic Brahmin with white hair and goatee.*)

GRAYSON: Senator Hitchcock. Senator Lodge.

LODGE: Ah, the inner sanctum! I haven't been privileged to visit these hallowed halls since Teddy Roosevelt had me in to dine on buffalo steak.

GRAYSON: The President will receive you in the bedroom.

LODGE: What better way to run a boudoir government than from a boudoir? Is the President convalescing in the Lincoln bed?

GRAYSON: He is.

LODGE: Tell me, does the Great Emancipator ever appear to the Great Pacifier?

GRAYSON: I must make it clear, Senator Lodge, that this is a social visit. You are not to talk to the President about government business, particularly the problems with the Treaty or the League. Any disturbance might cause serious physical consequences.

LODGE: Would I endanger the health of the President of the United States?

GRAYSON: That's a question better left unanswered.

(EDITH *appears at the door of the bedroom.*)

EDITH: Senator Lodge, Senator Hitchcock. Won't you come in?

(SENATORS LODGE *and* HITCHCOCK *enter the bedroom.* EDITH *gestures for them to stand on the right side of the bed. She takes up a position on the left.* GRAYSON *stands across the room, near the doorway.*)

WILSON: Welcome, welcome, gentlemen. Forgive my receiving you so informally—

LODGE: And you forgive our taking so long to come and pay our respects. We would have come sooner but—

GRAYSON: But his doctor forbade it.

WILSON: As you can see, I've been well taken care of.

LODGE: Yes. And you're fortunate to have so much assistance from your lovely wife.

HITCHCOCK: (*Interrupting*) It's good to see you, Woodrow.

(WILSON *extends his hand and* HITCHCOCK *shakes it.*)

HITCHCOCK: My, that's quite a handshake for an invalid!

LODGE: We have been praying for you.

WILSON: Which way, Senator?

LODGE: I see you haven't lost your wit!

WILSON: Or my marbles.

LODGE: Has there been any suggestion, Mister President, that you have lost your marbles?

WILSON: Not so much the suggestion—as the hope. Second only to the hope for my imminent demise.

LODGE: Now, now, Mister President. I wish you nothing but well. Just because I'm a Northerner while you're a Southerner doesn't mean I want to reduce by one the Dixie population.

WILSON: How magnanimous of you.

LODGE: In fact, we're all enjoying the rarity of having a Princeton man in the White House.

WILSON: You think it's the private preserve of Harvard?

HITCHCOCK: (*Interrupting again*) Woodrow, how are you feeling?

WILSON: A little like the Princess and the Pea.

LODGE: The Princess and the Pea?

WILSON: I'd rest more comfortably if it weren't for you and your amendments. Every one is a pebble underneath my mattress.

EDITH: Woodrow, this subject is forbidden—

LODGE: I apologize most humbly for the pebbles under your mattress, Mister President. But you know, the idea of this country joining the League of Nations is a great big lump in mine.

WILSON: How in the name of God can you stand there and pretend to be an educated man and be against the League?

EDITH: Now, now. No business, gentlemen, you promised—

LODGE: Because it usurps the prerogatives of the United States Congress, that's why! It would become a superstate above us all!

WILSON: Not so. There are safeguards in the charter.

GRAYSON: Gentlemen—

LODGE: Where in the charter?

WILSON: Chapter and verse?

LODGE: Chapter and verse.

WILSON: *(Having difficulty remembering)* Why, Article—Article—

EDITH: Article Five clearly states that—

(All stop and look at EDITH. *She cuts herself off.)*

EDITH: I beg your pardon.

LODGE: So you've studied the charter, have you, Mrs Wilson?

EDITH: Well, I—

LODGE: Then you're aware, of course, that the League is unconstitutional.

EDITH: That, Senator Lodge, is entirely a Republican opinion!

LODGE: Not at all. A sizeable number of Democratic Senators agree! I'm told the names of at least a dozen of them were brought up at last week's Cabinet meeting.

WILSON: Cabinet meeting?

HITCHCOCK: It was just informal, Woodrow—

WILSON: A Cabinet meeting can only be called by the President!

(He is beginning to get upset. EDITH *tries to calm him.)*

EDITH: Woodrow—

WILSON: I'll wager it was called by Lansing! Was it Lansing?

HITCHCOCK: Yes. It was Lansing.

WILSON: It's insu—insu—*(His speech begins to get cloudy.)*

EDITH: Insulting?

WILSON: In-su-bor-di-na-tion! It's wrong! How dare a Secretary of State, who is supposed to be loyal— *(His face begins to twitch, his hand to tremble. He accidentally throws back his covers, revealing his useless left hand.)*

(EDITH *calls out:*)

EDITH: Cary—!

(GRAYSON *steps forward.*)

GRAYSON: Gentlemen, that's quite enough! The interview is over.

(EDITH *covers* WILSON. HITCHCOCK *and* LODGE *begin to exit.*)

WILSON: You'll see I'm still a force to reckon with!

LODGE: Yes, I see you are. *(Glancing at* EDITH*)* You and your trusty Adjutant General.

(WILSON *gives* EDITH *a hard look. She pulls back from the bed.*)

HITCHCOCK: Take care of yourself, Woodrow.

(The SENATORS *exit.* WILSON *is extremely agitated.)*

WILSON: A Cabinet meeting—called by my Secretary of State without my permission. Did you know about it?

EDITH: Well, I—

WILSON: You knew and you didn't tell me!

EDITH: I don't like to upset you—

WILSON: What else have you been keeping from me?

GRAYSON: Woodrow, Edith has been doing her level best—to the brink of exhaustion—

WILSON: You've been hiding things from me—

EDITH: I've been using my judgement—

WILSON: I *thought* the work load had suddenly lessened. You've been shipping my work elsewhere, haven't you?

EDITH: Some things seemed better delegated to others while you recovered.

WILSON: And some things you've been taking on yourself—

EDITH: I've tried to spare you where I could—

WILSON: You let me lie here while you slowly but surely channelled things away—

EDITH: What you weren't up to doing, what I had no authority to do, I thought it best to—

WILSON: You've been making it seem—to Lansing and Lodge and everybody else—that I can't manage the work of this office!

GRAYSON: She's the one who held the office intact for you!

WILSON: Get Tumulty!

EDITH: Don't you think you ought to rest—

WILSON: Get me Tumulty! And get me up!

GRAYSON: You're not ready to get out of bed!

WILSON: I'm tired of taking orders from you. You knew what she was doing. You and she—in cahoots!

(EDITH *and* GRAYSON *exchange a look.* WILSON *shouts at* GRAYSON:)

WILSON: Go away! *(He rings a handbell at the side of his bed.)*

GRAYSON: *(To* EDITH*)* I'll look in later.

(GRAYSON *exits.* IKE *enters.*)

(WILSON *points to the armless wheelchair.*)

WILSON: Get me into that thing.

(IKE *starts to lift him into the wheelchair.*)

(TUMULTY *enters the living room.* EDITH *goes out to see him.*)

TUMULTY: He passed with flying colors! Lodge and Hitchcock both talked to the boys at the gate and told them he's just fine!

EDITH: If Senator Lodge says he's fine, it's because he wants to use my husband's weakness to some advantage. *(Then she says:)* The President wants to see you—

TUMULTY: At last—!

EDITH: He's had a hard day. However he seems to you, you must be careful what you say to the press—

TUMULTY: Look, you know I'd never say anything to hurt him. All I ever say to those guys is straight truth.

(IKE *wheels* WILSON *into the living room.* TUMULTY *becomes silent with shock. He is not prepared for the sight of the thin ill man wrapped in a blanket, his entire left side paralyzed, his left eye blind, the left side of his mouth hanging limp.*)

(TUMULTY *is blankly silent for a moment. Then he collects himself and says:*)

TUMULTY: Guv'nor,—it's—swell to see you! You look—swell—!

WILSON: Tumul—, Tumul—, Lansing is trying to us--, us--

EDITH: Usurp?

WILSON: I can say it! *(To* TUMULTY*)* He's trying to take over! Help me fire him! I want him out!

(WILSON *flings out his arm with emotional emphasis. The violent gesture unbalances him and he falls onto the floor.* TUMULTY *looks on in horror.)*

(EDITH *and* IKE *lift* WILSON *and get him back into the chair with difficulty.* IKE *secures* WILSON *in the chair by tying him in with the blanket.)*

(EDITH *takes her place behind the chair, holding* WILSON, *lovingly, on both sides of the head so his head will not fall over. She looks at* TUMULTY *and asks quietly:)*

EDITH: Well, Tumulty,—do you know what to say to the press now?

(TUMULTY *can't speak. He gives* EDITH *a deep look of sympathy and understanding.* WILSON *says:)*

WILSON: I want sun. Wheel me out of here and down to the portico.

(EDITH *starts to do so.* WILSON *stops her.)*

WILSON: Not you... Tumulty.

(EDITH *relinquishes her position.* TUMULTY *takes her place.)*

(IKE *opens both of the entrance doors.* TUMULTY *wheels* WILSON *out into the corridor as* EDITH *stands silently watching.)*

(Blackout)

END ACT ONE

ACT TWO

(Time: Early Spring, several months later)

(At rise:)

(WILSON is sitting in his new wheelchair—one with arms and a leg rest. TUMULTY is near him. From the light which flickers against their faces, we can tell they are watching a movie. EDITH is sitting at a distance from them, knitting. In her own light, she says to us:)

EDITH: Well, here I am—knitting. Having stuck my head above the surface of the sand without permission, I've been relegated to the doghouse! It seems the Great Peacemaker is raring for peace everywhere but on the homefront.

WILSON: *(Watching the screen)* What trash! Shut that damn thing off!

(TUMULTY moves to do so.)

EDITH: *(To us:)* I can't even choose the right movies!

WILSON: A heroine is stolen by gypsies, gets thrown over the falls in a barrel, tumbles over the rapids and lands on the shore at the feet of her lover—! It's ridiculous!

EDITH: Sorry, Woodrow. I thought it would amuse you. How about *Girl of the Golden West*?

WILSON: I've seen it so many times I'm beginning to feel I live in that saloon! ...Tumulty, come read me today's newspapers.

TUMULTY: But Guv! I just finished reading you six days' worth of the Congressional Record! I'm going hoarse!

EDITH: I'll read them to you—

WILSON: No, thank you.

TUMULTY: *(To EDITH:)* This is one of his porcupine days.

EDITH: Beware the quills.

WILSON: Am I going to hear the news or am I not?

TUMULTY: Sure, Guv'nor.

WILSON: They say good things about my firing Lansing, don't they?

TUMULTY: Oh, yes, Guv. They take it as evidence that the Captain is still at the helm.

WILSON: Still at the helm...

(GRAYSON *enters, carrying a spray of forsythia.*)

GRAYSON: What a day! It's beautiful out there! I've just been for a ride through Rock Creek Park with Altrude and the baby. I've brought you the first blossoms—

WILSON: *(Refusing to take them)* Flowers are for funerals.

EDITH: They're beautiful—

WILSON: Which is why they should have been left in Rock Creek Park.

GRAYSON: I prescribe a ride in the Spring air. Come. Both of you.

EDITH: Yes, let's go for a ride, Woodrow. You need to breathe the air away from 1600 Pennsylvania Avenue. If you did—

WILSON: If I did, what? It might help me forget that after all these months the Treaty is still stuck in Committee like the Tar Baby in tar and I cannot *dis-Lodge* it?

EDITH: It might give you some perspective.

WILSON: "Perspective" is what people say they want you to get when what they really want is for you to change your mind. *(He turns to* TUMULTY:*)* Go see what's happening on the Hill, will you? And if nothing's happening, make it happen!

TUMULTY: I'll try, Guv'nor.

(MARGARET *enters.*)

MARGARET: Hello, father. *(She brushes his cheek with a kiss.)*

WILSON: *(Distracted)* Margaret—

(*As* TUMULTY *puts together documents with* WILSON, MARGARET *says, aside, to* EDITH:)

MARGARET: Have you had a chance to ask him about McAdoo?

(EDITH *shakes her head.*)

WILSON: *(Who has overheard)* Ask me what about McAdoo? *(He waves* TUMULTY *off.)*

(TUMULTY *exits.*)

MARGARET: Father, ... Nellie's husband is thinking of trying for the Democratic nomination for President.

(WILSON *is silent.*)

EDITH: He wouldn't do it without your permission—

(Still, WILSON doesn't speak.)

MARGARET: Since McAdoo was Secretary of the Treasury on his own merits before he and Nellie married, he certainly has a right to run if he wants to. But he would like to have your consent. Do you approve?

(Once more, WILSON is silent.)

EDITH: Woodrow—? It would be such an advantage for you to help choose your own successor—

WILSON: Are you giving me advice?

EDITH: No. I am knitting. See? Knitting.

MARGARET: Father, what will I tell Nellie?

WILSON: Tell her I don't want to be asked this question!

EDITH: But, Woodrow, McAdoo has to know—

WILSON: I'd consider it a favor, Edith, if you'd stick to your knitting!

EDITH: If I could vote, I'd vote not to do knitting!

WILSON: What would you prefer to do? Have me appoint you Ambassador to the Court of Saint James?

GRAYSON: Woodrow, —I think it's time for your nap.

(He begins to wheel WILSON into the bedroom.)

WILSON: The President slumbered while Rome burned.

(In the bedroom, GRAYSON says to WILSON:)

GRAYSON: You're a little rough on Edith, don't you think, Woodrow?

WILSON: You're always taking her side. What are you two, lovers?

GRAYSON: Maybe I ought to wash your mouth out with soap. Or your mind.

WILSON: She always sleeps in her own room now.

GRAYSON: When she slept here on the couch, you said she was eavesdropping on your dreams!

WILSON: She spies on me—

GRAYSON: She is looking out for your welfare. There is no one more devoted, more loyal—

WILSON: No doubt she's repelled—

GRAYSON: You know, you've got enough problems without inventing ones that don't exist.

(In the bedroom GRAYSON helps WILSON onto the couch as, in the living room, MARGARET says:)

MARGARET: He's impossible!

EDITH: It's the illness. It's changed him.

MARGARET: I never realized how much you have to put up with.

EDITH: He's the one who bears the burden, not I.

MARGARET: You know, having somebody else marry my father was hard to get used to at first. But now I realize—he couldn't have made a better choice.

EDITH: Thank you, Margaret. I'm glad at least *you* think so.

MARGARET: And so do Nellie and Jessie.

EDITH: It's good to have a little support from the distaff side. ... Tell me, how are things going with the Amendment?

MARGARET: Just one more state and we're in.

EDITH: ...I'm rooting for you.

MARGARET: *(Surprised and touched)* Why, thank you, —Mother. *(She kisses* EDITH *lightly on the cheek, then goes.)*

(EDITH *is moved. Happy, she goes to the bedroom door to tell* WILSON.)

WILSON: Stop spying on me!

(EDITH *turns back into the living room.* GRAYSON *puts out the bedroom light and comes into the living room.)*

GRAYSON: I'm beginning to be sorry I put you two together in the first place.

EDITH: You mean you did it on purpose? You never told me that!

GRAYSON: I didn't want to be blamed for anything! I still don't!

(GRAYSON *takes his leave of* EDITH *and exits.)*

(The bedroom is dark. WILSON *is asleep.)*

(Lights change. Time passes.)

(Alone in the living room, EDITH *goes to a drawer, takes out the packet of letters tied with the lavender ribbon, and opens one after the other. One in particular arouses a warm remembrance. She goes into the bedroom where* WILSON *is lying in bed, not facing her, and says:)*

EDITH: Woodrow, I want to read you something. You wrote me this the week before we married. ... "I love you with all my heart. You are my ideal companion. The delightful chum of my mind. Only with you can I be joyous and mirthful. Until you, I was sinking in quicksand. You came and I know no one can help me as you can."

*(*WILSON *is silent.)*

EDITH: Do you remember that, Woodrow?

(No answer.)

EDITH: Woodrow—? *(She goes over to the bed; she sees that he's asleep. She comes into the living room, closing the bedroom door behind her.)* Asleep. Never mind. At this point, he'd probably claim that letter was forged. *(She puts the letter in a drawer.)*

(TUMULTY enters in a state of high excitement.)

TUMULTY: Mrs Wilson—

EDITH: I'm sorry, Tumulty. You can't see the President at the moment. He's taking his nap.

TUMULTY: I haven't come to see the President. I've come to see you.

EDITH: Me?

TUMULTY: I mean—Senator Hitchcock is on his way over to see you.

EDITH: To see *me*! I can't receive him! The President would be furious!

TUMULTY: But you have to see him.

EDITH: Why?

TUMULTY: Because—it's finally happening! This afternoon! They're going to take the vote!

EDITH: At last!

TUMULTY: Lodge has used up every tactic in his bag of tricks and there's nothing left for him to do but let the Senate make it's decision.

EDITH: This is wonderful!

TUMULTY: Not as wonderful as it could be.

(IKE enters.)

IKE: Mrs Wilson, Senator Hitchcock is here to see you—

(A moment, then EDITH nods. HITCHCOCK enters. IKE exits)

HITCHCOCK: Mrs Wilson—has Tumulty told you—?

TUMULTY: I haven't told her everything.

EDITH: What haven't I been told?

(HITCHCOCK and TUMULTY exchange a glance.)

HITCHCOCK: Mrs Wilson—the Treaty which is going to be voted on is the Treaty with the Lodge amendments.

EDITH: Oh, no—!

(GRAYSON enters.)

GRAYSON: I just heard—

(EDITH *gestures to him to be seated then turns to* HITCHCOCK *and* TUMULTY *asking:*)

EDITH: How do the numbers shape up?

HITCHCOCK: As I now see it, out of a total of ninety-six members of the Senate, Lodge has only twenty Republicans who will vote for the Treaty as he's presenting it. Fourteen to eighteen prefer it as it originally was. And twelve or thirteen won't vote for it in any form whatever.

EDITH: And the Democrats?

HITCHCOCK: One or two of those won't have it in any form whatever. Four or five will vote for it the way Lodge is bringing it to the floor—which gives him twenty-five. But forty loyal friends of the President are ready to vote according to Woodrow's instruction.

EDITH: That's good, isn't it?

HITCHCOCK: Oh, yes. That's good. We certainly can defeat the Treaty with the Lodge amendments.

EDITH: Well, then—!

HITCHCOCK: But if the Treaty *without* amendments is then presented, we don't have enough votes to get that to pass.

TUMULTY: Two-thirds are needed to ratify. So even if the few unpredictables come down on our side, it doesn't add up to a win.

HITCHCOCK: We've wined, dined, begged, traded—done everything short of bribery—but we still can't come up with sixty-four, which is the magic number.

EDITH: But if Lodge can't come up with sixty-four either—

HITCHCOCK: Then there'll be an impasse. The Treaty will be defeated. We will be out of the peace—and out of the League.

EDITH: Then what do you suggest?

(After a long pause, HITCHCOCK *says:)*

HITCHCOCK: The Treaty, as amended by Lodge, is still a viable treaty. It ends the war and brings us into the League of Nations on terms which, I believe, a two-thirds majority of the Senate can accept—can accept, that is, if the President instructs the forty Democrats who are faithful to him to vote for its acceptance.

EDITH: You're suggesting that Woodrow instruct his side to vote for Lodge's treaty?

HITCHCOCK: Yes.

EDITH: You can't believe he'd do that!

HITCHCOCK: The situation is very serious. It would be tragic if all these months of wrangling will have been in vain. The key to our entering the League is to enter it on Lodge's terms.

EDITH: No, no—!

HITCHCOCK: The entire outcome hinges on the forty of us faithfuls. If the President insists we must hold to the original document, without changes, then we will do so—and, today, the Treaty will definitely be defeated. Everything Woodrow worked so hard to achieve will crumble to dust—this afternoon.

EDITH: Is this the final vote?

TUMULTY: There's no way of going any further. It will be all over.

(EDITH *paces, saying nothing. At last* HITCHCOCK *speaks:*)

HITCHCOCK: I've come to ask you to convince the President to let the Democrats accept the Treaty with the Lodge amendments.

EDITH: To ask *me* to ask him! Why not Tumulty?

TUMULTY: You're closer to him—

GRAYSON: I think they're right, Edith. I think the best one to present this to him is you.

EDITH: I'm not exactly always in his good graces!

GRAYSON: Who is?

EDITH: You're afraid he might have a relapse, aren't you!

GRAYSON: I'll be frank with you: If his blood pressure rises there could be danger.

EDITH: I knew it.

GRAYSON: On the other hand, if the Treaty goes down to defeat, he might lose the will to live.

HITCHCOCK: If you could only try—

EDITH: He has forbidden me to talk to him about any political topics whatsoever!

GRAYSON: In spite of that, you're probably the only one on earth who has any chance of getting a favorable reply.

EDITH: You know he sees Lodge's changes as a perversion and betrayal of everything he fought for.

HITCHCOCK: Yes, we know.

EDITH: Then how can you ask me to go in and beg him to turn from everything he believes in—?

HITCHCOCK: I'm afraid that, isolated as he's been for many months, he's lost sight of the realities of politics. He forgets about the need to concede—

EDITH: To concede—to Lodge—! How bitter that would be for him!

GRAYSON: But think of the alternative.

(EDITH *is silent.*)

HITCHCOCK: I beg you, Mrs Wilson, with everything that's in your power—help us save the Treaty. Help us save Woodrow from himself.

EDITH: *(After a long pause)* ...I will do what I can.

(EDITH *goes into the bedroom and closes the door behind her.*)

(*In the living room,* HITCHCOCK *asks* GRAYSON *and* TUMULTY:)

HITCHCOCK: Would you bet she can persuade him?

GRAYSON: Would you?

TUMULTY: Fortunately, I'm not a betting man ... I am a *drinking* man, however. *(He looks into a few cabinets and finds no liquor.)* Oh, the hell with it! *(He takes a flask out of his pocket and pours out a small measure of whiskey for each.)*

(*Meanwhile, in the bedroom,* WILSON, *lying on the couch, has been told the situation by* EDITH. *He responds vehemently:*)

WILSON: I told you I don't want you interfering in affairs of state!

EDITH: Fine. I'll send in Hitchcock. *(She starts out.)*

WILSON: No!

(EDITH *comes back.* WILSON *says:*)

WILSON: We can't adopt the Treaty in such a bastardized form.

EDITH: Are all the changes that impossible to accept?

WILSON: No matter how many times I tell you, you don't seem to understand. There can be no changes! A treaty is a contract. It can't be changed unless the changes are agreed to by the other side.

EDITH: But if Congress can't agree to accept it as written—

WILSON: If I accept the Treaty the way Lodge has changed it, it means I was irresponsible to sign it the way I did.

EDITH: It only means you understand the necessity of being flexible, accommodating.

WILSON: No amount of desire to be accommodating can make the wrong course the right one.

EDITH: Are you positive this course is the right one?

WILSON: It's wonderful to see how little faith you have in me.

EDITH: I'm trying to help you.

WILSON: Ellen never "helped" me like this. Ellen never disagreed with me.

EDITH: Could we please, once and for all, exorcise the ghost of the Perfect Ellen! She would let you go down in flames just to keep domestic peace! I don't want you to go down in flames! I want to be able to say with you: "Grand! We did it!"

WILSON: *(With an edge)* "We" did it. You and I did it.

EDITH: Yes.

WILSON: ...Perhaps I chose the wrong successor to Ellen after all.

EDITH: Perhaps you did. That doesn't really matter at this moment. What matters is—everything you worked for, all your life, is going to be decided in the next few hours.

WILSON: I accept that. And I have every faith it's going to come out well. ... You see, it was promised to me. By God. *(Holding the khaki bible, he says to her almost feverishly:)* He didn't put me on earth to help me bring such a splendid concept almost to fruition and then snatch it away from me. ... This trial inflicted on my body and mind is a test—a test to see if I will hold firm and not turn from my principles. And I have held firm. I am still holding. No matter how difficult the burden I've had to bear, I can bear it—because I know He will not fail me.

EDITH: It will need a miracle—

WILSON: But there are miracles. *(He touches the bible.)* ...I am going to prevail. It's as sure as that God exists.

EDITH: For all of our sakes, I hope so. *(She exits. She re-enters the living room and says:)* He says no. No compromise.

HITCHCOCK: Certain?

EDITH: Absolute and final.

TUMULTY: *(Defeated)* That's it, then.

(Wearily, HITCHCOCK *picks up his briefcase.)*

EDITH: He believes that all will turn out well.

HITCHCOCK: He must have forgotten the ways of Lodge and the U S Senate.

GRAYSON: At least, in a few hours, everything will be decided.

EDITH: I thought only *criminals* had their fates decided in an afternoon.

*(*HITCHCOCK *and* TUMULTY *exit.* EDITH *says to* GRAYSON:*)*

EDITH: What can you say when someone brings on God to defend his position? Lodge isn't depending on God. Or maybe he is. You know what they say in Boston: "The Lowells talk to the Cabots and the Cabots talk only to God."

I'm sure Lodge is enough of a Cabot to think he has direct *entrée* to the Deity. Woodrow's going to be defeated. And there's nothing I can do about it.

(GRAYSON *shakes his head and exits.*)

(EDITH *sits on the sofa, picks up her knitting but cannot concentrate on it. After a moment, something occurs to her. Throwing down the knitting she says to us:*) Or maybe there is! (*She picks up the downstage phone.*) Line three-five, please. ... Ike? Listen. Go to Senator Lodge and say that Mrs Wilson wants to see him. ... Yes. You heard correctly. Senator Henry Cabot Lodge. Tell no one. Do whatever you have to do. But get him here at once. (*She puts down the phone and turns to us:*) If Woodrow's talking into God's right ear, Lodge is filibustering into the left—and who knows what promises Lodge is getting! Woodrow may think he can depend on a decision from heaven. I think a little something has to be done right here on earth!

(*Lights change. Time passes.*)

(EDITH *goes to the mirror above the mantel and arranges her hair. She remembers the "Votes for Women" sash in the drawer. She takes it out and tries it on, looking at herself in the mirror. She is pleased at what she sees.*)

(IKE *enters and, noticing the sash but not raising an eyebrow, announces with a certain trepidation:*)

IKE: Excuse me, Mrs Wilson, he's here. Senator Henry Cabot Lodge.

EDITH: Thank you, Ike. Show him in.

(EDITH *takes off the sash and puts it back in the drawer. But she retains the strength she has gained from it.*)

(EDITH *checks on* WILSON, *who is sleeping. Quietly, she closes the door between the rooms.*)

(LODGE *enters. With gentlemanly politeness, he bows his head.*)

LODGE: Madame President—

EDITH: Mrs Wilson.

LODGE: I'm flattered that you wish to see me.

EDITH: Senator Lodge, I've asked you here to see if I can accomplish what my betters have been unable to accomplish.

LODGE: You are too modest.

EDITH: I propose we talk directly, without drawing room manners.

LODGE: I'd be only too pleased.

EDITH: Your hatred for my husband is well known.

LODGE: And highly exaggerated.

EDITH: You don't hate him?

LODGE: Quite the reverse, I have the greatest respect —

EDITH: We said no drawing room chit-chat!

LODGE: You do me a disservice if you think I don't give your husband his due.

EDITH: Yet you oppose the League —

LODGE: It will be a dead issue before sundown.

EDITH: What a great sense of satisfaction that must give you!

LODGE: On the contrary, I am doing everything in my power to get it passed.

EDITH: You have a very strange way of accomplishing it!

LODGE: Mrs Wilson, I am not the villain of this piece. That role is being played by your husband. I don't have to tell you how intractable he can be —

EDITH: You don't expect me to concur in criticism of my husband —!

LODGE: Not out loud. It's enough that we both understand what we've had to put up with.

EDITH: His vision of international peace —!

LODGE: Couched in conditions which are unacceptable to a majority in the United States Government! Mrs Wilson, do you realize how extremely unusual it is for a head of state to spend six months abroad handling his own peace negotiations?

EDITH: He felt they were so important he should entrust them to no one but himself.

LODGE: Without consulting the chairman of his Foreign Relations Committee! *(He indicates himself.)*

EDITH: I'm sure no slight was intended.

LODGE: He should have gotten our approval *before* making any agreements, rather than presenting us with a fait accompli! If he had, he wouldn't be having so much difficulty now.

EDITH: One would think, at this point, we'd have moved beyond petty political considerations.

LODGE: You think I'm nit-picking, don't you. That these are only words. But, Mrs Wilson, do you have any idea what his words are asking us to agree to?

EDITH: I know it by heart, Senator.

LODGE: Then you aware that, the way things are stated, once we are in this thing we can never withdraw.

EDITH: Why should we want to?

LODGE: Because we don't know what will be asked of us—or forced on us—in the future.

EDITH: We have full voting privileges. That shouldn't be a problem.

LODGE: And what about the expense? Your husband is pledging us, now and forever, to shouldering a financial burden that is far more than our share. Can you see the drain on the Treasury as we try to bankroll setting everything right everywhere on the planet?

EDITH: You really think the world is depending almost solely on the United States?

LODGE: After our heroic role in this war? I'm certain of it!

(EDITH *listens carefully, beginning to understand* LODGE'S *point of view for the first time.*)

LODGE: ...And that's not the end of the abominations! Woodrow is asking us to freeze territorial rights exactly as they are now, for all time.

EDITH: That seems just.

LODGE: If the League existed in 1776, we'd still be a British colony!

EDITH: Woodrow only wants the League to guarantee some stability in the world—

LODGE: It is folly to try to deal with all possible questions that may arise in the unknowable future! It is folly to give an outside body jurisdiction over our internal affairs. What if the Navajos sue in World Court for possession of Arizona? Should we give it back to the Indians?

EDITH: Mister Lodge, I am part Indian. A direct descendant of Pocahontas.

LODGE: Then you probably expect me to hand you back Massachusetts.

EDITH: We might do something splendid with it.

LODGE: Mrs Wilson, once the United States gives up its right to determine its own destiny, that right will be gone forever!

(*In the bedroom,* WILSON *has awakened and heard the voice of his enemy. He calls out:*)

WILSON: Edith!

EDITH: *(To* LODGE:*)* Excuse me. *(She hurries into the bedroom.)*

WILSON: I had a terrible nightmare. I thought I heard the voice of Henry Cabot Lodge!

EDITH: It's not a nightmare. He's here. In the flesh.

WILSON: How dare he barge into my private quarters!

EDITH: I invited him.

WILSON: You invited my enemy into my house?

EDITH: If you're working so hard to get adversaries to talk, I thought we might as well begin in our own living room.

(WILSON *points to the wheelchair.*)

WILSON: Get me into that thing.

EDITH: I didn't mean that you should have to face him—

WILSON: *(Sarcastically, to her:)* Of course not. Why don't I leave it all to my co-President! *(He tries to struggle into the wheelchair.)* Help me!

EDITH: Woodrow, are you sure it's wise to—

WILSON: Damn it! Get me into this contraption! *(She begins to help him into the wheelchair.)* I suppose he's been filling your head full of drivel.

EDITH: Some of the things he's said seem not entirely unreasonable.

WILSON: Double negatives. Maybe you should have been a diplomat after all!

(EDITH *wheels him into the living room.* LODGE *rises.*)

LODGE: Mister President—

WILSON: Is the vote being taken now?

LODGE: It'll begin in a few minutes.

WILSON: If you've left the Senate floor, you must be very confident.

LODGE: Very.

WILSON: Confident that on this day you'll send the future of the planet straight to hell.

EDITH: Woodrow, some of Senator Lodge's points—

WILSON: Don't tell me the great orator has succeeded in converting the lady of the house—

EDITH: Of course he hasn't, but—

WILSON: *(To* EDITH:*)* I was sure, one day, I'd be fighting all alone.

EDITH: Woodrow—

WILSON: *(Turning to* LODGE:*)* How in the name of God can you be against people getting together to talk out their differences?

LODGE: I'm not against people getting together to talk out their differences. I'm here, you may notice.

WILSON: How can you be against *nations* talking?

LODGE: I'm not against nations talking. They're just collections of differing human beings—like you and me.

WILSON: Then how can you be against establishing a World Court?

LODGE: What would a World Court do if one country invaded another?

WILSON: It would declare an economic boycott.

LODGE: Suppose that didn't work. How would it enforce it's will?

WILSON: By force. A force made up of many nations.

LODGE: Only Congress has the right to send our men to war!

WILSON: They'd only go with Congressional assent.

LODGE: So they wouldn't have a legal obligation?

WILSON: Only a moral obligation.

LODGE: In other words, they wouldn't have to go.

WILSON: No.

LODGE: In that case, Mister Wilson, the entire proposition is a rope of sand!

(EDITH *reacts. It is a serious point, well taken.*)

WILSON: The League would send a moral message to all men everywhere—

LODGE: Please! Spare me the idealistic gibberish! Don't you think I know your main reason for espousing the League? It's so that you can head it! You see yourself going to Geneva and playing Lord and Master, not only over this nation, but over all the nations of the world!

EDITH: Senator Lodge, my husband has been ill. I beg you not to—

LODGE: Not since Napoleon has anyone on this earth had such dreams of conquest. You hate me because, if my efforts keep the United States out of the League of Nations, you'll be kept from ascending to your exalted place—beside God.

EDITH: Mister Senator! I must insist you have the courtesy, before the President of the United States, to—

WILSON: Silence, Edith. Let me fight my battles on my own. (*He turns to* LODGE.) I know you, too, Senator. It bothers you that I was born below the Mason-Dixon line, that I have a slightly Southern accent, that my ancestors didn't come over on the Mayflower, that I didn't go to Harvard.

LODGE: That you didn't go to Harvard is your misfortune, not mine.

WILSON: You were born superior and assumed that you would die superior. But somehow, Brahmin, you are not President—and I am. Every morning when you wake up that astounds you.

LODGE: If I were President, I would not give foreign powers the right to determine the course of the American Ship of State.

WILSON: That's not what I'm doing.

LODGE: You're moving us into the entangling alliances Washington warned us against.

WILSON: You don't seem to notice that the world has changed. In this last war our shores were reached by submarines. Next time, it will be by aeroplanes. Whether we like it or not, our days of isolation are over. We are completely involved with every other nation on this tiny planet.

LODGE: We ought not to undertake the task of policing the universe! The American people do not want our boys sent to die on far-flung battlefields for causes they do not understand and which are not our concern! They do not wish to go into an overseas war unless for a very great cause and where the issues are absolutely plain. *(To both* EDITH *and* WILSON:*)* I have never loved but one flag and I cannot share that devotion with a mongrel banner invented for some foreign League. Call me selfish if you like, but an American I was born, I have never been and will never be anything else but an American. I must think of the United States first. And when I think of the United States first, I am thinking of what is best for the world. For if the United States fails, the best hopes of mankind fail with it.

(EDITH *is almost convinced. She looks toward* WILSON. *He says:)*

WILSON: How strange it is, that with so much intelligence, you can oppose something so clear and so right. In everything you say, you have neglected one matter: Peace amongst the nations of the world. What did we fight for? For Democracy, for the rights of people to have a voice in their own governments. ... Before this war we were only a fledgling nation. Now we have taken our place as one of the foremost powers on the globe. To detach ourselves from world concerns now would be to sacrifice the greatest opportunity for human service that has ever come to any single people. ... When I was a boy swinging on a gate in Georgia, I saw crippled men come home from battle between the northern and southern states. Only a few months ago, I saw the battlefields of Europe, bloodstained from that other, greater, war. Such things must not happen again!

(WILSON *stops, seeming to lose strength.* EDITH *touches his hand, recalling him to himself. He continues, gaining strength:)*

WILSON: If we do not join in this great community of nations, there will come, some time in the vengeful Providence of God, another struggle, one which will be fought with such force and with weapons of such unimaginably destructive power that it will threaten the very existence of the human race. We must do everything we can to keep that from happening. ... The only way we can do it is to have one place on earth where every nation may bring its problems and seek for a solution—not through fighting, but through *talk*. Will you have it that all nations will join together for peace but the United States will stand separate and silent? No. We must not only *join*—we must *lead* that effort. It is our destiny.

(EDITH *looks at him with tremendous admiration.* LODGE, *unmoved, says:*)

LODGE: This is fascinating, of course, but it is all irrelevant. It's not a matter of principles, it's a matter of votes. If you don't release your votes, we will, today, be out of the Treaty for Peace and out of the League of Nations... It's your decision.

WILSON: I have already said—

EDITH: Woodrow—

WILSON: This is a matter between Senator Lodge and myself! (*To* LODGE:) You have my decision.

LODGE: Very well. Never let it be said I didn't do my best. (*He goes out.*)

WILSON: His best as an assassin!

EDITH: Woodrow, listen to me. There's still a chance to make it happen. Release your votes.

WILSON: And let them approve Lodge's version of the Treaty?

EDITH: There's still time. I beg you, compromise.

WILSON: Let Lodge compromise.

EDITH: Bend!

WILSON: Let Lodge bend.

EDITH: You're killing your own baby!

WILSON: You've gone over to his side—

EDITH: I'm only trying to help you—

WILSON: My wife—in collusion with my greatest enemy.

EDITH: How can you say that?

WILSON: In my entire life, I have never been so betrayed.

EDITH: Woodrow, release your votes.

WILSON: No!

EDITH: God in heaven, can no one ever make you change your mind about anything!

WILSON: You *Judas*! I'm married to a traitor!

EDITH: Enough! I'm fed up with these accusations! If I've done anything at all these past months it was only to try to help you. You were in no position to do these things so I did them. I thought you would be grateful. I thought, if I were criticized, you'd come to my defense! Instead, my reward is to find you constantly resentful, constantly pushing me away from your side. ... Before you, I was alive, but I had no reason for being. Now I have a reason for being. It's the same as yours. Five years ago I attached myself not only to you, but to your dream. And now I would do anything in this world to help you achieve it. Die for it—as you would die for it. Or, even worse, risk your shouting at me in a rage. ... I can't help my female state, or the fact that I'm only newly in your life, or the fact that I can walk around while you need wheels to get places. If it would help, I'd cut off my legs and give them to you. ... But don't—do not—think I have so little self-respect that I will stay here while you insult me. If you think, when I'm trying to do my best to help, that I'm betraying you, if you find my presence abhorrent, there is one thing I can definitely do—I can leave! Move back to my own house. I was happy there, I can return there!

WILSON: Go! And good riddance to you!

(Silence. EDITH *and* WILSON *look at each other.)*

(Before either can utter a word, TUMULTY, *looking very serious, enters. For a moment, he cannot speak, then:)*

TUMULTY: ...It's over.

(EDITH *and* WILSON *say nothing.)*

TUMULTY: They voted on the Treaty with amendments. It was defeated. They voted on the Treaty without amendments. It was defeated, too. A motion was made to begin to draft an agreement for a separate peace.

EDITH: But the League—

TUMULTY: We won't be in the League. Not now. Not ever.

(As WILSON *does not speak,* EDITH *says:)*

EDITH: Thank you for coming to tell us.

TUMULTY: I'm sorry, Guv'nor. We tried...

*(*TUMULTY *exits. After a moment,* WILSON *says to* EDITH*:)*

WILSON: Since you feel the way you feel, I won't expect you to come and live with me in Geneva.

EDITH: Didn't you hear him?

WILSON: Who?

EDITH: Tumulty... They said no. ... The United States isn't going to be in the League. Not now. Not ever. ... Woodrow—it's over.

WILSON: ...It isn't.

EDITH: But there's nothing more you can do.

WILSON: There is. I have a plan.

EDITH: What plan?

WILSON: I'm going to make the next election a solemn referendum. I'll say a vote for me is a vote for our joining the League.

EDITH: *(Stunned)* You don't intend to run for a third term—!

WILSON: I do. That's why I couldn't endorse my son-in-law. I have no doubt that at this summer's convention I'll be nominated by acclamation. As a man of honor, I can do no other than accept.

EDITH: You plan to go to Chicago? You plan to campaign—?

WILSON: I'm the only one who can carry my banner. The vote today proved it! I'll appeal directly to the people. I've always depended on them. They won't let me down now. You'll see. ... My third term is going to be my best!

(EDITH *looks at* WILSON, *struck dumb.*)

WILSON: Don't look so flabbergasted, Edith. I won't expect you to come campaigning with me. All I ask is that you still appear to be my wife through the election—

EDITH: *(Stunned)* Woodrow—

WILSON: I have to write my speech to the Convention. It's in my head. I want to get it down. *(He wheels himself into the bedroom and positions himself in front of the typewriter.)*

(*In the living room,* GRAYSON *enters.*)

EDITH: Cary,—he expects to run for another term! He expects to be nominated by acclamation! He expects to be elected to a third term and fight for the Treaty. Then, after his third term, he intends to move to Geneva and head up the League!

GRAYSON: He can't be serious!

EDITH: He's in there now, trying to write his speech to the Convention! It's as if, to survive, he's simply refusing to accept what's happened! He can't see it's the end. He thinks it's just another setback and now he will go onward! *(She is nearly hysterical, but she has to keep her voice down so* WILSON *won't hear her.)* What could I have done to make it turn out differently? What could I have done, what could I have said?

GRAYSON: You did all you could.

EDITH: All these months—all these long, long months since September—it's been like swimming underwater. All I lived for was to get him to the end of his term and out of this house alive! ...Now he tells me he's going to continue! This man—who can't walk, who's half blind, who sometimes can hardly speak --, plans to campaign from coast to coast, be elected, and spend another four years in office!

GRAYSON: Can he really think that—?

EDITH: I know what it is. He's trying to martyr himself. Die for the boys whose blood he still believes is on his hands. It's suicide!

GRAYSON: Edith,—he will never get the nomination. There are many in his party who have great affection for him—but they know he is incapable of standing for office one more time. It would be cruel, unbelievably cruel, to let him nourish the hope—the illusion—

EDITH: *(Her emotions rising and overflowing)* What you're saying is, I have to go in there and tell him it's over, truly over. ... How can I break his heart for him—more than it's already been broken? ...What in the name of God am I going to say?

(EDITH *breaks down and weeps.* GRAYSON *comforts her.)*

GRAYSON: Do you want me to be there when you—?

(EDITH *shakes her head.* GRAYSON *gives her an encouraging look, then exits.)*

(EDITH *goes into the bedroom.* WILSON *is sitting motionless, staring at the typewriter.)*

WILSON: I must be mad! I can't even see the letters on the keys!

EDITH: I'll type for you—

WILSON: Can't seem to organize my thoughts! Can't think clearly enough to put my ideas down on paper—*(He looks at her with the horrifying realization.)* Edith—even if they asked me—I couldn't manage it! *(His face reflects his anguish.)* It—really—is—over. ... My having another term in office, my getting us into the League—it isn't going to be. *(He turns his head away, stricken.)* It never occurred to me that I could fail. I thought—if I just held on long enough—I would have to succeed. *(Bitterly:)* But God, in His infinite wisdom, looked down and said, "This he shall not have!" *(He looks at her, his eyes reflecting great pain and emptiness.)* All my life I've felt that God and I had a pact together. I felt—privileged—to be warmed by His special affection. How cold it feels, to be without that now.

EDITH: You don't know that you are.

WILSON: I had—so many hopes.

EDITH: You've achieved more than most.

WILSON: But not the one thing—not the final thing—

EDITH: Most of us don't get all we try for.

WILSON: But it was a worthy thing, wasn't it?

EDITH: Worth a life. Attained or not.

WILSON: If it weren't for that damn Henry Cabot Lodge—! *(He looks at her then says:)* No. I can't blame him for everything. ... Maybe I should have compromised—. But I *couldn't*—. *(He looks at her again.)* It's hard—so very hard—to lose everything. The League. The White House. And you.

EDITH: You haven't lost me.

WILSON: Haven't I?

EDITH: If you'll have me, I'll stay—for your entire tenure on earth—and even in heaven. Will you have me?

(WILSON *takes* EDITH'S *hand, pats it for a moment, overcome with emotion, unable to speak. At last, understating his joy and relief, he says:*)

WILSON: I'll take it under advisement.

EDITH: ...Woodrow, listen—

WILSON: What?

EDITH: How would you like to move to a home where we're not just temporary tenants?

WILSON: I'd say that would suit me splendidly.

EDITH: I'll start right away to look for a place of our own.

WILSON: You won't mind living there with a porcupine?

EDITH: I have a great fondness for porcupines.

WILSON: This porcupine—has a very great fondness for you.

(EDITH *and* WILSON *look at each other with great love. She takes his hands in hers and kisses them.*)

(*The lights change. At a great distance there is the sound of snare drums.*)

(IKE *and* GRAYSON *enter. They begin to help* WILSON *into his dress suit.*)

(EDITH *goes into the living room.* TUMULTY *enters with empty boxes. He and she begin to pack the personal items in the room.*)

(*As she works on packing,* EDITH *says to us:*)

EDITH: The League has had its opening session in Geneva—without Woodrow, though they read his message. ... He has won the Nobel Prize for Peace. It means *something* to him—but if circumstances had been different, it would have meant much more.

(*The sound of a band playing patriotic music is distantly heard.*)

(*In the bedroom,* WILSON, *indicating the high top hat which accompanies his formal suit, says to* IKE:)

WILSON: You can force me into the suit, but you can't railroad me into that hat!

It makes me look ridiculous! I wore the damn thing for years and I always hated it. From now on, I go bare-headed.

(In the living room, TUMULTY *exits with full boxes.* EDITH *is packing the khaki bible).*

*(*MARGARET *enters.)*

MARGARET: Does he really insist on attending the inauguration?

EDITH: Yes. He does.

MARGARET: Stubborn to the last!

*(*MARGARET *goes into the bedroom.)*

(In the living room, EDITH *says to us, evenly, hiding her feelings:)*

EDITH: In this election, for the first time, women were able to vote! And what happened? Warren G Harding. This—Republican—has been elected President of the United States by the widest plurality ever compiled in the history of this country. ... The Democrats ran that insignificant James M Cox. What could they expect?

(In the bedroom, MARGARET *says to her father:)*

MARGARET: It's twenty degrees out there! Are you sure you want to do this?

WILSON: If Lodge is going to be there, I am going to be there!

*(*IKE *hands* MARGARET *the hat and she tries to give it to her father. He refuses to take it.)*

MARGARET: It's freezing outside!

WILSON: I say no to that chapeau!

(In the living room, EDITH, *putting on a formal coat, says to us:)*

EDITH: I've found us a house—on S Street—a town house—with a very pleasant garden. We've never lived together in any house but this one. *(She comes upon the love letters and carefully packs them.)* Woodrow plans to write his memoirs and—miracle of miracles—has actually agreed that I can help him! *(Making one last check to see if everything is packed, she finds her knitting buried within the pillows on the sofa. She drops it ceremoniously into the wastebasket. ... Then she opens the drawer, takes out the red sash, and packs it neatly in a suitcase.)* Last week I invited Mrs Harding to tea and she stayed eight hours! I went off and returned to find her already giving instructions to the kitchen staff! Oh, let her have it! Let her have it all!

(Wearing his formal coat, WILSON *is wheeled out of the bedroom by* IKE. GRAYSON *and* MARGARET *accompany them.* MARGARET *is holding the top hat.)*

(The clock begins to chime eleven. TUMULTY *enters. Trying to keep his emotions under control, he says:)*

TUMULTY: Mister Harding is waiting outside in the automobile to drive with you to the Capitol, Guv'nor.

WILSON: We'll be right down.

(EDITH *puts on a stylish wide-brimmed hat.* WILSON *looks at her with admiration.*)

WILSON: How lovely you are! Did you inherit that beauty?

EDITH: Yes. ... From my marriage.

(WILSON *smiles. They look fondly at each other.*)

(IKE *starts to wheel the chair toward the exit.* WILSON *stops him.*)

WILSON: Wait a moment. *(He looks toward* EDITH.*)* I have a surprise for you. Grayson and I have been practicing. ... You don't think I'm going to hand over the reins from a sitting position, do you?

(GRAYSON *comes over and assists* WILSON *out of the chair.*)

WILSON: The hell with being wheeled into the future. I'm going to walk!

(WILSON *stands unsupported and offers* EDITH *his arm. Overwhelmed, she takes it. They start to walk slowly toward the exit.*)

(TUMULTY *is near tears.* MARGARET *hands* TUMULTY *the hat and he tries to get* WILSON *to take it.* WILSON *pushes it away.*)

WILSON: I won't wear that damn hat!

(EDITH *takes the hat from* TUMULTY *and says to* WILSON, *pleasantly but firmly:*)

EDITH: You will.

(EDITH *holds it toward him. For a moment,* WILSON *refuses to take it. Then, as she stands unwavering, he takes it in hand. She waits. At last he raises it toward his head. All look on with approval.*)

(WILSON *doffs his hat once, to* EDITH, *in love and tribute. Then he puts it on his head.*)

(Once more WILSON *takes* EDITH's *arm. Together, they move slowly and proudly toward the exit.*)

(*Blackout*)

END OF PLAY

We Open In Florence

Reprinted from The New York Times Magazine Sunday 4 December 1977

New York, Tuesday, September 27, 1977

Several years ago, I wrote a play called "The Abdication," which is about Christina of Sweden, who renounced her throne in 1654 and went to live in Rome. First produced by the Bristol Old Vic at Bath, England, in association with Roger Stevens and Donald Albery, it was later made into the Warner Bros film starring Liv Ullmann and Peter Finch. Now the play is going to be produced in Italy. I don't speak Italian, but I've decided to go to Florence for the national premiere.

The play begins with Christina's arrival at the Vatican, where she is challenged by Cardinal Azzolino on the sincerity of her conversion to Catholicism. Alternating with scenes of her growing involvement with Azzolino are flashbacks dealing with her early life and the conflicts between her masculine and feminine natures that lead to her eventual abdication. I have never seen the work produced exactly as I would like it. I wonder what will face me this time.

Will the play be cut, as the film was? Will it be encrusted with history, as it was in the production in Bath? I'm planning to arrive two days before the opening. What will I find? If I want to protest, how will I communicate it? The production of a play is always a time of trial. How will I cope, in a foreign place, with no one I know, and in a language of which I am totally ignorant?

The inception of the production is unusual. Duilio Del Prete, the well-known Italian actor, was in Hollywood making a movie. One day he and actress Edmonda Aldini were walking down Wilshire Boulevard, where they happened to meet George Morfogen, their fellow actor and my friend. They said they had just come from seeing a film, "The Abdication". "We liked it," they said. "But there was something missing." George said, "You know, there's a play..."

Now, three years later, Duilio and Edmonda are putting it into production and starring in it. They've gotten Giuseppe Patroni Griffi as director; he is, I am told, one of Italy's leading directors (on a par with Zeffirelli). But the snippet of news from abroad that intrigues me most is that the setting is to be designed by Mario Ceroli, one of Italy's leading modern sculptors. "Modern" is the key word. That's the kind of production I've always wanted. I've never thought of my plays as historical dramas, but as plays that use history to communicate a contemporary idea.

Remembering Isabella d'Este's motto, "Neither hope nor fear", I've warned myself constantly against pre-thinking what's to happen. But a week before I'm to leave I find myself, unwillingly, nearly crazed with hope that *this* time, in *this* place, the play will be made to live and breathe the way I want it. I am nearly wild with hope. I tell myself I am a fool.

New York, Friday, September 30

Four days before I am to leave. Our agreement says I'm to approve the Italian translation of the play. I've bought a dictionary but the manuscript hasn't arrived yet. A letter comes to Audrey Wood (my literary representative) from her associate, Lea Danesi Tolnay, who is handling the play for us in Rome. It says, in part: "The title of the play could not be the straight translation of *The Abdication*, as in Italian *L'Abdicazione* phonetically sounded wrong. ... They decided on the following: *Confessione Scandalosa,* keeping the English title also in brackets. I hope Miss Wolff will be satisfied."

Scandalous Confession! My God! What are they doing? Changing the title without my consent is a breach of contract. And if this is how they think of it, what am I going to see when I arrive?

But the letter goes on—and gets worse. About the translation, Tolnay says, "They had a script, which was given to Aldini in New York, which was more like a script derived from the film than a play, while I gave her the regular stage version. Working on both scripts, they sort of combined both versions into one and I think the result is very fine, suitable to the Italian temperament, with the historical events which took place in the Vatican."

These sentences I don't understand at all. What two versions? Did they, somehow, get a copy of the film script and interpolate pieces of that? Did they throw in characters and scenes I added only for the screenplay? If so, I don't own them. What was added for the film is owned by Warner Bros. We will all be sued.

New York, Monday, October 3

I spend three sleepless nights. My husband and son, who are not to accompany me, try to fill me full of the strengths I'll need from them when I'm alone in Florence. My last words to them, as I get into the taxi that will take me to Kennedy Airport, are: "I think the play will be 'Vaticanized' beyond recognition. There will be half-a-dozen cardinals written in, running around saying lines I never wrote. All the controversial parts about the nature of woman will be cut. Everything sexual will be gone. This will be 'The Bowdlerized Abdication.'"

Totally without hope, like someone flying to her own beheading, I get on the plane.

New York to Florence, Tuesday and Wednesday, October 4 and 5.

The flight to Milan is three-and-a-half hours late in leaving. We are served dinner after midnight. Beside me sits an Italian stockbroker from Lucca who speaks nearly perfect English. A man who knows the value of symbols, he wears a five-carat diamond ring, drives a Mercedes-Benz and is a great-grandfather at the age of 79. He tells me this was his first trip to New York and his ambition was to go to "21". He did. He paid $22 for lunch and left a $10 tip — in the style, he says, of Frank Sinatra, who was there when he was. The grateful waiter asked if there was anything he wanted as a souvenir. The man said some "21" toothpicks. The waiter gave him a box of a thousand. The man gives me two.

At this point in the journey, I am not a playwright but a traveler, with all the traveler's preoccupations. Where will I change dollars into lira? How will I make myself understood so I can change from plane to bus to taxi to train to taxi, which I must do to get from the Milan airport to Florence. While, a month ago, I had cheerily studied my Italian phrasebook, as the time got closer to leaving the more I became convinced of the futility of learning a language in minutes. I'll have to depend on what I know of French and Latin. But not knowing Italian has left me without confidence in my ability to get around on my own.

My seatmate solves this problem by changing his plans and accompanying me all the way to Florence. It's almost as if he were sent, like a guardian angel, to smooth my way. Mysteriously, in the morning, he takes to speaking to me in Italian, and in some crazed way I almost think I'm understanding him. And he seems to *know* things: Although I spend three hours on the plane with my eyes firmly closed, my head jammed into the pillow, he says, "You didn't sleep, did you?" No, I answer. Later, on the bus from Malpensa Airport into Milan, I drop off for a second. He says, "You slept, didn't you?" I nod.

I don't tell him what I'm doing in Italy. Or rather, I did tell him, but he didn't hear. On the plane when he had told me of his life, I said, "I'm a playwright. I'm going to Florence because a play of mine is being done there." But he totally disregards that statement. Sudden deafness? Or is the idea too incomprehensible? I don't repeat it. I pretend to be someone traveling alone for pleasure.

Thanks to my dignified companion, I reach the Helvetia e Bristol Hotel in the Piazza Strozzi without a hitch.

Florence, Wednesday, October 5

The hotel is medium-sized, straightforward, unpretentious. I am given a room on the top floor with a ceiling 20 feet above my head. The furniture is unrelenting plain wood. The light bulbs are all 40-watt. The huge window looks out into a light well at the rear of the hotel. But the room has a private bathroom, and by standing on the toilet I can get a magnificent view of tiled roofs, distant hills and a nearby bell tower. I am, I tell myself, not here for the scenery.

The phone rings. It's Lea Danesi Tolnay, who has come up from Rome to see me through this ordeal. "Come out into the hall," she says. "I'll meet you there. My room is just down the corridor." We meet outside a door that says "Signori". She looks exactly as I expect. Mature, vibrant, talkative (like her letters), and with a mellifluous, pleasantly accented English.

In my room, she tells me details of the production. No expense has been spared. The costumes are extraordinary, the setting is superb. The sculptor built the set in an airplane hangar (does she mean "warehouse") outside of Rome. "He is the Henry Moore of Italy," she tells me. The actors drove out each day after he finished work and rehearsed from 5 PM. She goes on and on.

For some reason, I don't challenge her with any of my fears about the production. Is it her enthusiasm? My exhaustion? My natural dislike of battle? Or is it a certain fatalism, the fact that it's too late to do anything anyway?

I hear disconcerting things. "They've added a speech, his part wasn't big enough." (Whose part?) "The little girl is radiant. She's twelve but looks eight." (There is no little girl in my play.) But I say nothing. I will judge tonight when I see the dress rehearsal. When I'll have the confrontation I've been rehearsing. After I observe the facts.

I'm beginning to feel the effects of the trip. Tolnay says I should rest. She will go to the theater and find out what time they want me to come over. I'm to sleep for two hours, then she'll phone me. We'll have dinner together and go to the theater. "Everyone is delighted you've come and can't wait to meet you."

I climb into bed. The phone rings. It's Signora Da Prato, friend of my Boston friend Jane Fogg, who has given her my number. Can I have supper with her tonight? Can I get her tickets for tomorrow's performance? Will I have lunch with her on Tuesday? I wriggle out of it all. No supper, no tickets, no lunch. I am unable to combine the trial of a theater opening with social engagements. I promise to call her.

On a mattress with no resilience, which seems to accept my body like dead weight and force me into the arms of Morpheus, I fall asleep...

The phone rings. It's Tolnay. (I check my watch, it's three, not two, hours later.) She's at the theater. There's trouble with the costumes. They don't want me to see anything yet. Half asleep, I sputter something like, "But I've come all the way from America—"

"Tomorrow you'll come to the preview. You'll see it then. But tonight, *nothing doing."* (It must be a literal translation of "niente". It sounds harsh and cold.)

I feel myself tighten. "Get me the script," I say. "*Get me a copy of the script.*" I begin to sink under the weight of what I'm about to go through. I've come all this way and they won't even see me.

"I'll try," Tolnay says. "I don't know if there's a copy."

I begin to suspect all kinds of sinister machinations. I'm speechless, unable to cope, not knowing what to say because I can't grasp the situation. Then I hear Tolnay's voice. "Get yourself some dinner. I'm going to dine with friends."

Stunned, I hang up the phone. Tolnay and I were to have dinner together. I have no idea, in this city, where I am. I was here only once, for two days, over a dozen years ago. There's no restaurant in the hotel. With the trip and the time change, I am starving. Dimly, with the traveler's instinct for self-preservation, I know I must eat.

I go out of the hotel. It's dark, past 9 o'clock, and I don't know where I'm going. The streets and sidewalks are narrow. I'm lost and afraid. I go down one street, then another, then another, only to turn back halfway when I see they are leading nowhere, only into darkness. All the people are in couples. Or groups of men. I dare not meet anyone's eyes.

I pass a restaurant that looks acceptable. But nearly all the tables are empty. I hurry away. I avoid the lighted areas as well; their gaiety contrasts with my aloneness and upsets me even more. I hurry back toward the hotel. Handsome Italian men are at every street corner. It would be very easy to get a man in this city. All one would have to do is stand still a moment. I hurry on.

I reach the hotel and collapse in a chair in the lobby. Ashamed, but still afraid. My brain isn't functioning. If I have any thought at all, it's that I'll stay one day and fly home. Just get out of here.

I look up. There, hanging on a column in the middle of the hotel lobby, is an orange poster with red letters: "*Confessione Scandalosa (The Abdication) due tempi di Ruth Wolff.*" That—that poster person—that's me! This idiot huddled trembling in a chair in the lobby. I stare at the printed name. Maybe *I* could be capable of collapse, but *she* wouldn't. I keep staring at the poster. It has the usual credits, and it names the cast and all the characters. And as I stare at it, something penetrates through my dim brain. The list of the cast is *exactly* as it is in my play. No additional little girls. No gaggle of cardinals. They may be doing what I wrote after all.

I begin to feel like a human being again. I get up, go out of the hotel and force myself to go back to the promising but empty restaurant. I reach it, but it isn't empty anymore. It's jampacked. Every table is taken. I'm determined to eat there whether they have room for me or not. How I hate that moment when you walk in, a woman, and say, "One, please." The maître d'hotel repeats—a challenge and a question—"*Solo?*"

I am seated. *Solo.* I order a Cinzano, mispronouncing the "C". They don't have a Cinzano. Would I like a "martini"? Yes. "*Secco*" or "sui"? ("*Sui*" seems to be his English for "Sweet".) I order "martini secco". I get dry vermouth. It's exactly what I want.

As dozens of identical plates of pasta go by (that solves the mystery of the crowded tables: it's the eating stop for a bus tour), I reflect on my situation. I'm aware it's always a tense time when "they" show the production to the writer. Especially when it's the day before the first public showing. I'm sure the director, cast and crew are worried about what I'll think. If I wildly protest, what, at this point, could be done? I understand their nerves, the pressure, the tension. I understand, but I would like to be on the inside, not the outside, of the production.

Before I left the States I happened to see my horoscope. It began: "Emotionalism does not suit you." I take a vow, never broken, to accept whatever comes *without emotion*, to look whatever befalls directly in the eye and deal with it with calm, intelligence (according to my measure) and understanding.

Finishing my spinach omelet, I start to walk back to the hotel. I feel I've passed a crisis, just by forcing myself to get a meal alone in a foreign city. I fall asleep after reading a chapter of John Fowle's "The Ebony Tower". I love his sensibility and envy his use of psychological exposition, but often I can't tell who is saying what. Not like the way it is in a play.

Florence, Thursday, October 6.

In the morning I'm awakened by the insistent chiming of the picturesque bell tower just outside my bathroom window. I resonate as if I'm sleeping in the belfry. But I *have* slept. (Only those who've spent sleepless nights in strange beds in strange cities can know the mercy of that statement.) And I go downstairs to find that the script is waiting for me at the desk.

I go back to my room. On the title page I've been Virginia-ized to "Woolf", but it doesn't matter. I begin to turn the pages. I have no idea what's there. All I recognize is what I know from Italian opera. Yes, there are some *"basta, basta's"*, a few *"andiamo's"*, and even a *"piangere"*. This is almost like familiar country, yet totally incomprehensible. It's clear the only way I'll know what I'm reading is to compare the English and Italian scripts line for line. But I'm too impatient for that at the moment. This is Florence. In daylight. I decide to go and see the theater. I get out my map.

Florence of the present is just like Florence of the Medicis—except for automobiles and the people in modern dress. Past elegant shops featuring boots of honey-colored leather, I make my way to the Duomo. How huge it is! Horizontally striped green and white marble courses rise directly from the street. Traffic is intense. Huge buses veer down streets that look too narrow to contain them.

Winding behind the Duomo, I go to the left, past the Piazza Santa Maria Nuova and into the Via della Pergola, searching for the Teatro della Pergola. It was built, I know, in 1652, two years before Christina abdicated and journeyed southward. So it was here then. But there's no evidence she stopped in Florence on her way to Rome.

The Via della Pergola is a narrow street in what has become an unpopulated area of the city. The street is only wide enough for one parked row of small cars and one narrow lane for other small cars to pass. There's a sidewalk on only one side. I walk on that side, squeezed against the buildings, unable even to see a theater. Then suddenly I pass a glass doorway and catch a glimpse of an orange poster: "*Confessione Scandalosa*" posters all along the facade. So... It's really happening. At least *they* believe it. I walk back toward the hotel, behind three young men who have just bought tickets for the show.

I walk back taking a detour past the Arno. Everyone is scurrying into the Ponte Vecchio shops to buy things before the one to three midday closing hours. Some shopkeepers are already pulling down their gates. No one is looking at the Arno. Only me. It's a gray day. Small ringlets are forming here and there on the water. Is it rain? Is it fish? It doesn't seem to be raining. I reach the hotel.

It takes me all afternoon to "read" the first act, turning the pages of the English and Italian versions laid side by side on my bed. I haven't the patience to use a dictionary. But it looks like my play, it feels like my play. The rhythms of the Italian version seem perfect. Certain phrases intrigue me. Nightmares become *incubi*. "Dear Christina" becomes "*Cara Christina mia*". Even in my total ignorance I can feel a beauty in the sound of the lines, a caring for the meaning. There are only brief passages, here and there, where, for a line or two, the meanings of both versions do not seem to coincide. But in the main, it's my play—far more faithful to me, for example, than the English translations I've compared with the original French of the plays of Giraudoux.

Later I ask Tolnay what was this "other version" they combined with the play to make this script. There's surely nothing here from the movie. It turns out that script was the very first version of the play, the ur-text, which somehow found its way to Italy even before the Bristol Old Vic production. It differs from the final text only in small details. I think of those sleepless nights in New York. Too late to undo them. One of my biggest worries has melted away.

Still, I haven't seen the production and have no idea what surprises await me. This evening we're to go to the *anteprima*, a preview, sold out to groups of young college students. There will be just this one preview, then the opening tomorrow. Major critics are coming tonight.

Before the evening performance, I go to dinner with Tolnay at La Poste. She shows me some clippings from today's Florence papers. One talks about the opening of the play and how the American *autrice* is coming over to see it. Another complains that no new plays are being done in the Italian theatre. There's mine and that of some Hungarian. The rest are by Pirandello, Rostand, Shakespeare and Noel Coward. Tolnay asks me if it's true, as she has heard, that I'm writing a play on Jackie Kennedy. I assure her I'm not. I've no idea where this strange rumor comes from.

The performance is scheduled for 9 P M, but Tolnay somehow knows it won't begin until 9:30. We arrive at the theater by cab. There is a great crowd of people outside, mostly young. We enter the lobby. It's grand. Marble floors, marble columns, huge allegorical murals. In the foyer, more marble columns, walls of creamy white with gilded rococo. Then we enter the theater itself, through red velvet curtains.

I'm overwhelmed by the beauty and the grandeur of the space. Row after row of seats in red velvet. Five tiers of boxes arching in a horseshoe around them, rising to a ceiling painted with Tiepolo-like beauty and climaxing in a great crystal chandelier. A theater with twelve hundred seats. No New York theater has anything like its richness and loveliness. I'm told the theater was damaged in the flood of 1966 and has since been totally refurbished.

My play? In this place? But I mustn't be seduced by interior decoration. We are seated near the center aisle in the tenth row. I wait, impatiently, for the curtains to part. At 9:30, they do.

For a moment, I'm shocked—because we seem to be in a modern room that looks to me like a railroad station. I think: this must be some other play, a curtain-raiser before they do mine. There's a strange creature sitting on a balustrade downstage left, playing weird music. And downstage right, with one leg up on something, stands a silhouetted figure in a great cavalier's hat.

Then the person in the cavalier's hat begins to speak, in a deep masculine voice, and I know that it's Christina, that we're in the Vatican, not a railroad station. I wanted a modern production and here it is. A set totally of wood. Red vertical strips for walls, beamed ceiling, raked parquet floor. Upstage, and left and right, doors of natural wood, with carved silhouettes of hands, faces, bodies (the trademark of Ceroli, I am told later). From astonishment, I begin to be pleased.

I'm even more pleased when, at the first flashback to Christina's childhood, the rear wall disappears to reveal, behind it, a Swedish wood—a forest of white abstract birches against a pale blue sky. When this extraordinary view reveals itself, the audience becomes hushed—as it subsequently does at every performance. It's the moment, every night, when the play and the setting begin to reveal their magic. It never fails to move.

Edmonda Aldini, as Christina, is strong—a commanding stage presence. Duilio Del Prete, as the cardinal, is the perfect foil for her, possessing an inner intensity and strength. The dwarf is not a dwarf but a jester. He communicates with Christina not through dumb-show gestures but through ancient musical instruments, which hang about his neck. The masculine and feminine personae of Christina, played in England by two actresses in their mid-20's, are here played by two blondes, one in her mid-20's, the other aged 12. (The "little girl" Tolnay told me about.) The use of the youngster adds an unexpected poignancy to all her scenes. And Giuseppe Patroni Griffi's handling of the direction is so rhythmic, so well-paced, so lively, so constantly psychologically true, that I'm amazed.

What amazes me most, as the performance unfolds, is that I feel I'm "with it" —even without understanding a word of the dialogue. Of course, I am watching the work of talents who won't let anyone, me or anyone else, be removed from what is taking place onstage. There are broad scenes that shock me the first time I see them; rightly or wrongly, I take them to be in the *Commedia dell'Arte* tradition.

As for my fear of their cutting the "nature of woman" scenes—far from it. The sexual scenes are much more explicit than I'd actually conceived them. In the bedroom scene, while the woman is totally nude, the man wears a loincloth. This leads to some grumbling from a female contingent in the audience which complains that what *she* can do, *he* can do. But it's a question, fortunately, I don't have to solve.

I'm a little disturbed by the number of scenes that are played far downstage, where, because there is no before-the-proscenium lighting, I cannot clearly see the faces. At intermission, Tolnay explains the Italian preference for *tableaux*— for stage pictures, unlike our American predilection for "close-up" clarity on-stage. Del Prete has asked that I come onstage for a bow at the end. So that I can slip out noiselessly, for the second act Tolnay and I are seated in a box toward the rear of the house. From here I can see the stage pictures, often in silhouette, and they enchant me. They have to enchant me, for I haven't read the second act and find it much harder to follow than the first. I often have no idea what is happening.

Then, at a point where I don't expect it, I feel a hand on my shoulder. It's the company manager. I'm to come with him backstage. It's almost the end. Through the deserted foyer I follow him backstage—regretful at missing the ending. But I see the ending from the wings. Then the curtain comes down. And there's tremendous applause. Enormous applause from these young university students. Waves and waves and waves. The cast takes curtain call after curtain call. Duilio calls out the set designer, costume designer, director— then me. Hardly knowing what I'm doing, I dash through the Swedish wood and out onto the bright lights of the stage, where, to the tumultuous applause of hundreds and hundreds of cheering people, I first meet the cast and director—and they meet me.

What a way to meet! With waves of applause washing over you. The applause grows into an ovation. I bow with the rest. I don't know how many curtain calls we take—again and again—being pulled forward by Edmonda, who has that special energy actresses possess when they're onstage.

At last the curtains close, and I go backstage with my arms about my stars, who, a moment ago, had never met me.

After midnight, Duilio, Edmonda, Griffi, Tolnay and I take taxis across the Arno to a small restaurant in the Piazza Pitti. The entire cast is there, seated at great round tables. There's no room for us, so a table is placed beneath the stairs. Edmonda is a natural leader. People automatically look to her for direction, even where to sit at the table. She has a vibrancy and life, a quick intelligence. She traveled with Duilio when he was making several films for Peter Bogdanovich and, feeling left out of conversations, locked herself in a hotel room with an English grammar. Now she speaks it enviably well. Duilio, having attended law school in England, speaks it fluently. (He did the play's translation.) Darkly handsome, he reminds me of my first love, a boy I adored in the third grade. And he has the most perfect male body I have ever seen. Griffi, the director, and the one to whom I want to say the most, hardly speaks English at all. We communicate in French, in which we both have a limited vocabulary. (It's the language Christina and Azzolino used to communicate with each other.)

Even with the flowing of the brilliant white Tuscan wine, Griffi does not relax like the others. He is constantly speaking of the performance to the actors, correcting, shaping, perfecting, even through the arrival of the risotto, the spinach crêpes, the fried rabbit. I learn that Edmonda and Duilio are starting a production company with this play. They have gambled a great deal on it. Their doing my play is miraculous, considering the fact that the Italian Government subsidizes only works by Italian authors. If I needed any proof of their devotion to the play, aside from the meticulous production, this self-sacrifice is it.

We part after three A M. They're happy with this evening's reception of the play by the young people of Florence. But, of course, opening night tomorrow is the real test.

Florence, Friday, October 7

I wake late after a sound sleep and go to the Piazza della Republica for lunch in a sidewalk cafe where, surrounded by Americans, I pay $5 for a chicken sandwich. Then I return to the hotel to read the second act. I feel like someone preparing for an examination, trying to get it all read before the test begins. I find the added speech. It's for the man, a celebrated character actor, who plays Oxenstierna, the prime minister. Such a prominent actor, I have been told, must have a principal speech. At the Swedish Embassy, Duilio found a letter from Oxenstierna to Christina, begging her not to abdicate, and he inserted it. (I think it stops the action, but the audience listens closely every night.)

I go to have my hair washed. The girl who washes it looks, I think, exactly like Christina's friend Ebba. And I hear her call the man who set my hair "Azzolino". I think I may be losing my mind.

At five, I go to the theater, where Griffi is polishing, brushing up, perfecting the cast, even hours before the opening. He works with strength and unsentimentality, qualities I saw in the production. I think how marvelous it is that he holds the actors together in the tense hours before the opening. It's better that they run the risk of getting tired rather than dissipate their energies in rest or worry. A television crew comes to interview the cast. I leave.

I go back to the hotel to dress. Tolnay has ordered flowers from us for Edmonda. She tells me in Italy it's bad luck to say, "Good luck." Instead, one says, "*In bocca al lupo*". (The literal translation is "In the mouth of the wolf"; it's the equivalent of our "Break a leg".) That's what she's written on the card. Later, when I see the cast telegrams, I see that many other well-wishers had the same idea.

We take a cab to the theater. I have no feelings. I really don't believe it's happening. My play? Opening the theatrical season in Florence? In Italian? Me here? Facing an opening? With no one I know?

At the stage door there's a cable from my son and husband: "With you tonight and every night. Love, Evan and Martin." I choke up for a moment, my eyes fill with tears. Not "wish-you-were-here" tears. But tears that recognize the fact that they *are* here. Their strength is with me. I feel it constantly. I am not alone.

What will be, will be. But suddenly it all seems as crucial to me as a Broadway opening.

The house is sold out. No seats have been left for us at the box office. In total contrast to the audience of the night before, the lobby is now filled with the aristocratic *haute monde* of Florence. Men in dark suits. Women in high-fashion gowns, their *maquillage* a thing of Renaissance splendor. They mill about the foyer greeting each other for the first time after the summer season. By these Beautiful People we are to be judged.

At last the company manager rescues us and takes us to a second-tier box, where there are a few empty seats. It feels very "Italian opera", leaning over the red velvet railing, a carved wooden divider at my elbow. The manager whispers to Tolnay, telling her she must be sure to tell me something. Tolnay tells me. His message is this: I must not be upset by the reactions of the opening-night Florentine audience. They are the most difficult in the world. (He knows, he has traveled the world with the Teatro Piccolo di Milano.) The Florentines are cold, reserved, interested only in their gowns and their appearance. *Frigido.* They are very stingy with their applause and if they find something funny, they will do everything they can not to laugh. I am not to be upset if they don't respond at all. I nod. I am so preprogrammed to expect nothing that being told to expect nothing doesn't move me. At 9:30, fifteen minutes late, and after a spattering of impatient clapping by the audience, the curtain parts.

This time I am not shocked. I know I'm looking at the Vatican. I know that's Christina. I know what I'll see. As the play progresses, I can sense, even with the language barrier, that this is an extraordinary performance. Rhythms are much tighter than the night before. Edmonda and Duilio and the rest are in top form. Something holds, something magical, something remarkable is happening. And I feel, in spite of the warning about the audience, that they're very attentive, that they're *with* the play. They're listening, responding, and toward the end of the first act, when Christina says: "Find me a *man* who will bear my children!" applause breaks out spontaneously in the orchestra and carries the whole house with it.

At intermission, Tolnay tells me, "I'm not worried anymore." I say, "There's the second act..." She repeats, "I'm not worried." I only pray that whatever magic is infusing the cast will hold beyond the break.

During intermission, there is great exuberance and noise echoing off the marble surfaces in the lobby, but to me it's incomprehensible babble. The twelve year-old actress's mother comes by with squares of chocolate-covered ice cream in the shape of bon-bons. She says she heard somebody say, "It doesn't let down for a minute." But I understand nothing at all.

We go back to our seats. The second act begins. There's an audible gasp when Christina enters with her bosom bared. The reactions to the second act are far more subtle, and I cannot judge at all how it's being accepted. I wait breathlessly for the final scene to judge its effect on the audience. But just as Christina and Azzolino are coming to their final moment of love and renunciation, the manager silently enters the box and says I am to come. I have to go backstage again and make an appearance. I protest. I want to see the ending. But Duilio has requested it. Tiptoeing, and never yet having seen the ending of the play from the front of the house, I go.

Griffi is standing backstage. He whispers he'll take his bow and then will come back to get me. I suddenly realize I haven't dressed for this. I'm wearing black pants and a sheer ruffled blouse, an exact copy of the one Garbo wore in "Grand Hotel". It's flaming orange and cut to the navel. The audience will be getting an extra nude scene. But if they like the play, I don't care.

The curtains close. The manager reminds me of what he said before about this audience. For a moment there's total silence. Then—thunderous applause.

The curtains open to a world gone nearly mad with cheering. These "cold, reserved Florentines" call the cast back for bow after bow. Griffi goes out, then comes back and gets me—and I face the applause and the cheering. I forget to be self-conscious about my décolletage. Heaven help me, I love being there. It's so rare for a playwright to take part in the action. I feel part of the show, not part of the audience. I feel I belong—not out there, but up here.

Bows from us all. An ovation. Audience standing and applauding. It goes on for twenty minutes.

At last the curtains close and we go backstage. I am stunned. People are pouring in, saying it was a "*successo fantastico!*" The manager of the theater hurries back breathlessly and says, "Never before in the history of the Pergola! *Trionfo!*"

Trionfo! Trionfo! They're saying it everywhere. Tolnay comes back and she says it. I'm reserved. I don't believe it's really happening. I remember a Kipling phrase: "If you can meet with Triumph and Disaster, and treat those two imposters just the same..." I was ready for the imposter Disaster. But Triumph? Couldn't he be an imposter, too?

We go, once more, to the cafe in the Piazza Pitti. There's applause when we enter. Just like Sardi's. This time, we are seated with the rest at the round tables. Dinner begins with an enormous bowl of *crudités* and coarsely textured bread. Then a gigantic bowl of pasta. Then exquisitely spiced rolled ground meat. Everyone is so excited they can't slow down to speak English. I listen to the incomprehensible happy buzzing around me, and apply myself to the Tuscan wine, and smile. I smile and keep smiling, as if I understand, to keep them from the burden of having to communicate in my language. But then, success is the same in any language. I begin to reel with wine and joy.

Nearing 3:30 A.M., we are just getting up to leave when someone runs in with tomorrow's paper. La Nazione. There's a review. Duilio reads it aloud. (Again, just like opening night at Sardi's, except it's in Italian.) I understand only his smiles, the cast's applause and the happy sounds. "*Successo magnifico!*" it says. "*Incandescente!*"

Duilio hands me the paper to keep.

I go out into the dark early-morning hours as one does after an opening. But it isn't 44th Street. Before me looms the great majestic hulk of the Pitti Palace. We make our way, exhausted, back over the Arno, by the Ponte Vecchio, to bed.

Pisa Airport, Wednesday, October 12.

I stay four more days in Florence—to see the play. I keep wanting to see it, living. It continues to reach people. Signora Da Prato comes to see it after I've had lunch with her. She approaches me at intermission, looks at me with something like awe and says, "I can't believe you wrote this. Now that I know you—and you're so *simple*!" (I pray she means unassuming.) Later, someone says to me, "Doesn't everyone tell you you look just like Maria Callas? Before she died, of course." (How unlike ourselves we look to other people.)

One day, I take a bus trip to Siena and San Gimignano. As we are passing through a tiny town known only for its ancient monastery, I look out and see the facade of the local cinema. They're playing the "Abdication" film.

A day later, I part, reluctantly, from what has been, without exaggeration, the happiest experience of my life. I say farewell to Griffi, feeling I've found *my* director. (The playwright's eternal search.) So what if he doesn't speak my language? We'll communicate somehow. I think he would be perfect for other plays of mine and I tell him so. The world must eventually speak one tongue.

Edmonda and Duilio I leave with love—as if we had known each other forever. It's their devotion and force that were responsible for this miracle. Nothing I say can thank them sufficiently.

At Pisa, as I get on the plane at the beautifully named airport, Galileo Galilei, I still can't quite believe all this has happened.

It never occurred to me that when I finally achieved the production I wanted it would be in the shadow of the Duomo.

I don't believe my life.

* * *

"The Abdication" ("Confessione Scandalosa") played engagements in Livorno, La Sera, Arezzo, Vicenza, Verona, Torino, Bologna, Milan and Rome, where, due to popular demand, its engagement was extended by many weeks.

www.ingramcontent.com/pod-product-compliance
Lightning Source LLC
Chambersburg PA
CBHW071055230426
43666CB00009B/1716